Fodor's

ESSENTIAL VIETNAM

Welcome to Vietnam

With everything from superb cuisine to stunning landscapes, this corner of Southeast Asia dazzles the senses. Peaceful paddy fields give way to frenetic urban centers like Ho Chi Minh City and Hanoi, where the youthful population rushes to embrace the future. Boutiques fill the French colonial buildings in enchanting Hoi An; in the north, a world away, are Sapa's ethnic markets. Around Vietnam, lush jungles and jagged karst peaks beckon adventurers. Absorb it all but take time to relax, perhaps on the long, alluring coastline with its world-class beaches.

TOP REASONS TO GO

★ **History:** From Hue's Imperial City to the Cu Chi tunnels, Vietnam's past enthralls.

★ **Cuisine:** Fresh herbs, fiery chilies, fragrant noodle dishes—pho is just the beginning.

★ **Postcard Views:** Misty mountains, vibrant green rice paddies, and sapphire seascapes.

★ **Cool Cities:** The buzzing streets of Ho Chi Minh City and Hanoi reward exploration.

★ **Islands:** Isolated Con Dao, blissful Phu Quoc, and rugged Cat Ba are tropical escapes.

★ **Boating:** Cruises in Halong Bay, boat rides through the Mekong Delta—Vietnam is best by boat.

Contents

MAPS

Chapter 1

EXPERIENCE VIETNAM

18 ULTIMATE EXPERIENCES

Vietnam offers terrific experiences that should be on every traveler's list. Here are Fodor's top picks for a memorable trip.

1 Halong Bay

Thousands of limestone karsts jut skyward from emerald waters in this UNESCO World Heritage–listed seascape. The best way to see it is to hop by boat between islands, including scenic Cat Ba, home to a national park. (Ch. 7)

2 The Imperial City, Hue

The jewel of Hue's Citadel, this sprawling complex of majestic palaces and evocative temples brings the magnificence of Vietnam's royal dynasties to life. (Ch. 6)

3 Markets

From Hanoi's bustling Old Quarter to floating outposts in the Mekong Delta, markets reveal colorful slices of local life. Plunge right in, and haggle like you mean it. (Ch. 3–9)

4 Ho Chi Minh City

Rapidly modernizing, HCMC is a jolt of urban energy unlike anywhere else in the country. The frenetic pace (that traffic!) is tempered by peaceful pagodas, parks, and cafés. (Ch. 3)

5 Street Food

Devour a delicious bowl of pho on a bustling corner, or follow the fragrant smoke emanating from a sidewalk brazier, where marinated pork sizzles. (Ch. 3–9).

6 Vietnam War Legacy

Museums pay tribute, but for a different perspective on the war, look underground— the vast Cu Chi tunnel network is a monument to Vietnamese tenacity. (Ch. 3)

7 Phong Nha Ke Bang National Park

Untamed jungle, vast imagination-defying limestone caves, and underground rivers make this spectacular region irresistible to adventurers. (Ch. 6)

8 Rice Terraces

In the Northwest, motorbike or hike along verdant mountains and take in the vibrant, undulating rice terraces outside of areas like Sapa, Mu Cang Chai, and Tu Le. (Ch. 9)

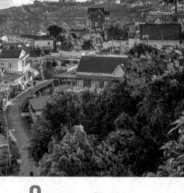

9 Hill Stations

Built by the French as health retreats, hill stations such as Dalat (pictured) make a cool contrast to the steamy lowlands—think misty peaks and rugged scenery. (Ch. 5)

10 Sapa

Home to ethnic minorities, this northern mountain town is also the jumping-off point for some compelling sights, including Fansipan, Vietnam's tallest summit. (Ch. 9)

11 Golden Bridge, Danang

Two giant stone hands appear to hold up this nearly 500-foot-long pedestrian bridge, which has become one of the biggest new tourist attractions in Danang's Ba Na Hills. (Ch. 6)

12 Mui Ne

The first major stop north of Ho Chi Minh City is Mui Ne, an international kitesurfing capital. Surfers come from all over to catch waves during the windy season from November to April. (Ch. 5)

13 Hoi An

French colonial architecture, historic traders' houses, and atmospheric temples are among the charms of Hoi An that are easily discovered on a riverside stroll. (Ch. 6)

14 Beaches and Islands

Two thousand miles of tropical coastline ensure that the white sands of a postcard are never far away. Islands like Phu Quoc combine idyllic beaches and diving. (Ch. 4)

15 Vietnam's Coffee Capital, Buon Ma Thuot

The capital of the Central Highlands is where you'll find Vietnam's best java, complete with a Coffee Village and local cafés where the coffee is so strong it's poured into shot glasses. (Ch. 5)

16 Hanoi's Old Quarter

Vietnam's capital is the center of culture and cool. In its most ancient section, the Old Quarter, stop into one of the many trendy restaurants or grab a beer on the bia hoi beer corner. (Ch. 8)

17 The Mekong Delta

This patchwork of waterways and floating markets, mangrove swamps, and brilliant green rice paddies is best explored by boat, but bike tours provide a fun alternative. (Ch. 4)

18 Tet, the Lunar New Year

Late January to early February is a good time to breathe in the excitement of the lunar new year. During Vietnam's largest festival, Hanoi's Old Quarter comes alive. (Ch. 8)

WHAT'S WHERE

1 Ho Chi Minh City.
Still called Saigon by many, Ho Chi Minh City is a rapidly expanding metropolis, one full of contrasts. The downtown core is quite walkable and most major sites—from the War Remnants Museum to the Reunification Palace—can be visited on foot.

2 The Mekong Delta.
Running through the upper delta is the Mekong River, dotted with small fertile islands where fruit grows in abundance. The rest is a patchwork of waterways, mangrove swamps, and brilliant green rice paddies that run into the emerald East Sea.

3 The South-Central Coast and Highlands.
Two of Vietnam's most popular resort towns are here—ocean-side Nha Trang and the cool mountain retreat of Dalat. On the East Sea, Nha Trang has a palm-lined boulevard running the length of its beach. If it's mountains and lakes you seek, head to temperate Dalat.

4 The Central Coast.
The towns of Hue and Hoi An provide a fascinating glimpse of Vietnam's history. UNESCO site Hoi An is

an ancient trading and fishing town where many buildings remain as they were 200 years ago. Hue's Imperial City and palatial royal tombs are impressive reminders of the country's regal past. In between Hue and Hoi An is Danang, the region's major transportation hub.

5 Halong Bay and North-Central Vietnam. A boat on Halong Bay or Bai Tu Long Bay, and kayaking among the islands of the Cat Ba archipelago are just two of the popular outdoor activities in the picturesque North Central region.

6 Hanoi. The capital of Vietnam is also its cultural hub. Despite the chaotic motorbike traffic, this city of majestic lakes, wide tree-lined boulevards, and hauntingly familiar French colonial architecture remains quite charming.

7 The Northwest. Hanoi is the jumping-off point for the rest of northern Vietnam, which is home to more than 50 ethnic minority groups. Many ethnic minorities live in the beautiful highlands of the north, where views of the rice terraces and surrounding fields are truly stunning.

Vietnam's Natural Wonders

HALONG BAY
Hop in a kayak and paddle around the emerald waters of UNESCO site Halong Bay, exploring caves and ogling the 1,600-some seemingly floating limestone formations crowned with rain forests. It's busy, yes, but one look at this otherworldly wonder, and you'll see why. (Ch. 7)

THE MEKONG DELTA
A manageable day-trip from Ho Chi Minh City, the agricultural Mekong Delta region covers an area of 15,600 square miles. Explore dozens of cities and towns along the water, peppered with floating markets, rice paddies, and Buddhist temples and pagodas. Start at Can Tho, a town at the heart of the region. (Ch. 4)

SAND DUNES OF MUI NE
Located near the palm-lined fishing village of Mui Ne lies an eye-catching system of red and white sand dunes that look like they came straight out of the Sahara Desert. These wonders are formed and shaped by gusts of wind over several years. Sand-sledding and sunset biking are popular activities here. (Ch. 5)

MARBLE MOUNTAINS
Twenty minutes' drive south of Danang are the five Marble Mountains, each of which are said to represent one of the five elements (metal, water, wood, fire, and earth). The climb to the summit of Thuy Son (water) is literally breathtaking; it's 150 steps (there's an elevator, too), but you'll be rewarded with shrines hidden inside caves and grottoes and sweeping views of Danang. (Ch. 6)

AN BANG AND CUA DAI
In addition to being a UNESCO site for its historical significance as an international port, Hoi An has two lovely white-sand beaches backed by low-key restaurants and resorts. An Bang is popular for surfing and paddleboarding, while Cua Dai's calm waters are perfect for swimming and relaxing. (Ch. 6)

NINH BINH
Located about 100 kilometers (62 miles) south of Hanoi, Ninh Binh is nicknamed the "inland Halong Bay." With towering limestone cliffs that merge into the surrounding rice paddies, this is a much less trafficked alternative to the natural wonder it is often compared to. Here, take boat tours to explore the wildlife-rich Van Long Wetland Nature Reserve or the Trang An Grottoes, encompassing dozens of cross-water caves and valleys. (Ch. 7)

Phu Quoc Island

BAN GIOC WATERFALL
Set in the northern Cao Bang province, this majestic duo of falls emerges from the Quay Son River in the towering karst limestone hills at the Chinese border. During the flooding season, the waters can rise high enough to join both sections together. Get panoramic views of the falls during a roughly 10-minute ride on a raft. Visitors are welcome year-round, and bringing a poncho and water shoes is recommended. (Ch. 9)

PHU QUOC ISLAND
Located off the coast of Cambodia, Phu Quoc is often referred to as the jewel of Vietnam, both for its gem-like shape and for its unmatched tropical beauty. Though what was once an untouched paradise is quickly becoming more developed, there are still stretches of beach with the immaculate white sand and cerulean waters of a postcard. Both boutique villas and big resorts can be found, but it's also worth venturing into Phu Quoc National Park for hikes, wildlife tours, and camping. (Ch. 4)

PHONG NA KHE BANG NATIONAL PARK
With its extensive cave system, karst rock mountains, and rivers, this national park in Central Vietnam offers some of the best outdoor activities in the country amid untamed jungle. The park is home to the gargantuan Son Doong Cave—only discovered in 2009 and believed to be the world's largest cave passage—as well as rich wildlife like tigers and elephants. Try your hand at ziplining, kayaking the rapids, or boating into a river cave. (Ch. 6)

SAPA'S RICE TERRACES
The people of Sapa built these stunning terraced rice fields to adapt to the mountainous northern highlands, sometimes known as the Tonkinese Alps. Once a French hill station, the area today is world-renowned as a hiking destination. (Ch. 9)

Vietnam's Temples and Pagodas

CAO DAI HOLY SEE
Located in the city of Tay Ninh roughly 80 km (50 miles) from Ho Chi Minh City, the Cao Dai Holy See is the headquarters of the Cao Dai religion, attracting thousands of worshippers clad in all white to partake in a daily ceremony of song and prayer. (Ch. 3)

PERFUME PAGODA
Located within an ancient complex of Buddhist temples and shrines carved into the limestone of the Huong Tich Mountains is the Perfume Pagoda (also known as the Inner Temple). Set inside the Huong Tich cave, it features statues of the Buddha and Bodhisattva Quan Am. (Ch. 8)

GIAC LAM PAGODA
Dating back to 1744, the Giac Lam Pagoda is one of the oldest Buddhist temples in Ho Chi Minh City, housing many of Vietnam's most treasured religious artifacts. Located in District 11, the pagoda remains a tranquil city escape for Buddhist worshippers today and has lovely views. (Ch. 3)

THIEN MU PAGODA
Also called the Pagoda of the Celestial Lady in honor of the local deity, this seven-story octagonal pagoda is a key religious and architectural symbol for the legendary imperial capital of Hue in Central Vietnam. Built in 1601 atop a forested hill on the northern bank of the Perfume River, the Thien Mu Pagoda features three statues representing Buddhas of past, present, and future. Arrive in the morning to enjoy the peaceful view before tourist groups arrive. (Ch. 6)

TEMPLE OF LITERATURE
Built in 1070 as a university, the Temple of Literature (Van Mieu) is a memorial to education and scholarly pursuits and a key example of classic Vietnamese architecture. Once site of the royal exams, the temple is now one of Hanoi's most popular attractions. The complex includes a maze of courtyards and trails connecting sites like the Lake of Literature, Well of Heavenly Clarity, and 116 carved stone turtles representing wisdom and longevity. There are also altars for worship of Confucius and numerous other philosophers. (Ch. 8)

LINH UNG TEMPLE
Set in Vietnam's third-largest city, the beach town of Danang, this gorgeous pagoda is famed for its towering Lady Buddha Statue, the tallest in Vietnam. The temple is located on Danang's scenic Son Tra Peninsula, with views of both mountains and sea. (Ch. 6)

Temple of Literature

BAI DINH PAGODA
Covering an area of some 539 hectares, the Bai Dinh Pagoda actually refers to a sprawling mountain Buddhist complex that includes an ancient pagoda, a newer pagoda built in 2003, plus parking, lakes, and gardens. Located in Ninh Binh province near Hanoi, the complex includes several attractions including a three-story bell tower, Bodhisattva temple, and a giant circular water well. Climb 300 steps to reach breathtaking views of cliffs, mountains, and caves. (Ch. 7)

TRAN QUOC PAGODA
Hanoi's oldest Buddhist pagoda, constructed in the sixth century, is set on a tiny island linked by bridges to Truc Bach Lake and West Lake. The ancient pagoda has a leafy garden and is a popular spot for watching the sunset. (Ch. 8)

VAN THUY TU TEMPLE
This mustard-colored temple is Vietnam's largest and oldest temple built in honor of Ca Ong, or the Lord Whale. Whale worship is distinct to Vietnamese culture, in which fishing and seafaring local people see the animals as guardians. Built in 1762 in the coastal southeast city of Phan Thiet, the temple houses the skeletons of some 500 whales amassed by local fishermen over the span of decades. The temple's key relic is a 20-meter-long whale skeleton, which is the largest in Vietnam. (Ch. 5)

HIEN LAM PAVILION
Also referred to as the Pavilion of the Glorious Coming, this temple is one of the most well-preserved buildings in the ancient imperial city of Hue. The pavilion pays tribute to the legacy of the Nguyen Dynasty, its emperors, and honorable mandarins. (Ch. 6)

What to Eat and Drink in Vietnam

BANH MI

A legacy of some 150 years of French occupation, banh mi refers both to the French baguette, as well as the signature Vietnamese style of meat sandwich made with the bread. The most popular variety is *banh mi thit*, a crisp-on-the-outside and fluffy-on-the-inside baguette with pâté, slices of sausage, cucumber, pickled carrot, chili, and more.

MI QUANG

Central Vietnam's Quang Nam province, including the cities of Hoi An and Danang, is home to some of Vietnam's most prized noodle soups. Mi Quang is a savory half-soup, half-salad noodle dish with pork, prawn, quail eggs, and rice cracker shards.

CA PHE SUA

Another legacy of French colonialism, coffee today is an integral part of Vietnamese daily life. Vietnam is the world's second largest producer of coffee, which grows in the highlands of Central Vietnam between cities like Dalat and Buon Ma Thuot. In Vietnam, ca phe sua is typically brewed through a stainless steel phin filter directly into a glass or mug with condensed milk.

COM TAM

Throughout Vietnam, rice restaurants offer cheap home-cooked meals. The signature com tam dish is barbecued pork marinated in fish sauce, garlic, and palm sugar, and a slice of Vietnamese quiche—an egg pie containing noodles, wood ear mushrooms, and ground pork.

RICE WINE

Rice wines have been distilled in Vietnam for centuries. There are many forms of rice wine, including the central Vietnamese *ruou can*, a sticky rice wine prepared in 6-liter vats and consumed communally through giant straws, and snake wine, in which whole snakes are infused in rice wine or grain alcohol, seen most often in tourist shops.

CHAO

Rice porridge is a breakfast staple and is often prepared with ginger as a comfort for simple ailments. Similar to Chinese *congee* and other Asian rice porridge dishes, *chao* can be prepared with *ca* (fish), *tom* (shrimp), *ech* (frog), *heo* (pork), *bo* (beef), *hai san* (seafood), or *chay* (vegetarian).

STICKY RICE

Sticky rice is a sweet anytime-of-day snack, although in Ho Chi Minh City it's most common to see food vendors pushing carts of colorful sticky rice—purple, black, and green—after dark. Rice is also used to make a range of delicious steamed crepes and savory cakes.

PHO

Often considered the unofficial national dish of Vietnam, pho (pronounced "fuh") is a tangle of silky rice noodles and beef (commonly served raw and sliced thin) or chicken in a fragrant broth with an instantly recognizable aroma of roasted onion, ginger, star anise, cinnamon, and cloves. Regional differences are worth noting: in Hanoi, the broth is clear and minimally garnished; whereas in southern Vietnam, pho is distinguished by bolder flavors and ample use of fresh herbs.

BUN CHA

Made widely known to westerners after a historic meal between President Obama and Anthony Bourdain, this beloved savory Hanoian specialty comes with rice noodles (bun), charcoal-grilled pork patties (cha), pork belly, and a plate of fresh herbs. Combine these ingredients at will, dunking meat and noodles into the sweet-sour fish sauce-based dipping broth.

What to Buy in Vietnam

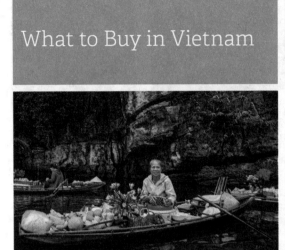

VIETNAMESE SILK
Relatively affordable, Vietnamese silk is often spun using manual looms. Destinations for silk include Hanoi's Silk Street and Hoi An, a city known for its tailoring as much as its history.

AO DAI
The traditional costume of Vietnam is a long two-piece tunic dress paired with loose silk trousers and a headband. Many stores in Ho Chi Minh City sell ao dai and can also custom tailor one.

FINE ART
The contemporary art scene in urban Vietnam is booming in the galleries of Hanoi and Saigon. In Hanoi's Old Quarter you'll find shops with all manner of traditional items, including paintings.

FLOATING MARKET FARE
When visiting a floating market, buying fresh fruit—and perhaps even seafood—is a must. The Mekong Delta city of Can Tho is a popular hub due to its proximity to numerous floating river markets including Nga Bay and Cai Rang markets.

POTTERY
Vietnam boasts a number of dedicated pottery villages, some of which have been perfecting their craft for hundreds of years. Ceramic aficionados will enjoy a visit to the Bat Trang Pottery Village, near Hanoi, which is known for its white clay goods.

CUSTOM TAILORED CLOTHING
Hundreds of small tailor shops line the streets in Hoi An. Here, made-to-measure clothing can be turned around in just 48 hours, but make sure to leave ample time for tailors to work their magic. The best way to get exactly what you want is to bring something to be copied.

SAPA HANDICRAFTS
Sapa, in northern Vietnam, is home to many of Vietnam's highland-dwelling ethnic minority tribes. The market in town is the place to go for the beautifully embroidered fabrics, indigo-dyed clothes, and silver jewelry of these groups.

Lanterns

LACQUERWARE

Believed to have been introduced by the Chinese in the first century AD, this art form features the resin of the lacquer tree, which is planted largely in Phu Tho in Northern Vietnam. Depicting both mythical and daily scenes, lacquered art can be found adorning everything from furniture to dishes, chopsticks, jewelry boxes, and vases.

LANTERNS

Hoi An's signature silk lanterns are particularly important to Vietnamese culture, signifying good fortune. Head to the picturesque lantern market to choose from myriad colors and patterns, each with its own meaning, and shapes including spherical and balloon-shaped.

CONTEMPORARY CLOTHING

The fashion scene in Ho Chi Minh City is growing rapidly, with new flagship showrooms for notable local designers like Moi Dien and Cong Tri. A local streetwear scene has also emerged, with young hometown labels sold at concept stores like The New Playground in Hanoi and Saigon. The centrally located Vincom Center Shopping Mall offers big-name luxury retailers, while Ben Thanh Market offers affordable tourist T-shirts and trinkets.

Vietnam Today

Vietnam is a place of lush, natural beauty, from the low-lying deltas of the south to the mountainous central highlands to the staggered layers of the rice terraces in the north. Over a thousand miles long and only 31 miles wide at its narrowest, with a total area slightly larger than New Mexico, Vietnam is home to an estimated 98 million people, with the majority born after 1975. Visitors will discover a vibrant culture: one that includes an elegantly crumbling European heritage and a delicious street-food scene. This is certainly the time to visit: Vietnam is a country obsessed with the future, rushing headlong toward a dream of first-world prosperity with an irrepressible energy. Despite centuries of war and poverty, the Vietnamese people have an obvious enjoyment of life. As in many places the locals add so much: their warm smiles, curiosity, and humor are what make a visit here so unforgettable.

GOVERNMENT

Since 1975, the Socialist Republic of Vietnam has been a one-party state, with the only legal political party being the Communist Party of Vietnam. Independent candidates are eligible to run for office but most are not permitted on the ballot.

In Vietnam, the prime minister is the head of government, responsible to the 500-seat national assembly, while the president is the head of state. Both are part of a 16-member Politburo, the nation's highest decision-making body, with the power to implement policy approved by the Communist Party's National Congress and parliament. The machinations of power are murky, and little reported in Vietnam, where the government or Communist Party directly or indirectly owns most of the media.

The government faces many challenges, including the widening gap between rich and poor, territorial disputes with its large and populous neighbor, China, and the pollution and environmental degradation that accompany modernization.

Human rights groups regularly chastise Vietnam for its one-party policy, and the zeal with which it imprisons citizens who make public comments about a multi-party state or call for political change. Visitors are highly unlikely to see any of this oppressive behavior, but don't expect any local tour guides to discuss politics in any depth, or even to speak on the topic at all. There is little prospect of political change in the near future. The stability of Vietnam's government is, in fact, one of the main attractions for foreign investors.

ECONOMY

Vietnam has one of the world's fastest growing economies. Development is most visible in the major cities, where soaring glass-and-chrome skyscrapers, new roads, bridges, and tunnels continue to be built alongside a plethora of new upmarket restaurants and five-star hotels. The other side of Vietnam's economic story is told outside the cities, where 70% of the population is still engaged in agriculture, often small-scale enterprises that provide only a subsistence living.

The vast economic divide continues to increase. The rise of urban overcrowding has led to rapidly growing shanty towns, particularly in Hanoi and Ho Chi Minh City, though residents' access to basic services is better than in many Asian cities. Meanwhile, private jets and high-end vehicles are now must-have accessories among the country's elite, and Rolls-Royce and Prada are the latest luxury brands to establish a presence in Hanoi.

Such displays of wealth are in stark contrast to the situation post-1975, when the nation was plunged into poverty after the imposition of a Soviet-style closed market economy. Realizing things weren't working, the government introduced *doi moi* (renovation) economic reforms in 1986, which included opening up a socialist market economy at home, allowing free trade, and renewing diplomatic relations to encourage foreign investment.

THE LEGACY OF WAR

Vietnam has been fighting off foreign forces for centuries, including China, France, and the United States. It was once part of Imperial China, before reverting to self-rule in the mid-1400s. France colonized Vietnam in the mid-1800s until the fall of France in World War II. In 1954 the Geneva Accord dictated the country be divided into the Communist North Vietnam and non-Communist South Vietnam. The governments of the North and South considered themselves rulers of the entire country, and tensions escalated until the United States joined what became all-out conflict, known as the Vietnam War outside of the country, and the American War within.

Despite the ongoing visible effects of the American use of Agent Orange, including third-generation birth defects and environmental devastation, the Vietnamese have moved on from the atrocities of the period of war that stretched from 1955 to 1975. (A Vietnamese victims' rights group failed to have their case heard in the U.S. Supreme Court in 2009, though efforts for compensation continue.) It comes as a surprise to some travelers that little resentment toward Americans remains among the general Vietnamese population, who are more interested in the future than the past. It is also the case that the government has encouraged this attitude. And with about 40% of the population aged under 25, the end of the Vietnam war in 1975 is practically ancient history. Vietnam's young people are more concerned with becoming rich (and sometimes famous), in order to buy the latest iPhones, cars, and fancy new apartments.

Some visitors to Vietnam are offended by the various Vietnamese museums and memorials dedicated to the last war, but it's important to remember that these government-owned facilities are designed to reinforce the government's own position domestically. The use of propaganda is still very much in evidence, for example in the War Remnants Museum in Ho Chi Minh City, where graphic images are displayed alongside explanatory text that presents the North Vietnamese side.

FAMILY

Vietnamese life still revolves around the family, even in the rapidly developing big cities. Modern Vietnamese society, like 1950s America, asks young people to study hard, complete a university degree, and then, as soon as possible, start a family. Children are often over-indulged, and older people are shown respect in a way that's not seen as often in Western society today.

A two-child policy exists in Vietnam. Enforcement is not as harsh as in China, but employees of state-owned enterprises who have a third or subsequent child are fined for their fertility, usually in the form of losing monthly bonuses and being denied promotions. Children are considered a blessing, sons more so than daughters because sons can carry on the family name through their children. (Vietnamese wives don't assume their husband's family name.) The eldest son is responsible for caring for his parents later in life, although often all the children contribute financially to the care of their parents. Most people still follow the tradition of expecting a new bride to move into her husband's family home after marriage, even nowadays with an estimated 70% of women of working age in paid employment.

If you're traveling with kids, expect them to be fussed over and touched (cheek pinches are common). If you're of grandparenting age, expect to be shown solicitous and attentive respect, and to be applauded for being healthy and wealthy enough to travel. However, if you are a childless or single woman of a certain age, you may be asked about your "bad luck."

The importance of family is illustrated by the mass migration of the population at Tet, the lunar new year. Everyone returns home for this important once-a-year national vacation, leaving the cities more or less deserted and transport systems gridlocked. It's also evident from the practice of ancestor worship, which is still widespread regardless of religion.

TRAFFIC GRIDLOCK

First-time visitors to Vietnam, who usually arrive in densely populated Hanoi or Ho Chi Minh City, are justifiably terrified by the traffic: the sheer volume of motorbikes and the seeming lack of any road rules whatsoever inevitably creates a first impression of utter chaos. This is only reinforced upon observing trucks and buses hurtling along poorly maintained highways, with their drivers leaning heavily on their horns to clear a path through the throngs of motorbikes.

As a matter of fact, road rules do exist, though not all make sense, such as the different speed limits imposed for motorbikes, and cars and trucks. The chaos in the cities is tempered by the fact that all this traffic moves quite slowly, only partially because of the number of vehicles sharing the roads. After a time, you will realize that the relentless tooting is actually more of a friendly "coming through" or "hey, I'm right here" rather than an outburst of aggression.

Motorcycle helmets became compulsory in Vietnam in 2008, but the death toll remains high, with an estimated 30 to 40 people dying on the roads every day in car and motorcycle accidents. Although traffic police, with their beige uniforms, are a common sight in the cities, motorcyclists still flout the rules quite openly, speeding, driving the wrong way, and wobbling about in obviously drunken states. In the cities, the traffic is best navigated by taxis, which edge their way slowly through the mess with minimal damage to the occupants. The traffic is also a compelling reason to schedule some time outside of the big cities (especially Hanoi) in order to discover the other, slower pace of Vietnam.

History You Can See

Ancient Vietnam and Chinese Domination

The origins of the earliest settlers in Vietnam are mostly lost in the mists of time. The first of the Hung Kings, Hung Vuong, came to power in 2879 BC, in the northern Red River Delta, naming his kingdom Van Lang. According to legend, Hung Vuong was the eldest son of an immortal mountain fairy called Au Co, who married a dragon lord with whom she had 100 children, the Bach Viet, also known as the ancestors of the Vietnamese people. The first Hung King is credited with teaching his subjects how to grow rice. The reign of all 18 Hung Kings is known as the Hong Bang period, which lasted for about 2,500 years until 258 BC.

Around this time, the Vietnam of today was divided into three states: Van Lang in the north, the Kingdom of Champa in the center, and the Indian-influenced Cambodian Kingdom of Funan in the south. For several centuries, these states waged ongoing battles for land and power. The first of four periods of Chinese domination of northern Vietnam began in 111 BC with the Han–Nanyue War and continued for 10 centuries, introducing the Chinese language, Confucianism, and advanced agricultural techniques to the area.

During Chinese domination, Vietnam was known as Annam, then Tinh Hai. Chinese rule ended in AD 938 when provincial governor Ngo Quyen took control of the military and fended off the Chinese in the Battle of Bach Dang River. The mandarin system remained in place for 1,000 years after Vietnam became a sovereign nation.

WHAT TO SEE

The Chinese influence on Vietnam can be seen in every temple and pagoda, and in every home, where the practice of ancestor worship continues to be observed. It's also evident in art, especially the techniques used to produce ceramics, as well as the visual references to themes of Confucianism, Mahayana Buddhism, and Taoism. Few actual relics remain, as sovereign Vietnam—past and present—does not like to be reminded of its domination by its populous northern neighbor. Instead, every city and town names its streets after the national heroes who helped *repel* the Chinese, Hai Ba Trung (the two sisters Trung), and Thi Sach (one of the Trung sister's husbands). You'll see these names frequently as you travel around Vietnam. Alexandre de Rhodes and Han Thuyen are also honored with street names in Ho Chi Minh City.

The Lost Kingdom of Champa

Little is known of the Cham, a powerful maritime empire that ruled the central and southern lowlands of Vietnam for more than 900 years, leaving behind exquisite temple complexes and fanciful Hindu sculptures. Like the Funan Kingdom, the Kingdom of Champa was based on strong trade links with India. The Cham culture adopted Indianized art forms and architectural styles as well as written Sanskrit. From AD 2nd to the 13th century, Amaravati, now known as Quang Nam province in central Vietnam, was the capital of the Kingdom of Champa, with the city of Lam Ap Pho the kingdom's center for sea trade. Lam Ap Pho, later called Faifo, and now Hoi An, was a key stop on the Spice Route between the Persian Gulf and China.

WHAT TO SEE

About 50 km (31 miles) from the former Cham port of Hoi An is the most famous of all the Cham temple complexes in Vietnam, **My Son,** which predates Angkor Wat in Cambodia. It was heavily damaged by carpet bombing during the Vietnam War. **The Po Nagar Cham Towers** in Nha Trang, the **Poshanu Towers** in Phan Thiet, and the **Thap Doi Cham Towers** in Quy Nhon are also relics of the mysterious kingdom. Locals still pay their respects at the old shrines, and the sites themselves are shown the same respect as temples and pagodas (when visiting, adults should have their knees and shoulders covered). The **Danang Museum of Cham Sculpture** houses the world's largest collection of Cham artifacts and sculptures, including many representations of the Hindu *linga* and *yoni* (male and female sex organs).

Dynastic Vietnam

Ngo Quyen's military defeat of the Chinese in AD 938 marked the start of the short-lived Ngo Dynasty. The Ngo Dynasty was followed by the Dinh Dynasty, during which time the country was renamed Dai Co Viet, literally Great Viet Land. Plotting and politicking was rife during these years, as was the ever-present threat of foreign invasion, leading to the rise and fall of many ruling families, now known as the Early Le, Ly, Tran, Ho, Le, and Nguyen dynasties. The emperors of these dynasties ruled with absolute power, in charge of the judicial system and the armed forces. During this time, the rulers were expanding south, battling the Kingdom of Champa in what is now central Vietnam and the Angkor Empire of modern-day Cambodia, as well as fending off incursions from the north, including several Mongol attacks ordered by Kublai Khan. In 1802 Emperor Gia Long united the country for the first

time, named the new nation Viet Nam (Southern Viet), and designated Hue the capital. This heralded the beginning of the 143-year Nguyen Dynasty, which ended in 1947 when Emperor Tu Duc ceded administration of the country to the French. This association with the French means Vietnam's current leaders don't favorably regard the Nguyen Dynasty, even though the founder of the dynasty, Emperor Gia Long (1762–1820), is credited with being the first to unify Vietnam's north and south.

WHAT TO SEE

The Imperial capital was moved to Thang Long (Ascending Dragon), now known as **Hanoi,** in the 11th century during the Ly Dynasty. The **Imperial Citadel of Thang Long** remained the capital of Vietnam for eight centuries, and the site was opened to the public to mark Hanoi's 1,000th anniversary. Hanoi's **Temple of Literature,** built by Ly Thanh Tong, the third emperor of the Ly Dynasty, remains in excellent condition, and is one of the city's most popular sights. **Ngoc Son Temple** in the middle of Hanoi's Hoan Kiem Lake is dedicated to Tran Hung Dao, the Supreme Commander of Vietnam during the Tran Dynasty, who helped repel the Mongol hordes in the 13th century. The former capital of **Hue** is now home to the country's highest concentration of Imperial architecture, including the UNESCO-listed **Citadel** and the **royal tombs** of the Nguyen Dynasty emperors Minh Mang, Gia Long, and Tu Duc.

French Indochina

The French had a presence in Vietnam from the early 17th century, when Jesuit missionaries arrived, quickly graduating from saving souls to involving themselves in diplomacy and politics. The ruling Nguyen Dynasty attempted to expel the Catholics, and in response,

France launched a military attack on Danang in 1847. Saigon was seized two years later and by 1883 Emperor Tu Duc had signed a treaty making north and central Vietnam a French protectorate. The French colonial era was to last until 1954. During this time the French divided Vietnam into three administrative areas—Tonkin, Annam, and Cochin-China—and set about ambitiously building roads, bridges, public buildings, and the Hanoi to Saigon railway, which is still used today. In 1941, the man born Nguyen Sinh Cung but better known by his assumed name of Ho Chi Minh, returned to Vietnam after decades abroad to lead the anti-French independence movement, the Viet Minh. After the fall of France in 1940 during World War II, Vietnam was provisionally administered by the Vichy Government and later occupied briefly by Japan. With Japan's surrender, Ho Chi Minh persuaded Emperor Bao Dai to abdicate and Ho Chi Minh declared himself leader of the Independent Republic of Vietnam. However, within weeks French rule was restored. The resistance that followed World War II, with Communist China supporting the Viet Minh, is known as the First Indochina War, which lasted until 1954. The Vietnamese defeated the French at Dien Bien Phu, marking the end of the French-Indochina War. Agreement was reached among France, Britain, the United States, and the Soviet Union as part of the Geneva Accords to cease hostilities in Indochina and to divide Vietnam temporarily at the 17th parallel. Hundreds of thousands of refugees, mostly Vietnamese Catholics worried that religious tolerance will not be practiced in the Viet Minh–controlled north, fled to the south with U.S. Navy assistance.

WHAT TO SEE

Colonial architecture can be found throughout Vietnam, some dilapidated and decrepit, some beautifully maintained. In Hanoi's **French Quarter,** crumbling colonial facades line the streets between landmark colonial buildings, such as the **Metropole** and the **Opera House.** Spanning the Red River is the cantilever **Long Bien Bridge,** designed by Gustave Eiffel of Eiffel Tower fame. In Ho Chi Minh City, the former **Hotel de Ville,** the **Central Post Office**—another masterpiece by the prolific Eiffel—and the Opera House are the most prominent public buildings from the colonial era. The existence of highland towns such as **Dalat,** with its large French villas, and **Sapa** are also credited to the former French rulers, who set up hill stations there to escape the oppressive heat of the lowlands.

War with the Americans

During the Cold War, the long-running military and political standoff between the United States and the USSR, much of the foreign policy of the United States was directed by the domino theory. This was the belief that allowing one country to fall to Communism would cause a stain of red to flow across the world's geopolitical maps, and Asia would be lost to Russian domination. Despite the forces on the ground in Vietnam since 1950, in the interest of "containment," American involvement in the North-South war through 1964 mainly involved financially assisting the French and then the South Vietnamese government in their conflict with Communist North Vietnam. By December 1965, however, there were more than 184,000 U.S. troops in Vietnam, and by 1967 there were almost half a million. Extensive carpet bombing did little to impede the growth and advance of the Communist Vietcong army, and both sides continued to suffer heavy casualties over the next four years. In the West, the public began questioning U.S. involvement in the war—and the government's claim it was winning—in the wake of the 1968 Tet Offensive, when the Vietcong launched coordinated surprise attacks against U.S. troops in more than 1,000 cities and towns throughout Vietnam. Public support for the war in the United States declined further when news broke of the brutal My Lai Massacre, a mass killing of unarmed Vietnamese civilians by American troops the same year (1968). After much negotiation, the Paris Peace Accords were signed, and on January 27, 1973, a ceasefire was called and the United States withdrew, leaving a skeleton ground crew to advise the South Vietnamese Army. On April 30, 1975, Vietnam was "liberated" when North Vietnamese tanks crashed through the Independence Palace in Saigon, marking the end of the war.

WHAT TO SEE

The tanks that remain guarding the front of the **Reunification Palace** in Ho Chi Minh City are perhaps the starkest reminder of the victory of the north over the south. Evidence of the brutalities of the last war abound at the various museums throughout the country, including Ho Chi Minh City's grueling **War Remnants Museum,** Hanoi's **Military History Museum,** the **Ho Chi Minh Museum,** and the **Son My Memorial,** 8 km (5 miles) from Quang Ngai city. You can also explore the **Cu Chi Tunnels,** the extensive network of underground tunnels used by the Vietcong just outside Ho Chi Minh City, as well as the horrific prisons used by the South Vietnamese government, including the infamous **tiger cages,** on Con Dao Islands.

REUNIFICATION AND AFTERWARD

A decade of brutal Communist rule followed the "liberation" of South Vietnam in 1975, with harsh reprisals for those linked to the southern government and military. The reprisals, the reeducation camps, and the grinding poverty of this period led to a mass exodus from South Vietnam, with an estimated 2 million people leaving the country. The so-called boat people who survived their sea journey, and the other Vietnamese refugees, settled in America, Australia, Canada, the United Kingdom, Germany, and France. Many used their culinary skills to support themselves with family-run restaurants. The tense relationship between the United States and Vietnam eased over the years, especially after Vietnam began moving toward a more open economy. In 1994 the United States lifted the trade embargo on Vietnam and a year later the two countries normalized relations. Vietnam's ascension to the World Trade Organization in 2006 further opened the doors to foreign investment and contributed to the resurgence of Vietnam's economy. Vietnam's move toward a market economy and the resumption of commercial flights between the two countries in 2004 also seemed to be the catalyst for many overseas Vietnamese, known as Viet Kieu, to return to Vietnam.

WHAT TO SEE

The gleaming skyscrapers in Hanoi, Danang, and Ho Chi Minh City, including the 68-story **Bitexco Financial Tower,** signify Vietnam's heady postwar rush toward capitalism. One of the most noticeable signs of international investment can be seen in the **food and retail landscape,** with foreign brands increasingly visible.

People of Vietnam

Visit any of the hill tribes and the variety of different ethnicities and cultures that make up Vietnam becomes readily apparent. The country has 54 ethnic groups recognized by the government, from the majority Kinh—who make up more than 85% of the population—to the tiny Brau group, who are believed to number fewer than 300.

The Kinh tend to live in urban areas and, socioeconomically, are at the top. The ethnic minority groups, however—especially the smallest—face a number of problems. These include lack of access to adequate education, health care, and public services. Without education, these groups—in particular those living in remote, mountainous regions with agrarian economies—are unable to acquire knowledge and increase production. Though there are government programs aimed at improving the lives of Vietnam's rural minorities, they are not very effective, and many live below the poverty line. For some ethnic minority groups, such as those in the hill tribes around Sapa, tourism has provided a major boon to the economy.

Many travelers in Vietnam make time for a motorbike trip into the mountains to visit local villages and get a glimpse of ethnic life. If you can't make it to the hill-tribe villages, the next best thing is a visit to Vietnam Museum of Ethnology in Hanoi. The fantastic exhibits showcase more than 15,000 artifacts, including photographs and objects including costumes, musical instruments, weapons, and hunting implements. On the museum's grounds are reconstructed homes from a dozen ethnic groups that visitors are welcome to explore. What follows is an overview of some of the groups you may see on your travels.

Kinh (Population: about 85,000,000) The Kinh originated from what is now southern China and northern Vietnam, and the Kinh living over the border in China are known as the Gin. The group originally settled in the deltas and coastal regions, both working in agriculture and eventually moving into industry. Today the highest concentrations of Kinh are in Ho Chi Minh City and Hanoi. You're unlikely to be able to recognize any Kinh by their outfits as they live in urban centers and dress just as in the West. Vietnam's majority ethnic group speaks standard Vietnamese.

Tay (Population: about 1,900,000) The country's second largest ethnic group makes up just 2% of the population. The Tay tend to live in Quang Ninh province, home to Halong Bay, and in Sapa, in Lao Cai province. Traditionally, the Tay society was an agrarian one, with most Tay living in fertile areas and growing rice and corn. Today, many Tay have intermarried and live in ethnically mixed villages or in towns. The group speaks Tay, a Tai language that includes standard Thai and Laotian. Traditional clothing is made from homegrown cotton, dyed with indigo, and usually without embroidery or embellishments. Women wear skirts or trousers.

Muong (Population: about 1,400,000) It's believed that the Muong are the most closely related to the ethnic Vietnamese (Kinh). They reside in northern Vietnam's mountainous regions, in Hoa Binh and Thanh Hoa provinces. Far from the Chinese border and high in the mountains, the Muong were not influenced by the Chinese as other ethnic minority groups were. The economy is agrarian and the Muong attend markets and trade goods. The group speaks Muong, closely related to Vietnamese. Women generally wear a plain white fabric headscarf, short blouses, usually with small side slits, ankle-length skirts with an embroidered floral border, and silver key chains hanging from the waist.

Khmer Krom (Population: 1,200,000) These are the indigenous Khmer (present day Cambodians) who live along the southern Mekong Delta. The group takes its name from the Khmer word "krom," which means "below," implying south of Cambodia. The area where the Khmer Krom live is not technically a disputed territory—it's considered Vietnam—but there are associations of exiled Khmer Krom who want self-determination for the Khmer Krom in Vietnam. The clothing worn in public by most Khmer Krom is unlikely to give them away; women are usually in a simple blouse and *sampot* (a long rectangular cloth worn as a skirt) and men wear shirts tucked into sarongs. Some Khmer Krom dress in Western clothing. Many practice Theravada Buddhism. They speak Vietnamese and Khmer, which differ from neighboring languages in that they aren't tonal.

Hmong (Population: about 1,100,000) The Hmong group, also known as the Mong, live in the northern mountainous regions of Thailand, Vietnam, and Laos, and over the border in southern China, where the government has lumped them into the larger Miao ethnic group. Within Vietnam, the Hmong have several subgroups, including the Red, White, Flower, Striped, Green, and Black Hmong. The Hmong economy was traditionally agrarian, but an influx of tourists into places like Sapa has helped jumpstart tourism. The Hmong wear and produce beautiful textiles with intricate embroidery. In their colorful embroidered skirts and jackets, the Flower Hmong women are the most recognizable. Other Hmong generally wear black skirts or trousers, a black jacket with colorful trim, and sometimes a peaked black turban. Depending on the group, the outfit is accessorized with an embroidered belt or waistband. At Sapa Market, dozens of Hmong women gather to sell jewelry, handicrafts, and textiles. In doing so, they've changed the traditional Hmong family structure; no longer is the man the head of every household. The Hmong/Mong speak Hmong.

Gia Rai (Population: about 500,000) This group, also known as the Jarai, lives primarily in Vietnam's Central Highlands (a few thousand live in Cambodia). The Gia Rai culture is matrilineal. It is an agricultural society, and the Gia Rai grow crops and raise pigs, chicken, buffaloes, oxen, and horses. Cloth and basket weaving are popular, and back baskets are often used to transport loads. The Gia Rai were originally animists (those who believe nonhuman entities have spirits), but visits by American missionaries have resulted in several thousand converts to Christianity. The Gia Rai speak Gia Rai, a Malayo-Polynesian language, as well as Vietnamese. Gia Rai men wear white or striped loin clothes (*toai*) and sometimes a short black jacket. Women dress in long indigo sarongs with designs on the hem and a long-sleeve black top with colorful sleeves.

Cham (Population: about 170,000) When the Ancient Kingdom of Champa was annexed by Vietnam, many Cham fled to present-day Hainan (China), Trengganu (Malaysia), and south to Cambodia. Today, the Cham in Vietnam live in the central part of the country, including in Ho Chi Minh City. Many are Hindu (compared to the Muslim Cham in Cambodia). In Vietnam, the group speaks Cham and Vietnamese. Most Cham living in urban centers dress in mostly Western clothing. Those who live in more rural areas wear a sarong, with men wearing a shirt on top and women wearing a form-fitting blouse. Both sexes use turbans or head wraps.

What to Watch and Read

RECOMMENDED READING
Historical texts on Vietnam War

Some of the most comprehensive histories of the Vietnam War are David Halberstam's *The Best and the Brightest,* Stanley Karnow's *Vietnam: A History,* Neil Sheehan's *A Bright Shining Lie,* and George C. Herring's *America's Longest War: The United States and Vietnam, 1950–1975.*

Frances FitzGerald's *Fire in the Lake* provides histories of the war from both the American and Vietnamese perspectives. Other insightful accounts of the war include Michael Herr's *Dispatches* and Nayan Chanda's *Brother Enemy: The War After the War,* which looks at the close of the Vietnam War and Vietnam's emerging conflicts with both Cambodia and China throughout the 1980s.

Novels and short fiction on Vietnam War

Several moving personal narratives (some fictionalized) have been written about the war, including *A Rumor of War* by Philip Caputo, *In Pharaoh's Army* by Tobias Wolff, *Fields of Fire* by James Webb, *Chickenhawk* by Robert Mason, and *The Things They Carried* by Tim O'Brien. A more recent account of the war is Karl Marlantes epic novel *Matterhorn,* which took the Oregon writer almost 35 years to write. For an altogether lighter read Ed Gaydos, who recounts his tour of duty in Vietnam in his memoirs *Seven in a Jeep,* injecting a good dose of humor and intelligence into otherwise intolerable conditions.

Tom Mangold's *The Tunnels of Cu Chi* describes the Vietcong movement based in the tunnels around Cu Chi. Michael Lanning's *Inside the VC* and the NVA examines the workings of the North Vietnamese army and the Vietcong. *When Heaven and Earth Changed Places* is Le Ly Hayslip's story of her life before, during, and after the Vietnam War.

In Robert Olen Butler's collection, *A Good Scent from a Strange Mountain,* each story is told by a Vietnamese immigrant in New Orleans, which gives provides a look at the war's aftermath from a non-American point of view, something that's not all that common in English language writing about the period. Tatjana Soli's penetrating novel *The Lotus Eaters* tells of an American war photojournalist involved in a love triangle as the fall of Saigon plays out. Meanwhile, the very 21st-century tragicomedy, *The Sympathizer,* by Viet Thanh Nguyen, uses the voice of a Vietnamese undercover agent to present a stark view of the end of the war and what followed.

Texts on present-day Vietnam

To learn more about contemporary Vietnam read Henry Kamm's *Dragon Ascending: Vietnam and the Vietnamese* and Justin Wintle's *Romancing Vietnam,* which depicts his fascinating experiences as one of the first writers to travel the country north to south after Vietnam first opened its doors to tourism. Look for an account of traveling through Vietnam by train in Paul Theroux's *The Great Railway Bazaar.* For a sense of Vietnam before you go, Walter Mason's *Destination Saigon* is a sometimes-funny tale of his travel experiences and people he met along the way. Andrew X. Pham's *Catfish and Mandala* is the Vietnamese American author's exploration of his roots, on a bicycle. If you're looking for a good insight into the street food culture of Vietnam, Tracey Lister and Andreas Pohl's *Vietnamese Street Food* takes readers on a colorful journey (with recipes) across a country obsessed with food. Included are a few helpful pointers on where you'll get the best pho.

For an intimate, visual rendering of the people and places of this beautiful and historical country, look to *Vietnam: Portraits and Landscapes,* featuring the stunning photography of Peter Steinhauer or *Passage to Vietnam: Through the Eyes of Seventy Photographers.* For images of the war, look for *Requiem,* a moving collection of war pictures by photographers who died at work in Indochina between 1954 and 1989.

FILMS
Films set in Vietnam

The Lover (1991), a Jean-Jacques Annaud film based on the Marguerite Duras novel, is the tale of a young French woman coming of age in colonial Vietnam and her relationship with her Chinese lover. Régis Wargnier's *Indochine* (1992), starring Catherine Deneuve, is another film set in Vietnam during the French colonial era; it showcases the beautiful scenery of North Vietnam and is credited for putting Halong Bay on the map. Graham Greene's 1955 antiwar novel *The Quiet American* yielded two movie adaptations of the same name. The 1958 film eschews Greene's antiwar message, while the 2002 remake by Phillip Noyce is more faithful to its source material. *Apocalypse Now* (1979) is Francis Ford Coppola's powerful look at the Vietnam War based on Joseph Conrad's *Heart of Darkness*; it stars Martin Sheen, Marlon Brando, and Dennis Hopper. Oliver Stone's *Platoon* (1986), with Tom Berenger, Willem Dafoe, and Charlie Sheen, is a harrowing, first-person tale of a young soldier's experience in the war. *The Deer Hunter* (1978) is a Michael Cimino film about three steelworkers from Pennsylvania who go off to fight in Vietnam; it stars Robert De Niro, John Savage, Meryl Streep, and Christopher Walken. Stanley Kubrick's *Full Metal Jacket* (1987) takes an unblinking look at the realities of the Vietnam War from the perspective of a U.S. army journalist. In Randall Wallace's *We Were Soldiers* (2002), Mel Gibson plays a colonel leading his soldiers in the first major, and bloody, battle of the Vietnam War.

Documentaries

Ken Burns's 18-hour documentary *The Vietnam War* is disturbing and compelling, with powerful first-person interviews. For an inside look at the making of *Apocalypse Now,* see the documentary *Hearts of Darkness: A Filmmaker's Apocalypse* (1991). Bill Couturié, in his documentary about the Vietnam War, *Dear America: Letters Home from Vietnam* (1987), uses newsreels, amateur footage, and letters read by Robert De Niro, Sean Penn, and others to portray soldiers' experiences.

Vietnamese films

Nhat Minh Dang's *When the Tenth Month Comes* (1984) documents the struggle of ordinary Vietnamese villagers in the years after the war. It focuses on a young mother's grief and guilt after her husband was killed during the fighting, and the difficulties of coping with loss. Following the story of Vietnam's boat people, Ham Tran's *Journey From The Fall* (2009) is an inspirational true story of one Vietnamese family's successful resettlement in the United States. Contemporary French-Vietnamese filmmaker Tran Anh Hung's beautifully filmed *The Scent of Green Papaya* (1993) follows the life of a young female servant in Saigon. Tran Anh Hung's *Cyclo* (1995) portrays the rough and violent life of a bicycle-taxi driver who is inducted into the mafia-world of postwar Saigon.

Chapter 2

TRAVEL SMART

Updated by
Shannon Brown

★ **CAPITAL:**
Hanoi

👥 **POPULATION:**
98,063,729

$ **CURRENCY:**
dong

$ **MONEY:**
ATMs common in cities; cash more common than credit.

💬 **LANGUAGE:**
Vietnamese

📠 **COUNTRY CODE:**
84

⚠ **EMERGENCIES:**
113 (Police), 114 (Fire), 115 (Ambulance)

🚗 **DRIVING:**
On the right

⚡ **ELECTRICITY:**
220v/50 cycles

🕐 **TIME:**
12 hours ahead of New York

✈ **MAJOR AIRPORTS:**
SGN, HAN, DAD, PQC

🌐 **WEBSITES:**
vietnam.travel

Know Before You Go

Do I need vaccines before my trip? Is it safe there? Do I need to carry cash? You may have a few questions before you head out on vacation to Vietnam. We've got answers and a few tips to help you make the most of your trip.

ENGLISH ISN'T ALWAYS SPOKEN

While English proficiency throughout Vietnam is low, and few foreigners visiting Vietnam speak Vietnamese, it is surprisingly easy to get around. English-speakers are most prevalent in Ho Chi Minh City and Hanoi, where the urban population is highly educated. Nearly all teenagers and university-aged people speak some English, and they're often happy to help. When in doubt, write it out: some locals can read English much better than they can speak it. For places that are on the tourist circuit, from Sapa in the north, to Phu Quoc in the south, vendors are used to speaking basic English. In places that see crowds of visitors, such as the big cities and Hoi An, even some taxi drivers understand simple English directions (left, right, stop). If you can't find anyone on the street, duck into a hotel catering to Westerners and you'll find staff members who know the area and tend to speak better-than-average English.

THE CONCEPT OF "FACE" IS IMPORTANT

Just as in other Asian countries, the concept of "face" is very important. You can give face, lose face, and help others save face. As face can be a tricky concept for foreigners, the safest way to give it is to compliment someone's family or their business acumen. When meeting people, you can shake hands as is done in the West, but locals may do so with both hands, and bow slightly as a sign of respect—especially if you're meeting someone elderly. When doing business it is polite to exchange business cards; do so with both hands. At religious sites, cover your shoulders and knees. Be sure not to raise your voice or gesture obscenely at staff; if you cause a scene or harass women, you may be asked to leave the premises.

VIOLENT CRIME IS RARE

Violent crime against tourists is extremely rare. Women traveling alone in Vietnam are unlikely to face any harassment. Most common is petty crime—pickpocketing, bag snatching, and scamming. A common scam is cab drivers telling new arrivals that the hotel they've booked is closed. They'll then drive to a hotel that will pay them commission. Insist on being taken to the hotel you've booked and make sure the meter is on. Beyond scams, the major safety hazard is Vietnam's chaotic traffic. Many intersections have no traffic lights; even if they do, the flow of traffic won't stop even though the light has changed. The safest way to cross the street is to latch on to locals; follow them closely and you'll get across safely.

GET YOUR VACCINES

All travelers should have routine vaccines up-to-date (these include MMR, diphtheria-tetanus-pertussis). Hepatitis A and typhoid can be contracted through contaminated food and water, so it's a good idea to get vaccinated for both; you shouldn't let this stop you from eating street food, but stick to bottled water. Hepatitis A vaccine is given in two doses six months apart. If you don't have time to get both doses, the Immunization Action Coalition says it's still well worth it to get just the first dose. The typhoid vaccine is 50%–80% effective and can be taken orally. The risk of malaria is low, but if you're planning to spend extensive time in rural areas and sleeping outdoors without a mosquito net, you should consult your doctor about taking malaria medication. Be vigilant with good quality bug spray to prevent bites. It's also a good idea to make sure your rabies and COVID vaccinations are up-to-date.

HEED THESE SIGHTSEEING TIPS

Always dress respectfully and cover shoulders and knees when visiting a place of worship. When entering temples and pagodas, remove your footwear. On the beach, bikinis and swimwear are perfectly acceptable but, for women, going topless is illegal. When traveling to and from the beach, always cover up. Begging is rare in Vietnam, though it's not unusual to be approached by children selling trinkets, and it's best not to encourage them by buying anything. The money will not go toward their education—the more money they make, the less time they'll spend in school.

SOME PLACES HAVE CURFEWS

Vietnam is a place where the sun rises at 6 am and sets at 6 pm year-round, which leads to a pretty predictable schedule for residents. Even in the cities, most restaurants and businesses close early and people turn in around 11 pm. In Hanoi, many bars and clubs operate with an official midnight closing time. Some smaller hotels and guesthouses close early as well—check with your front desk about the procedure if you'll be arriving very late in the evening or early in the morning.

PACK FOR THE REGION AND THE WEATHER

Vietnam is a tremendously long country with varied temperatures from the north to the south. Many people only pack for one season, and end up needing to buy more clothes if they travel through the entire country. Do your research on the average temperatures for the time you are visiting. One thing you don't need to pack are ponchos: the full-body hooded canvas ones that are sold inside Vietnam are spectacular and cost around $20 at roadside stands.

VEGETARIAN FOOD IS READILY AVAILABLE

Around 16% of the Vietnamese population identifies as Buddhist, with 10% following a vegan diet. The words *ăn chay* (ahn chai) mean vegan, and there are several restaurants in Hanoi and Ho Chi Minh City that cater to the meat-free. Cooking classes in Ho Chi Minh City and Hanoi are generally able to adjust their recipes if you are a vegetarian, and there are also stellar Indian restaurants in most major cities with plentiful options.

CASH IS KING

Most places in Vietnam are still cash only. You will want to have cash on hand for any excursions, especially if you are leaving the major cities, as ATMs are much harder to find in smaller areas. Vietnamese dong comes in plastic-covered bills of 500,000, 200,000, 100,000, 50,000, 20,000, and 10,000, and paper bills of 5,000, 2,000, and 1,000. Keep a note with the exchange rate of these bills in your pocket or on your phone.

WI-FI IS FAST AND RELIABLE

Almost all hotels and hostels provide very good Internet—even homestays in out-of-the-way Mai Chau have a great connection. The only places you may not be able to connect are on cruises in Halong Bay and treks in Sapa. If you're looking to work, large coffee shops and co-working spaces with high-speed Wi-Fi are common in most cities.

BE PREPARED TO PART WITH YOUR PASSPORT

Per Vietnamese law, your hotel will most likely ask to hold onto your passport. Politely insist that it be kept in a safe. Before you go, make several photocopies—if you rent a motorbike, take a bus or a train, or buy anything that needs to be shipped, these will come in handy.

VIETNAM'S RESPONSE TO COVID-19

In early 2020, Vietnam suspended all tourism and enacted mandatory government quarantines for any exposures to the coronavirus, while rolling out a highly effective contract tracing system. In 2021, Vietnam ranked 2nd in the world in successfully handling the pandemic, with the fewest number of deaths in Asia. However, by mid 2021 a wave of the virus brought more intense lockdowns. The effects of the pandemic on the tourism and hospitality industries are yet to be fully understood, but Vietnam's resilience will likely lend in their economic recovery.

Getting Here and Around

Vietnam is a narrow, S-shape country stretching more than 1,600 km (1,000 miles) from north to south and with nearly 3,200 km (2,000 miles) of coastline. Most visitors fly into Hanoi (in the north) or Ho Chi Minh City (in the south), which are separated by a 2-hour flight or a roughly 30-hour train ride. For some shorter trips out of major cities or towns, the best option is to take a train, but in many cases buses are the ideal form of transport.

Motorcycles and bicycles can be rented, but are not recommended for city travel—all of Vietnam's cities are notorious for their chaotic traffic. There are several options for getting around town, and although taxis are slightly more expensive, they are generally the safest and most efficient way to get from A to B. Taxi scams are not uncommon, but can usually be avoided by only riding with a trusted taxi company—Vinasun and Mai Linh are two of the country's more reputable companies. You can also download the Grab or Uber app on your phone, but be prepared to still pay the fare in cash. You may also need to direct your driver using Google Maps.

Addresses in Vietnam often contain words such as *huyen* (district), *duong* (road), or *pho* (street). Odd and even numbered addresses are usually on opposite sides of the street. Sometimes one address will be broken into several units (A, B, C, etc.).

Traveling during Tet, the Vietnamese New Year, means paying premium prices and should be booked as far in advance as possible. Public transportation like buses and trains are best avoided at this time as prices double and overcrowding is a problem; it's not unusual for a bus driver to pick up extra passengers and luggage along the way and delays are frequent.

✈ Air

International flights into Vietnam typically connect through hubs such as Bangkok, Singapore, Jakarta, Hong Kong, Kuala Lumpur, Phnom Penh, Siem Reap, Beijing, Seoul, Osaka, Tokyo, Dubai, Melbourne, Sydney, and Taipei and fly into Ho Chi Minh City and Hanoi. It's also possible to fly into the international airport in Danang, in central Vietnam, via Kuala Lumpur, Tokyo, Hong Kong, and Seoul. Vietnam Airlines is expected to offer direct flights between Vietnam and the U.S. by 2022. Otherwise, there are no direct flights between the U.S. and Vietnam. Hanoi and Ho Chi Minh City are the main hubs for direct flights to Vietnam from the United Kingdom.

Be aware that two airlines may jointly operate a connecting flight from an Asian hub, so ask if your airline operates every segment of your flight—you may find that your preferred carrier flies only part of the way. For instance, if you purchased a ticket through an international carrier such as Air France, Cathay Pacific, Delta, Japan Airlines, or Thai International Airways but are not flying directly to Hanoi or Ho Chi Minh City, it is possible that your connecting flight into Vietnam will be on Vietnam Airlines.

Some layovers require an overnight stay in a connecting city. Before buying your ticket, check to see who covers the cost of the hotel—you or the airline—if you have to stay overnight.

AIRPORTS

The major gateways to Vietnam are Hanoi's Noi Bai Airport (HAN), 44 km (28 miles) north of the city, Ho Chi Minh City's Tan Son Nhat Airport (SGN), 7 km (4 miles) from the center, and to a lesser extent Danang International Airport (DAD), 5 km (3 miles) from the center. As the main gateways for thousands of international visitors, Ho Chi Minh City and Hanoi airports have procedures that can involve more in-depth immigration checks and baggage searches, should customs officials have any cause for suspicion. If you have arranged for a visa on arrival (VOA) waiting times can be long, so allow for at least an hour prior to check-in if you have a connecting flight, and make sure all the required paperwork, photographs, and visa fee are easily accessible to avoid delays. If you have obtained your Vietnam visa in advance, you are more than likely to get through immigration, pick up your waiting bags, and breeze through customs quite quickly. All the international airports have free Wi-Fi and snack bars. For domestic air travel, major transportation hubs are Ho Chi Minh City, Hanoi, and Danang, but there is also service to Buon Ma Thuot (BMV), Ca Mau (CAH), Can Tho (VCA), Con Dao (VCS), Dalat (DLI), Dien Bien Phu (DIN), Dong Hoi (VDH), Haiphong (HPH), Hue (HUI), Nha Trang (CXR), Phu Quoc Island (PQC), Pleiku (PXU), Quy Nhon (UIH), Rach Gia (VKG), Tam Ky (VCL), Tuy Hoa (TBB), and Vinh (VII).

GROUND TRANSPORTATION

Airports in Vietnam are relatively small and easy to navigate, both Hanoi and Ho Chi Minh airports have two terminals, one for domestic and one for international arrivals and departures. For international passengers landing in Ho Chi Minh City, a short, shady walkway is provided between the domestic and international terminals. At Hanoi's Noi Bai airport a free shuttle bus runs every 10 minutes to ferry passengers between terminals; once you have cleared immigration and collected your baggage head for the shuttle bus station outside the terminal lobby, making sure you have proof of onward travel ready to present to staff. The short transfer takes approximately five minutes. Figuring out how to get into Hanoi or Ho Chi Minh City from the airport can be a little overwhelming when you first arrive. There are a few options: the easiest is to either have your hotel or tour company arrange to pick you up, but it's much more expensive than a taxi. If opting for a taxi, go to the taxi desk just inside the exit doors at either airport. Always ask your driver to turn on the meter rather than agreeing to a set fare, which tend to be set in the driver's favor, and have your hotel's name, address, and telephone number written down to present to your driver.

INTERNATIONAL FLIGHTS

For most international visitors, flying to Vietnam usually entails a nondirect flight, with popular layovers for U.S. travelers flying Delta, American Airlines, Cathay Pacific, Emirates, or Air Canada being either Bangkok, Tokyo, or Hong Kong. From the United Kingdom, Vietnam Airlines is the only carrier offering direct flights into the country. Nondirect flights with major carriers Emirates, Air France, and Malaysia Airlines are often serviced by two different airlines; flights connect from Paris, Doha, Bangkok, or Kuala Lumpur, before flying into Vietnam's Ho Chi Minh City, Hanoi, or, to a lesser extent, Danang. Silk Air and Vietnam Airlines offer daily services from Danang, Ho Chi Minh City, and Hanoi to several cities in Cambodia.

AIR TRAVEL WITHIN VIETNAM

The main operator for domestic routes in Vietnam is Vietnam Airlines, which offers the most reliable service. Its smaller competitors, Jetstar Pacific (owned jointly by Vietnam Airlines and Quantas) and the privately owned VietJet Air, service fewer aircraft and despite being slightly cheaper, tend to suffer the most delays and cancellations. Flights are short and very reasonably priced; when booked in advance the two-hour trip between Hanoi and Ho Chi Minh City can cost as little as $50.

Getting Here and Around

FLYING TIMES

There are no direct flights to Vietnam from the United States. Flying time to the Southeast Asian hub of Hong Kong is approximately 15½ hours from Los Angeles, 16 hours from Chicago, and 16 hours from New York; the onward flight to Ho Chi Minh City takes just under 3 hours. Flying direct to Ho Chi Minh City from London takes 12 hours and from Sydney it's about 8 hours.

Travel Times from Hanoi	By Air	By Train
Ho Chi Minh City	2 hours	34 hours
Dong Hoi	1½ hours	9–10 hours
Hue	1 hour	12 hours
Danang	1½ hours	14 hours
Nha Trang	1¾ hours	23 hours
Siem Reap Cambodia	1¾ hours	N/A

⛴ Boat

Traveling by boat in Vietnam is generally reserved for those who want to explore the Mekong Delta, Halong Bay, or the Perfume River. The slow pace, limited routes, and high costs make it not the most expedient way to get from point A to B. For many riverside or seaside towns in Vietnam, boat rides are a natural attraction, and a great way to get a view of life on, in, or near the water. In northern Vietnam and in the Mekong Delta, ferries are often the only way to get to destinations where bridges have not yet been built or have been destroyed, or to get to islands such as Cat Ba. Bicycles and motor vehicles can usually be brought on board for a fee.

Speedboats that make sea crossings to the islands are notoriously unsafe. Designed for use on rivers, they are often not seaworthy when the water gets choppy, and the companies that run them tend to take too many passengers. Do some research and make sure you book with a reputable company, or opt for a slower trip on a large dive boat or local supply boat. Life jackets are a legal requirement on all boats; if you are told you can take it off once the boat has passed the checkpoint, you have chosen the wrong company. Ignore them, and keep the jacket on throughout the crossing.

For travel between Cambodia and Vietnam, there's a speedboat service to Phnom Penh from Chau Doc (a 3–4 hour bus journey from Ho Chi Minh City). Although very few companies service this 5-hour transfer, one reputable company that does is Blue Cruiser. Tickets can be arranged at any of the tour offices in the main backpacker district (Pham Ngu Lao) in Ho Chi Minh City or online. Boats depart daily at 7 am and at 1:30 pm. You must arrange your visa beforehand.

📍 Border Crossings

Air travel is the recommended way to go between Vietnam and other points in Asia. Most travelers must obtain a visa to visit the countries near Vietnam—Laos, Cambodia, and China—which can be a difficult process; it's best to make visa arrangements before you go to Vietnam. Many countries, including China and Cambodia, offer e-visa services, though the process still takes several days. Cambodia and Laos currently provide visas on arrival at international airports (with a photo), but this is subject to change; inquire at these countries' embassies for the most up-to-date policies. In general, Thailand automatically grants short-term-stay visas to most Western visitors. Note also that tourist visas can be arranged quickly for most Asian countries from their respective embassies in Bangkok.

⊖ Bus

Air-conditioned buses catering to travelers can be a good option for long-distance travel in Vietnam. "Open tour" bus tickets allow you to make stops along the way and there are options for sleeper buses, which have reclining seats. For about $60, you can purchase an open ticket from Hanoi to Ho Chi Minh City with four stops at destinations in between. About a dozen tour operators offer bus service; reputable ones include Mai Linh and Phuong Trang. It's a good idea to book at least a day in advance (earlier if it happens to be a national holiday). One of the biggest conveniences of bus travel is that many companies offer the option of hotel pickup.

⊖ Car

Despite changes in Vietnam's traffic laws and a new law that recognizes international drivers' licenses, it's nearly impossible—and not recommended due to the hazard of locals driving dangerously—to rent a car without a driver. Many foreigners do drive motorbikes, though.

CAR RENTAL
Before 2015, tourists were not permitted to drive in Vietnam at all. Now, although international drivers' permits are accepted, the fact that the driver must have local insurance makes doing so virtually impossible.

It is, however, possible to rent a car with a driver. Cars and minivans with drivers are readily available from private and state-run travel agencies, tourist offices, and through most hotels in bigger cities. You are charged by the kilometer, by the day, or both. A daily rate runs about $100 per day, depending on a number of criteria: the city in which you rent the vehicle; whether it has air-conditioning; the make of the car; and your bargaining skills. The agreed price should include gas and tolls, but clarify all this before you set off. Travel agencies can also arrange for English-speaking guides to accompany you and the driver. For overnight trips you're generally responsible for the driver's lodging costs as well, which may or may not be included in the quoted price; make sure to clarify this up front.

Note that most rental cars lack seat belts and the provision of child seats is unusual. You should negotiate a price in advance and check out the vehicle before you rent it.

EMERGENCY SERVICES
If you have hired a car and driver and the car breaks down, you should not be held responsible for the cost of repairs. Make sure everyone is clear about this before you embark on a long journey. There are mechanics on virtually every block in the cities.

In case of a traffic accident, remember that the foreigner is always at fault. So, in minor accidents, even if you've done nothing wrong it's a good idea to stay in the car and let your driver do the talking or to try to get out of the situation as quickly as possible without involving the police. Even if the case seems crystal clear, you'll likely be fighting a losing battle and will probably be asked to pay

Getting Here and Around

damages immediately even if you are not to blame. Many of Vietnam's civil laws provide for the underprivileged, and as a foreigner you are automatically considered privileged.

PARKING

Any traveling by car you do will be with a hired driver, so they will be the one responsible for finding adequate parking. On many streets in Ho Chi Minh City and Hanoi it is illegal to leave an unattended car; the streets are simply too narrow or crowded. Instead, cars—and motorbikes and bicycles—are often parked in guarded lots, driveways, or even on roped-off pieces of sidewalk. A few streets have marked automobile parking, and some of the newer high-rises in Ho Chi Minh City and Hanoi have underground or elevated garages. In most small towns and at the entrance to beaches, private home owners and parking attendants will offer to look after bicycles and motorbikes for no more than 5,000d. These are the safest places to park bicycles and motorbikes and will prevent your bike or helmet from being stolen, or being removed by the police for parking illegally. At night always check what time the attendant's shift ends—if your bike is still there, he will most likely take it home for safe keeping overnight. If this happens you'll need to make other arrangements to get back to your hotel and return in the morning to be reunited with the bike.

ROAD CONDITIONS

Highways are the main transportation route for cars, public buses, trucks, tractors, motorbikes, bicycles, pedestrians, oxcarts, and a host of farm animals. Highway 1 is the primary north–south commercial route and is the backbone of Vietnam's road system. It has been upgraded along its entire length, which extends from near the Chinese border, north of Hanoi, through Ho Chi Minh City and to the heart of the Mekong Delta in the south.

Vietnam's major roads are for the most part paved and well-maintained but flooded during monsoon season. Road conditions in the north are worse than in the south, where the U.S. war effort built or paved many of the roads. Most dirt roads turn to mud during the rainy season and become impassable. Despite some stretches of highways having speed limits up to 100 kph (60 mph), road transportation is very slow in Vietnam. When working out approximate journey times by bus or car a more realistic average speed to work from is approximately 30 kph (20 mph).

When driving (or, more likely, being driven) around the country, try to travel during the day and be extra vigilant during rush hour—around 8 am and from 4 pm—when traffic is at its heaviest. Driving at night can be hazardous because many vehicles either don't have lights or drive with their high beams on at all times, and it is difficult to see bad spots in the road.

Driving in Ho Chi Minh and Hanoi should be left to the experts.

ROADSIDE EMERGENCIES

There is no motoring organization to provide emergency assistance in Vietnam. If you have a problem on the road and are driving a rented vehicle, call the rental company for help. Otherwise, phone the police emergency number: . Try to enlist the services of someone who speaks Vietnamese to tell the police where you are and the nature of your problem.

RULES OF THE ROAD

Considering that Vietnam's streets are a frenzy of motorists, bicyclists, motorcyclists, and pedestrians, it's no surprise that the country's traffic fatalities per capita are among the highest in the world. There seems to be a vague understanding among riders, drivers, and pedestrians that they're all in it together. But this doesn't make the streets much safer. Traffic police are treated with contempt, pedestrians seem oblivious to the flow—and danger—of vehicles, late-night construction workers play cards in the intersections, and children have been known to dart into streets without warning.

Though traffic lights are all over Hanoi and Ho Chi Minh City, you shouldn't put too much faith in them; red lights are often ignored, especially at night and especially in Hanoi. Right turns on red are forbidden, although you'd never realize this by watching an intersection. One-way streets are also dangerous, as there is usually a trickle of traffic flowing the wrong way. And although the Vietnamese technically drive on the right side of the road, the concept of lanes has yet to catch on. Road safety laws and speed restrictions do exist, but they change frequently, are poorly communicated and rarely upheld.

Driving a motorbike in smaller towns like Hoi An is easier than doing so in hectic Ho Chi Minh City and Hanoi, but driving skills remain poor throughout the country. When riding a motorbike or bicycle, use your skills of predicting, timing, and weaving. It is imperative that you use the horn, since most drivers rarely glance around before changing lanes. Unfortunately, since everyone uses the horn at every opportunity, it has become less of a warning and more of an announcement of one's status as a motorcycle rider.

Always give the right of way to trucks, army jeeps, and buses. It's not that they don't necessarily *want* to stop for you—they just might not have any brakes. The best way to get through traffic on foot, using extreme caution, is to walk at a steady pace across the street and watch out—oncoming vehicles will have a better chance of avoiding you if the drivers can get a sense of where you will be going next, and if you stop suddenly, it's harder for them to judge.

For border crossings into Vietnam from the neighboring countries of Laos, Cambodia, and China, it is not advisable to drive because Vietnam imposes heavy import taxes on foreign vehicles and formalities are rigorous, involving a lot of preplanning, paperwork, and luck—even armed with the appropriate import papers, visas, and permits, your vehicle is likely to be refused entry. Even major tour companies are not immune, and get around it by switching vehicles and drivers at border crossings. Vietnam does not issue visas on arrival, but many reputable travel agencies offer prearranged visas, which are available to citizens of most countries, including the United States, but only to those landing in Hanoi, Ho Chi Minh City, or Danang. This makes for a convenient option for those who don't live near a Vietnamese consulate, but note that in high season, you may be stuck waiting in line for some time. You'll need to pay your visa fee in cash; as of this writing, the cost for American citizens is $45 for a one- or three-month single entry visa, $65 for a 30-day multiple-entry visa, and $95 for a longer multiple-entry visa.

Getting Here and Around

ⓜ Motorbike

You can rent a motorbike in Vietnam if you have an International Drivers' License. It's not a good idea to do so, however, unless you have ridden one before. City traffic is chaotic, country roads may have human-size potholes, and local drivers are unlikely to stick to the rules of the road. If you're involved in an accident you, as the foreigner, will be blamed (whether it was actually your fault or not) and be liable for all costs, including hospital bills for any injured parties.

Today there is a good network of rental sources throughout the country, and most hotels will organize a rental for you. For a day rental, check what time you need to get back. You can rent motorbikes and scooters in major cities *(see individual city planners)* at most tourist cafés and some hotels and guesthouses for about 100,000d to 120,000d a day. A deposit is usually required, along with a passport or a photocopy of one (it's best to leave a copy). It is a legal requirement to wear a helmet; all agencies provide them at no extra cost, but a better quality helmet (look for the safety mark and hologram sticker on the back, showing that it's passed the minimum legal safety standards) can be picked up for around 250,000d—a wise investment.

Many rental bikes are not in good condition, so always check brakes, tires, and lights before agreeing to the rental; also check the gas tank, which may have been siphoned. If you're planning a long-distance ride, it's a good idea to take the bike to a mechanic to check the oil and the brakes.

If you rent a motorbike in Vietnam, be prepared to pay for parking in cities. You will be given a receipt of payment—always ask what time the parking lot closes in the evening. Do not lose your ticket—you may not get the bike back.

ⓣ Taxi

Metered taxis are common in Hanoi and Ho Chi Minh City and are becoming more common in Vietnam's smaller cities. Simply wave down a cab on the street, or ask the hotel or restaurant staff to call one for you. In Hanoi and Ho Chi Minh City, the moment you step into a cab the meter reads between 10,000d and 14,000d; after that the rate runs about 14,000d per km. Fares are always quoted in dong, and many drivers will complain if you try to pay with American dollars. Although tipping is not required, some cabbies have developed a habit of "not having change" in hopes you'll tell them to keep it.

Although many cabbies act like reckless kings of the road, taxis are the safest way to get around Vietnam's cities.

To find addresses in Vietnam it helps to know a few local practices. You may see addresses with numbers separated by a slash, such as "361/8 Nguyen Dinh Chieu Street." This means you should head for No. 361 on Nguyen Dinh Chieu Street and then look for an alley next to the building; you want No. 8 in this alley. When you see addresses with a number followed by a letter, such as "97A," this means there is more than one No. 97 on the street and you need to find the one numbered specifically with an "A." If you see "54bis," look for a building adjacent to No. 54; this is a leftover from the French that means 54½. Fodor's uses the English word *street* (abbreviated St.) rather than the Vietnamese words *pho* and *duong*. This was done to make sure street names are clear; in Vietnamese, the words pho and duong come before the names of the streets, which can prove very confusing when trying to find your way around. In addition, many Vietnamese refer to streets only by name (without adding pho or duong), so you may only see these words on street signs and maps.

MOTORBIKE TAXIS

Faster than regular taxis, but a less safe option, is the motorbike taxi (*xe om*). Many hang out on the streets with the most foot traffic, outside bus stations, and in busy tourist destinations. They will drive next to you as you walk down the street, offering their services. For a short distance it can be fun. Always wear a helmet, agree to a price before you get on, and make sure the driver knows where you want to go (your best bet is to have the address written down). Never take a xe om late at night, especially if you're on your own or have had one too many to drink. Quite often, a taxi will cost around the same. Expect to pay about 10,000d to 15,000d per km.

You can also download the very popular app called Grab, recently purchased by Uber. You can order a van, car, or motorbike through the app for a set price; in most cases, you will still need to pay the driver cash on arrival.

🚆 Train

The 2,600-km (1,612-mile) rail system, built by the French, runs north–south, servicing coastal towns between Hanoi and Ho Chi Minh City. The main drawback of rail travel is that it's slow. The quickest train from Ho Chi Minh City to Hanoi, the Reunification Express, takes about 34–41 hours, depending on how many stops it makes, though most people who choose this option make it a slower sightseeing route, getting on and off. Trains are better for the shorter hops between Hanoi and Hue; Hanoi and Lao Cai (which gets you close to Sapa); or Ho Chi Minh City and Nha Trang.

Train travel through Vietnam can be an enjoyable experience (not to mention a time saver if you take overnight trips), provided you can get a soft sleeper or at least a soft chair. Designed just for tourists, the more luxurious Livitrans that run between Hanoi and Danang, the Golden trains that connect Ho Chi Minh and Nha Trang, and the privately run tourist sleeping car services between Hanoi and Sapa make for a far more comfortable experience than the Reunification Express where, regardless of what class ticket you hold, the bathrooms are often dirty and noise is often a problem; day and night, when the train stops, vendors may pop into your compartment to try to sell you soda, beer, and cigarettes. Smoking is permitted in some compartments.

Security is another concern. At all times keep the metal grille over the window shut. If you are concerned about eating food from the local vendors who sell everything from rice crackers to soup, you should bring food and water with you, especially if you have cumbersome luggage that makes trips to the dining carriage impossible.

Getting Here and Around

CLASSES

There are several seating and sleeping options on the train and most come with air-conditioning: the best are soft-berth sleepers, which generally have comfortable, 4-inch-thick mattresses and contain only four bunks; next are the midrange soft sleepers, which also have only four bunks but with 2-inch-thick mattresses; then come hard-berth sleepers, which are exactly the same as soft sleepers, but come with six bunks (the top ones are cheapest); after that are soft seats, which are reclining soft seats, perfect for shorter trips; next are air-conditioned hard seats, which provide slightly uncomfortable wooden seats more attuned to short distance, daytime travel; and finally, hard seats, which are just what they sound like.

FARES AND SCHEDULES

As everywhere, fares vary based on the length of trip and the class of travel. You can purchase tickets at train stations, and travel agencies can also help you make reservations.

Train service runs daily between Hanoi and Ho Chi Minh City (34–41 hours, $99 for soft sleeper with air-conditioning), daily between Hanoi and Hue (12–14 hours, about $85 for a soft sleeper), daily between Hanoi and Lao Cai (8–11 hours, about $85 for soft sleeper), and daily between Ho Chi Minh City and Nha Trang (about 8 hours, $55). It's also possible to take a train from Hanoi to Nanning in China (12 hours, $45), from where you can continue to Beijing. The northeastern border crossing is at Dong Dang, just north of Lang Son. You can currently get a visa for China in China, but this could change.

The Victoria Sapa Resort and Spa's deluxe train carriages travels between Hanoi and Lao Cai daily except Saturday. There's a service fee for those not staying at the resort. Prices start at about $75 one way and $115 round-trip, depending if it's a weekday or weekend.

RESERVATIONS

It's a good idea to book ahead, especially for overnight travel, although for some trips you can only reserve a few days in advance. Tickets can either be booked at the train station, through a local tour company, or with an online booking resource such as Vietnam Impressive, Vietnam Train, or Vietnam Railways. Train tickets must be paid for in dong, unless you book through a tour company. Foreigners are charged higher fares than Vietnamese nationals. Once you disembark you may need to show your ticket again, so don't throw away your ticket stub or you may face major hassles when trying to leave the station, and may even be forced to pay again.

Essentials

🛏 Accommodations

The Vietnam National Administration of Tourism has instituted its own rating system, which vaguely conforms to international standards of quality, though hotels billed as five-star in Vietnam are often more like three- or four-star hotels in the United States.

In major cities and tourist destinations, the hotel industry continues to grow, with more and more international and smaller-size hotels opening. Many of the larger international hotels often aren't fully booked but it is rare that staff will have the authority to offer discounted rates; most will point you in the direction of the online booking agents that have the best deals. Smaller hotels and guesthouses may give you a better room rate than what's listed if you call or visit in person. Vietnam has a selection of other mid-size, mid-level hotels and guest houses, which go by the term "homestays." These privately owned, often family-run operations range from utilitarian to plush; they usually provide friendly service, spotless if basic rooms, and a homey environment. Although such amenities as swimming pools and exercise equipment are rare, and their restaurants may be a bit bland, guest rooms generally have air-conditioning and usually include satellite TV, Wi-Fi, and showers. They may also include lots of street noise.

In smaller towns or rural areas expect much more basic accommodations. Reservations are recommended during Christmas and New Year and during Tet, which is the lunar new year (January or February); prices can be more expensive at these times.

APARTMENT AND HOUSE RENTALS

Airbnb, Flipkey, and to a lesser extent, home-exchange directories, list rentals as well as exchanges.

Upscale beach villas and family rentals are a relatively new thing in Vietnam, but the quality of accommodations is high; some easily compete on a design scale with the private villas at four- or five-star resorts in the region, but come at less than half the price. The highest concentration is found in the popular coastal town of Hoi An. Hanoi and Ho Chi Minh City have a number of international-standard serviced apartments. Most of these are underused, and agents are only too happy to make deals with short-term occupants.

When renting an Airbnb, be sure to bring your own towels and toiletries.

GUEST HOUSES AND HOMESTAYS

Basically bed-and-breakfasts, though you won't see them advertised as such, and guesthouses flood the lodging market in many towns and country areas. Standards vary from small and basic in more rural areas to downright luxurious in popular tourist destinations. Wherever these are located, you can be certain they are the cheapest places to bed down for the night, with the nicest staff and generally awful breakfasts (there will always be other options nearby). You might want to ask if your room has a window with a view, as it is common for cheaper rooms to be nose-to-nose with the neighboring building, making rooms feel dark and claustrophobic.

Essentials

In recent years the government has linked up with various NGO and tour companies to set up sustainable homestays in remote minority villages, providing hill-tribe villagers the tools, training, and support to welcome overnight guests into their village homes. Accommodations are usually basic but full of character, and usually lack air-conditioning, en suite bathrooms, and, quite often, electricity—you're more likely to have shared bathroom facilities and a solar-powered fan. What rooms might lack in modern conveniences, though, they more than make up for with stunning settings, welcoming hosts, and village experiences that you are unlikely to find anywhere else in the country. Bring mosquito repellent and toilet paper.

⊕ Customs and Duties

When shopping abroad, keep receipts for all purchases. Upon reentering the country, be ready to show customs officials what you've bought. If you feel a duty is incorrect, appeal the assessment. If you object to the way your clearance was handled, note the inspector's badge number. In either case, first ask to see a supervisor. If the problem isn't resolved, write to the appropriate authorities, beginning with the port director at your point of entry.

Keep in mind that it is illegal to export antiques unless you get special permission to do so. If you purchase an item that looks like an antique, be sure to get a note from the owner of the store stating that it is not.

Do not attempt to bring anything that could be considered subversive (such as political or religious materials) into Vietnam, as you may receive a hefty fine, be detained, or, in extreme cases, jailed. It is a requirement to declare foreign currency

over $5,000 or Vietnamese currency in excess of 15,000,000d. Contact the Embassy of Vietnam for more information on customs requirements.

⊕ Dining

Vietnam has a variety of eateries, from street peddlers selling food and drinks from handcarts or shoulder poles to elegant international restaurants. In between are small, basic Western-style restaurants serving Vietnamese food; stalls or stands on the street, surrounded by small plastic stools, serving very inexpensive and quite good rice and noodle dishes; hip venues (including hotel restaurants) serving Vietnamese, Chinese, Japanese, French, American, Italian, or other international cuisines; and tourist cafés, which cater primarily to budget travelers and serve mediocre Western and Vietnamese dishes.

Keep in mind that Vietnam's best eating isn't only found in elegant restaurants or hotel dining rooms, but also at stalls on street corners and in marketplaces. To taste Vietnamese favorites, you need only step out of your hotel and onto the streets. These soup, rice, noodle, and seafood kitchens are usually run by several generations of a single family, and sitting down on the low plastic chairs at one of these sidewalk operations for a bowl of *bun cha* (chopped grilled meat over vermicelli-style rice noodles) is a quintessential Vietnam experience.

If you stick to local restaurants, food will constitute a minor part of your travel costs. Smaller restaurants—even those serving international cuisines—are surprisingly cheap. Expect to pay international prices at hotel restaurants.

Good, strong coffee and Vietnamese tea are served with breakfast, after dinner, and all day at local cafés. Traditional Vietnamese coffee is served black and bitter, or with half a can of condensed milk and sugar.

PRECAUTIONS

It's important to be careful of what you eat and drink in Vietnam. Fresh, leafy vegetables are known to carry parasites, so avoid those of dubious origin or those likely to have been washed in tap water. That said, dining at street-side food stands can be as safe as or safer than eating in restaurants, especially in cities. Ho Chi Minh City in particular has a celebrated street-food scene. The stands often serve fresher food than many restaurants because they have a faster turnover; they also prepare the food in front of you. Be more cautious with food stands once you are out of urban areas. It is imperative that you avoid drinking tap water, so ice is always made from pure, filtered water in large factories and then delivered to households, street food stands, and restaurants. Ask if you are unsure. Most decent restaurants either make their own ice using filtered water or buy ice in bulk from the freezer warehouses. Your best bet is to drink bottled water; be sure to check the seal on the cap to make sure the bottle hasn't been refilled.

Keep in mind that monosodium glutamate (MSG) is used in many dishes in Vietnam, particularly in the ubiquitous pho. If you don't want MSG in your food, ask—the cooks may not have already added it to the dish. Many people are unfamiliar with the term MSG, so try referring to it by a popular brand name, Ajinomoto, or in Vietnamese, *mi chinh.*

MEALS AND MEALTIMES

Locals tend to snack throughout the day, and unless you are in a very small village after 8 pm, you only need stand outside your hotel for two minutes before a mobile food vendor crosses your path. Breakfast vendors usually set up at first light, serving noodle soups like pho or bun bo, chao (rice congee), or banh mi

sandwiches on baguettes (most usually sell out by 9 am). Small local restaurants offering a similar menu open at around 7 am. Tourist restaurants generally open around 8 am, serving their full menu, including a few Western breakfast options like bacon and eggs and fresh fruit. Practically every hotel will include a breakfast buffet of Vietnamese and Western staples in their rates, although standards vary. Lunch is typically served between 11:30 and 2 and dinner is available anytime after 2:30 and usually before 8. Restaurants are generally open daily (except major holidays), and although the Vietnamese eat dinner fairly early, most city restaurants remain open well into the night, even after they are supposed to close.

Unless otherwise noted, the restaurants listed in this guide are open daily for lunch and dinner. As a rule the only restaurants that accept credit cards are the more upscale places. However, if you do pay with plastic, these places normally add a 5% service charge to your bill.

WINE, BEER, AND SPIRITS

You'll find Heineken, Carlsberg, Tiger, and San Miguel, along with Saigon Beer, Ba Ba Ba (333), Biere Larue, Huda, and Su Tu Trang (White Lion). Craft beers are a growing industry. Look for brands such as Pasteur Street Brewing Company, who have taprooms in Ho Chi Minh City and Hanoi, as well as a large presence throughout the country's fine dining establishments. In Ho Chi Minh City, enjoy Fuzzy Logic, East West Brewing Company, and Tete; in Hanoi, Furbrew offers the most unique craft beer.

Bia tuoi (also known as *bia hoi* in Hanoi and Hoi An), a watery draft beer, is available on many city street corners; look for low plastic stools occupied by jovial drinkers. The popular rice wine (*ruou gao* or *ruou de*), which is similar to sake, is highly inebriating. You may want to skip

Essentials

the snake rice wine (with a cobra in the bottle) made "especially for men." Imported French, Italian, Australian, Spanish, Californian, and even Chilean wines are available in all main tourist destinations. Brave souls may want to pop open a bottle of the locally produced wine, Vang Da Lat, which bears the label "Product of the Thanh Ha Fertilizer Company."

◉ Electricity

To use electric-powered equipment purchased in the United States or Canada, bring a converter and adapter. The electrical current in Vietnam is 220 volts, 50 cycles alternating current (AC). In the north and other parts of the country, wall outlets take the Continental-type plugs, with two round prongs; they use both the two round prong and flat-pin plugs in much of the south. Many of the international hotels can provide you with converters and adapters.

If your appliances are dual-voltage, you'll need only an adapter. Don't use 110-volt outlets marked "For Shavers Only" for high-wattage appliances such as blow dryers. Most laptops operate equally well on 110 and 220 volts and so require only an adapter and a surge protector.

Blackouts sometimes occur, especially in summer, when everyone uses fans and air-conditioners. Hotels usually have generators, but you may want to keep a flashlight handy.

◉ Emergencies

If something has been stolen from you, contact your hotel or guesthouse and ask them to help report the theft to the police or phone your embassy, especially regarding more costly items such as

expensive jewelry or laptop computers. Contact your embassy if your passport has been stolen or lost.

Pharmacies are found in every town and village and open daily from about 7 to 11:30 and 2 to 8. Most stock a limited range of prescription and nonprescription drugs (including antibiotics), which are available over the counter; always check the expiration date. Outside of these hours and for medical emergencies, seek assistance from local hospitals or clinics, or from your hotel.

⊕ Health

Temperatures in Vietnam can get extremely high; drink plenty of bottled water and use common sense to avoid dehydration, heatstroke, and sunstroke. Dengue fever and malaria are risks isolated to areas in the Central Highlands—if you're not taking a prophylaxis, make sure to use mosquito repellent. Most of Vietnam is quite humid; keep a close eye on small cuts and scrapes as they can easily get infected.

Using sunscreen is highly recommended, especially in the south and on the coast. It is sold in more upscale pharmacies and in stores featuring imported products but bring your own if you can. Pharmacies are plentiful and well stocked.

FOOD AND DRINK

Street food is one of the best and most authentic ways to enjoy the Vietnam experience and is usually clean and tasty. If you do decide to indulge in frequent street dining, keep in mind the risk of parasitic infection from eating improperly handled meat. The major health risk in Vietnam is traveler's diarrhea, caused by eating contaminated fruit or vegetables or drinking contaminated water. Drink only bottled water, or water that has been boiled for several minutes, even when brushing your teeth. It's recommended you avoid eating unpeeled fruit and uncooked vegetables or those you suspect have been washed in unboiled water. Mild stomach ailments may respond to Imodium (known generically as loperamide) or Pepto-Bismol, both of which can be purchased over the counter. Drink plenty of purified water or tea—ginger (*gung*) is a good folk remedy. In severe cases, rehydrate yourself with a salt-sugar solution (½ teaspoon salt [*muoi*] and 4 tablespoons sugar [*duong*] per quart of water); if symptoms persist or worsen, seek medical assistance.

MEDICAL CARE
International clinics and hospitals in major cities offer the highest quality care but also cost more. Local hospitals are not up to the standards of Thailand, Hong Kong, or Singapore, but they are decent and occasionally employ doctors who have been trained overseas. The language barrier is an issue in local hospitals, although some doctors can speak English and French.

Hospitals and pharmacies are often undersupplied and out-of-date. Foreign insurance is not accepted in local hospitals, so you should expect to pay immediately in cash on completion of treatment; keep all your receipts if you want to be reimbursed through your own insurance. The larger hospitals in Hanoi, Ho Chi Minh City, Hue, and Danang have experience treating foreigners (mainly due to motorcycle accidents, the biggest cause of injury or death of Westerners in Vietnam). Blood supply is a serious problem in Vietnam: the nation's blood banks are small and, according to Western doctors, insufficiently screened.

Foreign-run medical clinics provide basic treatment, 24-hour on-call services, and can arrange for emergency medical

evacuation to better hospitals in other countries in the region—medevac planes dedicated to Vietnam are on standby in Singapore. Embassies have duty officers on call to assist with logistics. If you get sick outside Hanoi or Ho Chi Minh City, get yourself to those cities as soon as possible.

Local hospitals can perform some serious emergency operations, but these hospitals are understaffed and aftercare is poor or nonexistent. If possible, it's best to avoid these hospitals altogether, but if you do end up in one, contact your embassy immediately and they will assist if you need to be evacuated to another hospital.

MEDICAL INSURANCE AND ASSISTANCE
Consider buying trip insurance with medical-only coverage. Neither Medicare nor some private insurers cover medical expenses anywhere outside of the United States. Medical-only policies typically reimburse you for medical care (excluding that related to preexisting conditions) and hospitalization abroad, and provide for evacuation. You still have to pay the bills and await reimbursement from the insurer, though.

Another option is to sign up with a medical-evacuation assistance company. A membership in one of these companies gets you doctor referrals, emergency evacuation or repatriation, 24-hour hotlines for medical consultation, and other assistance. International SOS Assistance Emergency and AirMed International provide evacuation services and medical referrals. MedjetAssist offers medical evacuation.

SHOTS AND MEDICATIONS
Tetanus-diphtheria and polio vaccinations should be up-to-date—if you haven't been immunized since childhood, consider bolstering your tetanus and polio vaccinations. If you have never contracted

Essentials

measles, mumps, or rubella, you should also be immunized against them. Immunizations for hepatitis A and typhoid fever are advised. According to the Centers for Disease Control and Prevention (CDC), there is a risk of contracting malaria only in rural areas of Vietnam, though in the Red River delta and the coastal plain north of Nha Trang, it is very rare and therefore considered safe. The CDC recommends taking mefloquine (brand name Larium) for malaria. Dengue fever occurs in Vietnam, but the risk is small except during periods of epidemic-size transmission; there is no vaccine to prevent it. Therefore, you should take precautions against mosquito bites. Malaria- and dengue-bearing mosquitoes generally bite at dusk and at night. No matter where you go, it's a good idea to protect yourself from mosquito-borne illnesses with a good insect repellent containing DEET, and if you're in susceptible regions, use aerosol insecticides indoors, wear clothing that covers the body, and bring mosquito nets.

If you're staying for a month or more and are traveling to rural areas, you should be vaccinated against Japanese encephalitis; for six months or more, against hepatitis B as well. Some of these vaccinations require staggered treatments, so plan ahead.

Bringing a first-aid kit with antacids, antidiarrheal, cold medicine, Band-Aids, antiseptics, aspirin, and other items you may need is a good idea. Also, know your blood type and bring enough medication to last the entire trip; you may be able to get common prescription drugs in Vietnam, but don't count on their availability or their quality. Just in case, however, have your doctor write you a prescription using the drug's generic name, because brand names vary from country to country.

OVER-THE-COUNTER REMEDIES

Pharmacies are almost as common as tea stalls in Vietnam, and many pharmacists in major cities speak English. Look for a shop with a green sign that reads *Nha Thuoc*. These usually stock painkillers (such as Panadol); eye-, nose-, and eardrops (such as Polydexa); cold remedies (such as Tiffy); and various antibiotics—for which no prescription is needed in Vietnam. Remember to check the expiration date when buying any sort of medication.

⊙ Hours of Operation

Vietnam has a tradition of afternoon siestas (especially in the countryside), which means that all activities except eating tend to stop during lunch, between 11:30 and 2. Urban life is changing rapidly in Vietnam, however, and more and more businesses are staying open during lunchtime to accommodate the increasing number of tourists and office-bound Vietnamese who use their midday break as a time to catch up on shopping or chores.

Cafés and restaurants are open all day, almost every day. Most sidewalk stalls serving breakfast and lunch finish by 2 and reopen for dinner about half an hour later. By 10 pm in Hanoi and 11 pm in Ho Chi Minh City, activity starts slowing down; smaller cities die down even earlier. In bigger cities more popular venues stay open much later. You can always find late-night noodle stands. Bars and nightclubs usually close at about 1 am or whenever the last customer leaves.

BANKS AND OFFICES

Vietnam for the most part has a five-day workweek. Some offices are open on Saturday morning, but many are not. Most government agencies and foreign-invested companies take the weekend off.

Banks are open on weekdays and on Saturday morning in some larger towns and cities, from 8 am to noon and then from 1:30 to 5 pm. Post offices are generally open five days a week; some are open on Saturday or Sunday.

GAS STATIONS
Vendors sell gas at many intersections in the cities, although you will have trouble finding gas stations open after 8 pm in smaller towns.

MUSEUMS AND SIGHTS
Most museums in Vietnam are closed on Sunday and Monday. Some are also closed on Saturday or are only open Saturday morning. It's also not uncommon to find some museums and galleries closed for a few hours at lunchtime. Pagodas are generally open from dawn to dusk, later if it's the 1st or 15th day of the lunar month.

SHOPS
Small family-run shops seem to stay open indefinitely, primarily because living and working quarters are often one and the same. Larger stores, such as supermarket chains and department stores, can stay open as late as 10 pm in major cities.

HOLIDAYS
The traditional lunar new year, known as Tet in Vietnam and celebrated throughout much of Southeast Asia, falls in January or February, depending on the lunar calendar. Note that accommodations are scarce and museums, offices, and some shops tend to shut down for days at a time during Tet. Other national holidays only tend to affect banks and government offices; these include International New Year's Day (Jan 1); Reunification Day (April 30), commemorating the day the North Vietnamese army took Saigon; International Workers Day, or May Day (May 1, the day after Liberation Day,

which means a two-day holiday); Ho Chi Minh's birthday (May 19); National Day (September 2); and Christmas Day (December 25).

📦 Mail

Main post offices (called *buu dien* in Vietnamese) are open daily from about 7 am to 7 pm; smaller and rural offices tend to close on weekends and between 11:30 and 1:30. There are mailboxes outside the post offices, but it's best to hand your mail over the counter. Sending a postcard or letter abroad should cost less than 50 cents. The local postal service is generally reliable, but for packages going abroad it's safer to use an international courier service. When mailing packages into and out of Vietnam, be aware that you usually need to show your passport and your parcels will probably be scrutinized at the post office. Note that videotapes, books, DVDs, and compact discs are especially sensitive items to ship or mail to and from Vietnam. It should take about two weeks, sometimes longer, for mail to arrive in the West from Vietnam, though postcards can take a while.

Note that Vietnam does not use postal codes.

OVERNIGHT SERVICES
The U.S. Postal Service, DHL, FedEx, and UPS all have express mail services to Vietnam. Unfortunately, the service isn't always that fast: it can take from four to seven days, depending on how long the package sits in customs. DHL, FedEx, and UPS can also ship from Vietnam. Because packages sent via regular mail can take up to three months to reach North America, courier services are a far better option.

Essentials

POSTAL RATES

Postage is based on weight. On average, a postcard or letter to the United States or Europe costs about $1 to $2. Stamps are sold at post office branches, and at many hotels and shops. Usually the postal clerk will cancel the stamps on your letter and give it back to you to put into the mail slot. This policy exists in part to eliminate any possibility of stamps being peeled off your letter for resale and your letter being thrown away.

RECEIVING MAIL

If you're receiving a parcel in Vietnam, don't be surprised if the parcel arrives already opened. Most parcels are opened as a matter of course, and sometimes the recipient in Vietnam is charged for the service of checking the parcel. In lieu of the parcel, you may receive a note providing information on where to collect a particular piece of mail. Sending items such as videos, books, compact discs, and DVDs through the mail is risky. Packages make many stops along the way, and opportunities abound for theft or loss. If these items do arrive, they're sometimes confiscated or checked for subversive material. Such "quarantines" for videos sometimes provide opportunity for replication by unscrupulous postal clerks or customs officials before they're handed over to you. Most letters and postcards will arrive within about two weeks of being mailed from abroad.

$ Money

U.S. dollars are the preferred currency of exchange, but other major currencies are easy to exchange at banks, exchange counters, and hotels.

Small businesses in more rural places often can't change 500,000d bills. This can be problematic because many ATMs

only give out bills in this denomination. Make sure you have plenty of small change on hand to avoid potentially awkward situations.

ATMS AND BANKS

Banks and ATMs are easily found in all major cities and most towns throughout Vietnam. If you are planning on visiting smaller towns take enough Vietnamese currency to cover your expenses. Despite the easy accessibility of ATMs, the withdrawal limit is low, with most offering a maximum of 4,000,000d per transaction in big cities and 2,000,000d per transaction in smaller places, though costs in Vietnam are also low. For limits of 5,000,000d look for ATMs of the major banks, like Donga and HSBC. Transaction charges are usually between about 20,000d and 55,000d and it's possible to make multiple transactions at a time, although most Western card companies frown upon this behavior and it's not unusual for the ATM to retain your card after the third attempt. Almost all ATMs have an English-language option and most accept Visa, Maestro, and Plus cards. MasterCard and Cirrus are less common. For larger sums you'll need to go to the counter inside the bank and show your passport and card.

AVERAGE COSTS

Be aware that Vietnam has an official dual-pricing system, so foreigners are often expected to pay more than double what locals do for trains, buses, flights, and other goods and services. In 1999 an official decree banned dual pricing at temples and tourist sites, but despite this rule, higher entrance fees for foreigners remain the norm.

It's standard practice throughout Vietnam for tourist businesses to pay commission to guides, hotel staff, drivers, and anyone who introduces you to their business. In most circumstances the business takes the rap for the fee, but may provide an inferior tour or service because of their outlay in commissions. The worst offenders are in the busiest tourist destinations; the Mekong Delta, Nha Trang, Hoi An, Hue, and Halong Bay. Before committing, always do your research and take advice from people who have used the company. Hoi An tailors have taken this one step further, and most will pay upward of 30% of your final spend in commission, which is added to your bill. Do not accept invitations to visit a "sister" shop and make it clear that the business was not recommended to you by anyone before you start bargaining over the price. Similarly, drivers of private cars and tour buses will park at restaurants or at shops where they have previously arranged commissions, meaning you will overpay. If it's a tour bus, you are unlikely to have a choice, but with a private car you can ask to be taken elsewhere if you're unhappy with the driver's choice.

CREDIT CARDS

Credit cards have yet to catch on as a form of payment in Vietnam, but Visa and MasterCard are accepted at most large international hotels, upscale restaurants, better shops, large tour operators, and airline agencies. Few establishments accept American Express or Diners International cards so it's best to check beforehand. For all credit card purchases you will be charged a 2%–3% transaction fee, although some restaurants, hotels, and shops sometimes insist on a service charge of up to 5%. Note that travelers' checks are accepted in Vietnam in very few places and especially not in rural areas and small towns.

CURRENCY AND EXCHANGE

The official currency is the dong. The largest denomination is 500,000 (approximately $21.75), followed by 200,000, 100,000, 50,000, 20,000, and 10,000, which all come as plastic-coated bills. Smaller (paper) bills come in 5,000, 2,000, 1,000, and to a lesser extent 500 denominations. Although banknotes come in various colors and sizes, some are difficult to differentiate. Two good examples of this are the blue 500,000d bill, which looks remarkably similar to the 20,000d, and the red 200,000d, which is easily confused with the 10,000d. Keep these larger bills separate to avoid expensive mistakes. The bank exchange rate remains fairly stable and the dong trades at approximately 23,000d to the U.S. dollar. Although some markets, local shops, hotels, and restaurants accept U.S. dollars, merchants set their own rate, which is usually lower than the bank. Sacom and Vietcom Bank have numerous branches all over the country and give the official government rate. International banks like HSBC and Citibank have a presence in Vietnam and provide extensive banking services, including currency exchange, cash transfers, and cash advances on credit cards. At currency exchange booths you can exchange money quickly without showing your passport, but rates for smaller bills are not competitive and they will not accept torn or marked notes.

In smaller towns where banks or exchange booths are not an option, you can exchange U.S. dollars to dong in gold shops but, because this practice is technically illegal, exchange rates can be poor. If there's no alternative, be sure to agree on an acceptable rate and check the currency for torn bills when it is handed over. It's also illegal for many smaller establishments to accept payments in anything but dong, but such rules are widely ignored. U.S. dollars are accepted at almost every private business, but many state enterprises—including trains—only accept dong. It's recommended that you carry both dollars and dong with you at all times.

Essentials

📷 Packing

You can get your laundry done very inexpensively (a dollar a kilo) at shops and stands outside most hotels. Temperatures vary hugely by region. Dress in Vietnam is generally informal.

You must remove your shoes when entering most temples, so you may want to bring ones that are hassle-free. A hat and sunblock are always good ideas.

You should also ask your doctor to write a spare prescription using the drug's generic name, because brand names may vary from country to country. Never pack prescription drugs or valuables in checked luggage. To avoid customs and security delays, carry medications in their original packaging.

Pack mosquito repellent and a first-aid kit. Diapers and baby formula are available in Vietnam, but you may not be familiar with the brands and they are surprisingly expensive.

🛂 Passports and Visas

It's highly recommended that you obtain your visa before you head for Vietnam; it's easy to apply for one online, with a standard turnaround time of three business days. As of this writing, the cost for American citizens is $80 for a one-month single-entry visa, $135 for a one-month multiple-entry visa, $110 for a three-month single-entry visa, $160 for a three-month multiple-entry visa, and $170 for a six-month multiple-entry visa.

Make two photocopies of the data and visa page of your passport (one for someone at home and another for you, carried separately from your passport). If you lose your passport, promptly call the nearest embassy or consulate and the local police.

U.S. passport applications for children under age 14 require consent from both parents, or legal guardians, and both must appear together to sign the application. If only one parent appears, he or she must submit a written statement from the other parent authorizing passport issuance for the child. A parent with sole authority must present evidence of it when applying; acceptable documentation includes the child's certified birth certificate listing only the applying parent, a court order specifically permitting this parent's travel with the child, or a death certificate for the non-applying parent. Application forms and instructions are available on the website of the U.S. State Department's Bureau of Consular Affairs.

📍 Restrooms

Hotels, guesthouses, and restaurants that cater to tourists usually have Western-style toilets, at least in bigger towns. In bus and train stations, on trains themselves, and in restaurants in the countryside, squat toilets are often your only option. Most of these do not flush; use the plastic ladle to splash water around and keep toilet paper handy. Many public toilets charge a 2,000d entry fee, which entitles you to a scrap of toilet paper.

➕ Safety

Although it is widely accepted that Vietnam is safe for tourists, pickpocketing and bag snatching are somewhat serious problems in Ho Chi Minh City, Nha Trang, and Hanoi; even Hoi An is beginning to see more petty crime. You may want to remove any jewelry that stands out. The rest of Vietnam's cities are safer—the biggest hassles are being stared at and being overcharged for purchases. You should take standard precautions, however.

In the big cities do not walk with your bag or purse on your street-side shoulder or leave it at your feet in a cyclo or in the basket of a bicycle, as the snatch-and-ride stealing method (on a motorbike or bicycle) is common. Children or elderly people may be acting as decoys or pick-pocketing you themselves. When sitting in a street café or in a cyclo, make sure you either hold your bag in your lap with your hands through the straps or put the straps around your neck; if you do put it at your feet, wrap its handles around your ankles so no one can grab it. If someone does steal your bag, don't pursue the thief—assailants have been known to carry knives. As for cyclos, motorbike taxis, and Easy Riders, be sure to negotiate a price before you get on, don't go with a driver you don't feel comfortable with, and don't travel by cyclo or motorbike taxi after dark, especially in cities. You should also avoid parks at night in large cities. If you carry a purse, choose one with a zipper and a thick strap that you can drape across your body; adjust the length so that the purse sits in front of you at or above hip level. Store only enough money in the purse to cover casual spending. Distribute the rest of your cash and any valuables between a deep front pocket, an inside jacket or vest pocket, and a hidden money pouch. Do not reach for the money pouch in public.

You should avoid leaving passports, cameras, laptop computers, and other valuables in your hotel room, unless the room has a safe. If it doesn't, consider leaving your valuables with the front desk. It is advised that you leave your passport in your hotel safe and carry only a photocopy with you while out exploring. In cheaper accommodations, it's normal for the reception desk to hold your passport for the duration of your stay. If they do, politely insist that it is kept in the hotel safe and not in an unlocked drawer with all the other guests' passports.

Vietnam is a relatively safe place for women travelers. Female travelers seem to encounter more hassles—such as grabbing and heckling—in the less visited, rural areas. Walking alone or taking a solo cyclo or motorbike taxi ride at night is best avoided; if you're taking a taxi alone at night, sit in the back seat. Finally, don't venture too far down deserted beaches alone.

Dozens of Vietnamese are killed every year by unexploded bombs left behind in central Vietnam. Most of these are located in Quang Tri and Quang Binh provinces, on protected national land. It is very unlikely you will visit any danger areas. If you are unsure, or you are visiting the caves in and around Phong Nha, travel with an experienced guide.

Though Vietnam is generally a peaceful country, it's a good idea to check the Department of State website for guidance or travel alerts before making plans to travel.

$ Taxes
VALUE-ADDED TAX

Vietnam's V.A.T. tax is 10% on items such as alcohol and cigarettes; 10% for hotels, bars, and nightclubs; and 5% for most other goods and services. Larger hotels, especially state-owned and joint-venture operations, often add another 5% service tax. Ask about added taxes before checking in or ordering.

A new V.A.T. refund program for tourists allows travelers flying out of international airports to be refunded for the V.A.T. value incurred on invoiced purchases of 2,000,000d (about $100) or more made in one shop, within the previous 30 days.

Essentials

You'll need to get a V.A.T. refund form when you're purchasing the items. A service charge of less than 15% of the V.A.T. refund is charged, and certain goods—especially those whose export is prohibited—are ineligible for the refund. Refund counters in the departure area provide travelers who have cleared immigration their refunds in dollars or other currencies.

⦿ Time

Vietnam is 7 hours ahead of Greenwich Mean Time, 15 hours ahead of Los Angeles, 12 hours ahead of New York, 7 hours ahead of London, and 3 hours behind Sydney. Daylight savings time is not observed.

⦿ Tipping

Tipping is a fairly new concept in Vietnam and is appreciated but not typically expected. Many higher-end restaurants and hotels in Vietnam include 5% service fees in the bill, but if you feel you've received good service, a tip is always welcome. Although it's not necessarily expected, tour guides are more than happy to receive a tip if you enjoyed their services. When tipping service staff, do so in dong.

⦿ Visitor Information

Free maps and tourist publications featuring up-to-date information on towns, cities, and events are available from most major airports, travel agencies, tourist cafés, and hotels. There are also plenty of useful online resources.

Tipping Guidelines for Vietnam	
Bartender	Not expected, but if service is good leave 10% of your final bill
Bellhop	20,000d to 40,000d, depending on the level of the hotel
Hotel Concierge	20,000d or more, if he or she performs a service for you
Hotel Doorman	20,000d to 40,000d if he helps you get a cab
Hotel Maid	20,000d to 40,000d a day (either daily or at the end of your stay, in cash)
Hotel Room-Service Waiter	20,000d to 40,000d per delivery, even if a service charge has been added
Porter at Airport or Train Station	10,000d per bag
Xe Om (motorbike) Driver	20,000d to 40,000d depending on distance traveled
Taxi Driver	10%, but round up the fare to the next dollar amount
Tour Guide	10% of the cost of the tour
Cyclo driver	20,000d for shorter journeys or 10% of the cost of a tour
Waiter	10% is the norm at high-end restaurants; nothing additional if a service charge is added to the bill
Restroom Attendant	Attendants in public facilities expect some small change or 5,000d

VIETNAM VETERANS

The office of the Vietnam Veterans of America Foundation (VVAF) in Vietnam is involved in building long-lasting ties and increasing understanding between Vietnamese and Americans. VVAF organizes cultural exchange programs and a prosthetics clinic. Veterans returning to Vietnam are encouraged to contact VVAF, either in Hanoi or at its Maryland office. At least once a year VVAF organizes tours to Vietnam; contact the Maryland office for information.

LANGUAGE

In large cities English is practically a second language, and is commonly used in the tourist trade; in the countryside, particularly outside tourist spots, communicating can be difficult if you don't speak any Vietnamese, so it's best to use a phrase book as a point-and-show device. A little Vietnamese goes a long way, and a few words—numbers and some important verbs and pronouns—you may find such matters as bargaining with cyclo drivers much easier. French is still spoken among an elite but shrinking crowd of older Vietnamese.

Ways to Save

Stay somewhere with a free breakfast. Many hotels offer free breakfast to guests.

Eat street food. Food stalls are cheap and plentiful and are a great place to try regional specialties.

Travel by cyclo. These three-wheeled bicycle taxis are among the cheapest way to get around Hanoi and Hoi An, though you won't find many in Ho Chi Minh City.

Stick to free attractions. If you're really tight for cash, many attractions have free days—check their websites. Hostels are great places to find free walking tours as well.

When to Go

High Season: Vietnam has two high seasons: November–March in the south and July and August in the north. Christmas and Western New Year are popular with travelers and rates will be higher, though the most expensive time to travel is during Tet, which falls in January or February.

Low Season: Because of Vietnam's different climate zones, high season in the south (November–March) is low season in the north, and vice versa. The Mekong Delta region is always hot and humid, but off-season travelers to the north will find temperatures pleasant.

Value Season: April–June and September–November offer the best value in Vietnam. You won't have to fight for accommodations or elbow room at major sites and you'll still be able to enjoy peak season weather in some parts of the country. The south is still very hot and it will rain, though not all day.

Great Itineraries

ESSENTIAL VIETNAM, 10 DAYS
DAYS 1–2: HO CHI MINH CITY

Spend the first day visiting top sites including the **Reunification Palace,** the **Central Post Office,** and the **Notre Dame Cathedral** in bustling District 1, as well as the controversial **War Remnants Museum.** Dine at **Ben Thanh market.** Take a **nighttime food tour** (book ahead) for an overview of the country's delicious and varied cuisine. On the second day, rise early to join an organized day tour to the **Cu Chi Tunnels,** accessible by car or boat on the Saigon River. Stretching from all the way to Cambodia, this network of underground tunnels was used by the Vietcong during the war.

DAY 3: MEKONG DELTA

(Full-day excursions from HCMC take 7–9 hours)

For richer insights into life on the delta, with its networks of waterways and narrow motorbike-only paths, fruit orchards, rice paddies, busy markets, and friendly locals, take a river cruise with a company like **Les Rives** (⊕ *lesrivesexperience.com*) or a reputable bicycle tour, such as those offered by **Mekong Bike Tours** (⊕ *www. mekongbiketours.com*).

DAY 4: NHA TRANG

(1 hour by plane from Ho Chi Minh City, about 7½ hours by train)

Take a one-hour flight from Ho Chi Minh City to **Nha Trang.** Check into one of the luxury resorts that line Nha Trang's coastline. Between spa treatments and beach walks, take a boat trip to the nearby island of **Hon Mun** for an afternoon dive or snorkel. Squeeze in a visit to the **Po Nagar Cham Towers** before dinner at one of Nha Trang's celebrated restaurants.

DAYS 5–6: HOI AN

(1 hour and 15 minutes by plane to Danang, then a 45-minute taxi ride to Hoi An)

Hoi An is home to French and Chinese architecture, tailor shops, art galleries, and the 16th-century **Japanese Covered Bridge.** Catch a flight from Nha Trang to Danang and then a taxi to Hoi An, and get lost in the **Old Quarter.** Sip Vietnamese coffee, get a custom-tailored suit, and shop to your heart's content. Visit the famed Chinese-built **Assembly Halls,** and take a bicycle tour of the surrounding countryside.

On Day 6, participate in a **cooking course** or join a culinary tour through the Central Market, the best place to try local dishes like cao lau (rice noodles) and *banh bao vac* (steamed dumplings). Spend the rest of the day at the **My Son Sanctuary,** the former religious capital of the Kingdom of Champa. Dating back to the 4th century, this archaeological site is an hour's drive from Hoi An. Or visit **An Bang Beach,** a favorite with locals, known for its warm waters, soft sand, and excellent seafood restaurants.

DAY 7: HUE

(About 2½ hours by train or 3 hours by bus from Danang)

A train ride to Hue sees the East Sea on one side and the Hai Van Pass on the other. Explore **The Citadel,** the **Thien Mu Pagoda,** and one of the impressive **mausoleums** that pay tribute to past emperors. Be sure to reach the pagoda by way of dragon boat along the **Perfume River.** Dine in the tourist district near Chu Van An Street, or venture to a converted colonial villa to dine at **Les Jardins De La Carambole.**

DAY 8: HANOI

(1 hour and 10 minutes by plane or 14½ hours by train from Hue)

Catch a morning flight from Hue to Hanoi. Account for a 45-minute drive from the airport to downtown. Wander the bustling streets of the **Old Quarter,** stopping along the way to shop or enjoy a cold one on **Bia Hoi corner,** the beer mecca of Hanoi. Visit the **Temple of Literature** and the nearby **Fine Arts Museum,** or stroll around the picturesque **Hoan Kiem Lake**; its northern shore is home to Jade Island where Ngoc Son Temple stands. Sample pho for dinner. End with a live performance at the **Hanoi Opera House** or the **Thang Long Water Puppet Theater.** The shuttle to Halong Bay leaves at 8 am. Most hotels will store luggage for guests who take day or overnight trips to the coast.

DAY 9: HALONG BAY

(Excursions from Hanoi take 11–12 hours round trip)

Travel by shuttle four hours to **Halong Bay.** Select a tour company offering trips to floating villages, historic caves, pristine beaches, and **Cat Ba Island.** As Halong Bay's largest island, Cat Ba is home to lakes, waterfalls, caves, and a national park where the endangered Langur monkey lives.

DAY 10: HANOI

Begin with a visit to **Ho Chi Minh's Mausoleum and Residence.** This memorial in Ba Dinh Square gets extremely crowded, so arrive early. Spend some time strolling through this area, which includes the pretty **One Pillar Pagoda.** Head back to the Old Quarter for dinner and a musical performance of Ca Tru. This ceremonial singing can best be enjoyed at the **Thang Long Ca Tru Theater.** Grab a nightcap at one of the rooftop lounge bars in this charming district.

SAPA EXTENSION, 4 DAYS

Follow days 1–10 of the Essential Vietnam itinerary.

(8 hours by train from Hanoi)

The former French hill station of **Sapa,** in the misty Tonkinese Alps near the Chinese border, is famous for its stunning scenery, the colorful traditional dress of the local ethnic minority people, and its proximity to **Mount Fansipan,** Vietnam's highest peak. Traveling through this region, on foot or by road, will take you past picturesque rice terraces, tiny ethnic villages, and cold, clear mountain streams.

Great Itineraries

PHU QUOC ISLAND EXTENSION, 2–3 DAYS
(1 hour by plane from Ho Chi Minh City)

A tropical island paradise with long, lovely beaches, warm turquoise water, and swathes of jungle, **Phu Quoc** is the perfect backdrop for winding down, no matter what form of relaxation you prefer. It makes for a great side trip from Ho Chi Minh City.

Follow days 1–2 of Essential Vietnam itinerary.

DAY 3

Fly from Ho Chi Minh City to Phu Quoc, just 12 km (7½ miles) from the southeast coast of Cambodia. If your idea of relaxation is the full five-star resort experience, spend today at your resort enjoying the amenities. If you're the type that can't stand still, organize some transport (motorbike, taxi, or car-and-driver) and set out to explore Phu Quoc's **beaches.** Watch the sun sink into the East Sea with a cocktail at **On The Rocks,** Mango Bay Resort's in-house restaurant at **Ong Lang Beach,** then enjoy some delicious Asian fusion cuisine as the waves caress the rocks under the deck.

DAY 4

Explore the undersea delights of Phu Quoc with a half-day diving or snorkeling tour with an outfitter like **Rainbow Divers** (⊕ *www.divevietnam.com*). Spend the afternoon recovering on a deck chair at **Rory's Beach Bar** and a long late-afternoon walk along the beach to your dinner destination, **The Spice House** at Cassia Cottage.

DAY 5

Allocate several hours to swimming, sunbathing, or spa-ing, then some laid-back exploring around some of Phu Quoc's sights. You could head south of **Duong Dong Town,** stopping at **Ngoc Hien Pearl** and the **Coconut Tree Prison** en route to the northern stretches of **Sao Beach.** After a bit of swimming, loop around to **Suoi Tranh** for a lovely rain forest walk to the waterfall. Get back to Duong Dong Town in time to watch the sun set from the pier near the **Dinh Cau Night Market,** then dive into the market for a local-style barbecue seafood dinner.

DAY 6

Fly back to Ho Chi Minh City, and take the ferry to Hai Tien to begin your Mekong Delta explorations.

CON DAO ISLANDS EXTENSION, 2–3 DAYS
(1 hour by plane from Ho Chi Minh City)

These islands offer some of the most unspoiled tropical landscapes in Vietnam, a short flight from Ho Chi Minh City.

Follow days 1–2 of Essential Vietnam itinerary.

DAY 3

Fly to these undiscovered and mostly undeveloped islands with beautiful beaches, clear waters, and a large **national park** teeming with exotic plants and animals, including the endangered green and hawksbill turtles. For a luxurious retreat, stay at the high-end eco-lodge, **Six Senses Con Dao,** and indulge in some pampering at the in-house spa and some serious relaxing in your private plunge-pool. After a long walk along the beach, enjoy a seafood dinner at the resort's **By The Beach** restaurant. Night owls can visit **Hang Duong Cemetery** for the atmospheric midnight ceremony honoring the martyred teenager Vo Thi Sau.

DAY 4

Organize some transport for a morning of island exploration, taking in **Van Son Tu Pagoda, Hang Duong Cemetery,** and the **Con Dao Museum,** where you can arrange to visit the nearby **Phu Hai Prison** the next day. If you're on Con Dao between

May and October you'll be able to take a **turtle-nesting tour,** which usually starts with a midafternoon pickup and includes an overnight stay on an outer island.

DAY 5

You'll be delivered back to the mainland midmorning after your nocturnal turtle nesting observations. Perk yourself up with a coffee at the **Café Con Son,** then begin some gentle ambling, stopping off at the **Old French Governor's House** on the way to **Phu Hai Prison.** Dine at the delightful **Thu Ba,** which specializes in fresh-caught seafood.

MEKONG DELTA EXTENSION, 4 DAYS

The lush Mekong Delta, with its fascinating river life, fruit orchards, and friendly locals, requires some time to explore, especially if you're keen to gain insights into local life.

Follow days 1–2 of Essential Vietnam itinerary.

DAY 3

(Can Tho is 3 hours by bus from Ho Chi Minh City)

Travel to the capital of the Mekong Delta, **Can Tho.** Break the journey in the charming town of **Sa Dec,** the childhood home of French author Marguerite Duras, and take some time to explore the streets fronting the river, the **Huynh Thuy Le Ancient House,** and the narrow pathways lined by flower farms. At the end of your long journey, stretch your legs in Can Tho with a walk along the river front, then watch the sun set from **L'Escale,** the rooftop restaurant at the **Nam Bo Boutique Hotel.**

DAYS 4–5

Spend Days 4 and 5 experiencing local Mekong Delta life with a **homestay** at Nguyen Shack Homestay or Green Village Homestay or an **overnight river cruise** with Bassac Cruises (www.luxurymekongrivercruise.com).

DAY 6

Travel to fascinating **Chau Doc** (3 hours), where the Cham people worship at the **Murbarak Mosque,** the local Buddhists pray at shrines on **Sam Mountain,** and river folk operate floating fish farms under their houses. Allocate several hours to exploring Sam Mountain, and finish your tour with a cocktail at **Nui Sam Lodge,** with its stunning views of the rice paddies and flood plains of the Mekong Delta. From Chau Doc, you can travel back to Ho Chi Minh City.

Follow days 1–10 of the Essential Vietnam itinerary.

DAY 11

Take the overnight train from Hanoi to **Lao Cai,** where minibuses await to run visitors farther up the mountain to Sapa, which overlooks misty rice terraces. If you want to avoid an early-morning arrival, consider taking the bus, which uses the new Noi Bai–Lao Cai Highway. Spend your first day exploring the town, which is full of international travelers as well as wandering vendors selling all manner of handicrafts.

DAYS 12–14

Rise early to start your **multiday trek** of the beautiful countryside that surrounds Sapa, past terraced rice fields and through a range of ethnic minority villages. Try to end your trek on a Saturday so you can spend Sunday doing a day trip to the **Bac Ha Market,** 110 km (68.4 miles) from Sapa, home of the very colorful Flower H'mong ethnic minority people. Then return to Hanoi.

On the Calendar

January–February

Tet: The Lunar New Year, or Tet holiday, is marked by family visits and special foods. It can be a tough time to travel through Vietnam, as many offices (including embassies and border crossings) shut down, and hotels and transportation can be hard to book. If you do decide to travel during Tet, you will enjoy locals lighting fireworks and beautiful flower stalls, and you may be invited to join the families on your block in street karaoke.

Lim Festival: Lim Festival occurs on the 12th and 13th day of the lunar year in Lim Village, Bac Ninh Province, 18 km (11 miles) from Hanoi. Highlights include quan ho folk singing, traditional costumes, and games like tug-of-war and human chess.

Perfume Festival: The perfume festival is a pilgrimage which starts on the 15th day of the lunar year. Pilgrims travel by boat along the Yen River to the base of the Huong Mountain, and then climb the stone steps toward Huong Tich Cave. The journey ends at the Perfume Pagoda, located about 60 km (37 miles) southwest of Hanoi.

April–June

Reunification Day: April 30th is observed as the day of liberation, and most schools and businesses are closed. Vietnamese flags are hung from every building, and in major cities there are shows and parades in downtown areas.

Hue Festival: Hue Festival takes place in Hue City every other year, and was created to preserve traditional customs. Expect a week of activities like the Hue Poetry Festival, Ao Dai fashion shows, and street performances.

Buddha's Birthday: While Buddha's birthday is recognized throughout the country, Hoi An holds a parade starting at Phap Bao Pagoda. In the evening, flower garlands and lanterns are placed along the riverbank.

Danang International Fireworks Festival: Usually held in June, this festival runs for several weekends. In the past, different countries have competed before a "final showdown" between the two best countries. You can buy tickets to a special standing area or riverboat cruise, or enjoy the show from the many rooftop bars that dot Danang.

August–September

Tet Trung Thu (Mid-Autumn Festival): This event marks the autumn harvest with moon gazing and special moon cakes. Also known as the children's festival, it's when parents celebrate their children by buying them lanterns, snacks, and masks. During this festival, and during Tet holiday, you can expect to see lion and dragon dancing in major cities.

Wandering Souls Day: Celebrated on the 15th day of the 7th lunar month (late August or early September), Wandering Souls Day is similar in spirit to the day of the dead. The night before, families will burn paper money and paper clothing for spirits to use in the afterlife. While practiced throughout the country, Hue's pagodas are a fantastic place to witness these rituals.

December

Ooc Om Boc Festival: The Khmer people living in the Mekong Delta celebrate with offerings to the moon, singing, dancing, and boat races.

Christmas and New Year's Eve: While the lunar new year is much more widely celebrated, Western holidays are also embraced. Motorbike parades to see Christmas decorations are common.

Contacts

✈ Air

AIRPORT INFORMATION
Cam Ranh International Airport. (*Nha Trang Airport*). ✉ *Nguyen Tat Thanh, Nha Trang* ☎ *258/398–9956* ⊕ *www.vietnamairport.vn.* **Cat Bi Airport.** (*Haiphong Airport*). ✉ *Le Hong Phong, Haiphong* ☎ *0225/397–6408* ⊕ *www.vietnamairport.vn.* **Con Dao Airport.** (*Co Ong Airport, Sang Bay Co Ong*). ✉ *Co Ong, Con Son* ☎ *0254/629–7981* ⊕ *www.vietnamairport.vn.* **Danang Airport.** ✉ *Duy Tan, Danang* ✛ *3 km (2 miles) southwest of Danang* ☎ *0236/382–3391* ⊕ *www.danangairportonline.com.* **Dong Hoi Airport.** ✉ *AH14, Loc Ninh* ☎ *0232/381–0898* ⊕ *www.vietnamairport.vn.* **Duong Dong Airport.** (*Phu Quoc Airport*). ✉ *Off TL 46, Phu Quoc* ⊕ *www.vietnamairport.vn.* **Lien Khuong Airport.** (*Dalat Airport*). ✉ *20 Lam Dong, Dalat* ⊕ *www.vietnamaiport.vn.* **Noi Bai International Airport.** (*Hanoi Airport*). ✉ *Vo Van Kiet, off QL 18, Soc Son* ☎ *024/3886–5047* ⊕ *www.hanoiairportonline.com.* **Phu Bai Airport.** (*Hue Airport*). ✉ *Huong Thuy, Phu Bai* ☎ *234/386–1131* ⊕ *www.vietnamairport.vn.* **Tan Son Nhat Airport.** (*Ho Chi Minh City airport*). ✉ *Hoang Van Thu Blvd., Phong 2, Binh Tan District* ☎ *028/3848–5383* ⊕ *www.vietnamairport.vn.*

WITHIN VIETNAM Japan Airlines. ☎ *800/525–3663* ⊕ *www.jal.co.* **Jetstar.** ☎ ⊕ *www.jetstar.com .* **Singapore Airlines.** ☎ *800/742–3333* ⊕ *www.singaporeair.com.* **VietJet Air.** ✉ *Hanoi* ☎ *01/900–1886, 28/3551–6220* ⊕ *www.vietjetair.com.* **Vietnam Airlines.** ☎ *1900–1100 in Vietnam* ⊕ *www.vietnamairlines.com.*

TO AND FROM THE UNITED STATES American Airlines. ☎ *800/433–7300* ⊕ *www.aa.com.* **Cathay Pacific.** ☎ *800/233–2742* ⊕ *www.cathaypacific.com.* **Delta.** ☎ *800/221–1212* ⊕ *www.delta.com.* **Thai Airways.** ☎ *800/426–5204* ⊕ *www.thaiairways.com.* **United Airlines.** ☎ *800/864–8331* ⊕ *www.united.com.*

⛴ Boat

BOAT INFORMATION
Blue Cruiser. ✉ *59/3B Pham Viet Chanh, District 1* ☎ *028/3926–0253, 090/985–7851* ⊕ *www.bluecruiser.com.*

🚌 Bus

Mai Linh Express. ✉ *Ho Chi Minh City* ☎ *028/3939–3939* ⊕ *www.mailinhexpress.vn.* **Phuong Trang FUTA Bus Line.** ✉ *80 Tran Hung Dao, Ho Chi Minh City* ☎ *1/900–6067* ⊕ *www.futabus.com.*

🇺🇸 Embassy

VISA OFFICES Vietnam Embassy to the U.S. ✉ *1233 20th St. NW, Suite 400, Washington* ☎ *202/861–0737* ⊕ *www.vietnamembassy-usa.org.*

🚕 Taxi

TAXI COMPANIES Mai Linh Taxi. ⊕ *www.mailinh.vn.* **Vinasun Taxi.** ⊕ *www.vinasuntaxi.com.*

🚆 Train

TRAIN INFORMATION
Danang Railway Station. ✉ *791 Hai Phòng, Danang.* **Dong Hoi Train Station.** ✉ *Tieu khu 4, Nam Ly, Dong Hoi.* **Hanoi Train Station.** (*Ga Hanoi*). ✉ *120 Le Duan St., Hoan Kiem District.* **Hue Train Station.** ✉ *2 Bui Thi Xuan, Hue.* **Saigon Railway Station.** ✉ *1 Nguyen Thong St., District 3.* **Victoria Sapa Resort &**

Spa. ☎ 0214/387–1522 ⊕ www.victoriahotels.asia.

BOOKING CONTACTS Vietnam Impressive Travel. ⊕ www.vietnamimpressivetravel.com.**Vietnam Railways.** ⊕ www.vietnam-railway.com.**Vietnam Train.** ☎ 098/8580–0614 ⊕ www.vietnamtrain.com.

📍 Emergencies

CONTACTS Ambulance. ☎ Area code plus/115. **Fire.** ☎ Area code plus/114. **Police.** ☎ Area code plus/113.

FOREIGN EMBASSIES Consulate General of the United States. ⊠ 4 Le Duan Blvd., District 1 ☎ 028/3520–4200 24-hr emergency hotline ⊕ www.vn.usembassy.gov/embassy-consulate/ho-chi-minh-city. **Embassy of the United States.** ⊠ 7 Lang Ha, Ba Dinh District ☎ 024/3850–5000 24-hr emergency hotline ⊕ www.vietnam.usembassy.gov.

➕ Hospitals

HOSPITALS AND CLINICS Family Medical Practice Ho Chi Minh City District 1. ⊠ 34 Le Duan, Ho Chi Minh City ☎ 028/3822–7848 ⊕ www.vietnammedicalpractice.com. **Family Medical Practice Hanoi.** ⊠ Van Phuc Diplomatic Compound, 298l Kim Ma, Hanoi ☎ 024/3843–0748 ⊕ www.vietnammedical-practice.com. **Hoan My Danang Hospital.** ⊠ 291 Nguyen Van Linh, Danang ☎ 0236/365–0676 ⊕ www.hoanmydanang.com. **Hue Central Hospital.** ⊠ 16 Le Loi, Hue ☎ 0234/382–2325, 0234/389-0888 ⊕ www.bvtwhue.com.vn; www.hueimc.vn.

📍 Insurance

MEDICAL ASSISTANCE COMPANIES AirMed International. ☎ 800/356–2161, 205/443–4840 ⊕ www.airmed.com. **International SOS Assistance Emergency.** ☎ 215/942-8226 ⊕ www.internationalsos.com. **MedjetAssist.** ☎ 800/527–7478 ⊕ www.medjetassist.com.

MEDICAL-ONLY INSURERS International Medical Group. ☎ 800/628–4664, 317/655–4500 ⊕ www.imglobal.com. **International SOS.** ☎ 215/942–8226 ⊕ www.internationalsos.com. **Wallach & Company.** ☎ 800/237–6615, 540/687–3166 ⊕ www.wallach.com.

Chapter 3

HO CHI MINH CITY

3

Updated by
James Pham

Sights
★★★★★

Restaurants
★★★★★

Hotels
★★★★★

Shopping
★★★★★

Nightlife
★★★★★

WELCOME TO HO CHI MINH CITY

TOP REASONS TO GO

★ **The buzz.** On every street corner there are people eating, drinking, and laughing, kids playing, old men napping, and someone selling something. The noise, the smells, the traffic, the honking—it's all part of the mesmerizing chaos that makes this city unforgettable to everyone who visits.

★ **The food.** Saigonese are the ultimate foodies, dedicating a large part of each day to discussing what and where to eat. This is evident in the proliferation of local joints, where style is unimportant, the options are almost endless, and everything is delicious.

★ **The history.** Chinese and French influence on the city is still in evidence—in the pagodas, the colonial architecture, and the food.

★ **The coffee.** Modern Ho Chi Minh City has a strong café culture. Everywhere you turn you'll see people at street-side cafés, watching the world go by over a glass of *ca phe*.

1 Around Dong Khoi Street. At the heart of Old Saigon in District 1, this historic thoroughfare is always bustling. It links the area around Notre Dame Cathedral to the Saigon River, with many of the city's main attractions along the way.

2 Around Pham Ngu Lao. This is the famous "backpacker area," long a magnet for budget travelers, which centers on the intersection of Pham Ngu Lao and De Tham streets. It's full of markets, hostels, lively bars, and travelers.

3 Around District 3. Stretching west from Nguyen Thi Minh Kai Street, the area bordering District 3 is also at the heart of downtown, but streets are narrower and it has a more residential feel.

4 Beyond the City Center. To the southwest of the central hub, Cholon is home to the city's large Chinese community, while the suburbs of Thao Dien in District 2 and Phu My Hung in District 7 have become expat enclaves of hip bars and great restaurants.

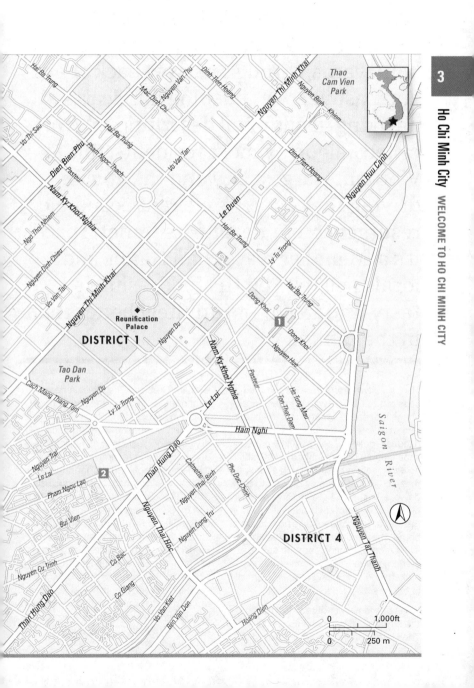

Ho Chi Minh City is a supercharged city of sensory overload. Motorbikes zoom day and night along the wide boulevards, through narrow back alleys, and past vendors pushing handcarts hawking goods of all descriptions. Still called Saigon by most residents, this is Vietnam's largest city and the engine driving the country's current economic resurgence, but despite its frenetic pace, it's a friendlier place than Hanoi, and locals will tell you the food—simple, tasty, and fresh—is infinitely better than in the capital.

This is a city full of surprises. The madness of the traffic—witness the oddball things that are transported on the backs of motorcycles—is countered by tranquil pagodas, peaceful parks, quirky coffee shops, and whole neighborhoods hidden down tiny alleyways, although some of these quiet spots can be difficult to track down. Life in Ho Chi Minh City is lived in public: on motorcycles, sidewalks, and in the parks. Even when its residents are at home, they're still on display, with many living rooms opening onto the street; grandmothers napping, babies being rocked, and food being prepared, are all in full view of passersby.

Icons of the past endure in the midst of the city's headlong rush into capitalism. The Hotel Continental, immortalized in Graham Greene's *The Quiet American*, continues to stand on the corner of old Indochina's most famous thoroughfare, the Rue Catinat, known to American G.I.s during the Vietnam War as Tu Do (Freedom) Street and renamed Dong Khoi (Uprising) Street by the Communists. The city still has its ornate opera house and its old French city hall, the Hôtel de Ville. The broad colonial boulevards leading to the Saigon River and the gracious stucco villas are other remnants of the French-colonial presence. Grisly reminders of the more recent past can be seen at the city's war-related museums. Residents, however, prefer to look forward rather than back and are often perplexed by tourists' fascination with a war that ended more than 40 years ago.

The Chinese influence on the country is still very much in evidence in the Cholon district, the city's Chinatown, but the modern office towers and international hotels that mark the skyline symbolize Vietnam's fixation on the future.

Planning

When to Go

The best time to visit the city is during the cooler dry season, roughly between November and April. Don't discount a visit during rainy season, which runs from about May through October, as most days dawn clear and blue and the afternoon rain showers can be waited out in a café or a museum. During the Christmas season, downtown is lit up with the most astounding Christmas lights and odd decorations, including nativity-themed "caves." The center of town becomes a traffic gridlock at night as people drive in to look at the lights. If you're traveling through Vietnam during *Tet*, the lunar or Chinese New Year (the date changes each year according to the phases of the moon), you are better off being in Ho Chi Minh City rather than a rural area, where everything will be shut. In the city, most tourist hotels and some eating places operate over this public holiday, during which 99% of the population travels home to spend time with their family. The lead-up to the celebration is also an interesting time to be in town to see the Flower Street display and the pop-up flower markets in the city's parks selling pots of bright yellow and red blooms and topiary trees. As Tet approaches, the city is gripped with excitement, with residents furiously cleaning, renovating, and shopping ahead of the holiday. The weeks leading up to *Tet* are also, unfortunately, when snatch and grab and petty theft become much more widespread, with impoverished city dwellers feeling immense social pressure to amass some big-city wealth to display when they go home for the annual family gathering. Police are also out in force at this time.

Getting Here and Around

Ho Chi Minh City sprawls across a large region, stretching all the way north to Cu Chi near the border of Tay Ninh Province, and south to the upper reaches of the Mekong Delta. The part of the city formerly known as Saigon covered only two of the 14 current districts of Ho Chi Minh City: Districts 1 and 3, which are home to the highest concentration of tourist sights, hotels, restaurants, and bars. Most areas of interest to visitors are here, although the city's Chinatown, known as Cholon, in District 5 and part of District 6, is also worth exploring. Outlying districts, including Districts 2 and 7, contain newer expat-centric areas, which warrant a visit for dining and entertainment rather than sightseeing.

Downtown Ho Chi Minh City is walkable nowadays, with mostly even sidewalks clear of parked motorbikes and street vendors. Outside of the main business area, however, the streets and sidewalks are chaotic, making a leisurely stroll a difficult proposition.

Traffic can often be quite hectic and very noisy, and taxis tend to be the best bet for getting around. Avoid taxi scams and unreliable meters by choosing Vinasun or Mai Linh taxis—one will cruise by within a few minutes no matter where you are in the city. Grab also operates in Ho Chi Minh City and can be a handy alternative to taxis. However, rumblings from authorities indicate ride-sharing companies may have their operations curtailed at some point.

Addresses in Ho Chi Minh City often contain words such as district (*quan*), ward (*phuong*), or road/street (*duong*). Odd- and even-numbered addresses are usually on opposite sides of the street. The ward name or number can be important because on many long streets, the numbering reverts to 1 at the ward boundary. Places located down a *hem* (alley) will have a sometimes-confusing address containing a multitude of numbers, such as 55/4 Le Thi Hong Gam. To find this address, go down the hem at 55 Le Thi Hong Gam Street and find building No. 4.

AIR

Ho Chi Minh City's Tan Son Nhat Airport, about 7 km (4 miles) north of the city center, is Vietnam's largest, with a domestic and an international terminal. Direct international flights are available from major cities in Europe, Australia, and other parts of Asia, including Cambodia's Siem Reap and Phnom Penh. It takes about 10 minutes to walk between terminals along a covered walkway, so it's a relatively easy airport in which to transit.

Ho Chi Minh City is also served by domestic flights from just about any airport in the country, including the major tourist destinations of Hanoi, Hue, Danang (for Hoi An), Dalat, Nha Trang, Phu Quoc, and Con Dao.

AIRPORT INFORMATION Tan Son Nhat International Airport. ✉ *Truong Son, Binh Tan District* ☎ *028/3848–5383* ⊕ *vietnamairport.vn.*

TRANSFERS

The cheapest way to get to the city is by bus. Route 109 and shuttle bus 49 pick up at column 15 at the international terminal. Bus 109 goes through the city center and terminates at September 23 Park near the backpacker area. Shuttle bus 49 is slightly more expensive because it stops at the major hotels, terminating at the Ben Thanh Bus Station. Hotels that offer airport transfers usually charge a premium for this service, and you'll probably pay two or three times what it would cost in a taxi. To take a taxi, ignore the touts who congregate outside the arrivals hall, turn left and look for someone with a clipboard and a Mai Linh or Vinasun taxi company uniform. Tell them your destination and they'll organize a taxi for you, although it might take some time and local travelers are likely to jump to the front of the line. It takes 20 to 45 minutes to get downtown, depending on the traffic, and the fare should be between 130,000d and 170,000d (slightly more if you have to negotiate peak hour traffic). There's a 15,000d taxi exit toll that will be added to the fare shown on the meter. Saigon Air Taxi has a monopoly at Tan Son Nhat airport and at some government-owned hotels in the city. If you purchase a prepaid Saigon Air voucher at the airport (not recommended), do not pay the driver any additional sum. Only take a Saigon Air taxi if you can't find a Vinasun or Mai Linh taxi.

TAXI CONTACTS Mai Linh. ☎ *028/3838– 3838* ⊕ *www.mailinh.vn.***Vinasun.** ☎ *028/3827–2727* ⊕ *www.vinasuntaxi. com.*

BIKE

Ho Chi Minh City was built for bicycles, though the sheer volume of motor traffic these days can make cycling a challenge. But once you work out how the traffic flows, cycling can be an enjoyable way to get around, especially if you want to explore some of the quieter reaches of the city. Consider a half- or full-day bicycle tour to get started. Bicycles can be rented from several shops, all outside the central business area, for about 300,000d a day, with the per-day rate dropping for weekly rentals. You can also rent panniers and racks. There are a few rental places south of the city. Saigon Cycles is in District 7, about 20 minutes by taxi from downtown, and this newer district has some cycling trails that are an easy introduction to pedaling in the city.

Similarly, Mr Biker is in a quiet residential location with little traffic, making the area well suited to cycling.

BIKE CONTACTS Mr Biker Saigon. ✉ *24 Street No. 6, Binh Chanh District* ⊕ *www.mrbikersaigon.com.***Saigon Cycles.** ✉ *Shop 51/1 Sky Garden 2, 44 Phan Van Nghi, Phu My Hung, District 7* ☎ *028/5410–3114* ⊕ *xedapcaocap.com.*

BOAT

Greenlines offers fast boat service between Ho Chi Minh City and Vung Tau while the public waterbus is a cheap, pleasant way to see the city from the Saigon River.

Greenlines DP
✉ *Bach Dang Speed Ferry Terminal, District 1* ☎ *0098/800–9579 cell phone* ⊕ *www.greenlines-dp.com.*

Saigon Waterbus
✉ *Bach Dang Pier, Ton Duc Thang, District 1* ☎ *1900/636–830* ⊕ *www. saigonwaterbus.com.*

BUS

There are several reputable bus companies that offer regular departures from Ho Chi Minh City on comfortable, air-conditioned coaches to major towns and cities in the Mekong Delta and points north. It pays to do a bit of research on the latest road conditions leading to a chosen destination before deciding whether to take the bus, the train, or a flight.

Ho Chi Minh City has a number of bus stations. More than 200 big and small bus companies operate out of Mien Dong Station, 7 km (4 miles) north of District 1, from destinations including Vung Tau, Phan Thiet, Dalat, Nha Trang, and places in the central highlands. Buses from the Mekong Delta arrive at and depart from Mien Tay Station. An Suong Station, a 45-minute taxi ride from downtown, serves Tay Ninh. Ho Chi Minh City bus stations have no central office. Instead each bus company that uses the bus station has a ticket office, most with

a waiting area. Disembarking passengers are accosted by an array of taxi and *xe om* drivers, but bus companies may offer a free minibus shuttle to bigger, more convenient bus stations. The shuttles can be very cramped, and information is very difficult to elicit if you don't speak Vietnamese, so if you plan to take the easier option of a taxi to downtown, consider pushing through the throng to find a trusted brand, such as Mai Linh or Vinasun. Some bus stations, including Mien Tay, have their own taxi company, which means you have to get past the "approved" drivers to find Mai Linh or Vinasun taxis, which will be waiting outside. Using public buses to get around the city can be a cultural experience. The city's department of transport lists bus routes and times on its website: buyttph-cm.com.vn.

In locations other than bus stations, the trick is identifying a bus stop (they're usually unmarked) and knowing where to get off. Commuters in Ho Chi Minh City are usually eager to help out their fellow travelers.

BUS CONTACTS An Suong Station. (*Ben Xe An Suong*) ✉ *Hwy. 22, Ba Diem, Hoc Mon District* ☎ *028/3883–2517.***Ben Thanh Station.** (*Tram dieu hanh Sai Gon*) ✉ *Ben Thanh Roundabout, District 1.***Cholon Station.** ✉ *46 Le Quang Sung, District 5* ☎.**Mien Dong Station.** (*Ben Xe Mien Dong*) ✉ *292 Dinh Bo Linh, Binh Thanh District* ☎ *28/3899–1607.***Mien Tay Station.** (*Ben Xe Mien Tay*) ✉ *395 Kinh Duong Vuong, Binh Tan District.***September 23 Park Station.** ✉ *Pham Ngu Lao, District 1.*

CAR

Even though the Vietnamese government now recognizes international drivers' licenses *(see also Travel Smart)*, self-driving is still not recommended in Ho Chi Minh City for those unfamiliar with the chaotic traffic. Most car-rental places offer car-and-driver rental, which can give you great freedom to explore the city and surrounding areas without the stress of driving in it. Hiring a car and driver for a full day starts at about 1,180,000d for a four-seater and 1,288,000d for a seven-seater, although the fee is based on where you want to go. For getting around within the city, taxis are often more useful; with a rented car, your driver will have to find somewhere to park in a city designed for bicycles, not automobiles. Most of the bigger hotels in Ho Chi Minh City can arrange short- or long-term car-and-driver rentals, or you can contact Drive Vietnam, Bali Limousines, or Avis, the latter with locations downtown and at the airport.

CAR CONTACTS Avis. ☎ 096/427–2009 ⊕ www.avis.com.vn.**Bali Limousine.** ☎ 028/3974–9749 ⊕ www.bali.limo.**Drive Vietnam.** ☎ 093/741–7938 ⊕ www.drivevietnam.com.

CYCLO

This form of travel is quite comfortable, and the slow and gentle rhythm of the pedaling makes for a strangely peaceful experience on the busy roads. Maika-tours offers reputable morning cyclo tours of the city (see Tours). Unless part of an organized tour, cyclos (xich lo) should be avoided at all costs. The freelance cyclo drivers who lurk at Ben Thanh Market and in the backpacker area in District 1 are notorious for ripping off trusting tourists.

MOTORBIKE

Motorbikes are available for rent all over Vietnam, but a Vietnamese motorbike license is required to drive one (see also Travel Smart). There are many motorbike rental places in the backpacker district, mostly catering to the backpacker brigade. Saigon Scooter Centre is a professional and reliable motorbike rental option set up by a British enthusiast, which has a fleet of well-maintained scooters and motorbikes ranging from classic Vespas to KTM touring bikes, available daily, weekly, or longer. Bikes can be rented here and dropped off at most towns and cities in Vietnam, and

a luggage service can be arranged. The motorbikes at Chi's Cafe are similarly reliable and the rental fees are very reasonable, from 120,000d a day. There are also outlets that advertise sales and repurchase for those who want to buy a motorbike in Ho Chi Minh City and sell it back to the company at their branch in Hanoi. The reliability of motorbike rental and sales places varies widely; most expect up-front payment, and some ask for a deposit or to hold your passport as security against the rented motorbike.

MOTORBIKE CONTACTS Chi's Café. ✉ 185/30 Pham Ngu Lao St, District 1 ☎ 0903/643–446 ⊕ www.chiscafe.com. **Saigon Scooter Centre.** ✉ 61 Nguyen Ba Huan, Thao Dien, District 2 ☎ 090/301–3690 cell phone ⊕ www.saigonscootercentrerentals.com.

TAXIS AND MOTORBIKE TAXI

One of the quickest—and scariest—ways around the city is riding on the back of a motorbike taxi, known as a Honda om or a xe om (xe means transportation, om means hug, and Honda is the most popular brand of motorbike in Vietnam). These days the xe om drivers who hang out in Ho Chi Minh City's tourist centers expect to be paid the same as a taxi fare for a journey that's far less comfortable and far more dangerous than in a taxi. A quick five-minute trip should cost no more than 20,000d.

For regular taxis, the recommended companies are Mai Linh and Vinasun. Mai Linh taxis are either all green or white and green, and Vinasun taxis are white with a red stripe. The drivers of both companies wear a uniform with a tie and should have an ID card on the dash. Meters start automatically—if you are trying to catch a taxi that has a passenger disembarking, you'll be asked to shut the door and then open it again to reset the meter. Fares are relatively cheap, but vary depending on whether you're in a four-seater or a seven-seater. Flagfall starts from 65 cents, plus 70–81 cents per kilometer; fares drop slightly at the 26-km (16-mile) mark. Waiting time is charged at 9 cents per four minutes.

■ TIP➔ **Check the name and the livery of the cab carefully as there are many fake taxis roaming the streets, often with one or two letters different from the company they're copying.**

TAXI CONTACTS Mai Linh. ☎ 028/3838–3838 ⊕ www.mailinh.vn.**Vinasun.** ☎ 028/3827–2727 ⊕ www.vinasuntaxi. com.

TRAIN

Trains connecting Ho Chi Minh City with coastal towns to the north arrive and depart from the Saigon Railway Station (Ga Sai Gon) in District 3, about 1 km (½ mile) from the downtown area of District 1. Two main train services depart from here. The Reunification Express travels along Vietnam's "spine" stopping at centers including Nha Trang, Danang, Hue, and finally—about 33 hours after leaving Ho Chi Minh City—Hanoi. A second train service runs from Ho Chi Minh City to Phan Thiet, 20 km (12 miles) from the resort town of Mui Ne. Hotels and travel agents can organize tickets for a small fee, which usually amounts to less than a taxi fare to the Saigon Railway ticketing office.

TRAIN CONTACTS Saigon Railway Station. (Ga Sai Gon) ✉ 1 Nguyen Thong, District 3 ☎ 1900–1520 for booking ⊕ www. gasaigon.com.vn.

Health and Safety

Ho Chi Minh City is safe for the most part, but traffic safety and petty theft are both issues to bear in mind when out and about, especially in the weeks before *Tet*. Always look in every possible direction when crossing the street, and be aware that motorcycles and even cars frequently use the sidewalks. Keep valuables out of view where possible, make sure your camera strap is around your neck or wrist, and consider minimizing what you carry around and wear, especially if going out at night. Patience and a pleasant demeanor are usually enough to sort out disagreements, but visible anger may attract threats or even violence.

Foreigners are often subjected to inflated prices for goods or services in Vietnam. This business tactic, which many Vietnamese consider reasonable, is often the source of disagreements between Vietnamese and tourists. Simple common-sense precautions, such as reconfirming a price before agreeing to purchase an item or service, can help avoid misunderstandings or mysterious new fees.

If you find yourself in need of medical attention in Ho Chi Minh City, there are several international clinics with internationally trained staff and modern medical technology.

Ho Chi Minh City is always hot—daily highs rarely dip below 90°F—so drink plenty of water and keep the risk of dehydration and sunstroke in mind when heading out. Apply sunscreen liberally. Ho Chi Minh City is also quite humid—keep a close eye on small cuts and scrapes as they can easily get infected. Mosquito-borne diseases such as dengue fever can ruin a trip. Make sure to use mosquito repellent, especially at dawn and dusk.

Money

International and local ATMs are scattered throughout the city. The local banks have a per-transaction limit of about 2 million dong (about $88) so to minimize international withdrawal fees, look for international bank ATMs, such as HSBC and Citibank. If exploring rural areas outside of Ho Chi Minh City's sprawl, it's a good idea to take plenty of low-denomination bills, as small shops and stalls frequently have difficulty changing large bills.

Sights

Ho Chi Minh City is a fascinating destination, but a chronic lack of infrastructure, not to mention oppressive heat and seasonal rains, can make navigation difficult. A fearless visitor might embrace the chaos by jumping on the back of a *xe om* with a hit list of cultural attractions and must-eat street food dishes, but most visitors prefer to traverse the city by taxi. Whatever your mode of transportation, spread your sightseeing over two or three days and let yourself unwind—despite the pulsating street life, this is also a city of soul-soothing spas, hidden cafés, and rooftop bars.

Restaurants

Dining options in Ho Chi Minh City run the gamut from fine dining in secluded air-conditioned splendor to sidewalk eateries where the food is cooked in makeshift open-air kitchens. The dynamism and energy of the city is reflected in a dining scene bursting with international options and a host of fusion choices in between.

The city's middle classes love nothing more than descending on the latest dining craze, so do note locals' recommendations and follow the crowds to the latest hot spot. Despite the Saigonese's love for the flashy "new next big thing," there's also a somewhat reluctant loyalty to the French cuisine of their former colonial rulers. Ho Chi Minh City is home to many French restaurants, from casual Parisian-style bistros to the full starched linen and paired wine experience. Most of Ho Chi Minh City's international restaurants are in and around Districts 1 and 3, although there are several excellent options in the expat areas of Districts 2 and 7.

Despite the international offerings, it's the mouthwatering Vietnamese cuisine that remains one of Ho Chi Minh City's major draws, whether eaten on the street or indoors in a tourist-friendly restaurant—the places with English menus are not always the most authentic, but can be the easiest when it comes to placing an order. But street food and no-frills, family-run restaurants offer incredible value, so after, say, a humble bowl of pho for breakfast and a host of southern specialties for lunch, you can easily justify a splurge for dinner.

Meals are serious business in Ho Chi Minh City, and between noon and 1 pm most office workers and public servants take a lunch break. Dinner is generally served any time after about 6 pm and eating (and drinking) can continue until 1 am or later.

What It Costs			
$	$$	$$$	$$$$
RESTAURANTS			
under 70,000d	70,000d– 270,000d	271,000d– 400,000d	over 401,000d

Hotels

Most visitors stay in Districts 1 and 3—the center of old Saigon—where the highest proportion of the museums, galleries, restaurants, bars, and nightclubs are found. The gracious old colonial hotels are here, too, as are many newer international hotels. Free Wi-Fi is ubiquitous, but service can be hit-or-miss. When in doubt, just remember that location trumps facilities. Look for bargains during Ho Chi Minh City's low season, from May to October, when some hotels discount their room rates to entice visitors during the rainy season.

At the higher end of the hotel spectrum, management strives to deliver international-standard four- or five-star service, and usually does so. Things can get interesting in the mid-range and budget options, especially if staff is unfamiliar with international service standards. Exercise patience because in most cases, intentions are good.

What It Costs

$	$$	$$$	$$$$
HOTELS			
Under 750,000d	750,000d –1 million d	1.1 million d–2.5 million d	over 2.6 million d

Nightlife and Performing Arts

As a thriving business hub, Ho Chi Minh City works hard and plays hard. You'll find plenty of lively bars and nightclubs all across District 1. The performing arts are largely represented by the Saigon Opera House and the French-government-funded Idecaf venue, which both hold regular concerts. English-language films either have Vietnamese subtitles or are dubbed (very loudly) into Vietnamese. If you want to see one, make sure you get a ticket to a subtitled screening so that you can hear the original soundtrack.

Shopping

There's a growing trend in Ho Chi Minh City's shopping scene of in-the-know locals and expats opening up enticing boutiques selling fair trade items, housewares, and very stylish locally made items, ranging from fashion to coffee cups.

Considered a traditional fine art of Vietnam, lacquerware is beautiful, long-lasting, and—best of all for those with luggage weight restrictions—light. Most tourist shops and markets hawk the same kind of budget lacquerware. Higher quality items come at a price and are usually found in specialty shops. Some of the newer high-rise shopping complexes in downtown Ho Chi Minh City are home to high-end international brands, such as Versace, Jimmy Choo, and Prada. On the other end of the scale, markets offer a cheap and cheerful experience. They are generally open from sunrise until sunset, although some vendors just outside the markets stay open later.

By law, all transactions should be completed using dong, even if prices are quoted in U.S. dollars.

Tours

Ho Chi Minh City has a two-tier tour industry, with older operations offering adventurous budget (and sometimes uncomfortable) options to the backpacker market, and a fledgling service catering to more upscale travelers. Reliability tends to come at a price. A number of companies offer city tours, on foot or by motorbike, and many reputable travel agencies can recommend an English-speaking guide to give you a personalized tour. Reliable new operators also offer food tours and bicycle tours. Day and multiday excursions outside of Ho Chi Minh City are easy to arrange, and an organized tour is sometimes the easiest option.

TOUR OPERATORS Back of the Bike Tours. ✉ *Ho Chi Minh City* ☎ *093/504–6910* ⊕ *www.backofthebiketours.com.* **Discova.** ☎ *0283/3820–8822* ⊕ *www.discova.com.* **Exo Travel.** ✉ *16-18 Hai Ba Trung, District 1* ☎ *028/3995–9898* ⊕ *www.exotravel.com.* **Les Rives.** ✉ *Ho Chi Minh City* ☎ *078/592–0018* ⊕ *www.lesrivesexperience.com.* **Maika Tours.** ✉ *5A/2 Tran Phu, District 5* ☎ *090/934–3760* ⊕ *www.maikatours.com.* **Saigon Craft Beer Tours.** ☎ *090/934–3760* ⊕ *www.saigoncraftbeertours.com.* **Saigon Photo Tours & Workshops.** ⊹ *Tours begin with a hotel pickup* ☎ *078/569–8144* ⊕ *www.saigonimaging.com.* **Saigon Street Eats.** ✉ *Ho Chi Minh City* ☎ *908/449–408* ⊕ *www.saigonstreeteats.com.* **Saigon Tourist.** ✉ *45 Le Thanh Ton, District 1* ☎ *028/3827–9279, 028/3822–4987* ⊕ *www.saigon-tourist.com.* **Vietnam Bike Tours.** ✉ *126 Dinh Bo Linh, Binh Thanh District* ☎ *0855/075–999.* **XO Tours.** ✉ *Ho Chi Minh City* ☎ *0933/083–727* ⊕ *www.xotours.vn.*

Dong Khoi Street is the center of the action in Ho Chi Minh City.

Visitor Information

While there are four official Visitor Information and Support Centers in Ho Chi Minh City operated by the city's Board of Tourism, some other places with signs claiming to offer tourist information might actually be travel agencies hoping to sell you a tour. Hotel tour desks are usually the best source of information, but be aware that some concierges and travel desks will only recommend activities that will pay them a commission.

Around Dong Khoi Street

District 1 is the center of old Saigon, and Dong Khoi Street, toward the eastern edge, is the neighborhood's historic main thoroughfare. It's a pleasant tree-lined street running down to the Saigon River from Notre Dame Cathedral and the Central Post Office. These buildings, among many other fine examples here, date from the French-colonial era, when the street was known as Rue Catinat. Another name change occurred in the 1960s and '70s, when, known as Tu Do Street, it was Saigon's red-light district. Since then, the seedy element has been replaced by plenty of chic shopping, eating, and drinking, but it tends to be more costly here than elsewhere in the city. Around Dong Khoi Street, broad Nguyen Hue and Le Loi boulevards converge at the Hotel de Ville (now the People's Committee building), the historic Opera House, and the Hotel Continental; the former presidential palace (now called the Reunification Palace) is on the northern boundary of the area. The unsightly and very behind-schedule metro construction project blocks some key streets downtown, making traversing the area much more difficult than it should be. The project was originally due for completion in 2014, but the latest schedule estimates the metro's first line won't be operational until 2022.

Ho Chi Minh City History

Bordered by the Thi Nghe Channel to the north, the Ben Nghe Channel to the south, and the Saigon River to the east, the city has served as a natural fortress and has been fought over by countless people during the past 2,000 years. The ancient empire of Funan used the area as a trading post, and the Khmer kingdom of Angkor transformed Prey Nokor, as Ho Chi Minh City was called, into a flourishing center of trade protected by a standing army. By the 14th century, while under Khmer rule, the city attracted Arab, Cham, Chinese, Malaysian, and Indian merchants. It was then known as the gateway to the Kingdom of Champa, the sister empire to Angkor.

In 1674 the lords of the Nguyen clan in Hue established a customs post at Prey Nokor to cash in on the region's growing commercial traffic. Saigon, as the Vietnamese called it, became an increasingly important administrative post. The building in 1772 of a 6-km (4-mile) trench on the western edge of old Saigon, in what is now District 5, marked the shift in control in the south from Khmer rule to Nguyen rule from Hue. Further Vietnamese consolidation came in 1778 with the development of Cholon, Saigon's Chinese city, as a second commercial hub in the area that is now District 5.

In 1789 the Nguyen lords moved their power base from Hue to Saigon, following attacks by rebels from the village of Tay Son. Unhappy with the way the Nguyen lords had been running the country, the rebels massacred most of the Nguyen clan and took control of the government—briefly. In 1802, Prince Nguyen Anh, the last surviving heir to the Nguyen dynasty, defeated the Tay Son ruler—with French backing—regaining power and uniting Vietnam. He moved the capital back to Hue and declared himself Emperor Gia Long.

In quelling the Tay Son rebels, Gia Long's request for French assistance, which was readily provided, came at a price. In exchange for their help, Gia Long promised the French territorial concessions in Vietnam. Although the French Revolution and the Napoleonic Wars temporarily delayed any French claims, Gia Long's decision eventually cost Vietnam dearly. In 1859, the French, tired of waiting for the Vietnamese emperor to give them what they felt they deserved, seized Saigon and made it the capital of their new colony, Cochin China. This marked the beginning of an epoch of colonial-style feudalism and indentured servitude for many Vietnamese in the highlands. The catastrophe that was to overtake Saigon and the rest of Vietnam during the latter half of the 20th century was a direct result of French-colonial interference.

👁 Sights

Bitexco Financial Tower

VIEWPOINT | A symbol of contemporary Ho Chi Minh City, the 68-floor Bitexco Financial Tower is the city's second tallest building, and you can enjoy high-altitude views from the Saigon Skydeck on the 49th floor. This deck features interactive screens that provide information about a selection of streets and sights below. ✉ *36 Ho Tung Mau, District 1* ☎ *028/3915–6156* ⊕ *www.saigonskydeck.com* 🎫 *200,000d.*

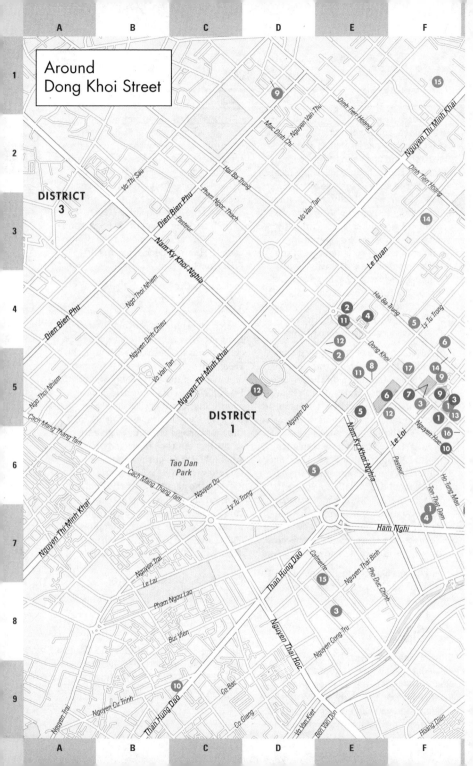

Around
Dong Khoi Street

DISTRICT 3

DISTRICT 1

Tao Dan Park

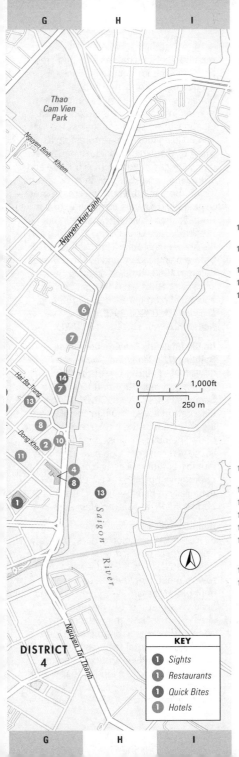

Sights ▼

1 Bitexco Financial
  Tower **G7**
2 Book Street............... **E4**
3 Caravelle Hotel.......... **G5**
4 Central Post Office **E4**
5 Ho Chi Minh City
  Museum **E5**
6 Ho Chi Minh City
  People's Committee
  Building **E5**
7 Hotel Continental **F5**
8 Hotel Majestic **G6**
9 Municipal Theater of
  Ho Chi Minh City (Saigon
  Opera House) **F5**
10 Nguyen Hue
  Walking Street **F6**
11 Notre Dame
  Cathedral **E4**
12 Reunification Palace ... **D5**
13 Saigon River............. **H6**
14 Ton Duc Thang
  Museum **G5**

Restaurants ▼

1 Anan Saigon............. **F7**
2 Au Parc **E4**
3 Bep Me In Farm.......... **E8**
4 The Elbow Room
  Bistro and Bar........... **F7**
5 4P's Pizza **E6**
6 Hoa Tuc **G5**
7 Hum Lounge and
  Restaurant.............. **G5**
8 Huong Lai................. **E5**
9 Loving Hut Hoa Dang... **D1**
10 Mad Cow
  Wine & Grill **C9**
11 Nous....................... **E5**
12 Propaganda **E4**
13 Racha Room............. **G5**
14 The Refinery............. **G5**
15 Secret House
  Vietnamese Restaurant
  and Cafe **E7**
16 Vietnam House.......... **G6**
17 Wrap and Roll........... **F5**

Quick Bites ▼

1 L'Usine **F5**

Hotels ▼

1 Caravelle Hotel.......... **F5**
2 Grand Hotel.............. **G6**
3 Hotel Continental **F5**
4 Hotel Majestic **G6**
5 InterContinental
  Saigon.................... **F4**
6 Le Méridien Saigon..... **H4**
7 Lotte Legend
  Hotel Saigon............. **G4**
8 The Myst Dong Khoi.... **G6**
9 Park Hyatt Saigon **F5**
10 Renaissance Riverside
  Hotel Saigon............. **G6**
11 The Reverie Saigon..... **G6**
12 Rex Hotel **E5**
13 Sheraton Saigon
  Hotel and Towers **F5**
14 Sofitel Saigon Plaza **F3**
15 Somerset
  Ho Chi Minh City **F1**

KEY

- 1 Sights
- 1 Restaurants
- 1 Quick Bites
- 1 Hotels

DISTRICT 4

Thao
Cam Vien
Park

Saigon River

Nguyen Binh Khiem

Nguyen Huu Canh

Hai Ba Trung

Dong Khoi

Nguyen Tat Thanh

0 — 1,000ft
0 — 250 m

Book Street

PEDESTRIAN MALL | This leafy 150-meter-long pedestrian-only street lined with bookshops and cafés is very close to the post office and the Notre Dame Cathedral. Some new and secondhand English-language books are available, but the real prizes here are the adult coloring books featuring Vietnamese scenes. ✉ *Nguyen Van Binh, District 1.*

Caravelle Hotel

HOTEL | Opened on Christmas Eve 1959, the Caravelle is one of the city's most iconic hotels, accommodating many foreign correspondents during the Vietnam War, with journalists chronicling the 1968 Tet Offensive from the hotel's rooftop bar. Extensive renovations in 2019 updated some of the rooms and event spaces while the 9th floor Saigon Saigon Bar still draws a crowd for its live music and city views. ✉ *19 Lam Son Sq., District 1* ☎ *028/3823-4999* ⊕ *www.caravellehotel.com.*

★ Central Post Office

(*Buu Dien Trung Tam*)

GOVERNMENT BUILDING | Be sure to go inside to check out the huge map of old Indochina in this classic French-colonial building, designed by French architect Alfred Foulhoux (and not Gustave Eiffel as some sources claim) and completed in 1891. In addition to the usual mail services, there are phones, fax machines, and a small gift shop. ✉ *2 Cong Xa Paris, District 1.*

Ho Chi Minh City Museum

(*Bao Tang Thanh Pho Ho Chi Minh*)

HISTORY MUSEUM | Completed in 1890, the building has been the residence for the French governor of Cochin China, the Japanese governor during Vietnam's brief Japanese occupation, and the envoy of Bao Dai, the last emperor of Vietnam, and also served as the Supreme Court. Since 1975, it's been a museum (formerly known as the Museum of the Revolution) with a strong focus on the Vietnamese struggle against the French and Americans. Displays focus on famous marches, military battles, and anti-French and anti-American activists. Exhibits include photos of historical events, uprisings, student demonstrations, and the self-immolation of the monk Thich Quang Duc as a protest against the war. The building itself is as interesting as many of the exhibits inside: a neoclassic design, it has huge columns outside and 19th-century ballrooms with lofty ceilings inside. Beneath the building are concrete bunkers and tunnels connecting to the Reunification Palace. It was here that President Ngo Dinh Diem (1901–63) and his notorious brother Ngo Dinh Nhu hid before being caught and eventually executed in 1963. Outside on the grounds are Soviet tanks, an American helicopter, and antiaircraft guns. ✉ *65 Ly Tu Trong, District 1* ☎ *028/3829–9741* ⊕ *www. hcmc-museum.edu.vn* ✉ *30,000d.*

Ho Chi Minh City People's Committee Building

(*Uy Ban Nhan Dan Thanh Pho*)

GOVERNMENT BUILDING | Built by the French between 1901 and 1908 to be Saigon's Hôtel de Ville (City Hall), this elaborate yellow-and-white colonial building now houses the city's main governing body. The building is not open to the public, so you can't get a peek at its ornate interior, but it remains one of the most photogenic buildings in Ho Chi Minh City, especially at night when it's floodlit. ✉ *86 Le Thanh Ton, at Nguyen Hue, District 1.*

Hotel Continental

HOTEL | In French-colonial days, the Hotel Continental's open-air terrace—then known as Café de la Hien—was the town's most sought-after lunch spot; during the Vietnam War, journalists and diplomats met there to discuss the latest events. Now, the terrace has been enclosed and renamed La Dolce Vita Café. The hotel features in Graham Greene's *The Quiet American* and the author himself was a long-time resident in room 214 and a regular at Le Bourgeois Restaurant. ✉ *132–134 Dong Khoi,*

The hall of Ho Chi Minh City's Central Post Office is architecturally stunning.

District 1 ☎ *028/3829–9201* ⊕ *www.continentalsaigon.com.*

Hotel Majestic
HOTEL | Built in the late 19th century, the Majestic was one of the first French-colonial hotels, and it still has the elegant style to show for it. Head to the rooftop bar for an excellent view of the Saigon River. ✉ *1 Dong Khoi, District 1, District 1* ☎ *028/3829–5517* ⊕ *www.majesticsaigon.com.vn.*

Municipal Theater of Ho Chi Minh City (Saigon Opera House) (*Nha Hat Thanh Pho*)
HISTORIC SIGHT | This colonial-style theater was built by the French in 1899 as Saigon's opera house. Later it housed the National Assembly of South Vietnam, the congress of the South Vietnamese government. After 1975, when South Vietnam ceased to be, it became a theater again. ✉ *7 Lam Son Sq., District 1* ☎ *028/3823–7419.*

Nguyen Hue Walking Street
STREET | During the daytime Nguyen Hue Walking Street, with its dearth of shade trees, is not very impressive, especially when it's not hosting an exhibition or event. But come evening, it's a charming microcosm of modern Saigon: wandering vendors, canoodling couples, and selfies galore. Ho Chi Minh City's first pedestrian street, which stretches from the People's Committee Building to Bach Dang Wharf, was a canal in colonial times, and the streets to either side were called Rue Rigault de Genouilly and Rue Charner. Tip: be careful when crossing the road to get to the walking section as the locals still aren't used to the traffic lights. ✉ *Nguyen Hue, District 1* 🎫 *Free.*

Notre Dame Cathedral (*Nha Tho Duc Ba*)
RELIGIOUS BUILDING | Officially known as the Basilica of Our Lady of Immaculate Conception, this neo-Romanesque cathedral, built by the French in 1880, was once a prominent presence on the city

At night, Saigon River reflects the lights of Ho Chi Minh City's skyline; see it up close on a Saigon Waterbus.

skyline. Spanish, Portuguese, and French missionaries introduced Catholicism to Vietnam as early as the 16th century and today there are approximately 8 million Catholics in Vietnam, the seventh-largest Christian population in Asia. Sunday mass can be quite a sight, as hundreds of faithful converge on the church and stand in the surrounding square. Some services include short sections in English and French. However, extensive renovations started on the cathedral in 2017, closing it off to tourists until at least 2023. ✉ *1 Cong Xa Paris, at top of Dong Khoi St., District 1* ✉ *Free.*

★ **Reunification Palace** (*Dinh Doc Lap*) **NOTABLE BUILDING** | This is one of the more potent symbols of the Vietnam War. On April 30, 1975, a North Vietnamese Army tank smashed through the main gate of what was then known as the Independence Palace, ending one of the bloodiest conflicts in living memory. The current boxy building replaced the elegant French colonial–style Norodom Palace, which was bombed by fighter jets in 1962 in an unsuccessful attempt to assassinate South Vietnam's President Ngo Dinh Diem. The jet, along with the tanks that ended the war, is on display on the grounds. Free guides are available inside the palace, which remains as it was on that fateful day in 1975, albeit slightly more worn. The time-capsule nature of the palace offers a fascinating insight into the high life of 1960s Saigon, when bigwigs would enjoy tea and movie screenings in plush rooms upstairs, while the war effort was directed from the spartan concrete warren in the basement. The gardens cover 44 acres of lush lawn and shady trees, and a large fountain in front of the palace redirects the bad luck that could flow into the palace from the broad boulevard of Le Duan Street, according to the principles of feng shui. ✉ *135 Nam Ky Khoi Nghia, District 1* ☎ *028/3829–4117* ⊕ *www.dinhdoclap.gov.vn* ✉ *40,000d.*

Saigon River
BODY OF WATER | You'll regularly catch glimpses of the Saigon River, which snakes its way through many districts of Ho Chi Minh City, while you're sightseeing. A Saigon Waterbus trip is a cheap and comfortable way to view the city from the river, and the "kissing bridge," aka Thu Thiem Bridge, has stunning views of the city at night. Sadly, the ancient shade trees that used to line part of the river along Ton Duc Thang Street were chopped down to make way for a new bridge.

Ton Duc Thang Museum
(*Bao Tang Ton Duc Thang*)
Dedicated to the first president of the unified post-war Vietnam, Ton Duc Thang, this stark museum is of interest mainly to avid historians and political junkies, who will relish the insights it offers into government propaganda in the downstairs section, featuring letters from family members. The museum contains items from Uncle Ton's personal life, such as his spectacles and a rattan trunk, as well as gifts from foreign leaders and replicas of various huts he lived in while fighting the French in the 1940s and '50s. ✉ *92 Le Thanh Ton, District 1* ☎ *028/3829–7542* 🌐 *www.baotangtonducthang.vn* 🎫 *Free* 🕒 *Closed Mon.*

🍴 Restaurants

★ Anan Saigon
$$$$ | **VIETNAMESE** | Voted one of Asia's 50 Best Restaurants in 2021, Anan Saigon puts a whimsically modern twist on Vietnamese street food. Talented Vietnamese-American chef-owner Peter Cuong Franklin is credited for pioneering Vietnamese fusion cuisine, often elevating Vietnamese flavors with French cooking techniques. **Known for:** the off-menu $100 banh mi and $100 pho; amazing chef's tasting menu; modern Vietnamese cuisine. [$] *Average main: d485,000* ✉ *89 Ton That Dam, District 1* ☎ *090/479–2920* 🌐 *www.anansaigon.com* 🕒 *Closed Mon.*

Au Parc
$$ | **MEDITERRANEAN** | **FAMILY** | Midway between the Reunification Palace and Notre Dame cathedral, overlooking the tall trees of April 30 Park, this is a great place to linger in exotic surroundings, whether for a meal or just a smoothie or coffee. The flavors are Mediterranean and Middle Eastern, the staff is attentive, and the location is prime. **Known for:** kids playroom on the top floor; Mediterranean cuisine; great location. [$] *Average main: d250,000* ✉ *23 Han Thuyen, District 1* ☎ *028/3829–2772* 🌐 *www.auparcsaigon.com.*

The Refinery
$$$ | **FRENCH** | With prints and paintings of old Saigon, this stylish bistro pays homage to its historic location within the former Manufacture d'Opium (built in 1881), yet the menu and the wine list are decidedly Continental. The Refinery's set lunch is great value, and its outdoor section is a great spot for a few sundowners. **Known for:** outdoor patio; historic location; bistro-style meals. [$] *Average main: d360,000* ✉ *Through the arch, 74/7c Hai Ba Trung, District 1* ☎ *028/3823–0509* 🌐 *www.therefinerysaigon.com.*

Bep Me In Farm
$$ | **VIETNAMESE** | **FAMILY** | Down a small street near Ben Thanh Market, this cute little eatery serves cheap and cheerful Vietnamese food at its finest. The staff are friendly, the food is tasty, and there's a range of interesting and refreshing drinks and desserts. **Known for:** refreshing drinks; cheap and cheerful home-cooked Vietnamese food; hidden entrance. [$] *Average main: d125,000* ✉ *165/50 Nguyen Thai Binh, District 1* ☎ *028/3824–4666* 🌐 *www.bepmein.com.*

The Elbow Room Bistro and Bar
$$$ | **AMERICAN** | **FAMILY** | This friendly little bistro, a fixture in the city's dining scene for many years, wouldn't be out of place in New York. The Elbow Room serves hearty all-day breakfast, burgers, sandwiches, pizzas, and pastas. **Known for:** friendly service; American-style

cuisine; decent portion sizes. $ *Average main: d300,000* ✉ *52 Pasteur, District 1* ☎ *28/3821–4327* ⊕ *www.shgsaigon.com/ elbowroom.html.*

★ 4P's Pizza

$$ | PIZZA | The centerpiece of this stylish, immensely popular Japanese-owned restaurant is not a sushi bar but a brick oven, and the focus here is Japanese-Italian fusion, targeted at the Vietnamese palate but equally loved by out-of-towners. You can opt for classic creations such as prosciutto margarita or something a little more experimental, like flower pizza (with edible blooms such as pumpkin, leek, and daylily), teriyaki chicken with seaweed or salmon miso cream. **Known for:** popular with locals; Japanese fusion pizza; homemade cheese. $ *Average main: d250,000* ✉ *8/15 Le Thanh Ton, District 1* ☎ *028/3622–0500* ⊕ *pizza4ps.com.*

★ Hoa Tuc

$$$ | VIETNAMESE | FAMILY | The name translates as opium poppy, and this chic little eatery is in a corner of the former La Manufacture d'Opium, the French-controlled opium refinery and warehouse. It offers contemporary Vietnamese cuisine with knockout flavors and a wine list that works with the local cuisine. **Known for:** outdoor dining; art deco interior; Vietnamese fare. $ *Average main: d300,000* ✉ *74/7 Hai Ba Trung St., District 1* ☎ *028/3825–1676* ⊕ *www.hoatuc.com/wordpress.*

★ Hum Lounge and Restaurant

$$ | VEGETARIAN | Classy surroundings, attentive staff, and amazing cocktails are good reasons to come here, but it's the mouthwatering pan-Asian food that's the highlight, regularly winning over meat lovers who have reluctantly accompanied their vegetarian partners and friends. The menu is full of health-conscious options, and the food is as visually appealing as it is delicious. **Known for:** stylish decor; vegetarian food; cocktails (try the cucumber ginger martini). $ *Average main: d170,000* ✉ *2 Thi Sach, District 1* ☎ *028/3823–8920* ⊕ *www.humvegetarian.vn.*

Huong Lai

$$ | VIETNAMESE | Huong Lai serves traditional Southern Vietnamese home cooking with a very high feel-good factor—all the staffers are orphans and disadvantaged young people, given a helping hand by the philanthropic Japanese owner, who calls his enterprise a training restaurant. The interior is delightfully rustic, the service is friendly, the English language skills excellent, the food is authentic, and over the course of more than a decade, Huong Lai has launched more than 60 young people into careers in the five-star hospitality sector. **Known for:** excellent service; Vietnamese cuisine; helping disadvantaged youth. $ *Average main: d160,000* ✉ *38 Ly Tu Trong, District 1* ☎ *028/3822–6814* ⊕ *www.huonglai2001saigon.com.*

Loving Hut Hoa Dang

$$ | VEGETARIAN | This is a bright and clean vegan restaurant catering to local Buddhists, who are full-time or part-time vegetarians—some just forsake meat twice a month, on the full and half moon. An extensive range of fresh and delicious Vietnamese vegan dishes features on the menu, many using mock meat made from tofu, lentils, or beans (meaning there's actually no beef in a dish labeled, for instance, beef with pepper sauce). **Known for:** English menu; local-style vegan food; mock meat dishes. $ *Average main: d160,000* ✉ *38 Huynh Khuong Ninh, District 1* ☎ *028/3820–9702* ⊕ *www.lovinghuthoadang.com.vn.*

★ Nous

$$$$ | FUSION | If Top Chef ever came to Vietnam, it would likely look like Nous. With just eight seats surrounding an open kitchen once per night, this modern minimalist space is all about elevating Vietnamese flavors to fine dining heights. **Known for:** exceptionally creative dishes using local ingredients; unique concept; chef's table experience. $ *Average main: d1,599,000* ✉ *42 Ly Tu Trong, District 1* ☎ *090/965–4096* ⊕ *www.nousdine.com* ☾ *Closed Mon.*

Ho Chi Minh City has plenty of enticing food options, from street stalls to internationally acclaimed restaurants.

Propaganda

$$ | **VIETNAMESE** | Serving what is described as "redesigned" Vietnamese cuisine with a focus on fresh ingredients, the sleek and artsy Propaganda does nontraditional takes on traditional dishes, especially fresh spring rolls. You can avoid menu confusion by choosing the 510,000d or 580,000d discovery menu of four courses, three glasses of wine, and organic green tea. **Known for:** fresh ingredients; Vietnamese food with a twist; propaganda art murals. [$] *Average main: d150,000* ✉ *21 Han Thuyen, District 1* ☎ *028/3822–9048* 🌐 *www.propagandabistros.com.*

★ **Racha Room**

$$$ | **ASIAN** | One of the hippest eateries in town, the Racha Room serves up Asian-inspired fusion food as well as artisanal cocktails (prepared by a mixologist imported from Melbourne, Australia) in a small but groovy space, with exposed brick walls, graffiti art, and funky music. The place has proved a hit with locals, expats, and travelers alike for its bold flavors and overall grooviness, so reservations are recommended. **Known for:** graffiti art; Thai fusion; artisanal cocktails. [$] *Average main: d300,000* ✉ *12–14 Mac Thi Buoi St., District 1* ☎ *090/879–1412.*

★ **Secret House Vietnamese Restaurant and Cafe**

$$ | **VIETNAMESE** | With a thriving indoor kitchen garden in the center of the restaurant, Secret House evokes the feeling of olden days Vietnamese countryside living; the home-style menu is short for a Vietnamese place, but every dish is reliably delicious with surprising attention to presentation. Schedule a visit early in your trip so you can return to try all the delicious dishes you couldn't fit in first time around. **Known for:** indoor garden (sometimes with chickens); home-cooked Vietnamese fare; shared dishes. [$] *Average main: d150,000* ✉ *55/1 Le Thi Hong Gam, District 1* ☎ *091/187–7008.*

Vietnam House

$$$ | **VIETNAMESE** | Australian celebrity chef Luke Nguyen has given this longtime tourist-centric restaurant a new

Ho Chi Minh City's Café Culture 🍴

Cafés aren't just for coffee in Ho Chi Minh City, they're an important part of the fabric of society. In this crowded city, jammed full of multi-generational homes, cafés offer an element of peace and privacy. They're cheap places for young people to hang out and for friends of all ages to meet and shoot the breeze. To attract the crowds among so much competition, all kinds of novelty and hidden coffee shops have sprung up. L'Usine in Dong Khoi led the charge, with its industrial-chic café and retail space hidden down an alley and up a flight of dingy stairs. Now "hidden" cafés are de rigueur; just about every old apartment block has one, and stylish cafés can be found in just about every street in town.

lease on life with an innovative "modern Vietnamese" menu and a stylish refit of the interior. The name, the central location, and the beautiful art deco building remain the same, but everything else is fresh and exciting. **Known for:** central location; Australian celebrity chef owner; modern Vietnamese cuisine made with quality Australian produce. [$] *Average main: d300,000* ✉ *93-97 Dong Khoi, District 1* ☎ *028/3822–2226* 🌐 *www.vietnamhousesaigon.com.*

Wrap and Roll

$$ | **VIETNAMESE** | This restaurant chain does a surprisingly good take on traditional Vietnamese street food, of which many dishes require wrapping or rolling. If actual street food freaks you out with its proximity to traffic, noise, and dirt, this is a quiet, clean, lime green, and air-conditioned alternative. **Known for:** slow service; wrap-your-own rolls; Vietnamese dishes. [$] *Average main: d98,000* ✉ *Level B3, Vincom Center, 72 Le Thanh Ton, District 1* ☎ *028/3993–9015* 🌐 *www.wraprollgrill.com.*

☕ Coffee and Quick Bites

★ L'Usine

$$ | **CAFÉ** | Industrial chic meets art house tucked away in a colonial villa at this well-loved café. The food is reliably good, offering a range of contemporary café fusion fare including salads, sandwiches, cold cut platters, and Western favorites. **Known for:** red velvet cake; balcony views of the Opera House; Vietnamese-style broken rice. [$] *Average main: d250,000* ✉ *151/1 Dong Khoi, 1st fl., District 1* ✥ *Turn into alley at 151 Dong Khoi and pass art shops. At parking area, turn right and walk toward stairwell where sign points up to L'Usine on 1st fl.* ☎ *0286/674–9565* 🌐 *www.lusinespace.com.*

🛏 Hotels

Caravelle Hotel

$$$$ | **HOTEL** | Extensive renovations in 2019 have freshened up this iconic hotel, which opened to the public on Christmas Eve 1959 and has entertained VIPs from around the globe throughout its storied history. **Pros:** convenient location; imbued with Vietnam War mystique; legendary bar. **Cons:** not the best value in its price range. [$] *Rooms from: d4,000,000* ✉ *19–23 Lam Son Sq., District 1* ☎ *028/3823–4999* 🌐 *www.caravellehotel.com* 🛏 *366 rooms* 🍴 *No Meals.*

Grand Hotel

$$$$ | **HOTEL** | Although more modest than the Majestic or the Continental hotels, this pleasant old colonial establishment evokes a bygone era of Francophone Saigon in the heart of the old Rue Catinat, where it's been since 1930. **Pros:** river views from some rooms on upper floors;

as locations go, this is as central as you get. **Cons:** service, while mostly good, can be indifferent at times. $ *Rooms from: d2,276,000* ✉ *8 Dong Khoi, District 1* ☎ *0283/915–5555* ⊕ *www.grandhotel. vn* ⤳ *251 rooms* |○| *No Meals.*

Hotel Continental
$$$ | **HOTEL** | History buffs head for this French-colonial-style hotel, where Graham Greene's classic *The Quiet American* was set and the author himself stayed (in room 214); it was also the meeting place of journalists and diplomats during the Vietnam War. The unique outdoor courtyard garden and dining area dates from the late 19th century—a delightful place to relax with a drink beneath frangipani trees, some of which were planted in 1880. **Pros:** it's one of the city's historic sights; central location; no extra charge added to its junior suite price tag for room 214. **Cons:** rooms facing the street are noisy—ask for one overlooking the inner courtyard. $ *Rooms from: d1,900,000* ✉ *132-134 Dong Khoi, District 1* ☎ *0283/829–9201* ⊕ *www.continentalsaigon.com* ⤳ *87 rooms* |○| *No Meals.*

Hotel Majestic
$$$$ | **HOTEL** | On the waterfront overlooking the Saigon River, this is one of Vietnam's truly great colonial hotels, steeped with nostalgia and old-world charm that has been accumulating since 1925. **Pros:** rooms have high ceilings; great central location; rooftop bar and pool on site. **Cons:** the fact that the government owns this hotel does occasionally peek through the usually professional service standards. $ *Rooms from: d3,300,000* ✉ *1 Dong Khoi, District 1* ☎ *0283/829–5517* ⊕ *www.majesticsaigon.com.vn* ⤳ *122 rooms* |○| *No Meals.*

Intercontinental Saigon
$$$$ | **HOTEL** | This luxe hotel wows with a flashy lobby and world-class amenities, but the rooms are warm and inviting, with understated elegance in neutral tones and floor-to-ceiling windows. **Pros:**

attentive service; central location; higher floors have great views. **Cons:** adjoins a labyrinthine shopping and dining complex, which can emit a bit of noise at night. $ *Rooms from: d4,200,000* ✉ *Corner Hai Ba Trung and Le Duan, District 1* ☎ *0283/520–9999* ⊕ *www.icsaigon.com* ⤳ *305 rooms* |○| *No Meals.*

Le Méridien Saigon
$$$$ | **HOTEL** | **FAMILY** | Part of the Marriott family, the well-located Le Méridien ticks all the boxes with its superior service, excellent club lounge facilities on the 22nd floor, ninth-floor pool deck, and comfortable rooms. **Pros:** close to tourist attractions; on bank of Saigon River; spa. **Cons:** no meals included in room rate. $ *Rooms from: d5,690,000* ✉ *3C Ton Duc Thang, District 1* ☎ *0286/263–6688* ⊕ *www.lemeridiensaigon.com* ⤳ *343 rooms* |○| *No Meals.*

Lotte Legend Hotel Saigon
$$$$ | **HOTEL** | Pleasant and luxurious, this riverfront business-centric hotel, part of the giant Korean-owned Lotte chain, has fancy marble bathrooms and spacious rooms with floor-to-ceiling windows for great views. **Pros:** professional and courteous staff; great location; extensive breakfast buffet. **Cons:** the noise of traffic and a bar next door can be heard in the lower rooms; nonsmoking floors may still smell smoke from other floors. $ *Rooms from: d3,600,000* ✉ *2A–4A Ton Duc Thang, District 1* ☎ *028/3823–3333* ⊕ *www.lottehotel.com/saigon-hotel* ⤳ *283 rooms* |○| *No Meals.*

★ The Myst Dong Khoi
$$$$ | **HOTEL** | The eclectic design of this hotel is almost as mysterious as its name. **Pros:** stylish rooftop pool; balcony Jacuzzis; rooms are comfortable, spacious, and full of character. **Cons:** construction next door will block the river views. $ *Rooms from: d4,190,000* ✉ *6–8 Ho Huan Nghiep, District 1* ☎ *0283/520–3040* ⊕ *www.themystdongkhoihotel.com* |○| *Free Breakfast* ⤳ *108 rooms.*

★ Park Hyatt Saigon

$$$$ | **HOTEL** | Arguably one of the top international luxury hotels in Ho Chi Minh City, the Park Hyatt Saigon has a hard-to-beat location close to the major downtown attractions. **Pros:** ideal location in District 1; world-class rooms and facilities; beautiful swimming pool. **Cons:** restaurants are a bit overpriced; standard rooms are on the small side. [$] *Rooms from: d6,000,000* ✉ *2 Lam Son Sq., District 1* ☎ *028/3824–1234* 🌐 *www.parkhyattsaigon.com* 🛏 *245 rooms* 🍴 *Free Breakfast.*

Renaissance Riverside Hotel Saigon

$$$$ | **HOTEL** | Part of the Marriott group, the Renaissance Riverside offers comfortable elegance in a central location; its relaxing pool area on the 21st floor has panoramic views of the city. **Pros:** accommodating staff; in walking distance of many downtown sights; great riverside location. **Cons:** the lobby café and rooftop bar are very expensive; city-view rooms look out on an office block across the way. [$] *Rooms from: d4,400,000* ✉ *8–15 Ton Duc Thang, District 1* ☎ *028/3822–0033* 🌐 *www.marriott.com* 🛏 *349 rooms* 🍴 *No Meals.*

The Reverie Saigon

$$$$ | **HOTEL** | Depending on your point of view, The Reverie's Italianate design is sumptuously ornate or completely over-the-top; nevertheless, the hotel, inside the landmark Times Square building, is bedazzling, and each of the spacious and comfortable rooms has glamorous bathrooms and stunning views of Saigon. **Pros:** personalized service; amazing views; unique decor. **Cons:** too opulent for some; meals not included. [$] *Rooms from: d8,155,000* ✉ *22–36 Nguyen Hue & 57–69F Dong Khoi, District 1* ☎ *028/3823–6688* 🌐 *www.thereverie-saigon.com* 🍴 *Free Breakfast* 🛏 *375 rooms.*

Rex Hotel

$$$$ | **HOTEL** | If it's history you're after, the Rex has it in spades: it played a major role in the Vietnam War, hosting the American Information Service's daily "five o'clock follies" press briefings, and the 1976 unification of North and South Vietnam was announced in the same room. **Pros:** friendly and helpful staff; a great sense of history; central location. **Cons:** like most five-star hotels, food and beverage prices can be extortionate. [$] *Rooms from: d3,100,000* ✉ *141 Nguyen Hue, District 1* ☎ *0283/829–2185* 🌐 *www.rexhotelsaigon.com* 🛏 *227 rooms* 🍴 *Free Breakfast.*

Sheraton Saigon Hotel and Towers

$$$$ | **HOTEL** | An older, but scrupulously maintained hotel in one of Ho Chi Minh City's premier streets, the Sheraton Saigon has all the amenities and standards of service you'd expect from a top international chain. **Pros:** exemplary service; central location; top-notch facilities. **Cons:**; some rooms don't have great views. [$] *Rooms from: d3,900,000* ✉ *88 Dong Khoi, District 1* ☎ *0283/827–2828/9* 🌐 *www.sheratonsaigon.com* 🛏 *485 rooms* 🍴 *No Meals.*

Sofitel Saigon Plaza

$$$$ | **HOTEL** | This superstylish hotel has elegant French and Vietnamese influences throughout, from the imposing lobby to the tasteful rooms to the sultry Boudoir Lounge on the ground floor. **Pros:** excellent fitness center; regular shuttle bus to Ben Thanh Market; has a boutique hotel feel, despite its size. **Cons:** closer to the zoo than the Reunification Palace; slightly out of the way on Le Duan Boulevard. [$] *Rooms from: d3,620,000* ✉ *17 Le Duan, District 1* ☎ *028/3824–1555* 🌐 *www.sofitel-saigon-plaza.com* 🛏 *286 rooms* 🍴 *No Meals.*

★ **Somerset Ho Chi Minh City**

$$$$ | | **FAMILY** | Serviced one-, two-, and three-bedroom apartments with fully equipped kitchens, only a short walk from the zoo and with on-site recreation amenities, make this a perfect choice for families. **Pros:** shuttle to city center; facilities and service standards of a five-star hotel; on-site restaurant; Wi-Fi. **Cons:** shuttle service is not free; slightly outside of the main business area and not close to the main sights. $ *Rooms from: d2,600,000* ⊠ *8A Nguyen Binh Khiem, District 1* ☎ *028/3822–8899* ⊕ *www. somerset.com* ⤤ *165 apartments* ⦿ *No Meals.*

🌙 Nightlife

BARS AND COCKTAIL LOUNGES

AIR Saigon

GATHERING PLACES | *AIR Saigon (formerly known as Air 360 Sky Lounge)* has fantastic views of Ho Chi Minh City, and is a great place to catch the sunset. Staff are usually attentive and the menu is a mix of Vietnamese and Western dishes. The drink prices are reasonable during happy hour (6–8 pm) but quite pricey otherwise. ⊠ *Rooftop, fl. 22 and 23, Ben Thanh Tower, 136–138 Le Thi Hong Gam, District 1* ☎ *097/458–7788* ⊕ *www.airsaigon.vn* ⤳ *Opens at 5:30 pm but starts serving at 6 pm.*

The Alley Cocktail Bar & Kitchen

COCKTAIL LOUNGES | Hidden down a little alley, this little speakeasy pays tribute to owner Minh Tan Pham's birthplace, the Mekong Delta. The Alley attracts a groovy young crowd, who come for the well-executed cocktails, the great food, and the friendly vibe. ⊠ *63/1 Pasteur, District 1* ☎ *093/565–3969* ⊕ *www.facebook.com/thealleysaigon.*

Blanchy's Lounge

COCKTAIL LOUNGES | Blanchy's Lounge is one of the city's most popular late-night haunts, attracting a mix of expats, tourists, and locals. If downstairs gets too crowded for your tastes, head for the rooftop terrace on the third floor. The three-hour-long happy hour on weeknights is a great value for a flash bar in a major city. For those curious about the peculiar name, it honors the moustache of Paul Blanchy, a colonial entrepreneur who made his fortune cultivating pepper and went on to become the first mayor of Saigon (1895–1901). ⊠ *95 Hai Ba Trung, District 1* ☎ *093/799–2636.*

Broma: Not A Bar

BARS | A small, trendy bar, Broma stocks an impressive array of bottled beers from all corners of the globe, and the bar staff mix an excellent cocktail. Make sure to sit in the open-air lounge on the top floor, where you will be right in between two of the city's flashiest skyscrapers (Saigon Times Square and Bitexco Financial Tower). The only drawback is the music, as customers often hijack the sound system. ⊠ *41 Nguyen Hue, District 1* ☎ *028/3823–6838.*

Firkin Bar

COCKTAIL LOUNGES | A cozy 27-seat bar focusing on "bespoking" whiskey- and whisky-based cocktails (and if you don't know about the different spellings, strike up a conversation with the bar staff) in a warm and welcoming atmosphere. Hundreds of specialty liquors from around the world line the bar (including over 250 types of whiskies), and a tasty menu of gourmet bar snacks complements the drinks. Ask about whiskey (and whisky) tasting flights. ⊠ *20 Mac Thi Buoi, District 1* ☎ *093/131–2723* ⊕ *www.facebook. com/firkinbar.*

The Gin House

COCKTAIL LOUNGES | A groovy little speakeasy down an alley, the Gin House has a strong focus on gins, with more than 20 of their own infusions behind the bar, including lavender and butterfly pea, seaweed and nutmeg, and green tea and pomegranate. The infused gins can be ordered as a gin and tonic, or something a bit wilder, like a gin and ginger beer.

Pasteur Street Brewing Co. draws locals and travelers alike for its American-style craft beer.

There's also a range of creative gin-centric cocktails, and with the cocktail menu divided into sections—sweet and sour; creamy; bitter and dry; herbal and spicy; and sling and fizz—there's sure to be something for every taste preference. ⊠ *28/3A Ton That Tung, District 1* ☎ *090/889–3660* ⊕ *www.facebook.com/ theginhousesaigon.*

Indika Saigon

CAFÉS | Welcome to Indika, the "house of curiosity" that's focused on chill, in the garden or the bar. Indika regularly hosts events, so check their Facebook page for the latest schedule of live music, "wine and words" book club, and film screenings. A rotating menu that includes authentic wood-fired pizzas and lots of vegan and vegetarian options will satisfy any hunger pains from 10 am to midnight. ⊠ *43 Nguyen Van Giai, District 1* ☎ *089/946–8370* ⊕ *www.facebook. com/IndikaSaigon.*

O'Brien's Factory

PUBS | An Irish pub with pool tables, exposed brick walls, friendly staff, daily happy hour, and pretty fine food, O'Brien's Factory is a great place to relax, meet new friends, watch sports, and enjoy live music on Friday nights. ⊠ *74a3 Hai Ba Trung, District 1* ☎ *028/3829–3198.*

★ Pasteur Street Brewing Co.

BREWPUBS | The place that really kicked off Saigon's craft beer scene, Pasteur Street is dedicated to combining American-style craft beer with uniquely Vietnamese flavors, such as jasmine, jackfruit, and chocolate. Do try a flight of beers to experience the full range of amazing flavors. Great-tasting American comfort food can be paired with the beer. The original taproom is tiny, but there's another taproom at 26A Le Thanh Ton with 12 taps and an open-air rooftop, while a third taproom with 150 seats is located at 23A Ngo Thoi Nhiem in District 3. ⊠ *144 Pasteur, District 1* ⊹ *Down alley and up stairs on left* ☎ *028/7300–7375* ⊕ *www. pasteurstreet.com.*

★ **Shri Restaurant & Lounge**
PIANO BARS | As well as great views and stylish decor, Shri has truly innovative food and beverage offerings, including a spectacular menu of Saigon-themed cocktails by artist / bartist Richie Fawcett. Don't just go for drinks—the food menu is excellent, making it the place for a special night out. ⊠ *Centec Tower, 72 Nguyen Thi Minh Khai, 23rd fl., District 1* ☎ *028/3827–9631.*

Xu
COCKTAIL LOUNGES | This posh lounge bar gets lively in the evening thanks to a generous happy hour 5:30–8:30 pm Monday to Saturday, with half-price cocktails. A classic martini, an oyster shot or something uniquely Vietnamese—the choice is yours. The bar menu is more extensive and surprisingly value-priced than elsewhere, focusing on modern cuisine. Smart-casual wear is expected. ⊠ *Ground floor, 71–75 Hai Ba Trung, District 1* ☎ *028/3824–8468* ⊕ *www.xusaigon.com.*

DANCE CLUB
Lush
DANCE CLUBS | Lush's longevity in the ever-changing nightclub scene of Ho Chi Minh City is a tribute to its eternal grooviness and cool beats, a combination that attracts a clientele of young Vietnamese, tourists, and expats. The indoor and outdoor sections can get crowded on Tuesday (Ladies Night), Friday, and Saturday. ⊠ *2 Ly Tu Trong, District 1* ☎ *028/3824–2496* ⊕ *www.facebook.com/LushSaigon.*

Performing Arts
FILM
BHD Bitexco (*Icon 68 cinema*)
FILM | Seven screens show local and international movies. ⊠ *2 Hai Trieu, Levels 3 and 4, District 1* ☎ *028/6267–0670* ⊕ *www.bhdstar.vn.*

MUSIC AND THEATER
idecaf
CONCERTS | Vietnam's institute of cultural exchange with France regularly hosts performances by local and visiting musicians and theater groups. Look for the *hoat dong van hoa* (cultural events) tab on the Vietnamese site for details of upcoming shows. ⊠ *31 Thai Van Lung, District 1* ☎ *028/3829–5451* ⊕ *www.idecaf.gov.vn (French and Vietnamese only).*

★ **Municipal Theater of Ho Chi Minh City (Saigon Opera House)**
THEATER | The French-colonial Opera House is one of the icons of downtown Ho Chi Minh City. It was built in 1897 and modeled on the Petit Palais in Paris, which was completed the same year. It was originally as lavish inside as it was out, with a revolving stage and a three-tiered, 800-seat gallery. Some of the more ornate fixtures were removed in the 1940s and from 1956 it was the home of the National Assembly of South Vietnam. It became a theater again in 1975 and is now the permanent headquarters of the Ho Chi Minh City Ballet and Symphony Orchestra. Check the website for details of upcoming ballet, musical, and cultural performances. As there are no tours, catching a performance is the only way to see the gorgeous interior. ⊠ *7 Lam Son Sq., District 1* ☎ *028/3823–7419* ⊕ *www.hbso.org.vn.*

Shopping

Continuing a tradition dating to the time when it was French Saigon's main shopping thoroughfare, Dong Khoi Street between Le Loi (also a shopping street) and the river, is lined with shops selling jewelry, clothing, art, lacquerware, wood carvings, and other souvenirs mostly to tourists—which doesn't mean there aren't good finds.

The ornate Municipal Theater of Ho Chi Minh City, also called the Saigon Opera House, was modeled after the Petit Palais in Paris.

ART

Couleurs d'Asie by Réhahn

ART GALLERIES | This is a permanent gallery featuring the work of French photographer Réhahn, who has been based in Hoi An since 2011. His award-winning photographs are mainly portraits, many featuring Vietnam's ethnic minorities. ✉ *151/1 Dong Khoi, District 1* ☎ *090/741–1771* ⊕ *www.rehahnphotographer.com.*

Craig Thomas Gallery

ART GALLERIES | This gallery regularly hosts exhibitions of painting, sculpture, and mixed media by emerging and mid-career Vietnamese artists. ✉ *27i Tran Nhat Duat, District 1* ☎ *090/388–8431* ⊕ *www.cthomasgallery.com.*

★ Galerie Quynh

ART GALLERIES | Vietnam's best-known contemporary art gallery showcases art from drawing and painting to video and installation over four spacious levels. Established in 2003 by Quynh Pham, who fled Vietnam for the United States at the end of the war, Galerie Quynh is known for its consistently focused programming and educational initiatives. ✉ *118 Nguyen Van thu, District 1* ☎ *028/3822–7218* ⊕ *www.galeriequynh.com.*

CLOTHING

Ninh Khuong

CHILDREN'S CLOTHING | The flagship store of a small local chain sells cute-as-a-button linen and cotton baby and kids; clothing and embroidered home wares. The fish-shaped baby sleeping bags are likely to make you squeal. ✉ *34 Le Loi, District 1* ☎ *028/3824–7456* ⊕ *www.ninhkhuong.com.*

Tuyet Lan Orchids Silk

MIXED CLOTHING | This cute little shop has a selection of ready-made clothing in Western sizes and a fast and efficient tailoring service. The clothing is mostly women's but there is a small range of men's items, including ties, as well as a range of handbags, scarves, and jewelry. ■TIP→ **Allow at least two days for tailoring, even though the shop assistants may tell you they can do a one-day turnaround—some extra fitting and final adjustments**

may make all the difference to your purchase. ✉ *217 Le Thanh Ton, District 1* ☎ *028/6274–8576.*

CRAFTS
Duy Tan - Saigon Artisan

SOUVENIRS | This innovative little souvenir shop sells quality bags, shoes, artwork, ceramics, and household items. Do check out Very Ngon home products featuring prints of colonial-era postcards. ✉ *84 Le Loi, District 1* ☎ *028/3824–4860* ⊕ *www.saigonartisan.com.*

★ Mekong Quilts

CRAFTS | Set up by an NGO to assist women in remote villages in Vietnam and Cambodia, Mekong Quilts stocks beautifully handcrafted items made from papier mâché, silk, bamboo (including seven models of bamboo bicycles), and water hyacinth as well as beautifully handmade quilts and cushions. ✉ *District 1* ☎ *028/2210–3110* ⊕ *mekongquilts.com.*

GIFTS AND SOUVENIRS
★ L'Usine

MIXED CLOTHING | This chic, capacious boutique stocks luxe gifts from an array of international brands like Rifle stationery, Izipizi sunglasses, and home accessories from design companies like Fritz Hansen and Hay. International travelers might be more drawn to the selection of stylish, made-in-Vietnam products from brands including Cochine, Avana, and Woo Cares. There are two larger locations at 24 Thao Dien (District 2) and in Crescent Mall (District 7). ✉ *First fl., 19 Le Thanh Ton, District 1* ☎ *028/3822–7138* ⊕ *www. lusinespace.com.*

Saigon Kitsch

SOUVENIRS | Just as the name implies, Saigon Kitsch offers a treasure trove of entertaining knickknacks—mugs, badges, stickers, coasters, laptop bags, shot glasses, ashtrays—all emblazoned with Socialist period slogans or quirky Vietnam-themed motifs. It's the perfect place to grab a sack full of souvenirs for friends and family back home. ✉ *43 Ton That Thiep, District 1* ☎ *028/3821–8019.*

HOUSEWARES
Authentique Home

HOUSEWARES | Authentique Home sells a range of beautifully crafted products made from wood, ceramic, and cloth from three workshops: Cam Kim carpentry, Cam Ha potteries, and Cam Giang textiles. ✉ *71/1 Mac Thi Buoi, District 1* ☎ *028/2210–3969.*

MALLS AND SHOPPING CENTERS
Diamond Plaza

DEPARTMENT STORE | One of the first modern department stores in town, Diamond Plaza has several floors of shopping as well as restaurants, a spa, and a mini-supermarket. The original building houses the department store, while two high-rise towers contain offices and serviced apartments. ✉ *34 Le Duan, District 1* ☎ *028/3822–5500* ⊕ *www.diamondplaza.com.vn.*

Lucky Plaza

MALL | Lucky Plaza spans an entire city block, with entrances in Nguyen Hue and Dong Khoi Streets, and is stuffed full of stalls selling clothing, shoes, handbags, lacquerware, watches, DVDs, jewelry, sunglasses, and souvenirs. ✉ *38 Nguyen Hue, District 1.*

Parkson Plaza

MALL | The first and most central of the Parkson chain of shopping centers, Parkson Plaza has a wide range of fashion, cosmetics, homewares, appliances, and kitchenware, as well as a small supermarket on the top floor. ✉ *35-45 Le Thanh Ton, District 1* ☎ *28/3827–7636.*

Takashimaya

DEPARTMENT STORE | The multifloor Takashimaya department store is the centerpiece of this glitzy new shopping mall, which features many international brands, restaurants, and cafés. Younger kids will enjoy tiNiWorld on the fourth floor. ✉ *92–94 Nam Ky Khoi Nghia, District 1* ☎ *028/3827–8555* ⊕ *www. takashimaya-vn.com/en.*

Vincom Center Dong Khoi

MALL | FAMILY | Five levels of retail therapy in a shiny new glass-and-chrome sky-scraper include an eclectic mix of high-end fashion brands, such as Jimmy Choo and Versace, and well-known midrange options, such as Gap and a branch of the British Debenhams department store. There are multiple dining options, a CGV movie theater on the sixth floor, and a Kids Zone on one of the basement floors, with a play area for young children and a large arcade for older kids. ⊠ *72 Le Thanh Ton, District 1* ☎ *097/503–3288* ⊕ *www. vincom.com.vn.*

MARKETS

Old Market

MARKET | Old Market, or Cho Cu, is a little glimpse of Old Saigon. It sells everything from fish to plastic toys, and some hit the market at 3 am to get the freshest of the fresh. ⊠ *Ton That Dam, District 1.*

Saigon Square I

MIXED CLOTHING | A huge conglomeration of tiny stalls hawking all kinds of clothing, footwear, accessories, and electronics, Saigon Square is a great place to restock on beachwear: shorts, T-shirts, swim-suits, flip-flops, children's clothing, sun-glasses, hats, and whatever else you may have worn out while on vacation. There are also lots of knockoffs on offer here, many claiming to use genuine mate-rials. Some haggling is required, even when an item has a price tag attached. Generally, the more you buy, the bigger the discount. Note that all transactions are cash-only. ⊠ *77 Nam Ky Khoi Nghia, District 1.*

SHOES AND LEATHER GOODS
Ipa Nima

HANDBAGS | The beautifully embellished handbags here, which are sold at high-end boutiques around the world, are considered by some to be the ultimate style souvenir from Vietnam. ⊠ *90 Le Loi, District 1* ☎ *093/882–6716* ⊕ *ipa-nima. com.*

Tran Quoc Lan

SHOES | This little cobbler shop can custom-make shoes in as little as a week, either copying an existing shoe or replicating one of the samples on display. Expect to pay 1,800,000d and up—not bad for a hand-stitched pair made with quality leather, likely to be a long-lasting reminder of your trip to Vietnam. ⊠ *97 Le Thanh Ton, District 1* ☎ *093/275–2275.*

TEXTILES AND SEWING
Catherine Denoual Maison

HOUSEWARES | French fashion edi-tor-turned-designer Catherine Denoual creates soft and luxurious hand-embroi-dered bed and table linens in elegant neutral colors, many with a dragonfly motif. The linen and other home wares in her flagship store have been described as contemporary heirlooms for their elegance and attention to detail. ⊠ *38 Ly Tu Trong, District 1* ☎ *028/3823–9394* ⊕ *www.catherinedenoual.com.*

XQ

CRAFTS | The hand-embroidered silk "paintings" created here have to be seen to be believed. They come in a range of styles, from traditional Vietnamese scenes to photograph-quality portraits. The artists work on the top floor, and the lower floors showcase their work, together with a small range of men's and women's clothes and accessories (scarves, ties, and fans). There are other locations in Dalat and Hanoi. ⊠ *106 Le Loi, District 1* ☎ *028/3822–7725* ⊕ *www. xqvietnam.com.*

Around Pham Ngu Lao

Pham Ngu Lao used to be the short-hand reference to the backpacker area, which is between September 23 Park along Pham Ngu Lao Street and Bui Vien Street. The area is still thriving and popu-lar with budget travelers of all ages, but many come here simply to experience the lively cultural mix of international travelers and locals going about their business. There are the requisite backpacker bars and eateries here, but also a growing number of upscale restaurants. Bui Vien Street is pedestrian-only on weekend evenings.

⊙ Sights

Ben Thanh Market
MARKET | This bustling market, which is more than a century old, has a bit of a Jekyll-and-Hyde personality, and if you are unlucky enough to encounter pushy vendors, scammers, and pickpockets it won't exactly be an enjoyable experience. Stay alert, though, and you can have a lovely time exploring the 3,000 stalls. The most interesting section is the wet market at the back. Cheap T-shirts and other tourist goods are for sale in the front section, fabric and haberdasheries in the middle, and some great food stalls spring up beside the market at night. ⊠ *Le Loi, District 1* ⊕ *www.ben-thanh-market.com.*

Ho Chi Minh City Fine Arts Museum (*Bao Tang My Thuat Thanh Pho Ho Chi Minh*)
ART MUSEUM | Spread over three floors in a reportedly haunted French-colonial villa known as Chu Hoa's mansion, the city's Fine Arts Museum offers a comprehensive run through the main stages of Vietnamese art. Strolling around is a pleasant experience as the building itself is architecturally beautiful. While there could be more information to enlighten visitors, the examples of wartime propaganda art and lacquer art are superb. ⊠ *97A Pho Duc Chinh, District 1* ☎ *028/3829–4441* ⊕ *www.baotangmythuattphcm.com.vn (Vietnamese only)* 🎟 *30,000d* ⊗ *Closed Mon.*

Ho Chi Minh Museum (*Nha Rong*)
HISTORY MUSEUM | This example of early French-colonial architecture in Vietnam, nicknamed the Dragon House (Nha Rong), could be considered more interesting than most of the displays within. Sitting quayside on Ben Nghe Channel,

at far end of Ham Nghi, it was constructed in 1863 as the original French customshouse; any individuals coming to colonial Saigon would have had to pass through the building once they docked at the port. Ho Chi Minh (1890–1969), who was known as Nguyen Sinh Cung as a child, Nguyen Tat Thanh as a schoolboy, and later Nguyen Ai Quoc as well as other aliases, passed through here in 1911 on the way to his 30-year sojourn around Europe and America. Inside are some of his personal belongings, including his journals, fragments of his clothing, and his rubber sandals. Uncle Ho, as he's now affectionately known, was an ascetic type of guy, known for wearing sandals made only from tires; these are now scattered in museums around the country. ⊠ *Ben Nha Rong (Dragon House Wharf), 1 Nguyen Tat Thanh, District 4* ☎ *028/3940–2060* 🎟 *2,000d* ⊗ *Closed Mon.*

Mariamman Hindu Temple (*Chua Ba Mariamman*)
TEMPLE | Vivid statues and colorful floral offerings at this Hindu temple create a microcosm of India in the streets of Saigon. Before the temple was returned to the Hindu community in the early 1990s, the government used it as a factory for making joss sticks (incense) and for processing dried fish. Today it serves a small congregation of Tamil Hindus, but some Vietnamese and Chinese locals also revere it as a holy space. ⊠ *45 Truong Dinh, District 1* 🎟 *Free.*

September 23 Park (*Cong Vien 23 Thang 9*)
CITY PARK | This long skinny park at the end of Ho Chi Minh City's backpacker district was built on the site of the city's former train station, which was demolished after the last war. The lush park, with its tall trees, is a pleasant spot to rest awhile after a long day of sightseeing. There's a small children's playground, a duck pond, and walking trails, which are full of locals exercising in the mornings and evenings. After dark, the park is where young

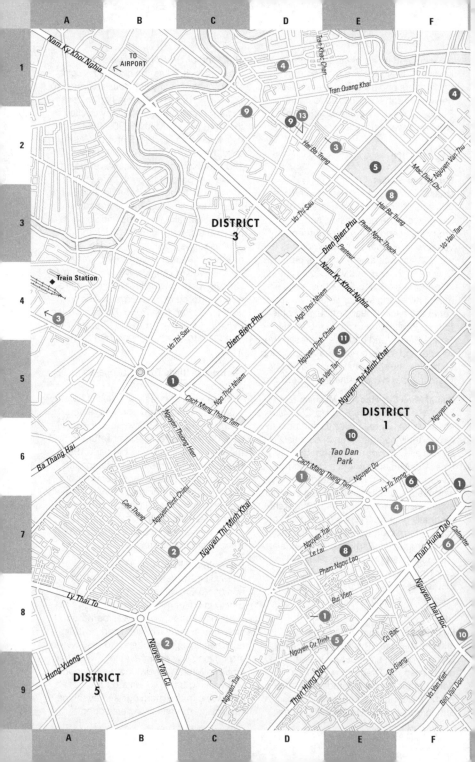

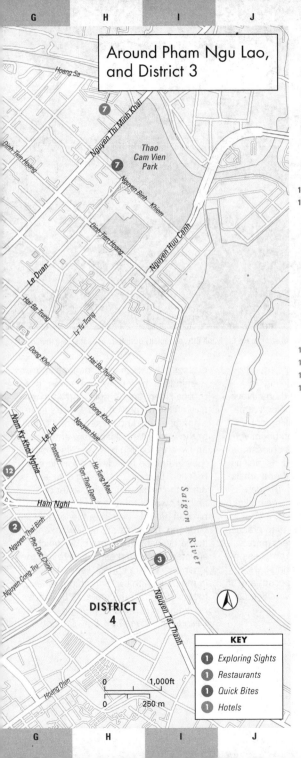

Around Pham Ngu Lao, and District 3

Sights ▼

1 Ben Thanh Market.................. F6
2 Ho Chi Minh City
  Fine Arts Museum G7
3 Ho Chi Minh Museum I7
4 Jade Emperor Pagoda F1
5 Le Van Tam Park E2
6 Mariamman Hindu Temple F6
7 Museum of
  Vietnamese History................ H2
8 September 23 Park E7
9 Tan Dinh Market D2
10 Tao Dan Park E6
11 War Remnants Museum E4

Restaurants ▼

1 Baba's Kitchen D8
2 Banh Cuon Hai Nam............... B7
3 Banh Xeo 46A E2
4 Cuc Gach Quan D1
5 Hum Café and Restaurant E5
6 La Fiesta F7
7 Lunch Lady H1
8 Noir.................................. E3
9 Pho Binh C2
10 Quan Ut Ut.......................... F8
11 Scott's Kitchen F6
12 Soul Burger.......................... G6
13 Tan Dinh Market
   street food stands D2

Quick Bites ▼

1 ID Café B5

Hotels ▼

1 Fusion Suites Sai Gon D6
2 Hotel Nikko Saigon B8
3 Ma Maison A4
4 New World Saigon Hotel F7
5 Pullman Saigon Centre............. E8

KEY

1 Exploring Sights
1 Restaurants
1 Quick Bites
1 Hotels

Tao Dan Park is a wonderful place to stroll in Ho Chi Minh City, especially during its annual spring festival.

couples sneak a bit of privacy, sitting on their motorbikes and cuddling. In the weeks leading up to Tet (Lunar New Year), the park is a blaze of color, with a temporary flower market selling potted flowers and shrubs, including bright yellow chrysanthemums, apricot blossoms, and miniature kumquat trees, as well as depictions of dragons and other animals made from fruit and flowers. The park's proximity to the backpacker area makes it popular with scammers, who try to open a conversation by asking to practice their English or claiming to recognize you. The conversation usually moves on to offers of card games, visiting bars, or going to their home. Never accept any of these offers. ⊠ *Between Pham Ngu Lao and Le Loi Sts., District 1.*

★ Tao Dan Park

CITY PARK | FAMILY | This huge park, a block behind the Reunification Palace, has a little something for everyone: walking paths for strolling or jogging; tall trees for shade; open areas where exercise classes are held in the mornings and evenings; a miniature Cham tower; a replica Hung King Temple; and an extensive children's playground. There's also a coffee stand, known as the bird café, at the Cach Mang Thang Tam entrance, and every morning bird fanciers bring their feathered friends here for singing practice. Do pull up a plastic chair and enjoy the ruckus and the theater of finicky owners trying to position their birds in order to generate the loudest birdsong. The birds are usually taken home by 9 am—by motorbike, which is a spectacle in itself. Leading up to Tet, the lunar new year, a spring festival is held in the park, with live entertainment and food and handicrafts stalls. ⊠ *Entrances on Nguyen Thi Minh Khai, Trung Dinh and Cach Mang Thang Tam Sts., District 1.*

🍴 Restaurants

Baba's Kitchen
$$ | **INDIAN** | Slap-bang in the heart of the backpacker district, this gem of an Indian restaurant serves a great selection of curries, tandoori, tikka, vegetarian dishes, breads, and Southern Indian specialties. It's an unassuming, clean, and friendly little place, but if you don't feel like venturing out, they deliver throughout Ho Chi Minh City. **Known for:** generous side dishes; high-quality Indian food; efficient service. [$] *Average main: d140,000* ✉ *274 Bui Vien, District 1* ☎ *028/3838–6661* 🌐 *www.babaskitchen.in.*

★ Banh Cuon Hai Nam
$ | **VIETNAMESE** | Always packed with locals, this narrow eatery serves up Ho Chi Minh City's best *banh cuon* (steamed rice flour crepes stuffed with minced pork and wood ear mushrooms) and an excellent version of the central Vietnamese *banh beo* (steamed rice flour pancakes topped with dried prawn). Just order the first three items on the menu and you'll be in foodie heaven in no time. **Known for:** limited menu; very local service (little English is spoken here); tasty local food. [$] *Average main: d60,000* ✉ *11A Cao Thang, District 3* ☎ *028/3839–3394* 💳 *No credit cards.*

Cuc Gach Quan
$$ | **VIETNAMESE** | Serving traditional Vietnamese dishes with an emphasis on healthy, environmentally friendly eating, Cuc Gach has succeeded in carving out its own niche in the city's dining scene. Set in an old French home that has received a modern makeover and is furnished with repurposed colonial-era furniture—including a wooden bed that's been converted into a dining table—this is Vietnamese with a green and design-y edge. **Known for:** very extensive menu; stylish decor; traditional Vietnamese cooking. [$] *Average main: d200,000* ✉ *10 Dang Tat, District 1* ☎ *028/3848–0144* 🌐 *www.cucgachquan.com.vn.*

La Fiesta
$$ | **MEXICAN** | **FAMILY** | La Fiesta, run by the effusive American-Vietnamese couple Scott and Duc, will satisfy all your Tex-Mex cravings, whether it's for tacos, chili con carne, enchiladas, sangria, or margaritas. This place is popular with locals, expats, and tourists for its big portions, big taste, strong drinks, and great service all at reasonable prices. **Known for:** great cocktails; Tex-Mex; friendly service. [$] *Average main: d200,000* ✉ *128 Ly Tu Trong, District 1* ☎ *94/429–1697* 🌐 *www.facebook.com/lafiestavietnam* 🕒 *Closed Mon.*

★ Quan Ut Ut
$$$ | **BARBECUE** | This American barbecue joint is wildly popular among locals, who love the tasty ribs, the craft beer, the cheeky menu, and the laid-back vibe. It was set up by an American, Australian, and French trio, who charm the local dining scene with shared plates, communal picnic-style tables, stripped-back surroundings, and reasonable prices. **Known for:** craft beer; American-style barbecue ribs; shared platters. [$] *Average main: d300,000* ✉ *168 Vo Van Kiet, District 1* ☎ *028/3914–4500* 🌐 *www.quanutut.com.*

Scott's Kitchen
$$ | **AMERICAN** | For those craving a taste of the USA, Scott's Kitchen serves big portions of soul-satisfying, home-cooked comfort food. There are more than 20 variations of mac-and-cheese alone on the menu including fun additions like Korean-style fried chicken, tuna melt, and BBQ pork. **Known for:** big, bold flavors; comfort food with a twist; good value portions. [$] *Average main: d185,000* ✉ *128 Ly Tu Trong, District 1* ✥ *Inside La Fiesta* ☎ *094/429–1697* 🌐 *www.facebook.com/scottskitchenhcmc.*

Soul Burger
$$ | **BURGER** | This hidden gem, run by Chicagoan Gabe Boyer, a runner-up in the second series of *Next Iron Chef Vietnam*, serves gourmet burgers named after the greats of America's soul scene,

such as the James Brown (200-gram house-ground U.S. beef glazed with sweet and spicy brown sugar barbecue sauce, topped with pulled smoked pork shoulder, cheddar cheese, crisp beer-battered onion rings, and a creamy coleslaw). Order a side of truffle garlic fries and wash it all down with one of the many international beers on the menu. **Known for:** awesome wings; gourmet burgers; extensive selection of bourbons. [$] *Average main: d250,000* ✉ *4 Phan Boi Chau, District 1* ☎ *0775/171–261* 🌐 *www.facebook.com/soulburgersaigon.*

Hotels

Fusion Suites Sai Gon
$$$$ | RESORT | Minimalist contemporary design, attentive staff, a daily spa treatment included in the room rate, and an "anywhere, anytime" breakfast policy, this all-suites hotel is something quite unique in Ho Chi Minh City. **Pros:** spacious, stylish suites; in-room massages; retreat from city. **Cons:** not many choices at breakfast. [$] *Rooms from: d3,100,000* ✉ *3–5 Suong Nguyet Anh, District 1* ☎ *028/3925–7257* 🌐 *www.saigon.fusionsuites.com* 🍴 *Free Breakfast* 🛏 *71 suites.*

Hotel Nikko Saigon
$$$$ | HOTEL | Minimalist Japanese elegance and attentive service are the hallmarks of this hotel, right on the border of District 1 and District 5. **Pros:** spa and fitness center; great outdoor swimming pool; spacious rooms; excellent dim sum at restaurant. **Cons:** even though the hotel is in District 1, it's 20 minutes from downtown by taxi, longer during peak hours. [$] *Rooms from: d4,330,000* ✉ *235 Nguyen Van Cu, District 1* ☎ *028/3925–7777* 🌐 *www.hotelnikkosaigon.com.vn* 🛏 *334 rooms* 🍴 *Free Breakfast.*

New World Hotel Saigon
$$$ | HOTEL | This was the first modern high-rise hotel in Ho Chi Minh City, and though it's looking a little tired these days, the central location, business amenities, gym, tennis court, and pool make it a good choice for business travelers. **Pros:** friendly staff; great location, opposite September 23 park and a short walk to the Ben Thanh Market. **Cons:** in some rooms you can hear noise from the street, the park across the road, and a nearby rooftop bar. [$] *Rooms from: d3,600,000* ✉ *76 Le Lai, District 1* ☎ *028/3822–8888* 🌐 *www.saigon.newworldhotels.com* 🛏 *533 rooms* 🍴 *Free Breakfast.*

Pullman Saigon Centre
$$$$ | HOTEL | One of the newer hotels in town, Pullman Saigon Centre has large, comfortable, and stylish rooms with great views, well-trained staff, and a convenient location close to the central business district and tourist sights. **Pros:** one of the best hotel breakfasts in town; great on-site restaurant. **Cons:** the partially open bathroom concept can be perplexing. [$] *Rooms from: d2,685,000* ✉ *148 Tran Hung Dao, District 1* ☎ *028/3838–8686* 🌐 *www.pullman-saigon-centre.com* 🛏 *306 rooms* 🍴 *No Meals.*

Nightlife

WINE BARS

Chill Skybar
WINE BARS | Far above the bustling crowds, Chill is an impressive open bar on the 26th floor of one of the city's modern office blocks. With unimpeded views of downtown Ho Chi Minh City and beyond, this is a dramatic vantage point to watch the sun go down and the metropolis's lights go on. It's a slick, pricey venue that attracts plenty of glamorous, well-heeled guests, but it's worth a splurge. ■ **TIP→ Gentlemen, make sure you slip on some casual wear lest you have to borrow the dreaded "trousers and shoes for lend."** ✉ *AB Tower, 76a Le Lai, rooftop* ☎ *093/882–2838* 🌐 *www.chillsaigon.com.*

📽 Performing Arts

FILM
Galaxy Cinema Nguyen Du
FILM | Five screens show local and international new-release films. ✉ *116 Nguyen Du, District 1* ☎ *1900–2224* ⊕ *www. galaxycine.vn.*

MUSIC
Conservatory of Music (*Nhac Vien Thanh Pho Ho Chi Minh*)
MUSIC | This is the only regular venue in town for classical music performances. The theater's main season is from September through June; it's generally closed in summer except when there are special concerts by visiting orchestras. Check the "notice" section of the website for performance times. ✉ *112 Nguyen Du, District 1* ☎ *028/3822–5841* ⊕ *hcmcons.vn.*

THEATER
Golden Dragon Water Puppet Theater
PUPPET SHOWS | Three times a day, talented water puppeteers perform this folk art from the Red River Delta in Vietnam's north. The show is narrated in Vietnamese by a troupe of singers, accompanied by traditional musicians. The 50-minute show does not tell just one story, but scenes from daily life and skits based on Vietnamese folk tales. Expect to get a little wet if you sit in the front row—it's okay to scream if you get splashed, it's all part of the fun. In high season, tickets are only available two weeks ahead. ■ TIP➔ **Explore the nearby Tao Dan Park before or after a show.** ✉ *55B Nguyen Thi Minh Khai, District 1* ☎ *028/3930–2196* ⊕ *www.goldendragonwaterpuppet.vn.*

🛍 Shopping

ANTIQUES AND ANTIQUE REPLICAS
Antique Street
ANTIQUES & COLLECTIBLES | The vendors in this short street crammed with shops might claim their wares are genuine, but the truth is they're mostly replicas—interesting and beautiful, but definitely not worth the first price quoted. It's a great street for browsing, especially if you're into old photographs, but it will test your negotiating skills. ✉ *Le Cong Kieu, District 1.*

GIFTS AND SOUVENIRS
★ Ginkgo
MIXED CLOTHING | A tiny little T-shirt shop that opened in 2007 has grown into a chain of stores featuring its own Ginkgo-branded clothing and backpacks. Their graphic T-shirts are especially popular souvenirs as many of them highlight whimsical aspects of Vietnamese culture. There is also a store at 10 Le Loi. ✉ *92–96 Le Loi, District 1* ☎ *028/3823-4099* ⊕ *www.ginkgo-vietnam.com.*

MARKETS
Ben Thanh Market (*Cho Ben Thanh*)
MARKET | Built in 1914 and renovated in 1985, the sprawling Ben Thanh Market has 3,000 booths. The outlets at the front are tourist-oriented, selling clothing, shoes, bags, and lacquerware; in the middle there's food and at the back fresh produce. The vendors can be incredibly pushy and pickpockets often roam the narrow aisles. There are better places to pick up souvenirs and much better places to eat. Once a must-see in Ho Chi Minh City, now it's a place best avoided, although it's a handy landmark, lying as it does between the central business district and the backpacker's area. ✉ *At intersection of Tran Hung Dao, Le Loi, and Ham Nghi Sts., District 1* ⊕ *www. ben-thanh-market.com.*

Yersin Market (*Cho Dan Sinh*)

MARKET | Once the go-to place for army surplus items and Vietnam War memorabilia, this market now has an eclectic range of hardware and camping supplies alongside the military-esque products. So if you're in the market for a Zippo cigarette lighter, a hand truck, an army-green hatchet, or a life jacket, this is the place for you. ⊠ *104 Yersin, District 1.*

Around District 3

The densely populated District 3 sprawls from the border of District 1 toward the airport. Its plethora of eateries draws Saigonese foodies from throughout the city to converge on the street food joints, drinking restaurants, and more upscale dining establishments from dusk until the early hours of the morning.

👁 Sights

Jade Emperor Pagoda (*Chua Ngoc Hoang, Phuoc Hai Tu, Chua Phuoc Hai*)

TEMPLE | The Cantonese community built this structure—the finest Chinese pagoda in Ho Chi Minh City—in 1909. A mixture of Taoist, Buddhist, and ethnic myths provides the sources for the small pagoda's multitude of statues and carvings, incorporating just about everything from the *King of Hell* to a *Buddha of the Future.* Slowly strolling around the interior to view them may be preferable to attempting to decipher the significance of each of the numerous, distinct deities. Take a moment to note the main altar, the side panel's depiction of hell, and, in the side room, the miniature female figures representing the range of human qualities. There are usually a few vendors at the entrance selling turtles. Buddhists believe that releasing these turtles into the pagoda's turtle pond will generate merit. ⊠ *73 Mai Thi Luu, District 1* 🏯 🖾 *Free.*

Le Van Tam Park

CITY PARK | In 1983, city authorities created this park by clearing the *Cimetière Européen,* which had been established in 1859 by the French navy as the final resting place for soldiers and sailors who died in the city. Some superstitious locals won't go to the park because of its previous incarnation and the ghost stories that have been circulating ever since the cemetery was decommissioned. Ghosts aside, with its large shady trees, this is a great spot for people-watching early in the morning, with games of badminton, ballroom dancing, aerobics, jogging, and stretching going on. The park, which occasionally hosts book and agricultural fairs, is also a popular spot for Vietnamese couples to steal some privacy after dark. ⊠ *Bounded by Hai Ba Trung, Vo Thi Sau, and Dien Bien Phu Sts., District 1.*

Museum of Vietnamese History (*Bao Tang Lich Su Quoc Gia*)

HISTORY MUSEUM | This fascinatingly eclectic museum is in a beautiful colonial building inside the grounds of Saigon Zoo and Botanical Gardens, with various galleries dedicated to different eras. Much of Vietnam's history, and consequently its identity today, has been influenced by outsiders. In ancient times the Khmer and Chinese empires occupied large portions of modern-day Vietnam, and in more recent times the country has been partially or completely occupied by French, Japanese, and American forces. The museum gives a Vietnamese perspective on these events. ⊠ *Saigon Zoo and Botanical Gardens, 2 Nguyen Binh Khiem, District 1* 🕿 *028/3825–8783* 🌐 *www.baotanglichsutphcm.com.vn* 🖾 *30,000d.*

Tan Dinh Market (*Cho Tan Dinh*)

MARKET | This authentic local wet market, full of stalls selling fresh flowers, fruit, vegetables, meat, and seafood, also has a strip of eating places fronting Nguyen Huu Cau Street. The narrow inside aisles are lined with stalls selling a range of haberdashery, clothing, and shoes, none of which would really appeal to Westerners unless they're seeking a quirky souvenir. ✉ *Corner of Hai Ba Trung and Nguyen Huu Cau Sts., District 3.*

War Remnants Museum
(*Bao Tang Chung Tich Chien Tranh*)
HISTORY MUSEUM | This is a grueling museum focused on the horrors of the Vietnam War, known as the American War in Vietnam, with indoor exhibitions featuring graphic photographs of dismembered bodies and dead children and infants. Outside the machines of war (fighter planes, tanks, howitzers, bombs) are displayed and there's a re-creation of the infamous tiger cages of Con Dao prison island. If you go, take Kleenex and a stoic demeanor. Expect to see the war from a different perspective than you might see in the United States. ✉ *28 Vo Van Tan, District 3* ☎ *028/3930–6664* 🌐 *www.baotangchungtichchientranh.vn* 🎟 *40,000d.*

🍴 Restaurants

Banh Xeo 46A
$$ | VIETNAMESE | A no-frills, family-run institution, Banh Xeo 46A is the go-to place for one of southern Vietnam's most cherished culinary creations: *banh xeo* (literally, "sizzling crepe")—a crispy pancake made with rice flour, coconut milk, and a smidgen of turmeric, and filled with bean sprouts, onion, shrimp, and pork. Break off a piece and wrap it up in a giant mustard leaf along with a handful of herbs and greens, and dunk it in a fish sauce-based dip laced with chilies. **Known for:** street-style dining; appearing on international television shows; banh xeo. [$] *Average main: d135,000* ✉ *46A Dinh Cong Trang, off Hai Ba Trung, District 3* ☎ *028/3824–1110* 💳 *No credit cards.*

Hum Café and Restaurant
$$ | VEGETARIAN | Just a few doors from the War Remnants Museum, this vegetarian restaurant is a calm oasis that starts to restore flagging spirits from the first step past the pond and lush greenery into the stylish interior. The fresh and healthy pan-Asian menu and the vibe are similar to Hum Lounge in District 1, but with a focus that's more on food than cocktails. **Known for:** proximity to a popular tourist sight; vegetarian food; inviting design. [$] *Average main: d170,000* ✉ *32 Vo Van Tan, District 3* ☎ *028/3930–3819* 🌐 *www.humvegetarian.com.*

Lunch Lady
$ | VIETNAMESE | A quirk of fate made the ever-smiling Nguyen Thi Thanh an international television superstar, yet fame has not wrought many changes to her humble food stand (although in a different location). The Lunch Lady, who famously served celebrity chef Anthony Bourdain on his *No Reservations* TV show in 2009, has a rolling menu of a different dish every day (which means no real choice). **Known for:** featured on an international television show; local-style folding tables and plastic chairs; street food menu. [$] *Average main: d40,000* ✉ *1A-B Nguyen Dinh Chieu, District 1* ☎ *093/388–7922* 💳 *No credit cards* 🕒 *No dinner.*

★ Noir
$$$$ | INTERNATIONAL | The concept of dining in pitch blackness, served by vision-impaired waiters, has been a huge hit since Noir opened its doors in mid-2014. The theory is that because sight is our dominant sense, if you take it away other senses are heightened, resulting in a more intense experience of the food's aromas and taste. **Known for:** surprising menu; blind waiters; pitch-black interior. [$] *Average main: d650,000* ✉ *180D Hai Ba Trung, District 1* ☎ *028/6263–2525.*

Pho Binh
$ | VIETNAMESE | Even today, long after the war, you couldn't guess this little pho shop's secret: in an upstairs room here, a resistance cell planned the Ho Chi Minh City attacks of the 1968 Tet Offensive. After a delicious bowl of beef or chicken

pho arrives, foreign visitors are usually presented with a photo album and guest book. **Known for:** flavorsome pho; historic links; small museum upstairs. [$] *Average main: d60,000* ✉ *7 Ly Chinh Thang, District 3* ☎ *028/3848–3775* 💳 *No credit cards.*

Tan Dinh Market street food stands (*Cho Tan Dinh*)
$ | VIETNAMESE | Sample some of Ho Chi Minh City's best street food from the vendors at the front of Tan Dinh Market (Cho Tan Dinh). The *bun rieu* (noodle soup with rice paddy crab and tofu) and *suon nuong* (grilled pork) are especially recommended, as is *che* , the Vietnamese dessert-in-a-glass that's a popular afternoon snack. **Known for:** authentic street food; regional specialties. [$] *Average main: d60,000* ✉ *Corner of Hai Ba Trung and Nguyen Huu Cau, District 3.*

Coffee and Quick Bites

ID Café
$$ | VIETNAMESE | Catering to the young switched-on set, ID Café is popular with digital nomads, bloggers, locals, expats, and tourists alike. They come for its groovy interior design, high-speed Internet, coffee, and very tasty food, including several vegetarian options. **Known for:** coffee; digital nomad hangout; cheerful food menu. [$] *Average main: d75,000* ✉ *61B Tu Xuong, District 3* ☎ *028/3932–0021* 🌐 *www.facebook.com/idcafe.net.*

Hotels

Ma Maison
$$ | B&B/INN | A small family-run boutique hotel outside the city center, Ma Maison is an affordable alternative to the city's international properties and a comfortable retreat from downtown that's ideal for solo travelers or couples. **Pros:** urban retreat with an affordable rate; excellent service; in-house restaurant. **Cons:** location can be inconvenient if you're spending a lot of time outside of District 3; house rules, such as removing shoes, rub some guests the wrong way; surrounding area has little to offer. [$] *Rooms from: d900,000* ✉ *656/52 Cach Mang Thang Tam, District 3* ☎ *028/3846–0263, 090/305–8888* 🌐 *www.mamaison.vn* 🍴 *Free Breakfast* 🛏 *12 rooms.*

Shopping

CLOTHING

Antonio De Torres Design Atelier
MEN'S CLOTHING | High-end bespoke menswear at this boutique features handmade shoes, suits, and shirts, as well as bags and sunglasses. If you can't make it to the District 3 store, you can arrange a consultation in your hotel room and be measured for gorgeous tailored clothing. ✉ *42A1 Tran Quoc Thao St., District 3* ☎ *028/3930–6212* 🌐 *www.facebook.com/antoniodetorresofficial.*

MARKET

Ban Co (Chessboard) Market
MARKET | This is a great example of a local wet market selling fresh fruit, vegetables, meat, seafood, and housewares. The aisles are narrow and crowded and full of locals doing their daily (sometimes second- or third-daily) market runs. Food, coffee, and other drinks are available if you need a recharge. It's all done by 4 pm. ✉ *664 Nguyen Dinh Chieu, District 3.*

Hatvala
OTHER FOOD & DRINK | A haven for tea lovers seeking the best Vietnamese brews, Hatvala offers tastings showcasing poetically named teas such as Mountain Mist White Tea, Fish Hook Green Tea, and Autumn Jade Jasmine Tea, which are available for purchase. All the teas are grown in Vietnam's misty and mountainous north, mostly by hill tribes who process the leaves using traditional methods. ✉ *5 Nguyen Van Mai, District 3* ☎ *090/243–1107* 🌐 *www.hatvala.com.*

Beyond the City Center

Several interesting sights lie outside of the center, some of them in far-flung areas of the city, such as the Buddhist-themed Suoi Tien amusement park and the Ao Dai Museum in District 9, and the Dam Sen pair of parks in District 11. There are modern residential suburbs in District 2 and District 7, where expats and wealthy Vietnamese live in large villas with swimming pools and gardens. Though they don't have any notable sights, these areas can be worth visiting for the shopping and dining options.

Southwest of central Ho Chi Minh City is Cholon, a Chinese sister-city-within-the-city, which takes up most of District 5 and a small part of District 6. This was and still is the heart of Chinese culture in the city. There's no discernible entry point into its rabbit warren of small streets with wall-to-wall houses, shops, and eateries. Hai Thuong Lan Ong Street is worth a peek for the aromatic apothecaries, and Luong Nhu Hoc—home to stores selling all kinds of ritualistic costumes, ornaments, and opera masks—is a great spot to pick up souvenirs.

The French supported the Chinese in Vietnam because of their success in commerce and their apolitical outlook—the Chinese seldom supported Vietnamese Nationalist struggles. The Communists, on the other hand, saw Cholon as a bastion of capitalism, and the area suffered greatly after 1975. Later, in 1979, during the war between Vietnam and China, Cholon was again targeted, because it was considered a potential center of fifth columnists (pro-Chinese agitators). Many of the first boat people to flee Vietnam were Chinese-Vietnamese from Cholon. Now, after having made money in Australia, Canada, and the United States, many have returned to Saigon and are among the city's wealthiest residents.

The pagodas concentrated around Nguyen Trai and Tran Hung Dao streets can be navigated on foot. Bright blue, yellow, red, orange, and gold cover the pagodas in a dazzling display that would put mating peacocks to shame. Getting lost in Cholon's backstreets can be interesting, but also hot, tiring, and noisy. For a good overview of the suburb, consider a motorbike tour that can whiz you through the crowded narrow alleys.

◉ Sights

★ Ao Dai Museum

OTHER MUSEUM | Honoring Vietnam's national dress, this private museum is set on stunningly picturesque grounds that are a very long way from downtown. Once you pay the admission fee, a guide will take you to the two beautiful wooden exhibition houses, which showcase *ao dais* from the 17th century to the modern day. Smaller kids will like feeding the fish and playing ao dai quoits (and generally letting off steam on the verdant lawns if they're all city-ed out). This place is—amazingly—still off the tourist radar. ✉ *206/19/30 Long Thuan, District 9* ☏ *0914/726–948* ⊕ *www.facebook. com/baotangaodaivietnam* ✉ *50,000d* ☉ *Closed Mon.*

Binh Tay Market

MARKET | This wholesale market, in a colonial-era Chinese-style building about a half-hour drive from downtown, is not so much a shopping destination (unless you want to buy spices, herbal medicine, or textiles) as a spectacle to behold, particularly if you get here before 8 am to savor the frenetic atmosphere at its peak. With more than 2,000 stalls, Binh Tay can get pretty chaotic. In the central courtyard a small shrine honors the market's founder, Quach Dam (1863–1927), a disabled Chinese immigrant who started out collecting scrap before making his fortune. The food court inside serves a wide variety of Vietnamese street food and Chinese-influenced dishes—great

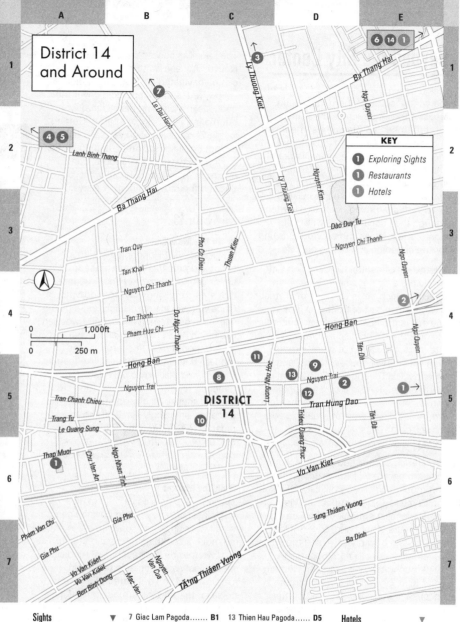

District 14 and Around

KEY

① Exploring Sights
① Restaurants
① Hotels

DISTRICT 14

for a replenishing brunch after an early arrival. ⊠ *57A Thap Muoi, District 6.*

Cholon Mosque

MOSQUE | Built in 1932 by Tamil Muslims, the Cholon Mosque now serves the city's Indonesian and Malaysian Muslim community. Notice how much simpler the mosque is than the pagodas in the area, which are characterized by exuberant ornamentation and bright colors. ⊠ *639 Nguyen Trai, District 5.*

Dai Nam

AMUSEMENT PARK/CARNIVAL | FAMILY | First opened in 2008, Dai Nam is a massive entertainment complex that includes Dai Nam Wonderland theme park, a sumptuous golden temple, a zoo, an artificial beach, 60-hectare racecourse, and a hotel. You'll probably need to rent a bicycle or golf cart to get around this sprawling complex, which has a recurring Buddhist theme, both peaceful and frightening. An example of the over-the-top-ness of Dai Nam: the racecourse has a 2,200-meter track for motorcycle and go-kart racing, a 1,600-meter track for greyhounds and horses, and a pool for Jet Ski performances. Dai Nam is about 40 km (25 miles) from Ho Chi Minh City, about 1 hour by car or 1½ hours by local bus 616 from Ben Thanh Market. ⊠ *1765A Binh Duong Blvd., Hiep An Ward, Thu Dau Mot* ☎ *0650/3896–389* ⊕ *www.khudulichdainam.vn* 🎫 *Entrance to The Golden Temple free. Entrance to racecourse and amusement park 200,000d. Individual rides from 20,000d; beach 200,000d; zoo 200,000d. Combo tickets available.*

Dam Sen Cultural Park

AMUSEMENT PARK/CARNIVAL | FAMILY | Next door to Dam Sen Water Park, this attraction has an amusement park as well as its cultural aspects, which makes it a good choice for a family outing. You can enjoy traditional Vietnamese handicrafts, games, and folk song performances and then view a range of cultural reproductions, which include an ancient Roman square and a Japanese teahouse and peach blossom garden. If the kids get restless, head for the roller coaster, bumper cars, Ferris wheel, and other rides. Tamer activities include swan boats to pedal, an extensive aquarium, animal enclosures, a bowling alley, and a movie theater. There are food and drink outlets throughout the park. ■ **TIP→ Trying to visit both the cultural and the water park in one day is not recommended.** ⊠ *3 Hoa Binh, District 11* ☎ *028/3963–2483* ⊕ *www. damsenpark.com.vn* 🎫 *120,000d for entrance only. Combo tickets including rides available.*

Dam Sen Water Park

WATER PARK | FAMILY | For a rollicking day out for kids of all ages, this park has a variety of slides and pools (one with a wave machine), a zipline, and a lazy river ride. Compared to water parks in more developed countries, Dam Sen is a little rough around the edges, but that doesn't prevent it from being an exhilarating day out. Children have to be taller than 4 feet 6 inches to go on the larger slides, but there's a range of medium slides for smaller kids and a toddler play area. ■ **TIP→ On weekdays there are usually no lines for the rides.** Lockers are available (15,000d) and you're given a small waterproof tube to hold your money, valuables, and the locker key. There are also several food kiosks within the park. It can take up to an hour to get here from District 1 when traffic is heavy, or about 40 minutes in light traffic. ⊠ *3 Hoa Bien, District 11* ☎ *028/3858–8418* ⊕ *www. damsenwaterpark.com.vn* 🎫 *Tickets from 190,000d before 4 pm, 150,000d after 4 pm; smaller people are 150,000d and 110,000d.*

★ FITO Museum (*Museum of Traditional Vietnamese Medicine*)

OTHER MUSEUM | The outside of this museum showcasing the history of traditional Vietnamese medicine might be plain, but inside it's a fabulous carved wooden wonderland, with the interior of an authentic antique house on the third floor and a re-created Cham-style gazebo on the rooftop. Displays, enhanced by audiovisuals and drawing on nearly 3,000 items in the collection, range from Stone Age pots to 3rd-century coins (for coin-rubbing therapy), ancient texts, bronze kettles, and a range of cutting, chopping, and storing utensils. The concluding part of the introductory film (subtitled in English) and the shop at the exit are a reminder that this is a private museum, set up by Fito Pharma. It's well worth a visit for the insight into traditional Vietnamese daily life through the ages. ☒ 41 Hoang Du Khuong, District 10 ☎ 028/3864-2430 ⊕ www.fitomuseum. com.vn ☝ 120,000d.

Giac Lam Pagoda

RELIGIOUS BUILDING | One of the oldest pagodas in Ho Chi Minh City, Giac Lam Pagoda was built in 1744 in the jungle outside of the city of Gia Dinh. Outside the walls of the pagoda now lies the urban sprawl of Ho Chi Minh City. Inside, however, are peaceful gardens containing a bodhi tree imported from Sri Lanka in 1953, a seven-story stupa, and the pagoda itself. Prayers are held every evening at 6 pm. ☒ 118D Lac Long Quan, Tan Binh District ☎ 028/3865-3933.

Ha Chuong Hoi Quan Pagoda

RELIGIOUS BUILDING | Like many other pagodas built by Fujian congregations, this one is dedicated to Thien Hau, goddess of the sea and protector of fisherfolk and sailors. It has four stone pillars encircled by painted dragons, brought from China when the pagoda was constructed in the 19th century. Also note the scenes in ceramic relief on the roof and the murals next to the main altar. ☒ 802 Nguyen Trai, District 5.

Nghia An Hoi Quan Pagoda

RELIGIOUS BUILDING | This pagoda, built by the Chaozhou Chinese congregation in 1872, is worth seeing for its elaborate woodwork. There are intricately carved wooden boats and a large figure of the deified Chinese general Quan Cong's sacred red horse, as well as representations of Quan Cong himself with two guardians. A festival dedicated to Quan Cong takes place here every year on the 13th day of the first lunar month. ☒ 678 Nguyen Trai, District 5.

Ong Bon Pagoda (Chua Ong Bon or Nhi Phu Hoi Quan)

RELIGIOUS BUILDING | Many deities are represented at this pagoda, but the main attraction is Ong Bon himself, the guardian of happiness and virtue. Ong Bong is also responsible for wealth, so people bring fake paper money to burn in the pagoda's furnace in his honor, hoping the year ahead will bring financial rewards to their families. The centerpiece of the pagoda is an elaborately carved wood-and-gold altar and a finely crafted statue of Ong Bon. Look for the intricately painted murals of lions, tigers, and dragons. ☒ 264 Hai Thuong Lan Ong, District 5.

Quan Am Pagoda

RELIGIOUS BUILDING | Busy scenes in lacquer, ceramic, gold, and wood illustrate traditional Chinese stories at this pagoda, built in 1816 by a congregation of Fujian refugees from China. Many legendary and divine beings, some dressed in elaborately embroidered robes, are portrayed, as are some simple rural scenes representing the birthplaces of the original members of the congregation. This is still one of Cholon's most active pagodas. ☒ 12 Lao Tu (parallel to Hung Vuong and Nguyen Trai Sts.), District 5.

Suoi Tien

AMUSEMENT PARK/CARNIVAL | FAMILY | Believed to be the world's only Buddhist-themed amusement park, Suoi Tien (the name means Fairy Stream) is certainly one of the quirkiest. On the outskirts of Ho Chi Minh City, about 20 km (12 miles) from District 1 and behind a giant pair of tusks, it's a vast, sometimes downright odd, complex that contains an amazing diversity of attractions, from waterslides, crocodiles, and dolphins—thankfully,

The world's only Buddhist-themed amusement park, Suoi Tien, is filled with waterslides and rides.

not all in the same place—to graphic depictions of hell, though there are not many signs in English to explain the more bizarre exhibits. There's also an ice palace, 4-D movie theater, fun fair rides for smaller kids, a go-kart circuit, and quad biking. Allocate a whole day to exploring the complex, and arrive early to get the land-based activities done before things heat up too much, then cool down in the water park, with its range of slides and pools to suit all ages. Food and drink kiosks can be found throughout the park. ■ TIP➜ The small zoo is depressing and best avoided. Doing the water park and then exploring the theme park is going to be a huge day out, so it's probably better to choose one or the other for a day trip. ⊠ 120 Hanoi Hwy., District 9 ☎ 028/3896–0260 ⊡ Theme park 120,000d; water park 140,000d.

Tam Son Hoi Quan Pagoda (*Chua Ba Chua*)
RELIGIOUS BUILDING | The Chinese Fujian congregation built this lavishly decorated pagoda dedicated to Me Sanh, the goddess of fertility, in the 19th century.

Women—and some men—pray to the goddess to bring them children. Many other deities are represented here as well: Thien Hau, the goddess of the sea and protector of fisherfolk and sailors; Ong Bon, the guardian of happiness and virtue; and Quan Cong, the deified general, depicted with a long beard and his sacred red horse. ⊠ 118 Trieu Quang Phuc, District 5 ☎ 028/3856–6655.

Thien Hau Pagoda (*Chua Ba*)
RELIGIOUS BUILDING | Sailors used to come to be blessed at this pagoda dedicated to Thien Hau, the goddess of the sea and protector of fisherfolk and mariners. On the main dais are three statues of the goddess, each flanked by two guardians. Note also the figure of Long Mau, guardian of mothers and babies. The turtles living on the grounds are considered sacred animals and are a symbol of longevity. The Cantonese congregation built this pagoda at the beginning of the 19th century. ⊠ 710 Nguyen Trai, District 5.

★ Van Thanh Park

CITY PARK | FAMILY | A large government-owned tourist park, Van Thanh is a lovely escape from Ho Chi Minh City's urban chaos, with its artificial lake, restaurants, swimming pool, and small children's playground. The food isn't brilliant but dining in a little hut over the lake is fun, and the grounds and buildings are picturesque "ancient Vietnam" style. Entry to the pool, which gets very crowded on weekends, is 70,000d. ✉ *48/10 Dien Bien Phu, Binh Thanh District* ☎ *28/3512–3026* 🌐 *www.binhquoiresort.com.vn.*

🍴 Restaurants

★ The Deck

$$$$ | CONTEMPORARY | A stylish lounge and restaurant on the banks of the slow-flowing Saigon River, The Deck is a place to spoil yourself with sublime seafood-focused pan-Asian cuisine, fine wines, and professional service. The beauty of the entry courtyard, with its tall trees, black marble pond, and potted lotus plants, is almost forgotten once you enter the restaurant, where the river views take center stage. **Known for:** river views; sumptuous high-end menu; stylish decor. [$] *Average main: d600,000* ✉ *38 Nguyen U Di, Thao Dien, District 2* ☎ *028/3744–6632* 🌐 *www.thedecksaigon.com.*

District Federal

$$$ | MEXICAN | FAMILY | There's a great atmosphere as well as great food at District Federal, the only place in town with a Mexican chef cooking authentic Mexican cuisine with fresh, high-quality local ingredients. Don't miss the Mexican drinks, including tepache juice, horchata, and frozen margaritas. **Known for:** great grills; Mexican cuisine (the chef is from Mexico City); lively atmosphere. [$] *Average main: d285,000* ✉ *84 Xuan Thuy, Thao Dien, District 2* ☎ *090/140–8998* 🌐 *www.dfed.vn* ⏲ *Closed Mon.*

Dtwo Sportspub

$$ | INTERNATIONAL | Non-sports fans are fully justified in hanging out in Dtwo Sportspub just for the awesome pub grub, including classic burgers, fish-and-chips, Cornish pasties, and beef stew. There's also distinctly non-pubby grub, such as a cheese board, salads, and eggs Benedict. **Known for:** selection of beers; sports broadcast on many screens; British pub grub. [$] *Average main: d270,000* ✉ *55–57 Thao Dien, Thao Dien, District 2* ☎ *028/3519–4138* 🌐 *www.facebook.com/dtwosportspub.*

★ La Villa

$$$$ | FRENCH | An experience rather than a meal, La Villa serves elegant but not pretentious fine French dining on a quiet street in District 2's Thao Dien area. Whether you sit in the garden by the pool, surrounded by fairy lights and greenery, or inside in the airy salon, the attentive service and the cuisine add to the memorable experience. **Known for:** beautiful setting; French fine dining; tasting menus. [$] *Average main: d1,290,000* ✉ *14 Ngo Quang Huy, Thao Dien, District 2* ☎ *090/771–9879* 🌐 *www.lavilla-restaurant.com.vn* ⏲ *Closed for lunch Sun.*

MAD House

$$ | SCANDINAVIAN | FAMILY | Serving northern European food with some local twists in a converted villa with lush gardens, Mad House is the work of two Danish chefs; "mad" is the Danish word for food. For the hungry, the mains, steaks, and burgers will satisfy; for the not-so-peckish there's an interesting selection of breakfast dishes and snacks. **Known for:** leafy garden setting; northern European cuisine; excellent selection of burgers. [$] *Average main: d270,000* ✉ *6/1/2 Nguyen U Di, Thao Dien, District 2* ☎ *028/3519–4009* 🌐 *www.madhousesaigon.com.*

The Posh Duck Kitchen

$$$ | TAPAS | A destination dining experience that's well worth the long journey out to the back lots of District 7, this restaurant produces Asian-inspired tapas platters in a hospitality supply showroom situated in an industrial zone. Don't miss the grilled pork chop glazed with soy and honey and the excellent duck confit. **Known for:** destination restaurant; spearheading the locavore movement in Ho Chi Minh City; Asian-inspired tapas. Ⓢ *Average main: d290,000* ⊠ *Lot DVTM-9, Rd. 7, Tan Thuan Export Processing Zone, 2nd fl., District 7* ☎ *096/112–4775* ⊕ *theposhduck.vn.*

Snap Café

$$ | CAFÉ | FAMILY | Serving a mishmash of international, Tex-Mex, and Vietnamese fare, Snap is an open-air family-oriented café-restaurant set in a large thatched hut overlooking a children's playground. Popular with the local expat community, Snap caters to non-families with its quieter library section tucked away on one side beside a manicured tropical garden. **Known for:** live music on Saturday night; kids playground out back; wide selection of cuisines available. Ⓢ *Average main: d270,000* ⊠ *32 Tran Ngoc Dien, Thao Dien, District 2* ☎ *028/3519–4532* ⊕ *www.snap.com.vn.*

Thai Street

$$ | THAI | Walk through a boutique shopping arcade and be transported to the streets of Bangkok with Thai Street's kitschy yet fun décor (think tuk tuks and a pay stand dressed up like a money exchange booth) and its authentic Thai street food dishes. Overseen by a Thai chef from Isaan, the dishes are prepared on the spot, so spice levels can be adjusted as well as made into vegan and vegetarian versions. **Known for:** customizable dishes; authentic Thai street food dishes; funky decor. Ⓢ *Average main: 130,000* ⊠ *32 Tran Ngoc Dien, District 2* ⊕ *At the very back* ☎ *028/6654–9525* ⊕ *www.thaistreet.com.vn.*

Union Jack's Fish & Chips

$$ | BRITISH | Belly-filling fish-and-chips, pork pies, battered black pudding, beef and ale stew, with sides of mushy peas, curry sauce, and Scotch eggs—you can't get much more British than that. Union Jacks's Fish & Chips is a firm favorite with Saigon's expats seeking a taste of home and some "kettle is always on" hospitality. **Known for:** proper "chippie" chips; fish-and-chips; English-style pork pies. Ⓢ *Average main: d180,000* ⊠ *10 Nguyen Ba Lan, District 2* ☎ *076/728–6183* ⊕ *www.union-jacks.co* ⊗ *No lunch Mon.–Thurs.*

☕ Coffee and Quick Bites

Ralf's Artisan Gelato

$ | ICE CREAM | FAMILY | This Italian-style Gelateria Artigianale is well-loved for its authentic gelatos and sorbets, all made by hand and fresh from scratch daily with no preservatives or additives. While there are traditional flavors such as chocolate, black currant, cinnamon, and rum raisin, try the Vietnamese-inspired flavors, including fish sauce and pho. **Known for:** tasting options before you buy; handmade Italian-style gelato; unusual flavors, such as pho and fish sauce. Ⓢ *Average main: d65,000* ⊠ *17 Le Van Mien, District 2* ☎ *097/932–7905* ⊕ *www.ralfs-artisan-gelato.com.*

Sweet and Sour

$ | CAFÉ | FAMILY | A pretty pink café specializing in cupcakes and macaroons, Sweet and Sour supplies many cafés and restaurants around town. Sweet and Sour has a little dollhouse to keep kids happy and a Champagne menu to keep the parents happy. **Known for:** party favors; Champagne menu; delicious cupcakes. Ⓢ *Average main: d50,000* ⊠ *9 Ngo Quang Huy, Thao Dien, District 2* ☎ *028/3519–1568* ⊕ *www.sweetandsour.vn.*

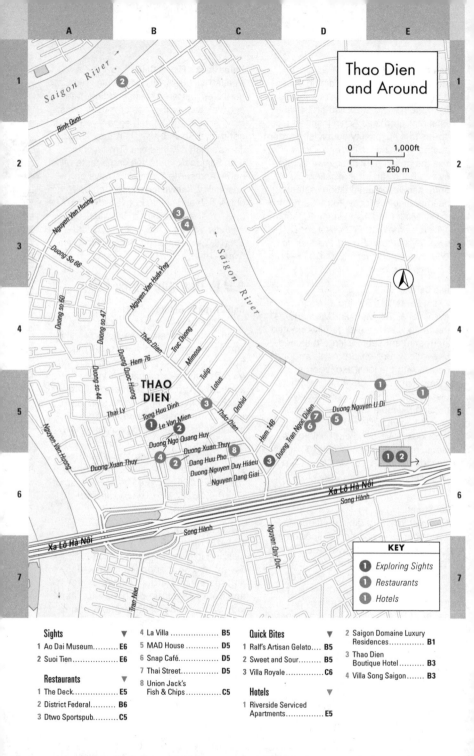

Thao Dien and Around

0 ————— 1,000ft
0 ————— 250 m

Saigon River

Binh Quoi

Nguyen Van Huong

Duong So 66

Duong so 60

Duong so 44

Nguyen Van Huong

Nguyen Van Huong

Nguyen Van Huong

Thao Dien

Truc Duong

Hem 76

Duong Quoc Huong

THAO DIEN

Thai Ly

Tong Huu Dinh

Le Van Mien

Duong Ngo Quang Huy

Duong Xuan Thuy

Duong Xuan Thuy

Dang Huu Pho

Duong Nguyen Duy Hiéu

Nguyen Dang Giai

Mimosa

Tulip

Lotus

Orchid

Thao Dien

Hem 14B

Duong Tran Ngoc Dien

Duong Nguyen U Di

Saigon River

Nguyen Duy Duc

Xa Lô Hà Nôi

Song Hành

Song Hành

Xa Lô Hà Nôi

Tran Nao

KEY

- **1** *Exploring Sights*
- **1** *Restaurants*
- **1** *Hotels*

Sights ▼
1 Ao Dai Museum.......... **E6**
2 Suoi Tien.................. **E6**

Restaurants ▼
1 The Deck.................. **E5**
2 District Federal.......... **B6**
3 Dtwo Sportspub.......... **C5**

4 La Villa **B5**
5 MAD House **D5**
6 Snap Café............... **D5**
7 Thai Street.............. **D5**
8 Union Jack's
  Fish & Chips **C5**

Quick Bites ▼
1 Ralf's Artisan Gelato.... **B5**
2 Sweet and Sour......... **B5**
3 Villa Royale **C6**

Hotels ▼
1 Riverside Serviced
  Apartments.............. **E5**

2 Saigon Domaine Luxury
  Residences.............. **B1**
3 Thao Dien
  Boutique Hotel **B3**
4 Villa Song Saigon....... **B3**

★ Villa Royale

$$ | **CAFÉ** | World-class tea, cakes, pastries, and Australian café-style comfort food is served among antiques, objets d'art, and other treasures collected by globe-trotting chef and hotelier David Campbell. It's a very exotic feeling to be sitting on a vintage couch surrounded by beautiful things, using the free Wi-Fi and sipping top-quality TWG teas. **Known for:** café-style food; high tea; dining among antiques. $ *Average main: d220,000* ✉ *3 Tran Ngoc Dien, Thao Dien, District 2* ☎ *028/3744–4897 cell phone* ⊕ *www. villaroyaletearoom.com* ☾ *Closed Mon. and public holidays. No dinner.*

🛏 Hotels

Alcove Library Hotel

$$$ | **HOTEL** | This is a great option if you're looking for a bit of glamour slap-bang in the middle of local life, and a stylish alternative to the big downtown hotels. **Pros:** bathrooms have rain showers; free Wi-Fi, mineral water, and beverages; a quiet retreat from the chaos of downtown. **Cons:** 20 minutes by taxi from downtown and the tourist attractions; with white paint being so difficult to maintain, the walls show every scuff mark. $ *Rooms from: d1,457,000* ✉ *133A Nguyen Dinh Chinh, Phu Nhuan* ☎ *028/6256–9966* ⊕ *www.alcovehotel.com.vn* ⇆ *26 rooms* ‖○‖ *Free Breakfast.*

Hotel Equatorial

$$$ | **HOTEL** | Part of a Malaysian-owned chain of five-star hotels, the Equatorial has spacious rooms, an excellent Pan-Asian restaurant, and impeccable service. **Pros:** excellent spa and health club; live entertainment in the lounge Thursday to Saturday; outdoor pool with swim-up bar. **Cons:** 15 to 20 minutes from downtown (but the hotel offers a regular free shuttle service). $ *Rooms from: d2,000,000* ✉ *242 Tran Binh Trong, District 5* ☎ *028/3839–7777, 028/3839–0011* ⊕ *hochiminhcity.equatorial.com* ‖○‖ *Free Breakfast* ⇆ *333 rooms.*

Riverside Serviced Apartments

$$$ | **APARTMENT** | **FAMILY** | True to its name, these riverside apartments house a mix of long-term expat residences and short-term visitors, and can be a great deal for families. **Pros:** river views; good amenities for families; feels like a resort. **Cons:** not all apartments have river view; removed from local life. $ *Rooms from: d1,950,000* ✉ *53 Vo Truong Toan, Thao Dien* ☎ *028/3744–4111* ⊕ *www.river-side-apartments.com* ⇆ *30 apartments* ‖○‖ *No Meals.*

Saigon Domaine Luxury Residences

$$$$ | **APARTMENT** | **FAMILY** | In this luxurious, peaceful, and private complex on Thanh Da Island, a 20-minute boat ride from downtown, apartments with one to four bedrooms come with a full kitchen and a washing machine, and there's a range of resort-style, family-friendly amenities including restaurants, bars, a swimming pool, children's play areas, a library, and a gym. **Pros:** friendly, knowledgeable staff; an escape from the chaos and energy of downtown; free bus and speedboat shuttles to downtown. **Cons:** nearby food stalls are the only off-site dining options; a 20-minute taxi or boat ride downtown. $ *Rooms from: d3,850,000* ✉ *1057 Binh Quoi, Binh Thanh District* ☎ *028/3556–6163* ⊕ *www. saigondomaine.com* ⇆ *54 apartments* ‖○‖ *Free Breakfast.*

★ Thao Dien Boutique Hotel

$$$$ | **HOTEL** | Part of the scenic riverfront Thao Dien Village complex, this welcoming boutique hotel on landscaped grounds is a celebration of textures, with a giant knitted installation in the lobby and rooms combining corduroy cushions, muslin drapes, and polished cement floors. **Pros:** restaurants overlook the river; friendly staff; visually appealing urban hideaway. **Cons:** there's no boat shuttle service, making downtown a long taxi ride away, especially during rush hours. $ *Rooms from: d4,500,000* ✉ *189–197 Nguyen Van Huong, District*

2 ☎ 028/3744–2222 🌐 *www.thaodienvillage.com* 🛏 *20 rooms* 🍴 *Free Breakfast.*

★ Villa Song Saigon

$$$$ | **HOTEL** | Channeling the elegance of the French-colonial era with soaring ceilings and wooden floorboards, the three-story Villa Song is an ode to art and interior design and is a favorite with discerning travelers. **Pros:** regular shuttle boats to District 1; all-day breakfast, free minibar, and the lush landscaped saltwater pool make relaxing all too easy; each room is unique. **Cons:** no elevator; the location outside of the main part of Thao Dien means there are few dining options within walking distance. [$] *Rooms from: d3,500,000* ✉ *197/2 Nguyen Van Huong, Thao Dien, District 2* ☎ *028/3744–6090* 🌐 *www.villasong.com* 🛏 *23 rooms* 🍴 *Free Breakfast.*

Nightlife

Saigon Outcast

THEMED ENTERTAINMENT | Saigon Outcast has a little something for everyone. It's an open-air café-bar, with a skateboarding section (free) and a rock-climbing wall (fee). Check the website to see what's coming up in the way of live music, movie nights, local theater, markets, charitable events, craft classes, and open mike sessions. The bar stocks local and craft beers, and the kitchen turns out some tasty international fare. ✉ *188/1 Nguyen Van Huong, Thao Dien, District 2* ☎ *090/236–5780* 🌐 *www.saigonoutcast.com.*

Performing Arts

FILM

CGV Crescent Mall

FILM | One of the newest movie theater chains in Ho Chi Minh City shows local and international movies, dubbed and subtitled. ✉ *Crescent Mall, Nguyen Van Linh, 5th fl., District 7* ☎ *1900–6017* 🌐 *www.cgv.vn.*

THEATER

Hoa Binh Theater (*Nha Hat Hoa Binh*)

THEATER | In an ugly Soviet-era palace, this theater is mostly used for local Vietnamese dramas, puppet shows, and the occasional fashion show. ✉ *240 Ba Thang Hai, District 10* ☎ *028/3865–5026* 🌐 *www.nhahathoabinh.com.vn.*

Shopping

ART

The Factory Contemporary Arts Center

ART GALLERIES | Established in 2016 by artist Ti-A, The Factory is dynamic destination for art, and home to curated exhibitions, workshops, live arts, talks, and film screenings. Check the website to find out what's on. ✉ *15 Nguyen U Di, Thao Dien, District 2* ☎ *028/3744–2589* 🌐 *www.factoryartscentre.com* ☞ *Admission 80,000d.*

VinSpace

ART GALLERIES | Regular art exhibitions are hosted in this boutique art studio in District 2's Thao Dien area, and it also runs workshops for adults and children. It's particularly popular with expats for its regular Wine and Canvas painting evenings. ✉ *6 Le Van Mien, Thao Dien, District 2* ☎ *090/772–9846* 🌐 *www.vinspace.com.*

CLOTHING AND SHOES

Anupa

HANDBAGS | Beautifully soft handmade leather handbags, resort wear, and accessories (including jewelry using semiprecious stones) here are all one-of-a-kind, often featuring intricate details, such as fish leather and tourmaline. Items are ethically produced, made in Vietnam from sustainable materials. ✉ *55 Ngo Quang Huy, District 2* ☎ *0913/989–747* 🌐 *www.anupa.net.*

Dominique Saint Paul

SHOES | Quality handmade leather shoes and accessories combining Italian leather, European techniques, and Vietnamese craftsmanship make this boutique worth

Ho Chi Minh City's flower market is the place to buy local specialties and goods.

the drive out to the suburbs. While there is a selection of ready-to-wear shoes in more than 20 styles (mostly for men but with some for women), the real value is in having a pair custom-made in the color of your choice, with some accents inspired by Vietnam. Shoes start at around $200 a pair and can be pre-ordered online or measured in person and shipped to your home. ⊠ *14A Road 9, Thao Dien, District 2* ☎ *028/3519–4595* ⊕ *shop.dominiquesaintpaul.com.*

ANTIQUES AND ANTIQUE REPLICAS
Villa Royale
ANTIQUES & COLLECTIBLES | This teahouse and antiques shop offers an eclectic mix of small, large, and very large collectibles, objets d'art, art, silverware, and vintage furnishings from Europe, North Africa, and Asia, collected by globe-trotting Australian chef and hotelier David Campbell. David exercises his chef muscles in the teahouse. ⊠ *3 Tran Ngoc Dien, Thao Dien, District 2* ☎ *028/3744–4897* ⊕ *www.villaroyaletreasures.com.*

LACQUERWARE
Huong Nga Fine Arts
CRAFTS | Finely crafted Vietnamese lacquerware in traditional and modern designs, as well as a range of wooden products, are all made at Nga's factory in District 9. ⊠ *240A Duong Dinh Hoi, District 9* ☎ *028/6679–0377* ⊕ *www. huongngafinearts.vn.*

MALLS AND SHOPPING CENTERS
Crescent Mall
MALL | One of Ho Chi Minh City's newest shopping complexes, Crescent Mall, in the Phu My Hung expat area, has just about everything you could want in one shopping experience: a supermarket, an eight-screen movie theater, fashion boutiques, specialty shops, restaurants and cafés, furniture and housewares, electronics, and a children's entertainment area. ⊠ *101 Ton Dat Tien, Phu My Hung, District 7* ☎ *90/879–3907* ⊕ *www.crescentmall. com.vn.*

SC VivoCity

MALL | Similar to Singapore's VivoCity, SC VivoCity has supermarkets, fashion outlets, cafés, restaurants, and cinemas. There's also a bowling alley and a rooftop kids play area. ⊠ *1058 Nguyen Van Linh, District 7* ☎ *28/3776–1018* ⊕ *www.scvivocity.com.vn/en.*

MARKETS

Flower Market

MARKET | Ho Chi Minh City's flower market is a vibrant and colorful affair. Busiest early in the morning when the bulk of the wholesale trade is conducted, the market continues to trade until midafternoon. The area is also home to a Khmer community, so break up your wandering with some Cambodian specialties like soup laced with the pungent *prahok* (fermented fish paste). ⊠ *Ho Thi Ky, District 10.*

🏃 Activities

Sporting amenities are somewhat limited within the city, but do include some unexpected facilities, and there are several golf courses in and around the city.

SPAS

Cat Moc Spa

SPAS | A calm and peaceful day spa a short distance from Ho Chi Minh City's backpacker district, Cat Moc Spa specializes in half-day pampering packages, with a menu of facials, massages, body treatments, hand and foot care, and a Japanese-style shampoo and blow-dry service. ⊠ *63 Tran Dinh Xu, District 1* ☎ *028/6295–8926* ⊕ *www.catmocspa. com.*

Jasmine Total Body Wellness Spa

SPAS | This boutique spa offers a range of face and body treatments, waxing, and manicures and pedicures for men and women. There's also a small hair salon on the ground floor. ⊠ *14E1 Street 38, District 2* ☎ *083/824–6693* ⊕ *www. jasminespa.vn.*

La Maison de l'Apothiquaire

SPAS | Down a dreamy, leafy lane, this is an elegant day spa in a beautifully renovated colonial villa. The spa has a full range of face and body treatments, manicures and pedicures, as well as a yoga studio and swimming pool. L'Apothiquaire also has a smaller salon downtown, at 41 Dong Khoi in District 1. Their chocolate fango wrap is amazing. ⊠ *64A Trung Dinh, District 3* ☎ *028/3932–5181* ⊕ *www.lapothiquaire.com.*

SQUASH

Landmark Squash Court

RAQUET SPORTS | The only squash court in downtown Ho Chi Minh City is at The Landmark serviced apartments. Lessons, opponents, and racquets are available from the health club, on the 16th floor of the apartment complex. Nonresidents of The Landmark need to reserve a court three days in advance. ⊠ *The Landmark, 58 Ton Duc Thang, District 1* ☎ *028/3822–2098* ⊕ *www.thelandmarkvietnam.com* ⊠ *From 240,000d.*

DIVING

Rainbow Divers

DIVING & SNORKELING | Established in the late '90s, Rainbow Divers is one of Vietnam's premier PADI dive centers. Guests can start their PADI training (classroom + pool) at the Ho Chi Minh City District 2 location before heading to one of their ocean centers in Nha Trang, Whale Island, Phu Quoc, or Con Dao to complete the course. ⊠ *231 Nguyen Van Huong, District 2* ☎ *0913/408–146* ⊕ *www. divevietnam.com.*

GOLF

Dong Nai Golf Resort

GOLF | It takes about an hour to reach this scenic course, about 50 km (30 miles) outside of Ho Chi Minh City. Designed by Ward W. Northrup, it's considered one of the most challenging courses in Southeast Asia, with hills and natural ponds. The location, at the bottom of a valley, ensures stable playing conditions year-round, with little wind. ⊠ *Off*

National Hwy. 1A, Trang Bom District ☎ *0251/866–1616* ⊕ *www.dongnaigolf. com.vn* ✉ *From 1,800,000d on weekdays* 🏌 *27 holes, 10,381 yards, par 72.*

Long Thanh Golf Club

GOLF | About 36 km (22 miles) east of Ho Chi Minh City, near Bien Hoa City—about 50 minutes from downtown when traffic is light—the two courses here, designed by Ron Fream, have rolling fairways, undulating greens, and several artificial lakes. The Hills Course is the more challenging of the two; the Lakes Course, although it has many bunkers and water hazards, is flatter. ⊠ *National Hwy. 51, Phuoc Tan* ☎ *0251/626–8989* ✉ *From 1,900,000d for 18 holes weekdays* 🏌 *Lakes Course: 18 holes, 6572 yards, par 72. Hills Course: 18 holes, 6400 yards, par 72.*

Saigon South Golf Club

GOLF | This compact 9-hole par-3 golf course and driving range is the closest golf course to downtown Ho Chi Minh City. The greens are well maintained and, while not the most exciting course around, it's very accessible from downtown. ⊠ *19 Ton Dat Tien, District 7* ☎ *028/5411–2001* ✉ *From 436,000d on weekdays, including caddy* 🏌 *9 holes, 1160 yards, par 3.*

Song Be Golf Resort

GOLF | This 27-hole USGA standard championship course, 20 km (12 miles) outside the city, was built on former fruit and coconut orchards and is considered one of the most challenging layouts in Vietnam, with 10 lakes. The 9-hole Desert Course is Song Be's most feared, with its long, narrow fairways and complex bunkers that require some strategy. The 9-hole Lotus Course and the 9-hole Palm Course are prettier than the Desert Course, with several lakes and large undulating greens. ⊠ *77 Binh Duong Blvd., Lai Thieu* ☎ *0274/3756–660* ⊕ *www.songbegolf.com* ✉ *1,950,000d weekdays, 3,000,000d weekends* 🏌 *27 holes, 6374 yards, par 72.*

Twin Doves Golf Club

GOLF | Visitors need to reserve a week or two in advance to play at this private club, but will be rewarded with a 27-hole international standard championship course featuring woodland, lakes, rolling hills, and tree-lined fairways. Of Twin Doves' three courses—Luna, Mare, and Sole—Mare is considered the most challenging. ⊠ *368 Tran Ngoc Len, Hoa Phu, Thu Dau Mot* ☎ *00274/386–0211* ⊕ *www. twindovesgolf.vn* ✉ *Visitor fees from 1,950,000d weekdays (1,750,000d on Mon.)* 🏌 *27 holes, 7282 yards, par 72.*

Vietnam Golf and Country Club

GOLF | This course, 20 km (12 miles) from downtown Ho Chi Minh City, was the country's first 36-hole golf course, set on a woodland estate. The 7,106-yard West Course, which features tree-lined fairways, has twice hosted the Vietnam Open Asian PGA Tour. The 6,946-yard East Course, designed by Lee Trevino, is more challenging, with many bunkers and water hazards and fast greens. ■ **TIP→ Fees are lowest on Monday but the promotional rate does attract the crowds.** ⊠ *Club House, Long Thanh My, District 9* ☎ *028/6280–0101* ⊕ *www.vietnamgolfcc. com* ✉ *Visitor fees from 1,900,000 weekdays including lunch or dinner* 🏌 *West Course: 18 holes, 7106 yards, par 36; East Course: 18 holes, 6946 yards, par 36.*

Side Trips from Ho Chi Minh City

Some of the destinations around Ho Chi Minh City can be visited as day trips; others may take a few days. Some excursions are more rugged, adventurous trips through forests and islands; others will take you to sandy beaches and seaside resorts.

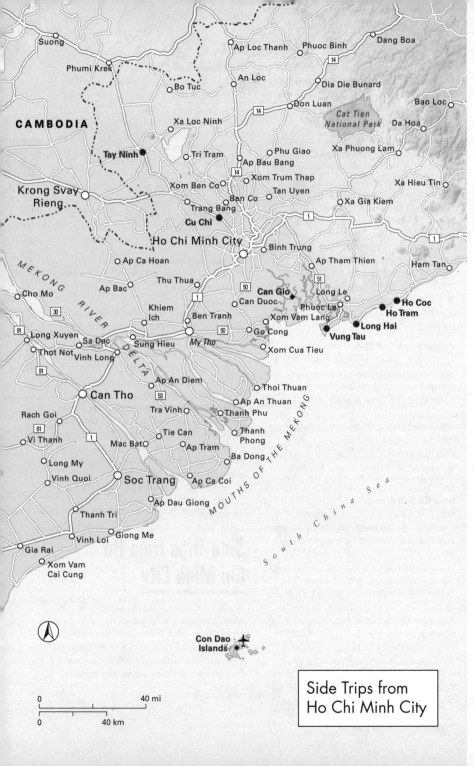

Side Trips from
Ho Chi Minh City

Cu Chi

70 km (44 miles) northwest of Ho Chi Minh City.

Cu Chi, now an outlying district of Ho Chi Minh City, was the Vietcong base of operations during the last war. The base was underground, in a vast system of tunnels that thwarted allied detection for most of the war. The tunnels are now regarded as a symbol of the resilience and enterprising nature of the Vietnamese people.

GETTING HERE AND AROUND

The easiest and best way to visit is on an organized tour, although it's possible to get to the tunnel complexes independently. It takes about 90 minutes to drive to Cu Chi in either a hired car with driver or a taxi. Negotiate a day rate with an operator at Mai Linh or Vinasun taxi companies rather than using the meter. Expect to pay around 1,500,500d.

Traveling from Ho Chi Minh City to the Ben Duoc and Ben Dinh sites by bus is possible but it's complicated, time-consuming, and the saving in cost over taking an organized tour is minimal. The easiest option is to take the No. 13 bus to the Cu Chi bus depot and then take a *xe om*. Expect to pay a *xe om* driver 215,000d to take you to one of the sites, each about 30 minutes away, wait for about an hour and a half, and return you to the Cu Chi bus depot. Bear in mind, when considering these options, organized tours start at around 200,000d.

TOURS

Organized tours can be arranged through reputable travel agents or hotel tour desks. The superbudget option involves strolling into any travel shop in the backpacker district—they'll be able to get you on a bus tour the following day for 110,000d or thereabouts, not including the entrance fee and lunch. Most bus tours offer the option of combining the Cu Chi Tunnels with a visit to the Cao Dai Holy See in Tay Ninh. Taking a boat tour to the Cu Chi Tunnels is faster and cooler, although more expensive, than going by road. Several companies offer boat tours, but Les Rives is probably the best.

Les Rives

This reputable river-based tour company, which operates small group tours, offers an insightful half-day tour to the Cu Chi Tunnels that starts with a 7·am hotel pickup, and includes a pleasant journey on their luxury speedboat, a guided tour of the Cu Chi site, and lunch. Les Rives also offers several full-day tour options that take in Cu Chi and include cycling, a countryside tour, or a Vesper tour of Ho Chi Minh City. ☏ *028/3827–5000* ⊕ *www.lesrivesexperience.com* ✉ *From 1,900,000d.*

Urban Adventures

Daily five- to six-hour day tours to the Cu Chi Tunnels complex are accompanied by local English-speaking guides. The tours, which include bus transportation, usually visit a family to learn about local life and culture. ☏ *0909/904–100* ⊕ *www.urbanadventures.com* ✉ *From 890,000d.*

Vietnam Bike Tours

For a more vigorous Cu Chi Tunnels experience, try this bike and cruise itinerary, starting with a leisurely cruise to Cu Chi, a visit to the complex, then some cycling through back roads, past rubber plantations and rice paper making operations, and transfers back to Ho Chi Minh City by private minivan. The tour price includes an English-speaking local guide, breakfast, lunch, bicycles, and safety gear, support vehicle, and boat and minivan transfers. ☏ *0855/075–999* ✉ *From 3,374,000d.*

At the Cu Chi Tunnels, a series of underground tunnels the Viet Cong used during the Vietnam War, visitors are invited to fit into the tight spaces.

⊙ Sights

★ **Cu Chi Tunnels** (*Dia Dao Cu Chi*)
MILITARY SIGHT | A 250-km (155-mile) underground network of field hospitals, command posts, living quarters, eating quarters, and traps, the Cu Chi Tunnels illustrate the Vietcong's ingenuity in the face of overwhelming odds. Work on the tunnels began in 1948 to combat the French and continued into the '70s. The extensive underground network made it possible for the Vietcong in the '60s not only to withstand blanket bombings and to communicate with other distant Vietcong enclaves but to command a sizable rural area that was in dangerous proximity (a mere 35 km [22 miles]) to Saigon. After the South Vietnam President Ngo Dinh Diem regime's ill-fated "strategic hamlet program" of 1963, disenchanted peasants who refused to move fled to Cu Chi to avoid the aerial bombardments. In fact, the stunning Tet Offensive of 1968 was masterminded and launched from the Cu Chi Tunnels nerve center, with weapons crafted by an enthusiastic assembly line of Vietcong-controlled Cu Chi villagers. Despite extensive ground operations and sophisticated chemical warfare—and even after declaring the area a free-fire zone—American troops were incapable of controlling the area. In the late 1960s B-52 bombing reduced the area to a wasteland, but the Vietnamese Communists and the National Liberation Front managed to hang on. There are two Cu Chi Tunnel tourist areas, which both have tunnels that have been expanded to accommodate tourists of all sizes. These larger tunnels are still claustrophobically small, however, and could be much too snug for some. Most guided tours go to **Ben Dinh**, where the firing range (M16 bullets are $1.50 each, AK47 bullets are $2 each) is right next to the souvenir shop. **Ben Duoc** is a much prettier site and is usually less crowded than Ben Dinh, with the added advantage of having its firing range farther away from the tunnel area. What makes Ben Duoc the more pleasant site is the on-site temple and restaurant: Ben Duoc Temple of Martyr Memorial is surrounded by

lush green gardens, while the Dia Dao Restaurant is a nice location for lunch. The ticket price includes an official guide, who will show you the tunnels, air vents, and living quarters. They will also explain the re-created booby traps, the mechanized mannequins making bombs and traps, and the real-life people making sandals from tires. Both sites are owned by the government and visiting both is not recommended, as the displays are the same. ⊠ *Phu Hiep Hamlet, Cu Chi District* ☎ *028/3794–8830 administration, 028/3794–8820 Ben Duoc site* ⊠ *105,000d for Ben Duoc site; 125,000d for Ben Dinh site.*

Tay Ninh

95 km (59 miles) northwest of Ho Chi Minh City.

Generally a visit to Tay Ninh is part of a day trip to the Cu Chi Tunnels arranged through one of the travel agencies in Saigon. A guide will accompany you, explain the history of the Cao Dai sect, and take you through the temple, usually to watch the midday service.

GETTING HERE AND AROUND
Tay Ninh's Cao Dai Holy See is usually an included stop on a Cu Chi bus tour (*see Cu Chi Tunnels for details*). Buses to Tay Ninh depart Ho Chi Minh City's An Suong bus depot regularly; the fare is about 65,000d each way. Getting to Tay Ninh by taxi or renting a car with driver will take about 2½ hours and a day trip will cost around 200,000d.

BUS CONTACTS Dong Phuoc.
☎ *028/3883–0477 in Ho Chi Minh City, 0276/377–7777 in Tay Ninh.* **Le Khanh.** ☎ *0971/521–313, 0971/831–313 in Tay Ninh.*

◉ Sights

Cao Dai Holy See (*Toa Thanh Tay Ninh*)
TEMPLE | The town of Tay Ninh is home to Cao Daism, an indigenous hybrid religion founded in 1926 by a mystic named Ngo Minh Chieu, and its impressive and brightly colored temple, the Cao Dai Holy See. The noon ceremony (others are held at 6 am, 6 pm, and midnight) at the temple is a fascinating and colorful religious vignette. A finely tuned hierarchical procession of men and women of all ages parades through the temple's great hall, where painted columns twined with carved dragons support sky-blue arched vaulting. Panels of stained glass with a cosmic-eye motif punctuate the walls. You are permitted to watch and take snapshots from the mezzanine. Ignore any feeling of complicity in what appears to be a collective voyeuristic sacrilege; the ceremony goes on as though you were not there. ⊠ *Hoa Thanh District, Tay Ninh* ⊕ *caodai.com.vn.*

Can Gio

60 km (37 miles) southeast of Ho Chi Minh City.

A maze of channels, inlets, and tiny hamlets hidden among swamp and forest, Can Gio has only appeared on the tourist radar within the last few years and so the amenities and services, set up to service the domestic tourist market, are quite basic. To make the most of a visit, going with a reputable tour company or a private tour guide is highly recommended. Tours usually include stops at the Rung Sac Guerilla Base, the Vam Sat eco zone, and sometimes the very brown Can Gio Beach. Without a guide, or at least someone who speaks Vietnamese, in your group, Can Gio can be a confusing and disappointing place to visit.

Cao Daism

Cao Daism incorporates elements of the major world religions—Buddhism, Confucianism, Taoism, Christianity, and Islam—as well as Vietnamese spiritualism. The religion fuses a Mahayana Buddhist code of ethics with Taoist and Confucian components. Sprinkled into the mix are elements of Roman Catholicism, the cult of ancestors, Vietnamese superstition, and over-the-top interior decoration that encompasses a fantastic blend of Asian and European architectural styles. Cao Daism has grown from its original 26,000 members to a present-day membership of 3 million. Meditation and communicating with spiritual worlds via earthly mediums or seances are among its primary practices. Despite its no-holds-barred decorative tendencies, Cao Daism emphasizes abstinence from luxury and sensuality as well as vegetarianism as a means of escaping the reincarnation cycle. Although the priesthood is strictly nonprofessional, clergy must remain celibate.

Key Beliefs

Perhaps most important, the Cao Daists believe the divine revelation has undergone three iterations: God's word presented itself first through Lao-tzu and other Buddhist, Confucianist, and Taoist players; then through a second set of channelers such as Jesus, Muhammad, Moses, Confucius, and Buddha. Whether because of the fallibility of these human agents or because of the changing set of human needs, the Cao Daists believe the divine transmission was botched. They see themselves as the third and final expression—the "third alliance between God and man." Because anyone can take part in this alliance, even Westerners like Joan of Arc, Victor Hugo, and William Shakespeare have been added to the Cao Dai roster.

Cao Daism and Politics

Cao Daism's presence wasn't always so tolerated. Although it quickly gained a large following after its founding, including Vietnamese officials in the French administration, it soon became too powerful. By the 1930s the Cao Daists had begun consolidating their strength in the region and recruiting their own army. During World War II, the Cao Daists were armed and financed by the Japanese, whom the sect saw as also fighting the government. After the war, the Cao Daists gained the backing of the French in return for their support against the Vietminh. After the French left in the late '50s, the South Vietnamese government made a point to destroy the Cao Daists as a military force, which caused many members of the sect to turn to the Communists, and the area became an anti–South Vietnamese stronghold. But when the Communists came to power in 1975, they repossessed the sect's land, and Cao Daism lost most of its remaining power. Today the religion is tolerated but is no longer involved in politics.

GETTING HERE AND AROUND

Can Gio is best visited with a tour guide or on an organized tour and there are many options for touring Can Gio's mangrove areas to view the wildlife. Driving here from Ho Chi Minh City takes about two hours and includes a ferry crossing. Hiring a taxi for a day trip will cost about 1,500,500d, plus the fee for the ferry crossing—10,000d each way.

TOUR CONTACTS
Les Rives

Take a luxury speed boat to Can Gio to explore the area with a knowledgeable English-speaking guide, who will introduce you to the local wildlife, including bats, monkeys, and crocodiles. The full-day small-group tour includes breakfast and lunch. ☎ 078/592–0018 ⊕ www. lesrivesexperience.com ⌛ 2,263,000d.

Saigon Riders

Leap onto the back of a motorbike cruiser and hit the highway (and a local wooden ferry) to explore Can Gio with local English-speaking guides/drivers. This full-day tour takes country roads to the biosphere reserve for some wildlife watching and lunch, with an option to travel farther to Monkey Island. ☎ 091/976–7118 ⊕ www. saigonriders.com.

◉ Sights

Can Gio UNESCO Biosphere Reserve

FOREST | This mangrove forest, officially part of Ho Chi Minh City, covers an area the size of Singapore. The old forest was destroyed by aerial bombing and defoliants—primarily Agent Orange—during the Vietnam War because it had been a regular hiding place for the Vietcong, who would fire mortars at the supply ships on the Saigon River. Residents of the area were forced to leave, and it wasn't until 1978 that surviving Can Gio families returned, replanted the forest, and gradually resettled. Surprisingly, the area's wild animals also returned, and today there are monkeys, wild boar, deer, leopards,

long-tailed macaques, crocodiles, birds, and giant fruitbats, although not all are easy to spot. In 2000, the area was declared a UNESCO Biosphere Reserve and the local economy is now supported by various eco-tourism ventures. Under the Can Gio Biosphere Reserve model, families live inside the reserve conducting small-scale aquaculture ventures to help preserve what's known as the "lungs of Ho Chi Minh City." The government-owned Saigon Tourist has an "eco forest park" on Monkey Island that includes a bizarre animal circus with monkeys and crocodiles which we do not recommend. ⊠ Rung Sac, Can Gio.

Vung Tau

130 km (80 miles) southeast of Ho Chi Minh City.

Known as Cap St-Jacques during colonial times, Vung Tau was a popular beach resort for the French and later, during the Vietnam War, it became a major United States and Australian army base. The area was later taken over by the Soviet Union as a concession for helping Hanoi win the war. The Soviets used the Vung Tau port as a navy base and drilled for oil off the coast. Following the collapse of the Soviet Union, many Russians left, although Vung Tau is still home to many, who are mostly still involved in the area's oil industry.

Vung Tau is an easy getaway from Ho Chi Minh City, although not as popular with foreigners as the resort town of Mui Ne farther along the coast. Tourism amenities are aimed at domestic tourists, who have a different set of expectations from international visitors. Vung Tau's quirkiness, rather than its beaches, makes it an interesting place to visit.

The city, which has made its fortune from the oil industry, is a good base for exploring the beaches along the coast: Long Hai and Ho Tram.

GETTING HERE AND AROUND

Buses leave at regular intervals during the day from Ho Chi Minh City to Vung Tau. The journey takes 2 to 2½ hours and costs about 100,000d. Minibuses run by Mai Linh Express and Rang Dong depart from Mien Dong bus station at 292 Dinh Bo Linh Street in Binh Thanh District. Hoa Mai buses depart for Vung Tau from 44 Nguyen Thai Binh Street in District 1. In Vung Tau, Hoa Mai offers a pickup service that must be reserved in advance.

It's possible to get to Vung Tau by taxi from Ho Chi Minh City. Agree to a rate with the taxi company operator rather than use the meter. A one-way trip should cost around 1,000,000d. Hiring a taxi for the day to take you to Vung Tau and back to Ho Chi Minh City should cost around 2,040,000d. Three reliable taxi companies ply the streets of Vung Tau. They can be hired on a daily basis.

BUS CONTACTS Hoa Mai. ⊠ *Ho Chi Minh City* ☎ *0889/200–200, 0909/200–200* ⊕ *www.hoamaicar.com.* **Mai Linh Express.** ⊠ *Ho Chi Minh City* ☎ *028/3511–7888* ⊕ *www.mailinh.vn.* **Vung Tau Bus Station.** ⊠ *192 Nam Ky Khoi Nghia, Vung Tau* ☎ *0254/385–9727.*

TAXI CONTACTS Mai Linh. ⊠ *Vung Tau* ☎ *0254/356–5656* ⊕ *www.mailinh.vn.* **Petro Taxi.** ⊠ *Vung Tau* ☎ *0254/381–8181.* **Vinasun.** ⊠ *Vung Tau* ☎ *0254/372–7009* ⊕ *www.vinasuntaxi.com.*

◉ Sights

Christ the King Statue (*Tuong Dai Chua Kito Vua*)

MONUMENT | Rio has Christ the Redeemer overlooking the city, Vung Tau has Christ the King, a 105-foot-high statue on a 13-foot-high platform atop Mt. Nho, looking out over the East Sea with his arms outstretched. Even though tackling the 847 steps up Mt. Nho is a challenge in the hot and steamy conditions, expect to be overtaken by tiny Vietnamese grandmothers in thick acrylic suits. Take plenty of water. There's a little shop at the top selling drinks and snacks, and an art gallery inside Jesus's legs, but the opening hours seem to change to suit the caretakers' own schedules. ⊠ *2 Ha Long, Vung Tau.*

Front Beach Park (*Cong Vien Bai Truoc*)

CITY PARK | One of Vung Tau's more quirky sights, Front Beach Park, sometimes called Statue Park, has a children's playground, fitness stations, walking trails, and an extensive collection of statues, including some that are quite racy for conservative Vietnam. ⊠ *4 Quang Trung, Vung Tau.*

Hon Ba Island

ISLAND | Only accessible at low-tide across treacherous slippery rocks, Hon Ba Island is home to the Mieu Ba (lady) temple, dedicated to the patron goddess of sailors and fishermen. If you visit, watch the tide carefully to make sure you don't get stranded. There's no food or fresh water on the tiny island. ⊠ *Off southern tip of Back Beach, Vung Tau.*

Long Tan Cross

MONUMENT | This marks the site of the Battle of Long Tan, which took place on August 18, 1966, between a regiment comprising 105 Australians and three New Zealanders and a Vietcong force estimated at between 1,500 and 2,500. The fierce battle fought during a torrential downpour in a rubber plantation left 18 Australians and 245 Vietnamese dead and 21 Australians and many more Vietnamese wounded. August 18 is now Vietnam Veterans' Day in Australia and every year on this date, and on Anzac Day (April 25), a small ceremony is held at the Long Tan Cross. People who want to attend one of these ceremonies should register their interest well in advance with the Australian Consulate in Ho Chi Minh City. The Long Tan Cross is politically sensitive and is on private land and should not be visited without an official tour guide. Those wishing to visit the site must notify the Dat Do District People's Committee in writing by fax 3 days in advance of their visit, either individually or through a travel agent. ✉ *Long Tan, Vung Tau* ⊕ *www.hcmc.vietnam.embassy.gov.au/ hchi/Visits_to_the_Long_Tan_Cross.html.*

Niet Ban Tinh Xa Pagoda (*Phat Nam Pagoda, Chua Phat Nam*)

RELIGIOUS BUILDING | Completed in 1974, this pagoda at the base of Nho Mountain is considered one of Vung Tau's most beautiful. The serene garden in front of the pagoda represents Buddha achieving the state of Nirvana. The most famous part of the complex, however, is the 39-foot-long Reclining Buddha statue. ✉ *66/7 Ha Long, Vung Tau.*

Our Lady of Bai Dau

MONUMENT | On the west side of Lon Mountain is a 25-meter (82-feet) high statue of the Virgin Mary holding aloft a baby Jesus. The statue is part of the Our Lady of Bai Dau (Mulberry Beach) church complex. There's a path that leads from near the statue to the peak of Lon Mountain. At the end of the path are the 14 Stations of the Cross. ✉ *140A Tran Phu, Vung Tau.*

Thich Ca Phat Dai Pagoda

RELIGIOUS BUILDING | This Theravada Buddhism temple, built between 1961 and 1963, is on the northwestern face of Lon Mountain. The highlights are a 33-foot-high gleaming white Buddha statue and the climb up the steps to its base, through beautiful gardens and jungle. Alongside the steps is a series of statues depicting Buddha's life. Pilgrims from all over Vietnam visit the pagoda, which has a Zen Buddhist monastery on-site. ✉ *608 Tran Phu, Vung Tau.*

Vung Tau Lighthouse (*Ngon hai dang Vung Tau*) ·

LIGHTHOUSE | Built by the French during colonial times to guide ships into the Saigon port, the still-operational 59-foot-high lighthouse sits at the top of Small Mountain, at the end of a steep and winding road, still protected by four old French cannons. If you take a taxi to the lighthouse, ask the driver to wait for you because there are not going to be any passing taxis to hail and it's a very long walk back down the mountain. The views on the way up are sensational, and there are a few cafés along the way for refreshment. ✉ *Hai Dang, Vung Tau.*

Whale Temple (*Lang Ca Ong*)

TEMPLE | Like many seaside villages in Vietnam, Vung Tau has a temple dedicated to *Ca Ong*, Mr. Whale, the guardian angel of the seas. This humble place of worship, with its small collection of whalebones, is an interesting place to visit, although there is no information in English to explain the beliefs and rituals of the temple. ✉ *Hoang Hoa Tham, Vung Tau* ⊠ *Free.*

White Palace (*Bach Dinh*)

HISTORIC HOME | Built in 1898, the White Palace has variously served as the French governor's residence, a retreat of Bao Dai, the last emperor of Vietnam, and the president of South Vietnam's summer house. The villa is now a slightly worn museum with a ground-floor exhibition of late-17th- and early-18th-century Chinese artifacts recovered from a shipwreck near the Con Dao Islands. On the upper floors there's the now-shopworn living quarters of the last resident. Despite its tired air, the White Palace is worth visiting for the views of the East Sea and the lush tropical grounds. ✉ *12 Tran Phu, Vung Tau* ☎ *0254/351–2560* ⊠ *15,000d.*

🍴 Beaches

Back Beach (*Bai Sau*)

BEACH | Vung Tau's most popular beach has golden sands that stretch for miles, but it's not the prettiest or the cleanest beach around. Quiet on weekdays, it's crowded on weekends, with locals who will be playing volleyball, football, and jogging. Back Beach is fine for swimming, but be aware that most of the locals swim fully clothed so parading around in a skimpy swimsuit may attract some stares. There are showers at the Imperial Hotel's Beach Club, which has a 250,000d entry fee. **Amenities:** food and drink; showers. **Best for:** sunset; swimming; walking. ✉ *Thuy Van, Vung Tau.*

Mulberry Beach (*Bai Dau*)
BEACH | A cramped beach below Ha Long Street, Mulberry Beach isn't really a place you'd travel miles to see, and despite the poetic name, it's not ideal for swimming. Legend has it that the hillside near the beach, where the Virgin Mary statue is now, was once a mulberry field, hence the name. **Amenities:** none. **Best for:** solitude; walking. ✉ *Ha Long, Vung Tau.*

🍴 Restaurants

Banh Khot Goc Vu Sua
$ | **VIETNAMESE** | *Banh khot* (tiny rice flour pancakes topped with shrimp that you wrap in baby mustard leaves) is Vung Tau's signature dish and locals rate Banh Khot Goc Vu Sua as the best in class. This is simple, inexpensive, and 100% delicious local street food—and adventurous foodies will enjoy the whole *banh khot* experience, sitting on tiny chairs in a big tin shed that fills with smoke every time a new batch is cooked. **Known for:** being a bit smoky; banh khot; local-style service. [$] *Average main: d50,000* ✉ *14 Nguyen Truong To, Vung Tau* ☎ *0254/352–3465* 💳 *No credit cards* 🕒 *No dinner.*

David's Pizzeria
$$ | **ITALIAN** | **FAMILY** | Wood-fired pizza, pasta, steak, and seafood with breezy sea views, David's Pizzeria is popular with tourists and locals. Service can be slow, but the pizzas are on point. **Known for:** pizza; ocean views from the upstairs terrace. [$] *Average main: d250,000* ✉ *92 Ha Long, Vung Tau* ☎ *0254/352–1012.*

Don Quijote
$$ | **FRENCH** | With superb European fusion dining in a rustic atmosphere, Don Quijote is the place for homemade pâté, foie gras, and Toulouse sausages, duck magret, and decadent desserts. The well-considered wine list complements the menu, and if you'd like to kick off a big night, try the meter of rum. **Known for:** decent wine list; homemade sausages and foie gras; European fusion dining. [$] *Average main: d265,000* ✉ *98C Xo Viet Nghe Tinh, Vung Tau* ☎ *0254/650–8033.*

★ **Ganh Hao**
$$$ | **VIETNAMESE** | This sprawling seafront eatery is regarded as the best seafood place in town. Like many Vietnamese places, the interior design takes a back seat to the food and the view. **Known for:** delicious spring rolls; ocean views; Vietnamese dishes. [$] *Average main: d275,000* ✉ *3 Tran Phu, Vung Tau* ☎ *0254/4355–0909.*

Kozac
$$ | **EASTERN EUROPEAN** | The interior is a bit worn around the edges, but this Ukrainian restaurant—Vietnam does have a knack for the unexpected—serves some tasty Eastern European, Western, and Asian dishes, along with Russian, Vietnamese, and imported beers. If you need a break from Vietnamese food, this will hit the spot. **Known for:** slow service; Ukrainian food; Russian beer. [$] *Average main: d250,000* ✉ *7 Nguyen Tri Phuong, Vung Tau* ☎ *0254/356–3776* 🌐 *www.facebook.com/KOZAK.VungTau.*

Lucy's Sports Bar
$$ | **BRITISH** | Great-tasting Western food with generous portions is served in a friendly sports bar, with giant screens showing all kinds of sports as well as a pool table. If you're not a sports fan, come for the food and the sea views from the balcony. **Known for:** sports broadcast on big screens; Western food; generous portions.

$ *Average main: d175,000* ✉ *138 Ha Long, Vung Tau* ☎ *0254/385–8896.*

Hotels

Binh An Village
$$$ | **RESORT** | With all the charm of a stylish and intimate lodging and the upscale amenities of an oceanfront resort, Binh An Village provides the best of both worlds. **Pros:** unique Quy An Bar, built into a cliff; a relaxing and stylish getaway with great views of the East Sea; beautifully manicured grounds with two pools. **Cons:** slightly too far from town to walk anywhere. $ *Rooms from: d2,700,000* ✉ *1 Tran Phu, Vung Tau* ☎ *0254/351–0732* 🍴 *Free Breakfast* 🛏 *9 rooms.*

Imperial Hotel
$$$ | **HOTEL** | With its slightly over-the-top French château interiors and large, sumptuous rooms, the Imperial is certainly the fanciest hotel in Vung Tau (you can even hire a butler!), and it has a private beach right across the road. **Pros:** sea views; prime location across from the beach, accessed via a pedestrian overpass; friendly staff. **Cons:** service doesn't always live up to the style; could be considered kitschy; breakfast is an additional fee. $ *Rooms from: d2,413,000* ✉ *159–163 Thuy Van St., Vung Tau* ☎ *0254/362–8888* 🌐 *www.imperial-hotel.vn* 🛏 *144 rooms* 🍴 *No Meals.*

Petro Hotel
$$$ | **HOTEL** | A friendly upscale business hotel, Petro Hotel is within walking distance to the beach, with great sea views from the higher floors (city view rooms look out over the dog track next door). **Pros:** spa, pool, and fitness center; 24-hour room service; rooms are large and comfortable. **Cons:** dog track view is not for everyone; some floors have a strong smell of cigarettes; rooms are a bit bland. $ *Rooms from: d1,700,000* ✉ *9–11 Hoang Dieu, Vung Tau* ☎ *0254/358–8588* 🌐 *www.petrohotel.vn* 🛏 *85 rooms* 🍴 *Free Breakfast.*

★ **Pullman Vung Tau**
$$$ | **HOTEL** | **FAMILY** | From the stunning atrium-style lobby to the bright and spacious rooms, the Pullman Vung Tau, the only five-star international hotel in town, is an oasis of style, elevated by friendly service and an exceptional breakfast buffet. **Pros:** the kids' club means parents can enjoy some alone time; exceptional service throughout the hotel. **Cons:** beach club is a 10-minute walk away (though there is a quick shuttle bus); the pool area is small and slightly awkward. $ *Rooms from: d2,300,000* ✉ *15 Thi Sach, Vung Tau* ☎ *0254/355–1777* 🌐 *www.pullmanvungtau.com* 🍴 *Free Breakfast* 🛏 *379 rooms.*

Sakura Hotel
$ | **HOTEL** | A neat and clean family-run hotel a little outside the main tourist area, Sakura Hotel has a Japanese-theme, friendly staff, and many charming details, such as a range of loofahs in the bathroom. **Pros:** great for budget travelers; helpful staff. **Cons:** a little too far to walk to where the action is. $ *Rooms from: d335,000* ✉ *H15 Hoang Hoa Tham, A Chau Area, Vung Tau* ☎ *0254/357–0465* 🛏 *9 rooms* 🍴 *No Meals.*

The Wind Boutique Resort and Hotel
$$$ | **RESORT** | **FAMILY** | Set halfway up a mountain with sweeping panoramic views, the spa-inclusive Wind Boutique Resort and Hotel is a wonderful home away from home, with large, beautifully designed rooms, modern facilities, and friendly staff. **Pros:** every room has a Jacuzzi with a view; free shuttle bus to take you anywhere in town; rate includes massage treatments for two people. **Cons:** slightly out of the way. $ *Rooms from: d1,620,000* ✉ *Bldg. B10, 84 Phan Chu Trinh, Vung Tau* ☎ *254/385–8859* 🌐 *www.thewind.com.vn* 🍴 *Free Breakfast* 🛏 *33 rooms.*

Nightlife

Vung Tau, unfortunately, has a seedy side at night, with lots of girly bars full of drunk and obnoxious patrons, but there are a couple of places that are more acceptable.

Cask

BARS | This is the only bar in Vung Tau serving Pasteur Street, East West, and Rooster craft beers from Ho Chi Minh City. It has great music and a friendly vibe, with a balcony overlooking Front Beach. ⊠ *12 Quang Trung, Vung Tau* ☎ *093/890–1009* ⊕ *www.facebook.com/ caskvungtau.*

Matilda's Pub

PUBS | A smart-casual bar run by an Australian couple, Matilda's Pub is one of Vung Tau's most popular watering holes for travelers and expats, with five TV screens showing sports. The pub offers a range of Western and Vietnamese comfort food at very reasonable prices, and does a great breakfast too. ⊠ *6 Nguyen Du, Vung Tau* ☎ *093/321–6425 cell phone* ⊕ *www.facebook.com/ MatildasPubVietnam.*

Activities

GOLF

Paradise Resort Golf Club

GOLF | This 27-hole golf course has a patchy track record when it comes to course maintenance but the caddies are regarded as some of the best in Vietnam. With a challenging links-style design, players must contend with sea breezes while enjoying great ocean views. ⊠ *1 Thuy Van, Vung Tau* ☎ *0254/385–9697* ⊕ *www.golfparadise.com.vn* ⛳ *From 1,800,000d for 18 holes weekdays* 🏌 *27 holes, 6840 yards, par 72.*

Long Hai

15 km (9 miles) east of Vung Tau, 170 km (105 miles) southeast of Ho Chi Minh City.

There's not much to Long Hai aside from a beautiful beach and an interesting temple with views of the beach. It's close enough to Vung Tau to make a nice day trip, but it's probably not worth the long drive from Ho Chi Minh City for the beach alone.

GETTING HERE AND AROUND

It takes about 30 minutes by car to Long Hai from Vung Tau, and a 3½-hour excursion by taxi will cost about 648,000d. It's also possible to hire a car with driver in Ho Chi Minh City for a day trip, a journey of about 2½ hours each way.

◉ Sights

★ Dinh Co Temple

TEMPLE | Le Thi Hong Thuy, a 16-year-old girl, washed up on Long Hai Beach nearly 200 years ago and the locals buried her on Co Son Hill. According to legend, her ghost began visiting seafarers and warning them of impending bad weather, and she is now regarded as a goddess who protects the local fishing fleet. This temple is dedicated to her, and every year, on the 10th, 11th, and 12th days of the second lunar month, the it hosts the Dinh Co Festival, which includes a colorful parade and boat races, and attracts thousands of people from surrounding regions. The views of Long Hai Beach and beyond from the temple terraces are magnificent. ⊠ *Off Rd. 6, Long Hai.*

Long Hai Beach

BEACH | This beach is about a 90-minute drive from Ho Chi Minh City and 15 km (9 miles) along the coast from Vung Tau, but it feels like it's worlds away. Opposite the Dinh Co Temple, a series of shacks offer deck chairs for rent, as well as food and drinks. The beach is not patrolled but the water is calm with no surf and the golden sand stretches for miles. **Amenities:** food and drink. **Best for:** sunsets; swimming; walking. ✉ *Rd. 6, Long Hai.*

Ho Tram

45 km (28 miles) east of Vung Tau, 113 km (70 miles) southeast of Ho Chi Minh City.

There's not much to Ho Tram apart from a very long—and very beautiful—stretch of golden sand beach. A growing number of upscale resorts front the beach but it's possible to find your own secluded little patch.

GETTING HERE AND AROUND

Some of the resorts at Ho Tram offer shuttle buses between Ho Chi Minh City and their properties, about a 2½-hour drive, starting at 500,000d. It's also possible to get a bus or shuttle from Ho Chi Minh City or Vung Tau. Hiring a seven-seat taxi in Vung Tau for a daylong (5½ hours) excursion to Ho Tram should cost around 1,400,000d.

Hotels

The Grand Ho Tram Strip
$$$$ | **RESORT** | **FAMILY** | This is a massive hotel, casino, and golf complex set along an exquisite white-sand beach. **Pros:** patrolled beach; gambling, golfing, and one of Vietnam's biggest spas are a few steps away; possibly Vietnam's best kids' and teen's club. **Cons:** not much in the surrounding area; to eat outside the complex your only option is to take a taxi to the other resort. [$] *Rooms from: d4,773,600* ✉ *Phuoc Thuan, Xuyen Moc* ☎ *0254/378–8888* 🌐 *www.thegrand-hotram.com* 🍴 *Free Breakfast* 🛏 *541 rooms.*

★ **Ho Tram Beach Boutique Resort and Spa**
$$$$ | **RESORT** | Capturing the romantic notion of a traditional Vietnamese village, Ho Tram Beach Boutique Resort's wood-and-tile bungalows and villas, along with two beautifully landscaped pools, a children's playground, a charming spa and Gecko Restaurant, are scattered throughout a casuarina forest that opens onto a beautiful stretch of beach. **Pros:** daily shuttle to Ho Chi Minh City; very relaxing setting; some villas come with private pools and a butler service. **Cons:** quite remote; if you want to eat elsewhere, the closest place is the Grand Ho Tram Strip resort. [$] *Rooms from: d2,585,000* ✉ *Phuoc Thuan, Xuyen Moc* ☎ *0254/378–1525* 🌐 *www.hotramresort.com* 🍴 *Free Breakfast* 🛏 *92 rooms.*

Activities

GOLF

The Bluffs Ho Tram Strip
GOLF | This Greg Norman-designed links-style course has stunning views of the East Sea from the dunes behind Ho Tram Beach. It's well worth the 120-km (75-mile) drive, which takes about 2½ hours, southeast of Ho Chi Minh City. The course flows over and around sand dunes and players must contend with strong sea breezes throughout the year. The golf course is associated with The Grand Ho Tram Strip integrated resort. ✉ *Phuoc Thuan, Xuyen Moc* ☎ *0254/378–8666* 🌐 *www.thebluffshotram.com* 🎫 *From 4,422,600d for 18 holes on weekdays* ⛳ *18 holes, 6855 yards, par 71.*

Ho Coc

51 km (32 miles) east of Vung Tau, 123 km (76 miles) southeast of Ho Chi Minh City.

Two and a half hours from Ho Chi Minh City, just past Ho Tram, this is a splendid, secluded area for anyone seeking an escape from the chaos of the city or wanting a higher class of beach to those in Vung Tau.

GETTING HERE AND AROUND

Buses run regularly from Vung Tau and Ho Chi Minh City to the Xuyen Moc bus depot (Ben Xe Xuyen Moc). Xe om drivers and taxis wait at the bus station to take passengers on to the seaside resorts at Ho Coc, Ho Tram, and Binh Chau. The taxi fare to Ho Coc is 300,000d. There are also several minivan shuttle services that make the trip. It's also possible to visit Ho Coc by taxi from Vung Tau—renting a seven-seater taxi for a 5½ hour excursion should cost about 1,400,000d.

Beaches

Ho Coc Beach

BEACH | This one of the most beautiful beaches in the area, and although two state-run resorts own part of the casuarina-lined golden sands, the remainder is available for strolling and swimming. There's a small collection of thatched huts containing deck chairs, which can be rented, as well as a few vendors selling drinks and snacks. **Amenities:** food and drink. **Best for:** swimming; walking. ⊠ *Ven Bien, Ho Coc.*

Hotels

Huong Phong Ho Coc Resort

$$$ | RESORT | The accommodations may be simple, but here you can enjoy a laid-back, local vibe right on one of the best beaches on this coast. **Pros:** on-site restaurants; some rooms have sea views; on weekdays this is a great budget option. **Cons:** limited English spoken; the resort is quite remote. $ *Rooms from: d1,230,000* ⊠ *Bung Rieng Commune, Xuyen Moc District, Ho Coc* ☎ *0254/387–8145* ⊕ *www.huongphonghococbeachresort.com* ❍ *Free Breakfast* ⇲ *44 rooms.*

Seava Ho Tram

$$$ | RESORT | Isolated and very large, this well-maintained state-run resort has a beautiful setting, right on Ho Coc Beach, but targets domestic travelers, so customer service, English language ability, and Western choices at breakfast are somewhat lacking. **Pros:** room rate includes free entry to the Binh Chau Hot Springs and 20% discount on the mud baths; beachfront location; shuttle bus to Ho Chi Minh City center for a reasonable fee. **Cons:** not much English is spoken; aside from the shuttle, it's nearly impossible to leave the resort if you don't have your own transportation. $ *Rooms from: d2,150,000* ⊠ *Hwy. 55, Bung Rieng Ward, Xuyen Moc, Vung Tau* ☎ *0254/379–1036* ⊕ *www.seava.vn* ⇲ *159 rooms* ❍ *Free Breakfast* ☞ *Round-trip shuttle van from Ho Chi Minh City is 400,000d.*

Con Dao Islands

100 km (62 miles) off the southern tip of Vietnam, about 50 minutes by plane from Ho Chi Minh City.

One of Vietnam's star attractions, this stunning archipelago of 16 islands has picturesque beaches, jungles teeming with wildlife, and a fabulous marine environment. In 1983, most of the archipelago was designated a national park to protect the flora, fauna, and marine life and, aside from a few national park personnel, most of the islands are uninhabited. They are an important nesting ground for green and hawksbill turtles, and every year from May to October it's possible to watch the turtles lay their eggs on the beaches of Bay Canh, Hon Cau, and Hon Tre islands.

Marco Polo called it Kondor when he stopped by in 1292, and it was known by the French as Poulo Condore, with Poulo believed to be a corruption of the Malay word for island, pulau. Emperor Gia Long ceded the islands to France in 1787 in exchange for military assistance, but the treaty didn't hold and 74 years later, when the islands officially came under French control, a penal settlement was established to house those accused of anti-French activities. Many of the

Fishing boats float near the Con Dao Islands, which are known for their beaches and jungles.

founding fathers of modern Vietnam spent time in the jails of Con Dao.

The South Vietnamese took over the prison in 1954, incarcerating their own political prisoners, and the Americans, with the South Vietnamese, built a prison camp here during the Vietnam War. For the 113 years the main island of this beautiful archipelago was used as a prison island, the place was known as "hell on earth," and all told, an estimated 20,000 people died miserable deaths on Con Dao—Nationalist and Communist prisoners as well as revolutionary insurgents and criminals from all over the French Empire. Some traces of the horror remain, but only one of Con Dao's cemeteries still exists; it alone has 2,000 graves, of victims of the struggles from the 1940s to the 1970s.

Con Son, also called Con Dao, is the main island of the archipelago and feels like a country town, with little traffic and a very laid-back air. The population currently stands at about 7,000, not including military personnel.

The Con Dao Islands today, with their fascinating history and beautiful natural environment, are still relatively unspoiled—and unknown. It's still possible to explore Con Son on foot and not see another non-Vietnamese person (unless you pop into one of the dive shops) or drive along deserted roads to deserted beaches. However, this will change soon. A secret this good doesn't keep.

GETTING HERE AND AROUND
The airport is on the northern end of the main island of Con Son (also called Con Dao) and most hotels provide a free pickup service. Taxis and shared minibuses are also available outside the terminal. Vietnam Airline Service Company (VASCO) operates several flights a day to Con Dao from Ho Chi Minh City, which take about 50 minutes and cost around 1,700,000d one way.

Traffic on Con Dao is fairly placid, making the prospect of driving a motorbike less daunting than in other places in Vietnam. Motorbike rentals can be arranged through the hotels.

AIR TRAVEL CONTACTS Con Dao Airport.
(*Co Ong Airport, Sang Bay Co Ong*)
✉ *Co Ong, Con Son* ☎ *0254/629–7981*
🌐 *www.vietnamairport.vn/condaoairport/en.* **Vietnam Airline Service Company (VASCO).** ✉ *Con Dao Airport, Con Son*
☎ *028/3833–0330* 🌐 *www.vasco.com.vn.*

 ## Sights

Bay Canh Island

ISLAND | This small islet east of Con Son, Con Dao's main island, is covered by rain forest and mangroves and its Cat Lon beach is a turtle nesting ground from April to September each year. Visitors can hike up to a small lighthouse in the island's northeast, built 740 feet above sea level by the French in 1884 and still operational today. Tours to the island can be organized through the national park headquarters. ✉ *Con Dao Islands* ☎ *0254/383–0669* 🌐 *www.condaopark.com.vn.*

Con Dao Museum (*Bao Tang Con Dao*)

HISTORY MUSEUM | This vast and relatively modern museum has interesting and impressive exhibits that explore the themes (with signs in English and Vietnamese) of Con Dao's natural environment and people, the island's history as a prison island, and Con Dao today. The displays provide some insights into the island's history and its role in Vietnam's long struggle for independence. ✉ *Nguyen Hue, Con Son* ☎ *0254/383–0517* 🏷 *10,000d.*

★ Hang Duong Cemetery

CEMETERY | The graves of more than 2,000 former prisoners (now considered war martyrs), who died during the 113 years Con Dao was used as a prison, are contained in this cemetery. The vast site, which covers nearly 2 square km (¾ square miles), contains victory monuments as well as marked, unmarked, and communal graves. For the longest time, Vietnamese pilgrims visited at midnight, bringing flowers, fruit, roast chickens, and paper offering to the grave of national heroine Vo Thi Sau, who was executed in 1952 at age 19. The cemetery now closes at 10 pm, but you can still witness pilgrims praying to Vo Thi Sau for special favors, such as money and improved social standing. It's a very atmospheric ritual and no one seems to mind visitors attending and taking (discreet) photographs. Cemetery attendants are on-site to ensure proper conduct. ✉ *Nguyen Anh Ninh, Con Son* 🏷 *free.*

Hon Cau Island

ISLAND | Other than Con Son, Hon Cau (Big Island) is the only island in the archipelago with a water source. It was also used as a prison island by the French—one of the more notable inmates was the late Vietnamese prime minister, Pham Van Dong, who was incarcerated here from 1930 to 1931. Hon Cau is home to a turtle nesting beach and the tours offered by the national park headquarters include a visit to the prison site, as well as snorkeling along the coral reefs just offshore. ✉ *Con Dao Islands* ☎ *0254/383–0669* 🌐 *www.condaopark.com.vn.*

Old French Governor's House (*Dinh Chua Dao*)

HISTORIC HOME | The former home of the Con Dao Museum, this house now contains somewhat confusing exhibits (signage in Vietnamese and French) outlining the history of Con Son's prisons. Admission is free and the entryway is presided over by a giant bust of Ho Chi Minh. Take time to stroll around the grounds, which have some exotic animals in pens at the rear. ✉ *Ton Duc Thang, Con Son.*

Phi Yen Temple (*An Son Mieu*)

TEMPLE | The original temple was built in 1785 to honor Phi Yen, one of the 21 wives of Nguyen emperor Gia Long. After the Tay Son rebellion, Gia Long fled to Con Son Island with his family and retainers. From there, he sent emissaries to France to ask for assistance in repressing the uprising. Phi Yen urged him not to deal with the French and was imprisoned for her efforts, suspected of sympathizing with the rebels. As the emperor sailed away from the island, her four-year-old son cried for her, angering his father, who threw him overboard (or so the story goes). A tiger and an ape freed Phi Yen from her prison and she stayed on the island, tending her son's grave, until taking her own life "after an unfortunate encounter with a man". The existing Phi Yen Temple was rebuilt in 1958 so pilgrims could pay tribute to the former queen, revered for her loyalty and honor. ⊠ *Hoang Phi Yen, Con Son.*

Phu Hai Prison

JAIL/PRISON | Con Dao's oldest prison, Phu Hai was built by the French in 1862. It is now a grisly monument to the appalling conditions in the prisons, with mannequins in some of the chambers providing a potent visual representation of the lives of the prisoners. The church inside the prison complex was never used. Guided tours of this and the other prisons on Con Dao can be arranged at the Con Dao Museum next door with one day's notice. ⊠ *Le Van Viet, Con Son* ☏ ⊠ *20,000d.*

Tiger Cages

JAIL/PRISON | A delegation of United States congressmen discovered the cramped tiger cages during an official visit to Con Dao in 1970, departing from their planned tour to follow a map drawn by a former prisoner. Photographs of the inhumane conditions were published in *Life* magazine in July 1970 and the international uproar that followed led to 180 men and 300 women being transferred from the cages to other prisons (or, in some cases, to psychiatric institutions). Mannequins rather than people now display the terrible conditions of the cages, which were hidden between a cluster of three prisons: Phu Tuong; Phu Son; and Phu Tho. Entry is through Phu Tuong Prison, built by the French in 1940. Guided tours of Phu Tuong and the other prisons on Con Dao can be arranged at the Con Dao Museum with one day's

notice. ⊠ *Nguyen Van Cu, Con Son* ☏ ⊠ *20,000d.*

Tre Lon Island

ISLAND | An important turtle nesting ground is here, and the jungle that covers the island is home to a variety of different species including some rare birds. Tours to the island, which can be booked at the national park headquarters, usually include snorkeling. Underwater highlights include giant clams as well as fish and coral. ⊠ *Con Dao Islands* ☏ *0254/383–0669* ⊕ *www.condaopark.com.vn.*

Tre Nho Island

ISLAND | Thousands of migratory sea birds nest on this island every year from May to September. It's also a nice spot for swimming, snorkeling, and exploring, lying 2 km (1 mile) off Ong Dung Beach. The national park office can organize a boat here. ⊠ *Con Dao Islands* ☏ *0254/383–0669* ⊕ *www.condaopark.com.vn.*

Van Son Tu Pagoda (*Nui Mot*)

TEMPLE | The name translates as Cloudy Hill Palace, and it's a picturesque place to visit, not so much for the temple—even though it is quite beautiful—but for the panoramic view it offers of Con Dao Town, An Hai Lake, and Con Son Bay below. The temple was built in 1964 for the prison officers and government officials stationed on Con Dao and is now considered a memorial to the martyrs who died during Vietnam's fight for independence. ⊠ *Nguyen Doc Thuan, Con Son* ⊠ *Free.*

🍴 Beaches

An Hai Beach

BEACH | The beauty of An Hai Beach is marred somewhat by the old stone and cement pier across from the Con Son Café. However, simply walk south along the casuarina-lined sand to get that deserted tropical island mood. **Amenities:** food and drink. **Best for:** solitude; sunrise; sunset; walking. ⊠ *Nguyen Duc Thuan, Con Dao Islands.*

Dam Trau Beach

BEACH | A few short years ago this was a pristine deserted wonderland of clear water and soft white sand. Now there's a collection of ramshackle huts on the beach hawking food, drinks, and deck chairs, but privacy can still be found by swimming around the rocks on the southern end of the beach. The beach is 200 meters down a rutted dirt track, which can be very slippery after rain. Look for the sign near the airport on Co Ong Street. It's a nice spot to watch the sunset, although traversing the track back to the main road in the dark can be treacherous if you're on a motorbike or bicycle. **Amenities:** food and drink. **Best for:** sunsets; swimming; solitude. ✉ *Co Ong, Con Dao Islands.*

Dat Doc Beach

BEACH | Most of this beautiful crescent of white sand and calm blue waters is the private domain of the luxurious Six Senses Con Dao resort. There is a steep and narrow track leading down to the beach, just north of the resort entrance, for those who'd like to (discreetly) explore the beach. **Amenities:** none. **Best for:** solitude; sunrise; swimming; walking. ✉ *Bai Dat Doc, Con Dao Islands.*

Lo Voi Beach

BEACH | Locals seem to prefer walking along Nguyen Van Cuu Street's sidewalk at dawn and dusk rather than on this long white-sand beach, which is usually dotted with the round basket-boats the fishermen use to get to shore. Despite being right in town, Lo Voi Beach is usually deserted during the day. Fishing boats moored just offshore make this beautiful beach even more picturesque. **Amenities:** none. **Best for:** solitude; sunrise; sunset; swimming; walking. ✉ *Nguyen Van Cuu, Con Dao Islands.*

Nhat Beach

BEACH | Check the tide times before heading to Nhat Beach, which only really exists at low tide. Then it's a smooth clear stretch of white sand, with waves just big enough to make things interesting. At high tide, the pebbles and rocks at the top of the beach rule out walking and swimming. There's not much shade at Nhat Beach, so be sure to cover up if low tide is in the middle of the day. **Amenities:** none. **Best for:** sunrise; sunset; swimming; walking. ✉ *Ben Dam, Con Dao Islands.*

🍴 Restaurants

★ Bar200

$$ | **CAFÉ** | More of a café than a bar, this tiny place makes fantastic sandwiches, salads, and pizzas, making their own pizza dough, sandwich bread, and burger buns in house. The interior is simple, yet welcoming, with wooden blinds, rattan tables and chairs, and photos and propaganda art on the walls. **Known for:** friendly staff; homemade bread; Italian coffee. [$] *Average main: d200,000* ✉ *Khu 6, Nguyen Van Linh, Con Son* ☎ *097/830–3025* 🌐 *www.divecondao.com* 🕒 *No lunch.*

By The Beach

$$$$ | **ASIAN** | Nonguests are welcome at the luxury Six Senses Con Dao's main restaurant, which is the perfect venue for a romantic meal of freshly caught local seafood and fine wine overlooking Dat Doc Beach. It's just as stunning by moonlight as it is during the day. **Known for:** fresh seafood; romantic dining; fabulous views. [$] *Average main: d500,000* ✉ *Dat Doc Beach, Con Dao Islands* ☎ *0254/383–1222* 🌐 *www.sixsenses.com.*

Infiniti Café & Resto

$$ | **CAFÉ** | Half a block north from the market, this bright, fan-cooled café has a rustic chic style featuring driftwood, rope, hessian, and a pool table. The menu is geared toward travelers, with pizza, burgers, and a small selection of Vietnamese dishes. **Known for:** Western dishes; best coffee on the island; homemade bread. [$] *Average main: d250,000* ✉ *Khu 8, Tran*

Phu, Con Son ☎ *0254/390–8909* 🌐 *www.facebook.com/Infiniticaferesto* 💳 *No credit cards.*

★ Thu Ba

$$ | VIETNAMESE | A visit to Con Son isn't complete without a meal at Thu Ba. Chef Thu Ba works her magic in the kitchen while her daughter Thuy works the guests in the homey front section, recommending dishes from the extensive menu full of Vietnamese seafood, pork, and beef dishes (the slipper lobster is highly recommended). **Known for:** takeout picnics; fresh seafood; friendly owner. [$] *Average main: d200,000* ✉ *Khu 7, Vo Thi Sau, Con Son* ☎ *0886/249–977* 💳 *No credit cards.*

Tri Ky

$$ | SEAFOOD | A spartan open-air local joint that's been the go-to place for domestic tourists to Con Dao for years, Tri Ky is worth a visit if you love fresh well-cooked seafood. The specialty is *oc ban tay* (hand snail); try it stir-fried with garlic—it tastes a lot better than it sounds! **Known for:** shedlike setting; lack of English-language skills; fresh seafood. [$] *Average main: d175,000* ✉ *5 Nguyen Duc Thuan, Con Son* ☎ *254/383–0294.*

Coffee and Quick Bites

Con Son Café

$ | CAFÉ | This is a cute and simple drinks-only café consisting of a few tables and umbrellas set under the trees in front of the former French Maison des Passagers (Customs House). The outdoor-only setup gives customers a great view of An Hai Beach, making it an ideal spot for sunset drinks, except when the staff turn up the V-pop volume or when it rains. **Known for:** sea views; sunset drinks; outdoor seating in front of a beautiful colonial building. [$] *Average main: d40,000* ✉ *Ton Duc Thang, Con Son.*

Hotels

Phi Yen Hotel

$ | HOTEL | Designed as a place to sleep only, this small and neat budget option somehow manages to be charming as well as functional, and the restaurant next door means the lack of in-house dining isn't a problem. **Pros:** relatively spacious rooms; the location is handy; staff is friendly. **Cons:** thin walls provide little protection from noisy guests; basic accommodations; amazing sea views blocked by construction. [$] *Rooms from: d570,000* ✉ *34 Ton Duc Thang, Con Dao Islands* ☎ *0254/363–0111* 🌐 *www.hotel-phiyen.com.vn* 🛏 *11 rooms* 🍴 *No Meals.*

Poulo Condor Boutique Resort & Spa

$$$$ | RESORT | Time really does seem to stand still at this luxuriously appointed resort, set between Lo Voi Mountain and a stunning 750-meter private beach (a great spot to catch the sunrise) with beautifully maintained gardens. **Pros:** weekly afternoon tea; daily free shuttle bus to Con Son Town makes the resort seem less isolated; infinity pool and spa on-site. **Cons:** the Bistro Des Iles Restaurant is quite pricey. [$] *Rooms from: d6,627,000* ✉ *Bai Vong, Co Ong Site, Con Son* ☎ *0254/383–1500* 🌐 *www.poulo-condorresort.com* 🛏 *36 rooms* 🍴 *Free Breakfast* ☞ *includes airport transfer.*

★ Six Senses Con Dao

$$$$ | RESORT | FAMILY | A luxurious yet laid-back eco-lodge on a stunning crescent of beach, Six Senses Con Dao's private villas are a heavenly retreat from everyday life with excellent amenities like private infinity pools. **Pros:** first-rate spa; superb dining; incredibly relaxing; family-friendly. **Cons:** 5 km (3 miles) from town, where you might want to seek out alternatives to the resort's high restaurant prices. [$] *Rooms from: d17,100,000* ✉ *Dat Doc Beach, Con Son* ☎ *028/3823–2229* 🌐 *www.sixsensescondao.com* 🍴 *Free Breakfast* 🛏 *50 villas.*

Villa Maison Con Dao Boutique Hotel

$$$ | RESORT | You almost feel like a time traveler when you step into Villa Maison, a lovingly restored colonial villa in the heart of Con Son village with elegant rooms, lush gardens, and an excellent on-site restaurant. **Pros:** warm staff; great restaurant; close to beaches. **Cons:** no pool. $ Rooms from: d1,500,000 ⊠ 46 Nguyen Hue, Con Son ☎ 0254/383-0969 ⊕ www.villamaisoncondaoboutiquehotel. com ❏❉ Free Breakfast ➪ 7 rooms.

☺ Activities

DIVING AND SNORKELING
Con Dao Dive Center

DIVING & SNORKELING | Con Dao Dive Center operates daily snorkeling and diving trips around the archipelago from a speedboat carrying a maximum of 5 divers and few more snorkelers. There are also "try" dives for first-timers and dive courses, including open water, advanced open water, and rescue certification. ⊠ The Den Coffee, Tran Phu, Con Son ☎ 097/594-7685 ⊕ www. divecondao.com ➪ 3,700,000d for a 2-dive trip, including all equipment, taxes, marine park fees, and snacks. Snorkeling starts at 1,000,000d.

HIKING

There are a number of (paved and unpaved) hiking trails on Con Dao. Maps and other information are available from the national park office. National park rangers lead guided treks on Con Son as well as the smaller islands, including multiday treks. Easy options on Con Son that don't need a guide include a hike up to So Ray plantation, now home to some quite aggressive long-tailed macaques, and then down to the rocky Ong Dong Beach and back. The hike takes about five hours.

Con Dao National Park Office

HIKING & WALKING | ⊠ Khu 3, Ma Thien Lanh, Con Son ☎ 0254/383-0669 ⊕ www.condaopark.com.vn.

WILDLIFE-WATCHING
National Park Turtle Nesting Tours

WILDLIFE-WATCHING | FAMILY | Green and hawksbill turtles come to 13 of Con Dao's beaches between May and October each year to lay their eggs. The national park offers overnight turtle nesting tours to Bay Canh Island on a join-in or private basis. The baby turtles hatch from mid-August to December and you can also organize turtle hatching tours through the national park office. ⊠ Con Dao National Park headquarters, Khu 3, Ma Thien Lanh, Con Son ☎ 0254/383-0150 ⊕ www.condaopark. com.vn ➪ From 1,800,000d per person to join a tour.

Chapter 4

THE MEKONG DELTA

Updated by
Joshua Zukas

⊙ Sights	🍴 Restaurants	🛏 Hotels	🛍 Shopping	🍸 Nightlife
★★★★☆	★★★☆☆	★★☆☆☆	★★★☆☆	★☆☆☆☆

WELCOME TO THE MEKONG DELTA

TOP REASONS TO GO

★ **Rice paddies.** There's something uniquely soothing about the Mekong Delta's rice paddies. Whether they're photogenically brilliantly green or postharvest brown, there's usually a buffalo standing around, accompanied by a white water bird. Sam Mountain, just outside Chau Doc, is the perfect vantage point.

★ **River life.** Get out on the water to see Mekong Delta life in action. Everything revolves around the water, which provides the region's main form of transportation.

★ **Floating markets.** Boats chock-full of locally grown produce congregate at certain points in the river to trade, advertising their wares by hoisting them up on a flagpole-like stick.

★ **Khmer culture.** The Mekong Delta used to be part of the Khmer kingdom, evidenced by the towering temples that punctuate the countryside. These structures are found across the region, but especially in Tra Vinh, Soc Trang, and Chau Doc.

The Mekong Delta stretches from the Plain of Reeds in the northern reaches to the wet mangrove forests of Ca Mau at the southernmost tip. Tours are a recommended way to travel around the delta for short trips. Most tour operators offer hotel pickup and transportation from Ho Chi Minh City, though bear in mind river cruises will not begin until you reach the top of the delta. You can continue your travels on to Phu Quoc Island (or even Cambodia) after exploring the delta.

1 My Tho. Closest Mekong Delta city to Ho Chi Minh City.

2 Cai Be. This Mekong Delta town and its nearby villages are a hive of market activity with floating markets.

3 Vinh Long. Capital of Vinh Long Province and transport hub of the Mekong Delta.

4 Chau Doc. A religiously diverse and picturesque border town with Kinh (Vietnam's ethnic majority), Khmer, Cham, and Chinese communities.

5 Sa Dec. Charming town home to a temple, pagoda, flower village, and market.

6 Ha Tien. Has a bustling waterfront market and a network of caves that have been converted into makeshift temples with Buddha images.

7 Phu Quoc Island. With white-sand beaches, turquoise waters, swaying palms, and a laid-back feel, this island is one of Vietnam's most popular resort destinations.

4

8 Can Tho. The main center of the Mekong Delta is this large riverside town with enough tourist facilities to make for a relaxing stay and the region's best hotels.

9 Tra Vinh. This fascinating and pretty township is home to a large population of ethnic Khmers who have built stunning Khmer temples here.

10 Soc Trang. On the western side of the Bassac is this town with a thriving Khmer population.

11 Ca Mau. Capital of Vietnam's southernmost province, this sleepy city with wide streets and laid back traffic is the jumping off point for visits to nearby bird sanctuaries and the Mui Ca Mau National Park.

The Mekong Delta (Cuu Long) is made up of innumerable rivers, canals, tributaries, and rivulets overflowing with fish; the rich alluvial soil helps produce an abundance of rice, fruit, and vegetables. Lush tropical orchards, floating markets, emerald-green rice paddies, and lazy brown rivers and canals add to its photogenic wonder.

Slicing through the heart of the delta is the Mekong River, also known as Song Cuu Long, or River of the Nine Dragons. Descending from the Tibetan plateau, the river runs through China, separates Myanmar (Burma) from Laos, skirts Thailand, passes through Cambodia, and flows through Vietnam into the East Sea. The river carries fertile soil deposits at a rate of 2,500 to 50,000 cubic meters per second, which created the delta and continues its expansion. As it enters Vietnam, the river divides into two arteries: the Tien Giang (Upper River), which splinters at My Tho and Vinh Long into several seaward tributaries, and the Hau Giang (Lower River or Bassac River), which passes through Chau Doc, Long Xuyen, and Can Tho en route to the sea. The river's many islands are famous for their beautiful fruit gardens and orchards, and the year-round hot and humid climate is ideal for tropical fruits.

Vietnam is now the world's fourth largest exporter of rice—a remarkable feat considering that as recently as the early 1990s the country was importing this food staple.

The northern delta, with its fruit farms and rice fields, is the most accessible from Ho Chi Minh City, with day trips possible to My Tho and Vinh Long. The south-central delta encompasses the Ca Mau Peninsula, which juts into the sea from Soc Trang. Can Tho is the major center, a pleasant town and convenient base with enough tourist infrastructure for a comfortable stay. In the Mekong's southern section, steamy mangrove swamps and thick palm forests thrive on the flat, flooded delta, creating a haven for water birds, including some rare species. A homestay or countryside lodge is recommended as it gives you access to local communities and river life.

MAJOR REGIONS

Northern Mekong Delta. My Tho, Ben Tre, Vinh Long, Sa Dec, and Chau Doc all make for interesting bases from which to explore the region. Farther along the coast, Ha Tien is the gateway to Phu Quoc Island.

Phu Quoc Island. This rapidly developing island has powder-white sand beaches and a growing number of luxury resorts. But there are still plenty of remote beaches and a luscious jungle interior.

South-Central Mekong Delta. Can Tho, at the heart of the Mekong Delta, is an ideal base for exploring the deeper parts of the delta. Southeast of Can Tho is Soc Trang and Tra Vinh, both with large Khmer populations, and farther south still is the pleasant city of Ca Mau.

Planning

When to Go

The best time to tour the Mekong Delta is during the dry season, from October to May. During the rainy season, from May to September, a large portion of the region is under water and inaccessible. The Khmer communities in Soc Trang and Tra Vinh hold the three-day Ooc Om Boc (or Ok Om Bok) festival each year on the 13th to 15th days of the 10th lunar month. The highlight of the festival, a combination of moon worship and prayers for a good harvest, is the racing of slender, wooden, snake-shaped Ngo boats. The Khmer communities in Soc Trang and Tra Vinh also celebrate the Khmer New Year, Chol Chnam Thmay, usually in mid-April (the date is determined by an ancient Khmer calendar, not the lunar calendar that guides most other celebrations in the region).

Getting Here and Around

AIR

There are three airports in the Mekong Delta—in Can Tho, Ca Mau, and on Phu Quoc Island. A taxi from any of the three to your hotel will be around 150,000d. Regular flights from Hanoi and Danang arrive at the Can Tho International Airport, 9 km (5½ miles) from the city center. Vietnam Airlines, VietJet, and Bamboo Airways fly to this airport, which only really becomes international when chartered flights arrive, usually during Tet. Round-trip fares start at $60 from

Danang and $80 from Hanoi. Ca Mau Airport is about 3 km (2 miles) from the center of Ca Mau. Vietnam Aviation Service Company (VASCO) operates one flight a day each way between Ho Chi Minh City and Ca Mau. Round-trip airfare starts at around $80.

Phu Quoc International Airport, 10 km (6 miles) from the main town of Duong Dong, is one of Vietnam's busiest airports. Direct flights arrive regularly from Hanoi, Ho Chi Minh City, Danang, and Can Tho, as well as an increasing number of destinations in Asia. Vietnam Airlines, VietJet, and Bamboo Airways operates daily flights between Phu Quoc and Hanoi, Ho Chi Minh City, Danang, and Can Tho. Airfares can be quite reasonable, especially if you snag a promotional deal. Most resorts have an airport transfer service, and taxis and *xe om* drivers meet scheduled flights.

AIRLINE CONTACTS VietJet. ☎ *1900–1886* ⊕ *www.vietjetair.com.* **Vietnam Airlines.** ☎ *1900–1800* ⊕ *www.vietnamairlines.com.*

AIRPORT CONTACTS Ca Mau Airport. ✉ *93 Ly Thuong Kiet, Ca Mau* ☎ *0290/383–3855* ⊕ *vietnamairport.vn/camauairport.* **Can Tho International Airport.** ✉ *179B Le Hong Phong, Can Tho* ☎ *0292/384–4301* ⊕ *vietnamairport.vn/canthoairport.* **Phu Quoc International Airport.** ✉ *Nguyen Truong To, Phu Quoc* ☎ *0297/384–8486* ⊕ *vietnamairport.vn/phuquocairport.*

BOAT

Despite improved infrastructure, traveling around the Mekong Delta may still require river crossings and boats can provide one of the most interesting and relaxed means of exploring. There are many tour operators, offering everything from short half-day to multiday cruises *(See also Tours).* Keep in mind that you get what you pay for, so it's worth a little extra cost to guarantee reliability and safety. In the case of ferries, if you're on a bus or in a private car, there's no need to do anything but enjoy the view. If you're traveling by motorbike, just follow the herd to the drive-up ticket window and wait for the next departure. Two ferry companies operate between Phu Quoc and the mainland. Superdong is the faster service, with three services a day between Phu Quoc and Ha Tien (about 1½ hours, 230,000d one way) and another three between Phu Quoc and Rach Gia (about 2 hours, 20 minutes; 330,000d one way). Thanh Thoi is the slower service, mainly for cars and heavy equipment. Thanh Thoi operates three services a day between Phu Quoc and Ha Tien, each taking 2 hours and 15 minutes; one adult ticket costs 185,000d and a ticket for a motorbike costs 80,000d.

FERRY CONTACTS Superdong. ⊠ *10 30 Thang 4, Phu Quoc, Duong Dong* ☎ *0297/398–0111* ⊕ *www.superdong. com.vn.***Thanh Thoi.** ☎ *1900/966–908* ⊕ *thanhthoi.vn.*

BUS

From Ho Chi Minh City, you can board buses for all major towns in the Mekong Delta at Mien Tay Bus Terminal (*395 Kinh Duong Vuong, An Lac Ward, Binh Tan District*). More than 750 buses depart daily for Mekong Delta provinces, serving about 13,000 customers. Bus transportation is extremely cheap and usually quite comfortable. A one-way ticket to Can Tho, for example, will cost around 129,000d, while a one-way ticket to Ca Mau will cost around 200,000d. Be aware that there's usually no toilet on these buses, but most journeys include regular stops at tourist centers with food, drinks, and washrooms. Phuong Trang, sometimes known as Futa Buslines, has the most extensive network of routes through the Mekong Delta, with smaller companies, such as Hoang Vinh and Thanh Buoi, specializing in certain routes.

BUS CONTACTS Hoang Vinh. ☎ *28/3853– 9268 Ho Chi Minh City, 299/362–7627 Soc Trang, 91/215–8168 hotline.***Hung Cuong.** ☎ *28/3857–2624.***Kumho Samco.**

⊠ *Ca Mau* ☎ *28/6291–5389 Ho Chi Minh City, 277/395–9797 Ha Tien bus station, 19006065 Hotline* ⊕ *www.kumhosamco. com.vn.***Phuong Trang.** ☎ *028/3838–6852 Ho Chi Minh City, 19006067 Hotline* ⊕ *futabus.vn.***Thanh Buoi.** ☎ *028/3833–3999* ⊕ *thanhbuoi.com.vn.***VeXeRe.** ⊕ *vexere. com.*

TAXI

Mai Linh is the most reputable taxi company throughout Vietnam, although you may find local taxis are cheaper in the Mekong Delta. If in doubt, ask your hotel to call you a cab.

CONTACTS Phu Cuong Taxi (Ca Mau). ⊠ *Ca Mau* ☎ *0290/383–7837.***Nam Thang Taxi (Ha Tien).** ☎ *0297/395–9595.***Mai Linh Taxi.** ☎ *0290/378–7878 Ca Mau, 0296/392– 2266 Chau Doc, 0292/382–8282 Can Tho, 0297/396–6966 Ha Tien, 0297/397–9797 Phu Quoc, 0299/386–8868 Soc Trang, 0273/387–8787 My Tho* ⊕ *www.mailinh.vn.*

Health and Safety

Malaria is not an issue in the Mekong Delta, but outbreaks of dengue fever can occur. Pack insect repellent and make sure you use it, especially at dawn and dusk.

As is the case throughout Vietnam, never drink anything but bottled or boiled water.

Restaurants

Expect both street stalls and fine dining, as well as wonderful seafood and quality vegetarian dishes throughout the Mekong Delta.

One renowned Mekong Delta specialty is *ca tai tuong*, a grilled "elephant ear fish." Rice is a staple, and the region is famous for its noodle soups, including *hu tieu* (pork, prawn, and usually some offal) and *bun nuoc leo* (a murky pork noodle soup with thin fresh rice noodles). *Banh mi* (baguettes) are another cheap and tasty option. Fruit sellers are in abundance here.

What It Costs

	$	$$	$$$	$$$$
RESTAURANTS				
	Under 60,000d	60,000d– 150,000d	151,000d– 250,000d	over 250,000d
HOTELS				
	Under 600,000d	600,000d– 900,000d	901,000d– 1,500,000d	over 1,500,000d

Hotels

While some parts of the Mekong Delta receive few foreign visitors, there's a growing number of boutique and luxury hotels and resorts in the delta. Many hotels in the parts of the Mekong Delta less traveled by Western ers are state owned.

For expanded reviews, visit Fodors.com.

Tours

Aqua Mekong

The decadent 205-foot *Aqua Mekong* cruises the Mekong between Ho Chi Minh City and Cambodia, with three-, four-, and seven-day itineraries. The floating five-star hotel, complete with luxurious suites, a plunge pool, spa, and a menu designed by one of Asia's best chefs, the award-winning David Thompson, stops at fascinating off-the-beaten-path places, where shore excursions give you authentic insights into local life. ⊠ *Singapore* ☎ *6270–4002* ⊕ *www. aquaexpeditions.com* ⊠ *3-night cruises from $4050.*

Bassac Cruises

Can Tho–based Bassac Cruises has a fleet of three elegant wooden cruisers with comfortable air-conditioned cabins, each with a cozy private bathroom, and public areas that are so well laid-out that it's possible to socialize with other guests or find some privacy in one of the covered or open lounge and dining areas.

All three vessels—*Bassac I* is a converted rice barge, while the *Bassac II* and *Bassac III* were purpose-built for touring the Mekong Delta—were designed with passenger comfort and safety in mind, with quiet engines and air-conditioning systems, and safety features throughout. ⊠ *144 Hai Ba Trung St., Can Tho* ☎ *0292/382–9540* ⊕ *transmekong.com* ⊠ *From 5,900,000d.*

Drive Vietnam

Explore local life in the Mekong Delta in a comfortable new vehicle with an experienced driver and a professional tour guide on Drive Vietnam's Unscripted private day tour. ⊕ *drivevietnam.com* ⊠ *From $122 per person for a private tour for 2 people.*

Exo Travel

The staff at this experienced and professional tour company can help with customized itineraries and join-in tours through the Mekong Delta. They can also provide personal tour guides for those who want to delve deep into the Mekong Delta where little English is spoken. ⊠ *261–263 Phan Xich Long, Phu Nhuan* ☎ *28/3995–9898 cell phone* ⊕ *www. exotravel.com* ⊠ *From $80 for a basic 1-day excursion.*

Innoviet

A Mekong Delta–focused boutique travel agency offering small group tours that take people off the beaten path, Innoviet has itineraries ranging from day trips from Ho Chi Minh City to five-day tours of the delta. Long-distance travel is by private car, while in the Mekong guests experience various forms of transportation, ranging from *xeo loi* bicycle trailers to bicycles and sampans. Private tours can also be arranged. ⊠ *5b Pho Quang, Tan Binh District* ☎ *967/931–670* ⊕ *innoviet.com* ⊠ *From $86 for a day excursion from Ho Chi Minh City to the Mekong Delta.*

Mango Cruises

Day trips from Ho Chi Minh City are available, as well as multiday cruises that take you off the beaten path into the "real" Mekong Delta. Some cruises include a night at a luxury homestay, with a cooking demonstration, and most itineraries include a range of transportation options, from sampans to *xe loi* (Mekong Delta bicycle trailers). Most tours begin with a hotel pickup in Ho Chi Minh City and a two-hour transfer by car to Ben Tre in the Mekong Delta. ☎ *096/7683–366 cell phone* ⊕ *mangocruises.com* ✉ *From 10,000,000d for a 2-day, 1-night cruise.*

Mekong Bike Tours

One- to seven-day all-inclusive bicycle tours of the Mekong Delta will take you along back roads and lanes that don't appear on any maps (not even Google Maps!). With friendly, experienced, English-speaking cycle guides, Mekong Bike Tours specializes in unique routes that show local life. All tours include vehicular backup, accommodations, drinks, snacks, and meals; most itineraries start in Ho Chi Minh City, with some trips meandering through the delta to Phu Quoc Island or Cambodia. ✉ *459/1 Tran Hung Dao, District 1* ☎ *0283/601–7671* ⊕ *vietnamcyclingtours.com* ✉ *From $150.*

Mekong Eyes

Spend one day to two weeks exploring the Mekong Delta aboard a luxurious wooden cruiser or a private houseboat. The boats, which combine local boat-building traditions with modern comforts, also travel to the Cambodian capital of Phnom Penh. ✉ *209 30 Thang 4, Ninh Kieu District, Can Tho* ☎ *0292/378–3586* ⊕ *www.mekongeyes.com* ✉ *2-day, 1-night cruises from 5,900,000d.*

Victoria Cruises

Private or join-in cruises are offered in one of three purpose-built sampans, including the *Cai Be Princess*, which seats up to 25 passengers and is used mainly for day trips, and the *Song Xanh Sampan*, with private cabins and spacious bathrooms for overnight cruises. The sampans are part of the Victoria Resorts chain, and day tours often stop at the company's elegant Le Longanier restaurant in Cai Be. ☎ *0273/392–4658* ⊕ *www.victoriahotels.asia/en/victoria-cruises* ✉ *From 2,200,000d, including transfers to and from Ho Chi Minh City.*

Vietnam Birding

Set up by British bird enthusiast Richard Craik, Vietnam Birding offers customized and join-in bird-watching tours throughout Indochina, including to the Mekong Delta. Vietnam Birding is also experienced in general tourism and so can help arrange an itinerary that includes relaxation, cultural sites, cruises, and other vacation activities. Make contact well in advance of your trip—their services are in very high demand. ✉ *BTT Building, 32–34 Ngo Duc Ke, District 1* ☎ *0283/827–3766* ⊕ *vietnambirding.com* ✉ *3-night, 2-day trips from $1000.*

My Tho

70 km (43 miles) south of Ho Chi Minh City.

The closest Mekong Delta city to Ho Chi Minh City, My Tho was the center of the ancient civilization of Funan from the 1st to 5th centuries AD, before the culture mysteriously disappeared—no one really knows the reason—and it wasn't until the 17th century that the modern city was established, by Chinese refugees fleeing Taiwan (then known as Formosa). During the Vietnam War, My Tho was one of the centers of operations for American and Australian troops. The largest battle in the Mekong Delta was fought in 1972 at Cai Lai, only 20 km (12 miles) outside the city. Today My Tho is known as a supplier of fruit and fish.

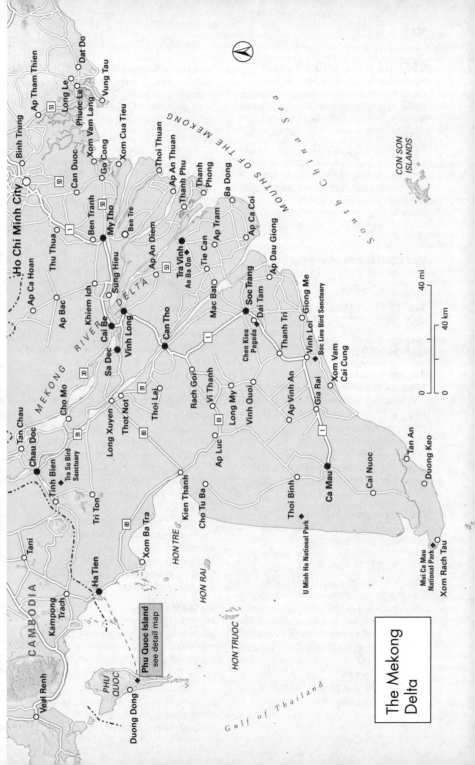

The Mekong Delta

GETTING HERE AND AROUND

Buses arrive here from Ho Chi Minh City and major centers in the Mekong Delta, and Phuong Trang (Futa) is one of the more comfortable and reliable bus companies that ply this route. The main bus station is Tien Giang, but most buses stop along Highway 1A to pick up and set down passengers. Xe om drivers wait near the set down point on the highway, but if you want a taxi and there are none there, the xe om drivers can summon one for you. My Tho's ferry station is on 30 Thang 4 Street.

BUS CONTACT Tien Giang Bus Station.
✉ *42 Ap Bac, Phuong 10, My Tho*
☎ *0273/385–5429.*

TAXI CONTACT Mai Linh Taxi.
☎ *0273/387–8787.*

 # Sights

Ben Tre

TOWN | A 20-minute ferry ride from My Tho (and then a 10-minute xe om ride) is Ben Tre, considered the Mekong Delta's coconut capital. Many Mekong Delta day trips from Ho Chi Minh City stop at Ben Tre, which has many interesting waterways and river islands to explore, as well as several coconut candy factories. ✉ *Ben Tre*

Cao Dai Temple

TEMPLE | Established in 1926 in the southern Vietnamese city of Tay Ninh, Caodaism is a monotheistic religion, in which Cao Dai is believed to be the creator of the universe. The temple in My Tho is a smaller offshoot of the main Cao Dai Temple in Tay Ninh (also called the Holy See Temple), and was built in the early 1970s. The colorful structure, which is done up in every shade of the rainbow and then some, has impressive wooden carvings of deities, immaculately painted iron grillwork, and handsome tiles. ✉ *85 Ly Thuong Kiet, My Tho.*

Island of the Coconut Monk (*Ong Dau Dua*)

ISLAND | About 2 km (1 mile) from My Tho, on the Mekong River, is Con Phung, or Phoenix Island, better known as the Island of the Coconut Monk. A religious sanctuary before the war, the island once had a garish, eclectic complex in a style similar to the Caodai Holy See in Tay Ninh. It was built in the 1940s by a French-educated engineer-turned-monk named Nguyen Thanh Nam, nicknamed the Coconut Monk by locals because he reputedly lived for some years on nothing but coconuts. The monk presided over a small community of followers, teaching a religion that combined elements of Buddhism and Christianity. He was imprisoned repeatedly, first by the Saigon regime and later by the Communists for antigovernment activities; he died in 1990. All that is left of the monk's utopian dreams are some dragons and gargoyles and columns with mythical creatures wrapped around them. Phoenix Island is one of My Tho's four islands named after mythical beasts—Dragon (Con Tan Long), Tortoise (Con Qui), and Unicorn (Con Lan) are the other three. Tours from My Tho usually visit all four, stopping at tourist pavilions where coconut candy, local honey, rice wine, and local musicians await. Organizing a visit through a reputable travel agency in Ho Chi Minh City is recommended but if you do take a local tour, be sure to explore the islands beyond the tourist centers by strolling the narrow lanes to see the fruit orchards and get glimpses of local life. Boats leave from Trung Trac Street, next to Mekong tributary. ✉ *My Tho.*

My Tho Market

MARKET | This large covered market is an interesting place to explore, especially if you haven't already wandered through a Vietnamese *cho* (market) before. Expect to see the usual Vietnamese wet market offerings of fresh fruit, vegetables, mounds of mysterious greens, meat, dried goods, clothes, shoes, and plastic paraphernalia. Do stop in for a bowl of the local specialty, *hu tieu My Tho* (pork-and-prawn noodle soup). ✉ *Corner of Trung Trac and Vo Tan Sts., My Tho.*

Vinh Trang Pagoda

TEMPLE | Delightfully fanciful, this pagoda built in 1849 features European and Asian design elements and is set within lovely ornamental gardens with bonsai and lotus ponds. Take some time to soak up the tranquil atmosphere of the pagoda, which was built in the shape of the Chinese character for nation, then tour the grounds to see the giant Buddha statues, including a very happy laughing Buddha. ✉ *Nguyen Trung Truc, My Hoa, My Tho* 🎟 *Free.*

🍴 Restaurants

Bo De Quan

$$ | **VEGETARIAN** | The setting of this charming vegan restaurant, which helps support the nearby Vinh Trang pagoda, is basic but pleasant with a tangle of potted plants. Service is not the fastest, but the food is truly delicious. **Known for:** tasty hotpot; vegan food; basic decor. [$] *Average main: d100,000* ✉ *69A Nguyen Trung Truc St., My Tho* ☎ *0273/397–6469.*

Hu Tieu Tuyet Ngan

$ | **VIETNAMESE** | Usually packed with locals, this big eating hall with metal tables and plastic stools is the best place in town to order *hu tieu My Tho*, a noodle soup that's the specialty of My Tho. The staff don't speak much English but the food more than makes up for any challenges with ordering. **Known for:** popular with locals; pork wonton soup; Hu tieu noodle soup. [$] *Average main: d40,000* ✉ *481 Ap Bac, My Tho* ☎ *0273/397–9224* 💳 *No credit cards.*

Loc Pho 2

$$ | **VIETNAMESE** | This garden restaurant is popular with locals. The specialty is whole chicken (including the head and feet), but if that's too adventurous, you can choose a beef, pigeon, or pork dish. **Known for:** chicken dishes; local-style eating; noisy drinking parties on weekends. [$] *Average main: d200,000* ✉ *151 Ly Thuong Kiet, My Tho* ☎ *0273/625–5139.*

Nha Hang Chuong Duong

$$$ | **VIETNAMESE** | The river side of this open-air hotel restaurant has a great view of sunsets behind the bridge. This is a great place to try the Mekong Delta specialty, elephant ear fish. **Known for:** elephant ear fish; views. [$] *Average main: d245,000* ✉ *10 Duong 30/4, My Tho* ☎ *0273/388–2352.*

🛏 Hotels

Happy Farm Tien Giang

$$ | **HOTEL** | **FAMILY** | At this charming little setup run by a lovely husband-and-wife team, Khoi and Oanh, the bamboo huts are quite basic, containing only beds and mosquito nets, but the big attraction here is the little hobby farm, which is home to chickens, ducks, horses, geese, dogs, cats, and a monkey. **Pros:** full itinerary of kids' activities; family-friendly; Vietnamese home-cooking. **Cons:** shared bathrooms; no air-conditioning or hot water. [$] *Rooms from: d600,000* ✉ *35 Ap Bo Xe, Xa Phu Thanh, Huyen Chau Thanh, My Tho* ☎ *909/991–218* 🌐 *happyfarmtiengiang.business.site* 🛏 *12 bamboo huts* 🍴 *All-Inclusive.*

★ The Island Lodge

$$$$ | **RESORT** | **FAMILY** | Only 2½ hours from Tan Son Nhat International Airport in Ho Chi Minh (where a luxury pickup can be arranged), this boutique riverside resort is a great place to rest and recharge in luxury at the start or end of a visit to Vietnam, with massages, pastries by the pool, drinks at the bar, or fishing off the pier. **Pros:** fabulous outdoor swimming pool; amazing on-site bakery; great river views. **Cons:** restaurant is quite pricey; isolated; breakfast finishes at 9:30 am. [$] *Rooms from: d5,000,000* ✉ *390 Ap Thoi Binh, Xa Thoi Son, My Tho*

☎ *273/651–9000* ⊕ *www.theislandlodge.com.vn* ⮌ *12 rooms* ⦿*⃝ All-Inclusive.*

Jardin du Mekong

$$$ | **B&B/INN** | Small and charming, this family-run guesthouse has nine cute bamboo bungalows set in a lovely garden area, well off the tourist trail, and is an ideal rural retreat for those seeking a glimpse of local life and a taste of excellent home cooking. **Pros:** truly friendly-family atmosphere; delicious home-cooked food; property has bicycles for exploring the area and hammocks for enjoying the gardens. **Cons:** about two hours from My Tho; isolated; no air-conditioning or fridge in the room. Ⓢ *Rooms from: d1,000,000* ⊠ *Cau Song Doc, Ben Tre* ☎ *090/314–9696 cell phone* ⦿*⃝ Free Breakfast* ⮌ *9 bungalows.*

Mango Home Riverside

$$$ | **B&B/INN** | A boutique homestay on the banks of the Ham Luong River, Mango Home Riverside has comfortable air-conditioned thatched bungalows set in a beautiful tropical garden. **Pros:** staffers are more than happy to suggest activities and tours; relaxing riverside retreat. **Cons:** isolated. Ⓢ *Rooms from: d1,100,000* ⊠ *Nghia Huan, Ben Tre* ☎ *98/323–2197 cell phone, Ho Chi Minh City office (English), 096/768–3366 cell phone, hotline* ⊕ *mangohomeriverside.com* ⮌ *9 rooms* ⦿*⃝ Free Breakfast.*

Mekong My Tho Hotel

$$$ | **HOTEL** | The fanciest place in town, this new four-star hotel is great value for money: the rooms—all with river views—are spacious, the swimming pool and fitness center are clean and new, and the rooftop café-bar is a great spot to watch the sunset. **Pros:** good fitness center; newly built; all rooms with river views. **Cons:** breakfast options are limited; staff can be inefficient; cleaners can be a bit lax. Ⓢ *Rooms from: d1,000,000* ⊠ *1A Tet Mau Than, My Tho* ☎ *0273/388–7777* ⮌ *114 rooms* ⦿*⃝ Free Breakfast.*

Cai Be

Spilling over from the land into the river, this Mekong Delta town and its nearby villages are a hive of market activity. Slip into a sampan and languidly cruise along the water with a stop at the floating market before ogling the town's handsome cathedral and eye-popping Caodaist temple.

GETTING HERE AND AROUND

You'll need a boat to visit Cai Be's floating market, but the rest of the town can be covered on foot or by bicycle. To go to My Tho and Vinh Long, hire one of the motorcycle drivers who are all around town; it's much easier to have the driver wait for you there than it is to hire another one to go back to Cai Be.

◉ Sights

Cai Be Cathedral (Nha Tho Cai Be)

CHURCH | This 1930s Gothic-Romanesque cathedral seems an anachronism in a small Vietnamese town, but it's a reminder of Vietnam's colonial past. The bell tower stands 171 feet tall and its bells, which were cast in France, weigh in at a whopping 400–2,000 kilos (880–4,400 lbs.). ⊠ *Just off the river, near Van Hoa K3, Cai Be.*

Cai Be Floating Market (*Cho Noi Cai Be*)

MARKET | The smallest of the Mekong Delta's floating markets, with only 10 to 12 boats, this is an easy excursion from most of the region's homestays. Be aware, however, that the floating markets around Can Tho are much bigger and livelier. The benefit of this market is that it runs all day, until about 5 pm. ⊠ *Off Cai Be Wharf, Cai Be.*

Dong Hoa Hiep Commune

MUSEUM VILLAGE | The most notable of the several hundred mid- to late 19th-century houses in this commune are those belonging to Tran Tuan Kiet and Nguyen Van Duc. The latter was built in 1850 and

Cai Be's floating market is one of the most famous in Vietnam.

combines French pillars and domes with more traditional Vietnamese style elements. This was the house of a wealthy family, and the trappings of their life are on display. ⊠ *Dong Hoa Hiep Commune, 22 Phu Hoa Hamlet, Cai Be.*

🍴 Restaurants

★ Le Longanier

$$$$ | VIETNAMESE | Reminiscent of an elegant colonial mansion, Le Longanier is a lunch-only restaurant set in tropical gardens that's part of the Victoria Hotels empire, and so is a regular stop on Victoria Cruises. Independent travelers can stop in (a reservation is required) to enjoy the set menu of Mekong Delta classics. **Known for:** lush gardens; beautiful colonial-style decor; set lunch. 💲 *Average main: d600,000* ⊠ *49 Hamlet 5, Phu An Village, Cai Be* ⊹ *If coming by road, follow sign just after the bridge. It's about a 200-meter walk along bike-only path* ☎ *1800/599–955* ⊕ *www.victoriahotels. asia/en/hotels-resorts/cantho/le-longani- er-restaurant.html.*

★ Mekong Lodge Restaurant

$$$$ | VIETNAMESE | FAMILY | The hotel restaurant uses only local ingredients and happily accommodates vegetarians. Specialties include crispy elephant ear fish and other local seafood. **Known for:** supporting the disadvantaged; elephant ear fish; good vegetarian options. 💲 *Average main: d720,000* ⊠ *An Hoa, Dong Hoa Hiep, Cai Be* ☎ *08/9663–3269 cell phone* ⊕ *mekonglodge.com.*

Mr Kiet's Ancient House

$$ | VIETNAMESE | The house of district chief Tran Tuan Kiet was built in 1838, its 108 poles made from the wood of *xylia xylocarpa* trees, and doors carved with illustrations of flowers and trees. On display within the house is beautiful carved furniture, some with mother-of-pearl inlays, ceramic pieces, and other antiques. **Known for:** seven-course set menu; historic setting; hyperlocal cuisine. 💲 *Average main: d250,000* ⊠ *22 Phu Hoa Village, Dong Hoa Hiep, Cai Be* ☎ *913/684–617 cell phone* ⊕ *kiethouse. com.*

Hotels

Mekong Lodge

$$$$ | ALL-INCLUSIVE | FAMILY | A great base for exploring the delta by bicycle or boat (the lodge is affiliated with Mekong Emotion cruise company), this eco-conscious resort, hidden among lush fruit plantations, has one of the biggest pools in the Mekong, lots of leafy paths to explore, and hosts regular cooking demonstrations and fruit art classes. **Pros:** large pool surrounded by loungers; riverside location; cooking classes available. **Cons:** parts of the property are a little tired; isolated. [$] *Rooms from: d2,270,000* ✉ *An Hoa, Dong Hoa Hiep, Cai Be* ☎ *089/663–3269 cell phone* 🌐 *www.mekonglodge.com* 🍴 *Free Breakfast* 🛏 *50 rooms.*

Mekong Riverside Boutique Resort and Spa

$$$ | RESORT | FAMILY | A delightful boutique resort on the river, with rooms in thatched bungalows, a pool, a spa, and excellent dining options, this is a great base for exploring the area and there are many walking, cycling, and boat tours on offer. **Pros:** friendly staff; eco-friendly; many on-site activities. **Cons:** limited outside dining choices; isolated. [$] *Rooms from: d1,500,000* ✉ *Hoa Qui Ward, Hoa Khanh subdistrict, Cai Be* ☎ *273/392–4466* 🌐 *mekongriversideresort.vn* 🍴 *Free Breakfast* 🛏 *50 rooms.*

Mekong Rustic Cai Be

$ | B&B/INN | FAMILY | Expect to be welcomed like visiting family at this friendly homestay, which for generations was a working fruit farm. **Pros:** great base for exploring; authentic countryside experience; delicious home-cooked meals. **Cons:** rooms in the main house provide limited privacy; as you would expect in the countryside, there's lots of insects, including mosquitoes. [$] *Rooms from: d275,000* ✉ *Tan Thien Hamlet, Tan Phong commune, Cai Lay district, Cai Be* ☎ *096/921–7586 cell phone* 🌐 *www.mekongrustic.com* 🍴 *Free Breakfast* 🛏 *15 rooms.*

Activities

Bike and Motorbike Rental

BIKING | You can get around Cai Be on foot, but it's hot, and that makes for slow going. A more fun and authentically Vietnamese way is to rent a bike or motorbike and take to the road, the sun on your face and the wind in your hair. Bicycles are usually built for one, but one or two people can fit on a scooter or motorbike. These can be rented from hotels, where you'll likely pay no more than 200,000d for a motorbike, and less for a bicycle. Helmets are available for motos but not for bikes, so watch where you're going. You're more likely to run into a pothole than another scooter, but it's your responsibility to get your vehicle back to the shop in one piece. ✉ *Cai Be.*

Vinh Long

74 km (46 miles) southwest of My Tho, 170 km (105 miles) southwest of Ho Chi Minh City.

The capital of the Vinh Long Province is the transport hub of Vinh Long, a midsize industrial town. Most of the tourist infrastructure is near the river, which is a short walk from the main market. Vinh Long can be used as a base to visit Sa Dec, 50 km (30 miles) away. Sa Dec is the modern-day home of many flower farmers and the 1920s home of French novelist Marguerite Duras—and the setting of her most famous novel, *The Lover.*

GETTING HERE AND AROUND

Vinh Long's main bus station is about 4 km (2½ miles) from downtown, with most buses providing a free shuttle service to hotels. The long-haul buses from Ho Chi Minh City stop here while the buses from Can Tho often let passengers off closer to the center of town. The main bus companies that operate out of the

Vinh Long bus depot are Phuong Trang (Futa) and Thanh Buoi.

BUS CONTACT Vinh Long Bus Station. ✉ *1E Dinh Tien Hoang, Vinh Long.*

Sights

Van Thanh Mieu Pagoda

TEMPLE | About 5 km (3 miles) from the Vinh Long Market, this large Chinese Confucian temple was built in the mid-19th century. It's decorated with multicolor dragons and statues of Confucius, which is odd because the monks here practice Buddhism. Added to the original structure is a different style of hall built in honor of a local fighter against colonialism, Phan Tanh Gian, who committed suicide in the 1930s rather than submit to French rule. Often the locals refer to the temple by his name rather than its official title. Although the temple has opening hours posted on the gate, it's often inexplicably closed. ✉ *Tran Phu, Vinh Long* 🎫 *Free.*

Restaurants

Meo U Kitchen

$ | **ASIAN FUSION** | This modern café on the ground floor of an apartment block serves Korean and Japanese-influenced dishes, including ramen and bi bim bap. The dual language menu is useful to travelers. **Known for:** interesting drink options; Japanese and Korean fusion fare. 💲 *Average main: d50,000* ✉ *1/7 Hoang Thai Hieu, Vinh Long* ☎ *0270/222–0168.*

Phuong Thuy

$$$ | **VIETNAMESE** | A plain and simple restaurant, associated with the Cuu Long Hotel across the road (which issues guests with tickets to the breakfast buffet), the riverside Phuong Thuy has a range of standard Vietnamese dishes, including hotpot, and a few Western choices. The main drawcards here are the English subtitles on the menu and the great river views, though service can be a bit slow. **Known for:** slow service; river views; simple Vietnamese fare. 💲 *Average main: d175,000* ✉ *1 Phan Boi Chau, Vinh Long* ☎ *0270/382–3765.*

Quan Pho 91

$ | **VIETNAMESE** | Locals will tell you that this is the best pho in town. There's no English menu, but they really only serve one thing (beef noodle soup), so there shouldn't be too many mishaps. **Known for:** open all day; tender beef; local favorite. 💲 *Average main: 50,000* ✉ *91 Hai Thang Chin, Vinh Long* 💳 *No credit cards.*

Vinh Long Market

$ | **VIETNAMESE** | Make your way through the bustling Ving Long Market to the food section at breakfast or lunchtime and inspect what the locals are eating. Point to what looks good and you will be chowing down on something cheap, authentic, and delicious in no time. **Known for:** budget dining; street food; early closing time (5 pm). 💲 *Average main: d40,000* ✉ *Nguyen Van Nha, Vinh Long* 💳 *No credit cards* 🕒 *No dinner.*

Hotels

Cuu Long Hotel

$ | **HOTEL** | This three-star hotel is probably the best in Vinh Long city, with a central location across from the Tien River and a block from the market. **Pros:** breakfast at nearby riverfront restaurant is included; great location; very reasonable price. **Cons:** housekeeping staff can heard in the corridors; occasional wailing from the karaoke place down the road. 💲 *Rooms from: d400,000* ✉ *1 Mot Thang Nam, Vinh Long* ☎ *0270/382–3765* 🍽 *Free Breakfast* 🛏 *48 rooms.*

Monks walk through Chau Doc, a religiously diverse and picturesque town.

Chau Doc

61 km (38 miles) from Long Xuyen, 245 km (152 miles) west of Ho Chi Minh City.

One of the Mekong Delta's most interesting destinations, Chau Doc is a religiously diverse and picturesque border town with Kinh (Vietnam's ethnic majority), Khmer, Cham, and Chinese communities.

GETTING HERE AND AROUND

Buses from major centers in the Mekong Delta arrive and depart at Chau Doc's main bus station, on the eastern outskirts of town. It's about seven hours by bus to Ho Chi Minh City and about 3½ hours to Can Tho. The main bus companies operating out of the bus depot are Phuong Trang (Futa) and Hung Cuong. There are taxis and xe om drivers waiting at the bus depot to take you into town. Most sites within town are a short taxi ride and it's best to use the meter rather than try to negotiate a price. If you're planning a longer trip, including to Sam Mountain,

see if your hotel can negotiate a rate for you. (Taxi drivers don't like driving up the mountain because it puts a strain on their engine.) Chau Doc is flat and the traffic is quite mild, making the city easy to traverse by bicycle. The Victoria Chau Doc Hotel and Murray Guesthouse both have free bicycles for guests, which can be rented for reasonable rates by nonguests. Xe loi are unique to a few Mekong Delta towns and are a fun way to get around, although the seats are low. Ask your hotel to organize a short xe loi tour of the town. It should cost about 50,000d for an hour.

Chau Doc is only a few miles from the Cambodian border and several companies offer boat transfers along the river to Phnom Penh. Hang Chau Tourist (⊕ *hang-chautourist.vn*) and Blue Cruiser (⊕ *www.bluecruiser.com*) provide the fast (4–4½ hours) daily speedboat service, including a stop to complete immigration formalities at the riverside Vinh Xuong border control station.

TRANSPORTATION CONTACTS Chau Doc Bus Station. ✉ *QL 91, Chau Doc* ☎ .**Mai Linh Taxi.** ✉ *Chau Doc* ☎ *0296/392–2266.*

 Sights

Ba Chua Xu Temple

TEMPLE | Ba Chua Xu is the prosperity goddess of the Vietnamese folk religion Thanism, and this is her temple. It was built about half way up Sam Mountain in the early 1800s after, legend has it, villagers discovered in the forest a female statue dating to the 6th century. The temple is constructed in what is commonly thought of as Chinese style, with four levels, and the tiled roofs have become green with age. Within is the statue of Ba Chua Xu, and locals come here to ask for protection. During the fourth lunar month, the 23rd–27th are festival days and locals celebrate with dances, praying, and by making offerings. Surrounding the temple are pleasant gardens and some small caves, and from up here there's a sweeping view of the surrounding countryside; on a clear day you can see neighboring Cambodia. ✉ *Nui Sam, Chau Doc.*

Floating Fish Farms

OTHER ATTRACTION | You can see some of the floating farms from 30 Thang 4 Park and the Chau Giang ferry terminal, off to the left across the river, but to visit one you need a guide. The fish farms are underneath the floating houses, in underwater pens accessed through the floors. A visit to a floating fish farm is usually on the itinerary of organized tours that come through Chau Doc. If traveling independently, ask your hotel for assistance. ✉ *Hau Giang River, Chau Doc.*

★ Mubarak Mosque

MOSQUE | One of nine mosques serving An Giang Province's Muslim population, Mubarak Mosque is a short ferry ride from Chau Doc's passenger pier. First built in 1750, the mosque is the spiritual heart of the area's Cham community.

Take some time wandering the surrounding streets to view the Khmer-style wooden houses. ✉ *Phu Tan, Chau Doc.*

★ Sam Mountain (*Nui Sam*)

MOUNTAIN | It's possible to walk to the smallish (230 meters) Sam Mountain, 5 km (3 miles) southwest of Chau Doc, although it is a long walk. Or you can get a xe om or a taxi to the top of the mountain and walk down (there's a surcharge for navigating the steep bumpy road; make sure you organize a round-trip unless you want to walk back to town). There are several interesting shrines on the mountain, known as Nui Sam in Vietnamese. The first, at its base, is Tay An Pagoda, originally constructed in 1847 and renovated several times since, with a mix of Vietnamese and Indian architecture. A little way past Tay An Pagoda is Ba Chua Xu (Lady Xu Pagoda), dedicated to a goddess whose origins have been lost in the mists of time and legend. Farther along is the Tomb of Thoai Ngoc Hau, an official of the Nguyen dynasty who died in 1829, and his two wives. Hang Pagoda (Cave Pagoda), at the top of 400 steps, has amazing views of the surrounding countryside, the flat rice paddies, and flood plains that stretch out beyond the Cambodian border. ✉ *Nui Sam, Chau Doc.*

Tra Su Bird Sanctuary

WILDLIFE REFUGE | The 2,088-acre Tra Su bird sanctuary, 25 km (15½ miles) southwest of Chau Doc, is home to more than 70 species of birds, including storks, egrets, and herons. The best time to visit is when the *cajeput* (paperbark) forest is flooded, from July to November. A three-hour exploration by boat includes a motorboat ride and then a peaceful cruise by rowboat through the brilliant green duckweed, lotus flowers, and water lilies. The tour usually includes a stop at a bird-observation tower that is 23 meters (75 feet) high. For most of the year, the sanctuary's narrow 12-km (7½-mile) track can also be explored by bicycle, with rentals available at the boat station. From Chau Doc, hotels and travel agents charge around 1,000,000d ($45) for a trip for two to Tra Su (including motorcycle ride out there and a boat), but the moto drivers outside Chau Doc Covered Market will take you there for around 175,000d ($8). There's one restaurant inside Tra Su and, next to where you'll hop in the boat, a few fruit stands and a small café where you can cool off with iced coffee. ✉ *Van Giao Commune, Tinh Bien District, Chau Doc* 🎫 *Boat tour 75,000d per person.*

🍴 Restaurants

★ Bassac Restaurant

$$$ | **VIETNAMESE** | The old-world charm of the Victoria Chau Doc Hotel extends to its in-house restaurant, which serves Western and Asian cuisine in a stylish riverfront setting. Take a seat on the terrace to enjoy the sunset (and happy hour at the bar) and the attentive but discreet service. **Known for:** attentive service; river views; finest dining in town. [$] *Average main: d250,000* ✉ *Victoria Hotel, 1 Le Loi, Chau Doc* ☎ *0296/386–5010* 🌐 *www.victoriahotels.asia/en/hotels-resorts/chaudoc.*

Bay Bong 2

$$ | **VIETNAMESE** | A basic Vietnamese joint, with a cafeteria-style interior and patchy English abilities, Bay Bong 2 does a range of standard but tasty Vietnamese dishes. The house specialty is *com ca kho to* (catfish in claypot) and sweet-and-sour soup with catfish or shrimp. **Known for:** claypot dishes; standard Vietnamese dishes. [$] *Average main: d150,000* ✉ *121 Trung Nu Vuong, Chau Doc* ☎ *0296/356–2747.*

Lien Phat

$$ | **VIETNAMESE** | Western tourists will find an English menu (with some very unusual translations) at this basic Vietnamese restaurant, where a range of standard dishes includes the local specialty, *lau mam* (fermented fish hotpot). A big plus is the air-conditioned room, in a town where many places are fan-cooled only. **Known for:** popular with locals; lau mam (fermented fish hotpot); air-conditioning. [$] *Average main: d145,000* ✉ *To 2A Trung Nu Vuong, Chau Doc* ☎ *0296/356–6868.*

Quan Mekong

$$ | **VIETNAMESE** | Alongside a French colonial villa once home to a Nguyen Dynasty official, Mekong serves up fresh and tasty Vietnamese dishes, has an English menu, and serves cheap cold beers. The location could be described as a courtyard if it didn't look so much like a parking lot, and the metal tables and chairs are rather basic, but the striped awnings and red tablecloths do give the place a certain touch of sophistication. **Known for:** limited English; street food-style dining; fresh seafood. [$] *Average main: d150,000* ✉ *41 Le Loi,* ☎ *0296/386–7381.*

Thanh Tinh

$ | **VIETNAMESE** | A pint-size eatery near the market and just in from the river, casual Thanh Tinh serves mostly vegetarian dishes. There's plenty to choose from, including a flavorful vegetarian pho made with coriander, tofu, diced vegetables, and tender noodles as well as a piquant dish of tofu stir-fried with citronella (safe to eat—it's a plant) and red peppers that pairs nicely with fried wontons in a fragrant broth. **Known for:** limited seating; good selection of vegetarian dishes; hit-and-miss service. [$] *Average main: d50,000* ✉ *12 Quang Trung, Chau Doc* ☎ *076/865–064* 💳 *No credit cards.*

Truong Van

$$ | **VIETNAMESE** | A simple roadside eatery where you'll see a good mix of tourists and locals, Truong Van serves standard but tasty pho, spring rolls, fish soup, and grilled beef in a sweet-and-sour sauce. Vegetarians can tuck into mixed sautéed vegetables (cauliflower, baby corn, red and green peppers, morning

glory) over wok-fried noodles. **Known for:** popular with backpackers; al fresco dining; great prices. $ *Average main: d60,000* ✉ *15 Quang Trung, Chau Doc* ☎ *0296/3866–567.*

🛏 Hotels

Hung Cuong Hotel

$ | **HOTEL** | One of the highest buildings in Chau Doc, this absolutely immaculate hotel has a great view of the town and the Mekong from its eighth-floor terrace. **Pros:** air conditioning works well; conveniently near street vendors and the market; good value. **Cons:** staff not great about helping to get tickets for boats, buses; rooms on lower levels susceptible to noise. $ *Rooms from: d570,000* ✉ *96 Dong Da, Chau Doc* ☎ *0296/3568–111* ❖ *Free Breakfast* ⇱ *45 rooms.*

Murray Guest House

$$ | **B&B/INN** | This family-run contender is fighting well above its price range, with large, clean, stylish rooms, comfortable beds, well-appointed bathrooms (with solar-heated water), and friendly staff. **Pros:** only a short walk from the riverfront and half a block from the ferry terminal; a much-welcome respite from the standard local-style budget hotels and guesthouses; staff can help organize tours. **Cons:** no elevator. $ *Rooms from: d730,000* ✉ *11–15 Trung Dinh, Chau Doc* ☎ *090/836–1344 cell phone* ⊕ *www. themurrayguesthouse.com* ❖ *Free Breakfast* ⇱ *10 rooms.*

★ Victoria Nui Sam Lodge

$$$$ | **HOTEL** | Halfway up Sam Mountain (Nui Sam in Vietnamese), this collection of charming stone cottages is a relaxing getaway from the bustle of Mekong Delta towns, but close enough to take day trips in and around Chau Doc—and it has stunning views over brilliant green rice paddies and flood plains. **Pros:** peaceful location; wonderful views; family rooms. **Cons:** isolated; the mountainside location and the many stairs make it unsuitable for people with mobility problems. $ *Rooms from: d2,200,000* ✉ *Vinh Dong I, Nui Sam, Chau Doc* ☎ *0296/357–5888* ⊕ *www.victoriahotels.asia* ⇱ *36 rooms* ❖ *Free Breakfast.*

★ Victoria Chau Doc Hotel

$$$$ | **HOTEL** | The French-colonial style Victoria Chau Doc, with its prime riverfront position, offers a touch of glamour in the Mekong Delta, along with international-standard service and a good restaurant. **Pros:** views of the river; great central location; pool on site. **Cons:** a little tired in places. $ *Rooms from: d2,240,000* ✉ *1 Le Loi, Chau Doc* ☎ *0296/386–5010* ⊕ *www.victoriahotels.asia* ⇱ *92 rooms* ❖ *Free Breakfast.*

Sa Dec

The former home of French novelist Marguerite Duras and the setting for her book *The Lover* (where said lover's house still stands), Sa Dec is small but interesting, especially in the weeks leading up to Tet, when the flower gardens are in full bloom. The leafy and charming waterfront is home to rows of shophouses built in different decades, a bustling market, an impressive Cao Dai temple, and a colorful Chinese pagoda.

GETTING HERE AND AROUND

Sa Dec is best enjoyed on foot, though as with anywhere in Vietnam, if you're tired of walking you can rent a bicycle or hop on one of the moto taxis parked on every corner. You'll need to get a lift out to Tu Ton Rose Garden.

👁 Sights

Cao Dai Temple (Sa Dec)

TEMPLE | A riot of color, this Cao Dai Temple, on the far side of the river, off Lac Hong, is pale yellow, with sky blue, red, and green accents, and inside the floor tiles change color from one to the next. At the front of the temple, on a

House Huynh Thuy Le Ancient House is the setting of Marguerite Duras's famous novel, *The Lover*.

carved wooden table with drawers, sit thick gilded candlesticks and offerings while ceramic egrets stand on either side. Established in 1926 in the southern Vietnamese city of Tay Ninh, Caodaoism is a monotheistic religion, and this temple is similar to the one in My Tho; both are branches of the main Cao Dai Temple in Tay Ninh, also called the Holy See Temple. Adherents worship Cao Dai, whom they believe is the creator of the universe. From the temples towers, take in the view of the river and surrounding countryside. ⊠ *102D Le Loi, Sa Dec.*

Huong Pagoda

TEMPLE | A Chinese-style pagoda built in 1838, Huong Pagoda sits behind teal wrought iron gates with a hint of art deco. Beautifully and brightly painted, the pagoda has red doors with gold floral designs, intricate scenes painted on the short walls between the second and third upturned roofs, and, resting on top, colorful animal figures. If you're lucky, a monk will be there and you can sit for tea and persimmons. ⊠ *75/5 Hung Vuong, Sa Dec.*

★ Huynh Thuy Le Ancient House
(*Nha Co Huynh Thuy Le*)

NOTABLE BUILDING | This house is famous for being the home of Huynh Thuy Le, upon whom French novelist Marguerite Duras based the title character of *The Lover* , a 1984 semiautobiographical book about a schoolgirl's love affair with a rich Chinese man. The house, built in 1895 by a wealthy Chinese family, was used as a government building for many years (which meant the 1992 film *The Lover* was shot at another colonial house in Can Tho). But it's been restored reasonably faithfully—without the original gold leaf decorations—and it's possible to stay in one of the bedrooms for about $25 a night, including dinner and breakfast. The architecture is interesting—French colonial on the outside but ornately Chinese on the inside—with many photographs of the "The Lover," both in real life and as he was portrayed on screen. ⊠ *255A Nguyen Hue, Sa Dec* ☎ *0277/377–3937* 🛏 *30,000d.*

Sa Dec Flower Village (*Làng hoa Sa Đéc*)

TOWN | For more than 100 years, people in this little village on the southern bank of the Tien River in Sa Dec have grown flowers, herbs, and ornamental plants, transporting them to markets around the region by river. The flower farms line a 2-km (1-mile) stretch of road, and most are open to the public. The village is at its most spectacular in the lead-up to Tet, the lunar new year. ⊠ *Tan Quy Dong, Sa Dec.*

Sa Dec Market

MARKET | This is a very typical Mekong Delta market where locals come to stock up on groceries, clothing, and homewares. To see how people really shop and earn a living, this is the place to come, and get here early. There's a wide variety of fruit and vegetables here, as well as snails, fish, eels, eggs in several sizes, chickens and ducks squawking and quacking, dry goods, and spices. Stop by the fruit stalls in front of the market, or wander inside for a bowl of something cheap and tasty. ⊠ *Lac Long Quan, Sa Dec.*

🍴 Restaurants

Night Market

$ | **VIETNAMESE** | This is a small outdoor market that sets up shop most evenings from 5 pm right on the riverside. You'll find Saigon beer for around 15,000d a bottle and stalls selling grilled meat and seafood as well as those with hotpot set-ups. **Known for:** wandering vendors; local-style alfresco dining; cheap prices. **$** *Average main: d30,000* ⊠ *Riverfront near Sa Dec Market, Sa Dec* ⊟ *No credit cards.*

🏨 Hotels

Thao Ngan Hotel

$ | **HOTEL** | A basic but immaculate hotel in the center of Sa Dec, this is an inexpensive place to stay the night. **Pros:** central; inexpensive; Wi-Fi throughout

the hotel. **Cons:** no breakfast; some will find the beds a bit firm. **$** *Rooms from: d300,000* ⊠ *4 An Duong Vuong, Sa Dec* ☎ *0277/277–4255* ➴ *26 rooms* ⦶ *No Meals.*

Ha Tien

112 km (70 miles) southwest of Chau Doc, 306 km (190 miles) west of Ho Chi Minh City.

Just 8 km (5 miles) from the Cambodian border, Ha Tien has an unusual and compelling history. Under Khmer rule it was a thriving trade hub, and in the 17th century the Nguyen lords gave the port to a Chinese lord, Mac Cuu, as a private, protected fiefdom. For the next few decades the Khmer, Siamese, and Vietnamese all struggled for control of the port and the trade that came with it. Ha Tien became an outpost of the Vietnamese Lords of Hue in 1780 before finally succumbing to French colonial rule. The Chinese, Khmer, Siamese, Vietnamese, and French impact can be felt throughout Ha Tien, notably in the Mac Cuu Tombs, Thien Dong Cave Pagoda, and fine colonial houses. The town, with its busy waterfront, bustling market, walkable backstreets, and towering swift farms, is undeniably charming.

GETTING HERE AND AROUND

Buses connect Ha Tien to the provincial capital of Rach Gia and to Chau Doc in nearby An Giang Province, with several services a day to each center. The bus depot is on the outskirts of town and the main bus companies that service the station are Kumho Samco and Phuong Trang. There are also a number of small minibus services that travel to Ca Mau, Vung Tau, Ben Tre, Soc Trang, Tra Vinh, and Can Tho. The ever-present Mai Linh taxi company has a fleet of taxis in Ha Tien. There are usually many taxis waiting at the ferry terminal when the Phu Quoc ferry is due in.

BUS CONTACTS Ha Tien Bus Station. ✉ *2 Thang 9 St., Ha Tien.*

TAXI CONTACTS Mai Linh Taxi. ✉ *Ha Tien* ☎ *0297/395–6956.*

Sights

★ Mac Cuu Tombs (*Linh Temple*)
TOMB | Sometimes referred to as the hill of tombs, this site is a garden cemetery containing the remains of General Mac Cuu and his family. Mac Cuu is credited with establishing Ha Tien in 1670, when the region was part of Cambodia. The family mausoleum, with its traditional Chinese tombs decorated with dragons, phoenixes, tigers, and lions, was built in 1809. There's a small temple dedicated to the family at the base of the complex. ✉ *Mac Cuu, Ha Tien* 🎟 *Free.*

Mui Nai Beach
BEACH | With its pebble-strewn brown sand, Mui Nai, 6 km (4 miles) west of Ha Tien, is definitely not the prettiest beach around, but the sea is calm and shallow and the water is relatively clean so it's a nice place to take a dip. There are deck chairs for rent and shacks selling seafood, and in the late afternoon the locals play volleyball and swim. There's sometimes an entrance fee, but usually only when the beach is busy. ✉ *Bai Tam Mui Nai, Ha Tien.*

Thach Dong Cave Pagoda
TEMPLE | On the road to the Cambodian border, 5 km (3 miles) northwest of Ha Tien, this atmospheric cave pagoda is in an echoey cavern in a limestone karst, with various chambers holding funerary tablets. The cave is home to a colony of bats (so keep your mouth closed when you look up), and the views from some of the openings across to Cambodia are just stunning. At the base of the mountain there is a small monument shaped like a clenched fist that commemorates the murder of 130 local civilians by the Khmer Rouge in 1978. ✉ *Off QL80, My Duc, Ha Tien.*

Restaurants

Ha Tien Market
$ | VIETNAMESE | There's a range of street food stalls in the streets surrounding Ha Tien's impressive market, which comprises several buildings, including one marked *"an uong"* ("eat and drink"). **Known for:** hot daytime temperatures; street food. [$] *Average main: d60,000* ✉ *Cho Ha Tien, Ha Tien* 💳 *No credit cards* 🕒 *No dinner.*

Oasis Bar
$$ | INTERNATIONAL | A plain and simple bar serving a range of drinks, including super cold beers, Oasis lives up to its name for the wealth of free travel information English owner Andy provides. (There is also a small travel agency inside the bar.) Oasis is the only place in town serving Western food, starting with breakfast, including the full English hot breakfast, and continuing through the day with bar-style meals such as chili con carne, baguettes, and Thai green chicken curry. **Known for:** Western food; travel tips; friendly service. [$] *Average main: d90,000* ✉ *Ha Tien*

Tran Hau Street
$ | VIETNAMESE | Tran Hau Street, which runs east from the market, is packed with delicious, local mom-and-pop establishments. These small eateries are usually named after what they serve, so look out for all manner of southern favorites, including *hu tieu* (chewy noodles with pork and seafood), *bun ca* (rice noodle soup with fish), *banh canh ghe* (thick tapioca noodle soup with crab), *com tam* (broken rice with grilled pork), and *che* (a Vietnamese dessert). **Known for:** local favorite; al fresco dining; cheap eats. [$] *Average main: 50,000* ✉ *Tran Hau St., Ha Tien* 💳 *No credit cards.*

Vinh Map
$$$ | SEAFOOD | As you'd expect from a seaside town, Ha Tien has excellent seafood restaurants, most of which line the river. Vinh Map is a good place to tuck into fresh shrimp, squid, clams, sea

snails, and oysters, which are usually sold by the kilo or half kilo. **Known for:** fun staff; fresh seafood; river views. $ Average main: 250,000 ✉ 8 Dang Thuy Tram, Ha Tien ☎ 097/585–5600 cell phone 🖃 No credit cards.

 Hotels

Bao Anh (Nha Nghi Bao Anh)
$ | **B&B/INN** | Close to the market, this guesthouse has large, neat-as-a-pin rooms with not-too-hard beds and bathrooms with shower cubicles rather than the usual Vietnamese splash room. **Pros:** clean and comfortable; cheap; close to the market. **Cons:** the language barrier can be frustrating. $ Rooms from: d350,000 ✉ Ha Tien Trade Center, Ha Tien ☎ 036/223–8440 cell phone ⏹ No Meals �’ 8 rooms.

Hai Phuong Hotel
$ | **HOTEL** | This is a pleasant enough option, close to the market, with spacious, clean comfortable rooms, all with windows and private balconies. **Pros:** private balconies; within walking distance of the market and the riverfront area; clean. **Cons:** the language barrier can create problems; slightly tired-looking bathrooms. $ Rooms from: d350,000 ✉ 52 Dang Thuy Tram, Ha Tien ☎ 0297/385–2240 �’ 43 rooms ⏹ No Meals.

River Hotel
$$$ | **HOTEL** | Ha Tien's only four-star hotel, in a prime location on the river, is understandably proud of counting Vietnamese and Cambodian prime ministers among its guests, and its seven floors have a small swimming pool, a restaurant, and a dance club. **Pros:** some rooms have river views; a step up from some of the more basic options in the Mekong Delta; good amenities. **Cons:** slightly sterile feel; limited English requires a degree of patience; expensive for what and where it is. $ Rooms from: d1,000,000 ✉ Tran Hau, Ha Tien ☎ 0297/395–5888 ⏹ Free Breakfast �’ 81 rooms.

Phu Quoc Island

45 km (28 miles) west of Ha Tien in the Gulf of Thailand.

The white-sand beaches, turquoise waters, swaying palms, and laid-back feel of this beautiful island in the Gulf of Thailand have made it one of Vietnam's most popular resort destinations.

Note: foreign passport holders who arrive on Phu Quoc via an international flight or boat will be eligible for a 30-day visa exemption. The exemption only applies to Phu Quoc, so any onward travel to the Vietnamese mainland requires a visa.

GETTING HERE AND AROUND
Phu Quoc International Airport is 10 km (6 miles) from the main town of Duong Dong. Direct flights arrive regularly from Hanoi, Ho Chi Minh City, Danang, and an increasing number of international destinations, including Singapore, South Korea, the United Kingdom, and Russia. Most resorts have an airport transfer service and taxis and xe om drivers meet scheduled flights. Superdong ferries leave Ha Tien and Rach Gia several times a day for Phu Quoc, arriving at the main passenger port of Bai Vong Port, 15 km (9½ miles) from Duong Dong Town. The journey takes 80 minutes from Ha Tien and 2 hours from Rach Gia. For ferry times, check the website.

Metered taxis are easy to get in Long Beach and Duong Dong Town but much more difficult to get in the more remote parts of the island. Mai Linh and Sasco have fleets on Phu Quoc. It's possible to negotiate a flat rate for a full day, exploring either the north or the south of the island, for about 1,000,000d. Most hotels and resorts can quickly and easily organize motorbike rentals. Expect to pay around 200,000d a day for an automatic motorbike (with helmet).

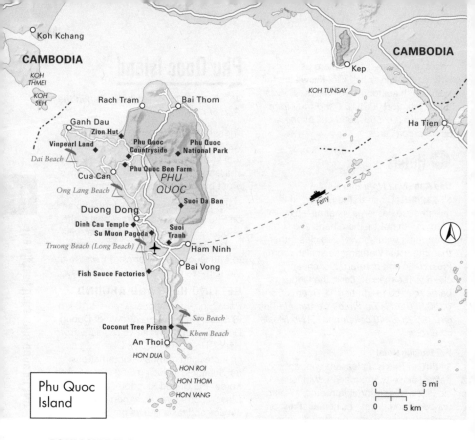

Phu Quoc Island

👁 Sights

Coconut Tree Prison

(*Nha Lao Cay Dua, Phu Quoc Prison*)
JAIL/PRISON | Established by the French and used by the Americans as well, the Coconut Tree Prison, also known as Phu Quoc Prison, is a chilling visual reminder of the atrocities the human race is capable of, as well as a stark record of history. Like many other war-related sites in Vietnam, the Coconut Tree Prison uses life-size mannequins to show the horrors committed in the past. The prison is right at the southern end of Phu Quoc. ✉ *350 Nguyen Van Cu, An Thoi* ☎ *0297/844–578* ⊕ *phuquocprison.org* 🎟 *Free, donations welcome.*

Fish Sauce Factories

FACTORY | Local tours often stop in at one of the very pungent fish sauce factories along the river in Duong Dong Town. It's possible to visit without an organized tour, although not much English is spoken at the factories and without any commentary, you're just looking at a hot and stinky shed full of giant wooden vats. Try Khai Hoan in Hung Vuong Street (☎ *0297/384 –8555*) and Hung Thanh at Khu Pho 3 (☎ *0297 /384–6124*).
■ **TIP→ Airlines that fly out of Phu Quoc will not allow fish sauce aboard, but it is possible to buy it at the departure lounge and have it shipped home.** ✉ *Phu Quoc* ⊕ *www.hungthanhfishsauce.com.vn.*

Phu Quoc Bee Farm

FARM/RANCH | **FAMILY** | This peaceful organic bee farm in the buffer zone of the national park has staff as sweet as their harvest. Tours of the farm's garden and orchards are free, and souvenirs and honey products are available at the little open-air café in a bamboo hut. ⊠ *Hamlet 2, Cua Can Ward, Duong Dong* ☎ *096/666–3365* ⊕ *www.phuquocbeefarm.com*.

Phu Quoc Countryside

FARM/RANCH | **FAMILY** | At this pepper farm you can take morning and afternoon cooking classes, where you prepare and, more importantly, eat four different dishes. Staff conduct free tours of the farm and their Kinh Beer brewery every 30 minutes, daily from 10 am. A range of local products are available, including a very tasty pepper tea, made with red pepper, cinnamon, and honey from their sister organization, Phu Quoc Bee Farm. Take time to taste the three types of beer and the Phu Quoc specialty, *ruou sim* (rose myrtle wine), at the little café, which has a short menu of simple Vietnamese dishes. ⊠ *Group 3, Xom Moi Hamlet, Bai Thom Ward* ✛ *10-min drive from Phu Quoc Bee-Farm* ☎ *091/167–7489 cell phone* ✍ *cookingclass.pqc@gmail.com* ⌨ *5-hr cooking class $50, including pickup.*

Phu Quoc National Park

(*Vuon Quoc Gia Phu Quoc*)
NATIONAL PARK | Covering most of the northern part of the island, the Phu Quoc National Park comprises mangroves, forest, and wetlands and supports many plant and animal species. It's an interesting place to explore by motorbike, or you could consider hiring a guide through your hotel that can tailor a trip based on your requirements. The cheaper local tour agents are best avoided or you might have a disappointing experience. The most beautiful parts of the national park are near Ganh Dau Beach in the island's northwest reaches. ⊠ ☎ *0297/384–6344* ⌨ *Free.*

Su Muon Pagoda

TEMPLE | This colorful temple, built in 1932, sits on top of a hill 4 km (2½ miles) east of Duong Dong Town. Access is via 40 stone steps, and it's more of a working temple than tourist destination. ⊠ *Off Tran Hung Dao.*

Suoi Da Ban

WATERFALL | This pretty stream and waterfall, about 6 km (4 miles) east of Duong Dong Town, suffers somewhat from its own popularity and has a serious litter problem, resulting from its use as a picnic spot among locals and Vietnamese tourists. If you want to visit, don't plan to swim. ⊠ *Off Nguyen Trung Truc.*

Suoi Tranh

WATERFALL | At the end of a 20-minute rain-forest walk, you'll reach this small but picturesque waterfall, which is much more spectacular in the rainy season but still worth visiting in the dry season. There are food and drink vendors and restrooms at the waterfall. ■**TIP**➜ **Suoi Tranh is popular with bus tours, so arrive early to avoid the crowds.** The entrance fee is used to pay trash collectors, so this site is much cleaner than some others on the island. ⊠ *Off TL47.*

Vinpearl Land

AMUSEMENT PARK/CARNIVAL | **FAMILY** | This 17-hectare amusement park in Phu Quoc's north has rides, a water park, an aquarium, and a 5-D cinema. There are food and drinks available throughout the park, and ATMs out in front. Free shuttle buses run regularly between Vinpearl Land and Duong Dong Town, stopping at several resorts along the way. ⊠ *Bai Dai, Ganh Dau Beach* ☎ *1900–6677* ⌨ *500,000d.*

Zion Hut

CRUISE EXCURSIONS | An offshore eco-retreat that's 19 km (12 miles) north of Duong Dong Town, this floating bamboo shack feels far away from it all and is a great base for swimming, snorkeling, fishing, or just general lounging.

Phu Quoc Island stuns with its white-sand beaches and jewel-toned water.

Good seafood is available at the hut.
■ **TIP→ Reservations are essential.** ✉ *4 km (2½ miles) offshore from Rach Vem village, Phu Quoc* ☎ *098098/421–8314 cell phone* ⊕ *www.facebook.com/zionhut* ✉ *$15 for transport to and from Zion Hut, life vest, and snorkeling gear.*

Dinh Cau Temple

TEMPLE | Part lighthouse, part religious building, Dinh Cau Temple is worth visiting while exploring Duong Dong town, its marina, and the night market. The temple sits on a rocky outcrop and was constructed during colonial times to honor the goddess of the sea, who would in turn protect the sailors and fisherman. ✉ *Dinh Cau, Duong Dong* ✉ *Free.*

🜂 Beaches

Dai Beach (Bai Dai)

BEACH | This beach in Phu Quoc's northwest used to be what tropical island paradises are all about—fine golden sand and warm turquoise water. Vinpearl Land and Vinpearl Resort now dominate this section of the island and it's no longer a secluded secret paradise. That being said, there are still beautiful stretches that are still accessible, with a few food shacks handy for refueling. **Amenities:** food and drink. **Best for:** sunsets; swimming. ✉ *Bai Dai.*

Khem Beach (Bai Khem)

BEACH | With powdery white sand and an ocean that seems to change colors throughout the day, this beach is just what you'd expect from a tropical island paradise. This is where the grandiose JW Marriott Phu Quoc is located, on the southern end of the island. If they are allowing guests (sometimes they don't) then you can spend a day enjoying their chairs and food, but you will have to pay for them. There is also a hard-to-find access road to the beach beside the Coconut Prison. **Amenities:** food and drink. **Best for:** walking; swimming. ✉ *Khem Beach.*

Truong Beach (Long Beach) (*Bai Truong*)
BEACH | The golden sand of the generically named Long Beach (not to be confused with Bai Dai, which also translates to "Long Beach") stretches for nearly 20 km (12 miles) along Phu Quoc's western coast, from just south of Duong Dong Town. This is where many of the island's smaller resorts and restaurants are located, which means some parts of the beach can be quite crowded with sunbathers and swimmers. It's still possible, however, to find deserted stretches of this beach. Cassia Cottage Resort, Long Beach Resort, May House Resort, Paris Beach Resort, Salinda Premium Resort and Spa, and La Veranda all front Long Beach. **Amenities:** food and drink; water sports. **Best for:** sunsets; swimming; walking. ✉ *Access via side streets off Tran Hung Dao.*

Ong Lang Beach (*Bai Ong Lang*)
BEACH | More of a series of coves than one long beach, Ong Lang is still very pretty, with its rocky outcrops and narrow strips of white sand. Mango Bay Resort, Bo Resort, and Phu Quoc Eco Beach Resort front the beach, so you can follow the signs to these resorts to enjoy wonderful views of the beach from their in-house restaurants. Public access to the beach is slightly tricky as the network of roads in this area aren't named. Head toward Mango Bay Resort and look for the "public beach" signs (in English) just south of the resort. **Amenities:** food and drink. **Best for:** snorkeling; solitude; sunsets; swimming. ✉ *Phu Quoc.*

Sao Beach (*Bai Sau*)
BEACH | This is one of Phu Quoc's prettiest beaches, but it's also one of the island's dirtiest. The northern tip of Sao Beach tends to be much cleaner than the rest, with crystal clear water and fine white sand. Make sure you take the third, northernmost entry to the beach—the first two entrances are where the tour buses go, so the beach gets crowded and noisy with Jet Skis buzzing about. To the north of all this activity, you'll find Paradiso Beach Club, which has free showers, food and drinks, and a massage service upstairs. **Amenities:** food and drink; showers. **Best for:** snorkeling; sunrise; swimming; walking.

🍴 Restaurants

DUONG DONG

Buddy Ice Cream and Info Café
$$ | **CAFÉ** | Across the road from the marina, this small, neat, and cozy café is a good place to stop for a coffee, ice cream, milk shake, or smoothie, as well as light meals such as salads, burgers, and Vietnamese dishes. It's probably the only place in town where you can get toasted Vegemite-and-cheese sandwiches, reflecting the owner's Australian roots. **Known for:** ice cream; tourist advice; Western food. [$] *Average main: d90,000* ✉ *6 Bach Dang, Duong Dong.*

Dinh Cau Night Market
$$ | **VIETNAMESE** | For fresh, cooked-before-your eyes seafood, head down to the Duong Dong Night Market. Dining at the street food stalls here, which set up around 6 pm, are a great experience, especially for group dinners. **Known for:** lively atmosphere; barbecued seafood. [$] *Average main: d80,000* ✉ *Bach Dang* 🕒 *No lunch.*

LONG BEACH

Ganesh
$$$ | **INDIAN** | **FAMILY** | For authentic Northern Indian cuisine, including great tandoor and naan, stop by this little restaurant, with simple style and friendly staff. Portions are generous and the masala tea is very delicious, although service can be on the slow side. **Known for:** friendly staff; slightly slow service; Northern Indian cuisine. [$] *Average main: d200,000* ✉ *97 Tran Hung Dao, Long Beach* ☎ *0297/399–4917.*

★ Peppertree Restaurant

$$$$ | INTERNATIONAL | La Veranda's in-house restaurant provides a full-sensory experience, with refined Pacific Rim cuisine, stunning views over the ocean, and elegant French colonial style. One of the priciest options on Phu Quoc, it's well worth it for the service, setting, food, wine list, and sunset views. **Known for:** sunset views; colonial-style decor; Pacific Rim cuisine. $ *Average main: d645,000* ⊠ *La Veranda Resort, Tran Hung Dao, Long Beach* ☎ *0297/399-4917* ⊕ *www.laverandaresorts.com.*

★ Rory's Beach Bar

$$$ | CAFÉ | Tasty bar food is available here day and night—think pizza, burgers, panini, salads, stir-fries, and pasta, served in a giant boat-shaped restaurant. Hosts Rory and Yoon preside over the café/bar, which has a genuinely welcoming atmosphere and fabulous views that stretch to Cambodia. **Known for:** Western-style bar food; good fun; friendly service. $ *Average main: d180,000* ⊠ *Cay Sao, Phu Quoc* ⊕ *www.facebook.com/RorysBarPhuQuoc.*

Saigonese Eatery

$$ | ASIAN FUSION | This cute little café has a short Asian fusion menu and a good selection of drinks, including local Pasteur Street craft beer on tap. Breakfast choices include a delicious eggs Benedict, as well as homemade granola. **Known for:** small courtyard at the rear; modern decor and menu; craft beer on tap. $ *Average main: d140,000* ⊠ *73 Tran Hung Dao, Duong Dong* ☎ *093/805-9650.*

★ The Spice House

$$$ | INTERNATIONAL | Cassia Cottage Resort's in-house restaurants have romantic settings: beside a pond filled with water lilies in a manicured tropical garden or right on the beach. This restaurant, which specializes in Vietnamese and international cuisine, uses fresh local produce, prepared with care and a bit of a French flourish. **Known for:** sunset views; romantic setting; fresh produce. $ *Average main: d175,000* ⊠ *Cassia Cottage, KP 7, Phu Quoc* ☎ *0297/384-8395* ⊕ *www.cassiacottage.com.*

Winston's Burgers and Beer

$$$ | BURGER | FAMILY | A popular stop for travelers seeking a break from Asian food, Winston's specializes in burgers, and all are made with Australian beef with all the fixings on homemade buns. Try the extra large "Big Freaking Burgers" if you dare, with such apt names as the Fat Bastard and the Terminator. **Known for:** no plastic straws; burgers and beer. $ *Average main: d185,000* ⊠ *121/1 Tran Hung Dao, Duong Dong* ⊹ *Down side street leading to Mango Resort* ☎ *076/390-1093* ⊕ *www.facebook.com/winstonsburgers.*

ONG LANG BEACH

Bamboo Cottages & Restaurant

$$$ | VIETNAMESE | The in-house restaurant at this friendly eco-lodge serves fresh local seafood, vegetarian dishes and *lau* (hotpots), which can be enjoyed with one of Phu Quoc's best views. Don't miss the house specialty, minted tempura shrimp, or book a beach barbecue for two. **Known for:** fresh seafood; ocean views; eco-friendliness. $ *Average main: d165,000* ⊠ *Vung Bau Bay, Duong Dong* ☎ *0297/2810-345* ⊕ *www.bamboophuquoc.com.*

Noname BBQ

$$ | BARBECUE | Fresh seafood, ribs, chicken, and vegetables are barbecued on sidewalk grills made from 44-gallon drums at this barbecue joint, where your food is selected from the blue canoe out front. The simple outdoor setting is even enjoyable in inclement weather, thanks to a canvas cover. **Known for:** lively atmosphere; very popular in peak season; barbecue. $ *Average main: d100,000* ⊠ *Cua Dong* ☎ *0937/760-779.*

★ On the Rocks

$$$$ | INTERNATIONAL | Mango Bay Resort's in-house restaurant serves excellent Asian and Western fusion cuisine from a wooden deck (with rocks peeking through) over the water. The views of the sunset over the Gulf of Thailand are fantastic, the cocktails delicious, the staff attentive, the music mellow, and the food, including the tapas, is some of the best on the island. **Known for:** excellent seafood platter; quality dining; sunset views. [$] *Average main: d350,000* ✉ *Mango Bay Resort, Ong Lang Beach, Phu Quoc* ☎ *0297/398–1693.*

Hotels

LONG BEACH

Cassia Cottage Resort

$$$$ | **RESORT** | This beachfront resort has a comfortable yet relaxing ambience, with its pretty little brick cottages, a modern and roomy extension, manicured gardens, a few swimming pools, and a charming garden restaurant, not to mention the helpful staff. **Pros:** free cocktail every afternoon; handy Internet lounge with a well-stocked bookcase; two pools help separate families and nonfamilies. **Cons:** new wing lacks the old wing's charm; limited breakfast menu; no TV. [$] *Rooms from: d4,400,000* ✉ *KP7, Duong Dong* ☎ *297/384–8395* 🌐 *www.cassiacottage.com* 🍴 *Free Breakfast* 🛏 *56 rooms, 2 2-bedroom beach houses.*

Famiana Resort and Spa

$$$$ | **RESORT** | **FAMILY** | Famiana Resort has two locations on either side of the main road: the beachside has bungalows, each with four rooms, plus a greenhouse that supplies Famiana Restaurant, a leisure center, kids' club, spa, and minigolf course, while the villa side, which doesn't have beach access, has bungalows overlooking a large pool, surrounded by loungers. **Pros:** great pool; many bars and restaurants within walking distance; family-friendly atmosphere. **Cons:** shrinking beach; crossing the main road between sections can be daunting. [$] *Rooms from: d4,000,000* ✉ *Tran Hung Dao, Duong Dong* ☎ *0297/398–3366* 🌐 *famianaresort.com* 🍴 *Free Breakfast* 🛏 *100 rooms.*

★ La Veranda

$$$$ | **RESORT** | Reminiscent of a colonial seaside mansion, with its swaying palms and wide verandas to catch the balmy sea breezes, La Veranda is an immaculately maintained haven of indulgent luxury on a quiet stretch of Long Beach. **Pros:** very attentive service; within walking distance to bars and restaurants; beautiful architecture and grounds. **Cons:** restaurants and bars are pricey; it's easy to get lost in the maze-like system of garden paths; the beach isn't what it once was. [$] *Rooms from: d5,000,000* ✉ *Tran Hung Dao, Long Beach* ☎ *0297/398–2988* 🌐 *www.laverandaresorts.com* 🛏 *70 rooms* 🍴 *Free Breakfast.*

Paris Beach Village

$$$ | **RESORT** | Choose a beachfront bungalow rather than one of the oddly laid-out rooms here, at one of Phu Quoc's older properties, which still manages to charm because of the friendliness of the staff. **Pros:** can be one of the more affordable options on the island; waterfront; pool with deckchairs. **Cons:** down a dirt track that buses can't negotiate; beach has eroded; a long (unlit at night) walk from the main area of Duong Dong Town. [$] *Rooms from: d1,200,000* ✉ *Tran Hung Dao, Phu Quoc* ☎ *0297/399–4548* 🛏 *33 rooms* 🍴 *Free Breakfast.*

Salinda Resort and Spa

$$$$ | **RESORT** | It may look like a giant shoebox from the street, but inside it's luxurious and elegant, with an emphasis on incorporating natural elements, such as coconut husks, bamboo, lacquer, and wood, into the design. **Pros:** infinity pool overlooking the ocean; great beachfront location; high-end dining options. **Cons:**; very expensive; the sheer size of the main building can make it seem impersonal. [$] *Rooms from: d11,600,000* ✉ *Tran Hung Dao, Phu Quoc* ☎ *297/399–0011* 🌐 *www.salindaresort.com* 🛏 *121 rooms* 🍴 *Free Breakfast.*

NORTHWEST TIP

Bamboo Cottages and Restaurant

$$$$ | **HOTEL** | The first "off-the-grid" and solar-powered resort in Vietnam, Bamboo Cottages has rustic bungalows set in a wild tropical garden, with one of the best views on Phu Quoc. **Pros:** many activities available; great on-site restaurant; daily yoga classes. **Cons:** a strange empty block sits in the middle of the property; isolated. [$] *Rooms from: d2,300,000* ✉ *Vung Bau Bay, Phu Quoc* ☎ *0297/2810–345* 🌐 *www.bamboophuquoc.com* 🛏 *22 rooms* 🍴 *Free Breakfast.*

Fusion Resort Phu Quoc

$$$$ | **RESORT** | This wellness-focused resort is one of Phu Quoc's most relaxing, where each villa has its own private pool and secluded garden and the spa is all-inclusive. **Pros:** all-inclusive spa; luxury self-contained resort; adults-only pool and restaurants on-site. **Cons:**; quite pricey; the property is very large. [$] *Rooms from: d9,800,000* ✉ *Vung Bao Beach, Phu Quoc* ☎ *0297/369–0000* 🌐 *www.fusionresortphuquoc.com* 🍴 *Free Breakfast* 🛏 *97 villas.*

Peppercorn Beach Resort

$$$$ | **RESORT** | This is a relaxed, simple, and secluded hideaway, only a few steps from the ocean, with enough creature comforts (air-conditioned beachfront bungalows!) to make a longer stay enjoyable. **Pros:** small and exclusive resort; complimentary use of mountain bikes to explore the nearby fishing village; complimentary airport shuttle when booking five nights or more. **Cons:** electricity and Wi-Fi can cut out; isolated. [$] *Rooms from: d4,400,000* ✉ *Ganh Dau, Phu Quoc* ☎ *0297/398–9567* 🌐 *www.peppercornbeach.com* 🛏 *12 bungalows* 🍴 *Free Breakfast.*

ONG LANG BEACH

Bo Resort

$$$$ | **RESORT** | With thatched wood-and-stone bungalows set on a hillside with lovely tropical gardens that overlook a bay of clear blue-green water, the focus of Bo Resort is a simple and "authentic" lifestyle right on the beach. **Pros:** laid-back vibe; gentle and harmonious atmosphere; quirky decor. **Cons:** hillside setting unsuitable for people with mobility challenges; isolated. [$] *Rooms from: d2,200,000* ✉ *Ong Lang, Phu Quoc, Phu Quoc* ☎ *0297/370–2446* 🛏 *17 bungalows* 🍴 *Free Breakfast.*

Chen Sea Resort and Spa

$$$$ | **RESORT** | Luxurious bungalows and villas overlook a private beach and the beautiful Gulf of Thailand at this polished resort from Thailand's Centara Hotels group, which promises simplicity, refinement, and some unique extras. **Pros:** on-site spa; infinity pool; range of leisure amenities. **Cons:** the resort is isolated; little within walking distance. [$] *Rooms from: d5,400,000* ✉ *Ong Lang, Phu Quoc* ☎ *0297/399–5895* 🌐 *www.chensea-resort.com* 🛏 *36 rooms* 🍴 *No Meals.*

★ Mango Bay Resort

$$$$ | **RESORT** | A collection of rammed-earth and wooden bungalows scattered through a vast stretch of jungle and gardens fronting Ong Lang Beach, this eco-lodge is the perfect location for low-key relaxing interspersed with the many activities on offer. **Pros:** low-season rates can be fantastic value; free airport transfers when booking three nights or more; solar-powered hot water. **Cons:** a long walk to other dining options; bungalows have no air-conditioning except in the canopy of the bed; no TV. [$] *Rooms from: d3,400,000* ✉ *Ong Lang, Phu Quoc* ☎ *0297/3981–693* 🌐 *mangobayphuquoc.com* 🛏 *44 rooms* 🍴 *Free Breakfast.*

Phu Quoc Eco Beach Resort
$$$$ | **RESORT** | Set on a hill with amazing ocean views and surrounded by tropical jungle, Eco Beach Resort is a small and friendly place, with Balinese-style decor throughout, from the breezy open-air restaurant to the swimming pool surrounded by sun loungers and white umbrellas. **Pros:** spa; free bicycle and kayak hire; spectacular ocean views. **Cons:** no dining options within walking distance; isolated. [$] *Rooms from: d2,300,000* ✉ *Ong Lang, Phu Quoc* ☎ *0297/398–6986* 🌐 *www.phuquocecobeachresort.com* 🛏 *34 bungalows* 🍴 *Free Breakfast.*

SOUTHERN TIP

JW Marriott Phu Quoc Emerald Bay Resort and Spa
$$$$ | **RESORT** | This grandiose beachfront resort, designed to look like a fictional French university from the 1890s, is a true flight of fancy filled with more than 5,000 European antiques and imaginative objets d'art, not to mention expansive villas. **Pros:** beautiful backdrops; villas have private pools; private white sand beach. **Cons:** sprawling layout makes for long walks between facilities; expensive; the interior design can feel over the top. [$] *Rooms from: d13,600,000* ✉ *Khem Beach, An Thoi Ward, Phu Quoc* ☎ *0297/377–9999* 🌐 *jwmarriottphuquoc.com* 🛏 *234 rooms* 🍴 *Free Breakfast.*

Nightlife

Phu Quoc's nightlife centers on the more heavily resorted part of Long Beach. The sprawling nature of Phu Quoc means that most people enjoy their resort facilities at night rather than heading out, though the Dinh Cau Night Market in Duong Dong is developing as an evening attraction.

Drunk'n Monkey
BARS | A sports bar with pool table, foosball table, and all kinds of football being broadcast, Drunk'n Monkey is usually a lively choice in high season and quieter in the off-season. The friendly staff add to the relaxed atmosphere, and the pizzas are pretty good, too. ✉ *Ong Lang, Phu Quoc* ☎ *090/925–9605 cell phone.*

★ **Rory's Beach Bar**
BARS | Relaxed, welcoming, and right on the beach, Rory's is a must-visit when on Phu Quoc for its chilled vibe, cold beers, friendly staff—especially Rory and his wife Yoon—and classic takes on café-bar food. Nighttimes can run late, with bonfires on the beach (weather permitting), foosball games, and general laid-backness. Rory's attracts all types, from families to backpackers to old-timers; expect to hear some interesting conversations at the bar, involving people with an interest in the world and its travelers. ✉ *Cay Sao, Phu Quoc* ☎ *091/933–3950 cell phone.*

Dinh Cau Night Market
GATHERING PLACES | Dinh Cau Night Market's atmosphere buzzes in the high season, with a growing number of bars and seafood restaurants, some with views of the river and of colorful fishing boats. ✉ *Dinh Cau, Duong Dong, Phu Quoc.*

Shopping

Dinh Cau Night Market
MARKET | Setting up just before sunset, the night market is an interesting place to explore and shop for souvenirs, such as shells, handicrafts, and wooden boats. Expect to bargain for souvenirs, but not for food. The jetty nearby and the Dinh Ba pagoda are popular spots for locals to watch the sunset. ■ **TIP→ Avoid the pearls; they're low-quality imports, not genuine Phu Quoc pearls.** ✉ *Dinh Cau, Phu Quoc.*

⚡ Activities

DIVING AND SNORKELING
Flipper Diving Club
DIVING & SNORKELING | This is one of Phu Quoc's most reputable tour companies, offering snorkeling and scuba diving trips as well as dive training courses. Trips include hotel transfers, lunch, and drinks, and—more importantly—do not include extra stops at tourist shops for the guide to get kickbacks. ⊠ *60 Tran Hung Dao, Phu Quoc* ☏ *093/940–2872 cell phone* ⊕ *www.flipperdiving.com* ✉ *Snorkeling tours from $25, scuba tours from $74.*

Rainbow Divers
DIVING & SNORKELING | With a seasonal presence on Phu Quoc from October to March each year, Rainbow Divers is a PADI-accredited dive center with daily boat-diving and snorkeling trips, as well as all PADI course offerings. ⊠ *The Rainbow, 11 Tran Hung Dao, Duong Dong* ☏ *091/340–0964 cell phone* ⊕ *www.divevietnam.com.*

GOLF
Vinpearl Golf Club
GOLF | Phu Quoc's first and only golf course is a challenging 27-hole course designed by IMG Worldwide, with rolling fairways set among trees and views of the jungle. The entire course covers more than 100 hectares (247 acres), and the caddies are friendly and knowledgeable. ⊠ *Bai Dai, Phu Quoc* ☏ *0297/384–4292* ⊕ *golf.vinpearl.com* ✉ *9 holes from 945,000d, 18 holes from 1,575,000d weekdays* ⚡ *Nha Trang Course: 9 holes, 3724 yards, par 36; Phu Quoc Course: 9 holes, 3521 yards, par 36; Quy Nhon Course: 9 holes, 3582 yards, par 36.*

Can Tho

34 km (21 miles) southwest of Vinh Long, 108 km (67 miles) southwest of My Tho, 170 km (105 miles) southwest of Ho Chi Minh City.

The meeting point of various waterways, Can Tho is the capital of the Mekong Delta. This bustling hub of activity is connected to other parts of Vietnam by the region's busiest airport and to other cities in the Mekong Delta by road and a system of waterways, making the city a convenient base from which to explore more far-flung corners of the region. Soc Trang and Tra Vinh, two centers of Khmer religion and culture and both with a remarkable collection of gleaming temples, are easy day trips, as are Sa Dec and Vinh Long. Can Tho is a desirable base for its centrality, but also its comfort. There are a number of elegant accommodation options, some of the delta's best restaurants, and several river cruise companies with trips ranging from half-day explorations of the nearby floating markets to multiday cruises through the region.

Can Tho retains a hint of its colonial past as one of the largest French trading ports in Indochina. This is best experienced on Hai Ba Trung Street around Can Tho Market, where several shophouses and colonial facades still survive and overlook a leafy park. During the Vietnam War, Can Tho was almost constantly surrounded by hostile Vietcong forces, but the city itself stayed loyal to the Saigon regime and many American and South Vietnamese troops were based here. It was the last city to fall to the North Vietnamese army, on May 1, 1975, a day after the fall of Saigon, as North Vietnamese forces moved south.

GETTING HERE AND AROUND

Regular flights from Hanoi, Phu Quoc, and Danang City arrive at the Can Tho International Airport, 9 km (5½ miles) from the city center. VietJet, Bamboo Airways, and Vietnam Airlines fly to this airport, which only really becomes international when chartered flights arrive, usually during Tet. A taxi to downtown Can Tho will cost around 150,000d. Can Tho Bus Station, southwest of Can Tho's main tourist area, is a regional hub. Buses arrive and depart here from Ho Chi Minh City's Mien Tay bus depot and most Mekong Delta centers, including Chau Doc, Long Xuyen, Vinh Long, and My Tho. The main bus companies operating from here are Phuong Trang and Thanh Buoi. Victoria Cruises offers river cruises to Soc Trang, which link to the new ferry service between Soc Trang and Con Dao Islands. Mai Linh operates a fleet of taxis in Can Tho. A daily fee of about 1,500,000d can be negotiated through the operator.

BUS CONTACT Can Tho Bus Station. ✉ 91b Nguyen Van Linh, Can Tho.

TAXI CONTACT Mai Linh Taxi. ✉ Can Tho ☎ 0292/3656–565.

TOURS

Mystic Sampans

The most popular Mystic Sampan cruises are the three-hour breakfast tours to visit either the Phung Hiep or the Cai Rang floating markets. Itineraries include stops at interesting places such as a fish sauce factory, a traditional apothecary, or a rice husking mill. The sampans also do sunset cruises and private tours, and the boats are all designed with safety and passenger comfort in mind. ✉ 144 Hai Ba Trung St., Can Tho ☎ 090/303–3148 cell phone ⊕ transmekong.com ✉ From 890,000d for a 3-hr floating market tour.

◉ Sights

★ Binh Thuy Ancient House

NOTABLE BUILDING | One of the very few remaining examples of 19th-century residences in the Mekong Delta, this house has been designated an official national relic by the Ministry of Culture. Built in 1870, the privately owned house is now managed by the sixth generation of the Duong family. The exterior looks French, but the interior is quintessentially Vietnamese, and all five rooms are furnished with antiques. The house appeared briefly in the 1992 film *The Lover*, based on the novel of the same name by French author Marguerite Duras, as the ancestral home of her Chinese lover (the actual home of *The Lover* still exists in Sa Dec but at the time of filming it was being used as a government office). Binh Thuy Ancient House is a 10-minute taxi ride from most hotels, and it's worth visiting Binh Thuy Temple, an ornate structure that predates Binh Thuy Ancient House, along the way. ✉ 144 Bui Huu Nghia, Binh Thuy ✉ Free.

Cai Rang Floating Market

(*Cho Noi Cai Rang*)

MARKET | A bigger market than Phong Dien and used by many wholesalers, Cai Rang is crowded and noisy (with many tourist boats), but still fascinating. The market, about 6 km (4 miles) or 40 minutes by boat from Can Tho, starts trading at around 4 am, in the dark, and is usually finished by 10 am. It really is worth making a superearly start to watch dawn break over the market. Coffee and breakfast are included in most floating market tours from Can Tho. ✉ Cai Rang, Can Tho.

Can Tho Museum

HISTORY MUSEUM | The Can Tho Museum has a large collection of artifacts from the local region. Displays illustrate the lives of former Chinese and Khmer occupants, and there's a life-size pagoda and a traditional teahouse. You will find a lot of

English signage here. ✉ *1 DL Hoa Binh, Can Tho* ☎ *0292/382–0955* 🎟 *Free.*

Munireangsey Pagoda

TEMPLE | This example of a Khmer Hinayana Buddhist pagoda was built in the 1940s to serve and provide spiritual well-being to Can Tho's Khmer community. Access to the interior is limited nowadays, but the pagoda is an emblem of one of the numerous ethnic groups that live side by side in the Mekong Delta. ✉ *36 Hoa Binh, Can Tho* 🎟 *Free.*

Ong Pagoda

TEMPLE | This picturesque 19th-century Chinese temple is inside the Guangzhou Assembly Hall, which is next to the redeveloped Ninh Kieu Pier waterfront park. Ong Temple is dedicated to Chinese military leader Kuang Kung (known as Quan Cong in Vietnam). Many of the decorative features of the temple, completed in 1896, were imported from China. ✉ *32 Hai Ba Trung, Can Tho* 🎟 *Free.*

🍴 Restaurants

The Cafe

$$$$ | **ECLECTIC** | Even if you're not staying at the Azerai, it's worth taking the free speedboat over to the islet for a leisurely lunch or a refined dinner. The menu ranges from Mekong specialties to Mexican favorites (the tacos are particularly good), or you can order one of two four-course set menus (625,000d). **Known for:** delicious food; quiet and rural setting; fabulous cocktails. [$] *Average main: d300,000* ✉ *Au Islet, get a speedboat from Azerai Arrival Pavilion* ☎ *0292/3627–888* 🌐 *azerai.com/resorts/azerai-can-tho.*

Hai San Binh Ba

$$$ | **SEAFOOD** | This casual seafood restaurant is popular with locals but sees few tourists, so you may have trouble finding someone that speaks English. Once the young and enthusiastic staff help break the language barrier, you'll be rewarded with mountains of fresh and delicious seafood, which comes grilled, steamed, or fried. **Known for:** fresh seafood; chao (rice porridge); lively atmosphere. [$] *Average main: d250,000* ✉ *110B Tran Van Kheo, Can Tho* ☎ *090/810–6088 cell phone* 💳 *No credit cards.*

★ L'Escale

$$$$ | **FRENCH** | The finest dining in town, on a beautiful rooftop terrace overlooking the Hau River, L'Escale serves a mix of French and Vietnamese dishes, accompanied by an extensive wine list and a jazz soundtrack, along with attentive service. The restaurant, in the Nam Bo Boutique Hotel, serves breakfast, lunch, and dinner, but you can also slide into a seat at the bar and enjoy a drink and the view. ■ **TIP→ Time your visit around 5 pm, when the light on the river is the most magical.** **Known for:** Vietnamese and French cuisine; attentive service; great sunset views. [$] *Average main: d400,000* ✉ *Nam Bo Boutique Hotel, 1 Ngo Quyen, 4th fl., Can Tho* ☎ *034/390–4735 cell phone.*

★ The Lighthouse

$$$ | **ASIAN FUSION** | The newest restaurant on Can Tho's tourist strip is also the city's most stylish, with elegant and comfortable furniture and a coveted terrace with views of the river. The menu is divided between European and Asian and both sections offer plenty of variety (try the chicken braised in coconut). **Known for:** baked goods; pretty park views; eclectic menu. [$] *Average main: d200,000* ✉ *120 Hai Ba Trung, Can Tho* ☎ *0292/3819–994.*

Nam Bo Restaurant

$$$ | **VIETNAMESE** | Part of the highly acclaimed Nam Bo Boutique Hotel, this all-day café-restaurant serves a variety of traditional Mekong specialties and European staples in a casual French bistro–style setting. For local fare, try the *lau* (a hotpot served with rice noodles, lean pork, seafood, and a pile of vegetables) or, if you're feeling adventurous, the snake set (*menu de serpent* in French). **Known for:** friendly service; casual setting; artsy interior. [$] *Average main: d200,000* ✉ *Nam Bo Boutique Hotel, 1 Ngo Quyen,*

Phuong Tan An, Quan Ninh Kieu, Can Tho ☎ *098/997–3070 cell phone.*

Ninh Kieu Night Market

$ | **VIETNAMESE** | There are two parts to the night market, one section selling clothes and tourist items and the other serving food from a variety of mobile stalls, with vendors who are well versed in the point-and-nod style of ordering. Most of the food can be munched while strolling and is more of a snack than a meal, but what's on offer can change from day to day, so it's best to just go and see what is available. **Known for:** lively atmosphere; street food; snacks. Ⓢ *Average main: d50,000* ✉ *Hai Ba Trung, Can Tho* 🚫 *No credit cards.*

Phuong Nam

$$ | **VIETNAMESE** | A basic riverfront restaurant targeted firmly at the tourist trade, Phuong Nam does a range of Vietnamese favorites and some of the Mekong Delta's more exotic specialties, such as field mouse, snake, and crocodile. The interior is basic, with check tablecloths and chunky wooden furniture, and the fan-cooled restaurant is open to the street. **Known for:** park views; backpacker-friendly fare; challenging dishes. Ⓢ *Average main: d150,000* ✉ *48 Hai Ba Trung, Can Tho* ☎ *096/343–9797 cell phone.*

Sao Hom

$$$ | **VIETNAMESE** | In a superb riverside setting inside Can Tho's beautiful old market hall, Sao Hom's friendly staff serves a range of Vietnamese and Western favorites, including the local version of *cha gio* (spring rolls). The service and venue are as relaxed as the river flowing by. Just a short walk from Ninh Kieu pier, Sao Hom is a great place to pause before exploring the local market beyond. **Known for:** spring rolls; river views; proximity to Ninh Kieu pier and local market. Ⓢ *Average main: d175,000* ✉ *Old Market Hall, Hai Ba Trung, Can Tho* ☎ *0292/381–5616.*

Vincom Plaza

$$$ | **INTERNATIONAL** | There are several dining options in this multilevel shopping complex adjacent to the Vinpearl Can Tho Hotel. Level 4 is where most of the eateries are, as well as an indoor kids' play center. **Known for:** Thai, Korean, Japanese and more; chain restaurants; on-the-go food. Ⓢ *Average main: d200,000* ✉ *2 Hung Vuong, Can Tho.*

🛏 Hotels

★ Azerai

$$$$ | **RESORT** | **FAMILY** | Like life in the Mekong, Azerai revolves around water: set on a pretty little islet on the Hau River, it's only accessible by boat, and it has its own serene lake. **Pros:** amazing spa services; very attentive staff; stylish contemporary design. **Cons:** the location away from the hustle and bustle of central Can Tho won't appeal to everyone. Ⓢ *Rooms from: d6,000,000* ✉ *Au Islet, Can Tho* ☎ *0292/362–7888* ⊕ *www.azerai.com* 🛏 *60 rooms* ⦿ *Free Breakfast.*

Green Village Mekong

$$ | **B&B/INN** | **FAMILY** | The family-run Green Village Mekong has two sites with simple bamboo bungalows and lush gardens: Green Village 1 is surrounded by rice paddies and banana trees, while Green Village 2, 3½ km (2 miles) away from the original property, is on a canal. **Pros:** comfortable yet rustic setting; superfriendly staff; provides insights into local life. **Cons:** no air-conditioning in the rooms; isolated. Ⓢ *Rooms from: d850,000* ✉ *Xeo Tre, Khanh Binh,* ☎ *091/977–2224 cell phone* ⊕ *www.greenvillagemekong.com* 🛏 *14 bungalows* ⦿ *Free Breakfast.*

Iris Hotel

$$ | **HOTEL** | Though it's outside the riverfront area, this shiny international-standard hotel has spacious, modern rooms with slick Western-style bathrooms. **Pros:** fitness center and massage services; great views from the rooftop bar; nice

new rooms at a great price. **Cons:** loud music from the bar can be heard on some floors; slight business hotel ambience; the cheapest rooms have no windows. $ *Rooms from: d890,000* ✉ *224 30 Thang 4, Can Tho* ☎ *0292/368–6969* ⊕ *www.irishotelcantho.vn* ➴ *66 rooms, 6 suites* ❢⊘ *Free Breakfast.*

★ The Lighthouse

$$$$ | **APARTMENT** | Little sister to the Nam Bo Boutique Hotel, The Lighthouse is a restored heritage building with seven serviced apartments and long-stay guests in mind. **Pros:** excellent on-site dining options; simple kitchen with pots and pans; ideal location on the river and close to markets. **Cons:** books out quickly with long-stay guests. $ *Rooms from: 2,400,000* ✉ *120 Hai Ba Trung, Can Tho* ☎ *0292/3819–994* ❢⊘ *No Meals* ➴ *7 apartments.*

Nam Bo Boutique Hotel

$$$$ | **HOTEL** | A true boutique hotel, the Nam Bo is small and personal with only seven large elegant suites (the corner suites are particularly delightful), friendly staff, great rooftop breakfasts, and many thoughtful little touches, such as local snacks left on the bed, a welcome cocktail, and a fruit platter. **Pros:** fabulous river views; central location; genuine boutique charm. **Cons:** when the party boat is cruising the river, the music can be heard in the rooms, although the cruise finishes at around 9 pm. $ *Rooms from: d2,400,000* ✉ *1 Ngo Quyen, Can Tho* ☎ *0292/381–9139* ⊕ *mekong-delta.com/en/1_nights/nambo* ➴ *7 suites* ❢⊘ *Free Breakfast.*

Nguyen Shack Homestay

$ | **B&B/INN** | This is a small, friendly, family-run operation designed to give guests an off-the-beaten-track experience from the home base of a bamboo shack over the Ong Tim River. **Pros:** reasonably priced food, boat, and bike tours; friendly atmosphere; complimentary bicycles. **Cons:** no air-conditioning in rooms; steep ladder leading to the bungalows could present problems for people with mobility issues; isolated (10 km [6 miles] from Can Tho). $ *Rooms from: d400,000* ✉ *Ong Tim Bridge, Thanh My, Cai Rang* ☎ *0292/628–8688* ⊕ *www.nguyenshack. com/cantho* ❢⊘ *Free Breakfast* ➴ *7 bungalows, 1 8-bed dorm* ▤ *No credit cards.*

Tay Ho Hotel

$ | **HOTEL** | There are neat, clean, freshly painted rooms in Tay Ho, one of Can Tho's few remaining colonial riverfront buildings, and despite state ownership, the hotel has a certain charm. **Pros:** heritage charm; affordable; central location a short walk from Ninh Kieu pier. **Cons:** no elevator; dim Vietnamese-style bathrooms; standard rooms have no windows. $ *Rooms from: d450,000* ✉ *42 Hai Ba Trung, Can Tho* ☎ *0292/382–3392* ⊕ *canthotourist.vn/khach-san/khach-san-tay-ho* ❢⊘ *No Meals* ➴ *18 rooms.*

★ Victoria Can Tho Resort

$$$$ | **RESORT** | **FAMILY** | Built in a style befitting French-colonial times, the Victoria Can Tho Resort comes replete with teak balustrades, hardwood floors, and bamboo ceiling fans. **Pros:** classic rooms with modern conveniences; exemplary service; excellent restaurant. **Cons:** a 10-minute walk from the main tourist strip (though it's a lovely riverside stroll). $ *Rooms from: d2,400,000* ✉ *Cai Khe Ward, Ninh Kieu District, Can Tho* ☎ *0292/381–0111* ⊕ *www.victoriahotels. asia/en/hotels-resorts/cantho.html* ➴ *92 rooms* ❢⊘ *Free Breakfast.*

Vinpearl Can Tho Hotel

$$$ | **HOTEL** | **FAMILY** | This 30-story hotel is the tallest in Can Tho, with great views from the upper floors, plus comfortable rooms, a large swimming pool, fitness center, spa, and dim sum restaurant. **Pros:** good views from upper floors; rate includes breakfast and access to sauna, steam room, and Jacuzzi; excellent swimming pool. **Cons:** feels slightly sterile. $ *Rooms from: d1,250,000* ✉ *209, 30 Thang 4 St., Next to Vincom Plaza Xuan Khanh, Can Tho* ☎ *0292/376–1888* ⊕ *vinpearl.com/vi/hotels/vinpearl-hotel-can-tho* ❢⊘ *Free Breakfast* ➴ *262 rooms.*

History and Culture of the Delta

Early settlement and ethnic disputes

The region was first mentioned in Chinese scholarly works as a part of the ancient kingdom of Funan. The Funan civilization was influenced by Hindu and Buddhist cultures and flourished between the 1st and 5th centuries AD. The Mekong Delta was settled by the Cham and the Khmer in the 7th century and was annexed by the Khmer civilization based at Angkor between the 9th and 10th centuries. Some Vietnamese settlers lived in the area even under Khmer rule, but with the defeat of the Cham in the late 15th century, more Vietnamese moved south. In the 17th century some of the Chinese fleeing one of the many northern dynastic autocrats appeared in the Mekong Delta. The Tay Son Rebellion in the late 18th century brought even more Vietnamese into the region. Allegiances were based on ethnicity—Cham, Khmer, Vietnamese, and so on—rather than on nationality. And there was feuding: the Khmer believed that over the centuries the Vietnamese had taken away their land, and they wanted it back.

20th-century conflict

French colonialism briefly put a stop to the disputes—and later contributed to them. The French encouraged the Vietnamese and the Chinese, who were much more commercially driven than the Khmer, to continue settling here. As more Vietnamese moved south, more Khmer left. Uncertainty over who would have sovereignty over the Mekong Delta lasted until 1954, when the French bequeathed the area to the new country of South Vietnam. Under Pol Pot's rule in Cambodia, the Khmer again laid claim to the delta as their ancestral land, and there were frequent skirmishes between Khmer Rouge and Vietnamese soldiers along the border.

During the Japanese occupation in the 1940s, colonial French and Vietnamese families fled from farther north to avoid the fighting. But the fighting eventually spread to the Mekong Delta, and these refugees were forced to fan out into the previously uninhabited mangrove swamps, hacking them down as they went.

A modern melting pot

Today the Mekong Delta is still populated by several cultures. The majority of people living in the area are Vietnamese, with the Khmer comprising the second-largest ethnic group. Nearly 2 million Khmer people live in the vicinity of the city of Soc Trang and on the Cambodian border, and the Mekong Delta is still often referred to as Khmer Krom by Cambodians. A small number of Cham also live close to the Cambodian border, but these Cham, unlike their counterparts in south-central Vietnam, are not Hindu but Muslim. Malay and Javanese traders who skirted the coast several hundred years ago converted the southern Cham to Islam. The Cham groups don't really mix with each other. The cultural diversity of the region accounts for the variety of religions practiced: Buddhism, Catholicism, Cao Daism, and Islam. Your travels throughout the delta will take you past examples of their remarkable coexistence.

Fishermen harvest at sunrise in Tra Vinh.

🛍 Shopping

Old Market Hall

MARKET | Can Tho's renovated old market, built in 1915, contains dozens of kiosks selling tourist-oriented items, including handicrafts, carvings, lanterns, silk items, and food souvenirs. ⊠ *Hai Ba Trung, Can Tho.*

Tra Vinh

200 km (124 miles) southeast of Ho Chi Minh City, 82 km (51 miles) from Can Tho.

Tra Vinh is a riverside town populated by friendly people, tall trees, and an amazing proliferation of temples used by the local Khmer and Chinese communities, as well as the dominant Vietnamese. In addition to pagodas, there's an eerily beautiful square pond outside of town, another relic of the Khmer kingdom that once ruled this area. Making the effort to visit this town, which welcomes few foreign tourists, can be a very rewarding experience and

an adventure in itself. It's also possible to visit as a day trip from Can Tho.

GETTING HERE AND AROUND

It takes about 4½ hours by bus from Ho Chi Minh City's Mien Tay bus station to Tra Vinh's bus depot, on the town's southern edge. There are a couple of local taxi companies in town, including Tra Vinh Taxi and the silver Taxi Thanh Thuy, as well as the omnipresent Mai Linh. Ask your hotel to help call a taxi.

BUS CONTACT Tra Vinh Bus Station. ⊠ *559 QL 54, Tra Vinh* ☎ *0294/384–0055.*

TAXI CONTACTS Taxi Thanh Thuy. ☎ *0294/361–2777.* **Tra Vinh Taxi.** ☎ *0294/3828–282.*

👁 Sights

Ang Pagoda (*Angkorajaborey Pagoda*)
TEMPLE | Originally built in the 10th century, Ang Pagoda has been rebuilt and restored several times. Set on 10 acres among ancient trees, the pagoda still retains its beautiful Khmer architecture.

Floating Markets of the Mekong Delta 🛍️

Before the modern roads and bridges were built, land travel here was difficult, and virtually impossible during the annual flooding season. This reliance on riverine life continues, with waterborne commerce, including several lively floating markets, an everyday occurrence.

Flying the Flag of Commerce

The unique feature of the Mekong Delta's floating produce markets is how the vendors advertise their wares—by running a sample up the flagpole. This means buyers aren't forced to waste time peering into the dark hulls of boats; if they're in search of pineapples, they just row or chug over to a vessel that's raised one of these fruits aloft. The abundance of the Mekong Delta is most apparent at these floating markets, where boats large and small are laden with coconuts, pineapples, pomelos, flowers, bananas, longans, onions, leafy greens, mangoes, and dragonfruit. Narrow boats, mostly rowed by women, wend their way through the market looking for good deals or offering coffee or food to those boat-bound. In the background, goods are transferred from seller to buyer in the time-honored tradition of throwing things from boat to boat. These markets provide a fascinating glimpse into lives lived aboard relatively small boats.

Visiting a Market

A visit to a floating market requires a certain amount of dedication. Their predawn start and early morning finish makes a day trip impossible to do from Ho Chi Minh City, although many travel agents will happily sell you such a tour and ignore your disappointment when you arrive at a virtually deserted stretch of river. The exception is the Cai Be floating market, which, because it's a wholesale market, operates for longer during the day, so it can be worth taking a trip here with one of the Ho Chi Minh City operators. Sadly, though, this market is a shadow of its former self because it's become easier to transport goods from here to Ho Chi Minh City by road. It's still better to access the Cai Be floating market from Vinh Long or Cai Be itself than from Ho Chi Minh City.

Sunrise Tours

Most floating markets are best viewed at sunrise, so an overnight stop in Can Tho is advised. Can Tho–based tour companies usually set out on floating market tours between 5 and 7 am. One of the bigger, livelier markets is close to Can Tho—the Cai Rang floating market. Cai Rang is just 6 km (4 miles) from Can Tho's main pier.

Ang Pagoda is 5 km (3 miles) from the center of Tra Vinh, a short walk from Ao Ba Om pond, and right across the road from the Khmer Culture Museum. ✉ *Luong Hoa, Tra Vinh* 🎫 *Free.*

Ao Ba Om

NATURE SIGHT | A relic of the glory days of the Khmer civilization, Ao Ba Om, which poetically translates as "square pond," is now a peaceful and serene body of water surrounded by tall trees. The pond, about 5 km (3 miles) from Tra Vinh, is a nice place to visit in the early morning, when the mists make the area seem even more romantic. Combine your exploration of the pond with visits to the nearby Ang Pagoda and Khmer Cultural Museum. ✉ *Ao Ba Om, Off Nguyen Du, Tra Vinh* 🎫 *Free.*

Hang Pagoda (*Chua Hang; Stork Pagoda; Kompom Chray*)
TEMPLE | This Khmer temple was built in 1637, and the tall trees on its 5-acre grounds are home to a small school and hundreds of storks, explaining one of its nicknames—Stork Pagoda. The pagoda, about 5 km (3 miles) from Tra Vinh, is also known as Cave Pagoda because of its cave-like entrance, as well as by its Khmer name of Kompom Chray (banyan tree wharf). It was once also called Bat Pagoda but bombing in 1968 scared the bats away and they've never returned. The monks here are famous for their woodworking skills and the intricate bonsai garden they tend while not studying, praying, and chanting. **■ TIP→ Hang Pagoda is a best visited in the late afternoon when the birds come home to roost, but try not to stand under a tree because the bird droppings come down like rain.** ✉ *Chau Thanh, End of Dong Khoi, Tra Vinh* 🎫 *Free.*

Khmer Culture Museum
OTHER MUSEUM | Housed in a blocky concrete building across the road from Ang Pagoda, the Khmer Culture Museum has four exhibition rooms containing re-creations of various aspects of traditional Khmer life, as well as collections of musical instruments and farming tools. All signs are in Vietnamese and Khmer. It's not the most interesting museum, but worth dropping by if you're just across the road anyway. ✉ *Opposite Ang Pagoda, Tra Vinh* 🎫 *Free.*

Ong Met Pagoda
TEMPLE | A Khmer temple has stood in this spot since 711 and the beautiful complex, also known as Bodhisalaraja, is now the center of Khmer spiritual life in Tra Vinh. A library with unique wooden features was added in 1916. The monks here are quite friendly and sometimes like to practice speaking English with male tourists. ✉ *50/1 Le Loi, Tra Vinh* 🎫 *Free.*

Ong Pagoda (*Phuoc Minh Palace*)
TEMPLE | A centuries-old Chinese pagoda that underwent a 20th-century renovation, Ong Pagoda, or Phuoc Minh Palace, is an important cultural and spiritual meeting place for Tra Vinh's Chinese community. The interior is shaped like the Chinese character for earth and the exterior represents the character for water, and throughout the pagoda mythical characters abound (some in front of a very pretty patch of artificial lawn). Every year on the 15th day of the first lunar month, this colorful pagoda hosts the Nguyen Tieu Festival, which marks the first full moon of the lunar new year. ✉ *44 Dien Binh Phu, Tra Vinh* 🎫 *Free.*

🍴 Restaurants

Bun Nuoc Leo
$ | **VIETNAMESE** | This basic street food outlet serves a great version of the local specialty, *bun nuoc leo*, a murky pork noodle soup. Patrons can expect celebrity treatment at this place, with extra plates of spring rolls, fried prawn cakes, and banana-leaf-wrapped roast pork offered, along with wide smiles. **Known for:** authentic local recipes; its namesake bun nuoc leo; extra helpings. [$] *Average main: d55,000* ✉ *48 Ly Thuong Kiet, Tra Vinh* 💳 *No credit cards.*

Phuong Hoang Restaurant
$$$ | **VIETNAMESE** | An eccentric tourist restaurant catering to domestic travelers, Phuong Hoang can be quite the experience, whether you choose to dine in a thatched hut, the fake floating restaurant, or the dining area that's in a giant cement reproduction of a helicopter cabin (minus rotor and skids). The menu offers a range of traditional Vietnamese dishes and a host of local specialties, such as bat, snake, and field mouse. **Known for:** quirky atmosphere; Vietnamese dishes; local specialties such as bat and field mouse. [$] *Average main: d250,000* ✉ *8 QL 60, Tra Vinh* ☎ *093/938–1188.*

Hotels

★ Coco Riverside Lodge
$$$$ | B&B/INN | FAMILY | Each of the lodge's spacious thatched-roof bungalows has a large patio overlooking the canal, perfect for a lazy breakfast or slowing down to the Mekong Delta pace. **Pros:** eco-conscious; great base for countryside tours; lush gardens. **Cons:** no other dining options nearby; lots of insects; isolated. [$] *Rooms from: d1,500,000* ✉ *Trung Nghia, Vung Liem, Vinh Long* ☎ *091/393–1193 cell phone* 🌐 *www.cocoriversidelodge.com* 🍴 *All-Inclusive* 🛏 *6 bungalows.*

Cuu Long Hotel
$ | HOTEL | The three-star Cuu Long Hotel is one the best places in town, and it does seem quite fancy compared to the other options. **Pros:** helpful staff; rooms are quite large; relatively close to town. **Cons:** style is a bit bland; the location isn't the best; popular with tour groups. [$] *Rooms from: d500,000* ✉ *210 Nguyen Thi Minh Khai, Tra Vinh* ☎ *0294/386–6867* 🍴 *No Meals* 🛏 *53 rooms.*

Thanh Binh 1 Hotel
$ | HOTEL | Basic but spacious, clean and functional, with dark wood furniture and Vietnamese-style bathrooms, the pastel-blue four-story Thanh Binh 1 Hotel is a good budget choice. **Pros:** cheap and clean; tidier than other hotels in the same price range; has the basic amenities. **Cons:** located slightly out of town; designed mostly for domestic tourists; very little English is spoken here. [$] *Rooms from: d350,000* ✉ *199 Nguyen Thi Minh Khai St., Tra Vinh* ☎ *0294/626–6789* 🛏 *38 rooms* 🍴 *No Meals.*

Soc Trang

63 km (39 miles) southeast of Can Tho.

Soc Trang is one of the centers of Khmer culture in Vietnam (the other being Tra Vinh). The town itself is unremarkable and the dining and accommodations options are limited, but it does have several interesting Khmer temples. The town is only an hour from Can Tho by car, so consider a day trip from there to take in the compelling temples. This was once a provincial capital of the Angkor Empire, which covered much of Indochina from the 9th to the 15th century. Vietnamese settlers did not appear here until the 17th century; later, in colonial times, they were encouraged to come by the French, who sought to develop agricultural production in the region.

GETTING HERE AND AROUND

If you're in a car coming from Tra Vinh, you will need to backtrack to Can Tho to get to Soc Trang, but if you're traveling by motorbike, there's a motorbike-only river ferry. Buses run regularly from Can Tho to Soc Trang, most continuing on to Ca Mau. The Superdong ferry company operates two services a day between Soc Trang and Con Dao. Soc Trang Bus Station is in the city's south, but most bus companies set down passengers on the side of the highway on the outskirts of town. Xe om drivers congregate at the bus stopping area, where there's a small stall selling drinks. The main bus companies serving Soc Trang are Phuong Trang and Hoang Vinh. The ever-present Mai Linh taxi company has a fleet in Soc Trang, and there's also a local company, Soc Trang Taxis. Expect to pay around 500,000d to hire a taxi for a day to see the local sights.

Farmers sell coconuts from their boats in Soc Trang.

BUS CONTACT Soc Trang Bus Station. ✉ *Le Duan, Soc Trang.*

TAXI CONTACTS Mai Linh Taxi. ✉ *Soc Trang* ☎ *0299/386–8868.***Superdong.** ☎ *0297/398–0111* ⊕ *www.superdong. com.vn.*

◉ Sights

Chen Kieu Pagoda
(*Xa Lon, Salon, Chen Kieu and Srolon*)
TEMPLE | Twelve kilometers (7.5 miles) outside Soc Trang, in the village of Dai Tan, this is the largest Khmer pagoda and religious school (for novice monks) in the area. The original pagoda, built in 1815, was destroyed during the Vietnam War and was rebuilt in 1969 using bowls and plates—hence the name (*chen* means bowl). The garden has several thatched huts in which pilgrims can meditate, and a lively market operates in front of the pagoda gates. ✉ *Dai Tam, My Xuyen, Soc Trang* 🍴 *Free.*

Dau Set Pagoda
(*Dat Set Pagoda, Buu Son Tu*)
TEMPLE | This is a vibrant Vietnamese temple that was built more than 200 years ago by a Chinese family called Ngo. A descendant, Ngo Kim Tong, who died in 1970, spent 42 years fashioning the pagoda's brightly colored statues, dragons, and gargoyles. Inside are candles so big and so broad—each about 40 feet high and so wide that two people extending their arms around it can barely reach each other—that have been burning continuously for more than 40 years. ✉ *286 Ton Duc Thang, Soc Trang* 🍴 *Free.*

Ho Nuoc Ngot
CITY PARK | The centerpiece of the cultural center of Ho Nuoc Ngot (Freshwater Lake) is an artificial lake with swan-shape paddleboats. The lake complex also includes garden cafés, a swimming pool, a movie theater, a children's funfair, and a playground. Ho Nuoc Ngot usually hosts the opening ceremony for the Khmer community's annual Ngo boat races on the lake on the 13th, 14th, and

15th days of the 10th lunar month. ✉ *Ho Nuoc Ngot, Off Hung Vuong, Soc Trang* ☎ ✉ *Free.*

Khmer Museum

HISTORY MUSEUM | In a large stucco French-Khmer colonial-style building, originally built as a Khmer school in the 19th century, the museum's collection includes Khmer statues and clothing, antique pots and utensils, and two long and colorful racing boats. During the French-Indochina War the building served as the headquarters for the local French militia, and during the Vietnam War it was a headquarters for American troops. ✉ *23 Nguyen Chi Thanh, Soc Trang* ☎ ✉ *Free.*

Kh'leang Pagoda

TEMPLE | The beautiful Khmer pagoda and nearby communal longhouse and meditation center are off the road behind graceful palm groves and huge banana trees. The richly worked interior of the pagoda houses extensive gilded wood carvings. Originally constructed in the 16th century, the pagoda was rebuilt in the French-Khmer style at the turn of the 20th century. It's an almost ethereal photo opportunity if you can snap monks posing in the foreground. ✉ *53 Ton Duc Thang, Soc Trang* ✉ *Free.*

Mahatup Pagoda (*Bat Pagoda, Chua Doi*)

TEMPLE | Legend has it that about 400 years ago Khmer monks constructed this pagoda, 3 km (2 miles) from Soc Trang, to honor the flying foxes (a type of bat) that live in the surrounding fruit trees. In Buddhism bats are considered sacred and, above all else, lucky. Strangely, the bats don't eat the fruit of the trees on which they live but feed on fruit trees several miles away. The best time to see these nocturnal creatures is dawn or dusk. Keep an eye out for the graves of five-hoofed pigs behind the temple; these creatures are believed to be bad luck so are given to the temple to be cared for until their death. ✉ *Van Ngoc Chinh, Chua Doi, Soc Trang* ✉ *Free.*

🍽 Restaurants

Bun Nuoc Leo Cay Nhan

$ | VIETNAMESE | This humble street food eatery is as good a place as any to try *bun nuoc leo*, a Mekong Delta specialty of broth made with fermented fish, served over fresh *bun* noodles, with slices of fish, roast pork, shrimp, and local greens. Pair it with a glass of sugarcane juice. **Known for:** no air-conditioning; bun nuoc leo; sugarcane juice. $ *Average main: d40,000* ✉ *Vo Dinh Sam, Soc Trang* ▭ *No credit cards.*

Café Que Toi

$ | VIETNAMESE | Offering very basic Vietnamese café fare, such as stir-fried noodles, pork and rice, and baguettes, this café associated with the Que Toi Hotel is a place more for satisfying hunger pangs than enjoying fine dining. Like most Vietnamese cafés, it's a place for people to meet, drink coffee, and smoke cigarettes. **Known for:** Vietnamese coffee; smoking allowed inside; basic Vietnamese café dishes. $ *Average main: d50,000* ✉ *278 Phu Loi, Soc Trang* ⊕ *quetoi.com.vn.*

🛏 Hotels

Ngoc Lan Hotel

$ | HOTEL | A clean and comfortable hotel, Ngoc Lan has a small, peaceful garden that's a great spot for relaxing. **Pros:** walking distance to Superdong ferry office; great value; walking distance to bus station. **Cons:** potential language barrier. $ *Rooms from: d300,000* ✉ *180 Le Hong Phong, Soc Trang* ☎ *0299/362–2696* ❙◐❙ *Free Breakfast* ⇩ *24 rooms.*

Que Toi Hotel

$ | HOTEL | The big selling point of the three-star Que Toi Hotel is its large, airy rooms and on-site swimming pool. **Pros:** rooms have TVs and a/c; a dip in the pool can be just the ticket after a long hot day of sightseeing; café and karaoke floor on site. **Cons:** oddly laid out bathrooms;

Mui Ca Mau National Park is set on a mangrove forest that's home to rare birds and reptiles.

rooms are a bit plain; can be noisy.
$ *Rooms from: d470,000* ☒ *278 Phu Loi, Soc Trang* ☎ *0299/627–8728* ⊕ *quetoi. com.vn* ⦿ *No Meals* ⤳ *55 rooms.*

Ca Mau

116 km (72 miles) southwest of Soc Trang, 360 km (224 miles) southwest of Ho Chi Minh City.

Ca Mau was once part of the Kingdom of Funan, then the Khmer Empire, and was only ceded back to Vietnamese control in 1757. On the Dai Dong River at the Phung Hiep Canal, some 50 km (31 miles) from the East Sea, it is the capital of Vietnam's southernmost province. Not many tourists make it this far down into the Mekong Delta, and this shows in the lack of foreigner-friendly infrastructure and English-language skills. The lure of sprawling Ca Mau is not the city itself, but the birdlife within the nearby *cajeput* (paperbark) and mangrove forests, and access to Vietnam's southernmost point within the Mui Ca Mau National Park.

GETTING HERE AND AROUND

Ca Mau Airport (camauairport.vn) is about 3 km (2 miles) from the center of town. Vietnam Aviation Service Company (VASCO) operates one flight a day each way between Ho Chi Minh City and Ca Mau. Expect to pay around 60,000d to get from the airport to the city center in a taxi. Ca Mau is pretty much the end of the line for bus service from Can Tho and Ho Chi Minh City. The main bus companies are Phuong Trang (Futa) and Kumho Samco, and they drop off at the main bus depot, near the airport on the eastern outskirts of town. Mai Linh taxis operate in Ca Mau.

BUS CONTACT Ca Mau Bus Station. ☒ *Ben Xe Ca Mau, Ly Thuong Kiet, Ca Mau.*

TAXI CONTACT Mai Linh Taxi. ☒ *Ca Mau* ☎ *0290/378–7878.*

Sights

Bac Lieu Bird Sanctuary

(*Vuon chim Bac Lieu*)

NATURE PRESERVE | In a mangrove forest about 5 km (3 miles) from the township of Bac Lieu is a large bird sanctuary that is home to 46 species of birds, including the endangered painted stork and small king cormorant. An estimated 40,000 birds live here, within a 951-acre mangrove ecosystem. The best time to visit is when the birds nest during the rainy season between May and October. Time a visit for dawn or dusk, when thousands of birds take to the skies. ✉ *Cao Van Lau, Bac Lieu* 🎫 *40,000d.*

Ca Mau Market

MARKET | The wet market here is small, but a bustling hive of activity from early in the morning to dusk. Few foreign tourists visit Ca Mau, so expect a lot of attention if you walk through. ✉ *Phan Boi Chau, Ca Mau.*

Mui Ca Mau National Park

NATURE PRESERVE | This 104-acre mangrove forest, which stretches to Vietnam's southernmost point, is a UNESCO World Biosphere Reserve that is home to many rare and endangered birds, animals, and reptiles. The national park is 110 km (68 miles) from Ca Mau City, about two hours by speedboat. No organized tours visit the park (at the time of writing), but it is possible to hire a speed boat to take you there. This should be arranged well in advance of arriving in Ca Mau (preferably from Ho Chi Minh City) and should include the services of an English-speaking guide. ✉ *Dat Mui Commune, Ngoc Hien* ☎ *0290/387–0545.*

U Minh Ha National Park

FOREST | The vast U Minh Ha National Park, 35 km (22 miles) from Ca Mau, contains swaths of swampland and pearl-white cajeput trees, also known as melaleuca or paperbark trees, as well as 32 mammal species, including deer and wild boar, and 74 bird species, including the endangered painted stork. A boat trip through the forest is breathtaking and eerily quiet. There are several "ecotourism" ventures in the forest, primarily in the Vo Voi area, which cater to domestic tourists rather than international visitors. Nevertheless, a visit can be interesting, but it's best organized well before arriving in Ca Mau. ✉ *U Minh District, Ca Mau* ☎ *0290/391–0029* 🎫 *10,000d.*

Restaurants

Huong Viet

$$ | **VIETNAMESE** | Popular with locals, this restaurant is designed to look like a bamboo village hut, and is a bit of a point-and-order eating adventure for visitors—the menu has no English, only a few photos on each page that vaguely correspond to the dishes listed below. The menu offers seafood, salad, beef, chicken, sparrow (*chim se*), and hotpot. **Known for:** photo menu; rustic setting; hotpot. [$] *Average main: d150,000* ✉ *126 Phan Ngoc Hien, Ca Mau* ☎ *0290/365–9999.*

★ Pho Xua

$$ | **VIETNAMESE** | This is a great find in Ca Mau, with nostalgic style (the name translates as "ancient street"), including quaint little wooden pavilions, a courtyard bonsai garden, and fish ponds. Serving Chinese-influenced dishes as well as Vietnamese cuisine, Pho Xua has a menu that contains English subtitles, although not much English is spoken by the staff. **Known for:** Chinese-influenced dishes; seafood; wooden pavilions. [$] *Average main: d165,000* ✉ *239 Phan Ngoc Hien, Ca Mau* ☎ *0290/367–7777 cell phone.*

🛏 Hotels

Anh Nguyet Hotel

$ | **HOTEL** | Anh Nguyet has spacious carpeted rooms with all the creature comforts, including air-conditioning, TV, fridge, writing desk, a small sitting area, not-too-hard beds, and slightly grimy bay windows; with the added advantage of staff that speaks some English. **Pros:** clean and comfortable; English-language ability of the reception staff; spacious rooms. **Cons:** bathrooms are a little tired; on-site karaoke can be loud, as can wedding parties held downstairs. $ *Rooms from: d550,000* ⊠ *207 Phan Ngoc Hien, Ca Mau* ☎ *0290/356–7666* ⊕ *www. anhnguyethotel.com* ↪ *83 rooms* ❙◯❙ *Free Breakfast.*

Dong Anh Hotel

$ | **HOTEL** | Small and serviceable, with heavy wooden furniture, Vietnamese-style bathrooms, and a central location, this is nevertheless a hotel for Vietnamese businessmen (who tend to smoke a lot). **Pros:** solid option if you don't mind business vibe; central location; within walking distance of local cafés and food stalls. **Cons:** rooms can smell smoky; can be noisy; very little English spoken. $ *Rooms from: d350,000* ⊠ *25 Tran Hung Dao, Ca Mau* ☎ *093/936–9369* ⊕ *donganhhotel.com.vn* ↪ *37 rooms* ❙◯❙ *No Meals.*

Muong Thanh Luxury Ca Mau Hotel

$$$ | **HOTEL** | This tidy hotel is the only branded hotel in town, with spacious rooms, understated decor, great views, a sizeable outdoor swimming pool, tennis courts, and a gym. **Pros:** outdoor swimming pool; relatively swanky compared to the other hotels in Ca Mau; great views. **Cons:** quite far from the city center; the spa isn't up to par; no room service. $ *Rooms from: d1,200,000* ⊠ *Unit C3A, Ca Mau Administration and Political Center, Ward 9, Ca Mau* ☎ *0290/222– 8888* ⊕ *luxurycamau.muongthanh.com* ↪ *177 rooms* ❙◯❙ *Free Breakfast.*

THE SOUTH-CENTRAL COAST AND HIGHLANDS

Updated by
James Pham

⊙ Sights   🍴 Restaurants   🛏 Hotels   🛍 Shopping   🍸 Nightlife

★★★★★   ★★★☆☆   ★★★☆☆   ★★★☆☆   ★★★☆☆

WELCOME TO THE SOUTH-CENTRAL COAST AND HIGHLANDS

TOP REASONS TO GO

★ **Nha Trang beach break.** Nha Trang's stretches of white-sand beaches are ideal for strolling and the warm waters are perfect for swimming, especially near Bai Dai Beach, where a string of food stalls sell the day's catch with a bucket of beer.

★ **Dalat, Le Petit Paris.** Head to the former French hill station of Dalat for long walks, serene lakes and pine forests, a visit to Emperor Bao Dai's summer palace, and fascinating temples.

★ **Vinh Hy Bay.** The South-Central coast's crown jewel, this lesser known beauty spot lies between the cities of Phan Rang and Cam Ranh, along a stretch of secluded road.

★ **Mui Ne resort hideaway.** Pamper yourself at one of Mui Ne's many five-star resorts, emerging only to view the spectacularly colored sand dunes at sunset or try your hand at kitesurfing.

★ **Coffee.** Buon Ma Thuot in the Central Highlands is Vietnam's coffee capital, and fantastic local coffee is available all through the region.

1 Phan Thiet. Heading northeast of Ho Chi Minh City by road or rail, the first notable stop is this fishing village, a thriving town full of smiling locals.

2 Mui Ne. The resort town of Mui Ne is the preferred beach getaway for expats living in Ho Chi Minh City, as well as a destination for thousands of international visitors seeking a beach break.

3 Nha Trang. The first major city you'll find heading north up the coast from Ho Chi Minh City is home to some of Vietnam's best beaches and dive sites.

4 Cat Tien National Park. Cat Tien National Park, which spans the lowlands and the start of the Truong Son mountain range, lies almost midway between Ho Chi Minh City and the mountain town of Dalat.

5 Dalat. This is the principal town of the southern Central Highlands region. It has an abundance of natural beauty and a good measure of kitschy tourist development targeted at the domestic market.

6 Lak Lake. The largest freshwater lake in the Central Highlands is set among picturesque rolling hills and reached via a beautiful journey through rural farmlands and mountain roads.

7 Buon Ma Thuot. The capital of the Central Highlands and Vietnam's coffee capital is a bustling town.

8 Pleiku. The capital of Gia Lai province is a practical mountain base.

9 Kon Tum. This is the best base for exploring the villages of the Central Highlands.

10 Quy Nhon. A seaside gem located midway between Nha Trang and Hoi An.

11 Quang Ngai. It's worth stopping at this town in order to visit the Son My Memorial at the site of the horrific My Lai Massacre.

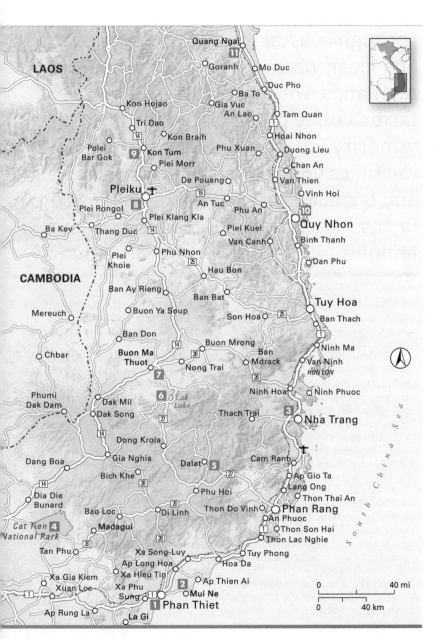

Vietnam's South-Central Coast and Highlands offer up a splendid contrast of attractions. Travel by road or rail through coastal towns with long beaches and clear, warm waters, to the cool misty highlands, with pine forests, flower farms, coffee plantations, and ethnic minority villages. Traveling by road or rail takes you past emerald rice paddies and terraces; Dr. Seuss–like dragonfruit farms; eerie salt flats; and resplendent temples.

The fishing village Phan Thiet and the resort town of Mui Ne are the first major coastal centers when heading northeast from Ho Chi Minh City. Although near-neighbors, the two towns are vastly different: Phan Thiet is a hive of local activity, with a picturesque fishing fleet and some cheap-and-cheerful seafood joints, while Mui Ne is a strip of hotels, B&Bs, and resorts fronting a narrow and often windy beach, popular with kitesurfers. The area is flanked by towering, desertlike sand dunes, belying the fact that the highlands are less than 160 km (100 miles) away. Farther north is the beach city of Nha Trang, with many luxurious five-star resorts and an enticing mix of eateries. Mui Ne and Nha Trang are joined by just over 322 km (200 miles) of stunning coastline, through the small cities of Phan Rang and Cam Ranh. High in the mountains to the west, where the air is crisp and cool, is Dalat, "Le Petit Paris." Founded by the French in the early 1900s as an escape from the steamy lowlands, the Central Highlands' biggest city still draws visitors from all over. Dalat can be the starting point for a deeper exploration of the Central Highlands, including the scenic Lak Lake, home to Vietnam's now retired elephant hunters, the coffee capital Buon Ma Thuot, the city of Pleiku where fighting raged during the war, and the riverside town of Kon Tum, a great base for treks to hill-tribe villages. Between Ho Chi Minh City and Dalat, at the base of the Central Highlands, is the Cat Tien National Park, home to gibbons, sun bears, and many other rare animals and birds. North of Nha Trang, on the coast, lies the truly hidden gem Quy Nhon. Just outside the coastal town of Quang Ngai lies a sobering reminder of the savage toll war often exacts on the innocent: the Son My Memorial, erected in memory of the victims of the My Lai massacre.

MAJOR REGIONS

The Southern Coast. The resort town of Mui Ne is the preferred beach getaway for expats living in Ho Chi Minh City, as well as a destination for thousands of international visitors seeking a beach break. For those interested in local life, Phan Thiet is a great place to explore and people-watch.

Nha Trang. The natural wonders of Nha Trang, which sits between a beautiful bay with warm, clear water studded with islands and green-clad mountains can be enjoyed by swimming, scuba diving, relaxing on the palm-lined beach, or exploring local waterfalls. More indulgent activities can be undertaken at the many resorts that overlook the bay.

The Central Highlands. Dalat, 1,500 meters above sea level, was founded in the early 1900s as a "sanatorium," or health retreat, for the French elite and remains a popular destination for local and international visitors. It is also the gateway to the Central Highlands, home to many ethnic minorities, dense jungle, waterfalls, and picturesque scenery. The towns of Buon Ma Thuot, Pleiku, and Kon Tum make good bases for exploration.

North of Nha Trang. Heading north from Nha Trang by rail or road takes you past some of the country's most picturesque scenery, including glimpses of lovely long white beaches, rocky coves, green-clad mountains, and bucolic countryside scenes. Quy Nhon is a quiet seaside city that's a great place to break the long 482-km (300-mile) journey between Nha Trang and Hoi An.

Planning

When to Go

The best time to visit Nha Trang is during the dry season, which usually runs from around January to May. It rains frequently in October, and November and can be chilly. With a temperate climate, Dalat is worth visiting any time of the year but provides the most relief from June through August, when the rest of the country is sweltering. Avoid visiting the coastal regions between October and mid-December during monsoon season.

Planning Your Time

Allocate a few days to Nha Trang—a visit to VinPearl Land takes a full day, as does an island tour or an excursion to one of the beautiful beaches outside of town. A beach break in Mui Ne or Quy Nhon should take several days. The major sights of Dalat can be taken in over a couple of days. The Central Highlands need more time, especially if planning to travel by road (or Easy Rider) between Lak Lake, Buon Ma Thuot, Pleiku, and Kon Tum. The back roads in this area are much more interesting and scenic than the main road, but take more time to traverse. Allow at least two days in Cat Tien National Park.

Getting Here and Around

AIR

Cam Ranh International Airport is 30 km (18 miles) from Nha Trang. Flights between Nha Trang and Ho Chi Minh City take about one hour. There are several flights a day to Dalat's Lien Khuong Airport from Ho Chi Minh City, Hanoi, Vinh, Danang, and more. Buon Ma Thuot is served from Ho Chi Minh City, Hanoi, and Danang, Vinh, and Haiphong. The former U.S. airbase at Pleiku is now the Pleiku Airport, which welcomes several flights a day from Ho Chi Minh City and Hanoi, and one flight a day from Danang. Quy Nhon has direct flights between from Ho Chi Minh City and Hanoi.

AIRPORT CONTACTS Cam Ranh International Airport. ✉ *Nha Trang* ⊕ *www.nhatrangairport.com.* **Lien Khuong Airport.** ✉ *QL20, Duc Trong, Dalat* ☎ *0263/384–3373* ⊕ *www.vietnamairport.vn/lienkhuongairport.* **Phu Cat Airport (Quy Nhon).** ✉ *Cat Tan,*

Phu Cat, Qui Nhon ☎ *0256/382–2953*
⊕ *www.phucatairport.vn.*

BUS

Daily and nightly buses run between Nha
Trang and Ho Chi Minh (some with a stop
in Mui Ne). The 10-hour trip costs around
400,000d. Several buses head north to
Hanoi, with stops in Hoi An and Hue,
or inland to Dalat by connecting in Phan
Rang. The trip between Nha Trang and
Hoi An takes about 10 hours and costs
around 250,000d. Sleeper buses have
bunk beds. Bus tickets are sold at most
tour offices and hotels throughout the
country. The northern station in Nha Trang
services towns in the Central Highlands,
including Buon Ma Thuot and Quang
Ngai. From the southern station, buses
depart for major centers throughout
Vietnam, including south to Ho Chi Minh
City, north to Hanoi, and west to the Central Highlands. Buses also run regularly
between Dalat and Ho Chi Minh City,
taking seven to nine hours during the
daytime and a slightly speedier (and scar-
ier) six hours by overnight bus. If you opt
for an overnight bus, double-check it has
sleeper beds rather than seats. A coach
between Dalat and Ho Chi Minh City
costs around 200,000d with limousine
buses and mini-vans costing more.

BUS CONTACTS Mai Linh Express. ⊠ *188
Nguyen Tat Thanh, Tan Lap, Buon Ma
Thuot* ☎ *1900/969–681* ⊕ *www.mailin-
hexpress.vn.***North Nha Trang Bus Station.**
⊠ *1 St. 2/4, Nha Trang* ☎ *0258/383–8788.*
Phuong Trang Bus Company. ⊠ *274–276 De
Tham, Ho Chi Minh City* ☎ *0283/838–
6852* ⊕ *www.futabus.vn.***South Nha
Trang Bus Station.** ⊠ *Km 6, 23/10 St., Nha
Trang, Nha Trang* ⊹ *near Metro Cash &
Carry* ☎ *0258/8356–2626.***Thanh Buoi bus
company.** ⊠ *266–268 Le Hong Phong
St., District 5, HCMC, Ho Chi Minh City*
☎ *1900–6079* ⊕ *www.thanhbuoibus.
com.vn.*

CAR

Hiring a private driver will cost you about
2,000,000d per day and is best arranged
through your hotel tour desk. Private cars
are much easier to organize for midrange
trips, with operators able to quote set
fees for certain routes. For example,
the mountainous, winding, but exceed-
ingly beautiful 140-km (87-mile) journey
from Nha Trang to Dalat costs around
2,500,000d total per car for the four- to
five-hour journey. From Dalat, Lak Lake
is an easy 150-km (93-mile) drive, again
along some winding mountain roads,
which often provide stunning views
of verdant valleys. Lak Lake to Buon
Ma Thuot is another easy drive, again
through very pretty countryside.

TRAIN

The Reunification Express runs six times
a day between Ho Chi Minh City and
Hanoi, stopping at five train stations in
the South-Central Coast region: Binh Thuan (you can take a taxi from here to Phan
Thiet or Mui Ne); Thap Cham (gateway
to Dalat); Nha Trang; Dieu Tri (10 km [6
miles] from Quy Nhon); and Quang Ngai.
From Ho Chi Minh City, the train takes
about 3½ hours to Binh Thuan, another
two hours to Thap Cham, another two
hours to Nha Trang, just less than four
hours from Nha Trang to Dieu Tri in Quy
Nhon, and just less than three hours
from Dieu Tri to Quang Ngai. A separate
twice-daily train service runs between
Ho Chi Minh City and Phan Thiet, which
takes about 3½ hours. Tickets begin at
$8, or 180,000d. Tickets can be pur-
chased online (⊕ *vietnam-railway.com*)
and at train stations, but by far the easiest option is to ask your hotel to arrange
tickets, rather than a travel agent. It's
best to book several days in advance to
ensure you get a comfortable seat or bed
(go for soft every time), and there's usually a small fee—44,000d or less—to get
your tickets delivered to your hotel.

Golden Express Train
✉ 1 Nguyen Thong, Ho Chi Minh City
☎ 0283/826–1685 ⊕ www.saigongolden-train.com.

Restaurants

Nha Trang and Mui Ne are famous for their seafood, which can be enjoyed local-style, in a noisy shack surrounded by beer-chugging Vietnamese, or in more sophisticated surrounds like a resort setting overlooking the beach. Outside of Nha Trang and Mui Ne, dining options are more basic; seafood is still the specialty along the coast, but in the Central Highlands the focus is on the locally grown vegetables and free-range village-raised chicken and pork. Local specialties are candied fruit, jam, artichoke tea, and Dalat wine. Beyond Dalat, Nha Trang, and Mui Ne, dining choices are mostly local but incredibly tasty, particularly in the tasting treasure trove that is Quy Nhon.

Hotels

Accommodation in this region runs the gamut from very basic government-run one-star hotels to backpacker hostels to international-standard five-star hotels with all the bells and whistles you could possibly imagine. Nha Trang and Mui Ne have, in recent years, experienced a boom in fancy beach resorts, while high up in Dalat, local entrepreneurs have been focusing on smaller boutique properties that take advantage of the area's cooler climate and natural beauty. Outside these centers the offerings are mixed, with many run-down budget hotels and a surprising number of quirky choices, from traditional long houses to charming new high-quality hotels. The coastlines both north and south of Nha Trang are shaping up to be some of Vietnam's next beach hot spots.

What It Costs

	$	$$	$$$	$$$$
RESTAURANTS	Under 60,000d	60,000d–150,000d	151,000d–250,000d	over 250,000d
HOTELS	Under 600,000d	600,000d–900,000d	901,000d–1,500,000d	over 1,500,000d

Phan Thiet

192 km (119 miles) northeast of Ho Chi Minh City.

Phan Thiet is a charming fishing town divided by the Phan Thiet River, where the colorful feline-eyed fishing fleet is moored. The town has some interesting sights and some excellent people-watching opportunities. It's a great place to see local life in action at a much slower pace than the major cities. Until 1692, the Cham controlled the area, as evidenced by the Cham towers. Many locals are ethnically Cham, descendants of these former rulers.

GETTING HERE AND AROUND
Two daily trains run from Ho Chi Minh City to Phan Thiet, which leaves the main north–south rail line at Binh Thuan. The journey takes four hours and there are many *xe om* (motorbike taxis) and taxis at the station to take you into Phan Thiet or to the resort town of Mui Ne 25 km (15½ miles) away (a 30- to 40-minute drive). It's also possible to take the main Ho Chi Minh City–Hanoi train, the Reunification Express, alight at Binh Thuan station, and get a taxi or xe om to your destination. Phan Thiet is 16 km (10 miles) from Binh Thuan and Mui Ne is 38 km (24 miles) away.

Note that the travel times advised by many bus companies can vary wildly: without traffic it's about four hours by road from Ho Chi Minh City to Phan Thiet and Mui Ne, not the three hours advertised by some companies. When traffic is bad it can take

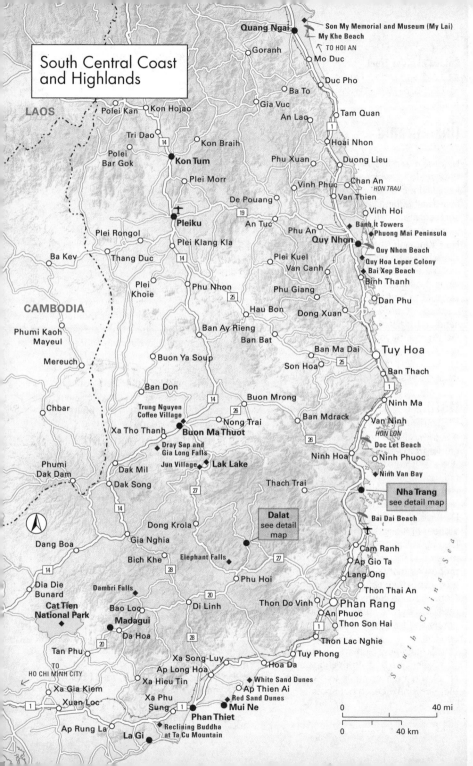

Inside Van Thuy Tu temple (The Whale Temple) is a 22-meter-long whale skeleton.

up to seven hours. Coaches and sleeper buses stop in Mui Ne and then continue north towards Dalat and Nha Trang.

There have been plans for the construction of an airport in Phan Thiet since 2009 but to date, plans have yet to materialize.

TAXI CONTACT Mai Linh Taxi. ✉ *Phan Thiet* ☎ *0252/3838–3838* ⊕ *www.mailinh.vn.*

TRAIN CONTACT Phan Thiet Railway Station. ✉ *Phong Nam, Phan Thiet* ☎ *62/383–3952.*

 Sights

Doi Duong Beach

BEACH | The narrow Doi Duong Beach, at the end of Nguyen Tat Thanh Street, is not the prettiest in the country, but it is well maintained and is loved by the locals anyway. It has a fantastic view of the bay and Mui Ne in the distance to the north. Crowds descend in the early morning and late afternoons, when the weather is not so hot. Couples stroll along the paved beachside walkway, families picnic in the adjacent park, and everyone eats snacks from the many itinerant food vendors. **Amenities:** food and drink. **Best for:** walking. ✉ *Nguyen Tat Thanh, Phan Thiet.*

Duc Thanh School

NOTABLE BUILDING | Ho Chi Minh (then known as Nguyen That Thanh) himself supposedly taught here in 1910 as he was making his way down to Saigon, from where he set sail for Paris and other foreign shores. History records him as teaching Chinese, Vietnamese, and martial arts to the second grade. The school is a beautifully tended and unusual monument, with interesting little placards marking out where Uncle Ho rested and read. ✉ *39 Trung Nhi, Phan Thiet* 🎟 *Free* 🕐 *Closed Mon.*

Ho Chi Minh Museum

HISTORY MUSEUM | This riverfront museum traces the life of Ho Chi Minh from his humble beginnings to his death in 1969, with displays of objects from his life. Some exhibits relate to the history of Phan Thiet and there are also some preserved specimens of local wildlife and large squid. The museum was built in 1986 on the site of Ho Chi Minh's former home, when he was a teacher at the Duc Thang School across the road. ⊠ *39 Trung Nhi, Phan Thiet* ☎ *0252/382–0574* 🎫 *Free* ⊗ *Closed Mon.*

Po Sah Inu Towers

RUINS | These three crumbling towers, relics from the 8th century when the Cham empire ruled this part of Vietnam, are not the best examples of such ruins—the towers in Nha Trang and Hoi An are more extensive and better preserved even though they pale when compared to the magnificence of Angkor Wat in Cambodia—but still worth spending an hour or so exploring. The towers, in front of a working monastery, are about 7 km (4½ miles) east of Phan Thiet on Ong Hoang Hill. Even if ancient history does not appeal, the hilltop where the towers are situated offers possibly the most panoramic view of the city of Phan Thiet and the ocean. ⊠ *Ong Hoang Hill, Phan Thiet* ⊹ *Off Nguyen Thong St. en route to Mui Ne* 🎫 *15,000d (an extra 5,000d for motorbike parking).*

Reclining Buddha at Ta Cu Mountain

(*Chua Nui Ta Cu*)

MONUMENT | The largest reclining Buddha in Southeast Asia is on Ta Cu Mountain, which dominates the skyline in an otherwise low-lying landscape. Located about 28 km (17 miles) southwest of Phan Thiet, the 49-meter-long and 18-meter-high white concrete Buddha is at the top of a large temple complex, past a range of other deities, and offers stunning views of the surrounding land. Access is via a cable car that provides stunning views of the area and then a long haul up some steep stairs. There are usually plenty of pilgrims praying and lighting incense for all of the deities, including the reclining Buddha (Thich Ca Nhap Niet Ban), depicted as he enters Nirvana and shown with the most serene smile on his face. Several years ago, when renovation work was underway, every visitor to the

site was asked to carry two bricks to the top of the complex for general absolution as well as to assist the construction workers. ⊠ *Hwy. 1A, Thuan Nam, Phan Thiet* ⊹ *Exit Hwy. 1 on Nguyen Van Linh* 🎫 *20,000d.*

Van Thuy Tu (The Whale Temple)

TEMPLE | The main attraction at this small temple, built in 1762, is the 22-meter-long whale skeleton. The temple honors the deity Nam Hai (the whale), who is believed to protect fishermen. There are two sections to the temple, a large room that houses the complete skeleton and a small temple with an interesting and colorful miniature ship and glass-fronted cabinets containing assorted whalebones. ⊠ *54 Ngu Ong, Phan Thiet* 🎫 *15,000d.*

🍴 Restaurants

Banh Xeo Cay Phuong

$ | **VIETNAMESE** | **FAMILY** | Opened in 1995, Banh Xeo Cay Phuong serves Central Vietnam–style *banh xeo* (sizzling pancakes), from 4:30 pm to 10 pm. A default order at this one-dish, family-run, off-street eatery is four palm-sized pancakes, but you can order as many as you like. **Known for:** authentic feel; iconic national dish; quaint environment. 💲 *Average main: d40,000* ⊠ *49 Tuyen Quang, Phan Thiet* ▭ *No credit cards.*

Khoa Cafe

$ | **INTERNATIONAL** | This contemporary café is a head-turner with its open-plan design, pop art posters, and semi-industrial decor. Spacious and centrally located, it's most notable for its very respectable Western-style coffee and freshly squeezed juices, as well as a small selection of cakes, at very reasonable prices. **Known for:** laid-back atmosphere; stylish decor; respectable Italian coffee. 💲 *Average main: d40,000* ⊠ *182 Thu Khoa Huan, Phan Thiet* ☎ *091/399–5868.*

Quan Cha Cuon

$ | **VIETNAMESE** | This basic spot specializes in roll-your-own fresh spring rolls. One serving includes a plate of various cuts of meat, sliced boiled egg, and Vietnamese sausage, a plate of herbs and cucumber sticks, a plate of fried spring rolls, and a stack of stiff rice paper. **Known for:** DIY dishes; jovial staff; tangy dipping sauce. [$] *Average main: d35,000* ✉ *122 Tuyen Quang, Phan Thiet* 💳 *No credit cards.*

Quan 49

$$ | **VIETNAMESE** | A basic seafood eatery fronting a river lined with fishing boats, Quan 49 serves barbecued seafood, conch salad, and, when in season, *dong* lizard. **Known for:** ice-cold beer and no-fuss food; local-style nightlife; view of fishing boats. [$] *Average main: d150,000* ✉ *49 Pham Van Dong, Phan Thiet* 💳 *No credit cards.*

Hotels

Green Organic Villas

$$$$ | **RESORT** | **FAMILY** | A tranquil and eco-friendly resort one hour from Phan Thiet, the beachfront Green Organic Villas has only two private air-conditioned villas, each with two bedrooms, two bathrooms, and a private pool. **Pros:** very relaxing atmosphere; discreet and attentive service; pool, open-air cinema, restaurant, and library on site. **Cons:** limited dining options outside of resort; isolated; must rent entire villa. [$] *Rooms from: d6,500,000* ✉ *Thon Tien Phu, Phan Thiet* ☎ *62/3846–546, 091/746–7068* 🌐 *greenorganicvillas.com* 🍴 *Free Breakfast* 🛏 *2 villas.*

Ocean Dunes Resort

$$$ | **RESORT** | **FAMILY** | An older but well-maintained property fronting a private beach, Ocean Dunes Resort has everything you're looking for in a resort—ocean views, white beaches, palm trees, beach bar, pool, spacious rooms—and all rooms have private balconies. **Pros:** spacious grounds; comfortable rooms with lovely views of the local fishing fleet; pool setup is great of families with kids. **Cons:** service standards are local, rather than international; requires a taxi to go into town; pool closes at 6:30 pm. [$] *Rooms from: d1,300,000* ✉ *1 Ton Duc Thang, Phan Thiet* ☎ *0252/382–2393* 🍴 *No Meals* 🛏 *123 rooms.*

Truong Thinh Hotel

$ | **HOTEL** | A basic hotel close to many local eateries, Truong Thinh Hotel is spacious, comfortable, central, and affordable. **Pros:** easy on the wallet; central location; air-conditioned rooms. **Cons:** can get noisy when karaoke is happening. [$] *Rooms from: d350,000* ✉ *26–28 Tuyen Quang, Phan Thiet* ☎ *0252/383–4567* 🌐 *truongthinhhotel.com.vn* 🍴 *No Meals* 🛏 *20 rooms.*

White Sand Resort

$$$$ | **RESORT** | **FAMILY** | One of the first resorts you'll encounter on your way out of Phan Thiet towards Mui Ne, White Sand is great for those seeking a bit of serenity. **Pros:** feels very secluded; private, sheltered beach; pet-friendly. **Cons:** some furnishings slightly dated; requires a taxi to the main tourist area; compact layout. [$] *Rooms from: d2,600,000* ✉ *Km 8, Nguyen Thong, Phu Hai, Phan Thiet* ☎ *0252/374–1175* 🌐 *www.whitesandresort.com* 🍴 *Free Breakfast* 🛏 *26 rooms.*

Mui Ne

225 km (140 miles) east of Ho Chi Minh City, 25 km (16 miles) east of Phan Thiet.

Twenty years ago, Mui Ne was not much more than a deserted road running along an equally deserted beach. Now there's a 15-km (9-mile) stretch of resorts, restaurants, and souvenir shops. Mui Ne town itself doesn't draw the crowds, but you may want to stop and capture the astoundingly large fishing fleet parked by the shore. The coastal stretch as a whole is a perfect reprieve from the buzz of Ho Chi Minh City or the chilly weather in nearby Dalat. For those traveling north of Ho Chi Minh, it's the first major stop and therefore the first taste of life outside the city. For those traveling south, it's often the last fix of sun, sea, and sand. Visitors usually hole up in luxurious resorts, boutique hotels, backpacking dorms, and even camping spots. The increasing popularity of Mui Ne has seen a miniboom in food and beverage options, and there are now plenty of respectable Western dining spots, as well as the popular local seafood and barbecue. In recent years, Mui Ne has also become an international destination for kitesurfers, who converge during the windy season from November to April.

GETTING HERE AND AROUND

Mui Ne usually takes at least four hours by bus or minivan from Ho Chi Minh City, although traffic in and out of the city can often delay arrival. The train is a comfortable alternative; the four-hour journey will get you to Phan Thiet Station, 25 km (16 miles) from Mui Ne. The final leg is easy to do by taxi, and many taxi drivers await the arrival of the daily train. Try to choose the Mai Linh taxis, which use a fair rate and a meter. Many hotels will offer a transfer service from the station if you ask, and will also be able to arrange bicycle or scooter rental. Be aware that Mui Ne is a hot spot for local police to catch foreigners driving illegally, so think twice before getting on a motorbike or scooter and make sure documents such as licenses and insurance are in order.

◉ Sights

Fairy Stream (*Suoi Tien*)
NATURE SIGHT | While it may not quite live up to its intriguing name, the highlight of this kitschy attraction is the miniature Grand Canyon-like cliffs that border the stream and whose red and brown layers create a nice backdrop for photos. It takes about 20 minutes to wade along the ankle- and knee-deep stream to a small waterfall that flows into waist-deep sections. Along the way, enterprising locals have set up make-shift rest stops, serving cool drinks and some snacks. There can sometimes

be a fair amount of trash at the start of the stream, but it gets cleaner the farther you go. ■ TIP→ Be aware that adults and children offering shoe-minding or guiding along the stream will expect to be paid, so negotiate a price first, or plan to tip about $1. ⊠ *12 Huynh Thuc Khang, Phan Thiet* 🖃 *15,000d.*

Red Sand Dunes
NATURE SIGHT | Around 15 minutes from the tourist strip of Mui Ne, the Red Sand Dunes are a very strange sight in a country renowned for its jungles, and provide great sunrise and sunset views. However, these are peak times for busloads of tour groups, so if you're after some more quiet, visit around 4 pm when the weather begins to cool a little and the sea breeze picks up. Children offer plastic mats for rent so tourists can slide down the dunes. Mats cost roughly 20,000d for an hour, plus tip. ⊠ *1 Hon Rom (off Vo Nguyen Giap)* 🖃 *Free.*

White Sand Dunes
NATURE SIGHT | These stunning, desert-like, white sand dunes are best seen at sunrise (before the noisy quad bikes start operating). If the lotus flowers are in bloom, take a photo as you approach the dunes of the adjacent blue lake. The pink flowers there, all backed by the white dunes, are especially striking. If you're more of a thrill-seeker, the quad bikes are a fun way to blow off some steam in the sand. However, the vendors who rent out the quads can be very pushy; beware of the "guides" who jump on the back of your quad who will demand a hefty tip at the end of the trip. The dunes are about an hour's drive from Mui Ne's main tourist area. ⊠ *Hoa Thang* 🖃 *15,000d.*

⑪ Restaurants

Breeze Restaurant and Bar
$$ | INTERNATIONAL | Located high up on a hill above the tourist strip, this restaurant serves a range of Western dishes as well as great local seafood. Use of the pool in the surrounding resort is free for paying customers. **Known for:** idyllic atmosphere;

generous range of dishes; excellent view of Mui Ne. $ *Average main: d140,000* ✉ *Mui Ne Hills Resort, 69 Nguyen Dinh Chieu* ☎ *0252/374–1682* 🌐 *www.muine-hills.com/breeze-restaurant.*

Cay Bang

$$$ | **VIETNAMESE** | About a mile outside the main tourist strip, Cay Bang commands a prime location right on the oceanfront, with a great view of Ong Dia Rock and the hordes of surrounding kitesurfers. Popular with tour groups, the unpretentious two-story local joint with seating for up to 1,000 guests specializes in live seafood cooked to order, including the local chisel fish (*ca duc*). **Known for:** popularity with locals; splendid oceanfront location; local specialty dishes. $ *Average main: d250,000* ✉ *2–4 Nguyen Dinh Chieu* ☎ *0252/384–7009* 🌐 *www.facebook.com/CayBangPT.*

Cham Garden Restaurant

$$$ | **ASIAN** | The small, romantic, fine-dining restaurant inside the boutique Cham Villas Resort adds an extra touch of class to a visit to Mui Ne. Overseen by a German chef, the kitchen prepares a range of Vietnamese and international dishes, including a nashi pear and shrimp cocktail, beef-and-prawn skewers, and spicy lemongrass beef served with fried *thien ly* flowers. **Known for:** spicy lemongrass beef; candlelit dining; upmarket standard. $ *Average main: d200,000* ✉ *Cham Villas Resort, 32 Nguyen Dinh Chieu* ☎ *0252/374–1234* 🌐 *www.facebook.com/chamgardenmuine.*

El Latino

$$ | **MEXICAN** | A Mui Ne favorite, El Latino serves up authentic, homemade Mexican eats with a very chill vibe. Warm and cozy with exposed brick, painted murals, and loads of color, the kitchen nevertheless takes its food very seriously, making fresh tortillas, breads, brownies to accompany the mainly slow-cooked meats that will melt in your mouth. **Known for:** friendly, relaxed vibe; authentic flavors; good value. $ *Average main: 120,000* ✉ *131A Nguyen Dinh Chieu* ☎ *0252/374–3595* 🌐 *www.facebook.com/el.latino.muine.vietnam* 🕒 *Closed Wed.*

Ganesh

$$ | **INDIAN** | Ganesh serves delicious North Indian and tandoori dishes and excellent naan bread. In its homey restaurant in the heart of Mui Ne's tourist strip, Ganesh offers a sometimes-welcome and comforting break from Vietnamese cuisine. **Known for:** perfect comfort food; top-notch curries; relaxed environment. $ *Average main: d140,000* ✉ *57 Nguyen Dinh Chieu* ☎ *0252/374–1330.*

★ **Joe's Cafe**

$$ | **INTERNATIONAL** | A staple in Mui Ne for live music and great food, Joe's Cafe's cavernous property is located right on the seashore in the heart of the strip. Filled with greenery and dappled sunlight, Joe's is open from early morning until late at night, so whether you're after a sea-view breakfast or dinner and a live music show, Joe's is a great place to be. **Known for:** serene ocean view; live music nightly; hearty Western dinners. $ *Average main: d150,000* ✉ *86 Nguyen Dinh Chieu* ☎ *62/384–7177* 🌐 *www.joescafemuine.com.*

Modjo Bar and Restaurant

$$ | **EUROPEAN** | This Franco-Swiss-owned resto-bar serves great European staples including Swiss fondue in a sophisticated, contemporary location right on the main strip. Sip wine and nibble on a board of cheeses and charcuterie in the fan-cooled space backed by a jazzy soundtrack. **Known for:** hot stone grilled meats; wine, cheese, and charcuterie; Central European staples. $ *Average main: d250,000* ✉ *139C Nguyen Dinh Chieu* ☎ *091/818–9014* 🌐 *www.facebook.com/modjo.muine.*

Did You Know?

Mui Ne is Vietnam's top kitesurfing destination, but it's also home to some spectacular red and white sand dunes.

★ Pit Stop Food Court

$$ | INTERNATIONAL | True to its motto of "Eat, drink, relax, be happy", Pit Stop Food Court is shaping up to be "the" place to eat and hang out in Mui Ne. Order anything from seafood hot pot and lobster grilled with cheese to Hungarian goulash and fish tacos and find a seat under the swaying palms with sweeping views of the water. **Known for:** relaxed vibe with lots of seating; central location by the beach; wide selection of international cuisines. $ *Average main: 150,000* ✉ *122 Nguyen Dinh Chieu* ☎ *092/841–9988* ⊕ *www.facebook.com/pitstopvietnam.*

Ratinger Lowe

$$ | GERMAN | Once the in-house restaurant at the Cham Villa resort, Ratinger Lowe's traditional German fare became so popular the eatery had to move to larger premises next door. The owner, who has been officially named the Phan Thiet culinary ambassador of his hometown of Ratingen, oversees a bountiful menu of German specialty dishes as a well as a selection of international and Vietnamese hits. **Known for:** good selection of imported German beers; charming rustic decor; superb Wiener schnitzel. $ *Average main: d200,000* ✉ *32 Nguyen Dinh Chieu* ☎ *0252/374–1234* ⊕ *www.ratinger-loewe.com.*

★ Sandals

$$ | INTERNATIONAL | Inside Sailing Club Resort Mui Ne in a high-ceilinged Bali-style pavilion overlooking the beach and the East Sea, Sandals is considered one of Mui Ne's best dining options even if you're not staying there. Sandals invites guests to linger a little bit longer with an excellent wine selection and a kitchen which can adapt to dietary requirements, including vegan and gluten-free options. **Known for:** elevated comfort food; fantastic fusion dishes; stunning sunsets. $ *Average main: d240,000* ✉ *Sailing Club Resort Mui Ne, 24 Nguyen Dinh Chieu* ☎ *0252/384–7440* ⊕ *www.sailingclubmuine.com.*

Sindbad

$$ | MIDDLE EASTERN | Fresh, tasty, and quite fabulous kebabs, salads, and dips: Sindbad's short and sweet menu is widely celebrated in the area. Everything on it is top quality. **Known for:** great value; unrivaled beef döner kebabs; speedy service. $ *Average main: d80,000* ✉ *133 Nguyen Dinh Chieu* ☎ *0359/328–950.*

☕ Coffee and Quick Bites

★ B&B Café

$ | CAFÉ | One of Mui Ne's best kept secrets is the beachside B&B Café. It feels out of place on the expansive grounds of Ca Ty Resort, but you can hang out here all day watching the kitesurfers and sipping reasonably priced fresh squeezed juices, blended coffees, and flavored sodas in shaded huts steps from the beach. **Known for:** lots of space to relax; reasonably priced drinks; prime beachside location. $ *Average main: d35,000* ✉ *Ca Ty Resort, 6 Nguyen Dinh Chieu, Phan Thiet* ✛ *Down side street leading to beach at Ca Ty Resort* ⊕ *www.facebook.com/cafecaty* ▭ *No credit cards.*

🛏 Hotels

Ananda Resort

$$$ | RESORT | In so far as luxury resorts in Mui Ne go, this is one of the more basic options, something which is reflected in the lower price. **Pros:** swimming pool, water-sports center, and restaurant on site; right on the beach; excellent location. **Cons:** service and amenities not as slick as some of the pricier resorts in Mui Ne. $ *Rooms from: d1,200,000* ✉ *48 Nguyen Dinh Chieu* ☎ *0252/374–1692* ⊕ *www.ananda.vn* ⤶ *28 rooms* ⃝ *No Meals.*

★ Anantara Mui Ne Resort and Spa

$$$$ | RESORT | Refined luxury and attentive welcoming service are the hallmarks of the Anantara Mui Ne Resort and Spa, the only international 5-star resort in Mui Ne. The beachfront resort boasts beautifully landscaped grounds (including

a lotus pond), a stunning infinity pool with a swim-up bar, an on-site spa, and an exceptionally wide beach. **Pros:** has a swim-up bar, spa, and exceptionally wide beach; stunning setting; staff really does go the extra mile. **Cons:** not pet-friendly; paths are dimly lit in deference to local fauna; no buggy service. $ *Rooms from: d3,600,000* ⊠ *12A Nguyen Dinh Chieu* ☎ *0252/374–1888* ⊕ *www.anantara.com/ en/mui-ne* ⫟ *Free Breakfast* ⤴ *90 rooms.*

Cham Villas

$$$$ | RESORT | This is an intimate, luxurious private paradise on the beach, with thatched-roof bungalows and villas set in a lush 2½-acre garden of coconut trees, orchids, tropical plants, and Cham-style sculptures. **Pros:** central location; charming setting; villas have private patios with daybeds. **Cons:** one of the pricier options in Mui Ne. $ *Rooms from: d3,500,000* ⊠ *32 Nguyen Dinh Chieu* ☎ *0252/374– 1234* ⊕ *www.chamvillas.com* ⫟ *Free Breakfast* ⤴ *18 villas.*

Full Moon Village

$$$$ | RESORT | Along a quiet beachside road 20 minutes outside of Mui Ne is the plush Full Moon Village, a collection of spacious, elegantly furnished one-, two-, and three-bedroom bungalows. **Pros:** beautiful grounds with a large swimming pool and beach bar; water sports available; a regular shuttle bus runs into Mui Ne proper. **Cons:** isolated location. $ *Rooms from: d2,700,000* ⊠ *Suoi Nuoc Beach* ☎ *0252/383–6099* ⊕ *www.fullmoon-vil-lage.com* ⫟ *Free Breakfast* ⤴ *17 villas.*

Grace Boutique Resort

$$$ | RESORT | A family-run three-story resort on the beach, Grace Boutique Resort provides a stupendously warm welcome. **Pros:** has an infinity pool, a tropical garden, and on-site restaurant with sea views; very helpful staff; reasonably priced. **Cons:** pool is small. $ *Rooms from: d1,900,000* ⊠ *144A Nguyen Dinh Chieu* ☎ *0252/374–3357* ⊕ *www.grace-boutiqueresort.com* ⤴ *24 rooms* ⫟ *Free Breakfast.*

La Marina Hotel

$$ | HOTEL | Located just a stone's throw from a less populated stretch of beach, and about 1 km (½ mile) from the busiest part of the tourist strip, La Marina is a modern boutique hotel with a bohemian feel. **Pros:** close to fairy stream and a local food market; good value; shaded outdoor swimming pool. **Cons:** could be maintained better. $ *Rooms from: d1,000,000* ⊠ *246/2b Nguyen Dinh Chieu* ☎ *0252/374–3848* ⊕ *www. lamarinamuine.com* ⫟ *Free Breakfast* ⤴ *18 rooms.*

Mui Ne Backpacker Village

$ | RESORT | With a mixture of value-for-money private rooms and 4-12 bed dormitories, Mui Ne Backpacker Village is a smash hit among visitors to Mui Ne on a budget. **Pros:** excellent social space; great value for money; exceptionally clean rooms and facilities. **Cons:** noisy in the evening. $ *Rooms from: d450,000 for private double room* ⊠ *137 Nguyen Dinh Chieu* ☎ *888/222–048* ⊕ *www. muinebackpackervillage.com* ⤴ *30 rooms* ⫟ *No Meals.*

Poshanu Resort

$$$ | RESORT | A Champa-influenced resort with a wonderful location overlooking the bay and Ong Dia Cape, Poshanu Resort is a tranquil getaway from the hustle and bustle of modern-day Vietnam. **Pros:** spacious rooms in bungalow-type buildings; one of the better priced resorts in the area; has a bar, restaurant, pool, spa, and spotless private beach. **Cons:** quite far from the main tourist area; lots of steps from the road down to the beach. $ *Rooms from: d2,300,000* ⊠ *Quarter 5, Phu Hai* ☎ *0252/381–2233* ⊕ *www.poshanuresort. com* ⤴ *24 rooms* ⫟ *Free Breakfast.*

★ Sailing Club Resort Mui Ne

$$$$ | RESORT | A stylish, tranquil boutique resort with a youthful vibe set in tropical gardens and located right on the oceanfront, Sailing Club Resort Mui Ne has beautifully designed, contemporary rooms, all with their own private terrace.

Pros: excellent, personalized service; central location, within walking distance to cafés and restaurants; free bicycles for guests to explore the local area. **Cons:** no gym; pricey; smallish swimming pool. $ *Rooms from: d3,200,000* ✉ *24 Nguyen Dinh Chieu* ☎ *0252/384–7440* 🌐 *www.sailingclubmuine.com* 🍴 *Free Breakfast* 🛏 *31 rooms.*

Serenity By The Sea

$$$ | **HOTEL** | **FAMILY** | This elegant, beautifully designed property is located right in the middle of the main tourist area and offers a sea-view swimming pool where you can watch kitesurfers flit about the bay. **Pros:** central location; beautiful new building; warm and considerate staff. **Cons:** depending on the tide, it isn't always possible to swim in the ocean. $ *Rooms from: d1,200,000* ✉ *88 Nguyen Dinh Chieu* ☎ *888/222–048* 🌐 *www.serenitybytheseamuine.com* 🍴 *Free Breakfast* 🛏 *17 rooms.*

Shades Resort Mui Ne

$$$ | **RESORT** | **FAMILY** | Run by a New Zealand couple, this small and friendly resort is homey with spacious and stylish accommodation options—studio rooms or self-contained apartments with private gardens. **Pros:** wonderful service; central location; great seafront setting. **Cons:** small pool; limited breakfast choices; some rooms aren't so private. $ *Rooms from: d1,100,000* ✉ *98A Nguyen Dinh Chieu* ☎ *0252/374–3236* 🌐 *www.shadesmuine.com* 🍴 *Free Breakfast* 🛏 *10 rooms.*

★ Victoria Phan Thiet Beach Resort & Spa

$$$$ | **RESORT** | **FAMILY** | With individual, thatch-roofed bungalows set on 7 hectares of lush gardens right along the 450m-long beach, Victoria Phan Thiet Beach Resort & Spa has all the requirements for a relaxing resort holiday, including two swimming pools (one is an infinity pool), a kids' club, night-lit tennis courts, lawn badminton, beach volleyball, and an excellent in-house spa. **Pros:** free use of bicycles to explore; great facilities including free kayaking and buggy service; service is truly excellent. **Cons:** taxi required to get to main strip; in-room furnishings slightly dated; beach is long but not very wide. $ *Rooms from: d3,000,000* ✉ *Km 9, Phu Hai* ☎ *0252/381–3000* 🌐 *www.victoriahotels.asia* 🍴 *Free Breakfast* 🛏 *57 bungalows.*

Villa Aria Mui Ne

$$$$ | **RESORT** | A bright, contemporary, and comfortable boutique resort on the Mui Ne strip, Villa Aria's lush gardens make it feel secluded even though it's in the middle of the tourist area. **Pros:** central location; boutique feel; caring staff. **Cons:** limited breakfast choices. $ *Rooms from: d3,000,000* ✉ *60A Nguyen Dinh Chieu* ☎ *0252/374–1660* 🌐 *www.villaariamuine.com* 🍴 *Free Breakfast* 🛏 *23 rooms.*

🍸 Nightlife

Mui Ne nightlife has often flitted erratically between relaxed beach bars and loud clubs catering to backpackers and fun-loving, superfit kitesurfers. However, the recent past has seen an emergence of a small core of more refined options, which offer an alternative to simply taking a seat at the bar of one's own resort.

Dragon Beach Bar & Lounge

DANCE CLUBS | A long-standing staple of the late night Mui Ne scene, Dragon Beach only really gets buzzing late at night. The bar staff have access to a wide range of drinks, but they prefer to stick to "buckets" of budget booze, a hit with most revelers at this hour. The club itself is actually rather nice to look at, and has a number of great waterfront loungers, where you can put your feet up and watch the waves crash just below you. ✉ *120/1 Nguyen Dinh Chieu* ☎ *093/804–7169* 🌐 *www.dragonbeachmuine.com.*

⚡ Activities

GOLF

Sea Links Golf and Country Club

GOLF | An 18-hole par 72 course designed by Ron Fream, set on sand dunes 80 meters above sea level, Sea Links Golf and Country Club is a beautiful course stretched over 7,700 yards, with undulating fairways, many water hazards, and strong winds for part of the year. It was the first links course designed in Vietnam and is considered one of the most challenging in Asia. ⊠ *Km 9 Nguyen Thong* ☏ *0283/930–4083* ☐ *From 1,800,000d for 18 holes on weekdays* 🏌 *18 holes, 7700 yards, par 72.*

WATER SPORTS

C2Sky

WATER SPORTS | One of the most trusted kitesurfing centers in the area, C2Sky offers private lessons for all levels of ability, from beginner to advanced. The purpose-built kite school is the only International Kiteboarding Association–affiliated school in Mui Ne. They also offer kitesurfing gear rental and storage. Lesson fees are approximately $55, around 1,200,000d. ⊠ *Seahorse Resort, 16 Nguyen Dinh Chieu* ☏ *091/655–5241* ⊕ *www.c2skykitecenter.com.*

Jibes

WATER SPORTS | The experienced international instructors at Jibes offer lessons in windsurfing, kitesurfing, surfing, and sailing, with all the equipment, including kayaks, stand-up paddleboards, and a beach catamaran to rent. The oldest kitesurfing school in Mui Ne (and the first in Vietnam), Jibes has a strong focus on safety and making water sports as enjoyable as possible. Lessons start at approximately $55, or around 1,200,000d. ⊠ *90 Nguyen Dinh Chieu* ☏ *0252/384–7405* ⊕ *www.jibesbeachclub.com.*

Manta Sail Training Center

SAILING | Vietnam's first and only official sailing school, Manta Sail Training Center offers sailing instruction for all levels, from introductory to advanced as well as race training. The courses are hands-on, with a focus on safety and good seamanship, as well as having fun. Stand-up paddleboarding is also available, as are special group discounts. ⊠ *108 Huynh Thuc Khang* ☏ *0908/840–0108* ⊕ *www.mantasailing. org* ☐ *Sailing instruction $60 per hour per person; boat rentals $40 per hour.*

Nha Trang

250 km (155 miles) northeast of Mui Ne.

Nha Trang is the first major city you'll find heading north up the coast from Ho Chi Minh City. Home to some of Vietnam's best beaches and dive sites, the coastal city is a magnet for those seeking sunshine and underwater adventure. The highlands loom off to the west and thus the beachside destination is backdropped by green-clad mountains, while the roads to north and south harbor some of the most beautiful coastline in Southeast Asia. Culture and history aren't as obvious here as they are in some other locations, for Nha Trang is eager to embrace both the present and the future. A destination for Russian vacationers, the main tourist area around Tran Quang Khai street features menus and signs in Russian as well as Vietnamese and English. The south side of Tran Phu Street, running along the beach, is where most of the action is to be found. For something more authentic, head north over the Tran Phu bridge (where you'll have wonderful views of the Cai River), toward the less tourist-oriented part of town. For more of a scene, head west of the beach toward Tan Lap ward around Bach Dang Street and enjoy great food, coffee, and an emerging creative scene. South of the city towards Cam Ranh airport, the once flawless Bai Dai Beach is undergoing some development, and while a lot of it is being taken up by glamorous resorts, some of the old pristine charm does remain. Major sites can be seen in a single day, but plan to tack on another day or two for island-hopping, scuba diving, or a visit to neighboring waterfalls and villages.

GETTING HERE AND AROUND

The traffic is bearable (by Vietnam's standards) in Nha Trang, but driving is not recommended. To get from Cam Ranh airport to the town center you can take a shuttle bus for around 70,000d, or a cab will cost 350,000d. Most hotels also offer a more expensive airport pickup. The best way to get around town is by foot or taxi, which are frequent and can be hailed all over the city. Bus companies and routes change all too often, so it's difficult to pin down any one company, but transport to any major destination from Nha Trang can be arranged by a travel agency, which can be found all over the tourist area. A bus to Mui Ne, Da Lat, or Quy Nhon from Nha Trang will usually cost around 200,000d. If you are staying outside of town near Bai Dai Beach, plan to spend about 320,000d for a one-way taxi trip from Nha Trang to your hotel.

Although not recommended, many travelers find motor biking to be an exciting way to explore Nha Trang. In 2013, after a spate of road deaths, Khanh Hoa Provincial authorities announced motorbikes could only be rented to foreigners holding a Vietnamese driving license. However, many agencies ignore this crackdown and don't ask for a local license. Motorbike rental starts at about 120,000d per day. Be aware in the case of an accident, regardless of who is at fault, the foreigner will always be held financially responsible.

Nha Trang also has local public buses running six routes in the city. This can be a cheap and fun way to get around if you have someone who can tell you which route to take. The main bus companies in Nha Trang are Phuong Trang, Mai Linh, and Khanh Hoa.

TAXI AND MINIBUS CONTACTS Mai Linh Taxi. ✉ Nha Trang ☎ 0258/3838–3838 ⊕ www.mailinh.vn.**Vinasun Taxi.** ✉ Nha Trang ☎ 0258/3827–2727 ⊕ www.vinasuntaxi.com.

TRAIN CONTACTS Nha Trang Railway Station. ✉ 17 Thai Nguyen ☎ 0258/382–2113.

TOURS

Smiling Easy Rider

The reliable and honest Mr. Duc is Nha Trang's Smiling Easy Rider, a knowledgeable and cheery guy who can arrange motorbike tours of Nha Trang and surrounds or longer multi-day trips throughout Central Vietnam down to Ho Chi Minh City. Tours include hotel or airport pickups. ☎ 093/577–4426 ⊕ www.vietnam-smiling-easyrider.com.

True Friends Easy Rider

As well as offering motorcycle tours of the staggering surrounding region and even further beyond, True Friends also offers a range of tours, from island-hopping to waterfalls, crowd-free snorkeling and private fishing trips. The guides are entertaining, warm, and very knowledgeable about the area. The company is very flexible and can usually customize trips and tours to meet your needs. ✉ 60 Nguyen Thien Thuat, Nha Trang ☎ 090/642–4266 ⊕ www.facebook.com/TrueFriendsEasyRider.

HEALTH AND SAFETY

Nha Trang is much safer than larger metropolises like Ho Chi Minh City and Hanoi. Crime is low and is usually limited to late-night pickpockets preying on drunken tourists. There are also anecdotal reports of drink-spiking at some of the seedier night venues. Secure passports and valuables in your hotel safe and be aware that taking motorbike taxis or walking at night sometimes exposes you to an increased risk of crime. Prostitutes sometimes approach in packs. Most local establishments—including police stations—close their doors by 11 pm, so keep a careful watch after dark.

Other than petty theft, the most common safety hazard is the traffic. Crossing the beach road can be daunting, and at times, you may think there is physically no way you'll ever reach the sand. When in doubt, wait for local pedestrians and cross together in a pack; there is power in numbers.

👁 Sights

The highlights of Nha Trang itself can easily be explored in a day or two and most of the sites are a short taxi ride away. Start the day with culture at the Po Nagar Towers and Long Son Pagoda, followed by a tour of traditional villages and rice paddies near Cai River. By midafternoon, you'll be ready for a swim or snorkel at one of Nha Trang's beautiful beaches. Watch the sunset at the trendy Sailing Club or Louisiane Brewhouse, the best spots to sink your toes into the sand while sipping a cocktail. If you've got the time, use Nha Trang as a base to explore neighboring hot springs, mud baths, and waterfalls. No visit to Nha Trang is complete without a boat trip to the surrounding scenic islands, such as Mieu Island (home to a quirky aquarium), Hon Mun (Ebony Island), and Hon Tam (Silkworm Island). Boat trips can be arranged through local hotels and travel agencies, and the waters around Mun Island are a popular stop on snorkeling and diving trips from Nha Trang.

Ba Ho Waterfalls and Cliff Jumping
WATERFALL | A stop often included in countryside motorbike tours, Ba Ho Waterfalls aren't the most impressive around, but the beautiful one-hour journey there can be quite an adventure. The entrance to the waterfalls is at the end of a long and bumpy dirt track, and the waterfalls themselves are at the end of long hike and short climb over large rocks (that requires sturdy shoes). You'll be hot, dusty, and perhaps a little tired after the journey and hike, so take a dip under the waterfalls to get reinvigorated. If you're in search of more of a thrill, you'll no doubt encounter tour groups flinging themselves from rock ledges into the deeper waters. To avoid injury, don't jump into areas not marshaled by tour guides.

✉ Ninh Ich, Ninh Hoa, Nha Trang ⊕ www.baho.vn 🖅 50,000d.

Hon Chong Promontory
VIEWPOINT | Just like the Po Nagar Cham Towers, this headland is on the north side of the Cai River. The promontory provides good views of the coastline and the surrounding islands and is a great spot to watch the sunset. Climb up for a view of Nha Trang and its islands. If you look northwest you can see Fairy Mountain (Nui Co Tien), said to resemble a reclining fairy. To get here from the Po Nagar ruins, head north on 2 Thang 4 Street and take a right on Nguyen Dinh Chieu Street. ✉ Nguyen Dinh Chieu, Nha Trang ✛ About ¾ km (½ mile) from intersection of Nguyen Dinh Chieu and 2 Thang 4 Sts. 🖅 22,000d.

I-Resort
HOT SPRING | While the mud baths are the main attraction at I-Resort, there are also warm mineral pools, mineral water spas, waterfalls, and a kids' play area, all set within landscaped grounds 20 minutes northwest of the main tourist area of Nha Trang. Some of the massages and mud bath package deals offer good value and include a "light bite" that's really a full meal. ✉ Vinh Ngoc, Nha Trang ☎ 0258/383–8838 ⊕ www.facebook.com/IRESORT.NHATRANG.

Islands
ISLAND | No visit to Nha Trang is complete without a boat trip to the surrounding scenic islands, such as Mieu Island (Tri Nguyen Island), Mun Island, and Tam Island. Boat trips can be arranged through local hotels and travel agencies or directly at the port on the south end of town, but note that there might be a language barrier this way. ✉ Nha Trang.

Long Son Pagoda (Chua Long Song)
RELIGIOUS BUILDING | Climb the 150 steps, breaking halfway to view the 262-foot-long white statue of sleeping Buddha. At the top of the hill, visit the Long Son Pagoda and sitting Buddha. This site is free to the public—watch out for the

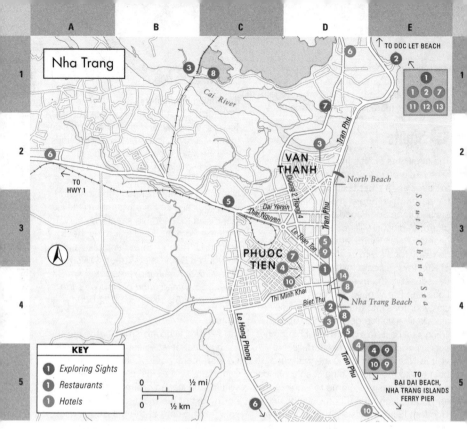

Nha Trang

TO DOC LET BEACH

South China Sea

VAN THANH

North Beach

PHUOC TIEN

Nha Trang Beach

Cai River

TO HWY 1

Dai Yersin

Tran Nguyen

Le Thanh Ton

Duong 2 Thang 4

Tran Phu

Tran Phu

Thi Minh Khai

Biet Thu

Le Hong Phong

TO BAI DAI BEACH, NHA TRANG ISLANDS FERRY PIER

KEY

1 Exploring Sights
1 Restaurants
1 Hotels

0   ½ mi
0   ½ km

Sights ▼

1 Ba Ho Waterfalls and Cliff Jumping **E1**
2 Hon Chong Promontory.............. **E1**
3 I-Resort **B1**
4 Islands **E5**
5 Long Son Pagoda........ **C3**
6 100 Egg Mud Bath **C5**
7 Po Nagar Cham Towers........... **D1**
8 Thap Ba Hot Spring Center........ **C1**
9 Vinh Hy Bay **E5**
10 Vinpearl Land **E5**

Restaurants ▼

1 Alpaca Homestyle Cafe......... **D4**
2 Galangal **D4**
3 Lac Canh................. **D2**
4 LIVIN Barbecue......... **D4**
5 Louisiane Brewhouse.. **D4**
6 Nha Trang Xua **A2**
7 Rainforest............... **D4**
8 Sailing Club.............. **D4**
9 Sandals **E5**
10 Sushi Kiwami............ **D4**

Hotels ▼

1 Amiana Resort **E1**
2 The Anam................. **E1**
3 Aroma Boutique Hotel **D4**
4 Evason Ana Mandara................. **D5**
5 InterContinental Nha Trang **D3**
6 La Paloma **D1**
7 Mia Resort............... **E1**
8 Novotel Nha Trang **D4**
9 Premier Havana Hotel...................... **D3**
10 Sheraton Nha Trang Hotel & Spa.............. **E5**
11 Six Senses Ninh Van Bay............. **E1**
12 Some Days of Silence Resort and Spa........... **E1**
13 Whale Island Resort..... **E1**
14 Zena House.............. **D4**

Vinpearl Land is an amusement park that can be seen from almost anywhere on the Nha Trang coastline.

hecklers and scammers asking for miscellaneous fees, and pushy vendors. The panoramic views of rice fields and the city below are absolutely breathtaking. ⊠ *Phat Hoc, Nha Trang* ⊕ *500 meters west of Nha Trang Train Station.*

100 Egg Mud Bath (*Tan Bun Cham Trung*)
HOT SPRING | These egg-shape private bathing capsules each accommodate two to three people, and are a 15-minute taxi ride away from the main tourist area. There are larger tubs for groups and a range of hot- and cold-water pools, as well as saunas and steam rooms and also a dining area. The purported youth-bestowing quality of the mud baths may or may not be a gimmick, but it's still worth spending a few hours here for a fun, albeit strange and messy, pampering session. ⊠ *Nguyen That Thanh, Phuoc Trung, Phuoc Dong, Nha Trang* ☎ *0258/371–1733* ⊕ *www.tramtrung.vn.*

Po Nagar Cham Towers
(*Thap Ba [Tower of the Lady]*)
RUINS | Perched on Cu Lao hillside overlooking the Cai River, the four remaining towers of an original seven or eight are reminiscent of those found at Angkor Wat and offer a glimpse of the Kingdom of Champa, who built the complex in the 8th century to praise their deity. It doesn't look like much from the main road outside, but up close it is a humbling site. The largest tower of the four stretches 75 feet high and contains a statue in honor of Goddess Ponagar, praised for her knowledge of agriculture and civilization. The center tower was built for Cri Cambhu, the god of fertility, and the south tower commemorates the god of success, Ganesh, recognizable by the human body and elephant head. The northwest tower is of the god Shiva. Visitors must cover knees and shoulders to enter the temple. If you happen to be in Nha Trang on the 20th to 23rd day of the third lunar month, you can catch the Po Nagar Festival that takes place near the

ancient towers. ✉ *2 Thang 4, at end of Xom Bong Bridge, Nha Trang* 🖂 *22,000d.*

Thap Ba Hot Spring Center

HOT SPRING | If your idea of relaxation involves soaking in a mineral mud bath, head to Thap Ba Hot Spring Center, on the northern outskirts of Nha Trang, 7 km (4½ miles) from the tourist area. In addition to mud baths there are hot mineral pools and a mineral swimming pool. You can choose to soak solo, with a partner, or in a group. ✉ *15 Ngoc Son, Ngoc Son, Nha Trang* ☎ *0258/383–7205* ⊕ *www. tambunthapba.vn* 🖂 *220,000d.*

★ Vinh Hy Bay

SCENIC DRIVE | Located 90 km (55 miles) south of Nha Trang, along a seldom-used stretch of astonishing coastline between Cam Ranh and Phan Rang, Vinh Hy Bay is a real crown jewel of the South-Central Coast. The entire road, named DT702, loops around the fringes of Nui Chua National Park on the west, and the East Sea on the east. There's not much to do around Vinh Hy except appreciate its beauty, but its beauty alone is worth the trip. Along the way, there are quite a few places to stop and grab a cool drink, as well as many tiny, unspoiled beaches. Only two resorts of note have taken up residence here so far: the eponymous Vinh Hy resort, which offers very comfortable and clean bungalows at low prices, and the opulent Amanoi Resort, which is nestled among the surrounding forest with great subtlety—were it not for the gate by the road, you might not notice it. ✉ *Vinh Hy Bay.*

Vinpearl Land

AMUSEMENT PARK/CARNIVAL | This amusement park on Hon Tre Island can be seen from almost anywhere along the Nha Trang coastline, due in large part to the huge Hollywood-style sign on the island's hillside. The park is accessed by cable cars which offer up striking views back over Nha Trang. Allow a full day to explore the amusement park, and take your swimsuit, because the complex is vast and includes a water park, rides, an electronic games arcade, dolphin and seal shows, an aquarium, and many shopping and dining options (the most varied food options are close to the water park). This is an excellent value for money and a truly fun day out for all ages. ■**TIP➔ Depart the island well in advance of closing time, as the vast crowds lead to very long waiting times for the cable car.** ✉ *Hon Tre Island, Nha Trang* ⊕ *www.vinpearl.com/en* 🖂 *880,000d.*

🅰 Beaches

Bai Dai Beach (*Long Beach*)

BEACH | Located 20 km (13 miles) south of Nha Trang center, Bai Dai Beach has fantastic sand and sea, but a deluge of luxury resort developments and bare-bones seafood shacks have damaged the aesthetic appeal. Another challenge is finding beach access without entering a seafood spot or resort, where you'll be expected to purchase food or leave. Some resorts might claim to own certain stretches of the beach, but they're actually open to the public (just don't enter through the resort itself). The best way to enjoy Bai Dai Beach is to go to one of the shacks and see what live seafood they have on offer, or indeed just have a few cold drinks between dips in the cool shallows. Jet Skis, surfboards, rafts, and kayaks are available for rent, and nearly every shack offers chairs, toilets, and showers with any food or drink purchase. This is one of the few spots where surfers can find waves through April. Bai Dai Beach continues 25 km (15½ miles) south to Cam Ranh Airport. ■**TIP➔ The best section is on the north end at the protected bay. Amenities:** food and drink; showers; toilets; water sports. **Best for:** surfing; swimming; walking. ✉ *Cam Hai Dong, Cam Lam, Nha Trang* ⊕ *East of roundabout on Nguyen That Thanh.*

Doc Let Beach

BEACH | About 45 km (25 miles) north of Nha Trang is the picture-postcard Doc Let Beach, a beautiful 10-km (6-mile) stretch of casuarina-lined fine white sand and azure water that welcomes few tourists. Like most beachfronts in Vietnam, it's seen a rise in development in recent years but fortunately, it's very low key, even the resorts themselves are much more humble and quaint than in many parts. Many of them are glad to welcome day guests for a very small fee. Overall, it's a great location for a laid-back beachy day trip from Nha Trang. It will take about an hour to get here from Nha Trang by taxi, which will cost around 500,000d. A much cheaper alternative is the local bus (No. 3), which will only set you back around 25,000d. **Amenities:** food and drink; water sports. **Best for:** walking; swimming; sunsets. ✉ *Bai Doc Let, Ninh Hoa.*

Nha Trang Beach (*Tourist Beach*)

BEACH | Because of its downtown location, the 5-km (3-mile) long Nha Trang beach is where the vast majority of visitors gather. The beach itself is free and open to the public, and sun loungers can be rented for around 70,000d. Plenty of amenities are available at the trendy Sailing Club, or you can simply bask in the sun on an open patch of sand and buy snacks from a passing vendor. A fine place to chill and soak up the sun during the day, the cooler hours between 4 pm and sunset are often a sight to behold, as droves of locals arrive to frolic in the milder conditions. Divers and snorkelers won't find much marine life here. To see clown fish, scorpionfish, and moray eels, it is better to organize a dive at the Sailing Club to the protected island of Hon Mun. The beach is not patrolled but authorities do raise red flags when conditions are unsafe. Do not ignore the red flags as the water can become very rough at certain times of the year. Amenities: food and drink; showers; toilets. Best for: partiers; swimming; walking. ✉ *Tran Phu, Nha Trang.*

North Beach

BEACH | Starting at Hon Chong beach just north of the Tran Phu Bridge and running 30 km (18 miles) north beyond Nha Trang city are several beautiful beaches that together are commonly referred to as "North Beach." This area mostly draws in college students who attend one of the five nearby universities. The most picturesque stretch of beach can be found past Ninh Hoa City, where shallow waters and powdery sand beckon swimmers and sunbathers alike. A handful of surfers paddle to the point break that whips up decent waves between October and April. Amenities are offered to those who buy food or drinks at neighboring properties such as Paradise Resort or White Sand Doclet Resort. **Amenities:** food and drink; toilets. **Best for:** surfing, swimming; walking. ✉ *Pham Van Dong, north of Tran Phu bridge, Nha Trang.*

🍴 Restaurants

Like most resort towns, Nha Trang has an abundance of dining options ranging from streetside banh mi hawkers to formal restaurants offering every type of Western cuisine imaginable. Catering to French residents are a handful of bistros that have created a fusion of Vietnam-meets-Paris. If time is limited, opt for local cuisine to experience authentic Vietnamese dishes like pork spring rolls, *cha ca* (fish patties), and seafood cooked in clay pot.

Alpaca Homestyle Cafe

$$ | **INTERNATIONAL** | A centrally located, quirky, chic café-restaurant, Alpaca captures the spirit of the more artful, creative modern day with its expressive atmosphere. It also boasts a versatile menu, all prepared with great care. **Known for:** Mexican fare; healthy food; vegan options. [$] *Average main: d150,000* ✉ *10/1B Nguyen Thien Thuat, Nha Trang* ☎ *0367/282–982.*

Galangal

$$ | **VIETNAMESE** | Tourist-friendly Vietnamese cuisine is served in a relaxing, relatively upmarket atmosphere here. The street food is cooked along the sides of the restaurant, giving the place a lively edge. **Known for:** lively atmosphere;

Nha Trang Beach may be quiet in the morning, but by the afternoon it's a popular place to swim and sunbathe.

street food dishes in a restaurant setting; tasting menus. [$] *Average main: d160,000* ✉ *1A Biet Thu, Nha Trang* ☎ *0258/352–2667.*

Lac Canh

$$ | VIETNAMESE | Join the locals at this popular and sometimes rowdy barbecue and hotpot joint that becomes quite smoky when the serious table-top barbecuing gets underway. The decor is very plain, the food is cheap and delicious, and there's an English menu. **Known for:** hotpot; DIY barbecue; good value. [$] *Average main: d150,000* ✉ *77 Nguyen Binh Khiem, Nha Trang* ☎ *0258/382–1391.*

★ LIVIN Barbecue

$$ | BARBECUE | This American-styled barbecue restaurant, complete with a smoker and long tables, serves up sweet, delicious barbecue and locally made craft beer. The hip, contemporary space also carries great gifts from local artists and designers. **Known for:** local craft beer; smoked barbecue; steak and burgers. [$] *Average main: d200,000* ✉ *77 Bach Dang, Tan Lap, Nha Trang* ☎ *091/863–8349* 🌐 *www.livinbbq.com.*

Louisiane Brewhouse

$$$ | INTERNATIONAL | An upmarket brewery, bar, and restaurant situated in huge beachfront premises, Lousiane Brewhouse even has its own pool and sun loungers. A good selection of well-priced European-style craft beer is on offer, as well as international, Vietnamese, and Japanese cuisine. **Known for:** international cuisine; wide drink selection; on-site brewery. [$] *Average main: d275,000* ✉ *Lo 29 Tran Phu, Nha Trang* ☎ *0258/352–1948* 🌐 *www.louisianebrewhouse.com.vn.*

Nha Trang Xua

$$ | VIETNAMESE | For some of the best authentic Vietnamese food around, head 6 km (4 miles) outside the city center to this 300-year-old house surrounded by rice paddies and lotus ponds. The menu, handwritten on cardboard, features fish barbecued in bamboo, banana flower salad, crispy prawn pancakes, and Asian spinach soup with basil-seasoned rice.

Known for: unique desserts; quaint decor; countryside surroundings. $ *Average main: d155,000* ✉ *6 km (4 miles) from downtown Nha Trang, Thai Thong, Vinh Thai, Nha Trang* ✛ *Left at light past Cau Dua Bridge, over railroad tracks, and right at Vinh Thai School, then follow signs to Nha Trang Xua Restaurant* ☎ *0258/389–6700* ⊕ *www.facebook. com/NhahangNhaTrangXua.*

Rainforest

$$ | **VIETNAMESE** | With a three-story jungle tree house decked out with swings and slides, as well as quieter alcoves and offbeat seating to enjoy local coffee and an array of food, Rainforest is certainly the most unique eatery in town. The theme might seem purely playful and wild, but the design of the place as a whole has a sophisticated feel. **Known for:** great coffee; secluded, peaceful atmosphere; unique design. $ *Average main: d120,000* ✉ *146 Vo Tru, Nha Trang* ☎ *098/698–1629* ⊕ *www.facebook.com/rainforestnt.*

Sailing Club

$$$ | **INTERNATIONAL** | Whether you're looking for some seaside relaxation, great meals, or a thumping party, the Sailing Club has you covered with its prime beachfront location and wide-ranging menu serving breakfast, lunch, and dinner. After dark it magically morphs into one of the plushest clubs in Nha Trang. **Known for:** first-rate breakfast; beachside relaxation; lively nightclub. $ *Average main: d300,000* ✉ *72–74 Tran Phu, Con Dao Islands* ☎ *0258/352–4628* ⊕ *www. sailingclubnhatrang.com.*

Sandals

$$$$ | **BARBECUE** | For the most romantic dining experience in Nha Trang, reserve a table for two and sink your toes into the sand at Mia Resort's beachfront barbecue restaurant, just a stone's throw from the water. Tiki torches and lanterns surround your private table. **Known for:** dining on sand is weather-dependent; fresh grilled seafood; intimate environment. $ *Average main: d420,000* ✉ *Mia Resort, Bai Dong,*

Cam Lam, Nha Trang ☎ *0258/398–9666* ⊕ *www.mianhatrang.com.*

★ Sushi Kiwami

$$ | **SUSHI** | With more than 30 years in the industry, chef Shoji Kajiwara is Nha Trang's sushi godfather. His small, cozy establishment nestles subtly along a quiet street a short walk from the tourist area, but behind the inconspicuous entrance, chef Shoji, the only Japanese sushi chef in Nha Trang, slices up fish with aplomb right in front of diners. **Known for:** revered Japanese chef; authentic sushi; intimate environment. $ *Average main: d180,000* ✉ *136 Bach Dang, Nha Trang* ☎ *0258/625–2595* ⊕ *www.facebook. com/kiwamijapaneserestaurant.*

🛏 Hotels

There is no shortage of resorts in Nha Trang, but only a select few offer a beachfront location with unobstructed views. If you plan on enjoying local sights, restaurants, and bars, stay close to the action near the center of town. For something a bit more private, choose one of the more remote resorts that offer daily shuttle service into Nha Trang.

★ Amiana Resort

$$$$ | **RESORT | FAMILY** | Located 15 minutes north of the main tourist area by car, this luxurious and private beach retreat has elegant villas, each with its own private terrace, outdoor bathroom, and handcrafted furniture. **Pros:** pool bar; saltwater and freshwater pools (with life guards on duty); free shuttle bus to the main tourist area. **Cons:** 15 minutes from downtown Nha Trang. $ *Rooms from: d5,200,000* ✉ *Pham Van Dong, Nha Trang* ☎ *0258/355–3333* ⊕ *www.amianaresort. com* 🛏 *153 rooms* ❘○❘ *Free Breakfast.*

The Anam

$$$$ | **RESORT | FAMILY** | Located right on Bai Dai Beach near Cam Ranh Airport, the classy Anam has rooms, suites, and villas across 12 palm-shaded hectares,

with a choice of garden, sea, or pool view, as well as villas with their own private pool. **Pros:** stunning facilities including a movie theater; pools, restaurants, and spa on site; lovely, attentive service. **Cons:** fee for breakfast; far from Nha Trang center. [$] *Rooms from: d5,000,000* ✉ *Lot D3, Cam Ranh Peninsula, Nha Trang* ☎ *0258/398–9499* 🌐 *www.thean-am.com* 🍴 *No Meals* 🛏 *213 rooms.*

Aroma Boutique Hotel

$$ | **HOTEL** | Just a few hundred meters from the Tran Phu beachfront and right in the heart of the tourist area, Aroma Boutique provides modern luxury accommodation at very reasonable prices. **Pros:** one of the nicer low-budget hotels; central location; rooftop pool with city view. **Cons:** not as luxe as other area hotels; area can be noisy at night. [$] *Rooms from: d900,000* ✉ *26A Tran Quang Khai, Nha Trang* ☎ *0258/388–5555* 🌐 *aromanhatrang.com* 🛏 *50 rooms* 🍴 *Free Breakfast.*

★ **Evason Ana Mandara**

$$$$ | **RESORT** | **FAMILY** | A secluded beachfront oasis with excellent facilities, but within walking distance of Nha Trang's main tourist strip, this resort has the best of both worlds, delivering the high service standards and quality amenities that make for a genuinely relaxing stay. **Pros:** central location; large rooms; kids' club. **Cons:** restaurants are somewhat pricey. [$] *Rooms from: d4,500,000* ✉ *Tran Phu, Nha Trang* ☎ *0258/352–2222* 🌐 *www.sixsenses.com/evason-resorts/ana-mandara/destination* 🛏 *74 rooms* 🍴 *Free Breakfast.*

InterContinental Nha Trang

$$$ | **HOTEL** | **FAMILY** | A luxurious high-rise across the road from the beach, the InterContinental has fabulous views of the East Sea, professional attentive staff, and just about every modern convenience you could possibly need, including a fitness center, kids' club, on-site spa, and a leafy pool deck overlooking the ocean. **Pros:** great central location; well-appointed bathrooms; balconies overlook Nha Trang Bay. **Cons:** very pricey considering it's not a resort; the large size and high-rise nature of the hotel can make it seem slightly sterile; fee for breakfast. [$] *Rooms from: d2,500,000* ✉ *32–34 Tran Phu, Nha Trang* ☎ *0258/388–7777* 🌐 *www.nhatrang.intercontinental.com* 🍴 *No Meals* 🛏 *279 rooms.*

La Paloma

$$$ | **B&B/INN** | A Spanish-looking family-run guesthouse with a carefully tended gardens surrounding a pool, La Paloma has simple spacious rooms with Vietnamese-style bathrooms and a sweet little breakfast area. **Pros:** close to Po Nagar and two of Nha Trang's three mud baths; affordable and friendly; pool. **Cons:** no phone in the room; beds are quite hard; 3 km (2 miles) from the main Nha Trang tourist area. [$] *Rooms from: d1,300,000* ✉ *1 Hon Chong, Nha Trang* ☎ *0258/383–1216* 🌐 *www.lapalomanhatrang.com* 🍴 *Free Breakfast* 🛏 *30 rooms.*

★ **Mia Resort**

$$$$ | **RESORT** | Thirty minutes south of Nha Trang, this immaculate resort of flat-roof villas is chiseled into cliffs that shelter a private bay and infinity pool that melds into the sea. **Pros:** free movies on demand; one-bedroom condos are an excellent value; private beach. **Cons:** hotel is often fully booked; far from central Nha Trang. [$] *Rooms from: d4,900,000* ✉ *Bai Dong, Cam Hai Dong, Cam Lam, Nha Trang* ☎ *0258/398–9666* 🌐 *www.mianha-trang.com* 🛏 *48 rooms* 🍴 *Free Breakfast.*

Novotel Nha Trang

$$$ | **HOTEL** | An international-standard high-rise hotel, the Novotel has airy, spacious rooms, each with its own balcony with great views of Nha Trang Bay, as well as courteous, well-trained staff and a private section of beach across the road. **Pros:** nice views; room rate includes access to private beach across the road from the hotel, with sun lounge; central location, close to main tourist area. **Cons:** not right on the beach; some noise at the front of the hotel; breakfast isn't included

in the rate. $ Rooms from: d2,000,000 ⊠ 50 Tran Phu, Nha Trang ☎ 0258/625–6900 ⊕ www.novotelnhatrang.com ¶◎¶ No Meals ⇨ 154 rooms.

Premier Havana Hotel

$$$$ | HOTEL | A classy beachfront hotel without the sky-high prices of some of its peers, the Premier Havana has more than 40 floors of luxury, culminating in the 360-degree skydeck and lighthouse, which can be seen from all over the city, as well as a skywalk, which allows daring visitors to gaze all the way down to the ground floor. Pros: safe beach access; cheaper than other similar hotels; rooftop beach club with stunning views. Cons: not as well-maintained as other similar hotels. $ Rooms from: d2,600,000 ⊠ 38 Tran Phu, Nha Trang ☎ 0258/388–9999 ⊕ www.havanahotel.vn ⇨ 1,060 rooms ¶◎¶ Free Breakfast.

Sheraton Nha Trang Hotel & Spa

$$$$ | HOTEL | FAMILY | The 30-story Sheraton Nha Trang has a wellness and relaxation focus, which is aided by the stunning views of Nha Trang's famous crescent bay, resortlike infinity pool on the sixth floor, state-of-the-art fitness center, kids' club, and on-site cooking school. Pros: excellent in-house dining options; central location, close to restaurants and shops; stylish rooms. Cons: across the road from the beach, rather than on the beach. $ Rooms from: d4,000,000 ⊠ 26–28 Tran Phu, Nha Trang ☎ 0258/388–0000 ⊕ www.sheratonnhatrang.com ¶◎¶ Free Breakfast ⇨ 280 rooms.

Six Senses Ninh Van Bay

$$$$ | RESORT | On a white sandy beach, backed by towering mountains, Six Senses Ninh Van Bay has 59 villas, each with two rooms, a garden terrace, private pool, and ocean views. Pros: excellent restaurant (open by appointment to nonguests); stunning beach; plenty of activities on site. Cons: 20 minutes from Nha Trang; expensive food and drinks; can be accessed only by boat. $ Rooms from: d21,865,000 ⊠ Ninh Van Bay,

Ninh Hoa, Nha Trang ☎ 0258/352–4268 ⊕ www.sixsenses.com/en/resorts/ninh-van-bay ⇨ 59 villas ¶◎¶ Free Breakfast.

Some Days of Silence Resort and Spa

$$$ | RESORT | Promising a peaceful retreat from everyday life, this boutique property has just nine bungalows, all with soothing views of the garden or the ocean. Pros: excellent in-house restaurant; friendly staff; two-bedroom bungalow is ideal for families. Cons: limited dining options outside the resort; isolated; sometimes quite a bit of trash washes up on the nearby beach. $ Rooms from: d1,980,500 ⊠ Dong Hai, Ninh Hoa - Hon Khoi, Doc Let Beach, Nha Trang ☎ 0258/367–0952 ⊕ www.somedaysresort.com ¶◎¶ Free Breakfast ⌀ Lunch and dinner available at USD 12 per meal. ⇨ 9 bungalows.

Whale Island Resort (L'Ile de la Baleine)

$$$ | RESORT | This tranquil beachfront eco-lodge in Van Phong Bay, about two hours north of Nha Trang, has basic but comfortable fan-cooled bamboo bungalows set among coconut palms. Pros: just enough activities to keep boredom at bay; diving offered seasonally; rate includes boat transfer. Cons: bugs and geckos are part of island life in the tropics; set meals are slighty pricey; no air-conditioning. $ Rooms from: d1,500,000 ⊠ Hon Ong ☎ 093/546–6245 ⊕ www.whaleislandresort.com ¶◎¶ Free Breakfast ⇨ 30 rooms.

Zena House

$ | APARTMENT | Straightforward, clean, and well-appointed studio apartments make Zena House perfect for travelers who are in search of simple, up-to-date accommodation in a convenient area. Pros: central location; great value; all studios have TV, private bathroom, and kitchen. Cons: basic accommodations. $ Rooms from: d350,000 ⊠ 19/1 Nguyen Thi Minh Khai, Nha Trang ☎ 093/546–6245 ¶◎¶ Free Breakfast ⇨ 30 rooms ⊟ No credit cards.

🍸 Nightlife

Sailing Club

GATHERING PLACES | From morning right up until the early hours, the Sailing Club is the place to be. After dinnertime, the space morphs into a sceney nightclub. Book a cabana or take a seat by the beachfront and sip good wine, beer, and signature cocktails, or just shake it on the dance floor. ⊠ *72–74 Tran Phu, Nha Trang* ☎ *0258/352–4628* ⊕ *www.sailingclub-hatrang.com.*

Skylight Nha Trang

MUSIC | On top of the Havana Hotel, Skylight boasts the most amazing view of the beach, the surrounding city, and the backdrop of the mountains. This high-end bar serves up artisanal signature cocktails, ice-cold beer, and tasty cuisine. Prices are high, but such a setting demands it. ⊠ *Havana Hotel, 38 Tran Phu, Nha Trang* ☎ *0258/352–8988* ⊕ *www.skylightnhatrang.com* 🍽 *220,000d.*

👜 Shopping

Dam and Xom Moi Markets

MARKET | Test your bartering skills at the local markets, where you can find everything from clothing and food to souvenirs and electronics. With its knockoff brands and cheap trinkets, Dam Market caters to tourists, while Xom Moi is more for locals who come for the fresh produce and dried goods, and makes for a great place to see local life in action. Xom Moi is at 49 Ngo Gia Tu. Dam Market is on the corner of Hai Ba Trung and Phan Boi Chau. Both are open daily 6–6. ⊠ *Xom Moi, 49 Ngo Gia Tu, Nha Trang.*

Nha Trang Center

MALL | This international style mall includes a bowling alley, movie theater, grocery store, and more than 100 brand-name shops that sell everything from clothing and jewelry to souvenirs and sunglasses. The top floor has a food court for those looking for a quick bite while bargain shopping, and the rooftop is home to Lunar Lounge, a bar and grill. ⊠ *20 Tran Phu, Nha Trang* ☎ *0258/626–1999* ⊕ *www.nhatrangcenter.com.*

🏃 Activities

Just 45 minutes by boat from Nha Trang, the island of Hon Mun is considered one of the best dive destinations in the East Sea. Further north at Van Phuong Bay is the more spectacular Whale Island, where Jacques Cousteau conducted his first Vietnamese explorations. Nha Trang has all kinds of water-related activities, including snorkeling, jet skiing, scuba diving, and boating. You can rent equipment through most hotels or operators right on the beach.

BOATING AND DIVING

Discova

BOAT TOURS | Specializing in tours for cruise ship visitors, Discova offers personalized day and half-day tours of Nha Trang and surrounds, including river and island tours. This is a more upmarket option for those wanting to avoid the party boat tour crowds. ☎ *0283/820–8822* ⊕ *www.discova.com* 🍽 *Half-day tours from d932,000, includes hotel pickup.*

Funky Monkey Tours

BOAT TOURS | For a fun and cheap day trip, join one of Funky Monkey's daily boat trip tours, which includes snorkeling, lunch, entertainment by the Funky Monkey Boy Band, and access to the floating bar. Note: the tour price doesn't include entry fees to two of the islands or the Tri Nguyen Aquarium. Funky Monkey has a range of other day tours, including city, river, and fishing tours. ⊠ *53/25 Nguyen Thien Thuat, Nha Trang* ☎ *090/849–8979* 🍽 *Full-day island hopping tours with lunch from d250,000.*

Rainbow Divers

DIVING & SNORKELING | The first PADI dive center established in Vietnam more than 25 years ago, Rainbow Divers is known for its diver training and progressive environmental practices. Daily two-dive boat trips cost 1,750,000d and take place at 7 am daily. Try dives and snorkeling tours are also available. The team here also offers instructor courses and trips to Whale Island. The outfit is open year-round but the best diving is from March to October. ✉ *132 Nguyen Thien Thuat, Nha Trang* ☎ *0258/352–4351* ⊕ *www.divevietnam. com* ✆ *1,750,000d for two-dive boat trip.*

Sailing Club Divers
DIVING & SNORKELING | This five-star dive center offers snorkeling tours, scuba-diving courses, and diving packages to Hon Mun Island. Trips take place daily 8am- 2pm. ✉ *72–74 Tran Phu, Nha Trang* ☎ *098/848–4416* ⊕ *www.sailingclubdivers.com* ✆ *1,450,000d for two-tank dive; 750,000d for snorkeling tour.*

GOLF
VinPearl Golf Club
GOLF | This 18-hole par 71 championship course, designed by IMG, is part of the Vinpearl complex on Hon Tre Island, accessible by (free) speedboat and a shuttle across the island. Every hole has spectacular views of Nha Trang Bay, with water in play on most holes. Practice facilities include a 300-yard driving range and an all-grass teeing area. ✉ *Hon Tre Island, Nha Trang* ☎ *0258/359–0919* ⊕ *www.vinpearl.com/en/vingolf* ✆ *9 holes from 1,010,000d, 18 holes from 1,680,000d on weekdays* ⚘ *18 holes, 6787 yards, par 71.*

Cat Tien National Park

150 km (93 miles) northwest of Ho Chi Minh City, 175 km (109 miles) southwest of Dalat.

This vast park, recognized as a UNESCO Biosphere Reserve, includes jungle, swampland, lakes, rivers, and hills, all of which are home to a multitude of exotic flora and fauna.

GETTING HERE AND AROUND
Cat Tien National Park is three hours by road from Ho Chi Minh City. Buses that ply the Ho Chi Minh City–Dalat route, including Phuong Trang, stop at the Tan Phu post office. From here, it takes 45 minutes by xe om or car to traverse the 24 km (15 miles) to the national park. Many of the hotels in and around the national park will offer to pick you up by car or minibus from the Tran Phu post office. This may come as part of the price of the hotel, but if not should cost around 300,000d one way. The national park office offers transportation around the park, as well as boat and bicycle rentals. There are several accommodations outside the park that offer transfers to the park, as well as tours and other activities within the park.

◉ Sights

Cat Tien National Park
NATIONAL PARK | The 72,000-hectare ruggedly beautiful Cat Tien National Park, one of nine biosphere reserves recognized by UNESCO in Vietnam, is home to hundreds of species of plants, birds, animals, and reptiles, including several species of endangered monkeys, Asian elephants, sun bears, and gaur. (Sadly, Vietnam's last Javan rhino was shot in the park by poachers in 2010.) The national park office has cars, bicycles, and boats available for hire and guests staying at the national park's hotel can book early-morning gibbon treks for 1,050,000d per person. The price includes breakfast at one of the two restaurants inside the park and a tour of the gibbon rehabilitation center. Accommodation within the park is basic, with small double rooms starting at 350,000d. There are nicer accommodation options outside the park, which can also arrange jungle excursions for you. ✉ *Nam Cat Tien, Tan Phu* ☎ *0251/366–9228* ⊕ *www.cattiennationalpark.com.vn* ✆ *60,000d.*

Those who explore Ca Tien National Park will spot many species of plants and wildlife in the jungle.

Dambri Falls

WATERFALL | The biggest waterfall in Lam Dong Province, the thundering Dambri Falls are 130 km (80 miles) southwest of Dalat and 19 km (12 miles) from the village of Bao Loc, near Cat Tien National Park. Like most of the falls in the area, they are surrounded by tasteless local "eco" tourism development, including trinket shops and a mini roller coaster. The 70-meter-high falls are still impressive, whether viewed from the paths in front of the waterfall, or from behind. According to local legend, the waterfalls are the tears of a girl called Bri who cried as she sat and waited for her love to return from the forest. The boy, Kdam, never did and when Bri died, her body turned to stone but her tears kept flowing. ■**TIP**➜ **Avoid Dambri Falls on weekends and public holidays when it's very crowded.** ⊠ *Ly Thai Tho, Bao Loc* ☎ *0263/391–1990* ⊕ *www.dambri. com.vn* 🎟 *200,000d including rides and attractions.*

🛏 Hotels

Forest Floor Lodge

$$$ | **B&B/INN** | Unlike most other accommodation options in the area, Forest Floor Lodge is located inside the national park itself. **Pros:** only privately owned lodging inside the national park; great views; rooms have a bathroom and a large balcony. **Cons:** much pricier than other options. 💲 *Rooms from: d2,200,000* ⊠ *Cat Tien National Park* ✛ *1½ km (1 mile) north of HQ* ☎ *0251/366–9890* ⊕ *www.forest-floorlodges.com* ➘ *16 rooms* ⊠ *Free Breakfast.*

Green Hope Lodge

$ | **B&B/INN** | Across the river from the national park, the family-owned Green Hope Lodge has basic but comfortable bungalows with mosquito nets (essential), spacious clean bathrooms, communal dining, and a range of tours and excursions in the park and surrounding villages. **Pros:** charming staff; peaceful and rustic setting; transport from Dalat or Ho Chi Minh for a fee. **Cons:** 10-minute walk to the pier to cross the river to the national park. $ *Rooms from: d400,000* ⊠ *Hamlet 4, Cat Tien Ward, Tan Phu* ☎ *097/218–4683* ⊕ *www.greenhopelodge.com* ⋈ *Free Breakfast* ⤢ *11 rooms.*

★ Ta Lai Longhouse

$ | **B&B/INN** | **FAMILY** | This traditional bamboo longhouse is a great base for adventurous travelers to experience all that Cat Tien National Park has to offer, as well as local village life. **Pros:** wonderful staff; authentic local experience; Wi-Fi. **Cons:** communal sleeping means little privacy. $ *Rooms from: d450,000* ⊠ *Ta Lai Village* ☎ *097/897–2734* ⊕ *www.ta-lai-longhouse.com* ⤢ *1 longhouse, sleeps up to 30 people; 1 minilonghouse, sleeps 15* ⋈ *Free Breakfast.*

Dalat

308 km (191 miles) north of Ho Chi Minh City, 205 km (127 miles) southwest of Nha Trang.

With an abundance of pine trees, the cool climate, and colonial architecture, the mountain resort of Dalat bears a vague resemblance to a European town. Its cool, misty mornings and chilly evenings provide a welcome respite from Vietnam's tropical heat. Well renowned as a romantic destination, it's a favorite among Vietnamese honeymooners. In recent years, it's also become a hot spot for young, hip, motorbiking Saigonese who seek somewhere less glitzy than Ho Chi Minh City to feed their souls. Dalat is as much about adventure as it is about romance, with hiking, cliff jumping, and canyoning on the itineraries of many visitors. Named for the "River of the Lat Tribe," after the native Lat people, Dalat was "discovered" in 1892 by Dr. Alexandre Yersin (1863–1943), a protégé of scientist Louis Pasteur. It quickly became a vacation spot for Europeans eager to escape the infernal heat of the coastal plains, the big cities, and the Mekong Delta. During the Vietnam War the city was a favored nonpartisan resting spot for both high-ranking North and South Vietnamese officers, before it capitulated to the North Vietnamese on April 3, 1975.

Dalat's prime sight is its market, an interesting place to poke around day or night, and the city also has a number of interesting temples and historical buildings that are worth exploring. For golfers, an 18-hole golf course originally set up by Emperor Bao Dai is now known as one of the best in the region.

GETTING HERE AND AROUND

Lien Khuong Airport is about 28 km (17 miles) from Dalat. Most taxis will have a flat fee of around 200,000d for 35 km (22 miles) so make sure you've confirmed a flat rate rather than using the meter. An airport bus, which meets every flight, also runs to Le Thi Hong Gam in Dalat. Tickets are 40,000d.

Dalat's main depot, 3 km (2 miles) south of the central market, is serviced regularly by buses from Ho Chi Minh City, Nha Trang, and Mui Ne, as well as points north. Hiring a 4-seater taxi for a full day (8 hours) to see the sights of Dalat (within city boundaries) should cost around 700,000d. Rates depend on the distance traveled and number of hours.

TOURS

Dalat Easy Rider

This outfit may or may not be the original Dalat Easy Rider group, so many Dalat-based motorbike touring companies make the claim. The truth is that most of the original easy riders have retired so there are no real originals out there anymore. This company, whatever its origins, is reliable and professional, but like any tour, your enjoyment hinges on how you relate to your guide. So do visit the Easy Rider headquarters and have a chat with potential drivers to make sure you get along. Dalat Easy Riders offer one-day countryside tours around Dalat for very reasonable prices. Longer tours, either as pillion passengers or self-driving with an easy rider guide, can be arranged at good prices. You can email to negotiate prices, and multiday tours will require a deposit. ✉ *Dalat* ☎ *090/454–4044* ⊕ *www.dalat-easyriders.com.*

Groovy Gecko Tours

Trekking, biking on or off road, rock climbing, canyoning, cycling—take your pick of athletic and adventurous tours with this fun and professional tour company that offers day tours as well as multiday trips from Dalat around the Central Highlands. Canyoning tours start from 1,650,000d per person. ✉ *14/1 3 Thang 4, Dalat* ☎ *0263/383–6521* ⊕ *www.groovygeckotours.net.*

Highland Sport Travel

A newer kid on the block, Highland Sport Travel is gaining a strong reputation for its guided tours, as well as its safety consciousness, using top-quality, modern gear. The main focus is on canyoning, mountain biking, cycling, and trekking, and it also offers motorbike tours, standup paddleboarding, and multiday trips. ✉ *Dalat* ☎ *0263/352–0521* ⊕ *www. highlandsporttravel.com.*

Phat Tire Ventures

This safety-conscious, fun-loving Dalat-based adventure tour company offers trekking, canyoning, cycling, rafting, kayaking, camping, and mountain-biking day and multiday trips, including cycling tours from Dalat down the mountain to either Nha Trang, Mui Ne, or Hoi An. Phat Tire also has a lakeside ropes course that's mainly used for team-building activities and school trips. ✉ *109 Nguyen Van Troi, Dalat* ☎ *0263/382–9422* ⊕ *www. ptv-vietnam.com.*

👁 Sights

Bao Dai's Summer Palace (*Dinh III*)

CASTLE/PALACE | Built in 1933, Bao Dai's Summer Palace, on the south side of Xuan Huong Lake, is a wonderfully preserved example of modernist architecture. The palace houses the original 1930s French furnishings of Emperor Bao Dai, the last emperor of the Nguyen dynasty, who ruled from 1926 to 1945 with the support of the French. With hundreds of visitors tramping through each week, the palace is showing its age. If you manage to avoid a big tour group, it's possible to find a quiet spot that feels like it's been suspended in time. For a kitsch souvenir, you can have your photo taken wearing a traditional royal getup. ✉ *1 Trieu Viet Vuong, Dalat* 💳 *30,000d.*

Central Market

MARKET | Originally built in 1929 and rebuilt in 1937 after a fire, the Central Market is the heart of Dalat. Locals and tourists come to the indoor–outdoor market to buy and sell fruit, vegetables, and local specialties such as dried fruit, fruit candy, flowers, mulberry wine, and jam. It's also a great place to check out the crops introduced by the French that only grow in Dalat's cool climate, like strawberries and artichokes. Unlike markets in a lot of Vietnam's other major destinations, the sellers here aren't pushy in the slightest, allowing browsers to browse. The main part of the two-story market is open from before dawn until nightfall. At sundown, a food town springs up outside the market and down the steps beside it. The specialty is *banh trang Dalat*, almost like a pizza on rice paper, barbecued, rolled up, and wrapped in a piece of newspaper. ✉ *4 Nguyen Thi Minh Khai, Dalat.*

Crémaillère Railway (*Ga Da Lat*)

TRAIN/TRAIN STATION | In 1933, 30 years after work started, a 105-km (65-mile) cog railway line was completed, linking Dalat to Nha Trang and Saigon. The line was closed in 1969 due to bomb attacks during the war, and the track ripped up sometime after the war ended in 1975. Twenty years later, a 7-km (4-mile) section of the track was restored and the wonderful art deco railway station renovated. Now it's possible to take the train (which now uses diesel traction) to the village of Trai Mat, home to the Linh Phuoc Pagoda. The round-trip takes two hours, although actually catching the train can prove tricky. It only departs once 25 people have bought tickets so it's best to get your hotel to call ahead to check the state of play. The railway station itself is architecturally interesting, with the three roofs representing the peaks of Lang Biang mountain while also paying tribute to the high pointed roofs of traditional Central Highlands communal houses. Vietnam's last steam locomotive sits at the station, serving as a basic coffee shop. The station and the locomotive are popular with wedding photographers, especially during the wedding "season" that runs from November to January. ✉ *1 Quang Trung, Dalat* ☎ *0263/383–4409* ✉ *5,000d to enter train station. Train tickets are 110,000d for nonresidents.*

Dalat Crazy House (*Biet thu Hang Nga*)
NOTABLE BUILDING | **FAMILY** | This psychedelic flight of architectural whimsy will probably be the wackiest thing you see in Vietnam, which is saying something, given the local penchant for quirkiness. Free-form stairs and tunnels wend their way through multistory Dr. Seuss–like concrete trees that contain 10 hotel rooms, unexpected sitting areas, and concrete animals. Its owner and designer, Dr. Dang Viet Nga, who studied architecture in Russia, built the structure to remind people of the importance of nature and the environment. Some of the staircases are very steep and the railings quite low. People who are unsteady on their feet or in charge of small children should be very careful. ✉ *3 Huynh Thuc Khang, Dalat* ☎ *0263/382–2070* ⊕ *www. crazyhouse.vn* ✉ *60,000d.*

Datanla Falls (*Thac Datanla*)
WATERFALL | One of Dalat's more easily accessible waterfalls, Datanla Falls is 5 km (3 miles) south of the city. The entrance is near the top of the falls and an easy 15-minute walk takes you down to the bottom. The more adventurous can reach the bottom by riding a toboggan through the trees down the valley (80,000d per person). ✉ *Deo Prenn, Dalat* ✉ *30,000d.*

Dinh An Village (Chicken Village)
TOWN | A K'Ho ethnic minority village, Dinh An has found itself on the tourist radar mainly because of its proximity to the highway and its giant concrete chicken. The village is often included in easy rider tours, and is only really worth visiting as one stop on a day-long exploration of the countryside surrounding Dalat. The village itself is quite spread out, with most families involved in small-scale farming of vegetables and flowers. The villagers don't wear their traditional dress, which disappoints some visitors, but keep in mind that they receive minimal benefit from tourists trooping through. There's a couple of small handicraft shops and a tiny grocery store across from the chicken statue. The chicken itself, which in its glory days was a fountain but is now propped up with an extra concrete leg, is from the local Romeo and Juliet legend for which the Langbian Mountain is named. Her Bian was a girl from a southern highlands village who fell in love with K'Lang, a boy from a northern highlands village. The villages were at war so the parents of the love-struck couple would not allow them to marry. Her Bian's parents finally relented, telling K'Lang he could marry their daughter if he found a chicken with nine spurs as the dowry. K'Lang went to the forest but he could not find a chicken with nine spurs (the rear-facing claw). So the couple eloped and lived in the forest until they died, cut off from their families. Dinh An Village is 9 km (5½ miles) from the airport and can be visited en route to

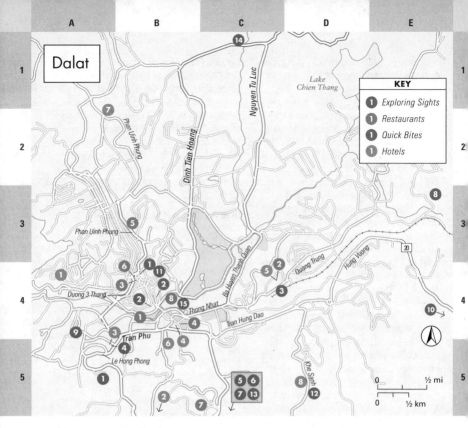

Dalat

KEY

- 1 Exploring Sights
- 1 Restaurants
- 1 Quick Bites
- 1 Hotels

Dalat rather than by making the 18 km (11 mile) trip from Dalat. ⊠ *Dinh An, Dalat.*

Elephant Falls (*Thac Voi*)
WATERFALL | About 30 km (19 miles) southwest of Dalat, these 30-meter-high waterfalls (one large and several smaller falls) are a popular stop on easy rider countryside tours. The mossy path down to the viewing area can be treacherous in the rainy season and challenging in the dry season, but once there, the views are impressive. It takes about 45 minutes to get the falls, which are just outside the village of Nam Ban. There's a coffee shop and handicraft shop at the waterfalls. Take the time to check out the textiles woven on-site by a K'Ho family. Also wander next door to the Linh An Pagoda, a peaceful working temple with hydrangeas and pine trees in the garden and a giant Happy Buddha (which doubles as a storage shed for garden supplies) out the back. The pagoda is closed for lunch from 12 to 1:30 pm. ⊠ *Gia Lam, Dalat* ✛ *Off road DT725* 🚇 *30,000d.*

Lake of Sighs (*Ho Than Tho*)
BODY OF WATER | **FAMILY** | The Lake of Sighs, northeast of town, takes its name from a tale of two star-crossed lovers, Hoang Tung and Mai Nuong. According to legend, Hoang Tung joined the army, but Mai Nuong thought she had been abandoned. Out of despair, she killed herself by jumping into the lake. On discovering her body, her lover did the same. Access to the lake is via a kitschy theme park that may entertain children for several hours. The extensive grounds contain flower gardens, statues designed for photo-posing, coffee stalls, concrete animals, and replica village huts. ⊠ *Ho Xuan Huong, Dalat* ✛ *About 5 km (3 miles) northeast of Dalat, following Phan Chu Trinh* 🕿 *0263/382–3800* 🚇 *50,000d.*

Lam Ty Ni Pagoda
RELIGIOUS BUILDING | The multitalented, multilingual monk Thay Vien Thuc, known as the Mad Monk of Dalat, resides in this small Lam Ty Ni Pagoda. An artist,

A View Worth Stopping For 👁

About 43 km (27 miles) southeast of Dalat, on the way to Nha Trang, along Highway 20, the Ngoan Muc Pass affords superb views of the surrounding lush countryside and, on a clear day, the Pacific Ocean in the distance, some 55 km (34 miles) away.

poet, landscape architect, craftsman, and religious scholar, Vien Thuc is a living legend. If you manage to visit when Vien Thuc is present, he will usually escort you through his rooms of watercolor paintings, replete with Zen poetry, and may even paint a picture for you in exchange for a small fee. When the monk is absent, the pagoda can be a bit disappointing. ⊠ *2 Thien My, Dalat* 🕿 *0263/382–2775* 🚇 *Free.*

Linh Phuoc Pagoda (*Chua Ve Trai*)
RELIGIOUS BUILDING | More commonly known as Dragon Pagoda, the gaudy Linh Phuoc Pagoda is in Trai Mat, a village 7 km (4½ miles) northeast of Dalat (accessible by road or the tourist train). Completed in 1952, the colorful pagoda is known for the inlaid pieces of broken glass throughout and the 49-meter-long dragon made from 12,000 beer bottles, as well as for its bell and 36-meter-high bell tower. This is an amazing piece of architecture worth exploring even by those suffering temple fatigue. ⊠ *120 Tu Phuoc, Trai Mat Village, Dalat.*

100 Roof Bar
BREWERY | Also known as the Maze Bar, this phantasmagorical labyrinth, featuring a popular bar at the top (if you can find it!), was designed by renowned architect Dang Viet Nga (designer of the Crazy House). It looks unremarkable from the outside, but upon entry you'll plunge down, up, and through winding corridors,

paradoxical pathways, and dead ends; if in doubt, just follow the noise to find the bar. The entrance fee is the price of a drink (a glass of beer starts at 30,000d). ✉ *57 Phan Boi Chau, Dalat* ☎ *090/304-0202* 🌐 *www.facebook.com/100roof.mazebar.*

Thien Vuong Co Sat Pagoda (*Tau Pagoda*)
RELIGIOUS BUILDING | The Chinese Thien Vuong Pagoda, southeast of town, sits atop a steep mountain with great views of the surrounding area. The pagoda was built in 1958 by the Chaozhou Chinese congregation. Three large, Hong Kong–made gilded sandalwood sculptures dominate the pagoda in the third of the three buildings, and peaceful gardens surround the complex. ✉ *385 Khe Sanh, Dalat.*

Truc Lam Pagoda & Cable Car
RELIGIOUS BUILDING | This peaceful Zen Buddhist pagoda, about 5 km (3 miles) from central Dalat, sits on top of Phuong Hoang Hill, and the best way to get here is via the beautiful cable car ride, with views of farmlands, pine forests, mountains, and lakes (100,000d round-trip). Completed in 1994, the 24-hectare complex includes a working monastery in a section that's closed to the public, as well as a meditation center. The public areas include a ceremonial hall, bell tower, beautiful flower garden, cafe, and vegetarian buffet restaurant. The pagoda is next to Tuyen Lam Lake, and the 15-minute stroll down to shore is pleasant. Day visits to the meditation center relatively easy to arrange, although are best done in person a day or two in advance, since every guest needs to be approved by the Grand Master. Longer stays are possible but require some complicated paperwork. The monks and nuns can explain the steps involved. ✉ *Cable car station, Ba Thang Thu, Dalat* ☎ *0263/383–7938.*

Valley of Love (*Thung Lung Tinh Yeu*)
CITY PARK | **FAMILY** | A superb example of how Dalat won its reputation as a kitschy destination, the Valley of Love is a pseudo theme park popular with honeymooning Vietnamese couples for photographs with "cute" man-made backdrops. Set in a valley that leads down to a lake, the park can keep younger kids entertained for quite a while, with fairground rides, a miniature train, swan-shaped pedal boats, and carriages drawn by very skinny horses. Older kids might enjoy paintball and jeep rides. The main attraction for adults is not the views but the opportunity to observe local life. ✉ *7 Mai Anh Dao, Dalat* ☎ *0263/355–8888* 🌐 *www.ttcworld.vn* 🎟 *250,000d (includes shuttle, rides and shows).*

Xuan Huong Lake (*Ho Xuan Huong*)
BODY OF WATER | **FAMILY** | Circumscribed by a walking path, Xuan Huong Lake is a hub of leisurely activity, including swan-shape paddleboats. Although there's traffic nearby, the lake provides a pleasant place to walk and bike. The dam-generated lake takes its name from a 17th-century Vietnamese poet known for her daring attacks on the hypocrisy of social conventions and the foibles of scholars, monks, mandarins, feudal lords, and kings. ✉ *Tran Quoc Toan, Dalat.*

🍴 Restaurants

Bingo Pizza
$$ | **PIZZA** | **FAMILY** | Although it's by no means the best pizza in Vietnam, Bingo nevertheless hits the spot after a long day trekking or canyoning with simple, run-of-the-mill toppings, thick crusts and decent sizes. Service can be a little slow, as is the way sometimes around here. **Known for:** comfort food; central location; generous sizes. [$] *Average main: d130,000* ✉ *2/43 Pham Ngu Lao, Dalat* ☎ *0263/351–2122.*

Dalat Train Villa & Cafe
$$ | **CAFÉ** | A quaint little café in a restored 1910 French train carriage that's now parked in lovely grounds next to a small guesthouse, this place serves up a selection of Western and Vietnamese dishes and a ton of charm. For trainspotters wanting to get a double train fix, the café and its

friendly staff are an easy walk along a main road and down a narrow local road from the old Dalat Railway Station. **Known for:** local coffee; charming atmosphere; historical feel. $ *Average main: d125,000* ✉ *Villa #3, 1 Quang Trung, Dalat* ✛ *From Xuan Huong Lake, take 1st left after old Dalat Railway Station* ☎ *0263/381–6365* ⊕ *www. facebook.com/DalatTrainVilla.*

Goc Ha Thanh

$$ | **VIETNAMESE** | This is a cheap-and-cheerful eatery serving up slightly Westernized versions of Vietnamese fare from a cute little place a short walk from the Central Market. The service can be a bit slow, but the food is reliably delicious and reasonably priced. **Known for:** good value; spring rolls; veggie curry. $ *Average main: d100,000* ✉ *51 Truong Cong Dinh, Dalat* ☎ *094/699–7925.*

Le Rabelais

$$$$ | **FRENCH** | Allow yourself to be transported to a French country estate, complete with chandeliers, period furniture, starched linens, gleaming silverware, flawless service, and fine French cuisine. With an extensive wine list and gentle live piano music, this is the place for a romantic—albeit expensive—evening in a superb setting. **Known for:** French cuisine; sumptuous high tea; colonial-era opulence. $ *Average main: d800,000* ✉ *Dalat Palace Heritage Hotel, 2 Tran Phu, Dalat* ☎ *0263/382–5777* ⊕ *www.royaldl.com.*

Nem Nuong Ba Hung

$ | **VIETNAMESE** | This plain but pleasant local eatery serves only one dish: *nem nuong* (barbecued pork skewers), with a range of edible accoutrements that are rolled up and dunked in a delicious dipping sauce. **Known for:** unfussy setting; one-dish specialty. $ *Average main: d50,000* ✉ *328 Phan Dinh Phung, Dalat* ☎ *0263/382–4344* ▭ *No credit cards.*

Nha Hang Chay Hoa Sen

$ | **VEGETARIAN** | This is the pick of Dalat's many vegan places, with a focus on fresh local produce rather than mock meat

(although that's on the menu too), served up in a bright, airy space with wooden furniture. Hoa Sen is very popular with locals for a good reason: the food is delicious. **Known for:** locally sourced produce; tom yum soup; banana leaf salad. $ *Average main: d60,000* ✉ *62 Phan Dinh Phung, Dalat* ☎ *02633/567–999.*

Oz Burgers

$$ | **BURGER** | Every now and then we just need a good old helping of home comfort, and this Australian-owned diner and takeaway is among the best Dalat has to offer, with a menu boasting a range of burgers, as well as hot dogs and even a cooked breakfast. **Known for:** cooked breakfast; big, juicy burgers; friendly service. $ *Average main: d140,000* ✉ *4 Dong Da, Dalat* ☎ *090/247–5923* ⊕ *www. facebook.com/ozburgersdalat.*

Thanh Thuy Blue Water Restaurant

$$ | **VIETNAMESE** | A stylish lakeside location for coffee, cocktails, or a meal, either on the deck under one of the purple umbrellas or inside, Thanh Thuy has an extensive menu (in English) of Vietnamese, Szechuan, and Vietnamese twists on Western dishes. The service can seem slow if you're not used to the local style of flagging a waiter down when you need one, rather than waiting for service. **Known for:** extensive menu; best view in town; slightly higher prices. $ *Average main: d140,000* ✉ *2 Nguyen Thai Hoc, Dalat* ☎ *0263/353–1668.*

☕ Coffee and Quick Bites

★ Bicycle Up Cafe

$ | **CAFÉ** | A cute and quirky little coffee shop serving a range of drinks, including beer, cakes, ice cream, and yogurt, Bicycle Up is a great place to rest and recharge with a book (check out the homemade book light fittings), a coffee, or a fruit smoothie while listening to mellow music. This quiet refuge is perfect for a rainy day. **Known for:** street art outside; cozy atmosphere; excellent coffee.

$ Average main: d50,000 ✉ 82 Truong Cong Dinh, Dalat ☎ 0263/370–0177 ⊕ www.facebook.com/Bicycleup ⊟ No credit cards.

Dalat Night Market

$ | **VIETNAMESE** | Sampling a fresh banh trang nuong, aka Dalat pizza, from one of the night market street vendors is a must—a great snack to sustain you while you explore all that the night market has to offer. *Banh trang nuong* is a circle of rice paper, brushed with an egg and dried prawn mixture, barbecued on an open brazier, folded, and wrapped in a square of newspaper. There are many *banh trang* sellers at the top of the stairs next to the market. **Known for:** barbecue snacks; "Dalat pizza"; rice porridge. $ *Average main: d40,000* ✉ *Near Dalat Central Market, Dalat* ⊟ *No credit cards.*

🛏 Hotels

★ Ana Mandara Villas Dalat Resort & Spa

$$$$ | **RESORT** | This charming resort, on a hill 5 km (3 miles) from downtown Dalat, comprises 17 French-colonial villas restored to capture the elegance of a former age, albeit with every modern convenience, including a spa for pampering. **Pros:** great breakfast and dining options; heated swimming pool; impeccable service. **Cons:** 10 minutes by taxi from all the downtown action. $ *Rooms from: d2,800,000* ✉ *Le Lai, Dalat* ☎ *0263/355–5888* ⊕ *www.anamandara-resort.com* ⌁ *87 rooms* ❍❙ *Free Breakfast.*

Binh An Village

$$$$ | **RESORT** | A misty mountain paradise near Tuyen Lam lake, about 20 minutes outside of Dalat, Binh An Village is a boutique resort that pays tribute to Dalat's French and hill-tribe heritage in its design and decor. **Pros:** use of kayaks; free shuttle into Dalat; lake views. **Cons:** isolated. $ *Rooms from: d4,000,000* ✉ *Tuyen Lam Lake, Dalat* ☎ *0263/380–0999* ⊕ *www.binhanvillage. com* ⌁ *26 rooms* ❍❙ *Free Breakfast.*

Dalat Crazy House (Hang Nga Guesthouse)

$$$ | **HOTEL** | Each of the 10 rooms has its own offbeat wildlife theme at this small guesthouse, which is also a tourist attraction in its own right, but beware: the Dalat Crazy House has the kitsch factor turned up so high it's almost off the scale. **Pros:** a unique experience, makes for an unusual travel tale. **Cons:** tourists knock on the doors of the hotel rooms and peer in the windows from 8:30 am to 7 pm when the attraction is open to the public. $ *Rooms from: d1,040,000* ✉ *3 Huynh Thuc Khang, Dalat* ☎ *0263/382–2070* ⊕ *www.crazyhouse.vn* ❍❙ *Free Breakfast* ⌁ *10 rooms.*

Dalat Palace Heritage Hotel

$$$$ | **HOTEL** | Retaining the splendor and charm of a bygone age with 15-foot ceilings, ornate fireplaces, artworks, beautiful manicured grounds, library, and spacious rooms with claw-foot bathtubs and original moldings, this historic property oozes old-world charm, matched by world-class service. **Pros:** genuine link to history; central location; great views over the lake. **Cons:** as you would expect in a property of this age, things malfunction from time to time. $ *Rooms from: d4,000,000* ✉ *2 Tran Phu, Dalat* ☎ *0263/382–5444* ⊕ *www.dalatpalacehotel.com* ⌁ *48 rooms* ❍❙ *Free Breakfast.*

Dalat Train Villa

$ | **B&B/INN** | A boutique guesthouse in a restored French colonial villa built in 1935, the Dalat Train Villa is associated with the Dalat Train Cafe, which is on the grounds. **Pros:** short walk from train station; intimate property; helpful and friendly staff. **Cons:** standard rooms are on the small side; ground floor rooms can be noisy if guests are staying in the rooms above. $ *Rooms from: d600,000* ✉ *1 Quang Trung, Villa #3, Dalat* ☎ *0263/381–6365* ⊕ *www.facebook.com/DalatTrainVilla* ⌁ *16 rooms* ❍❙ *No Meals.*

Du Parc Hotel Dalat

$$$ | **HOTEL** | Built in 1932 to take the overflow from the popular Langbian Palace Hotel (now the Dalat Palace Heritage Hotel), the art deco–style Du Parc Hotel Dalat is full of character, from the original metal-cage elevator and the ornate staircase in the lobby to the hardwood floors in the rooms. **Pros:** charming old-world feel; very reasonable prices; near the lake and restaurants. **Cons:** really showing its age; small rooms; breakfast is served across the road. [$] *Rooms from: d1,100,000* ✉ *15 Tran Phu, Dalat* ☎ *0263/382–5777* 🌐 *www.dalathotelduparc.com* 🛏 *140 rooms* 🍴 *Free Breakfast.*

★ **Terrasse des Roses**

$$ | **HOTEL** | This romantic boutique hotel, on a hill 3 km (2 miles) from downtown Dalat, is one of the city's best-kept secrets. **Pros:** incredibly helpful staff; the peaceful atmosphere is most conducive to relaxing; each spacious room has a balcony. **Cons:** Wi-Fi can be patchy in rooms. [$] *Rooms from: d900,000* ✉ *35 Cao Ba Quat, Dalat* ☎ *0263/356–5279* 🍴 *Free Breakfast* 🛏 *9 rooms.*

Zen Valley Dalat

$$$ | **B&B/INN** | Zen is a small and tranquil family-owned resort with lovely views of the valley, large, comfortable rooms with modern bathrooms, an excellent in-house restaurant, and a spa. **Pros:** peaceful and relaxing; personalized service. **Cons:** outside the city center. [$] *Rooms from: d1,300,000* ✉ *38 Khe Sanh, Dalat* ☎ *0263/357–7277* 🌐 *www.facebook.com/zenvalleydalat* 🛏 *28 rooms* 🍴 *Free Breakfast.*

Nightlife

Dalat's groovy cafés are ideal for quiet, reflective evenings, and there are also some newish bars featuring live music. These bars close relatively early here, and those wishing to stay out are limited to the karaoke joints, where little English is spoken.

B21 beer

BARS | Located along "Artists Alley" on Truong Cong Dinh Street, the first thing that is apparent about this bar is that it's a hit with the young, hip Dalat crowd. The recipe is fairly simple: the bar plays loud music and puts on entertaining live shows while serving cold, cheap beer. It's perhaps a little too loud to sit inside, but the terrace is a great place to watch the city go by in the evenings. ✉ *68 Truong Cong Dinh, Dalat* ☎ *091/938–2121* 🌐 *www.facebook.com/b21bar.*

V Cafe

CAFÉS | This is a cool little café that features good live acoustic music every evening from 7:30–9 pm and a range of Western and Vietnamese comfort foods. If you're lucky, the owner will join a jam session. ✉ *17 Bui Thi Xuan, Dalat* ☎ *0263/352–0215* 🌐 *www.facebook.com/vcafe.dalat.*

Activities

Dalat offers many activities to appeal to outdoorsy types, including the novelty swan-shaped paddleboats that are available to rent on Xuan Huong Lake. Bicycles, including tandem "love bicycles" and mountain bikes, can be rented along the main street, but check the size of the bikes before you commit to renting one, as some of them are very small. A number of adventure tour operators cover trekking, cycling, canyoning, and more.

See listings under Tours for more.

GOLF

Dalat Palace Golf Club

GOLF | The pristine and historic Dalat Pines Golf Club has an 18-hole championship course overlooking Xuan Huong Lake. Built in the 1930s with just six holes after Emperor Bao Dai encountered golf on a trip to France, the course was abandoned in 1945 and languished for nine years until a group of investors rebuilt it as an eight-hole course (with one sponsor per hole). In early 1966, Dalat Palace hosted professional golfers from around the world including Billy Casper, several months before he beat Arnold Palmer to win the U.S. Open at San Francisco's Olympic Club. The course was abandoned again in 1975, after the reunification of Vietnam, and initiated its second comeback in 1993 with a major renovation by a group of American investors. The original clubhouse, built in 1956, is still in use today. A full practice facility complements the golf course and clubhouse, with a 290-yard grass driving range, a putting green, and practice bunkers. ✉ *Phu Dong Thien Vuong, Dalat* ☎ *0263/382–1201* 🌐 *www.dalatpalacegolf.com* 🎫 *9 holes from 1,600,000d, 18 holes from 2,400,000d on weekdays, less for Dalat Palace and Du Parc guests* ⛳ *18 holes, 7009 yards, par 72.*

Lak Lake

150 km (93 miles) north of Dalat.

Lak Lake, the largest freshwater lake in the Central Highlands, is set among picturesque rolling hills and reached via a beautiful journey through rural farmlands and mountain roads. It is still an off-the-beaten-path destination, even though the last emperor of Vietnam, Bao Dai, saw fit to build a summer house overlooking the lake, which doubles in size in the rainy season. There's a laid-back feel to the lakeshore, where most visitors end up, with elephants awaiting passengers or strolling slowly around the lake and through the M'nong settlement of Jun Village. Treks and homestays can also be organized through Duc Mai Coffee.

GETTING HERE AND AROUND

Lak Lake is 154 km (96 miles) from north of Dalat and around 50 km (30 miles) south of Buon Ma Thuot. It's possible to rent a taxi for the day to visit the lake and return to Dalat. Expect to pay around 2,000,000d in a four-seater or 2,500,000d in a seven-seater for a round-trip lasting less than 11 hours. Local buses to Lak Lake run regularly between Lak Lake and Buon Ma Thuot's North Coach Station.

👁 Sights

Jun Village

TOWN | A small community of about 30 ethnic M'Nong households on the shores of Lak Lake, Jun Village is an interesting place for a stroll to see the traditional bamboo and wood longhouses and the more modern concrete versions, most with a collection of pot-bellied pigs, chickens, dogs, and children running around or napping nearby. There are two restaurants on the lakefront, both serving cheap Vietnamese fare, as well as some handicraft shops selling baskets, weaving, wind chimes, and other knickknacks. It's possible to organize a stay in one of the longhouses in Jun Village through Duc Mai Coffee, but this is best done with a guide. Be advised that bathrooms are outside. ✉ *Buon Jun, Lien Son.*

🛏 Hotels

Lak Tented Camp

$$$ | **B&B/INN** | Choose from elegant, rustic tents, luxurious bungalows with private balconies, a dorm, and camp grounds (gear included), all commanding stunning views from above Lak Lake at Lak Tented Camp. **Pros:** eco-conscious design; excellent food; lovely view over the lake. **Cons:** no A/C; natural setting means bugs can be present; higher price range (but great amenities) for the area. [$] *Rooms from: d2,200,000* ✉ *193 Nguyen Tan Thanh, Lien Son, Lak Lake* ☎ *0262/625–5552* 🌐 *www.*

laktentedcamp.com ❍❙ *Free Breakfast*
☞ *Rates include breakfast, boat transfer*
🛏 *19 rooms.*

Buon Ma Thuot

50 km (31 miles) north of Lak Lake.

Central Highlands towns are good bases from which to stage trips to the ethnic minority villages and jungles of the hinterland. Buon Ma Thuot, the capital of the Central Highlands and Vietnam's coffee capital, is a bustling town with a population of about 300,000 people. It was once the administrative and economic center of the region and its central location gave it strategic importance during the Vietnam War. Traveling here, and onward to Pleiku and Kon Tum, can be fairly rough going because of long driving distances and limited facilities, but they are great places to escape the tourist trail and meet some of Vietnam's 54 recognized ethnic minorities. An exploration of this area will take you past coffee plantations and should include regular stops at local cafés, where the strong coffee is served in shot glasses.

GETTING HERE AND AROUND
Nonstop flights to Buon Ma Thuot are available from Ho Chi Minh City, Danang, Vinh, and Hanoi. Buses arrive several times a day from Ho Chi Minh City, Nha Trang, Danang, Pleiku, Quy Nhon, Hai Phong, and Hanoi. Mai Linh operate a fleet of taxis in Buon Ma Thuot (262/381–9819).

TOURS
Vietnam Highland Travel
The friendly and knowledgeable team at Vietnam Highland Travel operates mostly private tours around the Central Highlands, including the regions surrounding Pleiku and Kon Tum, many of which include trekking and homestays at ethnic minority villages. ⊠ *24 Ly Thuong Kiet, Buon Ma Thuot* ☎ *0262/385–5009*
⊕ *www.vietnamhighlandtravel.com*
✉ *Tours from $90.*

◉ Sights

Dak Lak Museum (*Bao Tang tinh Daklak*)
HISTORY MUSEUM | This large, relatively modern museum highlights the history of Dak Lak Province with a focus on local ethnic minority people through its overall design and displays, which include artifacts from the 44 ethnic minority groups who live in the province. Exhibits are signed in Vietnamese, English, French, and Ede. ⊠ *12 Le Duan, Buon Ma Thuot* ☎ *0262/625–3636* ✉ *30,000d* ⊘ *Closed Mon.*

Dray Sap and Gia Long Falls
(*Thac Dray Sap*)
WATERFALL | These pretty waterfalls, 32 km (20 miles) southwest of Buon Ma Thuot, are a good place to break the journey from Lak Lake to Buon Ma Thuot. Trails lead to the bottom of the falls, where it's possible to take a dip in the slightly murky green water. ⊠ *Dak Sur, Dak Nong* ✉ *40,000d.*

Trung Nguyen Coffee Village
(*Lang Ca Phe Trung Nguyen*)
OTHER ATTRACTION | This tourist site, owned by the Trung Nguyen coffee behemoth, Vietnam's answer to Starbucks, is essentially a giant coffee shop with a beautiful replica "ancient house" at the front. There's a museum at the rear of the property, showcasing coffee paraphernalia from around the world. A gift shop at the front of the property sells a selection of coffees, including weasel coffee that goes for $50 per 225-gram box. ⊠ *222 Le Thanh Tong, Buon Ma Thuot* ☎ *0262/651–1168* ⊕ *www.facebook.com/langcaphetrungnguyen* ✉ *Free although guests are expected to buy a drink.*

Victory Monument
(*Tuong dai Chien thang Buon Ma Thuot*)
MONUMENT | Located in the center of Buon Ma Thuot's biggest roundabout, this monument honors the day the town was "liberated" by the North

Waterfalls at Dray Sap make for a beautiful excursion from Buon Ma Thuot.

Vietnamese army (the losing side would say that Buon Ma Thuot "fell") on March 10, 1975. The provincial administrative center was the first domino to fall as the northern army pushed south towards Ho Chi Minh City, which was liberated only a few weeks later, on April 30, marking the end of the Vietnam-American War. The monument features a replica tank and fighters with suitably victorious raised arms and guns. There's no need to make a special trip to the monument—you'll probably pass it as you enter the town. ✉ *Center of roundabout at Le Duan, Phan Chu Trinh, and Nguyen Tat Thanh Sts., Buon Ma Thuot.*

🍴 Restaurants

★ Nem Viet

$ | VIETNAMESE | This is a basic metal-tables-and-chairs joint that's open to the street, serving up a delicious version of *nem nuong* (barbecued pork) served with platters of rice paper, herbs, pickled vegetables, fried wonton wrappers (for crunch), fresh rice noodles, sliced green banana, and star fruit, which are rolled together and dipped into a pork-and-peanut sauce. This is a Central Highlands specialty that's best washed down with a cold beer. **Known for:** authentic, street feel; local specialty dish; no-fuss food. [$] *Average main: d40,000* ✉ *14–16 Ly Thuong Kiet, Buon Ma Thuot* ☎ *0262/381–8464* 💳 *No credit cards.*

Trung Nguyen Coffee Village
(*Lang Ca Phe Trung Nguyen*)

$$ | VIETNAMESE | The standout feature of what is essentially a giant café is the beautiful replica open-air ancient house, of a type that would have housed royalty in Imperial times, which serves Vietnamese dishes, such as *bo kho* (beef stew) and *bo luk lak* (shaking beef). Try a coffee in the ancient house, in the "cave" section, reached via concrete stepping stones over a pond, or on the deck overlooking the gardens. **Known for:** tasty desserts; ancient replica house; pretty garden view. [$] *Average main: d150,000* ✉ *222 Le Thanh Tong, Buon Ma Thuot* ☎ *0262/651–1168* 🌐 *www.facebook.com/langcaphetrungnguyen.*

Hotels

★ Coffee Tour Resort

$$ | **HOTEL** | Part of the Trung Nguyen coffee empire, Coffee Tour Resort is a cute boutique hotel a little more than 2 km (1 mile) from the center of Buon Ma Thuot with lovely grounds, an on-site restaurant, and clean, modern rooms (with fluffy bathrobes in the wardrobes). **Pros:** next door to Trung Nguyen Coffee Village and a short walk to Buon Ma Thuot's water park; very restful ambience; ideal for families. **Cons:** a long walk from downtown Buon Ma Thuot; no elevator access to second- and third-floor rooms. *[$] Rooms from: d773,000 ✉ 149–153 Ly Thai To, Buon Ma Thuot ☎ 0262/357–5575 🌐 www.coffeetour.com.vn 🍴 Free Breakfast 🛏 33 rooms.*

Damsan Hotel

$ | **HOTEL** | This three-star hotel is one of the finer options in town because rooms are comfortable, clean, and spacious, with decor accents in the form of textiles from local ethnic minorities. **Pros:** very reasonable price; central location, walking distance to the Victory Monument. **Cons:** showing its age (it opened in 1997). *[$] Rooms from: d550,000 ✉ 212–214 Nguyen Cong Tru, Buon Ma Thuot ☎ 0262/385–1234 🛏 70 rooms 🍴 Free Breakfast.*

Eden Hotel

$ | **HOTEL** | Clean and comfortable rooms, friendly staff, and a central location in a café-lined street make the unpretentious Eden Hotel popular with budget travelers. **Pros:** fridges in rooms; cheap price; helpful staff. **Cons:** the beds are very firm. *[$] Rooms from: d450,000 ✉ 228 Nguyen Cong Tru, Buon Ma Thuot ☎ 0262/384–0055 🍴 No Meals 🛏 52 rooms.*

Pleiku

180 km (112 miles) north of Buon Ma Thuot, 140 km (87 miles) west of Quy Nhon.

Pleiku, the capital of Gia Lai province, is smaller and less colorful than its neighbor Kon Tum, but it makes a practical base in this forested and mountainous region. Much of this area served as a major battleground during the Vietnam War.

GETTING HERE AND AROUND

Flights arrive at Pleiku Airport from Ho Chi Minh City, Hanoi, Vinh, Hai Phong, and Danang. The airport is about 5 km (3 miles) north of central Pleiku. Buses arrive daily in Pleiku from all over Vietnam, including Ho Chi Minh City, Hanoi, Dalat, and Nha Trang. It's an uncomfortable 12 hours from Ho Chi Minh City and 24 from Hanoi, but only 6 hours from Dalat and 1 hour and 40 minutes from Kon Tum. Taxis are the best way to get around town. Mai Linh operates a fleet in Pleiku (0269/383–8383).

TOURS

Gia Lai Eco-Tourist

This local outfit can help arrange trekking and tours of the Central Highlands ethnic minority villages with an English-speaking guide (Ms. Nga is highly recommended). Tours can start with airport pickup in Pleiku or Buon Ma Thuot, or even from further afield, such as Nha Trang or Hoi An. The company can also arrange car (and driver) hire. Hill-tribe treks start at about $100 per person per day, including transport, accommodation, guide, and some meals. *✉ 82 Huong Vuong, Pleiku ☎ 0269/376–0898 🌐 www.gialaiecotourist.com.*

Sea Lake (Bien Ho)

(Bien Ho, T'Nung, Ea Nueng)

About 6 km (4 miles) north of downtown Pleiku, Sea Lake is a flooded crater of an extinct volcano. A pine tree–lined road leads to a viewing area, which includes a female Buddha statue. It's clear why it's called Sea Lake, given that it's more than

200 hectares in size. Locals say the lake is at its best in the early morning when covered in fog that looks like strips of silk. ✉ *Access road off Ton Duc Thang St., Pleiku* 🎟 *10,000d.*

Hotels

Elegant Hotel

$ | **HOTEL** | Pleiku is not known for top of the range accommodation, but the Elegant Hotel keeps standards high enough while providing great value for money. **Pros:** great value for money; good location; friendly service. **Cons:** some rooms are windowless. [$] *Rooms from: d450,000* ✉ *64 Nguyen Tat Thanh, Pleiku* ☎ *0269/371–7799* 🌐 *www.facebook.com/KhachsanElegant* 🍴 *No Meals* 🛏 *30 rooms.*

Tre Xanh Hotel

$ | **HOTEL** | This three-star business hotel close to the central market has large clean rooms and reasonable bathrooms, making it a good choice for budget travelers looking for a place to crash in Pleiku. **Pros:** cheap rates; central location. **Cons:** noise from the in-house karaoke venue can be heard in some rooms. [$] *Rooms from: d600,000* ✉ *18 Le Lai, Pleiku* ☎ *0269/371–5787* 🍴 *Free Breakfast* 🛏 *116 rooms.*

Kon Tum

50 km (31 miles) north of Pleiku, 50 km (30 miles) west of Quy Nhon.

The best base for exploring the region, Kon Tum is a sleepy, relatively undiscovered gem on the banks of the Dakbla River, surrounded by interesting ethnic minority villages. The Bahnar and Jarai, two of the largest hill-tribe groups in the area, possess a fascinating culture with traditions that stretch back for centuries. You can join them in drinking the *ruou can* (rice wine) for which this region is famous. Of particular cultural interest are the wood carvings made by the Bahnar tribe (who have villages within walking distance of Kon Tum) to adorn the graves of their departed. The strong animistic beliefs of the Jarai tribe are expressed through traditional musical instruments, such as the wind flute and gongs with which they produce ethereal and entrancing hymns.

GETTING HERE AND AROUND

The most northern city in the highlands, Kon Tum remains relatively untouched by mass tourism. It's perhaps unfairly seen as just a place stay for a night while on a motorcycle tour, but is actually an excellent base to access the beautiful surrounding countryside and appreciate the country's recent warring history. The easiest way to get to Kon Tum is to fly into Pleiku airport and get a taxi or a private car for the one-hour drive. You can usually organize a private car (and driver) when you book your hotel in Kon Tum; otherwise just take a Mai Linh taxi from the rank at the Pleiku airport (*269/383–8383*). By bus, it's one hour and 40 minutes from Pleiku to Kon Tum. Getting to Kon Tum from anywhere by bus is arduous: trips take 11 to 13 hours from Ho Chi Minh City, 8 hours from Nha Trang, and 20 to 24 hours from Hanoi.

TOURS

Highlands Eco Tours

A well-regarded local tour company with guides that speak English, French, and several hill-tribe languages, Highlands Eco Tours offers cycling, trekking, boating, and adventure tours as well as tours of the hill-tribe villages around Kon Tum and further afield. This company also offers humbling insights into Vietnam's past, with a number of tours around former battlefields. ✉ *41 Ho Tung Mau, Kon Tum* ☎ *0260/391–2788.*

Sights

Konklor Suspension Bridge

BRIDGE | This bridge, about 2 km (1 mile) from downtown Kon Tum, spans the Dakbla River. The 292-meter bridge was completed in 1994, making it easier for people in Konklor village to get to town. If you're really lucky, you may see a "traffic jam" caused by a bullock cart crossing the bridge. Don't miss the rong house on the left side of the northern bank of the river. ✉ *Bac Can, Konklor Village.*

Kon Tum Seminary

RELIGIOUS BUILDING | Another picturesque wooden building, the three-story Kon Tum's Catholic seminary was completed in 1934. It contains a small minorities museum that shows the history of Christianity and conversion in the region, as well as exhibits from local hill tribes. It's open on Sunday. ✉ *146 Tran Hung Dao, Kon Tum* ☎ *090/920–1075* 🎫 *Free.*

★ **Rong Houses**

NOTABLE BUILDING | Each ethnic minority village in the region has its own rong house, which serves as a community hall. These tall stilted structures, with long pitched roofs, often thatched, are where meetings, weddings, and other community activities take place. The size of the rong house is an indication of how wealthy the village is—and the roofs can be as high as nearly 100 feet. The Bahnar people usually build their rong houses from wood and bamboo, with wooden stilts, while the Jarai people use corrugated iron for the roof and concrete for the supporting pillars. There are a few rong houses within easy reach of Kon Tum, including two near the suspension bridge in Konklor Village. ✉ *Kon Tum*

Wooden Church (*Nha Tho Go; Kon Tum Cathedral; Our Lady of the Immaculate Conception Cathedral*)

CHURCH | Also known as the Cathedral of Kon Tum, this church (completed in 1918) combines Roman and Bahnar architectural styles in a unique and beautiful building with wide verandas. The church is usually open, so you can go inside and admire the stained-glass windows that light up the airy interior. There's an orphanage behind the church that welcomes visitors and some interesting workshops in the grounds. Masses are held at the church daily at 5 am and 5:30 pm and on Sunday, at 5 am, 7:30 am, and 4 pm. ✉ *13 Nguyen Hue, Kon Tum* 🌐 *www.facebook.com/hnambayangtom.kontum.*

Coffee and Quick Bites

Eva Cafe

$ | VIETNAMESE | A beautiful, restful garden café, filled with carvings and sculptures, this is the place to come for excellent coffee, sweet egg coffee (a Hanoi specialty of whipped egg yolk and coffee), and fruit shakes. The English-speaking owner, Mr. An, is a fountain of knowledge about the local area and is available to lead multiday treks or tours through nearby ethnic minority villages. **Known for:** peaceful atmosphere; Hanoi-style egg coffee; local expert owner. [$] *Average main: d20,000* ✉ *5 Phan Chu Trinh, Kon Tum* ☎ *0260/386–2944* 💳 *No credit cards.*

★ **Indochine Coffee**

$ | CAFÉ | This stunning café was designed by international-award-winning Vietnamese architect Vo Trong Nghia, who specializes in structures made completely out of bamboo. Part of the Indochine Hotel, it's a local drinks-and-ice cream spot overlooking the Dakbla River, with soaring inverted cone-shaped bamboo columns and many peaceful fish ponds. **Known for:** river views; unique bamboo design. [$] *Average main: d25,000* ✉ *Indochine Hotel, 30 Bach Dang, Kon Tum* 🌐 *www.indochinehotel.vn.*

Hotels

Indochine Hotel Kon Tum
$$ | **HOTEL** | Billing itself as an international-standard three-star property, the eight-story Indochine Hotel has a commanding position overlooking the Dakbla River and surrounding countryside. **Pros:** offers a pickup service from Pleiku Airport, starting from 590,000d; central location; welcome flowers and fruit are a nice touch. **Cons:** some parts of the hotel are looking a bit tired. [$] *Rooms from: d753,000* ✉ *30 Bach Dang, Kon Tum* ☎ *0260/386–3334* 🌐 *www.indochinehotel.vn* 🍴 *Free Breakfast* 🛏 *81 rooms.*

★ **Konklor Hotel**
$ | **HOTEL** | An easy 2½-km (1½-mile) bicycle or motorbike ride from downtown Kon Tum, this charming family-run operation in Konklor Village has clean, spacious rooms with roomy private bathrooms in a series of bungalows, each a few steps from the central lounge area and restaurant, where you can have breakfast, lunch, and dinner at very reasonable prices. **Pros:** short walk to Kon Tum's suspension bridge and two Bahnar rong houses; great value for money; motorbikes and bikes available for rent. **Cons:** a long walk from downtown Kon Tum. [$] *Rooms from: d350,000* ✉ *38 Bac Can, Kon Tum* ☎ *0260/386–1555* 🌐 *www.konklorhotel.vn* 🍴 *No Meals* 🛏 *39 rooms.*

Quy Nhon

222 km (138 miles) north of Nha Trang, 296 km (184 miles) south of Hoi An.

Once the Cham capital of Vijaya, Quy Nhon is a seaside gem located midway between Nha Trang and Hoi An. People who come here often stay a day or two longer than planned; such is the charm of the city itself and particularly the surrounding environment. Tourism is growing and become more appealing for Westerners, so it won't stay secret forever. The laid-back atmosphere is perfect for those interested in exploring a town with no heavy industry and locals who aren't jaded by tourism, as well as sensational food.

GETTING HERE AND AROUND

The airport is about 30 km (19 miles) northwest of the main tourist area of Quy Nhon. Mai Linh and Phuong Trang buses run between Nha Trang and Quy Nhon (and onward to Danang/Hoi An). From Nha Trang it takes about six hours and there are some spectacular views along the way, though the trip can sometimes be quite nerve-wracking. Thuan Thao and Thanh Thuy bus companies run one or two buses a day between Quy Nhon and Dalat, and it's also possible to catch a minibus from Pleiku. The Reunification Express, which runs five times a day between Ho Chi Minh City and Hanoi, stops at Dieu Tri Train Station, which is about 10 km (6 miles) west of the main tourist area of Quy Nhon. The town is well serviced by taxis and most hotels will assist with motorbike rentals. Most tour operators cater to the domestic market and there are plenty of small-scale operations run by hotel owners. The best approach is simply to ask at any of the accommodation options listed below.

Sights

Bai Xep Beach
BEACH | Located 10 km (6 miles) south of Quy Nhon, via a beautiful stretch of coastline, Bai Xep village is a narrow, confusing warren of dwellings which intersect and descend until they eventually spit you out on a pristine little beach. The beach is now occupied by a handful of guesthouses and a resort, but this has barely taken away from the pristine feeling. ✉ *Khu Vuc 1 Bai Xep, Qui Nhon.*

Banh It Towers (*Bac Towers*)
VIEWPOINT | Around 30 minutes inland from Quy Nhon are the 11th-century Banh It Towers, yet another reminder

of the Cham empire who ruled this land. Set high on a hill with incredible 360-degree views of the surrounding land, the three towers have had some extensive restorations, but fortunately there are still plenty of original carvings left. ✉ *Dai Loc Hamlet, Phuoc Hiep, Qui Nhon* 🎟 *12,000d.*

Phuong Mai Peninsula
SCENIC DRIVE | Across the seemingly endless Thi Nai bridge (the second-longest sea crossing in Vietnam) is a vast, dusty landscape, which at first seems nothing more than industrial, but take the road south and be rewarded by delightful, traditional fishing villages. The village of Eo Gio is the most accessible, but just like Bai Xep, the "streets" are nothing more than tight, winding alleyways. This peninsula isn't the easiest to find your way around, so unless you're confident on a motorbike, inquire at the hotel first. Enabling Google Maps on your phone will also be helpful. ✉ *Phuong Mai Peninsula, Qui Nhon.*

Quang Trung Museum
HISTORY MUSEUM | About 40 km (25 miles) west of Quy Nhon, the Quang Trung Museum is dedicated to Emperor Quang Trung, one of the leaders of the Tay Son Rebellion, which began in 1772 as a peasant uprising and eventually led to the temporary overthrow of the Nguyen rulers in Hanoi. The museum has limited signage in English and is only really of interest to committed historians, given its out-of-the-way location. ✉ *Phu Phong, Tay Son, Binh Dinh* 🕾 *0256/388–0185* 🎟 *50,000d.*

★ Quy Hoa Leper Colony
TOWN | This tiny commune is a true example of preserved architecture amid a stunning backdrop. The pristine Quy Hoa beach is right through the trees, just a short walk away from the center of the colorful village. Most of the actual lepers are elderly now, and it's mostly their descendants who populate the village, some of whom work in a small clothing factory or as crab fishermen. The residents are friendly and don't seem to

mind foreigners wandering around. The village and its hospital is well-known among Vietnamese because one of the country's most famous poets, Han Mac Tu, died there in 1940 after contracting leprosy at age 38. The cemetery is interesting and colorful. ✉ *Quy Hoa, Qui Nhon.*

Quy Nhon Beach
BEACH | This white-sand beach is a long crescent dotted with basket boats that runs along An Duong Vuong Street. Like many parts of Vietnam, trash is a problem, but as of the present day the town seems to have made a real effort to look its best, and it's working. You can walk to the southern end of the beach, then up and over a headland to get to the more secluded but rocky Queen's Beach, then farther on to the Quy Hoa leper colony. Allocate half a day for this hike—it's a good 6 km (4 miles) or so. **Amenities:** food and drinks. **Best for:** walks; sunset; sunrise. ✉ *An Duong Vuong, Qui Nhon.*

Thap Doi Cham Towers
RUINS | These restored Cham towers, built some time between the 11th and 13th centuries, are some of the most easily accessible in southern Vietnam, set in a little park that's a popular meeting place for locals. The twin towers, with their intricate carvings of mythical animals, are considered unusual relics of the Cham empire because most other towers were built in clusters of three. In truth, there are more impressive towers to be found further out of town, but these are worth a visit at breakfast time simply for the wealth of cheap, delicious street food on offer right outside. ✉ *Thap Doi, Qui Nhon* 🎟 *20,000d.*

🍽 Restaurants

★ Banh Xeo Tom Nhay Anh Vu
(*Banh Xeo Gia Vy 2*)
$ | **VIETNAMESE** | Take your pick of *tom* (shrimp) or *bo* (beef) to fill your Binh Dinh–style rice pancake. The local rendition of *banh xeo* is arguably the best in

The Banh It Towers outside of Quy Nhon are reminders of the Champa kingdom.

the country; they come smaller and zestier here than in other parts of the country, and can be wrapped in rice paper and green mango (a must). **Known for:** local specialty dish; simple service; servings of two pancakes. $ *Average main: d40,000* ⊠ *14 Dien Hong, Quy Nhon* ☎ *093/279–8669* ▭ *No credit cards.*

Com Ga Bay Quan
$ | **VIETNAMESE** | Like a lot of eateries in Quy Nhon, this place does simple, but truly delicious meals, with minimum fuss and maximum care. A good idea is to sit outside on the street corner and watch the world go by as you tuck into dinner. **Known for:** great people-watching spot; com ga (delicious, filling chicken and rice); suon (grilled pork chops). $ *Average main: d50,000* ⊠ *47 Mai Xuan Thuong, Qui Nhon* ☎ *0256/381–2214* ▭ *No credit cards.*

Com Sau Thu
$ | **VIETNAMESE** | One of the most popular *com binh dan* (canteens) in town, Com Sau Thu has been making locals happy with their cheap and cheerful fare for more than 10 years. (The husband and wife Sau and Thu now have three shops, but locals agree the original one at this address remains the best.) The daily options are displayed in a glass case at the front of the restaurant, so you can just point to a range of dishes and then take a seat. Vietnamese people usually order one meat dish, one or two vegetable dishes, and a soup, and all are placed in the middle of the table and shared. **Known for:** local popularity; simple service—just point; sharing dishes. $ *Average main: d50,000* ⊠ *121 Tran Cao Van, Qui Nhon* ☎ *0256/382–3980* ▭ *No credit cards.*

Ngo Van So Food Street
$ | **VIETNAMESE** | Qui Nhon's "eating street" is lined with dozens of little local places which come alive in the evenings. Make your way to the top of the street and amble around to peruse the options. **Known for:** banh xeo; banh canh ca (peppery fish noodle soup). $ *Average main: d50,000* ⊠ *Ngo Van So, Qui Nhon* ▭ *No credit cards.*

Quy Nhon Sports Bar

$$ | **INTERNATIONAL** | Opened in 2018, this Australian-owned, coastal bar reflects the growth of tourism in Quy Nhon. The multistory bar is a relaxing place to grab a bite to eat and a beer, while the roof terrace has a fantastic view of the ocean and the mountains. **Known for:** beachfront location; excellent burgers; live sports. $ *Average main: d150,000* ⊠ *92 An Duong Vuong, Qui Nhon* ☎ *079/290–5201* ⊕ *www.facebook.com/TheQNSB* ⊟ *No credit cards.*

Surf Bar

$ | **INTERNATIONAL** | Curiously, there are two Surf Bars under the same ownership, within 100 meters of each other on Quy Nhon Beach. These shelters are the perfect places to relax in the early evening and take in the sunset, or to take some shelter from the sun during an afternoon on the beach. **Known for:** smoothies; reasonably priced beer; decent cocktails. $ *Average main: d30,000* ⊠ *Xuan Dieu, Le Loi* ☎ *094/209–0909.*

 # Hotels

★ Avani Quy Nhon Resort & Spa

$$$$ | **RESORT** | Ideal for a get-away-from-it-all break, this luxury hideaway (one of Vietnam's best-kept secrets) has comfortable, spacious rooms, all with private balconies overlooking the East Sea. The resort amenities, including the pool, restaurants, and bar, are international standard and there is also a range of interesting activities, including excursions and sunrise yoga. **Pros:** superb dining options; excellent massages at the in-house spa; spacious balconies. **Cons:** isolated; a one-hour drive from Phu Cat Airport and 20 minutes south of Quy Nhon. $ *Rooms from: d3,600,000* ⊠ *Ghenh Rang, Bai Dai Beach, Qui Nhon* ☎ *0256/384–0132* ⊕ *www.avanihotels.com/en/quy-nhon* ⇌ *63 rooms* ❍ *Free Breakfast.*

Casa Marina Resort

$$$ | **RESORT** | Opened in 2018, this four-star luxury resort is located right on Bai Xep beach; 56 rooms are spread out across 1.5 hectares of land, which is also populated by a restaurant, swimming pool, Jacuzzi, and a gym. **Pros:** the most modern resort around; great value for a resort; beautiful views from the restaurant. **Cons:** design is a bit sterile. $ *Rooms from: d2,050,000* ⊠ *Quoc Lo 1D, Khu Pho 1, Bai Xep, Quy Nhon* ☎ *0256/369–6868* ⊕ *www.casaresort.com.vn* ❍ *Free Breakfast* ⇌ *56 rooms.*

Haven Boutique Hotel

$ | **B&B/INN** | On the beach in the fishing village of Bai Xep, Haven underwent a renovation in 2020, now offering rooms and a mini-suite, many with sea views and balconies. **Pros:** right on Bai Xep Beach; boat trips can be arranged; relaxing vibe. **Cons:** can be hard to find. $ *Rooms from: d550,000* ⊠ *Khu Vuc 1, Bai Xep* ☎ *086/681–5105* ⊕ *www.havenvietnam.com* ⇌ *15 rooms* ❍ *Free Breakfast.*

John & Paul Inn

$ | **B&B/INN** | Run by extremely friendly Dalat natives John and Paul, this is now the most popular hotel and hostel in Quy Nhon itself. **Pros:** great music; excellent atmosphere; two-minute walk from the beach. **Cons:** limited reception hours. $ *Rooms from: d360,000* ⊠ *63 Chuong Duong, Qui Nhon* ☎ *098/429–2350* ⊕ *www.facebook.com/johnandpaulinn* ❍ *No Meals* ⇌ *10 rooms.*

★ Life's A Beach

$ | **B&B/INN** | Two British guys opened this rustic beachfront homestay in 2014 after falling in love with the small fishing village of Bai Xep, one of Vietnam's best-kept secrets. **Pros:** genuinely welcoming hosts; beachfront location with fresh seafood available; many opportunities to interact with locals. **Cons:** 10 km (6 miles) outside of Quy Nhon. $ *Rooms from: d460,000* ⊠ *Bai Xep, Qui Nhon* ☎ *097/893–1085* ⊕ *www.lifesabeachviet-nam.com* ❍ *No Meals* ⇌ *6 rooms.*

Seagull Hotel (*Khach San Hai Au*)
$$$ | **HOTEL** | An older establishment that's trying to keep up with the times, the sky blue–color Seagull Hotel retains a certain charm. **Pros:** price; location; fitness center. **Cons:** some rooms have a stale carpet smell. [$] *Rooms from: d1,400,000* ✉ *489 An Duong Vuong, Qui Nhon* ☎ *0256/384–6377* 🌐 *www.seagullhotel.com.vn* 🍴 *Free Breakfast* 🛏 *170 rooms.*

Quang Ngai

174 km (108 miles) north of Quy Nhon.

Quang Ngai itself is, unfortunately, no great shakes. However, it is worth stopping at in order to visit to the Son My Memorial at the site of the horrific My Lai Massacre.

GETTING HERE AND AROUND

Quang Ngai is a stop on the Reunification Express train between Quy Nhon and Danang. Taxis are the best way of getting around town.

TAXI CONTACT Mai Linh Taxi Company. ✉ *Quang Ngai* ☎ *0255/383–8383.*

TRAIN CONTACT Quang Ngai Train Station. ✉ *Tran Quoc Toan, Quang Ngai* ☎ *0255/382–0280.*

Sights

My Khe Beach
BEACH | About 15 km (9 miles) from Quang Ngai town, just past the My Son Memorial, lies the pretty casuarina-lined beach of My Khe. There are only a small handful of local guesthouses and homestays across the street from the beach, so it's best to plan to visit the beach, dine at one of the seafood shacks along the beach, and continue north to Hoi An or south to Quy Nhon to stay the night. **Amenities:** food and drink. **Best for:** swimming. ✉ *Hwy. 24B, Quang Ngai.*

Son My Memorial and Museum (My Lai)
MILITARY SIGHT | The Son My Memorial is dedicated to the victims of the massacre at My Lai and lies about 10 km (6 miles) east of National Highway 1A, just north of the town of Quang Ngai. The memorial itself is in the former hamlet of Thuan Yen, where many of the worst crimes occurred. The village, which was burned down after the attacks, has been re-created to look as it did immediately after the massacre, with the paths between the rice paddies containing the imagined footprints of the victims and their booted attackers, giving a chilling sense of the frenzy of killing that occurred. The nearby museum recounts the events of the day in vivid detail, with explanations in English and very graphic color photographs of some of the victims. English-speaking guides are available at the museum. In striking contrast to the terrible events that took place here, the memorial and the museum are located in a quiet and pastoral area. To get to the memorial, you can take public bus No. 3 from Quang Ngai bus station, or you can hire a taxi in Quang Ngai. Expect to pay around 200,000d each way for the taxi ride, and it's probably best that you ask the taxi driver to wait at the memorial. ✉ *Tinh Khe, Son Tinh, Quang Ngai, My Lai* ☎ *0255/384–3222* 🎟 *20,000d.*

Hotels

Central Hotel
$$ | **HOTEL** | The run-down hotel, which claims to be four-star, is one of the best options in town, which isn't saying much. **Pros:** central location; suitable base for exploring the My Lai site; pool on-site. **Cons:** noise of traffic filters into the rooms; dated property; limited English skills. [$] *Rooms from: d700,000* ✉ *1 Le Loi, Quang Ngai* ☎ *0255/382–9999* 🌐 *www.centralhotel.com.vn* 🍴 *Free Breakfast* 🛏 *90 rooms.*

Chapter 6

THE CENTRAL
COAST

Updated by
Agnes Alpuerto
and Vo Thi Huong Lan

⊙ Sights	🍴 Restaurants	🛏 Hotels	🛍 Shopping	🍸 Nightlife
★★★★★	★★★★☆	★★★★☆	★★★★★	★★★☆☆

WELCOME TO THE CENTRAL COAST

TOP REASONS TO GO

★ **Hoi An.** Discover the charm of Hoi An's Old Quarter with its historic sights, traditional architecture, flavorful cuisine, and lantern-strewn streets.

★ **Tee off on Vietnam's Golf Coast.** Soak in the splendid scenery while working on your handicap on three of Vietnam's award-winning golf courses, all within easy reach of Danang.

★ **Imperial City explorations.** Learn about past emperors by visiting the historic palaces and tombs in Hue.

★ **Take to the trails.** Rub shoulders with a Co-Tu hill-tribe king and overnight in Bho Hoong village, in a beautifully appointed stilt house deep in the jungle, a thrilling motorbike or jeep ride from Hoi An or Hue.

★ **Adventure beyond the cave.** Phong Nha is one of the most spectacular limestone regions in Southeast Asia. Explore untamed jungle, climb steep karst mountains, and sleep under a thousand stars.

The Annamite Mountain range that marks the border between Vietnam and Laos hugs the Central Coast, and it's relatively easy to travel around. South are the flatlands of Hoi An, an ancient port town surrounded by rice fields and organic farms, which are fed by tributaries of the Thu Bon River, carving the landscape into tiny rural islands out to the East Sea and the marine-protected Cham Island archipelago. An hour away to Hoi An's east, the Champa kingdom of My Son lies in the valley of the Truong Son Mountains, which continue all the way north, bordering the coastal city of Danang, a 40-minute drive from Hoi An. Farther north, the two-hour journey to Hue takes you through the mountain ranges of Bach Ma through sweeping, low-lying countryside and onward, to the karst mountain region of Phong Nha, a four-hour drive from Hue.

1 Hoi An. From the lantern-strewn streets of Old Town to the farmers shouldering their harvest in balanced baskets, the scenes of Hoi An capture what every traveler imagines Vietnam to be.

2 Marble Mountains. Five beautiful limestone peaks rise above the beach north of Hoi An and south of Danang.

3 Danang. Five iconic bridges have been built connecting the city in the west to picture-postcard beaches, 3 km (2 miles) to the east. Dazzling, modernist hotels, lofty skyscrapers, and gourmet restaurants have sprung up alongside the Han River, creating a dramatic new skyline.

4 Danang Beach. Encompasses several smaller beaches, including My Khe, which runs parallel to Danang City and Bac My An.

5 Lang Co Beach. An oasis with pristine, white, sandy beaches and tranquil lagoons lined with oyster shacks and seafood stalls.

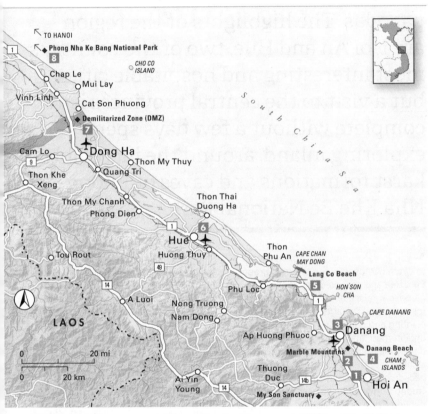

6 Hue. UNESCO World Heritage Site and reminder of Vietnam's Imperial past.

7 Demilitarized Zone (DMZ). Although the surrounding countryside is stunning in parts, tours to these far flung bases and former battlefields are best suited to military enthusiasts.

8 Phong Nha Ke Bang National Park. One of the most distinctive examples of karst landforms in Southeast Asia, with more than 300 caves and grottoes.

Vietnam's long, lovely Central Coast has iconic sandy beaches, ancient Cham ruins, and fascinating royal tombs and pagodas. The highlights of the region are Hoi An and Hue, two of the country's most interesting and hospitable cities, but a visit to the central provinces isn't complete without a few days spent exploring inland, around the incredible karst formations and caves of Phong Nha Khe Be National Park.

As you travel around this region, expect to catch glimpses of the emerald-green East Sea and scenes of traditional Vietnamese rural life as they have appeared for centuries. The age-old rhythm of planting and harvesting continues undisturbed, and you'll see families drying their rice in their front yards only inches from the road against a stunning backdrop: the dramatic peaks of the Truong Son Mountains cascading into the sea. The culinary curious will love Hoi An, an enigmatic but hip coastal town full of old-world charm, with some of the best street food and restaurants in the region. Originally a port trading village, it is incredibly well preserved. Amble around 200-year-old homes incorporating architectural elements from traditional Chinese, Vietnamese, and Japanese styles, reflecting those who populated Hoi An over the centuries. This is also Central Vietnam's gateway to diverse mountainous countryside, home to hill tribes.

Hugging the coastline north of Hoi An is 30 km (19 miles) of tropical white sandy beaches lined with some of the most luxurious beach hotels in the country. Just inland is the spectacular Marble Mountain range.

A little farther north is Danang, once an important U.S. Air Force base during the Vietnam War. Today it is the country's fastest growing city, with an international dining scene, stunning beaches, great street food, vibrant nightlife, and the region's gateway airport.

Once the capital of Vietnam and the home of its emperors, Hue, north of Danang, was once largely in ruins, the consequence of both French attacks in the late 19th century and American bombings during the Vietnam War. Only during the past decade have efforts been made to restore Hue's imperial architecture. Today the Imperial City continues to attract visitors with the grandeur of its royal past. From here it's a three-hour drive north across the DMZ to the limestone mountain, caves, and grottoes of Phong Nha Kha Be National Park, a bucket-list destination for adventurists and home to the biggest cave on the planet, Han Son Doong.

MAJOR REGIONS

Hoi An. Fast gaining status as Vietnam's culinary capital, the atmospheric river town of Hoi An is quite rightly one of Vietnam's top destinations. The big draw here is the Old Town Quarter, a lantern-lit labyrinth of ancient Indochine architecture, traders' houses, and temples, a short bike ride through rural countryside from Hoi An's other major draw—its beaches.

Danang and Around. Three kilometers (2 miles) from Central Vietnam's main airport is Danang City, a buzzy urban sprawl of skyscrapers and colonial architecture with a vibrant dining and nightlife scene. The luxury beach resorts along the city's coastline are the main attraction, along with the Marble Mountains.

Hue. The onetime Imperial Capital of Vietnam is the place to slow down and take in the country's regal past. Explore the Citadel, Imperial Palace, museums, and emperors' tombs, and take a cruise on the Perfume River. For a more rural vibe, a short drive through fishing villages and lagoons takes you to undeveloped beaches lined with seafood shacks.

DMZ. Once one of the most heavily militarized areas in the world and the setting for some of the bloodiest battles of the Vietnam War is the DMZ. Hamburger Hill, Khe San, the Rockpile, and the Vinh Moc Tunnels are all located here.

Phong Nha Ke Bang National Park. Hang Son Doong is the world's largest cave, but it's just one of many in this spectacular park, where a vast network of underground caves, awesome jungle scenery, and fascinating history form the perfect backdrop for outdoor adventure.

Planning
When to Go

The Central Coast has four distinct seasons. The monsoon season between September and January is plagued by unpredictable weather conditions. The low-lying coastal towns of Hoi An, Danang, Hue, and the mountain valleys of Phong Nha are particularly prone to flooding during October and November, but good warning systems and protocols are in place and, in most instances, this need not affect your trip. The cooler months of spring, which begins in February and ends in April, are generally dry and are a good time to travel if you want to avoid the intense heat and humidity of the summer months from April to July, which are the best months to visit if you are planning a beach holiday. During autumn, from August to September, humidity reaches its peak and thunderstorms roll in off the mountains most evenings, while the days are usually sunny and hot. Like the rest of the country, the central region comes alive during Tet, the celebration of the lunar new year, which takes place in January or February. Due to long national holidays, this can be a difficult time of the year to travel. Tet Trung Thu or the Mid-Autumn Festival, which takes place in August or September, is a far more tourist-friendly event, celebrated on a huge scale in the central town of Hoi An.

Getting Here and Around

AIR
Danang International Airport (serving Danang and Hoi An) is Vietnam's third busiest airport, and it makes for a great hub from which to hop between popular destinations within Vietnam. Few international flights service Danang; the most popular are direct services to Singapore,

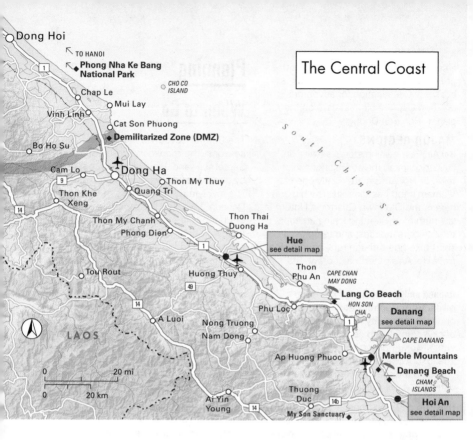

The Central Coast

Dong Hoi

TO HANOI

Phong Nha Ke Bang National Park

CHO CO ISLAND

Chap Le

Mui Lay

Vinh Linh

Cat Son Phuong

Demilitarized Zone (DMZ)

Bo Ho Su

Cam Lo

Dong Ha

Thon My Thuy

Thon Khe Xeng

Quang Tri

Thon My Chanh

Phong Dien

Thon Thai Duong Ha

Hue
see detail map

Tou Rout

Huong Thuy

Thon Phu An

CAPE CHAN MAY DONG

Lang Co Beach

HON SON CHA

Danang
see detail map

Phu Loc

A Luoi

Nong Truong Nam Dong

CAPE DANANG

Ap Huong Phuoc

Marble Mountains

Danang Beach

CHAM ISLANDS

LAOS

Thuong Duc

Hoi An
see detail map

Ai Yin Young

My Son Sanctuary

South China Sea

0   20 mi
0   20 km

Kuala Lumpur and Seoul. Although new destinations are slowly being added, most connect north in Hanoi or south in Ho Chi Minh City, both a 70-minute flight from Danang.

Hue's Phu Bai Airport serves as a popular hub for flights into central Vietnam. Most connect north in Hanoi (1 hour) or south in Ho Chi Minh (70 minutes). Phu Bai Airport is 20 minutes from central Hue.

Dong Hoi Airport is located in Quang Binh Province, about 500 km (311 miles) southeast of Hanoi. It is the closest gateway to Phong Nha-Ke Bang National Park, a UNESCO World Heritage site that contains a complex system of grottoes and caves. It operates regular domestic flights to Noi Bai International Airport in Hanoi (1 hour, 25 minutes) and Tan Son Nhat International Airport in Ho Chi Minh City (1 hour, 40 minutes).

AIRPORT CONTACTS Danang International Airport. ✉ *3 km (2 miles) west of Danang city center, Duy Tân, Hòa Thuân Nam, Hai Châu, Hai Chau District* ☎ *0236/353–9555* ⊕ *www.danangairportonline.com.* **Dong Hoi Airport.** ✉ *Loc Ninh Ward, Dong Hoi* ☎ *0232/381–0898* ⊕ *www.vietnamairport.vn.* **Phu Bai Airport.** ✉ *Zone 8, Phu Bai Ward, Huong Thuy District, Hue* ☎ *0234/3861–646* ⊕ *www.vietnamairport.vn.*

BUS

To reach Hoi An from Danang International Airport, catch the yellow Bus No. 1 at the roundabout where Dien Bien Phu and Nguyen Tri Phuong meet (a 10-minute walk). Buses run daily from 6 am to 6 pm, leaving for Hoi An every 20 minutes and terminate an hour later at Hoi An's main bus station on Le Hong Phong Street, a 15-minute walk from the

Old Town. Tourist minibus services run directly from the airport and train station. These cost approximately 80,000d and can be arranged at the information counter upon arrival.

Tour buses north to Hue take about 3½ hours, overnight buses south to Nha Trang take 10 to 12 hours, while tour buses north to Phong Nha take eight or nine hours. There are also Open Tour buses available for the route between Hoi An and Hue that include stops at Marble Mountain and Lang Co Beach. These take about five hours.

Hue's Phu Bai Airport runs a regular shuttle bus service into the city. The 15-km (9-mile) trip takes about 25 minutes and costs 30,000d. Only prearranged, private minibuses run the route between Dong Hoi airport and Phong Nha and the nearest public bus station is Nam Ly, which is just over 10 km (6 miles) away in the wrong direction, so it's best to book transfers through your hotel. Prices start at 125,000d.

Local buses ply the route between Danang's central bus station and Le Hong Phong Street in Hoi An, a couple of kilometers outside of the Old Town. Buses leave every 30 minutes from 5:30 am until 5:50 pm, taking approximately 45 minutes from door to door. Expect to pay extra for luggage.

Tour companies like The Sinh Tourist offer long-distance bus service to and from northern and southern provinces.

BUS CONTACTS Danang Central Bus Station. ✉ *201 Ton Duc Thang, 2½ km (1½ miles) north of junction with Highway 1A, Danang* ☎ *00511/3767–6789.* **Dong Hoi Bus Station.** ✉ *Nam Ly, To Huu, Dong Hoi* ☎ *0232/3822–018.* **The Sinh Tourist.** ✉ *646 Hai Ba Trung, Hoi An* ☎ *0235/386–3948* ⊕ *www.sinhtourist.com.*

CAR

With the Central Coast becoming a tourist hub, especially for travelers wanting to escape the hustle and bustle of big cities like Hanoi and Ho Chi Minh City, the number of car rental companies has grown over the years. You can easily book a vehicle. The price of a private car with a chauffeur starts at 2,000,000d per day. The coastal road linking Danang and Hoi An is manageable and takes about 50 minutes to drive 28 km (17½ miles), and should cost no more than 500,000d. From Hoi An to Hue the most direct route takes you through the Hai Van Tunnel; the 140-km (87-mile) journey takes 2½ hours and costs around 1,500,000d by taxi. An alternative and more scenic route takes you along coastal roads and over the Hai Van Pass, with a few stops to enjoy the view. This 160-km (99-mile) mountainous drive takes upward of four hours and costs 1,700,000d. The 227-km (141-mile) route from Hue to Phong Nha offers spectacular scenery and, outside of rush hour, the journey can be done in just over four hours, although during the rainy season, already poor road conditions around the national park area are prone to flooding and mudslides, which can add a good hour onto the journey time.

TRAIN

Danang Train Station serves as the main access point to Hoi An, a 40-minute drive from the Old Town. In startling contrast to the larger city train stations, Danang is easy to navigate, clean, and well serviced with a tourist help desk manned by English-speaking staff. As a stop between Ho Chi Minh and Hanoi, Hue's train station is near the river on the east side of Le Loi. If you're short on time (and money), overnight trains are a good way to travel while you sleep. Express trains are recognizable by the SE prefix. Local trains, which are much slower and cheaper, have the TN prefix. Trains between Ho Chi Minh and Hue cost about 500,000d and take 18½ hours. Those between

Hue and Hanoi cost around 300,000d and take 13 hours. There are also daily connections between Danang and Hanoi, with a stop in Hue and Dong Hoi.

The train ride between Danang and Hue is like passing through a postcard; it's one of most scenic coastal train routes in the country, taking in the Hai Van Pass, Son Tra Peninsula, Lang Co beach, and the jungle-clad mountains of Bach Ma National Park. Crossing mountainous landscape, the route gives way to patches of emerald and blue, where rice fields meet lagoons and bays. The public TN train takes four to five hours and includes stops at the smaller coastal stations including Lang Co, while the more expensive Reunification Express (SE train) takes 2½ hours. The latter costs roughly 300,000d and is offered four times daily. The SE trains also continue on to Dong Hoi—the main station for Phong Nha Ke Bang National Park. The journey from Danang takes 5½ hours, or three hours from Hue.

Hue's train station is conveniently located 1 km (½ mile) from the city center and serves as the central transit point for the country-long Reunification line, with daily services to Ha Noi (13 hours), Nha Trang (12 hours), and Ho Chi Minh City (19 hours). A licensed taxi (look out for the green Mai Linh cars) to centrally located hotels should cost no more than 50,000d, though most high-end hotels offer shuttle services to airports, railways and bus stations.

TRAIN CONTACTS Hue Railway Station. *On right bank at southwest end of Le Loi St., 2 Bui Thi Xuan, Hue ✛ 2.8-km (1.7-mile) walk from the entrance to Hue's Imperial Citadel ⊕ vietnam-rail-way.com.***Lang Co Train Station.** *Lang Co Town, Phu Loc District, Phu Loc ☎ 0236/3821–175.***Danang Train Station.** *202 Hai Phong St., Tam Thuan Ward, Thanh Khe District, Danang ☎ 0236/382–3810 ⊕ vietnamrailway.com.*

Restaurants

The Central Coast is known for its outstanding cuisine, with Hoi An now considered a culinary destination, full of trendy restaurants, cooking schools, and hipster cafés alongside the lively street food scene in Old Town. For Vietnam's fastest growing city, Danang, the future of the dining scene looks bright; recent years have seen an influx of design-savvy restaurateurs, talented bartenders, and top international chefs. Hue's imperial cuisine is richly diverse. *Bun bo* (a lemongrass-and-chili-infused beef and pork noodle soup) originated here as did the "kingly table," a sociable, family-style dining experience where tables are loaded and food is shared tapas style.

Hotels

The Central Coast is home to some of the most luxurious resorts and hotels in the country, with the highest concentration found in Hoi An and Danang. Small hotels and guesthouses (which are more commonly known locally as homestays) have also upped their game. For five-star experiences, you'll find your money goes a lot further in Hue, where luxury hotels and resorts are, for the most part, located just outside of the city. As long-stay beach vacations become more fashionable, coastal areas that were once considered remote have started to develop.

For expanded reviews, facilities, and current deals, visit Fodors.com.

What It Costs

$	$$	$$$	$$$$
RESTAURANTS			
Under 60,000d	60,000d– 150,000d	151,000d– 250,000d	over 250,000d
HOTELS			
Under 600,000d	600,000d– 900,000d	901,000d– 1,500,000d	over 1,500,000d

Tours

Handspan Travel Indochina

One of the oldest and most respected tour operators in Vietnam, Handspan Travel Indochina offers a wide range of tours and package holidays, and staff members are a great source for travel information on the region. Tours on offer are varied, well priced, and child friendly with great off-track options, licensed English-speaking guides, and high-quality transport. ⊠ 78 Ma May, Hoan Kiem District, Hanoi ☎ 024/3926–2828 Head Office ⊕ www. handspan.com.

Hoi An Express

Offering everything from visas to interpreters and chauffeur-driven cars to countrywide travel, Hoi An Express excels in customer service and competitive pricing. Tours on offer range from countryside rides in Hoi An on vintage Vespas to street food tours in Danang's liveliest night markets. Full-day group tours start at 2,500,000d. ⊠ 30 Tran Hung Dao St, Hoi An ☎ 0235/919–293 Hoi An Office ⊕ hoianexpress.com.vn.

Trails of Indochina

Trails of Indochina offers bespoke travel experiences around Vietnam, specializing in high-end and off-the-beaten-path adventures. With more than 20 years of experience, they take travelers to lesser-known destinations, where they experience local lifestyle and connect with communities. Tours vary in price; 3-day trips with a professional guide and accommodation start at 10,000,000d. ⊠ 21/1 Ngo Gia Tu St., Vinh Ninh Ward, Hue ☎ 0234/3836–525 Hue Office ⊕ www.trailsofindochina.com.

Hoi An

More than 500 km (310 miles) north of Nha Trang.

From the lantern-strewn streets of Old Town to the farmers shouldering their harvest in balanced baskets, the scenes of Hoi An capture what every traveler imagines Vietnam to be. It is the country's must-see destination, delivering culture, cuisine, history, and charm with the added bonus of a beach just minutes from the town center.

Preserved in pristine condition are its 18th-century shophouses, pagodas, and assembly halls built by early Fujian, Canton, Chaozhou, and Hainan-Chinese communities. The many galleries selling the works of local artists and artisans, and the numerous cafés lend a strong bohemian feel. Hoi An has great cuisine and is probably the most tourist-friendly town in the country, with English being widely spoken by the locals. The whole town can easily be navigated on foot in a half a day. Just outside of town is the pleasant An Bang Beach, which you can reach by taking a 5-km (3-mile) ride through a picturesque slice of rural Vietnam. Also nearby are the My Son Cham ruins, which evoke the ancient history of this region, and the coral-encircled Cham Islands that provide spectacular diving alongside some of the most underdeveloped beaches in Vietnam.

GETTING HERE AND AROUND

The closest airport to Hoi An is the one in Danang, 30 km (19 miles) north. The only way to get to Hoi An from Danang airport is by minibus or car, which takes about 40 minutes. The trip to Hoi An costs around 300,000d–400,000d and is a very scenic coastal drive through small towns

Hoi An History

Hoi An, or Faifo as it was called in previous centuries, is a composite of many foreign influences. From the 2nd to 10th century AD, the city was under the control of the Kingdom of Champa and was an important port town. During the 14th and 15th centuries, the Cham and the Vietnamese fought for control of Hoi An, and as a consequence the city ceased to be a trading center. Peace between the Cham and the Vietnamese in the 16th century once again made possible the accommodation of ships from all over Asia and Europe, bringing merchants in search of silk, porcelain, lacquer, and medicinal herbs. During the Tay Son Rebellion in the 1770s, Hoi An was severely damaged by fighting.

After a speedy reconstruction, the town managed to sustain a two-century tenure as a major international port town where Chinese, Japanese, Dutch, and Portuguese merchants came to trade. During the off-season, seafaring merchants set up shops, and foreigners' colonies began to develop along Hoi An's riverfront. To this day, ethnic Chinese, who settled early in Hoi An, make up a significant portion of the population.

The French arrived in the late 1800s and made Hoi An an administrative post. They even built a rail line to Danang (then called Tourane). By this time, the Thu Bon River, which connected Hoi An to the sea, had begun to fill up with silt, making navigation almost impossible. Danang gradually eclipsed Hoi An as the major port town in the area.

and rice paddies. You can rent a car with a driver from Danang or from any travel agency in Hoi An.

Hoi An has two bus stations, one on Hung Vuong and a second on the corner of Le Hong Phong for public buses servicing north and south routes. Taxis line Thu Bon River to the south of the Hoi An Peninsula. They can also be found outside most hotels or parked on Le Loi Street in Old Town. The going rate is about 1,000d per km. Bikes can be rented for around 20,000d per day from many hotels, and independent bike-hires can be found throughout the town and surrounding streets.

TOURS

Eat Hoi An Culinary Tours

Boost your culinary credentials and learn to pull up a plastic stool like a pro on this four-hour walking street-food tour, accompanied by local foodie Mr. Phuoc, also fondly called Mr. Happy. It's a meandering stroll through the alleyways and markets of the Old Town, allowing ample time to graze at Hoi An's tastiest food stalls, while learning about condiments, culture, and the history of the cuisine with plenty of fun interaction with the vendors. Tour prices start at 1,100,000d and run daily from 2 pm, finishing with sunset drinks by the river. ✉ *37 Phan Chau Trinh, Hoi An* ☏ *090/541–1184* ⊕ *www.eathoian.com.*

Hoi An Photo Tour

Learn the basics of composition, shutter speed, and light exposure while capturing images of farmers in rice fields during a sunrise or sunset tour to local villages. Tours are led by professional photographers, who are familiar and closely connected with locals and students, making tours as fun as they are diverse. The workshop includes boat transportation, coffee, and bikes for exploration. Tours start at 1,000,000d and are suitable

Hoi An is known for its Old Town's lantern-lit streets.

for all levels. ✉ *42 Duong Phan Boi Chau, Cẩm Châu, Hoi An* ☎ *090/567–1898* ⊕ *www.hoianphototour.com.*

Trails of Indochina

The custom package itineraries offered by Trails of Indochina range from Hoi An's historic sights to a romantic dinner set up in a vast rice field. Fees include luxury transportation and knowledgeable English-speaking guides. ✉ *21/1 Ngo Gia Tu St., Vinh Ninh Ward, Hue* ☎ *28/3535–0455 in Ho Chi Minh City, 234/3836–525 in Hue* ⊕ *www.trailsofindochina.com.*

Vespa Adventures Vietnam

One of the big names in Saigon, Vespa Adventures Vietnam offers a full range of vintage Vespa tours exploring the islands, countryside, and beaches of Hoi An, along with a hugely popular street-food night cruise through the lantern-lit streets lining the Old Town. ✉ *Alley 22/2, 170 Ly Thai To St., Hoi An* ☎ *077/299–3585* ⊕ *www.vespaadventures.com.*

◉ Sights

Most of the UNESCO World Heritage Sites, as well as restaurants and boutiques, are located in the Old Town, which can be explored in half a day. The Old Town is strictly reserved for pedestrians and bicycles, with motorbike access limited to a few hours each day.

Did You Know?

The Old House of Tan Ky is one of the oldest and best preserved houses in Hoi An.

Assembly Halls

NOTABLE BUILDING | As part of their cultural tradition, the Chinese built assembly halls as a place for future generations to gather after they migrated to new countries. Once a major Southeast Asian trading port, Hoi An is home to five such halls that date back to the 16th and 17th centuries; however, exact dates for the buildings are unclear from historic records as most have been subjected to newer 18th- and 19th-century improvements. Recognizable by their Chinese architecture, the assembly halls generally feature ornate gates, main halls, altar rooms, and statues and murals in honor of gods and goddesses. Four of Hoi An's assembly halls—Fujian, Hainan, Cantonese, Chinese—are located on Tran Phu Street near the river. The Chaozhou assembly hall is situated in the French Quarter, a short stroll east of Old Town on Nguyen Duy Hieu. Among them, the Fujian Hall, Phuc Kien, is considered the most prominent. Entrance to each assembly hall is one coupon from the five included in the Old Town ticket. ⊠ *46 Tran Phu, Cam Chau, Hoi An* ⊹ *near Thu Bon River* 🖃 *Included in 120,000d tourist-office ticket.*

Central Market

MARKET | This is one of the most enjoyable fresh markets in Vietnam, covering a large area, snaking its way around the French-colonial food hall, Cho Hoi An, down to the river on Bach Dang, with feeder lanes sprouting off down mossy side alleys. The merchants are friendly and a large selection of merchandise is available, but barter hard to strike a good deal—expect to come in at the midway point and haggle upward to around a third off the starting price. The stalls that surround the market are lined with fruit and flower sellers, while the small local shops opposite specialize in bamboo baskets and household wares; this is the best place to pick up the pretty blue-and-white dishware popular in Hoi An.

The fish market down by the river is best avoided during the pungent hours of midday; the best time to visit for ambience and photos is just before sunrise as the conical-hatted traders descend upon fishing boats laden with colorful fish, squid, and giant prawns. ■ **TIP→ Made famous by Anthony Bourdain, Banh Mi Phuong has a small stall here serving quite possibly the best banh mi in Vietnam. To find it walk 50 meters around the outside of Cho (Market) Hoi An, to the left of the well.** ⊠ *Intersection of Nguyen Hue and Tran Phu, Hoi An.*

★ Cham Islands (*Cu Lau Cham*)

ISLAND | **FAMILY** | The Hoi An coast is flanked by eight small, coral-fringed islands featuring beautiful seascapes, deserted white sandy beaches, and some of the best microdiving sites in central Vietnam. Despite their beauty, the islands have never been developed for tourism, and it wasn't until their 2009 designation as a World Biosphere Reserve by UNESCO that anyone took any interest. Those that did were dive companies, limiting visitors to just a couple of dives. From April to September, daily junk and speedboat services run the 18-km (11-mile) route between Cua Dai dock and Hon Lau Island, where you can arrange a homestay or camp on two of the main island beaches—though few visitors do, which makes it one of the most tranquil respites from the touristy beaches of Hoi An and also one of the most beautiful places to watch the sunset from your own private beach. Activities available include snorkeling, diving, swimming, camping, fishing, and trekking. ■ **TIP→ Local tour offices and hotels can arrange island tours. For camping, visit Cham Island Divers (Nguyen Thai Hoc Street) or the Blue Coral Diving (Nguyen Hung Dao Street) in Hoi An.** ⊠ *Hoi An* ⊹ *Daily boat services run from Cua Dai Harbour to Hon Lau Port* 🖃 *70,000 per person.*

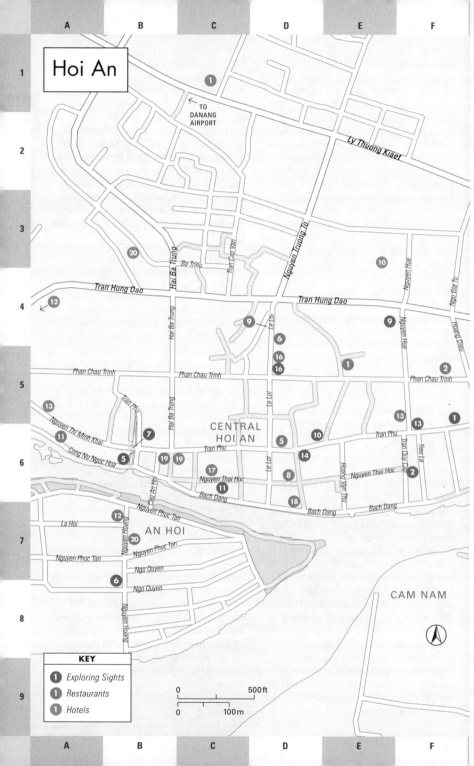

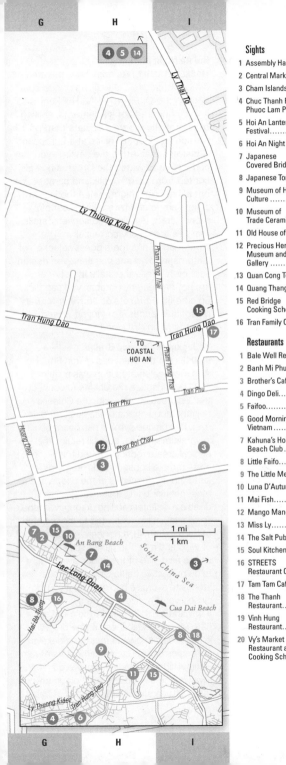

Sights ▼

1 Assembly Halls........... **F5**
2 Central Market........... **F6**
3 Cham Islands.............. **I7**
4 Chuc Thanh Pagoda and Phuoc Lam Pagoda..... **H1**
5 Hoi An Lantern Festival................... **B6**
6 Hoi An Night Market ... **B8**
7 Japanese Covered Bridge **B6**
8 Japanese Tombs........ **G8**
9 Museum of History and Culture **E4**
10 Museum of Trade Ceramics **D6**
11 Old House of Tan Ky..... **C6**
12 Precious Heritage Museum and Fine Art Gallery **H6**
13 Quan Cong Temple **F6**
14 Quang Thang House ... **D6**
15 Red Bridge Cooking School **I4**
16 Tran Family Chapel **D5**

Restaurants ▼

1 Bale Well Restaurant.... **E5**
2 Banh Mi Phuong......... **F5**
3 Brother's Café........... **H6**
4 Dingo Deli................ **G9**
5 Faifoo.................... **D6**
6 Good Morning Vietnam **D4**
7 Kahuna's Hoi An Beach Club **H7**
8 Little Faifo................ **D6**
9 The Little Menu **D4**
10 Luna D'Autunno......... **G7**
11 Mai Fish.................. **A6**
12 Mango Mango **B7**
13 Miss Ly................... **F5**
14 The Salt Pub............. **H7**
15 Soul Kitchen............. **G7**
16 STREETS Restaurant Cafe......... **D5**
17 Tam Tam Café **C6**
18 The Thanh Restaurant.............. **D7**
19 Vinh Hung Restaurant.............. **B6**
20 Vy's Market Restaurant and Cooking School **B7**

Hotels ▼

1 Almanity Hoi An Wellness Resort **C1**
2 An Bang Seaside Village Homestay **G7**
3 Anantara Hoi An Resort...................... **I6**
4 Boutique Hoi An Resort................... **H8**
5 Four Seasons Resort - The Nam Hai **H1**
6 Hoi An Ancient House Resort & Spa **G9**
7 Hoi An Beach Bungalows **G7**
8 Hoi An Beach Resort.... **I8**
9 Hoi An Chic Hotel....... **H8**
10 Hoi An Historic Hotel.... **E3**
11 Hoi An Riverside Resort & Spa **H9**
12 La Siesta Resort & Spa **A4**
13 La Tonnelle **A5**
14 The Moon Villa Hoi An.................... **H1**
15 Muca Hoi An Boutique Resort & Spa **H9**
16 Tra Que Mansion **G8**
17 Vaia Boutique Hotel Hoi An.............. **I4**
18 Victoria Hoi An Beach Resort & Spa **I8**
19 Vinh Hung Heritage Hotel........... **B6**
20 Vinh Hung Library Hotel............. **B3**

Chuc Thanh Pagoda and Phuoc Lam Pagoda

TEMPLE | Head north on Nguyen Truong To Street for approximately 1 km (½ mile) to the end, turn left, and follow the path until you reach Chuc Thanh Pagoda, the oldest and most revered pagoda in Hoi An. Founded in 1454 by Minh Hai, a Chinese Buddhist monk, the pagoda contains several ancient religious objects, including bells and gongs made of stone and wood. On the way back, stop at the Phuoc Lam Pagoda, built in the mid-17th century. Note the interesting Chinese architecture and the large collection of ceramics on its roof. ⊠ Hoi An ⊠ Free.

Hoi An Lantern Festival

PUBLIC ART | Every month on the 14th day of the lunar calendar, Hoi An closes Old Town to traffic, switches off its lights, and hosts the magical Lantern Festival. Domestic travelers flock to the streets, and temples and pagodas open their doors for ancestor worship. Most people choose to watch the festivities from a restaurant balcony, but to really get the best experience you need to tackle the crowds head on and mingle with the locals at street level. Festivities start at sunset and this is the best time to visit the candlelit pagodas (which are free to enter on full moon) and take in the street entertainment, pop-up poetry reading groups, and live music. As darkness falls, approach the small river boats that line Bach Dang and arrange for a half-hour cruise, ending at An Hoi, where a short stroll on quieter streets lined with restaurants leads you to the glowing night lantern market where you can pick up souvenirs and grab a taxi back to your hotel. ⊠ Hoi An ✛ The action is centered in the area between the Japanese Covered Bridge and the Cau An Hoi Bridge.

Hoi An Night Market

MARKET | FAMILY | As dusk falls, the area directly opposite the walking bridge connecting the Old Town to An Hoi Peninsula is lit by hundreds of silk lanterns, spilling out from little wooden chalets that wouldn't look out of place at a European Christmas market. In the daytime you can come here to watch the lanterns being crafted from wafts of silk and bamboo, but it's not until night, when the lantern sellers are joined by a whole host of mobile craft, jewelry, and souvenir stalls, that this area really comes alive. The night market has the biggest selection of lanterns in town and you can even design your own. While the stalls in between are not particularly notable, you can pick up cute little trinkets as souvenir for very reasonable prices. ⊠ Nguyen Hoang St., Phuong Minh An, Hoi An.

★ Japanese Covered Bridge

BRIDGE | On the west end of Tran Phu, Hoi An's most celebrated icon was built in 1593 by Japanese merchants to connect the Japanese quarter with the Chinese neighborhood on the other side of the river. This unique symbol has been rebuilt several times since, but still retains the original ornate roofing, arched frame, and small temple housed inside. Legends surround the functions of the bridge, the most popular being that it was built to disable a disaster-causing dragon, with the small altar inside dedicated to the worship of Bac De Tran Vu, a northern god in charge of wind and rain. The pair of spirit dogs on the east side of the bridge are thought to be protective deities, placed on altar stones to exorcise bad omens. If you look closely you'll notice they are different sizes: a boy and a girl. Some say the monkeys here represent Japanese emperors. What is not widely known is that the monkeys are copies carved by the carpenters of Kim Bong Village; the original pair were swept away during a flood and washed up beyond repair 20 years later. ⊠ West end of Tran

Phu St., Phuong Minh An, Hoi An ⊞ *Included in the 120,000d tourist-office ticket.*

Japanese Tombs

CEMETERY | Erected in the 1600s, these are the few remaining tombs of Hoi An's old Japanese community. Although the tombs—tombstones, really—are not nearly as grand as those in Hue, it's worth the trek if only to see the "suburbs" of Hoi An. En route you'll encounter families sitting in their front yards and field workers harvesting rice. Buried in the first tomb along the dirt path clearly visible in the front yard of a family home is a Japanese merchant named Masai. About another 1,500 feet ahead is the most famous of Hoi An's Japanese tombs, the burial place of a Japanese merchant named Yajirobei, who died in 1647. Perched right in the middle of a working rice field, his tomb has an almost supernatural feel. The main tombs are easily accessible by bicycle—just head along Hai Ba Trung Street and go north of Old Town. To find the tombs, keep your eyes peeled for the white-and-yellow signs positioned along the right side of the road. (Cars are not recommended because the tombs are at the end of narrow, rugged paths.) ■ **TIP→ Continue 5 km (3 miles) to the end of Hai Ba Trung for a refreshing dip and lunch at one of the bohemian seaside shacks on An Bang beach.** ⊠ *North of Old Town, Hai Ba Trung, Cam Son, Hoi An.*

Museum of History and Culture

HISTORY MUSEUM | This small museum—housed in just one large room—provides a small insight into Hoi An's history and culture. On display are ancient bowls, cups, and other ceramics, many of them archaeological artifacts dating back to the Cham. A collection of traditional Chinese objects includes pagoda bells and the "watchful eyes" placed above doorways for protection. Information is scant, so you are likely to leave underwhelmed and none the wiser, but the old black-and-white photos of 20th-century Hoi An make for an interesting comparison to the town today. The connecting door to the back of Quang Ong Temple provides a more interesting view. ⊠ *7 Nguyen Hue St., Hoi An* ⊞ *Included in 120,000d Old Town ticket.*

Museum of Trade Ceramics

HISTORY MUSEUM | The ancient Diep Dong Nguyen House has been converted into a small museum dedicated to the history of ceramics in Hoi An. The collection includes ancient wares, some of them recovered from shipwrecks in the surrounding waters, and a large assortment of household objects, such as bowls and vases. Possibly the most interesting thing you'll find here are the maps that date back as far as the 13th century, detailing the various marine trade routes. There are also detailed architectural drawings of the restored town houses, which provide helpful explanations of the different architectural influences throughout the Old Town. ⊠ *80 Tran Phu St., Hoi An* ⊞ *Included in 120,000d Old Town ticket.*

★ Old House of Tan Ky

HISTORIC HOME | One of the oldest and best-preserved private houses in Hoi An, this structure has remained largely unchanged in the 200 years since it was built in 1741. Seven generations of the Tan Ky family have lived here. The house incorporates Chinese, Japanese, and Vietnamese styles. Chinese poetry is engraved in mother-of-pearl on the walls, each character formed in the shape of birds in various stages of flight. Look up into the eaves and you will see symbols of dragons, fruit, crossed sabers, and silk intricately carved into the wooden framework. The back door was constructed to open onto the river so that waterborne goods could be easily transported into the house; look out for the marks etched in to the wall recording the height of the annual flood waters. ⊠ *101 Nguyen Thai Hoc, Minh An Ward, Hoi An* ⊞ *Included in 120,000d Old Town ticket.*

Did You Know?

The Gate of Phuc Kien Assembly Hall was built by the Chinese in the late 17th century and is one of the most popular spots to photograph in Hoi An.

★ Precious Heritage Museum and Fine Art Gallery

ART GALLERY | FAMILY | This museum offers a wonderful look into the cultural identity of Vietnam's ethnic minority communities. Each placard gives facts about the region, population, and traditions of several minority groups in English, French, and Vietnamese. The museum's curator, Réhahn, is a professional French photographer who has been snapping portraits of these amazing individuals and collecting their stories and artifacts since 2013. The coffee shop inside sells K'ho coffee, harvested by the K'ho people in the central highlands. ⊠ 26 Phan Boi Chau St., Hoi An ☎ 094/982–0698 ⊕ www.rehahnphotographer.com.

Quan Cong Temple

TEMPLE | FAMILY | Founded in 1653 by the Chinese community, this impressive temple is dedicated to Quan Van Truong, a revered general of the Chinese Han dynasty. The temple is divided into four parts: the front hall, the left and right sections, and the main sanctuary. The entrance leads through a large garden to the temple, where the main altar is, along with a gilt-and-papier-mâché statue of the general standing between two life-size, jolly-looking horses. Quan Cong lends itself to contemplation and meditation, and you get a real sense of that in the rear courtyard, gazing up at the unicorns and dragons perching on the colorful ceramic tiled roof or watching the small school of fish that happily dart around in the pond out front. The carp, symbolic of patience in Chinese mythology, is displayed throughout. Every year, on June 24 of the lunar calendar, Hoi An organizes a ceremony for Quan Cong, and pilgrims, especially merchants, come to the temple to make offerings. ⊠ 24 Tran Phu, Cam Chau, Hoi An ⊠ Included in 120,000d Old Town ticket.

Quang Thang House

HISTORIC HOME | FAMILY | One of Hoi An's ancient family homes, Quang Thang was built about 300 years ago by the current owners' Chinese ancestors. This house has some beautiful wood carvings featuring peacocks and flowers on the walls of the rooms that surround the mossy courtyard. These were sculpted by the craftsmen from the Kim Bong carpentry village, who are renowned for their intricate craftsmanship of the Hue garden houses. It's a beautiful and very well-preserved example of a trader's house, popular with large tour groups. ■ TIP→ If Quang Thang House is busy, wait it out with a coffee at Lantern Town restaurant across the road. ⊠ 77 Tran Phu St., Hoi An ⊠ Included in 120,000d Old Town ticket.

Red Bridge Cooking School

SCHOOL | FAMILY | Learn the secrets of Vietnamese cuisine at this cooking school located beside Thu Bon River. Half- and full-day cooking classes are available and include a market tour, boat transportation, and either lunch or dinner. Courses cost $23–$59 (550,000d–1,300,000d) and commence at Hai Café in Old Town, where they also run evening cooking classes daily (111 Tran Phu Street). ■ TIP→ Take your bathing suit and grab a hammock by the pool; complimentary access is offered to all diners and students. ⊠ Thon 4, Cam Thanh, 2 km (1 miles) outside of Hoi An, Hoi An ⊹ along the banks of the Thu Bon River ☎ 0510/3933–222 ⊕ redbridge.visithoian. com ⊠ starts at 550,000d.

Tran Family Chapel

NOTABLE BUILDING | FAMILY | This elegantly designed house was built in 1802 by Tran Tu Nhuc, a 19th-century Mandarin and Chinese ambassador, as a place of worship for the Tran family's deceased ancestors. It's packed with interesting antiquities. In the morning, light floods down through a glass tile in the roof, illuminating the family altar that stands behind three sliding doors—the left for men and the right for women. The central door (designed for deceased ancestors to return home) is opened only at Tet and other festivals; it's an architectural touch common for older residential houses throughout the country. The altar houses a box with pictures and names of dead relatives, a 250-year-old book that records the Tran family history, and a bowl of Chinese coins representing yin and yang—toss one for good luck. Tours are given in English by members of the Tran family. ☒ *21 Le Loi, Phuong Minh An, Hoi An* 🌐 *Included in 120,000d Old Town ticket.*

🅐 Beaches

★ An Bang Beach

BEACH | FAMILY | The locals' favorite beach, An Bang is one of the few remaining public beaches on the long Hoi An–Danang coastline. Locals flock here for sunrise swimming and sunset family picnics, leaving this lovely stretch of beach almost deserted during the day. The beach offers stunning views of the neighboring Marble Mountains, Danang Bay, and Cham Island. A row of palm-thatched restaurants borders the clean, sandy beach, offering free use of beach loungers and umbrellas if you buy food or drinks. Competition is fierce and staff can be pushy. Development has been slow but steady, with only a few homestays and holiday cottages, but plans for large resorts at both ends of the beach are set to change this over the next few years. **Amenities:** food and drink; showers. **Best for:** swimming; sunsets; families; surfing; walking. ☒ *D. Hai Ba Trung, 7 km (4½ miles) north of Hoi An, An Bang.*

Cua Dai Beach

BEACH | FAMILY | Ten minutes from the Old Town is Hoi An's main public beach, where clear water and warm surf beckon tourists and locals alike. This 3-km (2-mile) stretch of white, powdery sand makes for a perfect place to bask under the sunshine. Though the area has been developed and resorts have been built along the shores, there are still a

few quieter stretches. The public beach area to the north has retained much of its sand and the beach is clean. It's the perfect spot to escape the sweltering humidity of Old Town during the hottest months. Walking beach vendors can be a problem, heckling people to buy fresh fruit and crafts, but most are easily rebuffed with a firm "no, thank you." Food shacks sell fresh fish, squid, and shellfish, and offer amenities. Bikes can be rented for about 20,000d per day; Jet Skis start at 1,200,000d for half an hour. **Amenities:** food and drink; parking (free); toilets; showers; water sports. **Best for:** surfing; swimming; walking. ■ TIP➜ **If Cua Dai Beach is crowded, walk or bike 3 km (2 miles) north to An Bang beach.** ☒ *Cua Dai Beach, Hoi An.*

Ha My Beach

BEACH | FAMILY | A little way outside of Hoi An, this peaceful beach, located midway between the award-winning Nam Hai and Le Belhamy resorts, is the best place to head to escape the hawkers and crowds that frequent the more famous Cua Dai Beach. With just a few incredibly good seafood restaurants and a couple of loungers and umbrellas, this regularly cleaned, gently shelving beach offers great swimming conditions, a chilled-out atmosphere, and plenty of space for children to run around safely. **Amenities:** showers; toilets; food and drink; parking (free). **Best for:** swimming; walking; solitude; sunset. ☒ *6 km (3½ miles) north of An Bang along Danang coastal road, Dien Duong Village, Cam An, Hoi An.*

🅧 Restaurants

Offering a delightful collision of flavors, Hoi An has everything from classic Vietnamese restaurants and noodle shacks to gourmet delis and charitable cafés. There's no shortage of eateries in the Old Town, where menus lean heavily on Vietnamese fusion with reasonable prices, considering the location. Cross over Thu Bon River to experience Hoi An Peninsula

An Bang Beach is a great spot for surfing and swimming right outside of Hoi An.

where an outcrop of trendy restaurants and bars add life to Nguyen Phuc Chu Street. Bordering the Old Town is the central market, packed with vendors selling everything from fish and noodles to flowers and produce. This is the best place to try local dishes like *cao lau* (rice noodles topped with pork and herbs) and *banh bao vac* (rose-shape steamed dumplings). For a more in-depth look at Hoi An's cuisine, try a cooking course or culinary tour.

OLD TOWN

Bale Well Restaurant

$$$ | **VIETNAMESE** | **FAMILY** | Local families who come in droves to this popular no-frills diner make out-of-town visitors feel warmly welcome, even if you don't master the art of rolling the perfect *banh xeo*. There's no menu; just pull up a stool and within minutes you'll be presented with pork skewers, crispy pancakes stuffed with bean sprouts, deep-fried shrimp spring rolls, rice paper, various greens, a satay-style dip, and an array of condiments. **Known for:** delicious local food; tourist spot; roll-your-own rolls. $ *Average main: d175,000* ✉ *Cut down alleyway near Le Loi end of Phan Chau Trinh, 45 Ngo 51 Tran Hung Dao, Phuong Minh An, Hoi An* ☎ *023/5386–4443* ⊕ *www.facebook.com/BaleWellrestaurant* ▭ *No credit cards.*

★ Banh Mi Phuong

$ | **VIETNAMESE** | **FAMILY** | Madam Phuong, the shop owner, serves from a simple little take-away counter, next door to a bakery on the edge of Old Town. When famed foodie Anthony Bourdain visited, he declared the banh mi served here to be quite possibly the best in Vietnam; and he might just have been right. **Known for:** chef recommended; delicious banh mi; Old Town staple. $ *Average main: d30,000* ✉ *2b Phan Chu Trinh, Phuong Minh An, Hoi An* ☎ *090/574–3773* ▭ *No credit cards.*

Brother's Café

$$$ | **VIETNAMESE** | **FAMILY** | The standard but good Vietnamese food served here—spring rolls and fried rice—may not be spectacular, but the setting is:

a beautifully restored colonial villa on the banks of the Thu Bon River. In the evenings you can sit and sip a drink in the lovely garden out back as you watch local fisherfolk ply their trade. **Known for:** Vietnamese classics; river view; vegan and vegetarian menu. [$] *Average main: d350,000* ✉ *27-29 Duong Phan Boi Chau, Cam Chau, Hoi An* ✣ *Across Precious Heritage Museum and Fine Art Gallery* ☎ *0235/391–4150.*

Dingo Deli

$$ | **SANDWICHES** | **FAMILY** | A popular rainy-day hangout for expats and families, this homey Western bakery, restaurant, and delicatessen midway between Cua Dai beach and the Old Town offers a large adventure playground and a menu packed with huge portions of home favorites, including delicious Aussie meat pie, home-baked cakes, and a great kids' menu. **Known for:** gourmet sandwiches; bottomless coffees; digital nomads. [$] *Average main: d79,000* ✉ *463 Cua Dai Rd., Cam Chau, Hoi An* ☎ *070/600–9300* 🌐 *dingodelihoian.com.*

Faifoo

$$ | **VIETNAMESE** | **FAMILY** | Faifoo has brilliant service and the staff have been known to give excellent recommendations. Come here for refreshing fruit shakes, as well as a great multicourse sampler menu of chicken and pork dishes, all for next to nothing (the five-course tasting menu is only 140,000d). **Known for:** street views; cold wine; shrimp dumplings. [$] *Average main: d150,000* ✉ *104 Tran Phu St., Hoi An* ☎ *0235/386–1548.*

Good Morning Vietnam

$$$ | **ITALIAN** | **FAMILY** | This traditional Italian restaurant is a popular spot in the Old Town center for those looking for a break from the standard Vietnamese fare. During the day, the welcoming, homely environs make for a quiet rest stop, where you can enjoy a good Italian coffee or a light bite from the second-floor balcony overlooking the streets. **Known for:** giant pizza; street views; decent Italian food. [$] *Average main: d200,000* ✉ *11 Le Loi St., Phuong Minh An, Hoi An* ☎ *0235/391–0227* 🌐 *gmviet.net.*

★ Little Faifo

$$$ | **VIETNAMESE** | **FAMILY** | Fusing art, music, history, and cuisine, this 19th-century house in Hoi An's Old Quarter has been beautifully restored and offers silver service at remarkable prices. Slightly overshadowed by the setting, the menu is Vietnamese-meets-modern cuisine with such dishes as bean sprout dumplings, mango and lotus salad, caramelized pork, and wok-fried ancient noodles. **Known for:** art collection; four-course set menu; amazing balcony seating. [$] *Average main: d325,000* ✉ *66 Nguyen Thai Hoc St., Hoi An* ☎ *0235/391–7444* 🌐 *www.littlefaifo.com.*

Mai Fish

$$$ | **VIETNAMESE** | **FAMILY** | In the Japanese Quarter, beside the river, is this classic Vietnamese restaurant resembling an upscale residence with its ornate armoires, wooden chairs, and a lantern-lit courtyard where you can listen to soft jazz. Lighter menu items such as baguettes, spring rolls, and salads are offered alongside duck or prawn curry, tofu, rice platters, and seafood dishes. **Known for:** slow-cooked duck curry with taro; green papaya salad with grilled prawns; open-air kitchen. [$] *Average main: d300,000* ✉ *45 Nguyen Thi Minh Khai, Phuong Minh An, Hoi An* ☎ *0235/392–5545* 🌐 *www.facebook.com/maifishhoian.*

Mango Mango

$$$ | **ASIAN** | **FAMILY** | A spinoff of the original Mango Rooms in Old Town, this Vietnamese fusion restaurant is located along the river directly across from the Japanese Covered Bridge. Owner-chef Duc has created an innovative menu of modern-Asian-meets-the-world, inspired from his 20-plus years of travels abroad. **Known for:** view of Hoi An's Old town; classic Vietnamese cuisine with

ingredients like giant prawns, mangoes, and cilantro; open-air terrace. $ *Average main: d400,000 ✉ 45 Nguyen Phuc Chu, Phuong Minh An, Hoi An ☎ 0235/391–1863 ⊕ www.facebook.com/mangomangorestaurant.*

Miss Ly

$$ | VIETNAMESE | FAMILY | Miss Ly was one of the first cooks in town to open her humble, market-edge restaurant to the trickle of travelers astute enough to have put Hoi An on their itinerary almost 20 years ago. Two decades later, Ly is still in the kitchen pouring her heart and soul into each dish served. **Known for:** a wait that's worth it; White Rose, steamed pork-and-shrimp dumplings; cao lau, chewy udon-like noodles with a thick five-spice gravy. $ *Average main: d100,000 ✉ 22 Nguyen Hue St., Phuong Minh An, Hoi An ☎ 090/523–4864.*

STREETS Restaurant Café

$$$ | VIETNAMESE | FAMILY | Street youth are given the opportunity to refine their hospitality skills during an 18-month training program here through the non-profit organization STREETS International, which employs orphaned and disadvantaged Vietnamese teens, many of whom go on to work at five-star restaurants and hotels. The restaurant café lives up to the highest standards of contemporary Vietnamese and international cuisine. **Known for:** 10 options customizable for vegetarians; delicious food; a good cause. $ *Average main: d150,000 ✉ 17 Le Loi St., Phuong Minh An, Hoi An ☎ 0235/391–1948 ⊕ www.streetsinternational.org.*

Tam Tam Café

$$ | CAFÉ | FAMILY | In a tastefully restored former teahouse, this café-restaurant is the perfect place to unwind over a coffee and French pastry or a cold beer during a busy day of sightseeing. For people-watching grab a balcony table; for shady seclusion there's a quiet courtyard garden; and for rainy days there's a pool table and games room. **Known for:**

charming architecture; relaxed ambience; central town location. $ *Average main: d75,000 ✉ 110 Nguyen Thai Hoc St., Hoi An ☎ 0235/386–2212 ⊕ www.tamtamcafe-hoian.com.*

The Thanh Restaurant

$$ | VIETNAMESE | FAMILY | This open-air restaurant makes a splendid flounder (or whatever whitefish happens to be fresh that day) cooked in banana leaves, as well as a refreshing squid salad prepared with lemon, onion, peanuts, and cucumber. The view of the lantern-lit street and the Thu Bon River a couple of meters away add to its authentic Vietnamese vibe. **Known for:** fresh food; candle-lit riverfront dining; cheerful service. $ *Average main: d100,000 ✉ 76 Bach Dang, Phuong Minh An, Hoi An ☎ 0235/386–1366.*

Vinh Hung Restaurant

$$$ | VIETNAMESE | FAMILY | This peaceful restaurant serves seafood and local specialties such as "white roses," the delicious shrimp dumpling that resembles a rose. Chinese lanterns and lacquered chairs decorate the place, which caters primarily to tourists. **Known for:** quick service; people-watching; traditional Hoi An delights. $ *Average main: d180,000 ✉ 01 Chau Thuong Van, Phuong Minh An, Hoi An ☎ 0235/386–2203 ⊕ www.vinhhungrestaurant.com.*

★ Vy's Market Restaurant and Cooking School

$$ | VIETNAMESE | FAMILY | As the first fully interactive street food experience in Vietnam, this buzzy, upscale food hall, owned by local-celebrity chef Ms. Vy, attracts a steady stream of enthusiastic foodies keen to take a culinary tour of Hoi An's gastronomic classics. The menu here is visual, and diners are invited to wander among the various food stations where traditional dishes like *cau lao* noodles, banh mi, and savory country pancakes are made to order, to be devoured on simple bench seating arranged in the central courtyard. **Known for:** traditional market setting; loads of tour groups; ad hoc cooking demonstrations. $ Average main: d120,000 ✉ 03 Nguyen Hoang St., Hoi An ✛ 3-min walk from the Japanese Covered Bridge ☎ 0235/392–6926 ⊕ www.tastevietnam.asia.

ON THE BEACH

From bia hoi (local draft beer) and barbecued seafood snacks through to fine French and Italian cuisine served from a chic palm-thatched cabana looking over the glittering white sand, Hoi An's beaches make for a year-round dining destination away from the crowds in the Old Town. An Bang beach is home to the highest concentration of family-friendly dining opportunities, with large grassy garden areas where kids can play safely. In the summer months from March through to October at sunset, locals flock to the beach, setting up seafood barbeques and food stalls in the sand, hawking delicious, cheap beach snacks like squid, shellfish, and crab.

Kahuna's Hoi An Beach Club

$$ | INTERNATIONAL | FAMILY | Managed by the Vietnam Backpackers Hostel, this beach bar offers a complimentary pool, bocce ball court, and great music, as well as alcoholic slushies for 50,000d. The cheeseburger spring rolls are an interesting fusion, and the buffalo chicken sandwich is definitely worth the money. Known for: paddle boards available; beach access; extremely helpful staff. $ Average main: d100,000 ✉ Nguyen Phan Vinh, Cam An, An Bang ✛ Between An Bang and Cua Dai beaches ☎ 093/675–6755 ⊕ www.vietnambackpackerhostels.com.

Luna D'Autunno

$$$ | ITALIAN | FAMILY | Clay-oven pizza, pasta, antipasti plates, and fine wines, all sourced from Italy, can be enjoyed on a tropically planted beachfront garden, or, on wintery days, holed up in a cozy corner by the kitchen. The sesame-coated tuna with salad, Pecorino cheese, and olives are to die for, as are the Italian homemade desserts. Known for: beach view; attentive service; the best pizzas in Hoi An. $ Average main: d200,000 ✉ 6 Cam An, An Bang ☎ 0359/470–374 ⊕ www.facebook.com/lunahoian.

The Salt Pub

$$$ | INTERNATIONAL | FAMILY | Run by an international team, the Salt Pub is a super family-friendly restaurant with a touch of artistic flavor. They've got rotating (and amazing) breakfast options, and interesting margarita flavors like watermelon-mint and pineapple-coconut. Known for: backyard beach; spicy pho; balcony seating. $ Average main: d100,000 ✉ 32 Nguyen Phan Vinh, An Bang ☎ 0235/375–7777 ⊕ anbangbeachside.com.

★ Soul Kitchen

$$ | ASIAN | FAMILY | The most social spot on the beach, Soul Kitchen attracts a year-round mix of expats and local visitors, with frequent live music and open mic events. During the day the shady grass frontage, pool table, and board games keep kids entertained, leaving parents free to relax in raised cabanas with a Vietnamese-French menu, wine list, and cold draft Tiger beer. Known for: live music; standouts like the mixed fish carpaccio or beef bourguignon served with freshly baked bread; beach access. $ Average main: d100,000 ✉ Far left at beach intersection, An Bang Beach, An Bang ☎ 090/644–0320 ⊕ www.soulkitchen.sitew.com.

🛏 Hotels

Beachfront resorts cater to discerning travelers with spa treatments and infinity pools, while those closer to the center are near restaurants, shops, and historic sights. Better value can be had by staying in one of the many hotels and resorts situated among the rice fields and riverways midway between town and beach. Most provide free use of bicycles, and taxis are inexpensive.

If you plan to stay in town, opt for a hotel with a river view or one that offers daily shuttles to the beach.

OLD TOWN

★ Almanity Hoi An Wellness Resort

$$$ | **HOTEL** | **FAMILY** | The spa-focused Almanity Hoi An Wellness Resort offers contemporary, luxurious digs with a focus on wellness, just a 10-minute stroll from Old Town. **Pros:** the herbal-infused cocktail menu; largest resort spa in Hoi An; heated pool. **Cons:** lax policy on guest noise; street-facing rooms are noisy (a few overlook a nightclub); out-of-town location. [$] *Rooms from: d1,099,000* ✉ *326 Ly Thuong Kiet, Tan An Ward, Hoi An* ☎ *0235/366–6888* 🌐 *almanityhoian.com* 🍴 *Free Breakfast* 🛏 *138 rooms.*

Anantara Hoi An Resort

$$$ | **RESORT** | **FAMILY** | Situated in low-rise buildings, rooms here have an apartment-like feel, with small living areas and three stairs leading to king-size beds. **Pros:** complimentary bikes, yoga, and beach shuttle; great location near Old Town; helpful staff. **Cons:** daybed patios lack privacy; thin walls; flood-prone area. [$] *Rooms from: d2,400,000* ✉ *1 Pham Hong Thai St., Hoi An* ☎ *0235/391–4555* 🌐 *www.anantara.com/en/hoi-an* 🛏 *94 rooms* 🍴 *Free Breakfast.*

Hoi An Ancient House Resort & Spa

$$$ | **HOTEL** | **FAMILY** | Tucked away in a tropical garden, this thin-walled hotel pays tribute to Vietnamese culture with its rice paper factory and a 200-year-old house, where fifth-generation family members still live today. **Pros:** newly renovated; great breakfast; local charm. **Cons:** tall bathtubs are awkward for exiting; no elevator; not suitable for those with mobility issues. [$] *Rooms from: d800,000* ✉ *377 Cua Dai, Cam Chau, Hoi An* ☎ *0235/392–3377* 🌐 *ancienthouseresort.com* 🍴 *Free Breakfast* 🛏 *56 rooms.*

★ Hoi An Chic Hotel

$$$ | **HOTEL** | **FAMILY** | Surrounded by rice fields and duck ponds and a short jeep ride from town and beach, this eco-chic countryside pad is a perfect romantic bolthole without the heavy price tag of an Old Town address. **Pros:** rooftop pool with awe-inspiring views; quiet; complimentary jeep transportation. **Cons:** far from city center; mosquitoes; distance to restaurants/beach. [$] *Rooms from: d1,400,000* ✉ *Lane off Cua Dai Rd., Nguyen Trai St., Hoi An* ☎ *0235/392–6799* 🌐 *www.hoianchic.com* 🛏 *17 rooms* 🍴 *Free Breakfast.*

Hoi An Historic Hotel

$$$ | **HOTEL** | **FAMILY** | This tour-group darling and one of Hoi An's oldest resort hotels is renowned for its friendly staff and fantastic location, a five-minute walk from Old Town. **Pros:** family-friendly; wonderful staff; town location. **Cons:** hard beds; pool and street-facing rooms can be noisy; Wi-Fi connection is poor. [$] *Rooms from: d1,241,625* ✉ *10 Tran Hung Dao St., Hoi An* ☎ *0235/386–1445* 🌐 *www.hoianhistorichotel.com.vn* 🛏 *150 rooms* 🍴 *Free Breakfast.*

Hoi An Riverside Resort & Spa

$$$$ | **RESORT** | **FAMILY** | Midway between the town of Hoi An and Cua Dai Beach, the Hoi An Riverside Resort & Spa may be the most peaceful accommodation in Vietnam. **Pros:** quiet pool; free transport to town and beach; spectacular views. **Cons:** mosquitoes; distance from restaurants; rooms and facilities are showing age. [$] *Rooms from: d2,400,140* ✉ *3 km (2 miles) from Hoi An Town, 175 Cua Dai, Cam Son, Hoi An* ☎ *0235/386–4800* 🍴 *Free Breakfast* 🛏 *64 rooms.*

★ La Siesta Resort & Spa

$$$ | **RESORT** | **FAMILY** | With two swimming pools—a saltwater and freshwater—and staff who make a point to learn your name and preferences, this beautiful resort offers the very best in customer service and design. **Pros:** well-appointed rooms; perfect service records; private spot near An Bang Beach. **Cons:** a little far from airport or train; thin walls. [$] *Rooms from: d2,294,725* ✉ *132 Hung Vuong,*

Phuong Cam Pho, Hoi An ☎ *0235/391–5912* ⊕ *www.lasiestaresorts.com* ⮂ *107 rooms* ⦿ *Free Breakfast.*

La Tonnelle

$$ | B&B/INN | FAMILY | This small family-run B&B, a short walk from the Japanese Bridge, has a bohemian vibe, with just two artfully styled en suite guest rooms and a three-bedroom family house (complete with lounge and kitchen) set above a shady terraced café. **Pros:** great restaurant scene on the doorstep; family-friendly; Old Town pedestrian location. **Cons:** bathrooms could do with an upgrade; no TVs in rooms; better options for the same price. ⑨ *Rooms from: d488,372* ✉ *44 Nguyen Thi Minh Khai, Hoi An* ☎ *016/3405–8534* ⊕ *www.facebook.com/latonnellehoian* ⮂ *3 rooms* ⦿ *No Meals.*

The Moon Villa Hoi An

$$ | B&B/INN | FAMILY | This budget homestay on the outskirts of town offers fantastic accommodations, incredible service, and exceptional tailoring on-site, without the hassle of endless fittings in town. **Pros:** great value; free cooking classes; free bikes. **Cons:** street noise; 5 km (3 miles) from the beach; 15-minute walk to Old Town. ⑨ *Rooms from: d441,860* ✉ *157 Thai To, Cam Son, Hoi An* ☎ *0385/051–081* ⊕ *www.themoonvillahoian.com* ⮂ *5 rooms* ⦿ *Free Breakfast.*

Muca Hoi An Boutique Resort & Spa

$$ | RESORT | FAMILY | Laid-back, intimate, and set amid lush tropical gardens, the Muca sits on the river's edge under the shade of coconut trees, just 4 km (2 miles) from Old Town and the beach. **Pros:** comfortable beds; great value; on-site spa. **Cons:** mosquitoes; unwalkable distance to beach or town; light sleepers should be aware that village community announcements sometimes start up at 5 am. ⑨ *Rooms from: d545,455* ✉ *115-117 Alley, Cua Dai St, Cam Thanh Village, Hoi An* ✣ *30km from Da Nang International Airport*

☎ *0935/930–222* ⊕ *mucahoian.com* ⮂ *36 rooms* ⦿ *Free Breakfast.*

Tra Que Mansion

$$$ | B&B/INN | FAMILY | Started as a bed-and-breakfast in Saigon, Tra Que Mansion has evolved into a respectable and ethical chain focused on treating every guest like a neighbor and every team member like a friend. **Pros:** energetic and hip design; halfway between the beach and town; free bicycles. **Cons:** on-site parking limited; village can get rowdy on holidays or during celebrations; no elevator. ⑨ *Rooms from: d1,400,000* ✉ *Tra Que Vegetable Village, Hoi An* ☎ *093/240–0899* ⦿ *Free Breakfast* ⮂ *7 rooms.*

Vaia Boutique Hotel Hoi An

$$ | HOTEL | FAMILY | If you have come to Hoi An to shop, the fashion-savvy Vaia Boutique Hotel, a well-located, affordable but chic mini-hotel owned by tailor giants Yaly (staying here gets you 10% off at any of their shops in the Old Town), is an excellent choice. **Pros:** tailor shop discounts; great value and location; free bikes. **Cons:** limited facilities; street-facing rooms can be noisy; average amenities. ⑨ *Rooms from: d431,818* ✉ *489 Cua Dai, Cam Chau, Hoi An* ☎ *0510/391–6499* ⊕ *www.facebook.com/vaia.boutique.hotel.hoian* ⮂ *18 rooms* ⦿ *Free Breakfast.*

★ Vinh Hung Heritage Hotel

$$$ | HOTEL | FAMILY | Made famous for providing Michael Caine with a dressing room (the decadent Suite 208) during the filming of *The Quiet American*, this charming 200-year-old timber merchant house has the best address in the city: right in the heart of the Old Town. **Pros:** welcoming staff; complimentary use of sister hotel (the Vinh Hung Resort) pool; the central Old Town location. **Cons:** dark rooms; heritage suites with front-facing balconies are noisy; bathrooms could be improved. ⑨ *Rooms from: d1,627,907* ✉ *143 Tran Phu St., Hoi An* ☎ *0235/392–0757* ⊕ *www.vinhhungheritagehotel.com* ⮂ *6 rooms* ⦿ *Free Breakfast.*

Vinh Hung Library Hotel

$$$ | HOTEL | FAMILY | The sweeping city views from the rooftop pool are a bonus for travelers in search of a great-value base close to the Old Town. **Pros:** boutique hotel ambience; pool; library. **Cons:** ground-floor rooms can be noisy at times; standard rooms have no windows; limited breakfast menu. [$] *Rooms from: d794,500* ⊠ *96 Ba Trieu, Phuong Minh An, Hoi An* ☎ *0376/700–700* ⊕ *www. vinhhunglibraryhotel.com* ⇆ *26 rooms* ⦿I *Free Breakfast.*

ON THE BEACH

An Bang Seaside Village Homestay

$$$ | B&B/INN | FAMILY | These family-friendly residences, scattered among a tropical fruit grove 4 km (2½ miles) from Old Town combine luxurious living with quirky An Bang beach style. **Pros:** great for kids; beach location; near bars and restaurants. **Cons:** village life starts early; no pool; books up quickly. [$] *Rooms from: d1,767,442* ⊠ *An Bang Village, Cam An, An Bang* ☎ *090/523–6122* ⊕ *www. anbangseasidevillage.com* ⇆ *9 houses* ⦿I *Free Breakfast.*

Boutique Hoi An Resort

$$$$ | RESORT | FAMILY | For beach villa stays, the colonial-style Boutique Hoi An Resort located on the sandy coastal stretch between Cua Dai and An Bang Beach is one of the most decadent in town. **Pros:** beautiful beach; good local restaurants nearby; free transfers to Old Town. **Cons:** spa privacy could be improved; books up well in advance; expensive. [$] *Rooms from: d4,000,000* ⊠ *34 Lac Long Quan St., Cam An, Hoi An* ☎ *0235/393–9111* ⊕ *www.boutique-hoianresort.com* ⇆ *110 rooms* ⦿I *Free Breakfast.*

★ Four Seasons Resort - The Nam Hai

$$$$ | RESORT | FAMILY | Set on an idyllic beach on Vietnam's culturally rich Central Coast, Four Seasons Resort The Nam Hai harmoniously combines sultry resort vibes and inspiring ancient traditions to form a luxury property now regarded as one of Vietnam's finest. **Pros:** superb restaurant and spa; pool villas include personal butler, cocktail bar, and private pool; excellent service. **Cons:** minimum three-night stay during holidays; 15 minutes from Old Town Hoi An; expensive resort. [$] *Rooms from: d13,309,550* ⊠ *Block Ha My Dong B, Dien Duong Ward, Hoi An* ☎ *0235/394–0000* ⊕ *www. fourseasons.com/hoian* ⦿I *Free Breakfast* ⇆ *100 villas.*

Hoi An Beach Bungalows

$$$ | B&B/INN | FAMILY | Get as close as possible to village life in these stylishly designed, cozy "fisher houses," tucked away in lush tropical gardens filled with fruit trees and flowers, a stone's throw from the beach. **Pros:** close to beach restaurants and bars; great value; good for families with small kids. **Cons:** 6 km (4 miles) from town; neighborhood roosters set early morning alarms; dark rooms. [$] *Rooms from: d1,849,000* ⊠ *Left at beach intersection, Cam An, An Bang* ☎ *090/811–7533* ⊕ *www.hoianbeach-bungalows.com* ⇆ *2 bungalows* ⦿I *Free Breakfast.*

Hoi An Beach Resort

$$$ | RESORT | FAMILY | The best feature of Hoi An's oldest beach resort is its riverside setting, and river views somewhat make up for the lack of beach (rapid coastal erosion took the last of the beach). **Pros:** lovely pool area overlooking the river; some rooms have river views; impeccable service. **Cons:** restaurant is average; you have to cross a busy road to get to what's left of the beach; expensive considering beach is not easily accessible. [$] *Rooms from: d1,507,275* ⊠ *Cua Dai Beach, 01 Cua Dai St., Hoi An* ☎ *235/392–7011* ⊕ *www.hoianbeachresort.com.vn* ⇆ *121 rooms* ⦿I *Free Breakfast.*

Victoria Hoi An Beach Resort & Spa

$$$$ | RESORT | FAMILY | Public spaces at this popular, family-friendly resort are well positioned to take in the panoramic

coastal view, and all rooms come luxuriously appointed with beautiful bathrooms and traditional Asian furnishings. **Pros:** good on-site dining; kids' club; large pool. **Cons:** coastal erosion means limited beach frontage; riverview rooms are road facing, which can be noisy; rooms are showing age. $ *Rooms from: d3,257,688* ✉ *Cua Dai Beach, Hoi An* ☎ *0235/392–704* ⊕ *www.victoriahotels.asia* ➟ *109 rooms* ⊚ *Free Breakfast.*

Nightlife

The energy of the town fades by 11 pm, leaving only a handful of bars and restaurants catering to night owls under the light of their lanterns. The few spots that remain open in the Old Town usually close by midnight, narrowing down options to a few late-night backpacker venues across the river on An Hoi peninsula.

Before & Now
BARS | Lively tunes, a pool table, and a 5–9 pm happy hour pull in crowds late into the night at this lively bar in Old Town. Cheerfully grungy street art plasters the walls surrounding the bar, where service can be slow and conversation almost impossible. Quieter surroundings can be found upstairs in the sofa-strewn lounge bar. ✉ *51 Le Loi St., Hoi An* ☎ *0235/391–0599* ⊕ *beforeandnow.net.*

Dive Bar Hoi An
BARS | Great cocktails and live music are the reason people come here, yet the excellent Italian menu and shady rear courtyard make for some of the calmest lunchtime dining in the center. Slightly more upscale than the brimming-with-backpackers Before & Now, the Dive Bar is a favorite hangout for expats and travelers looking for a relaxed vibe. The bar is also where diver-wannabes or enthusiasts can book for courses and escapades on Cham Island. ◾TIP➔ ✉ *88 Nguyen Thai Hoc, Phuong*

Minh An, Hoi An ☎ *0235/391–0782* ⊕ *www.vietnamscubadiving.com.*

Mango Rooms
BARS | This restaurant-lounge-bar makes an array of refreshing cocktails with—you guessed it—mangoes. This place is often chock-a-block with expats and tourists, and happy hour starts at 8 am and ends at 7 pm. A full menu with starters, salads, mains and desserts is served, complemented by an innovative cocktail selection. Bypass the front busy dining room for a low table in the back beside the river. It's best at sunset. ✉ *111 Pho Nguyen Thai Hoc, Phuong Minh An,* ☎ *0235/391–0839* ⊕ *www.facebook.com/mangoroomshoian.*

White Marble Wine Bar & Restaurant
WINE BARS | One of the few nightlife spots in the heart of Old Town, this corner wine bar has cocktails, beer, spirits, and quality wines by the glass. The cheese platter and various tapas pair well with a chilled Sauvignon Blanc on a hot day. Grab a table on the top floor for views of the Thu Bon River. ✉ *98 Le Loi St., Hoi An* ☎ *0235/391–1862* ⊕ *www.facebook.com/whitemarblehoian.*

Performing Arts

Hoi An Arts and Crafts Manufacturing Workshop
ARTS CENTER | **FAMILY** | One of the local attractions offered through the Heritage Pass, this 200-year-old house has 30-minute musical performances daily. In the workshop, children and adults can make Hoi An's traditional silk lanterns or paint masks at additional costs. Tickets are available on the corner of Bach Dang and Chau Thuong Van beside the Japanese Covered Bridge. ◾TIP➔ **The hour-long craft workshops run daily (bookable on-site), and are great for kids.** ✉ *9 Nguyen Thai Hoc St., Hoi An* ☎ *0235/391–0216* ▱ *Included in the 120,000d Old Town ticket.*

🛍 Shopping

As the garment capital of Vietnam, Hoi An is the place to have a clone of your favorite designer outfit tailored while you vacation. From suits and dresses to jackets and shoes, any garment you fantasize about can be replicated for you. Simply show the masters a photo of your desired item, select the fabric, get fitted, and voilà, it's yours—and usually within 48 hours. The designer boutique–lined Nguyen Thai Hoc is where you'll find off-the-peg fashion, boho arts, and unique souvenirs. Beyond fashion, wander over the bridge to Hoi An's Japanese Quarter, where cheap rental prices have proved a honeypot for Hoi An's most bohemian local artists. Family-run galleries showcase everything from traditional to abstract sculptures, paintings, and crafts. You can pick up unique pieces with unbelievably cheap price tags while watching the artisans in action; they'll even commission artwork for you if you have a particular design in mind. For knickknacks including ceramics, embroidery, trinkets, and knock-off "antique" opium paraphernalia, take your bargaining skills to the stalls that line the roads and alleyways that snake around the Central Market. Worth bearing in mind is that every other stall here is a clone of another, so if the price seems too high at one, move on to the next and ask again: Of all Hoi An's bespoke crafts, the one trade that slips under the radar is the talented jewelers (reputed to be some of Asia's best) scattered throughout the outskirts of town. They can melt down and revamp an old heirloom, or fashion something new from a photo or a scribbled design.

CLOTHING AND SHOES

Avana

MIXED CLOTHING | This off-the-peg, edgy fashion boutique stocks everything a fashionista could wish for and won't find anywhere else in Vietnam. The seasonal collections of clothes and accessories are designed by the in-house expat designer Ava, and crafted by Hoi An weavers, tailors, and leather makers. ∎ **TIP→ If you love the design but don't like the color, you can choose from a bespoke selection of fabric; they'll run up a one-off design tailored to your preference.** ✉ *57 Le Loi, Hoi An* ⊕ *www.avanavietnam.com.*

Friendly Shoe Shop

SHOES | FAMILY | If it's custom shoes you're after, this is Hoi An's top destination for leather boots and sandals. After you select your design and material, the staff will take your measurements and have the item tailored within 24–72 hours. Then they will deliver it to your hotel or ship it directly to your home. Their motto is "No Like. No Pay," which they back up with a 180-day money-back guarantee, as well as a generous warranty of six months for shoes and one year for bags. ✉ *18 Tran Phu St., Hoi An* ☎ *093/521–1382* ⊕ *shoeshop-hoian.com.*

Hot Chili

MIXED CLOTHING | This funky little traders house on Nguyen Thai Hoc stocks a truly Hoi An–inspired collection of casual resort- and swimwear. Each fashion-forward piece is professionally printed and stitched in Vietnam. Hot Chili focuses on producing apparel, swimwear, and accessories made from a fusion between handmade art and screen printing technology. ✉ *86 Nguyen Thai Hoc, Cam Ha, Hoi An* ☎ *093/527–7712* ⊕ *www. hotchilihoian.com.*

Lana Tailor

MIXED CLOTHING | While the city at large has garnered a reputation for its custom-made suits, Lana Tailor stands out among Hoi An's dozens of tailors because of its stylish selections and satisfaction guarantee (you won't be asked to pay until you see the finished product and are happy with it). Choose from a showroom of in-vogue dresses, suits, jackets, and skirts, and if you don't find what you're looking for, just show them a photo of it online and they'll make it within 24 hours. Choose from fabrics including leather, cotton, cashmere, and wool. Tailored dresses range from $45 to $85 in U.S. dollars, while suits cost between $79 and $200. Items can be shipped internationally for an additional fee. ⊠ *90 Le Loi St., Hoi An* ☎ *0235/392–9559.*

Metiseko

MIXED CLOTHING | This small high-end, ethical slow fashion brand produces one-of-a-kind clothing and accessories made from premium and organic materials. Metiseko also sell quilts and home decor, all with lovely prints and fabrics, drawing inspiration from Vietnamese culture, folk traditions, and landscapes. ⊠ *142 Tran Phu, Minh An, Hoi An* ☎ *0235/392–9278* ⊕ *www.metiseko.com.*

Mr Xe

MIXED CLOTHING | Feel *GQ*-worthy with a custom suit from this leading men's tailor, where jackets, suits, and coats are all made within 24 hours. Materials and fabrics are a cut above the other shops in Hoi An, and somehow Mr. Xe manages to get you a perfect fit on the first attempt—maybe because he and his staff are meticulous with measurements. A three-piece suit will set you back around $150; it's okay to haggle for the price. ⊠ *71 Nguyen Thai Hoc, Phuong Minh An, Hoi An* ☎ *0235/391–0388.*

★ The O Collective

SOUVENIRS | **FAMILY** | A consortium of Vietnam's contemporary designers all under one roof, O is the Vietnamese word for umbrella. This fashion-savvy boutique on the trendy Nguyen Thai Hoc sells everything from funky propaganda art posters and Saigon Kitsch trinkets, to funky cushion art, luxury resort wear, and bohemian fashions. ■**TIP→ Kids can be entertained in the make-your-own monster workshop.** ⊠ *85 Nguyen Thai Hoc, Hoi An* ☎ *090/589–3740* ⊕ *www.facebook.com/ OCollectiveHoiAn.*

Yaly Couture

MIXED CLOTHING | From leather boots and silk scarves to high fashion dresses and corporate suits, Yaly Couture can re-create practically any designer item within two days. The shop's own designs have plenty of character and style, thanks to the owner's passion for workmanship. It is one of the most professional and ethical tailoring businesses in town, with the largest selection of high-quality fabrics. Find them at 47 Tran Phu, 47 Nguyen Thai Hoc, and 358 Nguyen Duy Hieu. ⊠ *47 Nguyen Thai Hoc, Hoi An* ☎ *0235/221– 2474* ⊕ *www.yalycouture.com.*

FOOD

Cho Hoi An (Central Market Food Hall)

MARKET | **FAMILY** | Wander through the labyrinth of vendors serving up freshly prepared Hoi An specialties including *cao lau*—a regional dish made with noodles, pork, and greens that can only be found in Hoi An—alongside a good range of other Vietnamese favorites like pho, *banh zeo* (savory pancakes), and bun bo hue. This is where the locals shop, so expect a lot of activity in some cramped quarters, especially if you arrive for early-bird specials. Once you've chosen your stall you are welcome to order dishes and fruit juices from other vendors who will bring them to your table. Prices are fixed and displayed, and the food vendors follow strict food hygiene rules, making this one of the best spots to sample a vast array of dishes normally only available on the street. ■**TIP→ Wander past the vendors to find market stalls packed with local spices, coffee, the famous Quang Nam Chili jam, and cooking utensils, but be prepared to barter hard with the friendly yet business-savvy stallholders in this area of the market.** ⊠ *Tran Phu St., Hoi An* ✥ *Intersection of Tran Phu St and Nguyen Hue.*

GIFTS AND JEWELRY

Lotus Jewellery

JEWELRY & WATCHES | Choose from a stunning range of high-quality jewelry designs, handcrafted locally by Quang Nam's finest artisans. Take your pick from a selection of intricate Vietnam-inspired

Cycling is a popular way to tour Hoi An, and many hotels offer complimentary bikes.

pendants, earrings, bracelets, and rings, or tailor your own personal design from a selection of jade, turquoise, opal, amethyst, citrine, blue topaz, or freshwater pearls. ■ TIP→ **They can also reset and remold jewelry brought from home.** ⊠ *82 Tran Phu St., Hoi An* ✢ *Additional location at 53A Le Loi St.* ☎ *0235/391–7889* ⊕ *www.lotusjewellery-hoian.com.*

🏃 Activities

BICYCLING
Most hotels in Hoi An offer complimentary bicycles, or you can hire one for roughly 20,000d–40,000d per day. For a low-impact, highly scenic workout, rent a bicycle and ride 20 minutes from the center of town to An Bang Beach, a splendid place to catch a breeze and relax in the sun. To get to An Bang, ride 5 km (3 miles) northeast of the town center along Hai Ba Trung Street, all the way to the beach. If you are feeling really energetic, turn right at the An Bang beach intersection and follow the road out to the Victoria Hoi An Resort and

continue on it until you arrive at Cua Dai lighthouse where a small dirt road to the right leads through a picturesque small village.

Hoi An Cycling
BIKING | FAMILY | If ricocheting between rocks and potholes on two wheels built for city shopping inspires less than comfortable thoughts, Hoi An Cycling offers international branded, full-suspension mountain bikes for rent, as well as helmets. Offtrack tours include a rather challenging 80-km (50-mile) loop to the top of the Son Tra Peninsula north of Danang. More relaxed itineraries take in the countryside and waterways closer to home, with the option to return to an action-packed cooking class guided by *Master Chef Vietnam*'s runner-up, chef Hung. ⊠ *132/7 Tran Phu St., Hoi An* ☎ *091/988–2783.*

BOATING
Exploring this 15th-century trading port by boat on the Thu Bon River, once used to transport goods along the old Marine Silk Road, is a highlight of a visit to Hoi

An. Depending on the type of boat you hire, fees range from 30,000d for a row-boat to 100,000d for an hour-long sunset cruise to a fishing village. There are plenty of riverfront sailors along Bach Dang Street, but be sure to negotiate the price in advance. Short bike ferries across to the neighboring Cam Kim Island, home to the Kim Bong Carpentry Village, and some stunning rural bike rides, run every 10 minutes from the market end of Bach Dang Street and cost around 10,000d each way. Speedboats over to the Cham Islands can be arranged through most hotels and travel companies in town and depart 7–11 am from Cua Dai Harbour, 7 km (4½ miles) from the Old Town. Return boats leave for Hoi An at around 3 pm taking upward of 45 minutes, with a return ticket costing around 350,000d. Half- and full-day boat tours to either Danang or Son My can be arranged through Rose Travel Service.

Rose Travel Service

BOATING | FAMILY | Safety comes first with this Hoi An tour company. Its fleet of transport options are not only good value, but are also maintained to international standards. Transportation options include speedboats, luxury spa fishing boats, retro jeeps, and air-conditioned cars and minibuses. Itineraries bring tourists closer to rural Vietnam; for example, they combine a minivan adventure to My Son and a boat tour with a meal on the Thu Bon river, allowing travelers to observe daily life of the waterway systems and the villages that border it. This company is particularly recommended for half-day boat trips from Hoi An. ⊠ 37–39 Ly Thai To St., Hoi An ☎ 0235/391–7789 ⊕ www.rosetravelservice.com ✉ Tours from 777,000d (boat, bus, lunch, and My Son Sanctuary tour).

KAYAKING, SURFING, AND SUP

Hoi An's water sports are governed by the weather. From March to September the tranquil sea, river waterways, and tiny tributaries are perfect for idle sunset paddling while observing the flow of local life on the water. A few companies based on the An Hoi peninsula provide both kayak rentals and tours. Stand-up paddle and surfboard rentals, classes, and tours can be organized throughout the year.

Hoi An Kayak Center

CANOEING & ROWING | FAMILY | Based out of a small riverside arts and crafts café on the An Hoi Peninsula, Hoi An Kayak Center can arrange a whole host of kayak and canoe adventure tours designed to get you close to nature and far from the crowded streets of the Old Town. Tours are offered for every level of paddler and include instruction, safety equipment, and trained guides to help unravel the mysteries of life on the river. Kayaks of all sizes can also be rented outside of tour hours, from as little as 200,000d for two hours. ⊠ Nam Tran Art Craft Village and Cafe, 125 Ngo Quyen St., An Hoi Islet, Hoi An ☎ 090/505–6640 ⊕ www.hoiankayak.com ✉ Tours start at 574,075d per person.

SUP Monkey

STAND UP PADDLEBOARDING | FAMILY | Hoi An's first stand-up paddleboarding and surf company, SUP Monkey offers lessons, board rentals, and completely unique tours. Tours are suitable for beginners through the most adventurous explorers, from an easy sunrise coastal paddle from the beautiful Ha My to An Bang beach to paddles through the rapids on a full-day adventure north of Danang. ⊠ 111 Lac Long Quan, Cam An, Hoi An ☎ 0235/395–9253 ⊕ www.facebook.com/SUPMonkeyVietNam ✉ SUP Paddleboarding Sunrise Adventure 688,890d (breakfast included).

SCUBA DIVING AND SNORKELING

Having gained UNESCO recognition as a global biosphere reserve in 2007, the seven islets that make up the Cham Islands just 10 nautical miles off the Hoi An coast are home to more than 165 hectares of coral reefs and some 947 aquatic species. The scenic underwater landscape is rich in macro life, making it a popular spot for underwater photographers, scuba diving, snorkeling, and swimming. Scuba diving, as well as PADI-certified courses, are available during the dry season that runs from April through September, with prices starting at as little as 1,550,000d for a fun dive to more than 7,000,000d for a three-day open-water course. Snorkeling trips are widely available, with most speedboats running the route over to the islands and offering the use of equipment and a short reef stop. However, due to overcrowding and the lax safety measures applied by speedboat staff, it is better to tag along with one of the dive companies where all-inclusive prices for snorkel day trips start at 1,000,000d.

Blue Coral Diving

DIVING & SNORKELING | FAMILY | This professional five-star IDC diving center offers snorkel and scuba-diving day trips to the Cham Islands that include stops at two dive sites and a seafood buffet lunch on the beach. PADI certification courses are available for all levels with prices starting at 6,600,000d for two days, and underwater photography equipment is available to rent. Blue Coral also sells a small range of diving and snorkeling equipment. ✉ *33 Tran Hung Dao St., Hoi An* ☎ *093/585–7578* ⊕ *www.divehoian.com* ✏ *One-tank fun dive from 1,400,000d* ☞ *It is recommended to dive between March and September, with the best weather between June and August.*

Cham Island Diving

DIVING & SNORKELING | FAMILY | "No troubles, make bubbles" is the mantra for this friendly five-star PADI dive center with over 15 years of experience under its belt. Slickly professional, the outfitter offers daily boat and speedboat transfers over to the coral-fringed Cham Islands, taking breaks along the way at the various dive and snorkel sites. All levels are catered to. ■TIP➔ **For seriously good sunsets, book an overnight camping trip**

with a seafood barbecue on the incredible Cham Island Beach. ✉ *88 Nguyen Thai Hoc, Hoi An* ☎ *0235/391–0782* ⊕ *vietnamscubadiving.com* ✏ *Private tours from 10,333,350d.*

Marble Mountains

19 km (12 miles) north of Hoi An, 11 km (7 miles) southwest of Danang.

Five beautiful limestone peaks, known as the Marble Mountains, rise above the beach north of Hoi An and south of Danang. Over the centuries, the *dong* (caves) in the Thuy Son Peak have been turned into temples and shrines. The first to use them were the Cham, who converted them into Hindu shrines. The Buddhists have since taken over, adorned, sanctified, and inhabited them.

The climb up the path leading to the various cave-pagodas is not particularly strenuous, unless attempted in the middle of a hot, sunny day, when it is preferable to take the 15,000d elevator that takes you two-thirds of the way to the top.

GETTING HERE AND AROUND

The Marble Mountains are easily accessed by taxi from either Hoi An or Danang. Onward journeys are catered to by a taxi rank at the base of the mountains. An alternative would be to hire a private car and driver for half a day and include a seafood lunch at Ha My beach a few kilometers further south, just past the Nam Hai Resort. Hoi An Express offers this service for approximately 600,000d. Day tours to Hoi An generally stop here, but it's rare that you will be accompanied by a guide. For more information and to make sure you don't miss anything, ask for the 15,000d map at the ticket office.

Cham Artifacts of the Central Coast

Despite nearly 12 centuries of ascendancy over a large swath of what is present-day Vietnam, very few records remain confirming the existence of the Kingdom of Champa. Because this area served as the seat of the Kingdom of Champa from the 2nd to the 15th century, it has the greatest concentration of Cham art and architecture in the country. You can savor the glories of the ancient kingdom at the excellent Cham Museum in Danang. Exploring the grand remnants of the Imperial City of Hue

and the magnificent Imperial Tombs will introduce you to the history of Vietnam's emperors. In Hoi An, the well-preserved houses and pagodas have hardly changed in the last 200 years, giving you a sense of 17th- and 18th-century Vietnamese life.

The Chams, today an ethnic minority in Vietnam, still speak about the ancient legends, their glories and splendors. They continue to practice their religions and traditional customs.

Sights

Linh Ung Pagoda

TEMPLE | After entering through Ong Chon Gate, the main entrance of the Marble Mountains, you'll see the Linh Ung Pagoda, a Buddhist shrine inside a cave, filled with a large collection of Buddha statues. Built in 1825, this sacred structure also features small lotus ponds, bonsai plants, and intricate tilework. It bears many of the same motifs found in the UNESCO-listed tombs in Hue. ⊠ *81 Huyen Tran Cong Chua, Ngu Hanh Son* 🖽 *Included in the 40,000d entrance ticket to Marble Mountains.*

Marble Mountains (*Ngu Hanh Son*)

MOUNTAIN | **FAMILY** | Tourists come to these five historic mountains to see ancient pagodas, Buddhist sanctuaries, sacred caves, spectacular views of the eastern beaches, and villages where artisans carve marble sculptures. Each of the primarily limestone formations are named after the five elements— *kim* (metal), *moc* (wood), *hoa* (fire), *thuy* (water), and *tho* (earth). At Thuy Son Mountain, you can explore several 17th-century pagodas and caves by

climbing 156 steps from the base—or take a glass elevator that eliminates a third of the steps in the initial climb, transporting you straight to the foot of Linh Ung Pagoda. Bring plenty of water and take your time, as the steps can be slippery after it rains. It is common to be hassled by locals in Non Nuoc Village who live solely on the production of their stone statues, jewelry, and artwork. Entrance to the Marble Mountains costs 40,000d plus the optional 15,000d one-way elevator ride. ⊠ *14 km (7 miles) southeast of Danang City, Ngh Hanh Son* 🖽 *40,000d; elevator ride 15,000d each way.*

Tam Thai Tu Pagoda

TEMPLE | Across the "Water" Mountain of the Marble Mountains, you'll see the tiny but charming Tam Thai Tu Pagoda, where monks still live. The pagoda is dedicated to the bodhisattva Phat Di Lac, and was rebuilt more than 400 years ago by King Minh Mang of the Nguyen Dynasty. Tam Thai offers a serene view of the landscape below, especially during early morning. ⊠ *81 Huyen Tran Cong Chua, Hoa Hai ✣ Ngu Hanh Son* 🖽 *Free; donations accepted.*

Danang

30 km (19 miles) north of Hoi An, 972 km (603 miles) north of Ho Chi Minh City, 108 km (67 miles) south of Hue.

Danang became a significant port city at the end of the 19th century, when silt filled up the Thu Bon River and eliminated neighboring Hoi An's access to the sea. The ancient Kingdom of Champa existed in the region from the 2nd to the 17th centuries, but Cham domination was significantly weakened by the Viet and Khmer in the 15th century; the last Cham king fled to Cambodia in 1820. Then in 1888, the French gained control of Danang (which they called Tourane), taking it by force from Emperor Gia Long—he had promised it to them in exchange for their help but had reneged on his agreement. In its heyday, during the first half of the 20th century, the city was second only to Saigon as Vietnam's most cosmopolitan center. During the Vietnam War, Danang was the first place U.S. Marines landed in March 1965, and it subsequently became home to a large U.S. Air Force base. Only 200 km (124 miles) south of the DMZ, the city was an ideal location for launching bombing missions. The influx of army personnel brought enormous growth, numerous refugees, and all kinds of entertainment, including movie theaters, bars, and prostitution. Soldiers would take time off at the nearby R&R resort of China Beach. By March 1975, Danang was in a state of total chaos as people tried to escape the fast-encroaching North Vietnamese army and had to fight for space on any boat or plane leaving the city. Today there are remnants of the American presence in the city, as well as vestiges of the French in the wide avenues and old villas.

Of late, Danang has seen extensive modern development, with top sights now including man-made wonders. The Ba Na Hills to the west, which features the picturesque 500-foot long arched Golden Bridge, opened a whole new world for tourism in the city. Beaches, museums, and pagodas round out the offerings.

◉ Sights

★ Ba Na Hills and Golden Bridge

VIEWPOINT | FAMILY | A former French hill station left abandoned until after the war, Ba Na is a local favorite, nicknamed "Da Lat in Danang." Accessible via the world's longest single-track cable car (5,801 meters), traversing above jungle and waterfalls, Ba Na presents remarkable panoramic views of the East Sea. At the top is a kitsch, fairground-themed park with a roller coaster, bumper cars, and a very entertaining wax museum—all popular with kids. Also nestled 1,400 meters above sea level is the **Golden Bridge,** an iconic architectural wonder that has made headlines since it opened in 2018. The bridge, which appears to be held by two giant concrete hands, spans nearly 150 meters long and leads to the **La Jardin D'Amour Gardens,** another must-visit spot. When you're done taking in the beauty from the top, take the smaller cable car down to the second, more spiritual level where you can either take a funicular or hike up the mountain to visit the temples and pagodas that line the route. If you have the energy, climb the 17-story tower inside the statue of Buddha Guanyin—the largest in the country at 67 by 35 meters (the equivalent of a 30-story building). The site to save until last is tucked away behind the Shakamuni Buddha statue: the Debay Wine Cellar, which was tunneled into the mountain in the 1920s by the former French residents. Inside is a large fully stocked bar and the chance to do a little wine tasting. ⌫ *42 km (26 miles) west of Danang, An Son Village, Hoa Ninh Commune, Hoa Vang District, Danang* ☎ *0236/374–9888* ⌑ *750,000d for adults; 60,000d for children.*

Two giant stone hands seem to lift up Golden Bridge, one of the most photo-worthy spots in the Ba Na Hills.

Bho Hoong Village

SPECIAL-INTEREST TOURS | **FAMILY** | Tours to the ethnic minority villages southwest of Danang take you out into the jungle-clad Truong Son mountains bordering the Ho Chi Minh Trail. About two and a half hours from Danang by private car or public bus, Bho Hoong Village is a small valley hamlet of the ethnic hill tribe, the Co Tu. Unlike many of the more popular ethnic villages along the trail, Bho Hoong and the surrounding area have retained their charm. It's a spiritual, timeless place, rich in flora, fauna, stunning landscapes, and culture. In the heart of the village, a circle of rong houses have been carefully restored to offer luxurious overnight stays with the Co Tu as your hosts, cooking up delicious organic meals and allowing visitors a glimpse into their lives. On-site activities include tribal dance performances, trekking or mountain biking to the nearby hot springs, crossbow shooting, and craft tours of nearby villages. Or you can just kick back in a hammock on the river deck, enjoying a slice of Vietnam few get to experience. ⊠ *Bho Hoong 1 Village, Song Kon Commune, Dong Giang District* ☎ *091/6866–041* ⊕ *www. bhohoongbungalows.com.*

Cao Dai Temple

TEMPLE | **FAMILY** | Touted as the largest of its kind in central Vietnam, the colorful Cao Dai Temple lies 1 km (½ mile) west of the Song Han swing bridge, on the Bach Dang side of the Han river, and is a peaceful spot to escape the madness of the city. Built in 1920, the impressive temple is still in use today and serves as a place of worship for approximately 50,000 followers. During the day, visitors are welcome to tour the gardens, temple, and a small building behind that holds a display of historic artifacts and statues of popular saints. The main temple is sparsely furnished and, beyond the impressive divine eye that towers from behind the altar, most visitors are left unimpressed. But venture up the staircase at the entrance and you'll be treated to a beautiful view of the city that spans all the way across to the East Sea. ⊠ *63 Hai Phong, Thach Thang, Hai Chau,*

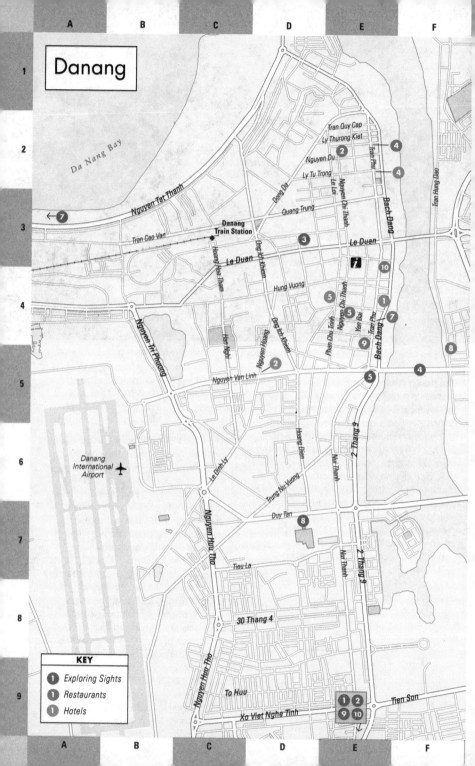

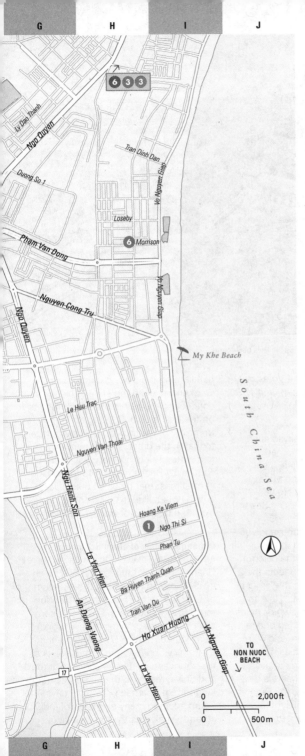

Sights ▼

1	Ba Na Hills and Golden Bridge....	**E9**
2	Bho Hoong Village..................	**E9**
3	Cao Dai Temple	**D3**
4	Danang Bridges.....................	**F5**
5	Danang Museum of Cham Sculpture.....................	**E5**
6	Goddess of Mercy & Linh Ung Pagoda..................	**H1**
7	Hai Van Pass	**A3**
8	Ho Chi Minh & Zone 5 Military Museum..................	**D7**
9	My Son Sanctuary.................	**E9**
10	Sun World Danang Wonders Amusement Park	**E9**

Restaurants ▼

1	Happy Heart Cafe..................	**H7**
2	Kushiyaki Banjiro	**E2**
3	La Maison 1888	**H1**
4	Luna Pub Danang..................	**E2**
5	Merkat	**E4**
6	My Casa Fusion Restaurant	**H3**
7	Namaste Omar's Indian Restaurant..................	**E4**
8	Olivia's Prime Steakhouse	**F4**
9	Red Sky Bar & Restaurant.........	**E4**
10	Retro Kitchen and Bar	**E3**

Hotels ▼

1	Brilliant Hotel.......................	**E4**
2	Danang Boutique Hotel	**D5**
3	InterContinental Danang Sun Peninsula Resort	**H1**
4	Novotel Danang Premier Han River	**E2**
5	Sanouva Danang Hotel	**E4**

Castles sit above the clouds in the Ba Na Hills of Danang.

Danang ☞ Prayers are held 4 times daily at 5:30 am, 11:30 am, 5:30 pm, and 11:30 pm.

Danang Bridges

BRIDGE | FAMILY | For all the skyscrapers and modern architectural landmarks that now grace the city skyline, it's the bridges that have become the pride of Danang. As the sun sets, crowds gather along riverside Bach Dang Street to watch the spectacle as the four bridges are illuminated by thousands of LED lights that flow through the color spectrum. Farthest north is the colorful Thuan Phuoc Bridge that connects the district of Son Tra to the city, the largest suspension bridge in Vietnam. Next to that is the Han Song Bridge, which holds the title of Vietnam's first swing bridge; every morning between 1 am and 4 am the bridge is closed to traffic as it swings on its axis to allow large ships to pass along the Han River. At the heart is the most impressive of them all, the Dragon Bridge (*Cau Rong*) a national symbol of power, nobility, and good fortune, highlighting the city's growth. Every weekend at 9 pm the six-lane highway connecting the city to the beach resorts on the east side of Danang closes to traffic and huge crowds take their place to watch the dragon spout plumes of fire and water. The bridge farthest north, the Tran Thi Ly Bridge, has a 145-meter-high central mast that holds a striking sail, which, when illuminated, can be seen from the beaches of Hoi An. ⊠ *Bach Dang, Danang*.

Danang Museum of Cham Sculpture

ART MUSEUM | FAMILY | On display at the Cham Museum, founded by the French in 1919, are artifacts from the Kingdom of Champa, which ruled this region for more than 1,000 years. The highly sensual, innovative, and expressive works from Tra Kieu's reign (7th century) and that of My Son (8th–9th centuries), and the abundant sandstone carvings of the god Shiva, testify to the prosperity of the Kingdom of Champa in its glory days. The Cham adopted many elements of Indian art and Sanskrit as their sacred language.

Note the Cham Buddha depicted on a throne in an imperial pose, with his feet flat on the ground, in contrast to the traditional image of Buddha seated in the lotus position. The symbol of fertility, Uroja (meaning "woman's breast"), which you will also see throughout the museum, reveals the esteem afforded women in Cham culture. The central Tra Kieu Altar in the Tra Kieu Room—in the middle gallery, opposite the entrance and across the courtyard—illustrates in relief-sculpture part of the Hindu *Ramayana* epic story. This is the museum's best-preserved relief. The galleries are arranged into a cohesive itinerary, and a performance and education space is on the second floor. Performances are listed on the website. English-speaking guides can lead you on tours of the Cham Museum. ⊠ *At the intersection of Bach Dang and Trung Nu Vuong, So 02 D. 2 Thang 9, Binh Hien, Hai Chau, Danang* ☎ *236/357–4801* 🔗 *60,000d.*

★ Goddess of Mercy & Linh Ung Pagoda

RELIGIOUS BUILDING | Vietnam's largest Goddess of Mercy statue dominates Danang's coastal skyline in a similar way to Christ the Redeemer in Rio de Janeiro; on a clear day you can see her silhouette from coastal Hoi An, 40 km (25 miles) away. The 17-story, 67-meter "Lady Buddha" statue stands on Son Tra Peninsula in the grounds of Linh Ung Pagoda, one of the most significant destinations for Buddhists in the area. The views from here are stunning. Equally charming is the journey along the winding coastal road leading to the peak of Son Tra, nicknamed "Monkey Mountain" by U.S. Troops stationed there during the war, due to the mischievous monkeys that hang out in the jungle cliffs. The best way to get here is to hire a car and driver (or a motorbike for more experienced riders). The whole trip should take no more than a couple of hours, but it's well worth making a day of it and incorporating a seafood lunch and swim in one of the secluded coves below, followed by a stop off at Bai Tien, a small fishing port town littered with crumbling French military remains including pillboxes, a lighthouse, and a small graveyard—the final resting point for many French soldiers defeated by the Vietnamese during their short-lived occupation of Danang during the first Indochine war. ⊠ *Hoang Sa, Tho Quang, Son Tra* 🔗 *Free.*

Hai Van Pass

SCENIC DRIVE | For adrenaline-filled road adventures, jungle-clad mountains, hairpin bends, and incredible views, you can't top the 21-km (13-mile) long, ex-military feeder road known as the Hai Van Pass. Although cyclists have tried it, it's advisable to take a motorbike (experienced riders only) or driver to take on the winding incline to the pillboxes at the pass's peak, where you can stop for photos. After, you can descend towards the lagoon on the Lang Co side where you can pull up a plastic chair for delicious seafood at one of the stilt restaurants, before returning via the Hai Van Tunnel. ⊠ *Head north out of Danang on the old QL1A (Nguyen Tat Thanh St.), Danang.*

Ho Chi Minh & Zone 5 Military Museum

HISTORY MUSEUM | FAMILY | These two museums are located in the same complex, a few kilometers outside of the city. Although neither compare with their larger contemporaries, the Ho Chi Minh Museum in Hanoi or the War Remnants Museum in HCMC, a visit here is a great way to learn about the anti-French and anti-American wars and the weaponry utilized, from a purely Vietnamese mindset. The smaller of the two, the Ho Chi Minh Museum has a small replica of Ho Chi Minh's home in Hanoi and three display rooms documenting the life and career of the nation's hero. Information is sparse, but the photo display is worth a look, even if it's just to get a glimpse of a pre-war Vietnam. Adjacent is the military museum courtyard where you can amble around a huge collection of aircraft, tanks, cannons, and armored vehicles confiscated from the enemy by the Vietnamese Fifth Division. Inside, twelve showrooms house a collection of photos, weapons, and artifacts representing the struggle and victory of the Vietnamese, including the very slippers Special Task Force member Phan Thi Mua used to smuggle enough dynamite powder to blow up the U.S. Fuel Depot in Danang in 1972. ✉ *Duy Tan, Hoa Cuong Bac, Hai Chau, Danang* ☎ *0511/362–4014* ✉ *40,000d* ⊙ *Closed 11 am–1:30 pm.*

My Son Sanctuary

RUINS | FAMILY | About 70 km (43 miles) southwest of Danang, or 45 km (28 miles) due west of Hoi An, are the My Son Cham ruins: former temples and towers dedicated to kings and deities, particularly Shiva, who was considered the founder of the Kingdom of Champa. Construction first began in the 4th century under the order of the Cham king Bhadresvara and continued until the 13th century. With more than 70 brick structures, of which some 20 remain in recognizable form today, My Son was the most important religious and architectural center of the Kingdom of Champa and was declared a UNESCO World Heritage Site in 1999. Although extensively damaged during World War II and the Vietnam War, extensive conservation work has ensured that the My Son complex still displays vestiges of its former glory. An interesting small museum and performance stage that hosts ad hoc Aspara dance and music performances is located at the entrance. ■TIP→ **The best tours incorporate a visit to the Danang Museum of Cham Sculpture. From Hoi An it's possible to take a boat tour to the ruins.** ✉ *Thon, My Son, Duy Xuyen, Danang* ☎ *0235/373–1309* ⊕ *disanvanhoamyson.vn* ✉ *150,000d.*

Sun World Danang
Wonders Amusement Park

AMUSEMENT PARK/CARNIVAL | FAMILY | For the best panoramic views of the city and the coastline beyond, forget the expensive skybars and instead take a ride on the Sun Wheel in city-central Asia Park. Scaling 110 meters (it's the 10th biggest in the world) and designed by famous U.S. architect Bill Bensley, the Sun Wheel is a great way to view the geography of Vietnam's fastest-growing city. Beside the all-time favorite Ferris wheel, there are other entertainment spots worth trying. ■TIP→ **If you are in Danang on either a Friday or Saturday night, time your ride to coincide with the fire-breathing display at the Dragon Bridge at 9 pm.** ✉ *Asia Park, No. 01, Phan Dang Luu, Hai Chau, Danang* ✚ *The Sun Wheel is 4 km (2½ miles) from the Cham Museum. Continue south along 2 Thang 9 for 4 km (2½ miles) and take the signposted left-hand street (towards the river). The best way to get here is by taxi.* ☎ *0236/368–1666* ⊕ *asiapark.sunworld. vn* ✉ *150,000d.*

🕊 Beaches

Non Nuoc Beach (*Truong Sa*)

BEACH | FAMILY | Just 14 km (9 miles) from either Danang or Hoi An lies Non Nuoc beach, a stunning stretch of white sandy beach overlooking the Son Tra Peninsula to the north and the stately Marble Mountains to the west. Once a popular fishing beach, the area has now become the private playground of some of the finest beach resorts in the area, leaving the surrounding pockets of beach land fenced off for future development. You can see why it's such a sought-after area (it even has international golf courses)—the deserted white sand beaches seem to go on forever and the sea is clean and perfect for swimming during the long dry season that runs from April to September. **Amenities:** food and drink; lifeguards; showers; toilets; water sports. **Best for:** solitude; sunrise; sunset; surfing; swimming; walking. ✉ *Truong Sa, Danang.*

🍴 Restaurants

Like everything in Danang, the city's culinary scene has been taken up a notch or 10 in the last few years. This is mostly thanks to an influx of talented chefs from Hanoi and Ho Chi Minh, who have established the international-standard bars and restaurants that line riverside Bach Dang on Han River's west bank, and neighboring Tran Phu, a scene that is slowly stretching out over to the east banks of the river. For fresh seafood, head to My Khe Beach or stay inland near Han Market where locals come for sizzling *be thui* (grilled veal). Authentic and affordable fare can be found on the avenues skirting Tran Phu, Dong Da, and Hai Phong Streets.

★ Happy Heart Cafe

$$ | DINER | FAMILY | There's nothing fancy about this charity-run diner, just good Western food at cheap prices and heartwarming service. Repurposed from an English center, this café employs minority and deaf workers, and is a favorite among expats and visitors. **Known for:** vegetarian chili; helping the deaf community; good breakfasts. [$] *Average main: d129,000* ✉ *57 Ngo Thi Sy, An Thuong, Danang* ☎ *2036/388–8384* 🌐 *www.facebook.com/happyheartdanang* 🕓 *Closed Sun.*

★ Kushiyaki Banjiro

$$ | JAPANESE | FAMILY | Don't be shocked when you walk through the door of Kushiyaki Banjiro to find the kimono-clad staff yelling in Japanese; it's the way they do it in Japan. Try the omakase set, a plate piled high with sashimi that includes blue lobster, tuna, and salmon, or authentic chicken or beef yakitori. **Known for:** business clientele; sushi; sake brewed in Hue and served in carafes. [$] *Average main: d150,000* ✉ *23 Nguyen Chi Thanh, Thach Thang, Danang* ☎ *0236/384–9880* 🌐 *www.banjiro.net* 🕓 *Closed 2–5 pm.*

★ La Maison 1888

$$$$ | FRENCH | FAMILY | As one of Vietnam's leading fine-dining experiences, this restaurant resembles an old French mansion with elaborately decorated themed rooms. The aesthetics have earned La Maison a spot among the World's Top Ten Designed Restaurants in *Architectural Digest*, and the cuisine of three-Michelin-star chef Pierre Gagnaire only adds to the illustrious status. **Known for:** gorgeous setting; creative menu; six-plate grand dessert. [$] *Average main: d1,999,000* ✉ *Intercontinental Danang Sun Peninsula Resort, Bai Bac, Son Tra Peninsula, Danang* ☎ *0236/393–8888* 🌐 *www.danang.intercontinental.com/la-maison-1888* 👔 *Formal.*

★ Luna Pub Danang

$$$ | ITALIAN | FAMILY | One of Danang's hippest hangouts, this industrial-style, open-fronted warehouse pub-restaurant wouldn't look out of place in New York City. The ever-changing menu of authentic Italian fare includes specials such as risotto alla Milanese, pizza, pasta, and steaks. **Known for:** changing menu; wood-fired pizzas; gas station-themed bar. [$] *Average main: d180,000* ✉ *9A D. Tran Phu, Thach Thang, Hai Chau, Danang* ☎ *093/240–0298* 🌐 *lunapubdanang.com.*

Merkat

$$$ | SPANISH | FAMILY | Pitch-perfect sangria is the best way to start a meal at Merkat. This restaurant, owned by Mamen and Dani from Spain, is the genuine article; and their open kitchen design allows customers to see the masters at work. **Known for:** perfect sangria; authenticity; delicious jamon. [$] *Average main: d200,000* ✉ *263 Nguyen Chi Thanh, Hai Chau, Danang* ☎ *0236/364–6388* 🌐 *www.merkatrestaurant.com* 🕓 *Closed 2–6 daily.*

My Casa Fusion Restaurant

$$ | FUSION | FAMILY | This garden restaurant with mostly outdoor seating is an expat favorite. Founded by ambitious Spanish and Italian natives, My Casa blends the two cuisines together to create a unique array of options. **Known for:** wild-bread pizzas; homemade pastas; excellent tapas. $ *Average main: d180,000* ✉ *53 Morrison, Phuoc My, Son Tra, Danang* ☎ *0769/900–8603* ⊕ *www. mycasa-danang.com.*

Namaste Omar's Indian Restaurant

$$ | **INDIAN** | **FAMILY** | This simple contemporary Indian restaurant a five-minute walk from the Old Town serves up and delivers the best northern Indian cuisine in town. The rara mutton and Kashmiri chicken are definitely worth coming back for, along with the Delhi street food breakfasts, served 9–11 am. **Known for:** cozy atmosphere; solid Indian cuisine at affordable prices; outstanding Tandoori oven dishes. $ *Average main: d120,000* ✉ *6 Thái Phiên, Phuoc Ninh, Danang* ☎ *0762/539–166* ⊕ *www.namasteomar. com.*

Olivia's Prime Steakhouse

$$$ | **AMERICAN** | **FAMILY** | American businessman Scott, who hails from Louisiana, decided to get into restaurants with his Vietnamese partner Olivia, and the result is a steak house devoted to Southern-style hospitality. Overlooking Han River, this brick-and-bamboo establishment caters to families and groups and has the best steaks in town, along with killer sides. **Known for:** killer side dishes; Australian and Japanese beef; personalized service. $ *Average main: d1,085,000* ✉ *505 Tran Hung Dao, Son Tra, Danang* ☎ *090/163–352* ⊕ *oliviasprime.com.*

Red Sky Bar & Restaurant

$$ | **AMERICAN** | Don't be fooled by the street view. The (red) sky's the limit at this trendy restaurant with some of the best Western food in Vietnam. **Known for:** great service; happy hours; delicate desserts. $ *Average main: d150,000* ✉ *248 Tran Phu St., 1 block from Han River, Danang* ☎ *0236/389–4895* ⊕ *redsky-danang.com.vn* ◷ *Closed daily 2–5 pm.*

Retro Kitchen and Bar

$$ | **ASIAN FUSION** | This modern two-story loft boasts 35 red wines from nine countries and would be a superb spot to host a party. Tall ceilings, large bay windows, and creative seating beckon. **Known for:** delectable seafood; open design; shareable meat plates. $ *Average main: d150,000* ✉ *85-87 D. Tran Phu, Hai Chau, Danang* ☎ *090/999–8587* ⊕ *www.retrokitchenbar.com.*

🛏 Hotels

Danang's luxury resorts are located on the coast outside the city center. These beachfront properties are the best option for exploring nearby attractions while still getting a taste of the urban life at city restaurants and night spots. If you are set on staying in the city, there are plenty of business hotels (with good weekend discounts) lining the river along Bach Dang Street on the west bank. More affordable lodging can be found one block south on Tran Phu Street or east in the quieter section of town.

If you plan on visiting the Son Tra peninsula, Marble Mountains, golf courses, or nearby Hoi An, you're better off staying at a beachfront resort and branching off from there. The added benefit is that you won't have to deal with city traffic when accessing attractions outside the center.

Brilliant Hotel

$$$$ | **HOTEL** | **FAMILY** | Luxurious rooms, central location, fantastic staff, and spectacular river views make this the most appropriately named hotel in Danang. **Pros:** Sothys spa; good discounts; soundproof rooms. **Cons:** mediocre decor; small pool; breakfast options need improvement. $ *Rooms from: d3,166,000* ✉ *162 Bach Dang, Hai Chau, Danang* ☎ *0236/322–2999* ⊕ *www.brillianthotel. vn* ⮌ *102 rooms* ◉| *Free Breakfast.*

Danang Boutique Hotel

$$$ | B&B/INN | FAMILY | This small hotel offers giant rooms designed with business travelers in mind. **Pros:** 3 minutes to the airport; big rooms and showers; outdoor pool. **Cons:** some service hiccups; hard-to-find entrance; noise from top floor. $ *Rooms from: d795,455* ✉ *150–156 Nguyen Van Linh, Danang* ☎ *091/459–7057* ⊕ *www.danangboutiquehotel.com* ❑ *No Meals* ⤺ *14 rooms.*

★ InterContinental Danang
Sun Peninsula Resort

$$$$ | RESORT | FAMILY | Ocean views await at this luxurious resort that is nestled on rain forest slopes and is accessed by a funicular train that descends to a private bay on the Son Tra Peninsula. **Pros:** daily shuttle to Danang and Hoi An; complimentary water sports; excellent French restaurant. **Cons:** remote location; property is poorly lit at night; pricey food and drinks. $ *Rooms from: d8,835,783* ✉ *, Danang* ☎ *0236/393–8888* ⊕ *www.danang.intercontinental.com* ❑ *Free Breakfast* ⤺ *201 rooms.*

Novotel Danang Premier Han River

$$$ | HOTEL | FAMILY | Attracting a mainly business crowd, the 36-story Novotel towers over the river on central Bach Dang street. **Pros:** complimentary shuttle bus to the airport and beach; five restaurants on-site; convenient location. **Cons:** small pool; slow Wi-Fi; poor service. $ *Rooms from: d1,446,795* ✉ *36 Bach Dang, Danang* ☎ *0236/392–9999* ⊕ *www.novotel-danang-premier.com* ⤺ *323 rooms* ❑ *Free Breakfast.*

Sanouva Danang Hotel

$$ | HOTEL | FAMILY | Four blocks west of Bach Dang, the Sanouva is a stylish city retreat offering contemporary Asian design, good service, and business-class facilities at competitive prices. **Pros:** free bicycles; walking distance from most sights; good weekend discounts. **Cons:** restaurant a bit hit-or-miss; rooms on low-level floors can be noisy; bathrooms

could use a refresh. $ *Rooms from: d652,800* ✉ *7 minutes from Danang International Airport, 68 Phan Chau Trinh, Hai Chau, Danang* ☎ *091/920–1468* ⊕ *www.sanouvadanang.com* ⤺ *84 rooms* ❑ *No Meals.*

✦ Nightlife

Bamboo 2 Bar

BARS | This lively dive bar draws a vast and varied crowd of visitors, and is big enough to accommodate them all. With three floors and wraparound balconies, there is always a seat somewhere. The pool table is located on the second floor, TVs broadcasting sports are located on the ground level, and there is a great selection of imported beer. It's the bar for river views and late-night food. Open 10 am til late. ✉ *216 Bach Dang St., Phuoc Ninh, Danang* ☎ *0873/887–790* ⊕ *bamboo2bar.com.*

Dirty Fingers Danang

PUBS | Set to be Danang's premier live-music venue, this establishment is the place to be. The warehouse comes complete with murals of pin-up girls and a giant wraparound wooden bar. There's ample seating both inside and out. Expect finger-picking music and finger-licking good food. ✉ *406 Vo Nguyen Giap, Danang* ☎ *0236/355–2297* ⊕ *www.facebook.com/dirtyfingersdanang.*

7 Bridges Brewing Company - Taproom

BREWPUBS | This rooftop bar offers amazing views of the skyline, great service, and delicious frosty beverages. The seven-beer flight will excite your taste buds, and if you get hungry, the sloppy joe and chicken wings will satiate your appetite. There's also a pool table on the third floor. ✉ *493 Tran Hung Đao, An Hai Tay, Danang* ☎ *961/917–066* ⊕ *7bridges.vn.*

Sky36

COCKTAIL LOUNGES | Taking cocktails to new levels, the 36th floor of the Novotel Danang Premier Han River, to be precise, Sky36 is a glitzy, glam, neon hangout with fantastic views of the whole city. Floor-to-ceiling windows on three sides give way to sparkly city views. The high-energy (and extremely loud) nightclub is a great place to see and be seen. It may be pricey, but the cocktails and dancing are worth it. ⊠ *Novotel Danang Premier Han River, 36 Bach Dang, Thach Thang, Danang* ☎ *090/115–1536* ⊕ *sky36.vn* ☞ *Dress code: smart casual.*

🛍 Shopping

Strangely, for a city as dynamic as Danang, the shopping here is still mostly based around the local market tradition. A recent influx of modern stores, fashion boutiques, and designer clothes shops that cater mainly to the Asian market can be found along the roads surrounding the large grocery shopping mall, the Big C, on Hung Vuong. Fabric shops and tailors in the upper level of Han Market on Bach Dang can make clothes for you cheaply and quickly. Shirts and pants should cost less than 324,000d apiece and the quality of craftsmanship is generally better than you would find in neighboring Hoi An.

Han Market

MARKET | FAMILY | Located right in the center of the city, this sprawling multi-story local Vietnamese market is a good place to head if you want to sample some good old-fashioned Danang specialties. It's very much like a miniature version of Ben Tanh Market in Ho Chi Minh City. There's an indoor food court near the meat section that offers the freshest and tastiest dishes. Worth trying are *mi quang* (noodles with pork, shrimp, and a light broth) or *com hen* (baby clams and rice). Venture upstairs for fabric, clothes, cosmetics, and housewares. ⊠ *Entrances at Bach Dang, Hung Vuong, and Tran Phu Sts., 119 D. Tran Phu, Danang.*

Danang Beach

Nicknamed "China Beach" by U.S. and Australian troops during the war, Danang Beach stretches for over 30 km (18 miles), and encompasses several smaller beaches, including My Khe, which runs parallel to Danang City and Bac My An. To the north, scores of glitzy Vietnamese seafood restaurants and karaoke bars act as a magnet for nouveau riche Vietnamese and visiting businessmen. Amble south and you hit rows of humble seafood shacks and Danang's public beach, a wide, white, sandy stretch that is almost always deserted during the daytime.

Accommodations along My Khe were once limited to dilapidated government-run hotels, but as with the rest of the city, huge redevelopment is in progress and luxury resorts are quickly popping up in their place. To the south of My Khe, Bac My An has the highest concentration of luxury beach resorts in the area (as well as the city's first casino resort). The tranquil, palm-fringed beaches here attract an international crowd and offer wraparound views of the bay. At the Marble Mountains is Non Nuoc, a quaint sculpture village that spills out onto 4 km (2 miles) of breathtaking beaches, luxury resorts, and golf courses.

GETTING HERE AND AROUND

Most city hotels provide free transfers to and from the beach, or you can cover the 3–5 km (2–3 miles) from the city center to the beach by metered taxi, which should cost approximately 70,000d. For a *xe om* (motorbike taxi), expect to pay no more than 40,000d and be sure to wear a helmet.

Fishing creels sit on the shore of My Khe Beach at sunrise.

Beaches

Bac My An Beach

BEACH | FAMILY | Bac My An is a small, gently sloping, white sandy stretch of beach located 7 km (4½ miles) east of Danang, just south of My Khe. Thanks to its pristine natural landscapes and clear water, Bac My An is a certified crowd-pleaser. Several luxury resorts have sprouted on the beach over the years. Water sports like canoeing, windsurfing, or diving are often complimentary experiences at the resorts. **Amenities:** food and drink. **Best for:** walking; swimming; solitude; sunrise. ⊠ *Bac My An Ward, Bac My An Ward.*

Danang Beach

BEACH | FAMILY | This 30-km (18½-mile) stretch starts at My Khe beach, which runs from the foot of the Hai Van Pass to the north, and ends at Non Nuoc beach near the Marble Mountains to the south. In the middle, south of the Furama Resort, lies Bac My An, the R&R resort spot for U.S. soldiers during the war.

Five-star resorts now line the pristine and quiet sandy stretches south of My Khe, leaving only a handful of beaches accessible to the public. There are a lot of water sports you can try, and some of the region's freshest seafood to devour at the small restaurants that line the beach road. It's best to come between April and August, when the water is placid. Waves can be very large at other times—in fact, the first international surfing competition in Vietnam was held here, in December 1993. **Amenities:** food and drink; toilets; parking. **Best for:** swimming; surfing; walking. ⊠ *Danang.*

My Khe Beach (*China Beach*)

BEACH | FAMILY | Part of the 30 km (18½ miles) of Danang's coastline is the city's most popular beach, My Khe Beach. After the arrival of American soldiers in 1965, it became popular with GIs who came here over their holidays. Sandwiched between Monkey Mountain and the nearby Marble Mountains, My Khe Beach is home to several international resorts, including the Pullman, A La

Carte, and Furama resort. It has fine white sand and warm water, and is surprisingly clean and isolated on weekdays. Beachfront vendors sell coastal specialties like shrimp, crab, and fish. There are palapa umbrellas and restrooms, and it's one of the few beaches with lifeguards on duty year-round. Rip currents and waves mean this is not a swimmer-friendly beach. **Amenities:** food and drink; toilets; lifeguards; water sports. **Best for:** surfing; walking, sunbathing. ⊠ *3 km (2 miles) southeast of Danang City.*

🛏 Hotels

BAC MY AN BEACH
Pullman Danang Beach Resort
$$$$ | RESORT | FAMILY | Supremely comfortable rooms and beach bungalows are elegant with little touches of local art dotted about, and they come with bathrooms suitable for the most serious groomers, plus lounges and balconies with sea views. **Pros:** plenty of kids' activities; free transfers to Danang, Hoi An, and the golf clubs nearby; beach. **Cons:** seasonal sea swimming—the water can get rough in the winter months; some staff don't speak much English; expensive spa. $ *Rooms from: d2,128,512* ⊠ *101 Nguyen Giap St., Danang* ☎ *0236/395–8888* ⊕ *www.pullman-danang.com* ⌁ *186 rooms* ⦿| *Free Breakfast.*

MY KHE
A La Carte Danang Beach
$$$ | HOTEL | FAMILY | The hippest address on the beach boulevard, A La Carte embodies its name perfectly—guests pay a base rate for their room and customize their experience from an all-encompassing menu, only paying for the things they use. **Pros:** near local restaurants; beach; reasonably priced dining. **Cons:** construction around the area can get noisy; pool area can get busy; pool area is slippery when wet. $ *Rooms from: d1,225,000* ⊠ *200 Vo Nguyen Giap, Son Tra District,* *Son Tra* ☎ *0236/395–9555* ⊕ *alacarte-danangbeach.com* ⦿| *Free Breakfast* ⌁ *202 rooms.*

Furama Resort Danang
$$$$ | RESORT | FAMILY | French Vietnamese–style villas surround an artificial tropical swimming lagoon right on the Bac My An beach. **Pros:** free shuttles; restaurants nearby; water sports. **Cons:** old-fashioned; expensive dining on-site; does not live up to five star rating. $ *Rooms from: d1,593,451* ⊠ *7 km (4½ miles) to Danang airport, 103–105 Vo Nguyen Giap St., Ngu Hanh Son District, Danang* ☎ *0236/384–7333* ⊕ *www.furamavietnam.com* ⦿| *Free Breakfast* ⌁ *196 rooms, 70 pool villas.*

★ TIA Wellness Resort
$$$$ | RESORT | Formerly Fusion Maia Danang, TIA Wellness Resort offers an inclusive wellness experience, integrating activities like yoga, spa treatments, and healthy dining into the experience. **Pros:** kids' spa and play area; emphasis on health and relaxation; all spa treatments included in room rate. **Cons:** some spa treatments are hit or miss; pool can get congested; pricey restaurant. $ *Rooms from: d10,466,583* ⊠ *Vo Nguyen Giap St., Ngu Hanh Son District, Danang* ☎ *0236/396–7999* ⊕ *tiawellnessresort.com* ⌁ *87 pool villas* ⦿| *All-Inclusive* ⌂ *2 spa treatments included per night.*

NON NUOC BEACH
Hyatt Regency Danang Resort & Spa
$$$$ | RESORT | FAMILY | Right in the middle of the coastal strip between Hoi An and Danang, the fabulous Hyatt Regency is the perfect beach compromise for those that can't decide between the two cities (both are within a 25-minute drive). **Pros:** beautiful beach; complimentary shuttles to Danang, Hoi An, Marble Mountains, and nearby golf courses; on-site bakery. **Cons:** impersonal; expensive; club upgrade downgrades your breakfast. $ *Rooms from: d3,000,000* ⊠ *5 Truong Sa St., Hoa Hai Ward, Danang*

☎ 0236/398–1234 🌐 www.hyatt.com 🛏 375 rooms 🍴 Free Breakfast.

Ocean Villas Danang

$$$$ | RESORT | FAMILY | Sitting at the midway point between Hoi An and Danang, between a beach and a golf course designed by Greg Norman, the state-of-the-art pool villas, beach, and facilities at Ocean offer the perfect compromise for non-golfers. **Pros:** good for families; two international golf courses nearby; beautiful beach. **Cons:** expensive for quality of service; isolated (unless you like golf); lacking in local flavor. [$] *Rooms from: d4,285,714 ✉ Truong Sa St., Hoa Hai Ward, Danang ☎ 0236/396–7094 🌐 www.theoceanvillas.com.vn 🛏 114 villas 🍴 Free Breakfast.*

Activities

Short of hiring a Jet Ski, surfboard, or bodyboard from one of the large resorts, water sports are fairly limited along Danang's coastal stretch. This isn't a bad thing when you take into consideration the strong rip tides and undercurrents that are common in the area. Lifeguard stations are set up at both public and private beaches, as these are the safest areas for swimming. Danang, fortunately, is home to two of Vietnam's finest golf courses.

BRG Danang Golf Resort

GOLF | Located midway along the coastal road between Danang and Hoi An, this is an 18-hole links course designed by Greg Norman with a 3,000-square-meter grass tee area, a 1,600-square-meter chipping/putting green, two practice bunkers, and a driving range. Packages are on offer for every level (and age) including lessons and video analysis of your swing. Golf packages and transfers are available from nearby resorts. *✉ Hoa Hai Ward, Ngu Hanh Son, Danang ☎ 0236/395–8111 🌐 www.dananggolfclub.com 🎫 4,950,000d ⛳ 18 holes, 7190 yards, par 72.*

Montgomerie Links Golf Course

GOLF | Colin Montgomerie designed this magnificent 18-hole golf course that links the bordering Marble Mountains to the East Sea with sweeping fairways and ocean views. Its facilities include a well-equipped sheltered driving range, pro shop, and par 5 clubhouse overlooking the 18th hole. There is also a PGA golf academy that caters to players of all ages and abilities. Golfers can also enjoy the newly-opened Montgomerie Links Hotel & Villas—five star accommodations featuring stunning fairway views. **■ TIP→ Look out for sunset driving range specials.** *✉ Coastal Road Dien Duong ☎ 0235/394–1942 🌐 www.montgomerielinks.com 🎫 4,100,000d for guests on weekends/holidays ⛳ 18 holes, 7090 yards, par 72.*

Lang Co Beach

35 km (22 miles) north of Danang, 73 km (45 miles) south of Hue city center.

In the dry season that runs from April through to August, Lang Co makes for an oasis from the modern construction along the Danang coastline with pristine, white, sandy beaches and tranquil lagoons lined with oyster shacks and seafood stalls. The quickest route from Danang takes you through the Hai Van tunnel and knocks a good hour off the journey, while the most scenic involves a sometimes hair-raising drive on a winding mountain road—but it's worth the effort for the spectacular views from the **Hai Van Pass** (Deo Hai Van). The panoramic view of the East Sea and Truong Son Mountain range is unparalleled in Vietnam. (If you look closely, you can make out the Marble Mountains in the distance beyond Danang.)

Transport options are plentiful, but the cheapest (and most uncomfortable) is to get the 75,000d public bus from the central bus station on Hai Phong Street in

Danang, which operates on a rather haphazard schedule with the bus departing only when full. For a more comfortable, air-conditioned service, opt for one of the 100,000d tourist buses heading for Hue with a stop at Lang Co Beach. Both of these services take you through the tunnel, so you'll miss out on the views. Lang Co train station is just 3 km (2 miles) from the beach and four public trains a day (trains TN2 and SE22) serve the coastal route from Danang. The journey takes just under two hours at a cost from 30,000d. Taxis and xe oms (motorbike taxis) are available at the station, although the walk through the friendly fishing village to the beach is worthwhile. Unless you ask otherwise, a taxi will take you the most direct route along the highway and through the Hai Van tunnel. This 35-km (22-mile) journey takes just 45 minutes and costs under 500,000d. Although this isn't the most scenic route, it makes the attractions of Danang easily accessible if you plan to base yourself in Lang Co. Only the most confident motorbike drivers should consider taking on the pass, but if you do, hire a geared bike and check that brakes and headlights work before you set off.

For the spectacular and sometimes hair-raising drive along the Hai Van Pass, you will need to hire a private car and driver, as very few taxi drivers will volunteer to take on the hairpin bends. This should cost upward of 600,000d and will include a stop at the old army lookout at the peak.

TAXI CONTACT Lang Co Taxi. ✉ *Lang Co* ☎ *0234/369–6969.*

Sights

★ Laguna Lang Co Golf Club

GOLF COURSE | **FAMILY** | Rolling rice fields, natural streams, a beautiful beachfront, and impressive rock formations are just some of the landscapes that make up the 18-hole Nick Faldo championship golf course and driving range. Located 35 km (22 miles) north of Danang or 55 km (34 miles) south of Hue, the course is an easy commute for those not staying in the area, though for those in search of a golfing vacation, the Angsana and Banyan Tree share the same beach cove. ■ **TIP→ Nongolfers might want to use Angsana and Banyan Tree resorts' spa, restaurants, kids' club, pools, and beach.** ✉ *Cu Du Village, Loc Vinh Commune, Phu Loc District, Phu Loc* ☎ *0234/3695–880* 🌐 *www.lagunalangco.com.*

Beaches

Lang Co Beach

BEACH | **FAMILY** | A convenient stopover on the trip from Hue to Danang, Lang Co is an idyllic hamlet on a peninsula jutting out into the East Sea. Lang Co Beach is a good place to have lunch and spend the day, and for the true sun worshipper, it's absolutely worth considering if you plan a couple of nights of beach indulgence at the Banyan Tree or its budget friendly little sister, Angsana, which is about 20km away from Lang Co Township. Take the turn off Highway 1 at the sign for the Lang Co Beach Resort; this will lead you to the long, sandy beach. **Amenities:** food and drink. **Best for:** sunsets; walks; swimming. ✉ *Lang Co.*

Hotels

Angsana Lang Co

$$$$ | **RESORT** | **FAMILY** | On a 3-km (2-mile) sandy beach, hugged by the Truong Son mountain range, this resort offers golf, quad bikes, water sports, a kids' club, and a beach club, and despite daily excursions to Hue and Hoi An, it's easy to see why most guests don't venture off the property. **Pros:** 18-hole Nick Faldo–designed golf course; idyllic beach; great for families. **Cons:** expensive tours; remote. $ *Rooms from: d3,719,000* ✉ *Cu Du, Loc Vinh Commune, Phu Loc*

☎ *0234/3695–881* 🌐 *www.angsana.com* 🍴 *Free Breakfast* 🛏 *215 rooms.*

★ Banyan Tree

$$$$ | RESORT | About as paradisal as it gets, the incredibly romantic Banyan Tree is the ultimate beach stop midway between Danang and Hue, with fabulous villas, azure ocean views, a tranquil lagoon, and a wraparound mountain backdrop. **Pros:** the food and views from Thai restaurant Saffron; 18-hole Nick Faldo–designed golf course; lagoon spa. **Cons:** better for summer stays; remote; expensive on-site dining. [$] *Rooms from: d10,626,000* ✉ *Cu Du, Loc Vinh Commune, Phu Loc* ☎ *0234/3695–888* 🌐 *www.banyantree.com* 🛏 *70 villas* 🍴 *Free Breakfast.*

Lang Co Beach Resort

$$ | RESORT | This has the feel of a state-owned hotel, though the facilities and beach location are first-rate. **Pros:** huge discounted rates for weekday stays; beach; large villas. **Cons:** thin walls; can be noisy; can be crowded on weekends and holidays. [$] *Rooms from: d900,000* ✉ *463 Lac Long Quan St., Lang Co Town, Phu Loc District, Lang Co* ✣ *Off Hwy. 1* ☎ *0234/3873–555* 🌐 *www.langco-beachresort.com.vn* 🍴 *Free Breakfast* 🛏 *128 rooms.*

Hue

93 km (58 miles) north of Danang, 240 km (149 miles) south of Phong Nha Ke Bang National Park.

Hue (pronounced hway), 13 km (8 miles) inland from the East Sea in the foothills of the Annamite Mountains (Truong Son Mountains), stands as a reminder of Vietnam's imperial past. The seat of 13 Nguyen-dynasty emperors between 1802 and 1945, Hue was once Vietnam's splendid Imperial City. Although it was devastated by the French in the 19th century and again in the 20th (as well as enduring much suffering because of its close proximity to the DMZ), the monument-speckled former capital has a war-ravaged beauty. One can still imagine its former splendor, despite gaping holes in its silhouette. Hue is a UNESCO World Heritage Site, and the city's gems are slowly being restored. Although much of the Imperial City was reduced to rubble, many sections still exist, and Hue's main draw continues to be the remnants of its glorious past. Today tourists keep the city thriving, drawn by the ancient Citadel, mausoleums, pagodas, and palaces. Winding through this historic capital is Perfume River (Song Huong), overshadowed by the Citadel on its north bank. Built under Emperor Gia Long in 1805, this fortress covers 10 km (6 miles) of Hue's waterfront. Equally appealing are the tombs scattered throughout the city, including the Khai Dinh mausoleum that stands out from the pack due to its detailed mosaic work. With so many attractions, Hue should not be rushed. Avoid visiting Hue during the worst of the rainy season, between November and late December.

Although initially daunting, Hue can easily be navigated once you get your basic bearings. The Citadel lines the northern banks of the Perfume River, the main landmark of the city. Four bridges connect the north to the south, where you'll find the train station and the city's newer hotels and restaurants. The south banks also house the backpacker district near Le Loi ("Side Street 66") and Pham Ngu Lao Streets. Most hotels outside this city center have free shuttle service to Chu Van An Street, which runs parallel to Pham Ngu Lao. This is the city's highest concentration of restaurants, shops, and budget properties. The best way to explore the tombs and pagodas on the outskirts of Hue is with a private tour, which includes transportation and a guide, as you are likely to get lost using the less-than-detailed maps available from the tourist offices.

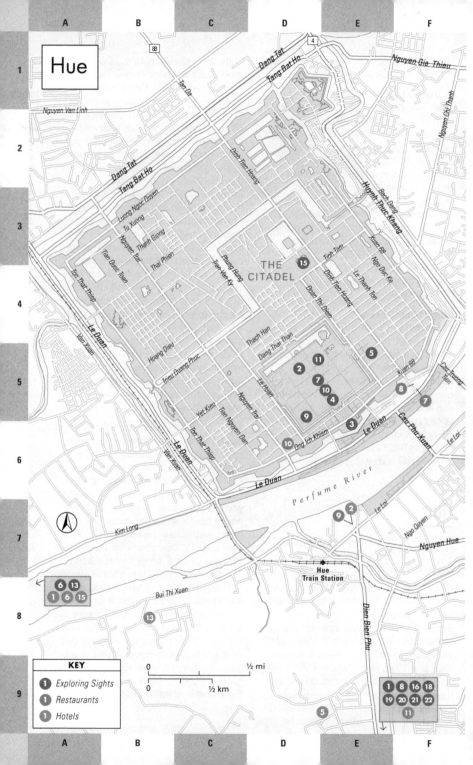

Hue

THE CITADEL

Perfume River

Hue Train Station

KEY

- Exploring Sights
- Restaurants
- Hotels

0 ——— ½ mi

0 ——— ½ km

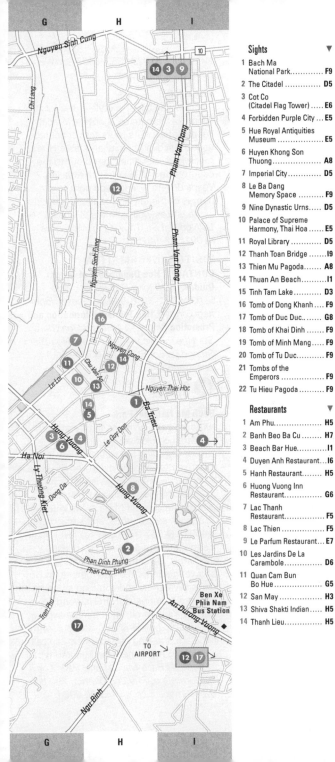

Sights ▼

1 Bach Ma National Park............ **F9**
2 The Citadel **D5**
3 Cot Co (Citadel Flag Tower) **E6**
4 Forbidden Purple City ... **E5**
5 Hue Royal Antiquities Museum **E5**
6 Huyen Khong Son Thuong................... **A8**
7 Imperial City............. **D5**
8 Le Ba Dang Memory Space **F9**
9 Nine Dynastic Urns..... **D5**
10 Palace of Supreme Harmony, Thai Hoa **E5**
11 Royal Library **D5**
12 Thanh Toan Bridge **I9**
13 Thien Mu Pagoda....... **A8**
14 Thuan An Beach...........**I1**
15 Tinh Tam Lake **D3**
16 Tomb of Dong Khanh **F9**
17 Tomb of Duc Duc........ **G8**
18 Tomb of Khai Dinh **F9**
19 Tomb of Minh Mang..... **F9**
20 Tomb of Tu Duc........... **F9**
21 Tombs of the Emperors **F9**
22 Tu Hieu Pagoda **F9**

Restaurants ▼

1 Am Phu.................. **H5**
2 Banh Beo Ba Cu **H7**
3 Beach Bar Hue............**I1**
4 Duyen Anh Restaurant...**I6**
5 Hanh Restaurant......... **H5**
6 Huong Vuong Inn Restaurant............... **G6**
7 Lac Thanh Restaurant............... **F5**
8 Lac Thien **F5**
9 Le Parfum Restaurant... **E7**
10 Les Jardins De La Carambole............... **D6**
11 Quan Cam Bun Bo Hue **G5**
12 San May **H3**
13 Shiva Shakti Indian..... **H5**
14 Thanh Lieu............... **H5**

Hotels ▼

1 Alba Wellness Valley by Fusion......... **A8**
2 Azerai La Residence Hue **E7**
3 Duy Tan Hotel **G6**
4 Eldora Hotel **G6**
5 Hillside Homestay Hue **E9**
6 Hue Riverside Boutique Resort and Spa.......... **A8**
7 Huong Giang Hotel **G5**
8 Indochine Palace....... **H6**
9 Lapochine Beach Resort **I1**
10 Moonlight Hotel......... **G5**
11 Pilgrimage Village Boutique Resort & Spa **F9**
12 Rosaleen Boutique Hotel **H5**
13 Sahi Homestay Retreat................... **B8**
14 The Scarlett Boutique Hotel **H5**
15 Tam Tinh Vien Homestay................ **A8**
16 Than Thien (Friendly) Hotel.......... **H4**
17 Vedana Lagoon Resort & Spa **I9**

GETTING HERE AND AROUND

Travelers reach Hue with air connections from Hanoi or Ho Chi Minh City, or via a two-hour drive from Danang. Tour company The Sinh Tourist runs sleeper buses twice daily between Ho Chi Minh City and Hanoi, with a stop in Hue. Public buses from major cities arrive at An Cuu Station from the south and An Hoa Station from the north. There's no shortage of taxis in Hue, but make sure you hail the green Mai Linh or yellow Vang cabs. Rates start at 14,000d.

The most pleasant way to explore Hue is by bicycle, which can be rented for 50,000d a day from hotels and guesthouses. Adventurous travelers might enjoy exploring by cyclo (three-wheeled bike taxi) or xe om (motorbike taxi). Rates vary, so don't be afraid to negotiate.

CONTACTS Mai Linh Taxi. ✉ *177 Phan Dinh Phung St., Phu Nhuan Ward, Hue* ☎ *0234/389–8989.* **The Sinh Tourist.** ✉ *37 Nguyen Thai Hoc St., Phu Hoi Ward, Hue* ☎ *0234/384–5022.* **Vang Taxi.** ✉ *138 Truong Gia Mo St., Hue* ☎ *0234/379–7979.*

TOURS

Hue Dragon Boat Station

Daily tour boats shuttle visitors between the citadel and the further-flung tombs. Several different packages are available, including guided tours. It's not the quickest way to get around, and in the wet monsoon months it's not even pleasant, but during the heat of the summer, the cool river breezes, relaxed pace, and views make it the perfect choice for those wanting to get the most from the journey. There's a second Dragon Boat station at 5 Le Loi Street, next door to Azerai La Residence Hue. ✉ *Toa Kham landing, 49 Le Loi St., Hue.*

Trails of Indochina

As the most reputable tour company in Vietnam, Trails of Indochina offers custom tours to Hue's main attractions and has highly experienced English-speaking guides. ✉ *21/1 Ngo Gia Tu St., Vinh Ninh Ward, Hue* ☎ *0234/383–6525* ⊕ *www.trailsofindochina.com.*

Vespa Safari

You now can travel in style in the former capital of Vietnam on a vintage Vespa. Vespa Safari offers tours that encourage you to discover the city and taste Hue's renowned specialties, or go out to the countryside and experience rural life. Vespa drivers will ride you right to the homes of friendly and welcoming locals in the city as well as in the villages. ✉ *64 Le Ngo Cat St., Thuy Xuan Ward, Hue* ☎ *091/547–5875.*

VISITOR INFORMATION

CONTACTS Hue Department of Tourist Guides. ✉ *23 Tong Duy Tan St., Hue* ☎ *0234/351–3818* ⊕ *www.hueworldheritage.org.vn.* **Hue Tourism Information and Promotion Center.** ✉ *4 Hoang Hoa Tham St., Hue* ⊹ *At corner of Hoang Hoa Tham St. and Le Loi St.* ☎ *0234/382–4037* ⊕ *visithue.vn.*

◉ Sights

Bach Ma National Park

NATIONAL PARK | With its temperate climate, rich biodiversity, and exquisite views, Bach Ma National Park is a must-see for wildlife lovers and those who want a break from Vietnam's heat. In 1932, the French built a hill station around the summit of Bach Ma with 139 villas, a post office, and a market, all 1,450 m (4,757 ft.) above sea level. Today it's the ultimate getaway for trekking in the jungle, swimming in pristine streams, showering under the 300-meter-high Do Quyen Waterfall, and admiring stunning sunsets or sunrises from Hai Vong Dai on Bach Ma's summit. The ultimate experience at Bach Ma is a private tour with Mr. Cam, the king of birds, who can call and talk to more than one hundred types of birds. ✉ *Bach Ma National Park, Loc Tri Commune, Phu Loc District, Phu Loc* ⊕ *bachmapark.com.vn* 🎟 *60,000d.*

★ **The Citadel**

CASTLE/PALACE | If there is only one sight you visit in Hue, make sure this is it. Constructed in 1805 under the rule of Emperor Gia Long, this fortress is sheltered by an outer wall spanning 10 km (6 miles). Marking its entry are the Nine Holy Cannons and a flag that stands 121 feet high, the tallest in the country. Inside the sprawling complex are temples, ruins, shops, and galleries paying tribute to the past. Something of an eyesore are the scaffoldings of sections still being restored from the severe damage caused during the 1947 and 1968 battles. Just beyond the main gate is the Supreme Harmony House, where the emperor addressed officials. Approximately 90% of this main building is still original, including the two unicorns at the base of the throne, symbolizing loyalty. In the Resting House to the left of the courtyard, bullet holes on the front steps leave traces of a battle during the American (Vietnam) War. ⊠ *North Bank, Hue* 🎫 *Free.*

Cot Co (Citadel Flag Tower)

NOTABLE BUILDING | This 170-foot structure, Vietnam's tallest flagpole, is one of the symbols of Hue. It was originally built in 1807 to serve as the Imperial Palace's central observation post. Like much of Hue, it has a history of being destroyed. The Flag Tower was toppled during a typhoon in 1904 and rebuilt, then, destroyed again in 1947, and rebuilt anew in 1948. When the North Vietnamese occupied the city during the Tet Offensive of 1968, the National Liberation Front flag flew from the Flag Tower. The interior is closed to the public. ⊠ *In front of 23 Thang 8 St., facing Ngo Mon Gate, Hue.*

Forbidden Purple City (*Tu Cam Thanh*)

RUINS | Built at the beginning of the 19th century, the Forbidden Purple City, inside the Imperial City, was almost entirely destroyed during the Vietnam War; now it's slowly being restored to its former glory. The preserved open corridors, which were used to connect the main palaces in the Forbidden Purple City together, are ornately adorned with lavish red and gold paint. Paintings and photographs about Nguyen Dynasty and old Hue are also exhibited in these open corridors. In its glory days the Forbidden Purple City housed members of the Imperial family and the concubines and eunuchs who served them. Anyone else who entered was executed. After the 1968 Tet Offensive, only the Royal Theater on the right-hand side and the intimate and restored Royal Library remained intact. ⊠ *In Imperial City, Hue* 🎫 *200,000d admission to Imperial City includes Forbidden Purple City.*

Hue Royal Antiquities Museum

HISTORY MUSEUM | The reason to visit this museum is to see the beautiful wooden structure that houses the antiques, rather than the displays themselves. Built in 1845, the small garden house is an architectural wonder, with walls inscribed with Vietnamese poetry and ceilings festooned with beautiful carvings. Inside there are miscellaneous royal knickknacks, such as wooden incense boxes, many inlaid with mother-of-pearl, plus statues, old weapons, and jewelry. Unfortunately, the whole experience is let down by lackluster guides and limited information available. ⊠ *3 Le Truc, Thuan Thanh Ward, Hue* 🎫 *Included in 200,000d citadel ticket.*

Huyen Khong Son Thuong

TEMPLE | Nestled at the foot of Hon Vuon Hill, Huyen Khong Son Thuong is a monastery and the serene home of about 60 Theravada monks. Founded by Ven. Silaguna in 1989, the monastery sits in a beautiful garden with five water lily and lotus ponds and is surrounded by pine trees. Unlike the majority of Buddhist temples in Hue in which designs are influenced by the Nguyen Dynasty's royal style, its architecture is simpler and is decorated with calligraphy poems that are composed by the monks and written

Hue's stunning Citadel is sheltered by an outer wall that's 6 miles long.

in Vietnamese rather than traditional Chinese characters. Apart from beautiful bonsai trees, hundreds of orchid plants bloom here year round. If you'd like to venture further, take a one-hour hike to the top of Hon Vuon Hill, where you'll get a stunning view of hills, lakes, the iconic Huong River, and Hue's cityscape expanding into the horizon. ⊠ *Dong Cham, Huong Ho Ward, Huong Tra Township, Hue* ✛ *7km to the west of Thien Mu Pagoda* ☜ *Free.*

Imperial City (*Hoang Thanh*)

RUINS | The Imperial City, also known as the Imperial Enclosure, was once a complex of palaces and pavilions where civil and religious ceremonies took place. Inside it was the **Forbidden Purple City,** where the royal family lived. Now the Imperial City has buried the few remnants of its past glory beneath the sporadic vegetation that has taken over the ruins, but restoration work is in progress and the site still conveys a sense of splendor. There are four gateways into the enclosure: the **Gate of Peace** (Cua

Hoa Binh), **the Gate of Humanity** (Cua Hien Nhan), the **Gate of Virtue** (Cua Chuong Duc), and the **South Gate** (Ngo Mon). You can only get to the Imperial City after you have entered the citadel. ⊠ *Inside citadel, Hue* ☜ *200,000d* ⚲ *Discounted tickets for multiple sites are available at ticket office.*

Le Ba Dang Memory Space

ART MUSEUM | Established in the memory of artist Le Ba Dang, who was born in nearby province Quang Tri and became successful in Paris, Le Ba Dang Memory Space is one of the country's best art museums. The main building of this private contemporary space, located on 4 acres near Thien An Hill, is modeled after one of the artist's paper works. The museum showcases Le Ba Dang's varied talents, from painting to sculpture to paper-cutting and printing. ⊠ *Kim Son Hamlet, Thuy Bang Commune, Hue* ☎ *0234/627–4771* ⊕ *www.facebook. com/lebadangmemoryspace* ☜ *269,000d (Discount for a group of over 10 people)* ☾ *Closed Mon.*

Nine Dynastic Urns (Cuu Dinh)

HISTORIC SIGHT | Each of these urns within the Imperial Enclosure, weighing approximately 5,000 pounds and cast in 1835, is dedicated to a ruler of the Nguyen dynasty. The central urn, the most elaborately decorated of the nine, features Emperor Gia Long, the founder of this dynasty. Nature motifs cover the urns, including the sun and moon, rivers and mountains, and one or two bullet pocks. Every urn has a name transcribed in traditional Chinese characters. ⊠ The southwest corner of Imperial Enclosure, Hue 🖃 200,000d admission to Imperial City includes Nine Urns.

Palace of Supreme Harmony, Thai Hoa (Thai Hoa Dien)

CASTLE/PALACE | Located within the Imperial Enclosure, this richly decorated wooden palace painted gold and red was constructed in 1805. In its imperial glory in the 19th century, it was where the emperor held special events, ceremonies, and semimonthly meetings. This is also where the emperor received dignitaries. Throngs of mandarins paid their respects to his highness while he sat on his elevated throne. Now the palace houses a seating area where an excellent 20-minute audiovisual display gives an in-depth overview of the history and architecture of the citadel. ⊠ In Imperial City, Hue 🖃 200,000d for admission to Imperial City (includes Palace of Supreme Harmony).

Royal Library (Thai Binh Lau)

NOTABLE BUILDING | The Royal Library, a wooden structure east of the Forbidden Purple City, is one of the few largely intact buildings in the Imperial City. The delicately carved architecture has survived, although there are no books or other library-like objects left. ⊠ In Imperial City, Hue 🖃 200,000d admission to Imperial City includes Royal Library.

Thanh Toan Bridge

BRIDGE | Resembling Hoi An's Japanese Bridge, this covered walkway was built in 1776 as a shrine to the local Tran Thi Dao, who bequeathed her life savings for its construction. Childless, she offered her funds to the Thanh Toan Village for a new bridge to connect villagers on both sides of the canal. In 1925, Emperor Khai Dinh had an altar set up in her honor in the center of the bridge, which is still used by villagers who come to show their respect. Located 8 km (5 miles) outside Hue, this bridge is reached by way of the peaceful countryside, making it a pleasant escape from the bustling city. On the far side of the bridge is a small museum displaying villagers' used farming equipment. ■TIP➔ If you visit independently, park your bike at the market 100 meters from the bridge. ⊠ Thuy Thanh Commune, Huong Thuy District, Hue ✢ 8 km (5 miles) east of Hue 🖃 Free.

Thien Mu Pagoda

TEMPLE | Overlooking the Perfume River, this pagoda constructed in 1601 under Lord Nguyen Hoang has impressive Buddha statues, a seven-tiered monument, a two-ton bronze bell, and a marble turtle dating back to 1715. Take note of the engraved graffiti covering the turtle's shell, most of which dates back to the 1950s, when refugees from northern Vietnam inscribed notes of their whereabouts. As Hue's oldest pagoda, this structure still functions as a monastery and is perched on a hill above the river at the narrowest point in Vietnam. Housed inside the grounds is the Austin car once used by Buddhist monk Thich Quang Duc, who lit himself on fire in protest of the persecution of Buddhists by the South Vietnamese president Ngo Dinh Diem in 1963. The best way to reach this official symbol of Hue is by dragon boat up the Perfume River. ⊠ 3½ km (2 miles) west of Phu Xuan Bridge, Ha Khe Hill, Hue 🖃 Free.

Thuan An Beach

BEACH | FAMILY | For now, Thuan An Beach, which lies out on a peninsula 14 km (8 miles) from central Hue, has only one beach resort, leaving an unspoiled, long, sandy stretch of coconut- and casuarina-tree-lined beach all but empty. In the summer months the tranquil turquoise sea and gentle breeze make for the most idyllic break from the city, while in winter it makes for wildly romantic walks, with scatterings of family temples, fishing villages, and Vietnam's largest lagoon to explore. **Amenities:** food and drink. **Best for:** walking; swimming; sunset. ⊠ *Thuan An Ward, Hue.*

Tinh Tam Lake *(Ho Tinh Tam)*

BODY OF WATER | For much of the year Tinh Tam Lake is hardly worth the bother, but during the spring and summer months this little lake in the citadel comes alive with lotus flowers that cover it entirely. Do as the emperors once did and walk across one of the bridges to the island for a brief respite. The best way to see it (and find it) is by asking your driver to include it in a cyclo tour of the citadel. ⊠ *Dinh Tien Hoang and Tinh Tam Sts., Hue.*

Tomb of Dong Khanh

TOMB | Dong Khanh was a despised puppet emperor of the Nguyen Dynasty who died during the French rule at the age of 24. This tomb complex, originally built for his father, took over 35 years and four kings to complete. The result is a unique fusion of traditional imperial Vietnamese and colonial design. Emperor Dong Khanh's final resting place was built near Ngung Hy Temple, an elaborate triple temple complex typical of the citadel. Look for the well-preserved lacquer art and Chinese calligraphy that adorn the walls, and the illustrations featuring the 24 filial sons and daughters taken from the Chinese story Nhi Thap Tu Hieu. The surrounding area is the colonial-style graveyard that was constructed between 1916 and 1923. ⊠ *Northeast of Tu Duc on right side of river; follow road that leads to Tomb of Tu Duc about ½ km (¼ mile) around corner, Hue* ⌹ *50,000d.*

Tomb of Duc Duc

TOMB | This partially renovated tomb has a story that beats any soap opera. It begins with the death of Emperor Tu Duc in 1883, when Duc Duc (one of three of Tu Duc's adopted sons) was controversially declared his successor. Duc Duc's reign of the Nguyen Dynasty was to last only three days before he was stripped of his title and incarcerated. The reasons for this are unclear, but it is believed that the three regents responsible for the appointment of Duc Duc, feared that he would strip them of the power they had enjoyed under the weak rule of Tu Duc. In modern history, Duc Duc is considered the first of a long line of "puppet emperors" whose short reign was thought to have been controlled by French colonialists. ⊠ *2 km (1 mile) from Le Loi St. on right bank of river, Hue* ⌹ *Free.*

★ Tomb of Khai Dinh

TOMB | An unbelievable concoction of glitzy Vietnamese and French colonial elements, the Tomb of Khai Dinh, completed in 1931, is a contender for Hue's most impressive mausoleum. Khai Dinh became emperor in 1916 at the age of 31 and died in 1925. The entrance is guarded by a row of impressive stone elephants and imperial soldiers. A climb up a steep flights of steps, flanked by dragons, takes you to a surprisingly colorful tomb heavily decorated with tile mosaics. Scenes from the four seasons welcome you into the central compartment of the building. It's best to visit this tomb by car, since it's not directly on the river. ■ **TIP→ Climb to the top for some incredible views of the countryside and the Annamite Range.** ⊠ *About 16 km (10 miles) south of Hue and about 1½ km (1 mile) inland on right bank of Perfume River, Hue* ⌹ *100,000d.*

The Tomb of Khai Dinh showcases stone elephants and imperial soldiers.

Tomb of Minh Mang

TOMB | A Hue classic, the Tomb of Minh Mang, emperor from 1820 to 1841, was completed in 1843 by his successor. His tomb is one of the most palatial, with numerous pavilions and courtyards in a beautiful pine forest. The burial site is modeled after the Ming tombs in Beijing. Sculptures of mandarins, elephants, and lions line the route to the burial site. The mountainous backdrop and crumbling structure make it one of the most eerie, yet beautiful, tombs to visit. ⊠ *About 11 km (7 miles) south of Hue and 1½ km (1 mile) inland on left bank of Perfume River,* ☎ *150,000d.*

★ Tomb of Tu Duc

TOMB | FAMILY | The Tomb of Tu Duc, one of Hue's most visited tombs, has its own lake and pine forest, and is easily accessed by bike. Built in 1864–67 by thousands of laborers, the tomb was once the second residence of Tu Duc, emperor from 1848 to 1883. Despite having more than 100 wives and concubines (but no children) Tu Duc somehow found

the time to escape here to relax and write poetry. Further along is Hoa Khiem Temple where Tu Duc and the Empress Le Thien Anh were worshipped. Behind is an old theater, now home to a vast wardrobe of imperial dress and some interesting props for photo opportunities. One of Tu Duc's favorite spots was the Xung Khiem Pavilion on the pond filled with lotus blossoms. If your schedule allows, stop by the Vong Canh Hill top to enjoy the stunning view of Huong River and the mountains at sunset. ⊠ *About 6 km (3 miles) south of Hue on right bank of Perfume River, Hue* ☎ ⊠ *150,000d.*

Tombs of the Emperors

TOMB | South of Hue along the Perfume River, these scattered tombs—the ego-boosting mausoleums erected by emperors in the late 1800s and early 1900s—can easily be explored in a day, although it's likely you'll experience tomb-overload by your second site—visually and historically they are a lot to absorb. The most impressive one is the Tomb of Khai Dinh due to its ornate architecture reflecting Buddhist imagery. Between 1920 and 1931, the tomb was built with money from a 30% tax increase forced on the people. To construct the final mosaics surrounding the tomb, fine china and ceramics were broken into pieces. Take note of the dragon eyes made from Champagne bottles, and the flower petals made from ceramic spoons. The most respected emperor was Thieu Tri, remembered for his compassion for the people, evidenced by his unadorned 1848 tomb. If you plan to see the Tomb of Tu Duc, Thieu Tri's son, allow plenty of time to explore the grounds, which once housed 50 buildings in a sprawling lakefront compound. The Tomb of Gia Long is 20 km (12½ miles) outside the city, which means you're likely to have the place entirely to yourself. ✉ *South of Hue, Hue* 🎫 *From 50,000d to 150,000 per tomb; discounted packages are available for multiple tomb touring at Citadel Ticket Office.*

Tu Hieu Pagoda

TEMPLE | One of Hue's most beautiful and peaceful pagodas is accessed via a junglelike path off the road, past a half-moon-shape pool. Built in 1843, the temple houses a large Buddha and it is the root pagoda of Zen master Thich Nhat Hanh. It's a good place for quiet meditation. The monks live in simple rooms off to the side and hold services several times a day. At the far corner of the pagoda is a cemetery for the Nguyen Dynasty's eunuchs who made contribution to building and renovating the pagoda. ✉ *About 5 km (3 miles) south of Hue on way to Tu Duc Tomb, Hue* 🎫 *Free.*

🍴 Restaurants

Leaning on Hue's history, the city's traditional cuisine incorporates the art of food carving, at royal dinners fit for a king. It's customary for restaurants to serve dishes with intricately designed flowers, dragons, and fish carved from carrots and other vegetables. To maximize this cultural experience, dine at one of Hue's many restaurants that offer royal dinners, including traditional music and dance.

Am Phu

$ | **VIETNAMESE** | A favorite with locals, Am Phu ("hell restaurant"), has been in operation for more than 80 years, serving excellent Vietnamese cuisine. It's famous locally for *com am phu,* a colorful rice, pork, shrimp, and herb specialty dish—the seven colors of this dish represent the first seven steps of Buddha. **Known for:** centrally located; authentic Hue food; family-style dining. [$] *Average main: d70,000* ✉ *51 Nguyen Thai Hoc St., Hue* ☎ *0234/382–5259* 💳 *No credit cards.*

Banh Beo Ba Cu

$ | **VIETNAMESE** | Don't be put off by the grungy interior of this restaurant. The quality of the decor is in inverse proportion to the quality of the food. **Known for:** low-budget; local specialties; small but excellent menu. [$] *Average main: d30,000* ✉ *23/177 Phan Dinh Phung St., Hue* ✥ *Right beside An Dinh Palace* ☎ *0234/383–2895* 💳 *No credit cards.*

Beach Bar Hue

$$ | **VIETNAMESE** | **FAMILY** | This inspired little beach club 15 km (10 miles) from Hue has shady beach cabanas, hammocks, and a large cobalt-blue fishing boat that serves as the bar. It's a laid-back place, with a simple Vietnamese seafood menu, where you feel a world away from the annoyances of the city. **Known for:** far away from the city; pristine beach; fresh seafood. [$] *Average main: d100,000* ✉ *Phu Thuan Beach, Phu Vang, Hue* ☎ *0917/673–656* 🌐 *www.beachbarhue.com.*

Duyen Anh Restaurant

$$$ | **SEAFOOD** | **FAMILY** | At Duyen Anh Restaurant you can pick up your own live fish, shrimp, or lobsters from the tanks, and vegetables are homegrown in the nearly 5,000-square-foot garden viewable from your dining table. All dishes are designed to share. **Known for:** spacious and tranquil setting; fresh seafood; homegrown vegetables. $ *Average main: d500,000* ⌨ *Tinh Lo 10A, Vinh Ve Hamlet, Phu My Commune, Phu Vang District, Hue* ☎ *0234/385–0195* ⊕ *www.duyenanhres. com.vn.*

Hanh Restaurant
$$ | **VIETNAMESE** | It might be overcrowded during lunch and dinner, but this open restaurant's wide range of Hue specialties such as *nem lui* (grilled pork sausage on lemongrass stick), *banh khoai* (savory pancake), tapas like *beo, nam, loc,* and noodles with grilled pork and salad are all worth the wait. **Known for:** grilled pork sausage on lemongrass; wide range of Hue specialties; local favorite. $ *Average main: d75,000* ⌨ *11 Pho Duc Chinh St., Hue.*

Huong Vuong Inn Restaurant
$$ | **VIETNAMESE** | Fresh daily ingredients are the pride of this small restaurant located near the iconic Truong Tien Bridge. While the restaurant's menu features a wide range of Vietnamese and local cuisines, their pizza is the best in town. **Known for:** thin-crust pizza; à la minute cooking; grilled pork rib rice. $ *Average main: d90,000* ⌨ *20 Hung Vuong St., Hue* ☎ *0234/3827–899.*

Lac Thanh Restaurant
$ | **VIETNAMESE** | Packed with tourists and teeming with easy riders and souvenir hawkers, this basic restaurant located near the entrance to the citadel is run by guidebook sweetheart, Mr. Lac. Sadly, what once was a great little local spot churning out a couple of delicious staple Hue dishes has turned into a giant enterprise with an equally giant menu and following. **Known for:** close to Hue Citadel; friendly service; giant menu. $ *Average main: d25,000* ⌨ *6A Dinh Tien Hoang St., Hue* ☎ *0234/352–4674* ▭ *No credit cards.*

Lac Thien
$ | **VIETNAMESE** | This busy little café is one of the oldest in Hue. On a busy corner by the side of the river, it specializes in just one dish: banh khoai, crispy pancakes stuffed with bean sprouts, shrimp, and little mounds of pork, served up with herbaceous side salads and a spicy peanut sauce. **Known for:** local specialties; amiable and fun staff; shaded sidewalk seating. $ *Average main: d50,000* ⌨ *6 Dinh Tien Hoang, Hue* ☎ *0234/352–7348* ▭ *No credit cards.*

Le Parfum Restaurant
$$$$ | **FRENCH** | Inside the historical Azerai La Residence Hue, this pricey brasserie rivals anything you might find in Paris. The French fusion degustation menu (which must be requested eight hours in advance) features six exquisite courses, ranging from smoked duck carpaccio to beef tenderloin with rosemary. **Known for:** elegant setting; professional staff; multicourse wine pairing. $ *Average main: d500,000* ⌨ *5 Le Loi St., Hue* ☎ *0234/383–7475* ⊕ *azerai.com.*

★ Les Jardins De La Carambole
$$ | **FRENCH** | Neighboring the historic Imperial City, this French-Vietnamese restaurant is fashioned after a colonial villa with green shutters, arched doorways, tile floors, antiques dating back to 1915, and artwork depicting pastoral scenes. Slightly pricey by local standards, the enormous menu features green mango salad, fresh spring rolls, beef in banana leaves, and grilled sea bass with a Mediterranean sauce, as well as sandwiches, pasta, and pizza. **Known for:** close to Imperial City; chic colonial architecture; enormous menu. $ *Average main: d180,000* ⌨ *32 Dang Tran Con St., Hue* ☎ *0234/354–8815.*

Quan Cam Bun Bo Hue
$ | **VIETNAMESE** | No visit to Hue is complete without sampling the city's most famous breakfast dish, *bun bo Hue,* a glorious lemongrass-and-chili infused

beef broth, served with slippery round noodles, beef, pork shank, and a fistful of fragrant herbs. It's not unlike fiery northern pho, and is best slurped from specialty kitchens; the best in Hue is Quan Cam, a tiny family-run noodle shop on Le Loi Street. **Known for:** central location; the best bun bo Hue in town; breakfast only. [$] *Average main: d50,000* ✉ *In front yard of Century Hotel on Le Loi St., 49 Le Loi St., Hue* ☎ 💳 *No credit cards.*

San May

$ | **VEGETARIAN** | San May is a small decent vegetarian restaurant on the quiet Thanh Tinh Street. Dine amid soothing music in a *nha ruong* (Hue's traditional panel house) surrounded by a beautiful garden. **Known for:** tasty and fresh pomelo salad; peaceful ambience; plant-based dishes. [$] *Average main: d55,000* ✉ *8 Thanh Tinh St., Vy Da Ward, Hue* ☎ *093/199–9972.*

Shiva Shakti Indian

$$ | **INDIAN** | There are times when only a good old-fashioned curry will do, and the talented Indian chefs here make some of the best. Highlights of the menu include anything from their tandoori oven, soft buttery naan, mixed vegetable or meat grilled dishes, and tikka. **Known for:** central location; authentic Indian food; tandoori dishes. [$] *Average main: d110,000* ✉ *27 Vo Thi Sau St., Hue* ☎ *0234/393–5627.*

Thanh Lieu

$ | **VIETNAMESE** | This vegetarian food stall is located right on the edge of Hue's Night Pedestrian Zone. This is the cheapest food stall in town with tasty plant-based dishes starting from 10,000d. **Known for:** fresh ingredients; the cheapest vegetarian restaurant in town. [$] *Average main: d30,000* ✉ *50 Nguyen Cong Tru St., Hue.*

Hotels

Most of Hue's upscale, full-service hotels are on Le Loi Street near Perfume River. Close to the sights, these properties are your best bet for service with a view. A few midrange hotels are clustered around the area between Truong Tien and Phu Xuan bridges, the main access bridges to the Citadel. Hotels of all sizes have travel services and can arrange boat tours to the tombs and pagodas as well as guided tours in and around Hue.

Alba Wellness Valley by Fusion

$$$$ | **RESORT** | With a hot spring running through its property and the backdrop of Annammite Range, this resort is an all-season wellness retreat. **Pros:** complimentary round trip airport transfer by shuttle bus; complimentary onsen, foot massage, guided hiking and biking tour, zip line, and high wire; family friendly. **Cons:** far away from the city center; crowded on weekends; mosquitoes at dusk. [$] *Rooms from: 2,900,000* ✉ *Phong Son Commune, Phong Dien District* ☎ *0234/355–6666* 🌐 *fusionhotelgroup.com* 🍴 *Free Breakfast* 🛏 *56 rooms.*

★ **Azerai La Residence Hue**

$$$$ | **HOTEL** | Built in the 1930s, this swanky hotel near the river (a French-colonial mansion and two newer wings) is recognized for its service as well as its art deco, jazzy panache. **Pros:** excellent service; central location; river views: tour service. **Cons:** newer rooms are small; not child friendly. [$] *Rooms from: d6,192,000* ✉ *5 Le Loi St., Hue* ☎ *0234/383–7475* 🌐 *azerai.com* 🛏 *122 rooms* 🍴 *Free Breakfast.*

Duy Tan Hotel

$ | **HOTEL** | Despite its large and semi-grand appearance, this hotel functions as a glorified minihotel. **Pros:** location; value; service. **Cons:** firm mattresses; popular with tour groups; uninspiring design. [$] *Rooms from: d700,000* ✉ *12*

Hung Vuong St., Phu Nhuan Ward, Hue ☎ *0234/3825–001* 🌐 *www.duytanhotel.com.vn* 🛏 *135 rooms* 🍴 *Free Breakfast.*

Eldora Hotel

$$$ | **HOTEL** | Aspiring starlets will love the Moulin Rouge stylings of this grandiose hotel in central Hue—it's all ooh-la-la French elegance with a bohemian twist. **Pros:** pool; close to all the city attractions; very good value. **Cons:** the best breakfast choices go quickly; some ongoing construction in the area. [$] *Rooms from: d1,570,000* ✉ *60 Ben Nghe, Hue* ☎ *0234/386–6666* 🌐 *www.eldorahotel.com* 🛏 *81 rooms* 🍴 *Free Breakfast.*

Hillside Homestay Hue

$ | **B&B/INN** | Huyen Lisa Truong who used to work for some luxury hotels in town is a very professional and caring host of this spacious and gracefully designed hotel. **Pros:** washing machine and kitchen are free to use; complimentary bicycle rental; close to the imperial tombs. **Cons:** might be hard to find this homestay if you come on your own. [$] *Rooms from: d550,000* ✉ *No 6 Alley 111 Tran Thai Tong St., Thuy Xuan District, Hue* ☎ *094/248–5454* 🛏 *4 rooms* 🍴 *Free Breakfast.*

Hue Riverside Boutique Resort and Spa

$$$$ | **RESORT** | **FAMILY** | All 40 of the riverfront rooms of Hue Riverside Boutique Resort and Spa sit in a verdant 10-acre pomelo garden and line the Huong River. **Pros:** complimentary fresh fruits; all rooms have private balcony with river view; complimentary shuttle boats to the city's center, kayak, fishing, and guided bicycle tour. **Cons:** uninspiring room design; far away from the city center. [$] *Rooms from: d1,950,000* ✉ *588 Bui Thi Xuan St., Thuy Bieu Ward, Hue* ✣ *Opposite Temple of Literature across river* ☎ *0234/397–8484* 🌐 *www.hueriversideresort.com* 🛏 *40 rooms* 🍴 *Free Breakfast.*

Huong Giang Hotel

$$$ | **RESORT** | Although not the swankiest, this huge riverside property offers all the benefits of resort facilities, a central location, and pool, all at low prices, while the helpful staff make this one of the most pleasant places to stay in Hue. The large rooms come decorated in traditional Vietnamese style, with rattan furniture. **Pros:** city-centered; exceptional travel office; good restaurants. **Cons:** ; popular with tour groups. [$] *Rooms from: d1,000,000* ✉ *51 Le Loi St., Hue* ☎ *0234/382–2122, 0234/384–5555* 🌐 *www.huonggiang-hotel.com.vn* 🛏 *163 rooms* 🍴 *Free Breakfast.*

Indochine Palace

$$$$ | **HOTEL** | **FAMILY** | One of the most luxurious hotels in Hue, this 17-story property blends modern Vietnamese with colonial elegance to avoid the chain-hotel effect. **Pros:** attentive English-speaking staff; live music all nights except Monday; excellent beds and showers. **Cons:** 20-minute walk to closest sights; open bathroom design lacks privacy. [$] *Rooms from: d2,660,000* ✉ *105A Hung Vuong St., Hue* ☎ *0234/393–6666* 🌐 *www.indochinepalace.com* 🛏 *222 rooms* 🍴 *Free Breakfast.*

★ **Lapochine Beach Resort**

$$$$ | **RESORT** | **FAMILY** | Hue's most beautiful luxury resort, perched on one of the best beaches in the region (you can see it just beyond the infinity pool as you check in), has sumptuous rooms with Indochine styling, imperial silks elegantly draped over oversize beds, and colossal bathrooms housing roll-top tubs. **Pros:** family-friendly; great discounted spa packages; on the beach; free daily transfers to Hue. **Cons:** seasonal, it's not quite as idyllic during the monsoon months; remote location. [$] *Rooms from: d2,500,000* ✉ *15 km (9 miles) east of Hue, Thuan An Town, Hue* ☎ *0234/3983–333* 🌐 *lapochine-beachresort.com* 🛏 *78 rooms* 🍴 *Free Breakfast.*

Moonlight Hotel

$$$ | **HOTEL** | All rooms at Moonlight Hotel have big windows and wood floors; some of the river view rooms have a bathroom well-lit with natural light. **Pros:** friendly and helpful staff; located in city's center; close to many restaurants and bars. **Cons:** a bit noisy at night, especially during weekends. $ *Rooms from: d1,470,000* ⊠ *20 Pham Ngu Lao St, Hue* ☎ *0234/397-9797* ⊕ *www.moonlighthue.com* ⊋ *90 rooms* ⦿ *Free Breakfast.*

★ Pilgrimage Village Boutique Resort & Spa

$$$$ | **RESORT** | Reminiscent of a rural Vietnamese village, this peaceful property has artisan shops lining a brick pathway that lead to spacious villas with hardwood floors, private balconies, and marble bathtubs framed with river stones. **Pros:** complimentary yoga, tai chi, and shuttle service; wonderful breakfast buffet; enormous swimming pool. **Cons:** poor lighting; pricey cocktails; popular with tour groups. $ *Rooms from: d3,045,000* ⊠ *130 Minh Mang Rd., Hue* ☎ *0234/388-5461* ⊕ *www.pilgrimagevillage.com* ⦿ *Free Breakfast* ⊋ *173 rooms and villas.*

Rosaleen Boutique Hotel

$$ | **HOTEL** | What the rooms here lack in style, they make up for with comfort, but the reason to stay here is the giant outside pool, a rarity at such a well-priced city-center location. **Pros:** walking distance to restaurants, bars; pool; great balcony views from deluxe rooms. **Cons:** lackluster breakfast. $ *Rooms from: d800,000* ⊠ *36 Chu Van An St., Phu Hoi Ward, Hue* ☎ *0234/394-6555* ⊕ *www.rosaleenhotel.com* ⦿ *Free Breakfast* ⊋ *56 rooms.*

Sahi Homestay Retreat

$ | **B&B/INN** | Designed by its owner who is also an architect, Sahi Homestay Retreat is more than a just a hostel but also a zen getaway with eco-friendly, creative spaces. **Pros:** quiet neighborhood; all rooms are flooded with natural light; swimming pool. **Cons:** polycarbonate walls of the dorm rooms give a feeling of less privacy. $ *Rooms from: d190,000* ⊠ *So nha 27 Hem 245A Bui Thi Xuan, Phuong Duc Ward, Hue* ☎ *036/780-0737* ⊘ *sahihomestay@gmail.com* ⦿ *No Meals* ⊋ *6 rooms* ▤ *No credit cards.*

The Scarlett Boutique Hotel

$$$ | **HOTEL** | Inspired and named after the heroine of "Gone with the Wind," the Scarlett Boutique Hotel is suitable for honeymooning couples and for those who try to avoid tour groups. **Pros:** professional and caring staff; chic art deco rooms and modern amenities; right in the city center. **Cons:** hard to find; not family-friendly. $ *Rooms from: d1,200,000* ⊠ *17/1 Ben Nghe St., Phu Hoi Ward, Hue* ☎ *0234/393-0888* ⊕ *www.thescarlettho-tels.com* ⊋ *17 rooms* ⦿ *Free Breakfast.*

Tam Tinh Vien Homestay

$$ | **B&B/INN** | Artful wooden garden house accommodations in a little oasis on the edge of the city, Tam Tinh Vien makes for a wonderfully relaxing base. **Pros:** bicycles; quiet, relaxing getaway; good local restaurants nearby; great tours. **Cons:** 5 km (3 miles) from the citadel; no TVs. $ *Rooms from: d850,000* ⊠ *Kiet 23 Nguyen Trong Nhan St., Huong Ho, Huong Tra District, Hue* ☎ *091/401-9983* ⦿ *Free Breakfast* ⊋ *2 deluxe rooms, 2 mezzanine rooms.*

Than Thien (Friendly) Hotel

$ | **B&B/INN** | A couple of streets removed from the late-night goings-on of Pham Ngu Lao, the peaceful Than Thien has rooms that offer outstanding value for money. **Pros:** customer service; Wi-Fi; flat-screen TVs; close to dragon boat station. **Cons:** breakfast choices are limited. $ *Rooms from: d400,000* ⊠ *10 Nguyen Cong Tru St., Hue* ☎ *0234/383-4666* ⊘ *thanthienhuehotel@gmail.com* ⦿ *Free Breakfast* ⊋ *38 rooms.*

Vedana Lagoon Resort & Spa

$$$$ | **RESORT** | On a peaceful lagoon halfway between Danang and Hue, this 67-acre luxury resort is the only property to offer over-the-water villas in Vietnam. **Pros:** free tai chi and yoga classes; enormous beds; one of Vietnam's most peaceful properties. **Cons:** mosquitoes at dusk; 50-minute drive to Hue. $ *Rooms from: d4,900,000* ✉ *41/23 Doan Trong Truyen St., Phu Loc District, Phu Loc* ☎ *0234/368–1688* ⊕ *www.vedanalagoon.com* ↪ *141 rooms and bungalows* ⚓ *Free Breakfast.*

⭐ Nightlife

Nightlife centers on the lively backpacker district near Le Loi and Pham Ngu Lao Streets. During happy hour, this south-bank bar scene has 25-cent beers, which can be borderline dangerous, considering the amount of tourist traffic on the block. For something a bit more local, a string of local beer joints line Dong Da near Le Hong Phong Street. If you are looking for a quiet cocktail with a view in more refined environs, head for the upscale hotels on the south bank of the river.

Ben Xuan Garden House Theatre

THEMED ENTERTAINMENT | This opulent theater is nestled in a verdant garden on Huong River shore between Temple of Literature and Thien Mu Pagoda. You'll feel like you've gone back to the golden time of the Nguyen Dynasty. The graceful hosts, Huyen Ton Nu Camille, one of the sixth generation descendants of Emperor Minh Mang, and her husband, Ngo, welcome you to their home in this experience that's best suited to groups. Camille and her band treat you to East-meets-West variations on Hue royal tunes and Vietnamese folk melodies; Camille sings both English and French songs while the musicians accompany her with traditional instruments. The performance is followed by a six-course dinner meticulously created by the hostess herself. The whole package is private. The best way to experience this haven is via boat on the Perfume River right before sunset. Make a reservation through your travel agency or directly with the owners at least one day in advance. ✉ *Van Thanh St, Huong Ho Ward, Hue* ☎↪ *benxuan.ngo@gmail.com.*

Brown Eyes

DANCE CLUBS | With a motto like "From 5 pm 'til the last one passes out," it's no wonder that this joint has become one of the most popular bars in Hue. If the street promoters with flyers don't grab your attention, the blaring sound system with pumping bass certainly will. There's a dance floor, pool table, and happy hour that generally lasts all day. This expat and backpacker hangout is small and crowded, but the cool air-conditioning and garden patio make it bearable. ✉ *56 Chu Van An St., Hue.*

DMZ Bar

CAFÉS | Located in the heart of the tourist zone, this hopping spot is Hue's longest running bar. Cheap eats are overshadowed by the atmosphere and drinks that are ridiculously cheap during happy hour, offered three times daily. This backpacker's hangout is where everyone comes to dance the night away to loud and outdated hits. For a drink with a view, head upstairs to the balcony overlooking the bustling avenue. It's tradition for patrons to add some graffiti to the wall before leaving. ✉ *60 Le Loi St., Hue* ☎ *0234/382–3414.*

Dragon Boat Night Cruise

CRUISES | A culturally enlightening way to spend an evening in Hue is to take a night cruise on the Huong River. Boats with musical groups performing traditional Hue folk songs can be rented through most tourist agencies or directly at Toa Kham landing near the Huong Giang Hotel. If you still have the energy after a day of visiting Hue's tombs and pagodas, don't miss this enchanting experience. ✉ *49 Le Loi St., Hue.*

Night Pedestrian Zone

GATHERING PLACES | Curious where the locals gather on weekend nights? Check out Hue's Night Pedestrian Zone, which is open from 6 pm to 2 am Friday to Saturday; on Sunday they close at midnight. The streets of Pham Ngu Lao, Vo Thi Sau, and Chu Van An are turned into a huge outdoor night club where music, street food, and beer flood this watering hole with delight after dark. ⊠ *Pham Ngu Lao St., Chu Van An St., and Vo Thi Sau St., Hue.*

🛍 Shopping

Shoppers have plenty of options, from lacquer paintings and calligraphic artwork to painted silk and handmade ceramics. For a local keepsake, conical leaf hats are available at souvenir shops and markets throughout Hue, the original birthplace of these national symbols. For military paraphernalia, wood carvings, and replicas of antique compasses and teapots, you are better off swerving around the pop-up stands lining the park near the boat station, and heading to some of the smaller shops on the northern end of Le Loi. If you didn't get your designer fix in Hoi An, your best bet for tailor-made clothing is in the backpacker's district on Chu Van An Street and Pham Ngu Lao Street.

Boi Tran Gallery

ART GALLERIES | Nestled on Thien An Hill, artist Boi Tran's gallery is an exquisite garden where some of Vietnam's best painters' work is housed in a more than 100-year-old nha ruong (Hue traditional panel houses) and a French-colonial-style building. Boi Tran together with Le Thi Luu (1911–88) are the only two female Vietnamese artists whose paintings are sold in Sotheby's and Christie's auctions. Boi Tran also owns a collection of masterpieces by artists such as Tran Quang Tran (Ngym), Nguyen Sang, To Ngoc Van, Hoang Tich Chu, Nguyen Trung, and others. The gallery also serves local dishes with artistic presentation. Reservations should be made at least one day in advance. ⊠ *Thien An Hill, Hue* ☎ *0234/388–4453* ⊕ *www.boitran.com.*

Bo's Tailor

MIXED CLOTHING | With more than 20 years of experience in fashion and customer service, Bo is the person to turn to if you need a dress or a shirt tailor-made in four hours. A true professional who speaks fluent English and French, Bo consults with you about design, material, and budget, ensuring you end up with the custom-made piece of your dreams tailored in house. Hats, silk, and cashmere scarves as well as embroidered clothes are available. ⊠ *67 Vo Thi Sau, Hue* ☎ *070/809–9502.*

Dong Ba Market

MARKET | Hue's main market, Dong Ba, situated north of the Citadel just beyond the central Hue bus station, is the place to go for street food, souvenirs, clothing, and knockoff brands. It's enormous and packed to the rafters, so it can feel cramped and hot, especially near the food stalls in the center. Unlike many other local markets in the central region, this one comes alive as the sun goes down, when crowds descend for dinner and a line of *bia hoi* (beer) stalls set up parallel to the river. Bargaining is expected at the market stalls. ⊠ *Tran Hung Dao St., north of Truong Tien Bridge, Hue.*

TA Gallery

ART GALLERIES | Owned by painter and fashion/interior designer Quang Tan, TA gallery is a collection of paintings by young artists in Hue. While the first floor is more for "touristic" art pieces, the second and third floors house themed exhibitions with a focus on Hue City; there is also a chic coffee shop and bakery. The themes of the exhibitions change every two months. ⊠ *44 Pham Ngu Lao St., Hue* ☎ *091/419–6992* ⊕ *tagallery.com.*

Truc Chi Art Gallery

ART GALLERIES | Taking cues from traditional paper-making techniques, artist Phan Hai Bang and his colleagues created the modern visual art form, Truc Chi. The process involves using water sprays to etch patterns layer by layer onto wet pulp that films on a fine silk frame. Truc Chi artworks are displayed in a detached house with garden inside Hue Citadel. A Truc Chi Art class is also available, starting at 380,000d. Reservations should be made at least one hour in advance. ⊠ 5 Thach Han St., Thuan Hoa Ward, Hue ☎ 096/290–1518.

XQ Hand Embroidery Art Museum

ART GALLERIES | More than just a gallery or museum, XQ is a serene oasis for embroidery artists and enthusiasts, with works of art crafted meticulously out of multicolor thread. The museum's front yard is a forest filled with orchids and birdsong (broadcast out of hidden speakers). Guests can sit here and enjoy complimentary tea or a Vietnamese zither performance every evening from 7 to 9. Most of the embroidery artworks here are for sale. ⊠ 1 Pham Hong Thai St., Vinh Ninh Ward, Hue ✛ At corner of Le Loi St. ☎ 0234/383–4441.

Demilitarized Zone (DMZ)

100 km (60 miles) north of Hue.

Hue is a convenient location from which to visit the former Demilitarized Zone (DMZ), a popular site for history buffs. A trip here can be combined easily with a visit to the Vinh Moc Tunnels and the Mine Action Museum in Dong Hoi. Little remains of the numerous former battlefields of the war that dot the area inland and travel time can be slow. Although the surrounding countryside is stunning in parts, tours to these far flung bases are best suited to military enthusiasts.

The origins of the DMZ (Demilitarized Zone) date to the Geneva Accords of 1954. It served as a cease-fire and interlude in the extensive fighting for control of Vietnam, which divided the country in half at the 17th parallel at the Ben Hai River. The northern half of the country became the Communist-led Democratic Republic of Vietnam, and the south became the Republic of Vietnam (led by Ngo Dinh Diem and supported by the United States). The DMZ, which consisted of an area extending 5 km (3 miles) on either side of the borderline, was supposed to have been a temporary measure, enforced only until the Democratic Republic of Vietnam and the Republic of Vietnam could be reunited following elections in 1956. The elections never took place, and the inaptly named DMZ was only abolished after many years of fighting that culminated in the victory of the North Vietnamese forces in 1975. Almost as soon as it was created, the DMZ was militarized, and by 1965 it had become a key battleground in the fight between north and south. The fighting forced virtually all the inhabitants of the area to flee and rendered the DMZ a wasteland. Despite the DMZ being heavily bombed, most of the land has been cleared and the risk of treading on unexploded ordnance is negligible, but sticking to the marked paths and staying out of remote areas is still advisable. The area south and west of the DMZ was the scene of some of the most bitter fighting of the war. Some names that may be familiar from the war are Con Thien, Camp Carroll, the Rockpile, Hamburger Hill, Quang Tri, and Khe Sanh. Hiring a guide in Hue or Dong Ha is advisable if you want to stand any chance of understanding the historical importance of any of the sites you are likely to visit.

GETTING HERE AND AROUND

Virtually all the tour agencies in Hue can arrange trips to the DMZ, Khe Sanh, and the Vinh Moc Tunnels. Given the scattered locations of these sites, time spent is little more than a point-and-shoot drive by, usually with little in the way of explanation. For the more in-depth tours, shop around and ask for detailed itineraries or invest in a private car and guide. Tours generally leave Hue early in the morning and return about 12 hours later. A better option if you plan on a few days visiting the caves in Phong Nha Khe Bang National Park, is to take one of the transfers between Hue and Phong Nha that include stops at the DMZ and Vinh Moc Tunnels. For military enthusiasts and war vets, specialist guides makes for a worthy investment. Not only will they have the best itineraries, but in most cases they will give unbiased information (something you will appreciate if you have already visited any of the war museums throughout the country). Most two-day tours will involve an overnight stay in Dong Ha, a soulless (almost lawless) town not comfortably navigated alone at night and with very little of interest beyond the exceptionally good Mine Action Visitor Center and Tam's Café (which offers very good guided tours in the DMZ area).

CONTACTS Annam Day Tours. ⊠ *207B Nguyen Du, Dong Ha* ☎ *090/514–0600* ✎ *annamtour@gmail.com* ⊕ *www.facebook.com/annamtourvietnam.* **Oriental Sky Travel.** ⊠ *Hue* ☎ *054/393–3199* ⊕ *orientalskytravel.com.*

◉ Sights

Camp Carroll

MILITARY SIGHT | Camp Carroll was one of the nine U.S. artillery bases located along the DMZ. It was home to the 3rd Marine Regiment and the most powerful artillery used during the war. Many battles were fought here, but the biggest and bloodiest of all was the Easter Tet Offensive when the North Vietnamese stormed the camp and the firebase fell into enemy hands. The site was cleared shortly after the war and is now a pepper plantation. The only visible remains of Camp Carroll are a small concrete platform and a few overgrown trenches. The turn-off to Camp Carroll is 5 km (3 miles) west of Cam Lo, 24 km (15 miles) northeast of Dakrong Bridge, and 37 km (23 miles) east of the Khe Sanh bus station. ⊠ *Hue*

Con Thien Firebase

MILITARY SIGHT | Can cu Con Tien was known as the Hill of Angels, or "Meat Grinder" to the United States Marine Corps stationed here during the fierce fighting and artillery strikes of 1967–1968. Con Thien Firebase was the northwest anchor of the famed (and failed) McNamara Line, where over 500 million landmines and 20,000 listening devices were dropped along the south Vietnam border by the U.S., in an attempt to detect and prevent incursions by the North Vietnam army across the DMZ. Nothing much remains (it's now a peaceful rubber plantation) except some big circular duck ponds to represent the thousands of troops from both sides who lost their lives here, but the hauntingly beautiful location and the expansive views from the top make it a worthwhile stop on a tour of the DMZ. ⊠ *Near Vietnamese DMZ, about 3 km from North Vietnam in Gio Linh District, Dong Ha.*

Demilitarized Zone (DMZ) Museum

MILITARY SIGHT | Tour groups flock to the DMZ to walk across the old French bridge, Hien Luong, and wander around the small museum on the north side of the bridge. They also take photos of the flag tower and an odd-looking reunification sculpture, which symbolizes the communication that developed between families divided by the river. Unable to communicate verbally (witness the loudspeakers pocked with bullet holes on display in the museum), they improvised with signals—a white scarf around the head meant someone had been killed and hands crossed behind the back announced that someone had been arrested. ⊠ *Dong Ha* ✛ *Ben Hai River.*

Hamburger Hill

MILITARY SIGHT | The battle of Hill 937 (Hamburger Hill) raged between the U.S. 101st Airborne Division and the North Vietnamese for 10 long days in May 1969 and marked the beginning of the end for the U.S. involvement in Vietnam. The senseless battle claimed many lives, both Vietnamese and American, and despite the battle being called a victory for the U.S., 16 days later troops were pulled off the hill. Like many of the old U.S. bases along the DMZ, there's little to mark the atrocities that took place here and you need a permit to enter the area. But with a specialist, military guide (for translation and to keep you on the right path) and equally good level of fitness, the 7-km (4-mile) uphill hike through beautiful Ca Tu hill-tribe villages and jungle paths to the base and the steep 900-meter (3,000-foot) climb to the top are rewarded by views stretching over the Laos border to the west and Quang Tri to the east. The drive from Hue takes two hours; on a DMZ tour Aluoi would normally be one of the last photo stops. If you plan on doing the guided trek, leave early and keep further sightseeing plans for other bases in the vicinity—Cunningham, Ershine, and Razor, as well as Hill 1175. Due to the small risk of unexploded ordinance in the area, a guide is recommended. If going it alone, take enough water and keep to the paths. ■TIP➔ **The military specialist, Mr. Vu at Annam Tours, provides excellent day trips from Hue to Hamburger Hill and can arrange your permit in advance. Apply three days in advance.** ✉ *Aluoi, 60 km (37 miles) from Hue.*

Khe Sanh

MILITARY SIGHT | One of the biggest battles of the war—and one of the most significant American losses—took place on January 21, 1968 at Khe Sanh, the site of a U.S. Army base 145 km (90 miles) northwest of Hue. Khe Sanh lies in a highland valley not far from Highway 9, which links Vietnam with southern Laos.

General William Westmoreland, the commander of U.S. forces in Vietnam from 1965 to 1968, became convinced in late 1967 that the North Vietnamese were massing troops in the area in preparation for a campaign to seize South Vietnam's northernmost provinces. Relying on an analogy with the French defeat at Dien Bien Phu, he reinforced Khe Sanh with thousands of Marines and ordered the dropping of more than 75,000 tons of explosives on the surrounding area. The North Vietnamese suffered horrendous casualties—estimates are that as many as 10,000 North Vietnamese soldiers and hundreds of U.S. Marines lost their lives, a sacrifice that seems senseless given the fact that the American forces abandoned the base shortly after, in June 1968. Although the debate continues, many military experts believe that the battle at Khe Sanh was merely a feint designed to pull American forces away from the population centers of South Vietnam in preparation for a massive assault by the North Vietnamese in the Tet Offensive of early 1968. Although there is only a small museum commemorating the battle at Khe Sanh, a visit to the base provides a sense of how isolated and besieged the U.S. Marines must have felt as they were bombarded from the surrounding mountains. In the museum, which opens whenever tours come through the area, there are a number of interesting pictures of the battle and a book for visitors' comments that reflects the continuing debate about the American presence in Vietnam. ✉ *3 km (2 miles) north of Huong Hoa, Khe Sanh.*

★ Mine Action Visitor Center

HISTORY MUSEUM | Around 15 million tons of U.S. munition were dropped over Vietnam between 1965 and 1975 and at least 10% of those failed to detonate. Since 1975, this unexploded ordnance have been the cause of more than 100,000 injuries and fatalities, a large percentage of these victims were children. With the U.S. focus on defending the demilitarized zone (DMZ) that separated the two countries, Quang Tri Province was the most heavily bombed—more than 72 million square meters of land have been mapped as hazardous. The Mine Action Visitor Center in Dong Ha is a joint venture between the international NGO–operated Project RENEW and the Department of Foreign Affairs, providing visitors with constantly updated information on the devastation caused, as well as heart-warming stories of recovery and survival. Unlike many of military sites along the DMZ, the center provides expert English speaking guides, which makes it an absolute must on any DMZ itinerary, especially if you have chosen to go without a guide. The site is about 150 meters (492 feet) after Ly Thuong Kiet Street intersects with Hung Vuong Street. Turn left into the Kid First Village where the visitor center is located. ✉ *Alley 185, Ly Thuong Kiet St., Đông Hà, Dong Ha* ☎ *0233/385–8445* 🌐 *www.landmines.org.vn* 🎟 *Free* 🕓 *Closed weekends, Lunar New Year.*

Rockpile

MILITARY SIGHT | Once an important observation point for the U.S Marines, the Rockpile (a 755-foot karst formation know in Vietnamese as Thon Khe Tri) was used for tracking the north Vietnamese army crossing in to the south and directing U.S military fire at their suspected positions. Other than the Rockpile, nothing remains in memorial to the site, but it's worth a stop for the scenery alone if you are traveling onwards to the Khe San Combat base. ✉ *26 km (16 miles) west of Dong Ha just off Hwy. 9, Cam Tuyen, Cam Lo District, Dong Ha.*

Truong Son Martyrs Cemetery

CEMETERY | Stretching over 202 acres, 27 km (8 miles) northwest of Dong Ha, this somber memorial site marks the final resting place for over 10,000 Vietnamese soldiers and civilians who lost their lives defending and maintaining the Ho Chi Minh Trail during the Vietnam War. Each tomb is marked with the word "liet si" ("martyr"); some are adorned with pictures or sculptures of the deceased, and others lay empty, a mark of respect to one of the 300,000 soldiers that remain missing in action to this day. Along the way to Truong Son you'll pass Con Thien Firebase, an old French bunker located 1.5 km (1 mile) down a dirt track to the east of the road, barely visible through the rubber plantation that has taken over the area. ✉ *On Hwy 15 near the village of Ben Tat, northwest of Dong Ha, Vĩnh Truong, Gio Linh District, Dong Ha.*

Vinh Moc Tunnels

TUNNEL | **FAMILY** | Local villagers built the 2-km-long (1½-mile-long) Vinh Moc Tunnels during the early 1960s to escape American bombing. The tunnels were later used by the North Vietnamese army to transport goods to Con Co Island. Less claustrophobic than the ones at Cu Chi near Ho Chi Minh City, these tunnels are a testament to the determination and ingenuity of the Vietnamese people under extreme circumstances. Guides are available at the small museum on-site; we suggest grabbing one to get the most out of your visit. ■ **TIP→ If you have time, head down to the beautiful beach that runs along the eastern perimeter of the tunnels.** ✉ *20 km (12 miles) north of the DMZ, Vinh Thach, Vinh Linh District, Ben Hai.*

🍴 Restaurants

★ Tam's DMZ Café

$ | **VIETNAMESE** | No visit to Dong Ha is complete without a visit to this cheerful spot in the heart of town. It's both a charity café (Mr. **Known for:** charity cafe; DMZ guided tours; chance to talk with war veterans. [$] *Average main: đ50,000* ✉ *Just off Tran Hung Dao, a short walk from Mine Action Visitor Center, 211 Duong Ba Trieu, Đông Hà, Dong Ha* ☎ *090/542–5912* 🌐 *tamscafe.jimdofree.com.*

Known as the King of Caves, Son Doong Cave is the largest cave in the world.

Hotels

Saigon Dong Ha Hotel

$$ | **HOTEL** | **FAMILY** | Dong Ha's biggest hotel has modern, spacious rooms with comfortable beds, decent bathrooms (although water pressure can be a bit hit or miss), and pleasant river views. **Pros:** river and city views; quiet; easy access to military sites. **Cons:** basic breakfast; the lack of completed facilities; staff lack English abilities. [$] *Rooms from: d782,609* ✉ *01 Bui Thi Xuan, Phuong 2, Dong Ha, Dong Ha* ☎ *0233/357–7888* 🌐 *saigondonghahotel.com* 🛏 *98 rooms* 🍴 *Free Breakfast.*

Phong Nha Ke Bang National Park

240 km (149 miles) north of Hue, 53 km (32 miles) north of Dong Hoi.

Part of the Annamite mountain range on the northwest Central Coast, Phong Nha Ke Bang National Park was listed as a World Heritage Site in 2003. Covering more than 800 km (497 miles), it's thought to be one of the most distinctive examples of karst landforms in Southeast Asia, with more than 300 caves and grottoes including Son Doong, the world's largest cave, only discovered in 2009. There are three cave systems in the national park, and one outside. Phong Nha Cave System includes Hang En, Hang Phong Nha, Hang Son Doong, and the Dark Cave. Von Cave System includes Paradise Cave. Nuoc Mooc Cave System is one of the most unique in the world. The park is incredibly beautiful, full of crystal clear blue waters and lush jungle wildlife, and tourism has (to date) been managed with sustainability in mind.

The best months to visit for trekking and caving are March, April, and May, before the draining humidity of summer kicks in. From the end of September, Phong Nha can get very wet with the chance of typhoons. Some services wind down during October and November as caves can flood, and roads become thick with mud, making it difficult to get around.

GETTING HERE AND AROUND

There are now many ways to get to Phong Nha by bus, as tour companies have taken note of its popularity. However, the safer and more scenic options involve taking a plane or train to Dong Hoi, and then a bus, taxi, or private transfer onto Phong Nha. Taxis meet all incoming flights, but it's a good idea to pre-arrange transfers with your hotel if you decide to go through Dong Hoi. Taxis have been known to ask for 600,000d to 1,000,000d; bartering can usually take them down to 400,000d. The price for a private transfer is around 500,000d for one person, but the price goes down considerably when you add people to the car.

Dong Hoi's airport is 46 km (28 miles) east of Phong Nha. From Ho Chi Minh City, there is one daily flight; from Hanoi, there are three. By far the most beautiful way to get to Dong Hoi is by train. The scenic coastal route takes you through breathtaking landscapes. To avoid turning up in the wee hours of the morning, the best trains are the SE2 leaving Danang at 12:45 pm and Hue at 3:30 pm, or the SE4 leaving Danang at 12:10 pm and Hue at 4:45 pm.

The local bus from Dong Hoi departs every 15–30 minutes and takes around 90 minutes to reach Phong Nha. You can catch it from outside the Nam Ly Bus Station or at any bus stop on Tran Hung Dao with a blue and white sign. The bus number is B4 (it's yellow and green and says "Dong Hoi–Hoan Lo–Phong Nha" across the windshield). If you are booking a long-distance bus, it's best to get dropped directly in Phong Nha (buses stop in front of the Easy Tiger hostel). There are three buses from Hue, which cost 150,000d: the Tan Nhat bus departs from the Why Not bar at 6:30 am and drops off in Phong Nha around noon. The DMZ bus leaves the DMZ bar at 2 pm and arrives in Phong Nha at 6:30 pm. The Hung Thanh bus leaves from 49 Chu Van An at 4:30 pm and arrives in Phong Nha around 10 pm. If you are coming from the north, there is a sleeper bus from Hanoi. The bus leaves around 6 pm, makes a stop in Ninh Binh to pick up more tourists around 11 pm, and terminates in Phong Nha around 4 am.

TRAIN CONTACT Dong Hoi Train Station.
✉ *Subregional 4, Tieu Khu 4, Dong Hoi* ☎ *1900–6469.*

TOURS

Jungle Boss

Jungle Boss is a spin-off tour company (the owner worked long-term with Oxalis) offering affordable treks through the national park and caves. They have six tours to choose from, but the most popular is the Abandoned Valley day trip. ✉ *DT20 Son Trach, Phong Nha Village, Phong Nha* ☎ *091/780–0805* ⊕ *www. jungle-boss.com* ✉ *From 1,350,000d.*

Oxalis

The best place to head for tours, Oxalis is the most professional outfit in town. The company has specialized in adventure caving tours since 2011, and focuses on sustainability. The impressive team includes Howard and Deb Limbert from the British Cave Research Association, the couple that helped put Phong Nha on the map and later discovered Hang Son Doong with the help of Oxalis porter Ho Khanh. Oxalis is the first and only tour company to have gained permission to take visitors through the world's biggest cave on a seven-day adventure tour. Tours range from full day trekking, swimming, and climbing out to Tu Lan, to two-, three-, four-, and five-day treks assisted by a support team of guides and porters. ■ TIP→ **A must-do is the two-day Hang En Cave Adventure that includes a night camping out in one of the cave's biggest chambers.** ⊠ *Son Trach office, Phong Nha Commune, Phong Nha* ☎ *0232/3677–678* ⊕ *www.oxalis.com.vn.*

VISITOR INFORMATION

CONTACTS Phong Nha Ke Bang Tourism Services. ⊠ *Son Trach, Bo Trach, Phong Nha* ☎ *023/267–7110* ⊕ *www.phongnha-tourism.com.vn.* **Quang Binh Tourism** ⊠ *1 Me Suot* ☎ *0232/3822–018* ⊕ *www.quangbinhtourism.com.*

◉ Sights

Phong Nha town is tiny and easily manageable on foot. To explore the Bong Lai Valley or the national park, you'll need a bike. For independent touring, Phong Nha cave is accessed by dragon boat via the small pier in the center of town. Tickets are available at the nearby tourism center. Visitors are now allowed to enter the national park, but you must stick to the roads unless you have a guide. There are several safety concerns in the jungle, and it's in your best interest to stay on the road. For a full hour of useful information, check out Easy Tiger's 9 am talk about the area. Each tour operator is designated specific caves and trails so that the sites don't get overrun by tourists.

★ Hang Son Doong

CAVE | This astounding cave was discovered in 2009 by a British Cave Research team led by Howard and Deb Limbert and guided by the "King of the Caves" Ho Khanh. Hang Son Doong has been distinguished as the largest cave in the world—a 747 could fit in its largest chamber. A lucky few (the government only releases a handful of visitors

permits a year) can now take thrilling seven-day trek through remote ethnic villages and deep jungle, and across rivers before exploring the entire length of this otherworldly cave, passing enormous stalagmites and fossil passageways to the "Great Wall of Vietnam" and beyond. ■ TIP→ **You'll need to have a good level of fitness and you may have to wait years to get in. Oxalis Adventure is the only company with access and tours cost $3,000 USD.** ⊠ *Xuan Trach, Bo Trach District, Phong Nha* ☎ *091/990–0357* ⊕ *son-doongcave.info.*

★ Paradise Cave

CAVE | FAMILY | The must-see Paradise Cave is one of the most beautiful park caves you can visit on a day trip. Tours and transport can be arranged from the Tourism Center in town, but if you are feeling energetic you can cycle along the stunning 16-km (10-mile) Nuoc Mooc Spring Eco Trail within the national park (tickets are available at the entrance gate). The scenic trail takes you all the way to Paradise Cave where you'll find another ticket booth. It's a long trek from here to the cave entrance, but an electric golf cart is available to whisk you to the stairs (all 500 of them) or the ramp that leads up to the cave entrance. The mouth of Paradise Cave is small, hidden behind the cliffs and trees. From there, more stairs will lead you down into the cave's magnificent chambers, linked by a wooden walkway that winds around majestic rock formations deep into the belly of the cave. To get to Paradise Cave, follow the road through town past the Phong Nha ticket office. Continue on that road for 16 km (10 miles) until you reach the intersection; take a right at the huge billboard. ⊠ *Km 16, Ho Chi Minh Highway - West Branch, Nhanh Tay, Bo Trach, Phong Nha* ☎ *0232/350–6777* ⊕ *www.dongthienduong.com* ☞ *Nuoc Mooc Spring Eco Trail: 180,000d; Paradise Cave: 250,000d.*

Phong Nha Cave

CAVE | **FAMILY** | Up until the discovery of Son Doong, the beautiful Phong Nha Cave was the national park's most famous treasure. It's the park's easiest cave to navigate and there really is no need to visit it with a guide. Buy tickets from the Tourism Center in the village and hop on a dragon boat from the small pier nearby. The boat takes you on a picturesque journey along the Son River right into the giant river cave where you disembark to explore 1,500 meters inside. Here you'll view the most splendid formations, stalagmites, and stalactites, enchantingly lit in a rainbow of colors. The boat to the cave costs about 350,000d, but this can be split among passengers (maximum of 10 passengers). Don't forget to tip your rower. ✉ *Phong Nha, Bo Trach District, Phong Nha* ☎ *091/884–1455* ⊕ *phongnhatourism.com.vn* ✉ *150,000d.*

🍴 Restaurants

★ Bomb Crater Bar

$ | **VIETNAMESE** | **FAMILY** | A great place to stop for a midday drink and refreshing splash in the river, this bar sits between two large bomb craters left during the American war. Run jointly by a Vietnamese couple and Australian couple, the bar is halfway between Phong Nha village and Farmstay Village. **Known for:** hammocks; gin and tonics; Vietnamese snacks. $ *Average main: d50,000* ✉ *Cu Lac 1, Bo Trach District, Phong Nha* ⊹ *3 km (2 miles) from Phong Nha along the river* ☎ *036/541–0230.*

Bong Lai Swing Nature Farm

$$ | **VIETNAMESE** | A couple of kilometers downstream from the Pub With Cold Beer, this rustic jungle hut, formerly called *Wild Boar Eco Farm,* is run by local tour operator Captain Cuong. The scenery here is awe-inspiring—swinging hammocks overlook the wilderness and Cuong's prize collection of free-range Euro-Asian wild boar. **Known for:** pork dish cooked in bamboo shoots; amazing views; traditional jungle dishes. $ *Average main: d100,000* ✉ *Bong Lai, Phong Nha, Phong Nha* ☎ *096/901–3681* ⊕ *www.facebook.com/WildBoarEcoFarm.*

★ Capture Vietnam

$$ | **AMERICAN** | Quite possibly serving the best Western food in all of Vietnam, this café captures the hearts of all who eat here. There is nothing on the menu that disappoints, but the complete winners are the veggie lasagna, meatball subs, and carrot cake. **Known for:** perfect service; wood-fired pizzas; good vegetarian options. $ *Average main: d120,000* ✉ *Son Trach, Phong Nha Village, Phong Nha* ☎ *0164/515–3869.*

Phong Nha Bamboo Cafe

$$ | **VIETNAMESE** | **FAMILY** | Hai, from Hai's Eco Conservation Tour, runs this bamboo restaurant with his family and serves delicious dishes every day from 7 am until 10:30 pm. Try the fresh fruit smoothies. **Known for:** nature vibe; beef stew; Phong Nha volcanoes. $ *Average main: d50,000* ✉ *Duong tinh 20, Phong Nha, Phong Nha* ☎ *096/260–6844* ⊕ *www.facebook.com/phongnhabamboocafe1.*

★ The Pub With Cold Beer

$$ | **VIETNAMESE** | At the midway point of one of the most incredible (and strenuous) 22-km (13½-mile) bicycle loops in the Bong Lai Valley, with views over rice fields and the river, the Pub With Cold Beer has hammocks, a pool table, and, in season, tubes for floating down the river. It's a beautiful spot to unwind and regain energy for a few hours, which is how long your chicken lunch is going to take to prepare once you've chosen your live bird. **Known for:** river tubing; chicken lunch; free cooking classes. $ *Average main: d180,000* ✉ *Hung Trach, Bo Trach District* ☎ *397/428–778.*

Hotels

Chay Lap Farmstay

$$$ | **B&B/INN** | **FAMILY** | Chay Lap is a remote and peaceful location for those seeking nature at the doorstep of the national park. **Pros:** ideal base for national park exploration; beautiful scenery and lodgings; on-site pool and sauna with acupressure options. **Cons:** remote location means most of your meals are eaten at the hotel; bicycles cost money after two hours; insects and geckos can get into the rooms. [$] *Rooms from: d1,920,000* ✉ *Thon Chay, Bo Trach District, Phong Nha* ☎ *091/103–0057* 🌐 *www.chaylapfarmstay.com* 🛏 *39 rooms* 🍴 *Free Breakfast.*

★ **Ho Khanh's Homestay**

$$ | **B&B/INN** | **FAMILY** | On the banks of the Son River, on the edge of Phong Nha town, this ornately carved wooden traditional homestay provides family-friendly lodgings hosted by Mr. Ho Khanh, the original discoverer of the world's biggest cave. **Pros:** perhaps the most knowledgeable guide in the province; quiet, riverside location; a short walk to bars and restaurants. **Cons:** gets booked up weeks in advance; shared bathroom in cheaper rooms; mosquitoes. [$] *Rooms from: d750,000* ✉ *Near the Phong Nha tourism center, Son Trach, Bo Trach District, Phong Nha* ☎ *091/679–4506* 🍴 *Free Breakfast* 🛏 *4 bungalows, 3 rooms.*

★ **Pepper House Homestay**

$$ | **B&B/INN** | For romantic retreats, it would be hard to find anything as charming as the four enchanting French-colonial eco-villas at Pepper House Homestay, set amidst a pepper plantation, 6 km (4 miles) from town. **Pros:** great tours; idyllic location; impeccable service. **Cons:** isolated location; mosquitoes; dark rooms. [$] *Rooms from: d860,465* ✉ *Just off the HCM Hwy., 6 km (4 miles) south of Phong Nha, Hung Trach, Bo Trach District, Phong Nha* ☎ *0167/873–1560* 🌐 *www.facebook.com/PepperHouseHomestay* 🛏 *4 rooms* 🍴 *Free Breakfast.*

Phong Nha Farmstay

$$$ | **B&B/INN** | **FAMILY** | This small and stylish family-run colonial villa, a short distance from the national park, is probably the best deal in town. **Pros:** complimentary Jeep or Ural motorbike transfers to town; great Western/Vietnamese restaurant; live music and movie nights. **Cons:** remote; overpriced for quality of service; presence of insects. [$] *Rooms from: d1,200,000* ✉ *1 km (½ mile) east of Ho Chi Minh Highway, Khoung Ha, Bo Trach, Phong Nha* ☎ *0944/759–864* 🌐 *phong-nha-cave.com* 🍴 *Free Breakfast* 🛏 *17 rooms.*

Phong Nha Lake House Resort

$$$$ | **HOTEL** | **FAMILY** | Sheltered in the mountain valleys of Lai Chau, overlooking the beautiful lake Dong Suon, the Lake House makes for an idyllic base within easy reach of Phong Nha Ke Bang National Park. **Pros:** incredible views; lake swimming; great food and wine menu. **Cons:** mosquitoes; remote; steps down to the lakeside bungalows a little steep. [$] *Rooms from: d1,906,095* ✉ *Khuong Ha hamlet, Hung Trach, Bo Trach, Phong Nha, Phong Nha* ☎ *0232/367–5999* 🌐 *www.phongnhalakehouse.com* 🍴 *Free Breakfast* 🛏 *16 rooms.*

Phong Nha Mountain House

$$ | **B&B/INN** | **FAMILY** | Run by brother and sister An and Ai, this homestay offers beautiful wooden stilt houses and balconies overlooking the river and mountains. **Pros:** welcoming family atmosphere; free bikes; comfortable rooms. **Cons:** not ideal for rainy season; remote location; stairs can be slick when it's raining. [$] *Rooms from: d750,000* ✉ *Son Trach Bo Trach, Phong Nha Village, Phong Nha* ☎ *093/593–1009* 🛏 *4 mountain houses, 1 family room* 🍴 *Free Breakfast.*

★ Victory Road Villas
$$$$ | **B&B/INN** | **FAMILY** | For luxury and long-term comfort, there is no better choice than the Victory Road Villas. **Pros:** family-oriented; impressive architecture and design; comfortable beds. **Cons:** expensive; stone floors can be cold in winter months; limited breakfast options. [$] *Rooms from: d3,150,000* ✉ *DT 20 Victory Road, Phong Nha Village, Phong Nha* ☎ *0232/367–5699* 🌐 *www.victoryroadvillas.com* 🛏 *6 villas, 1 penthouse* 🍴 *Free Breakfast.*

Nightlife

Phong Nha is an up-and-coming destination, with a couple of places in town now serving cold beer (it's a new thing here) and a resident Filipino band performing ad hoc live music evenings at a few venues.

Activities

BIKING AND MOTORBIKING

The roads around the national park are often in terrible, muddy condition, and although motorbikes are available to rent from many places in town, unless you are an experienced rider, it's inadvisable to tackle them on your own. Experienced riders can hire everything from a standard Japanese scooter to a Russian Ural from Phong Nha Farmstay, where excellent motorbike tours are also available that take you through remote villages, incredible karst landscapes, and waterfalls that you would not find on your own.

Phong Nha Adventure Cycling
BIKING | **FAMILY** | For thrills and maybe the odd spill, local villager and tour guide Private Shi runs a professional mountain bike adventure tour company, exploring the trails, villages, and water holes of Phong Nha Ke Bang National Park. The tours range from a 20-km (12½-mile) village ride to a thigh-burning 70-km (43½-mile) adventure trail along the Ho Chi Minh Trail, through rice and peanut fields, war remnants, and river crossings in an old B52 boat. Private Shi is an exceptional guide. ✉ *DT20, Son Trach, Bo Trach, Phong Nha* ☎ *098/555–5827* 🌐 *www.facebook.com/PhongNhaAdventureCycling* 🎟 *Tour prices start at 1,538,655d.*

Chapter 7

HALONG BAY AND NORTH-CENTRAL VIETNAM

Updated by
Hiezle Bual

● Sights	🍴 Restaurants	🛏 Hotels	🛍 Shopping	🍸 Nightlife
★★★★★	★★★★☆	★★★☆☆	★★★☆☆	★★☆☆☆

WELCOME TO HALONG BAY AND NORTH-CENTRAL VIETNAM

TOP REASONS TO GO

★ **Views from the water.**
Cruise among thousands of limestone karsts and deserted islands where sandy coves, hidden caves, and floating villages abound.

★ **Exploring Cat Ba Island.**
At this national park the endangered langur monkey finds refuge among lakes, waterfalls, and limestone cliffs that are now prized territory for rock climbers.

★ **Luxury at sea.** You don't have to spend the earth to enjoy a Halong Bay cruise, but the ever-growing selection of sumptuous vessels with top-class amenities that ply the waters make it worth splashing a few dollars more on the experience.

★ **Laid-back café culture.**
Haiphong may not get the same press as other major Vietnamese hubs, but the city's tree-lined boulevards and colonial-era architecture are easily appreciated from one of its many friendly coffee shops.

One of the most appealing aspects of this part of Vietnam is how easy it is to get to all the major points of interest from Hanoi. Although the 3½-hour journey from the capital to Halong Bay may seem like an inconvenience, it is a mere trifle in a Vietnamese context. Likewise, Haiphong and Ninh Binh are an easy hop from the big city, with plenty of comfortable and convenient transportation services operating the routes. In fact, if your time is very limited, you can even take in a selection of attractions in a (long) day trip from Hanoi. However, such is the visual manna on offer, a few days to absorb the area's splendor is far preferable.

1 Ninh Binh. The karst scenery that surrounds this provincial capital is some of the country's loveliest.

2 Phat Diem. Home to Phat Diem Cathedral, the country's most distinctive—and arguably most storied—Catholic church.

3 Cuc Phuong National Park. The park makes up for its relative shortage of wildlife with lush peaks and peaceful lakes.

4 Haiphong. Vietnam's third-largest city has a wonderful café culture.

5 Halong Bay and Around. A boat trip through the calm waters and more than 3,000 limestone karsts is one of best experiences in Northern Vietnam.

6 Cat Ba Island. One of Halong Bay's most remarkable formations.

7 Bai Tu Long Bay. Less crowded, laid-back alternative to Halong Bay with karsts that are just as beautiful.

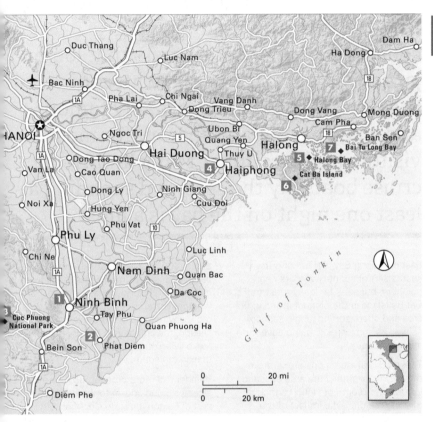

There is no disguising the stature of Halong Bay among Vietnam's tourist draws. The UNESCO World Heritage–listed seascape, a mind-blowing collection of limestone karsts that loom jaggedly from the emerald waters of the Gulf of Tonkin, is justifiably famous and a key part of an itinerary for most visitors to the country. Many luxurious cruise boats ply the seas, and spending at least one night on the bay is a must.

East of Halong Bay, Bai Tu Long Bay shares similar scenery with its near neighbor, but sees far less tourist traffic. Cat Ba Island is the biggest island in the area and offers stirring jungle scenery as well as some trekking and adventure sport options.

These coastal attractions are far from the only highlights in the area east and immediately south of Hanoi. Although missing the dramatic impact of the mountains of the far north, the sprawling Red River delta, the leafy port town of Haiphong, and the spectacular inland scenery at Ninh Binh are worthy additions to any schedule.

Even though the region has borne the brunt of centuries of war—first Chinese invaders, then French colonialists, the Americans, and once again the Chinese—and bomb craters still pockmark the Red River delta, much of this area of Vietnam has maintained its beauty.

The Red River delta is the most densely populated area of Vietnam, with more than 1,000 people per square mile, compared with approximately 400 per square mile in the Mekong Delta. Extreme weather patterns—too much rain and too many damaging storms in the wet season, too little rain in the dry season—make living off the land more difficult than in the south.

Haiphong is more prosperous. Once the sleepy second cousin to the booming port of Saigon (now Ho Chi Minh City), Haiphong is emerging as more than just Vietnam's second-largest port. The city is awakening to the prospect of the rapid development of import-export channels. Tree-lined boulevards, expansive green parks, and impressive—if a little shopworn—French-colonial architecture fill the downtown. To the north of the city center, 10,000-ton freighters unload containers bound for Hanoi and load up with Vietnamese exports.

Farther northeast, natural beauty and nationalized industry share the spotlight. In Quang Ninh Province an ever-expanding coal-mining industry is counterbalanced by the scenic splendor of forested peaks and Halong and Bai Tu Long bays.

Around 100 km (62 miles) south of Hanoi, the provincial town of Ninh Binh is the gateway to more quintessentially Vietnamese karst scenery. Although there's a steady trickle of foreign tourists, local visitors are the primary market. Attractions here include the grottoes of Trang An and Tam Coc as well as the nation's biggest pagoda.

MAJOR REGIONS

Ninh Binh and Nearby. A short trip (around 100 km or 62 miles) south of Hanoi, the provincial city of Ninh Binh is pleasant enough, but it is the quintessentially Vietnamese limestone karst scenery surrounding the city that puts it on the tourist map. Dive headlong into the landscape while getting rowed along lazy rivers and through intricate cave systems.

Haiphong. Overlooked by many visitors, Haiphong is well worth a day of anyone's time. Although it is one of Vietnam's most important ports and an industrial center, the city's tree-lined boulevards, colonial architecture, and excellent transportation links with Hanoi make it a fine addition to a travel itinerary.

Halong Bay and Nearby. The karst-studded seascape of Halong Bay (around four hours by road from Hanoi) is one of the world's most arresting sights and a trip here is an absolute must if you are in northern Vietnam. Farther east, Bai Tu Long Bay showcases virtually the same visual splendor, but welcomes a fraction of the tourists. Cat Ba Island is a rugged, jungle-clad paradise that has become a favored center for adventure sports.

Planning

When to Go

Around Halong Bay, the season runs from early summer to mid-autumn. From July to September beware of tropical typhoons; flooding in Haiphong and Hanoi is common during these storms. The capital is hot and extremely humid in summer, which makes it a popular time for residents to head for the hills or the coast.

During Tet, the lunar new year, you'll find northern Vietnam cold and drizzly but extremely festive. If you're coming during this time, make flight and hotel reservations very early. Also understand that many tour operations, such as trips to Halong Bay, are limited or suspended during this period.

Getting Here and Around

AIR

There are between 11 and 30 daily flights from Ho Chi Minh City to Haiphong's Cat Bi Airport, operated by Vietnam Airlines, Jetstar Pacific, and VietJet Air. Vietnam Airlines operates a daily service to Haiphong from Danang.

BOAT AND FERRY

There is no boat service from Hanoi to Haiphong, but ferries, high-speed boats, and hydrofoils link many of the coastal destinations. However, with roads much improved these days, most travelers find it more convenient to go overland when possible.

Unless you're a guest of the Vietnamese military, the only way on and off Cat Ba Island is by boat or hydrofoil. There is a ferry service from Halong City to Cat Ba, but the more common route is from Haiphong.

FERRY CONTACT Mekong Hoang Yen. ✉ *6 Cu Chinh Lan St., Haiphong* ☎ *04/3926–2730, 091/915–9968.*

BUS

Frequent buses travel from Hanoi to Haiphong, Ninh Binh, and other points in the area. Highly recommended companies operating the route include Hai Au, which is widely held to have the best service and cleanest buses. Buses depart from Gia Lam bus station near Hanoi's Old Quarter and take around 2½ hours to complete the journey to Haiphong's Niem Nghia bus station. The fare is about 85,000d each way and there are 11 buses each day. Good Morning Cat Ba, Cat Ba Express, and Dai Chi Buses are also good options.

BUS CONTACTS Hai Au Bus Company. ✉ *16 Ton Duc Thang St., Haiphong* ☎ *022/5371–7717.***Hoang Long Bus Company.** ✉ *28 Tran Nhat Duat, Hanoi* ☎ *024/3987–7225.*

CAR

Renting a car and driver from one of the many travel agencies and tourist cafés in Hanoi or going with an organized tour by minivan are the easiest ways to get around the northeast. The condition of the roads in the area has improved significantly over the last few years, making travel much more comfortable than it once was.

Renting an air-conditioned car with a driver for a day's drive to Haiphong and back to Hanoi will run from 1,200,000d to 1,500,000d and will take about two hours each way. Of note on your way are the half-dozen pagodas set back in the rice fields along Highway 5.

Halong Bay is a 3½-hour drive from Hanoi. Your driver will most likely head east on Highway 5. Halfway to Haiphong, just before the city of Hai Duong, you'll turn left onto Highway 18. Although crowded, the road has one of the better surfaces in the north and the journey is rarely anything less than smooth. Renting

an air-conditioned car with driver from Hanoi costs between 2,400,000d and 2,600,000d for a two-day, one-night trip to Halong, including all car and driver expenses. If it's not the weekend, or if it's in the dead of winter or peak summer, bargain hard—you can usually get a better deal.

TRAIN

Four trains per day (from 6 am to early evening) leave Hanoi bound for Haiphong from one of two stations: Hanoi Railway Station (Ga Hanoi) and Long Bien Station. Tickets for all trains can be purchased at the Hanoi Railway Station, but you must ask at the ticket booth whether your train leaves from there or from Long Bien Station. The cost is 90,000d for travel in a soft sleeper carriage and 115,000d for travel in an air-conditioned soft sleeper carriage. The unspectacular trip takes just over two hours. There are two stations in Haiphong. The first, Thuong Li Railway Station, is west of the city. You should detrain at the Haiphong Railway Station, which is the end of the line on the Hanoi route.

TRAIN STATION Haiphong Railway Station. ✉ *75 Luong Khanh Thien St., Ngo Quyen* ☎ *031/392–0500.***Vietnam Railway System.** ✉ *Hanoi* ☎ *04/3513–5136* ⊕ *www.vietnam-railway.com.*

Tours

Traveling independently is not particularly difficult in Vietnam. However, the presence of several reputable tour operators that specialize in itineraries in the north of Vietnam supplies succor and security for those who prefer to leave the legwork to others. Whether it's flight tickets, hotel reservations, or luxurious multiday voyages out on the pristine waters of Halong Bay, these specialists major in making life easy for travelers.

Backyard Travel

The consultants here pride themselves on their insider knowledge of Asia, and their Vietnam itineraries deviate from the tried and tested to offer something a little different for the adventurous traveler. In northwest Vietnam, tours include a three-day, two-night cruise around Bai Tu Long Bay. ⊠ *Hanoi* ⊕ *www.backyardtravel.com* ☒ *Bai Tu Long cruise from 8,880,000d.*

Handspan Travel

One of the most respected tour operators in Vietnam, Handspan can organize everything from luxurious cruises on Halong Bay to more offbeat adventures such as bike tours and kayaking itineraries. ⊠ *78 Ma May St., Hanoi* ☎ *024/3926–2828* ⊕ *www.handspan.com* ☒ *2-night Halong Explorer and Kayak Discovery Tour from 6,975,000d.*

Tonkin Travel

Founded by two native Hanoian women in 2002, Tonkin Travel has built a formidable reputation in the intervening years. In common with the other top operators in Vietnam, Tonkin is as comfortable directing tourists to the main sights and attractions in the country as it is designing more imaginative bespoke itineraries to off-the-beaten-track destinations around Lan Ha Bay, Ninh Binh, and Bai Tu Long Bay. ⊠ *164 Xuan Dieu St., Hanoi* ☎ *024/3719–1184* ⊕ *www.tonkintravel. com* ☒ *Halong Bay/Ninh Binh/Mai Chau tour (4 days/3 nights) from 11,300,000d.*

Restaurants

With the emerald waters of the Gulf of Tonkin lapping the coastline, fresh seafood is the undoubted star in this part of northern Vietnam. In fact, the Vietnamese set great store by the ritual of plucking a delicious morsel out of a giant tank and having it prepared for them—and so should you. Delicious fruits of the ocean can be found all the way along the coast, purveyed in venues ranging from simple family-run establishments to more

ostentatious (and expensive) options. Aside from seafood, there are some solid Vietnamese restaurants in the region serving specialties including *thit de* (goat meat) and other local favorites. Larger cities such as Haiphong have a growing selection of international restaurants with Indian, American, and Mexican among the cuisines available.

Hotels

If it's the height of luxury you're after, you probably won't find it in many places outside Hanoi in the north of Vietnam. However, the pretourism days of mainly dank and dingy accommodations are long gone and even less vaunted destinations tend to have at least one highly acceptable hotel. Clean and friendly (if a little low on character) family-run hotels are the norm, but more luxury and individuality are creeping in as tourist flow increases.

For expanded reviews, facilities, and current deals, visit Fodors.com.

What It Costs			
$	$$	$$$	$$$$
RESTAURANTS			
Under 60,000d	60,000d– 150,000d	151,000d– 250,000d	over 250,000d
HOTELS			
Under 600,000d	600,000d– 900,000d	901,000d – 1.5 million d	over 1.5 million d

Ninh Binh

94 km (58 miles) south of Hanoi.

Dubbed as "Halong Bay on Land," Ninh Binh is a provincial capital on the main road between Hanoi and Hue that's most notable for being within easy striking distance of some of Vietnam's most stunning limestone karst scenery. With its easy transportation links to destinations

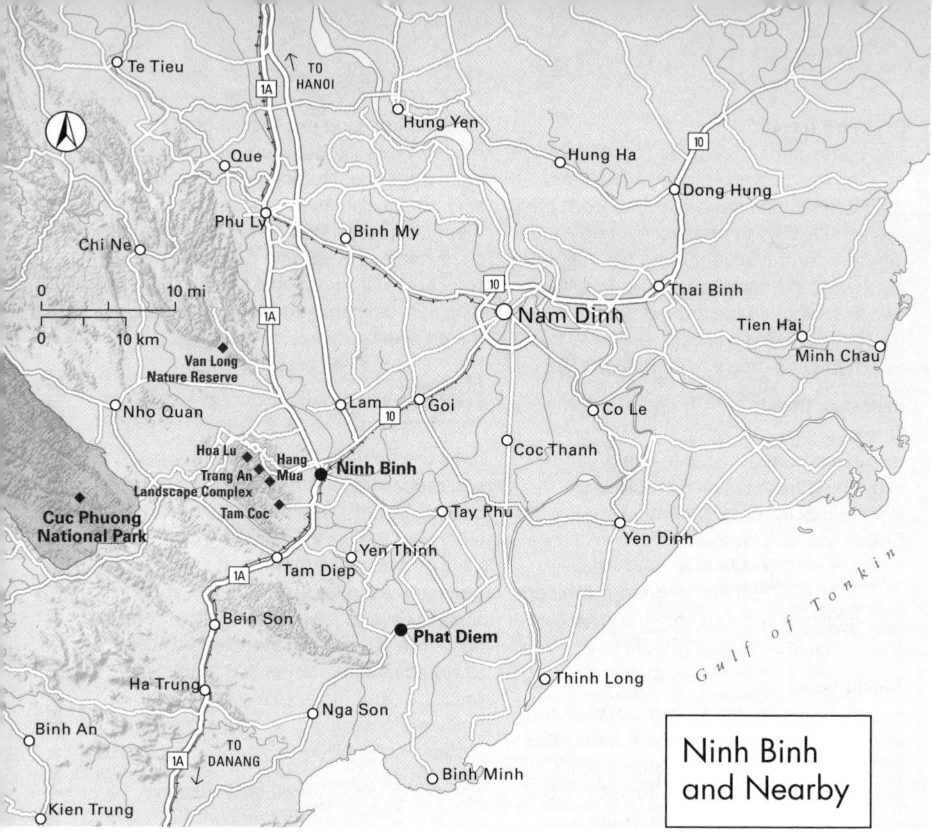
Te Tieu
TO
HANOI
1A
Hung Yen
10
Que
Hung Ha
Dong Hung
Phu Ly
Binh My
Chi Ne
10
Thai Binh
0
10 mi
0
10 km
1A
Nam Dinh
Tien Hai
Minh Chau
Van Long
Nature Reserve
Nho Quan
Lam
10
Goi
Co Le
Coc Thanh
Hoa Lu
Hang
Mua
Trang An
Landscape Complex
Ninh Binh
Cuc Phuong
National Park
Tam Coc
Tay Phu
Yen Dinh
Yen Thinh
Tam Diep
1A
Gulf of Tonkin
Bein Son
Phat Diem
Thinh Long
Ha Trung
Nga Son
Binh An
TO
DANANG
1A
Binh Minh
Kien Trung
Ninh Binh
and Nearby

both north and south, it makes a perfectly amenable base from which to explore the surrounding splendor. Much of the area to the west comes within the UNESCO World Heritage Site of Trang An Landscape Complex, including a series of caves accessible by boat and the fascinating remains of Vietnam's first capital, Hoa Lu, 12 km (7½ miles) northwest of town. Just to the south of Trang An are the more famous Tam Coc caves.

GETTING HERE AND AROUND

There are regular buses, leaving every 15 minutes or so, from Hanoi's southern Giap Bat bus terminal to Ninh Binh. A one-way journey takes between 1½ and 2½ hours, depending on the traffic, and the fare is 80,000d. Ninh Binh is a regular station on the north–south train route. The fare for a one-way journey from Hanoi is 45,000d and the trip takes 2½ hours. Taxis can be chartered for the journey from Hanoi and cost 1,448,000d from the city center.

If you are approaching from the opposite direction, an open tour bus from Hue to Hanoi can drop you off in Ninh Binh by request. This is a service offered by various tour companies including The Sinh Tourist, one of the longest-running operators in the country. The buses leave Hue at 5 pm and the journey takes around 10 hours, meaning an extremely early arrival in Ninh Binh. A one-way ticket costs 400,000d. There are three trains daily from Hue to Ninh Binh. They leave Hue at 5:39 am, 1:36 am, and 9:33 pm and take approximately 11 hours. A one-way fare for a comfortable soft sleeper is 1,090,000d.

Most hotels can organize a motorbike and driver to take you round the sights. These should cost around 325,000d for the day.

TOURS
The Sinh Tourist
A day trip from Hanoi by minibus will take you to the Tam Coc caves for a rowboat tour in the morning and to Hoa Lu in the afternoon. The outfitter also offers three-day tours for a more in-depth exploration of the area. ✉ *66 Hang Than St., Hanoi* ☎ *028/3838–9597* ⊕ *www.sinhtourist.vn* 💲 *Day trips from 630,000d.*

⊙ Sights

Hang Mua
CAVE | While the cave itself is not that impressive, the views from the top of the mountain are breathtaking, featuring Tam Coc River on one side and rice paddies on the other. The climb and its 486 steps are steep but worth it. There are several parking lots outside the entrance where you will be charged 10,000d for a bicycle and 20,000d for a motorbike. The views are the best on a clear day and comfortable footwear is suggested. If you are visiting for only a short time, skipping the cave is advised. ✉ *Hang Mua (Mua Cave), Ninh Binh* 💲 *100,000d.*

Hoa Lu
HISTORIC SIGHT | This ancient town is an interesting excursion on a number of different levels. Significantly, it was the first capital of independent Vietnam, and equally arresting is its stirring location amid the karst scenery that distinguishes Ninh Binh Province. Both the stunning natural surroundings of limestone outcrops and meandering streams and Hoa Lu's status as a former seat of power make for a worthy addition to any travel itinerary. Consider hiring a guide to enhance your experience. The Dinh Tien Hoang Temple at Hoa Lu honors the emperor who established the capital here. The musty, dimly lit back chamber

here houses statues of the king and his three sons. The main hall has been heavily restored, and much of the wood construction visible today is from reno-vations done in the 17th century. In the temple, courtyard stands a 3-foot-high sculpture made of stone. The dragon lying atop it is meant to symbolize the king sleeping, while unicorns stand guard on each side to protect him. To the left of the temple is a small structure containing three stone stelae inscribed with the king's blessings and details about various restorations. In 1696, the entire temple compound was shifted from its original northward orientation, the direction of evil according to Taoist belief, to face the more auspicious east. In 1898, Emper-or Nguyen Thanh Thai had the temple raised 2 feet as a gesture of respect to Dinh Tien Hoang. The entire walled-in compound was designed in the shape of the Chinese character meaning "coun-try." The Le Dai Hanh Temple is named after the general who became the first emperor of the dynasty in 980. The back chamber here houses ornate wooden statues of Le Dai Hanh, his son Tri Trung, and one of his five wives, Duong Van Nga, arguably the most interesting of the three figures. Upon the emperor's death, Duong Van Nga beseeched the head military mandarin of the time to prevent Chinese invaders from entering the country. She promised that she'd take away the rule of her six-year-old son and put it in the mandarin's hands, marrying him if he succeeded. When the mandarin repelled the Chinese, she made good on both promises. Her lifetime saw her become the wife of two kings, as well as the mother of two kings—the only woman with such a distinction in Viet-namese history. Depending on the angle from which you view her statue, her face will appear to reflect one of three feel-ings: seriousness over her daily affairs, sadness for the death of her husbands, and a half-smile of satisfaction after the military mandarin defeated the invading

There are many cliffs and rice paddies to see on a traditional boat ride down the river to Tam Coc.

Chinese forces and reinstalled her as queen. ⊠ *Hoa Lu* 🖃 *20,000d.*

Tam Coc

SCENIC DRIVE | Only a short bus or car ride away from Ninh Binh (drivers and tour group operators know exactly where to go) is a trio of caves accessible by a traditional boat ride down the Hoang Long River, a peaceful stream that winds through rice paddies after cutting its path through the steep cliffs around nearby Hoa Lu. Kind village women paddle your boat the the 2 km (1 mile) through Tam Coc, a series of three caves, one of which has a cement plaque on its far side commemorating Nguyen Cong Cay, a Vietnamese weapons maker who lived in Hoa Lu from 1947 to 1950 and plotted with other resisters against the French. At the far end of the boat ride, other women in similar boats are waiting to sell you soft drinks, bananas, and even embroidery. Another cave, Bich Dong, can also be reached by boat; you can disembark to visit the 17th-century pagoda here. Tam Coc has recently become

a small tourist epicenter and there are several hostels and restaurants located around the boat harbor. ⊠ *Ninh Binh* 🖃 *Entrance ticket 120,000d, boat rides 150,000d.*

★ Trang An Landscape Complex

RUINS | Closer to Ninh Binh city than Tam Coc, UNESCO World Heritage-listed Trang An offers a very similar experience to its more famous near neighbor. Although it is very popular with Vietnamese tourists, most visitors find it less crowded and more hassle-free than Tam Coc. Boat trips leave from the garish main office and take around 2½ hours, although the ticket operators will ask if you would like the 2-hour "short" tour instead. Boats will depart when they have four passengers. The journey by rowboat takes you through nine caves, some of which are very low and twisting, and along beautiful waterways lined with limestone karst. The landscape is of high historic and archaeological importance. Several pagodas can be visited on the boat tours, while the highest altitude caves dotted

Vietnam's First Capital

After three decades of internal strife following the expulsion of the Chinese by Ngo Quyen in 938, Dinh Bo Linh, also known as Dinh Tien Hoang, unified the country. (A colorful festival on the 12th day of the third lunar month commemorates this successful reunification.) The new king moved the capital to Hoa Lu, in a valley whose maze of narrow streams and inhospitable limestone outcroppings served as natural protection for the fledgling nation; he had numerous fortifications built around his citadel in order to avert another Chinese invasion, and word quickly spread of his ruthless treatment of prisoners. (The king reportedly fed enemies to tigers and then boiled their bones in ceremonial urns.) Despite such tactics, the Dinh dynasty was short-lived; bodyguards assassinated Dinh Tien Hoang in 979. The killers were discovered and put to death, and General Le Dai Hanh ascended to the throne, establishing the Early Le dynasty. Upon Le Dai Hanh's death in 1009, Ly Thai To became the first king of the Ly dynasty and moved the capital to Thang Long, the site of present-day Hanoi.

around the area have archaeological traces of human activity dating back almost 30,000 years. Unfortunately, it is not yet possible for visitors to access these higher altitude caves. Your boat operator will ask if you would like to stop and view the pagodas, and you can opt-in or -out (but if you say yes, the rower's arms will get a break). There are bathrooms at these small stops, and using them costs 2,000d. There has been increasing pressure put on these rowers to deliver good customer service, so don't be surprised when they hand you a survey to indicate your opinion of the tour. Tips are not mandated but still appreciated. **■TIP→ If you're already in Ninh Binh, there is no need to book a reservation for any of the boat trips. Just show up and hop on!** ✉ *Ninh Binh* 🎫 *200,000d.*

Van Long Nature Reserve

NATURE SIGHT | FAMILY | Van Long offers shorter boat rides than both Tam Coc and Trang An (they only take an hour or so), but they're far more secluded and serene. This wetland reserve has 32 grottoes and 39 animal species, including rare monkeys and birds. In the dry season, Van Long is the wintering place of migratory birds from the north, making this a great spot to bring those binoculars. ✉ *Gia Van, Gia Vien, Ninh Binh* ✥ *23 km (14 miles) from Ninh Binh on way to Cuc Phuong* ☎ *046/672–9191* 🎫 *80,000d.*

🍴 Restaurants

The Banana Tree Hostel-Kitchen-Bar

$$ | INTERNATIONAL | FAMILY | Located only a few meters away from Tam Coc Harbor, The Banana Tree Hostel-Kitchen-Bar is a large social hub and outdoor restaurant that offers spectacular Italian coffee and a range of comfortable seating options. Their menu is small but expertly executed. **Known for:** delicious Vietnamese snacks and salads; fire pit in winter; excellent travel information. [$] *Average main: d100,000* ✉ *Bich Dong Rd., Ninh Binh* ✥ *6W8P+XQ Hoa Lu District, Ninh Bình Province, Vietnam* ☎ *037/636–7982.*

Minh Toan Restaurant - Father Cooking

$$ | VIETNAMESE | FAMILY | A family operation, Minh Toan is located very close to the Tam Coc boat harbor. Tourists keep the kitchen quite busy, so be prepared for a slightly longer wait when the

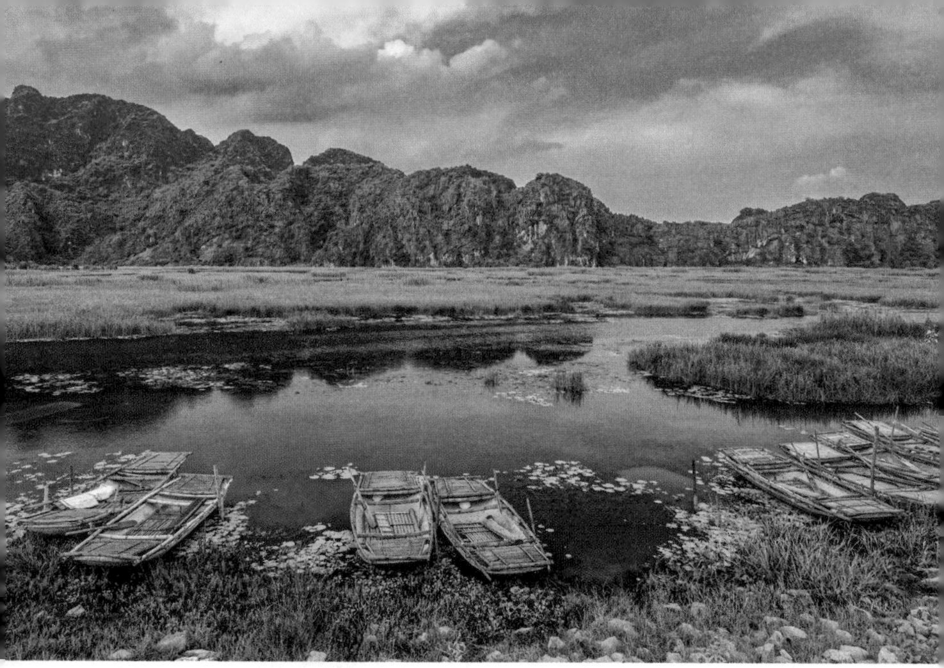

Boat tours in Van Long Nature Reserve wind past wetlands filled with wildlife.

restaurant is full. **Known for:** kind service; goat with lemongrass and chili; vegetarian options. [$] *Average main: d150,000* ✉ *Bich Dong Rd., Van Lam, DT491C, Hoa Lu* ☎ *0168/416–7388.*

Hotels

★ Dragon Boat Rock Homestay
$ | **B&B/INN** | Built right into the limestone, this cozy homestay near the Trang An heritage site and the Van Long Nature Reserve is unique and welcoming. **Pros:** free bicycles; peaceful location free of tourists; will help to arrange pickups from wherever you're coming from. **Cons:** a bit far from Tam Coc. [$] *Rooms from: d500,000* ✉ *Xa Ninh Giang, Hoa Lu* ☎ *096/366–1928* 🍴 *Free Breakfast* 🛏 *5 bungalows.*

★ Emeralda Resort
$$$$ | **RESORT** | The most prestigious address in Ninh Binh Province, this plush resort luxuriates in a bucolic location on the outskirts of the city. **Pros:** wide selection of leisure facilities; great outdoor swimming pool; chic and contemporary. **Cons:** expensive on-site restaurants; no nearby dining options. [$] *Rooms from: d2,695,000* ✉ *Van Long Reserve, Gia Vien District* ☎ *096/869–9690* 🌐 *www.emeraldaresort.com* 🛏 *172 rooms* 🍴 *Free Breakfast.*

Hang Mua Ecolodge
$$ | **B&B/INN** | These small but quite nice bungalows lie at the foot of the mountain that houses the Hang Mua or Mua Cave. **Pros:** reasonably priced on-site restaurants; free ticket to the cave; bungalows have porches and outdoor showers. **Cons:** area is full of tourists; loose commitment to maintaining a clean environment; some garish decor. [$] *Rooms from: d650,000* ✉ *Khe Ha, Ninh Xuan, Hoa Lu* ☎ *016/7869–9330* 🌐 *www.hangmua.vn* 🛏 *12 bungalows* 🍴 *Free Breakfast.*

Ninh Binh Hidden Charm Hotel & Resort
$$$$ | **HOTEL** | Many of the rooms at this elegant resort overlook beautiful rice paddies and rock formations, and the service is excellent. **Pros:** top-notch restaurant and outdoor bar; great location

near Tam Coc; luxurious spa. **Cons:** full of tour groups from Hanoi on weekends. Ⓢ *Rooms from: d1,750,000* ✉ *No. 9 Bich Dong, Tam Coc, Hoa Lu* ☏ *0229/388–8555* ⊕ *www.hiddencharmresort.com* ⇄ *100 rooms* ⦿ *Free Breakfast.*

★ Ninh Binh Legend Hotel

$$$ | **HOTEL** | The closest thing to a luxury option in Ninh Binh city, this sparkling hotel doesn't disappoint. **Pros:** large rooms; comfortable beds; great resident guides. **Cons:** some garish touches; by Ninh Binh standards, it is a little out of the way. Ⓢ *Rooms from: d1,290,000* ✉ *Ly Thai To, Tien Dong Zone* ☏ *0229/389–9880* ⊕ *www.ninhbinhlegendhotel.com* ⇄ *108 rooms* ⦿ *Free Breakfast.*

★ Tam Coc Garden Resort

$$$$ | **B&B/INN** | A boutique retreat in the heart of the beautiful Ninh Binh countryside, this is a great place to get away from it all; in fact, you may want to forsake the nearby tourist attractions in favor of a day by the pool. **Pros:** the location is heartbreakingly beautiful; complimentary bikes; close to the attractions. **Cons:** breakfast is a surcharge (but the restaurant is good quality); ceramic bathtubs cool down hot water rather too quickly. Ⓢ *Rooms from: d3,400,000* ✉ *Hai Nham Hamlet, Hoa Lu* ☏ *0246/273–3615* ⊕ *www.tamcocgarden.com* ⇄ *16 rooms* ⦿ *No Meals.*

Tam Coc Rice Fields Resort

$$ | **B&B/INN** | These bungalows offer amazing views, indoor and outdoor bathrooms, live traditional music on Saturday, and an outdoor pool and barbecue garden. **Pros:** high commitment to guests; beautiful bungalows; live music Saturday. **Cons:** communication can be sporadic; only one unpaved and slick mud road to get here. Ⓢ *Rooms from: d805,000* ✉ *Hai Nam Hamlet, Ninh Hai, Hoa Lu* ☏ *030/656–9656* ⊕ *www.tamcocricefields.com* ⇄ *24 bungalows, 1 dorm* ⦿ *Free Breakfast.*

★ Vancouver Hotel

$$$ | **HOTEL** | It is all about the welcome at this smart, family-owned hotel, overseen by manager David, who studied in Canada—hence the hotel's name. **Pros:** manager has fantastic knowledge and impeccable English; central location; clean rooms with private bathrooms. **Cons:** tucked away on a side street, so it can be hard to find; breakfast nook is a little small. Ⓢ *Rooms from: d1,090,000* ✉ *No.1 Alley 75 Luong Van Tuy St., Ninh Binh* ☏ *0229/389–3270* ⊕ *www.thevancouverhotel.com* ⇄ *10 rooms* ⦿ *Free Breakfast.*

Phat Diem

30 km (19 miles) from Ninh Binh, 121 km (75 miles) southeast of Hanoi.

Phat Diem's hulking cathedral is prominent among Vietnam's religious buildings. Unique both for its vast dimensions and also an architectural mélange that incorporates both European and Sino-Vietnamese influences, it is a formidable sight and also possesses a fascinating history. Although the cathedral is undoubtedly the main selling point of the area, there are other points of interest, including a covered bridge dating from the late 19th century.

GETTING HERE AND AROUND

Phat Diem is incorporated into many tour itineraries from Hanoi and Ninh Binh, but not all tours that go to Hoa Lu stop here, so check before you book. Most travelers who visit the cathedral independently choose to do so by renting a motorcycle in Ninh Binh. The cathedral is in the town of Kim Son, which is an easy ride. Motorcycle rental from a hotel costs around 200,000d per day. It is easy to charter a taxi from Ninh Binh, and the fare should cost approximately 600,000d for a round-trip. You can also hire and car and driver, which shouldn't cost more than 1,080,000d for the round-trip (although

Phat Diem Cathedral combines both European and Vietnamese architectural styles.

finding a driver prepared to get you there for the 5 am Mass might not be easy).

◉ Sights

★ Phat Diem Cathedral

CHURCH | It took 24 years (from 1875 to 1898) to build Phat Diem Cathedral, a complex comprising a lake, a cathedral, a stone church, Phuong Dinh (bell house), and three artificial grottoes. The cathedral, a hulking edifice made of local stone and hardwood, was designed by a Vietnamese priest named Father Sau, who died the same year the cathedral was completed. He is now interred in the narrow courtyard behind the bell tower, which was immortalized by Graham Greene in a description of a battle that took place here between French and Vietnamese forces in *The Quiet American*. The third floor of this tower supports a two-ton bronze bell that purportedly can be heard from 10 km (6 miles) away. The cathedral is flanked on both sides by four small chapels, all built in the late 19th century and dedicated to various saints.

The prayer hall is a wooden marvel; almost the entire interior is made of Vietnamese ironwood, with 48 massive pillars supporting arched ceiling beams in what is truly an artist's loving creation. The curved eaves are a nod to Sino-Vietnamese architecture, but the crosses and saints (all sitting in the lotus position) reflect the fervor of the 150,000-strong congregation. Many of Phat Diem's Catholics fled to the south in 1954 when Vietnam was divided. A great deal of restoration work has been done on the complex, which was bombed heavily by American B-52s in 1972. Catholicism has experienced a comeback in these parts, and because a more liberal tone has been adopted toward religion by Hanoi, Sunday Mass is now extremely popular. Services are held at 5 and 9 am, and by 10 everyone's already out in the fields. On holidays such as Christmas and Easter, expect crowds of 10,000 or more. ☒ *Kim Son* ⊕ *phatdiem.org*.

Cuc Phuong National Park

40 km (25 miles) from Ninh Binh, 130 km (81 miles) southwest of Hanoi.

The first national park in Vietnam and still one of its most important, Cuc Phuong is a refuge for diverse animal and plant life and an idyllic place to spend a couple of days. Hiking is a major draw and there are numerous trails that cut through the forest. Bird watchers flock here to catch a glimpse of silver pheasants and red-collared woodpeckers among other species. In the early part of the last decade the Ho Chi Minh Highway was rerouted through the park, cutting off some 371 acres from the main area of the park. The construction of the road has aided connectivity, but environmentalists maintain it has also harmed the biodiversity of the park.

GETTING HERE AND AROUND

It is relatively straightforward to travel here from Hanoi. Most of the reputable tour operators such as Handspan, Exo Travel, and Buffalo Tours run trips here. If you are traveling under your own steam, there's a regular bus from Hanoi to the park that departs Giap Bat station daily at 3 pm. The return bus to Hanoi leaves at 9 am and the journey takes around three hours. From Ninh Binh, the best option is to rent a motorbike or to engage the services of a motorbike and a driver for the journey.

◉ Sights

★ Cuc Phuong National Park

NATIONAL PARK | Established in 1962 by President Ho Chi Minh, Cuc Phuong National Park is Vietnam's oldest national park. Cuc Phuong consists of 220 square km (85 square miles) of heavily forested subtropical lowlands sheltering 97 mammal species, including nine species of civet, a kind of barking deer called the muntjac, as well as the extremely rare Delacour's langur. Approximately 336 bird species and 76 types of reptiles and amphibians live here as well, along with nearly 2,000 species of flora. The Endangered Primate Rescue Center, which can be visited with staff accompaniment, focuses its rescue efforts on channels of illegal trade, then tries to establish populations in captivity. Although Cuc Phuong's habitat would seem to be the perfect place to see Vietnam's wildlife in full splendor, mammal- and bird-watching are sadly not particularly successful pastimes in the park. Despite Cuc Phuong's status as a protected preserve, the primary forest habitat has been heavily denuded during the past few decades, and officials believe the park's wildlife numbers are dwindling due to increased hunting and high tourism pressures, which have led to the creation of in-park facilities, hiking trails, and paved roads. Despite the misfortunes of northern Vietnam's animals, Cuc Phuong is quite beautiful. In April, it's particularly lovely with swarms of butterflies. Dozens of miles of trails lead to such highlights as cascading Giao Thuy waterfall, a 1,000-year-old tree, and Con Moong Cave—the "cave of early man"—where evidence of prehistoric humans has been discovered. Longer hikes lead to some Muong villages. Many trails are well marked, but exploring this thick forest would be foolish without a guide. Be sure to bring lots of mosquito repellent, especially if you plan to stay the night. ☎ *0229/384–8018 park headquarters* ⊕ *www.cucphuongtourism.com.vn* 🖾 *50,000d.*

🛏 Hotels

You can overnight in one of three areas in the park: the Park Headquarters, Mac Lake just 2 km (1 mile) beyond the main gates, or Park Center in Bong, a tiny village 20 km (12 miles) into the park. If you plan on staying overnight, you may wish to consider going on a weekday, as

Cuc Phuong's proximity to Hanoi makes it a favorite weekend retreat among Vietnamese student groups. The Park Center in Bong, secluded as it is, occasionally fills with a boisterous crowd of 100 to 200 students. Culinary refinement is not a feature of the national park, but visitors can fill up on adequate fare at the restaurants attached to the accommodations sites within the park.

Mac Lake

$ | B&B/INN | The bungalows at Mac Lake are possibly the nicest in the park with good facilities including hot water and en suite bathrooms complementing the idyllic surroundings. **Pros:** beautiful location; traditional music and bonfires are a regular occurrence; convivial atmosphere. **Cons:** things can get noisy on weekends when young Hanoians descend on the area; dorm-style accommodations aren't for everyone; no hot water in the stilt house. $ *Rooms from: d500,000* ⊠ *Cuc Phuong National Park* ☎ *0229/384–8088* ✉ *vqgcucphuong@gmail.com* ⊕ *cuc-phuongtourism.com.vn* ❍| *No Meals* ⤶ *4 rooms.*

Park Center (Bong Sub-station)

$ | B&B/INN | Two stand-alone bungalows, beside a large, algae-green pool, feel far from civilization but are equipped with en suite bathrooms, air-conditioning, and hot water. **Pros:** practical, budget lodging; feels remote but idyllic; air-conditioning in bungalows. **Cons:** reservations are recommended; stilt house bathrooms are shared; electricity limited to evening in Bong. $ *Rooms from: d500,000* ⊠ *Cuc Phuong National Park* ☎ *0229/384–8006* ✉ *vqgcucphuong@gmail.com* ⊕ *cuc-phuongtourism.com.vn* ❍| *No Meals* ⤶ *2 bungalows, 1 stilt-house dorm.*

Park Headquarters

$ | B&B/INN | Tour operators usually guide people to the facilities at Park Headquarters, which now has a wide range of rooms, from those within detached bungalows and basic accommodations in a large stilt house to deluxe rooms with amenities such as television, air-conditioning, and hot water. **Pros:** most luxurious accommodations within the national park; bike rentals available; lots of activities like kayaking, trekking, and bird watching. **Cons:** seasonal (don't stay during rainy season); it's a tour group favorite, so is frequently busy. $ *Rooms from: d400,000* ⊠ *Cuc Phuong National Park, Ninh Binh* ☎ *0229/384–8006* ✉ *vqgcucphuong@gmail.com* ⊕ *cuc-phuongtourism.com.vn* ❍| *Free Breakfast* ⤶ *16 rooms.*

Haiphong

103 km (64 miles) east of Hanoi.

Vietnam's third-largest city, with a population of more than two million, has been a hub of industrial activity for the last century and one of the most significant seaports since the Tran dynasty's rule (1225–1400). Haiphong's reputation as a dingy industrial port is by no means justified. This is indeed the largest and busiest port in the north, and container trucks rumble through town on the way to Highway 5 and Hanoi. But the port itself is on the northern edge of the city and hugs the Cam River, away from the heart of the city. As you cross the Lac Long Bridge into the city center, you leave the dusty, industrial outskirts and slip into a quaint, clean downtown. Here huge banyan trees and blossoming magnolias line wide boulevards, and Vietnamese play badminton in the stately Central Square (Quang Truong). Walking through the city center feels like stepping into a time warp: portraits of revolutionary heroes, especially Ho Chi Minh, hang elegantly from the eaves of buildings; socialist-realist propaganda posters announce the latest health-awareness campaign, and swarms of bicycles fill the streets.

Today you are most likely to use Haiphong as a transfer point to destinations like Halong Bay, Cat Ba Island, and many popular islets nearby.

Here you can catch a cyclo to the port, and take the first boat out. If you have time, however, settle into an enjoyable two-day stay in Haiphong before moving farther afield. Some say it is what Hanoi was like not too long ago: a sleepy northern city with less traffic and less nightlife, but bursting with potential. It's very easy to navigate central Haiphong. Sidewalks on the main boulevards are wide, and the parks and gardens provide ample room to roam. If you've come to Haiphong by car and plan on a day of leisurely sightseeing, have the driver park at a hotel and then go for a long walk.

GETTING HERE AND AROUND

There are daily direct flights from Ho Chi Minh City and Danang to Haiphong. The airport is an easy 5-km (3-mile) journey from Haiphong. You probably won't need to take a taxi except to get from the airport or train station to your hotel, or to the ferry landing. Taxi companies have figured this out, and plenty wait outside the airport, train stations, and at the ferry landing.

Seeing downtown Haiphong by bike is almost idyllic, and many of the city's hotels have their own supply of bikes, which can be rented for around 100,000d per day.

TAXI CONTACT Mai Linh Taxi. ⊠ *Haiphong* ☎ *0225/383–3833.*

VISITOR INFORMATION
Haiphong Tourism Office. ⊠ *18 Minh Khai St., Haiphong* ☎ *098/322–2201.*

Sights

An Bien Park
CITY PARK | FAMILY | Shady and green, this park is the site of early morning tai chi classes and nighttime strolls, where locals sit at sidewalk stalls drinking fruit shakes and eating sweets and roller skaters zoom by. Near the southwestern

edge stands a massive statue of local heroine Le Chan, and there's a colorful daily Flower Market. Kids enjoy the playground and amusement rides in the attached Children's Park. ⊠ *Tran Phu and Tran Hung Dao Sts., Haiphong.*

Du Hang Pagoda
RELIGIOUS BUILDING | Some beautiful pagodas stand in the southern and eastern districts of the city, and this is the most impressive and moving of all. The 300-year-old temple is a good example of traditional Vietnamese architecture, with a gate and three buildings surrounding a stone courtyard crowded with flowers, statues, and bonsai plants. In front and to the right of the compound is a round pond with lotus flowers encircled by white statues of the Buddha and scholars. One of the 10 monks who live here may be chanting her daily prayers and tapping on a round wooden drum in the richly gilded main sanctuary. Occasionally in the afternoons, the senior monk holds one-on-one healing sessions with the sick. Hundreds of Buddhists fill the courtyard on Buddhist holy days, the 1st and 15th of every lunar month. To get here follow Cat Cut Street south until you hit Chua Hang Street. After a few alleyways, you'll see the pagoda set back on the left. It can be a bit tricky to find on your own, so use a GPS or guide to help you find it. ⊠ *Off Chua Hang St., Haiphong* ☞ *Free.*

Haiphong Museum
(*Bao Tang Thanh Pho Hai Phong*)
HISTORY MUSEUM | In the heart of the city, a huge shuttered French villa with creaky wooden staircases, musty corners, and occasionally rotating ceiling fans houses this museum—an underrated gem of a building that rivals the Opera House in classic design. Although it attempts to cover all of the history, geography, archaeology, agriculture, and wildlife of the region (the stuffed owl with a rodent in its claws is rather macabre), the museum's main focus is on Vietnam's struggle

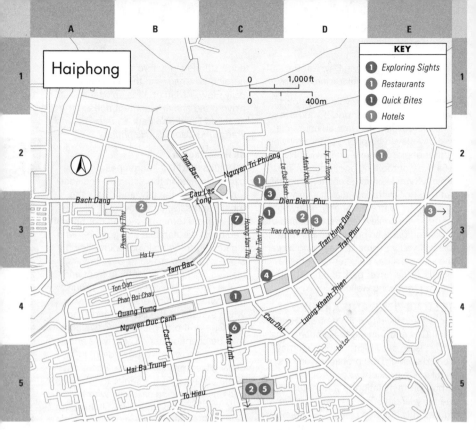

Haiphong

KEY

1 *Exploring Sights*
1 *Restaurants*
1 *Quick Bites*
1 *Hotels*

0 — 1,000 ft
0 — 400 m

Tam Bac
Nguyen Tri Phuong
Le Dai Hanh
Minh Khai
Ly Tu Trong
Cau Lac Long
Bach Dang
Pham Phu Thu
Dien Bien Phu
Hoang Van Thu
Dinh Tien Hoang
Tran Quang Khai
Tran Hung Dao
Tran Phu
Ha Ly
Tam Bac
Ton Dan
Phan Boi Chau
Quang Trung
Nguyen Duc Canh
Cat Cut
Me Linh
Luong Khanh Thien
Cau Dat
Hai Ba Trung
Le Loi
To Hieu

Sights ▼

1 An Bien Park **C4**
2 Du Hang Pagoda **C5**
3 Haiphong Museum **C3**
4 Haiphong
   Opera House **C4**
5 Navy Museum **C5**
6 Nghe Temple **C4**
7 Queen of the Rosary
   Cathedral **C3**

Restaurants ▼

1 BKK Trendy Thai **C2**
2 Indian Kitchen........... **D3**
3 TexGrill **D3**

Quick Bites ▼

1 No. 1986 Cafe............. **C3**

Hotels ▼

1 AVANI Haiphong
   Harbour View Hotel **E2**
2 Lac Long Hotel **B3**
3 Sea Stars Hotel **E3**

for independence from various forces. In recent years, the museum has closed its doors to visitors except for prearranged tours. ⊠ *66 Dien Bien Phu St., Haiphong* ☎ *0225/382–3451* ⊠ *5,000d.*

Haiphong Opera House (*Nha Hat Thanh Pho*)

PERFORMANCE VENUE | One of the most beautiful buildings in Haiphong, the Opera House, built by the French in 1907, has all the exterior designs of a classic, except for its coat of splendidly yellow paint. Once the site of lavish French and Vietnamese productions, the 400-seat theater was taken over by the Vietminh following World War II. President Ho Chi Minh addressed the world's youth from the steps in June 1946, and a huge portrait of him, visible from hundreds of yards away, hangs above the wooden front doors, making this feel eerily like the focal point of the city. In a way it is; the Haiphong People's Committee now holds its major meetings and assemblies here. Stage productions and concerts do take place, but they're rare. If you're not attending a show, you need written permission from the authorities to step inside, although tourists have been known to be waved in on occasion. The stone courtyard in front of the opera house is a popular place for families on weekends and couples after sunset. ⊠ *Between Hoang Van Thu and Dinh Tien Hoang Sts., Haiphong* ☎ *0225/3745–5763.*

Queen of the Rosary Cathedral (*Nha Tho Lon, Queen of the Rosary Cathedral*)

CHURCH | Haiphong's pagodas are tucked into the city's alleyways or off in the suburbs; no major religious structures except the city's main Catholic cathedral stand out in the middle of town. The cathedral was built in 1880 by missionaries from Spain. Regular Masses are still held. ⊠ *46 Hoang Van Thu St., Haiphong* ⊠ *Free* ☞ *Ask the guard if you can take a look inside.*

Navy Museum

HISTORY MUSEUM | As might be expected of a city whose name means "sea defense," much of Haiphong's more intriguing history is documented in the Navy Museum. Here you can see the Bach Dang stakes—the sharp wooden poles driven into the riverbed that impaled Kublai Khan's boats in 1288. A room dedicated to the Vietnam War houses a (presumably deactivated) MK-52 mine pulled from the waters of Haiphong Harbor in 1973, the lighthouse lantern that warned of impending bombing raids, and the antiaircraft gun that brought down a dozen American planes. ⊠ *353 Street, Anh Dung Commune, Kien Thuy, Haiphong* ☎ *0225/381–4788* ⊠ *Free.*

Nghe Temple (*Den Nghe*)

HISTORY MUSEUM | This temple is *more than just a religious site. Nghe Temple is* dedicated to Le Chan, the founder of Haiphong City, a heroic peasant woman who helped organize the popular revolt against the Chinese that was led by the two Trung sisters in AD 40. Ceramic reliefs at the top of the front wall depict the Trung sisters in royal carriages. Ancestral altars and chapels are to the right, through the courtyard. ⊠ *Corner of Me Linh and Le Chan Sts., Haiphong* ⊠ *Free.*

🍴 Restaurants

For a city with more than two million people, Haiphong doesn't have many upscale restaurants. That said, the once sleepy port has been sharpening up its culinary act in recent times and a range of alternative options spanning everything from Indian to Pan-Asian fusion cuisine now bolsters the city's indigenous restaurants. Local seafood is excellent, cheap, and available at any number of small, nondescript, family-run establishments. Just follow the crowds and remember the adage that "busier is better." Restaurants specializing in fish cluster around the north end of Rau

Haphong History

Early history

With its old-time aura, Haiphong feels very Vietnamese compared to the country's other big conurbations, and appropriately so, because the port city has played a key role in the nation's tumultuous history. Because of its strategic coastal location, it has witnessed the coming and going of many foreign invaders. The Bach Dang River, on the outskirts of the city, was the site of one of Vietnam's greatest victories against its old foe China when, in 1288, Kublai Khan's 300,000-man army and navy were soundly trumped by the Vietnamese, under the command of Tran Hung Dao.

20th-century conflicts

Six centuries later, the French settled into Haiphong and began turning it into a major industrial and shipping center. Later, following the German occupation of France during World War II, the Japanese muscled in, and began redirecting valuable Vietnamese exports to Japan. Once again in control of the port city after the war, the French bombed Haiphong over a bizarre customs dispute, killing up to 1,000 Vietnamese civilians and precipitating the eight-year war between the Vietminh and the French.

Haiphong figured prominently in the war against the Americans as well and, because of its strategic location on the northeast coast, the city was frequently bombed during the conflict. President Richard Nixon ordered the mining of Haiphong Harbor in May 1972, and during the holiday season that same year, the city suffered particularly devastating attacks, which became known as the Christmas bombings. The following year, as part of the agreement between the U.S. government and Vietnam in the Paris peace talks of 1973, the U.S. Navy was asked to help clear the mines.

Chinese exodus

In 1979, following conflicts between Vietnam and China, as many as 100,000 ethnic Chinese, who had lived for generations in the Haiphong area, piled into barely seaworthy boats and fled from what they expected to be deadly reprisals by their Vietnamese neighbors. In fact, few acts of retribution took place, but the damage had been done. And because the departing Chinese represented a large section of the city's merchant class, Haiphong has struggled to gain back the economic power lost as a result of their departure.

Its history may be littered with contentious incidents, but there's little sign of disharmony in modern Haiphong, and the most prominent remnant of foreign interlopers is the graceful French architecture that's sprinkled throughout the city center.

Bridge (Cau Rau), a few miles from the city center on the road south to the nearby beach town of Do Son.

BKK Trendy Thai

$$ | THAI | This Thai eatery was opened by Daniel Takianchan, a native of Bangkok, in 2006. With a big menu and wine on display from around the world, the open wooden dining area welcomes many expats and tourists. **Known for:** must-try chicken pandanus; first and only authentic Thai restaurant in town; delicious tom yam koong. $ Average main: d150,000 ✉ 22A Minh Khai, Haiphong ☎ 093/652–8133.

Indian Kitchen

$$$ | **INDIAN** | **FAMILY** | This little venue doesn't let you down. From the ornate Sanskrit-style lettering on the door to a menu well balanced with meat and vegetarian options, the restaurant is as authentic as they come. **Known for:** excellent breads; fiery curries; juicy meats. Ⓢ *Average main: d160,000 ⊠ 22 D Minh Khai St., Haiphong ☎ 0225/384–2558.*

TexGrill

$$$ | **AMERICAN** | **FAMILY** | If it's hearty Western comfort food you are after, there is no better place in Haiphong. All the staples you would expect, such as pizza, steak, chicken wings, tacos, ribs, and nachos, are present and correct. **Known for:** pizza; Tex-Mex; extensive menu. Ⓢ *Average main: d180,000 ⊠ 27 Minh Khai St., Haiphong ☎ 0225/382–2689 ⊕ texgrill.vn.*

Coffee and Quick Bites

No. 1986 Cafe

$ | **CAFÉ** | This intricately designed café is a feast for the eyes. Its sharp angles, giant staircases, and glowing skylights make it feel more like an architectural display than a place to eat, but the coffee and sandwiches are worth the visit. **Known for:** stunning architecture; good coffee; ample seating. Ⓢ *Average main: d60,000 ⊠ 33 Dinh Tien Hoang, Haiphong ☎ 090/880–1986 ⊕ www.facebook.com/no1986cafe.*

🛏 Hotels

Although its hotel portfolio cannot compare to that of Hanoi or Ho Chi Minh City, Haiphong has a pretty handy selection of accommodations nowadays. Family-run hotels rub shoulders with a smattering of international brands as well as some more unique boutique-style options, meaning that there is variety across the price spectrum. If you're shopping around for hotels in person, ask to see the room before you hand over your cash. Room standards are generally pretty decent, but you may find that some have a better view or amenities than others in the same price bracket. Also keep in mind that almost none of the rates are written in stone—meaning you may be able to make a deal.

★ AVANI Haiphong Harbour View Hotel

$$$$ | **HOTEL** | With its French-colonial architecture and smart, well-appointed rooms, this hotel is Haiphong's one and only luxury lodging choice. **Pros:** on-site restaurants serve some of the best food in town; beautiful architecture and smart rooms contribute to overall salubrious atmosphere; hotel can arrange tours. **Cons:** not much in the way of harbor views. Ⓢ *Rooms from: d2,840,000 ⊠ 4 Tran Phu St., Haiphong ☎ 0225/382–7827/8 ⊕ www.avanihotels.com ⏰ Free Breakfast ⇨ 122 rooms.*

Lac Long Hotel

$$$ | **HOTEL** | Some lapses in style aside, this centrally located hotel is a very solid option—in the heart of Haiphong, within easy walking distance of the city's main attractions, and not far from the ferry for Cat Ba Island. **Pros:** giant rooms; on-site Vietnamese restaurant; central location. **Cons:** interior design may not be to everybody's taste. Ⓢ *Rooms from: d1,170,000 ⊠ 83 Bach Dang St., Haiphong ☎ 0225/382–0777 ⊕ www.laclonghotel.vn ⏰ Free Breakfast ⇨ 34 rooms.*

Sea Stars Hotel

$$$$ | **HOTEL** | This imposing hotel is an archetypal Vietnamese business hotel, and though aesthetes won't go for the garish decoration throughout, it's convenient for exploring and has some good amenities. **Pros:** several good seafood restaurants nearby; health club with gym, swimming pool, and massage facilities; clean rooms and good service. **Cons:** not the most tasteful decor; highway outside can mean noisy traffic intrusion. Ⓢ *Rooms from: d2,000,000 ⊠ 1/3A Le Hong Phong St., Ngo Quyen ☎ 0225/355–6998, 090/600–4089 ⊕ www.seastarshotel.vn ⇨ 91 rooms ⏰ No Meals.*

☱ Nightlife

It may never be regarded as a party town, but Haiphong has some more than adequate options for letting your hair down. A smattering of smart café-bars caters to an upwardly mobile, youthful market, with regular live music adding to the conviviality. For a more local experience, Haiphong is blessed with numerous *bia hoi* venues, where gallons of low-price, pilsner-style beer are consumed on a nightly basis. Also, fun are the city's nightclubs and karaoke venues, where pumping house music and enthusiastic crooning are the order of the day.

Beaumont Coffee & Bar

CAFÉS | A club that promises dance music by night and espresso in the morning, Beaumont is the go-to choice if you are celebrating. The wooden ceiling beams and low lighting add to the ambience, and the comfortable armchairs are a perfect place to kick back with a hookah to share. There are several whisky and Champagne options as well. Open from 7 am to 2 am. ☒ *50A Dinh Tien Hoang, Haiphong* ☎ *0225/351–5979.*

Buzz Pub

PUBS | Buzz Pub is a smoky brick club that sells the regular spirits along with 14 types of cigars. Reminiscent of a London dive bar, there are vintage touches scattered here and there. There is also a small stage, where you can find live music on Saturdays from 9 to 11 pm. They serve beer and cocktails and have a nice regular crowd of businessmen. Open 2 pm to 1 am. ☒ *27 Hoang Van Thu, Haiphong* ☎ *096/514–0400.*

Mya Bar

PUBS | A funky coffee shop during the day, Mya Bar gets crowded in the evenings with locals and travelers alike. There are high wooden tables, a large fully stocked bar, and friendly staff waiting on your every need. The walls are covered in one-of-a-kind graffiti and art projects. Try the zombie cocktail and enjoy the vibe. It's open from 4 pm until 2 am. ☒ *134 Van Cao, Haiphong* ☎ *0225/373–0179.*

Halong Bay and Around

55 km (34 miles) northeast of Haiphong, 175 km (109 miles) east of Hanoi.

A visit to the north is not complete without a trip to Halong Bay, where placid waters give way to more than 3,000 limestone karsts and wind-sculpted limestone formations that jut from foggy lagoons. Dotting the bay are tiny islands bordered by white sandy coves and hidden caves, adding to the majestic landscape of this UNESCO World Heritage Site. Adding to this naturalist's dream is the biodiversity of islets, grottoes, and Cat Ba Island National Park. The bay, however, shows tourism's impact: the clearing of mangrove forests to make way for jetties and piers, marine life threatened by game fishing, and garbage from passenger boats and fishing villages washed up on the shores.

Beyond its geological uniqueness are activities like hiking, kayaking, rock climbing, or exploring one of the many floating villages where fishermen bring in their daily catch. The downside to all this allure is the large number of unlicensed boats it draws to the bay each day.

Boat trips out onto the bay are the main tourism stock in trade farther north, but a more multifaceted side of the area can be experienced at Cat Ba Island. The largest island in Halong Bay, Cat Ba is very much its own entity. Its national park offers incredible biodiversity, with more than a thousand species of plants having been recorded here. Animal life is slightly thinner on the ground, but alert visitors may spy inhabitants such as the endangered golden-headed langur, wild boar, deer, civets, and several species of squirrel. Trekking through the wilderness is a highlight, with a number of fascinating trails to follow.

Cat Ba Island has also become a firm favorite with the adventure sports set. Indeed, along with Railay Beach in Thailand, it is recognized as one of the top spots in the region for rock climbing. Other outdoor pursuits include sailing and kayaking around Lan Ha Bay. Although Halong Bay has arguably been tainted by overexposure, Bai Tu Long Bay, farther east toward China, retains all the majesty of Vietnam's premier bucket-list natural attraction but sees a fraction of the traffic of its immediate neighbor to the west. Here, visitors will find islands of substantial size with deserted beaches and untamed jungle.

Halong Bay's 3,000 islands of dolomite and limestone cover a 1,500-square-km (580-square-mile) area, extending across the Gulf of Tonkin nearly to the Chinese border. According to legend, this breathtaking land and seascape was formed by a giant dragon that came barreling out of the mountains toward the ocean—hence the name (Halong translates into "descent of the dragon"). Geologists are more likely to attribute the formations to sedimentary limestone that formed here between 300 and 500 million years ago, in the Paleozoic Era. Over millions of years water receded and exposed the limestone to wind, rain, and tidal erosion.

Today the limestone formations are exposed to hordes of tourists—but don't let that discourage you. Hundreds of fishing trawlers and tour boats share space on these crystal waters, yet there seems to be room for everyone. Most people use the main population center, Halong City, as a base from which to venture into the bay. Although it's now officially one municipality, Halong City was, until 1996, two separate towns: Bai Chay is now Halong City West, where Halong Road winds its way around the coast and past the lifeless central beach; Hon Gai is Halong City East, where a coal transportation depot dominates the center of town. Locals still refer to the towns by their old names, but they are now inexorably lassoed together by a bridge. Boat trips through Halong Bay are the main attraction. Little of the majesty of this region can be found in the city, so head out onto the water and start exploring. Countless 10- and 30-foot fishing boats have been converted into Halong Bay's formidable tourist-boat fleet. Hotels or travel agencies in Halong City or Hanoi can arrange boat trips for you (often they are part of organized tours from Hanoi). It is still possible to go down to the wharf and bargain yourself onto a boat for the day, but you are likely to be charged (sometimes significantly) more than you would pay for a prebooked tour, so this is not advised. Self-sufficient travelers have fallen victim to the old bait-and-switch: they've arranged a next-day boat tour with local fishermen, only to be told in no uncertain terms the following morning that they could not board their chosen boat, but they could take a different one for quite a bit more money. You may have no choice in the end. Travel agencies, however, have their tried-and-true favorites.

GETTING HERE AND AROUND

The most common way to reach Halong Bay is by taking a four-hour shuttle bus from Hanoi's Old Quarter. However, it is possible to reach Halong Bay directly from Hanoi's main airport by hiring a private transfer. Since most boats depart from the dock at noon, only passengers with early arrival times into Hanoi Airport should pursue this method. All shuttles to Halong Bay depart from Hanoi at around 8 am. They stop midway at art galleries that double as rest stops, where restrooms, shops, and restaurants are available. Passengers are finally dropped off at Halong City's bustling port between 11:30 and 12:30 daily.

AIR

There are now two ways to fly directly from Hanoi to Halong Bay. The most exciting—and accessible—way of transferring is via a new seaplane service launched last year by Hai Au Aviation. Travelers are flown from Hanoi's Noi Bai Airport to Tuan Chau Marina in Halong City in a Cessna Grand Caravan seaplane. The flight takes just 45 minutes and costs $175 (around 4,000,000d) per person for a one-way flight. Round-trip tickets cost $350 (7,875,000d) per person; it's also possible to tag on an extra 15-minute scenic tour over Halong Bay for an additional $175 (around 4,000,000d). Another way of flying direct is by private helicopter between Hanoi's Gia Lam Airport and Halong's heliport on General Giap Hill. Round-trip tickets cost between $1,058 and $10,170 per person, depending on the number of passengers and the category of helicopter that is chartered. Cat Bi Airport in Haiphong opened a new terminal and runway in May 2016 and now has daily flights to Ho Chi Minh City, Danang, Dong Hoi, Nha Trang, and Phu Quoc, as well as select flights to Thailand, Korea, and China.

AIR TRAVEL CONTACTS Hai Au Aviation.
✉ Fl. 9, 70–72 Ba Trieu St., Hoan Kiem District ☎ 09/6206–9689 ⊕ www.sea-planes.vn.**Luxury Travel Vietnam.** ✉ Halong Bay ☎ 024/3927–4120 ⊕ luxtraveldmc.com.**Northern Airport Flight Service Company.** ✉ Gia Lam Airport, 173 Pho Truong Chinh St., Hanoi ☎ 24/3827–1535 ⊕ www.petitfute.com.

BOAT

Take your pick from more than 600 boat operators that cruise Halong Bay. Standards vary from cheap "get 'em in, get 'em out" passenger boats to high-end luxury vessels that aim to make relaxing your main priority. Package tours usually include round-trip transportation from Hanoi, with bay excursions like kayaking, cave tours, and island expeditions. Overnight trips include the above, plus meals,

a private cabin, a visit to floating villages, and a day at Cat Ba Island (two-night tours only). If you are paying less than 3,400,000d for a two-night, three-day trip, then expect some subpar services.

For package tours, see Exploring.

Day trips to Halong Bay are extremely rushed and should only be booked if time is limited. Ranging from about 800,000d for budget tours to about 1,800,000d for higher-end ones, these day trips are rather exhausting considering the four-hour drive from Hanoi. For those short on time and money, it's possible to take a ferry from Halong City to Cat Ba Island for 150,000d. This will give you a glimpse of the landscape and an afternoon on the island before returning to Haiphong City by hydrofoil.

CONTACTS Au Lac Quang Ninh Company. ✉ Tuan Chau Ward, Halong Bay ☎ 0203/384–2134 ⊕ www.tuanchau-halong.com.vn.

BUS

Buses depart for Halong Bay from Hanoi's Gia Lam Bus Station. The four-hour ride costs 120,000d. Most boat tours include shuttle service to/from Halong Bay with an 8 am pickup at your hotel and noon drop-off at Halong City port. A number of public shuttles depart from Hanoi's Old Quarter, offering round-trip transportation for about 216,000d.

CAR

Like elsewhere in Vietnam, although the law is changing and international driving permits will be accepted, the details are still under discussion, and certain restrictions may be applied to foreign drivers. Check the situation before considering renting a vehicle. Hiring a private car or taxi should cost about 1,900,000d–2,500,000d from Hanoi to Halong Bay (four hours). Round-trip shuttle service is generally included for overnight cruise passengers, or it might be tacked on for an added fee.

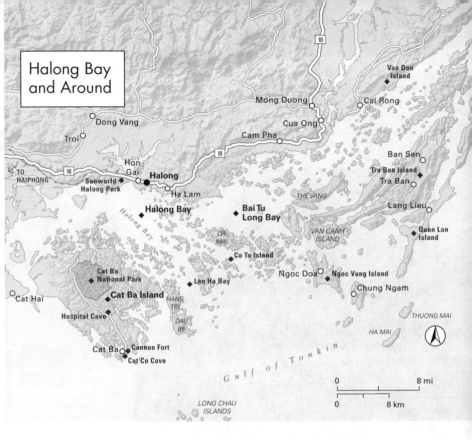

Halong Bay and Around

TO HAIPHONG

Dong Vang

Troi

Hon Gai

Halong

Sunworld Halong Park

Ha Lam

Halong Bay

Bai Tu Long Bay

DA MAI

Co To Island

Cat Ba National Park

Lan Ha Bay

Cat Ba Island

HANG TRI

DAU BE

Hospital Cave

Cat Hai

Cat Ba

Cannon Fort

Cat Co Cove

LONG CHAU ISLANDS

Mong Duong

Cua Ong

Cam Pha

Cai Rong

Van Don Island

Ban Sen

Tra Ban Island

Tra Ban

THE VANG

Lang Lieu

VAN CANH ISLAND

Quan Lan Island

Ngoc Doa

Ngoc Vung Island

Chung Ngam

THUONG MAI

HA MAI

Gulf of Tonkin

0   8 mi

0   8 km

TAXI

A taxi from Cat Bi International Airport in Haiphong to Halong Bay takes 2½ hours and costs about 863,000d. A metered taxi from Hanoi to Halong Bay will cost at least 2,159,000d.

TRAIN

Several daily trains run from Hanoi to Haiphong. The two- to three-hour train ride costs 90,000d–135,000d in person, or 340,000d if you book online. From the Haiphong Ferry Terminal, passengers can catch a hydrofoil to Cat Ba Island.

◉ Sights

So much to sail, so little time … Halong Bay is a destination not to be rushed; you need several days to do it justice. Day cruises will only whet your appetite, and an overnight trip will simply get you in the zone moments before it's over. If your schedule allows, opt for a two-night, three-day trip to properly explore the waters. Halong's must-sees include a visit to a floating village, kayaking, caving, and a day at Cat Ba Island. The eons of erosion have left countless nooks and crannies to explore: secluded half-moon beaches lie at the base of steep untouched forest canopies, and grottoes of all shapes and sizes—some well tramped, others virtually unknown—are open jaws of stalactites and stalagmites. One of the largest and most visited is the Grotto of the Wooden Stakes (Hang Dau Go), claimed to be the 13th-century storage spot for the stakes that General Tran Hung Dao planted in the Bach Dang River in order to repel the invasion of Kublai Khan. This cavernous grotto has three distinct chambers and is reached by climbing 90 steps. Another quite popular

Did You Know?

Halong Bay, a UNESCO World Heritage Site, is home to about 1,600 islands and limestone karsts.

destination in the bay is the Grotto of Bewilderment (Sung Sot), a stalagmite cave, estimated to be 1 million years old, with 29 chambers inside.

The best way to hit all destinations is through a reputable tour company.

★ Paradise Line

CRUISES | With 10 years of experience in the luxury tourism industry, Paradise is both a pioneer and a trendsetter. Paradise owns and operates four ships on Halong Bay: *Luxury, Elegance, Peak,* and *Delight.* The newest of these, with 31 spacious cabins (including balconies) is the *Delight.* It also boasts a live piano bar and walk-in closets. The *Peak*'s signature feature is a commitment to wellness and romance. This boat has eight suites, a sauna, Jacuzzis for couples, a library, and a wellness room. *Paradise* offers half-day lunch and sunset cruises starting at $120, around 2,800,000d. For packages, prices for each boat differ, but start from $547 to $1,205 (12,450,000d–27,400,000d). ⊠ *Tuan Chau Island, Halong Bay* ☎ *0203/3384–2368* ⊕ *www.paradisecruise.com.*

★ Heritage Line

CRUISES | This company operates two cruise boats on Halong Bay—*Violet* and *Jasmine.* The more luxurious of the two is the 12-passenger *Violet,* which parades the waters in style by combining classical French design with Vietnamese allure. It offers tours from one to three nights, and destinations include Tien Ong Cave, the Cua Van fishing village, and Ti Top Island. Each of its six suites has a private balcony, Jacuzzi tub, hardwood floors, ornate furnishings, and a flat-screen TV. Set menus and à la carte cuisine are included in the rate, and there's also a gym, sauna, library, sundeck, and spa on board. The 30-passenger *Sunset* also offers a one-day excursion, subject to availability (check in advance), which explores the southern part of Halong Bay to Cat Ba Island. A restaurant on board serves brunch shortly after passengers embark. The highlight of the voyage is Cat Ba Island, where passengers can explore small coves, fishing villages, mangrove forests, limestone cliffs, and the main town. Both vessels offer tai chi, cooking workshops, and spa treatments as part of the on-board activities. ⊠ *22 Slot C, Cai Dam, Garden Villa, Bai Chay* ☎ *0203/351–2446* ⊕ *www.heritage-line.com.*

★ Quang Ninh Museum

HISTORY MUSEUM | Modern and massive, this three-story museum rises out of nowhere and is a must-visit for anyone interested in Vietnamese history, culture, or environment. On entering, visitors are greeted by a suspended skeleton of a giant whale that washed up on the shores of Vietnam some years ago, and are taken on a journey of discovery through exhibits that seem to cover everything. The first floor mainly focuses on plant and animal life, with a few nods to boat builders and sea traditions. The second floor displays an array of anthropological artifacts and an interesting walkable cave that pays homage to the coal industry in the region. The third floor showcases Vietnam's military past and dedicates one room to the venerated Ho Chi Minh. If you can only visit one museum in Vietnam, make it this one, as it has the most information under one roof. ⊠ *Tran Quoc Nghien, Tuan Chay, Halong* ☎ *0203/382–3045* ⊕ *www.baotangquangninh.vn* ✉ *30,000d* ◷ *Closed Mon.*

Sunworld Halong Park

THEME PARK | FAMILY | This giant theme park has taken over much of Halong City bay and runs a cable car over the ocean next to the Bai Chay bridge. There are two main areas to the park: a beach water park and the Mystic Mountain complex, which includes the large Ferris wheel you can see from the boats. Tickets for the cable car and sun wheel are 300,000d. ⊠ *Ha Long St., Bai Chay, Halong* ☎ *09/8920–0699* ⊕ *halongcomplex.sunworld.vn* ✉ *560,000d for 3 parks.*

Halong Bay Safety Tips 👁

When visiting Halong Bay, make sure your operator follows safety regulations, including life jackets, and provides experienced guides and admission to designated sites. You get what you pay for, so choose your cruise operator wisely, including opting for higher-end operators that have stringent safety standards and that insist passengers wear life jackets during bay activities. Incidentally, the increased number of boats on the water led to a rise in boat collisions, so the government issued a ruling that all Halong boats were to be painted white in an effort to decrease the number of accidents. Another thing to keep in mind is that most land-based activities require some level of fitness. Access to caves and coves have slippery stone steps devoid of guardrails. Wear suitable footwear when exploring the area, especially on island trails that are narrow and somewhat arduous. And remember, the government is doing its best to clean up the water in the bay, so keep your trash on you or dispose of it suitably on board.

🍴 Restaurants

Halong City, the launching point for Halong Bay, is not known as the place to come for fine cuisine. In fact, you might be better off suppressing your appetite until you dine aboard ship. However, since the opening of the Sunworld theme park, a string of coffee shops, bars, and restaurants has sprung up along the coast. If you want to try something local, *tu hai* is a shellfish specialty from Van Don Island. Other Halong dishes include dried shrimp, steamed cuttlefish, sea snails, and *gat gu* (steamed pancake made from rice flour). On the other side of the bridge, make sure to hit up Wander Station after visiting the Quang Ninh museum.

Wander Station
$ | CAFÉ | Trung and Linda Nguyen accomplished a dream by opening this excellent restaurant and coffee shop across the river from Bai Chay in Hong Gai. The couple purchases their beans from the mountainous Dalat and roasts them on-site. **Known for:** projector for movies and sports; espresso; staff that loves to help travelers discover the area.

Ⓢ *Average main: d75,000* ✉ *32 Van Lang, Tuan Chau, Halong* ☎ *093/206–2186.*

🛏 Hotels

Most visitors who choose to overnight here do so in Halong City West. The larger hotels, some of which are listed below, are slightly less tacky than the average downtown minihotel, and many offer a 50% discount in the steamy summer months.

Halong Plaza Hotel
$$$ | HOTEL | A glass-fronted entryway looks out onto the bay from the spacious front lobby at this modern luxury hotel close to the ferry landing. **Pros:** tremendous views of Halong Bay; sunken bath in deluxe rooms; range of decent on-site dining and drinking options. **Cons:** fittings and interiors need some TLC; some rooms face industrial rear side rather than the bay; surcharge for buffet breakfast. Ⓢ *Rooms from: d1,515,000* ✉ *8 Halong Rd., Halong* ☎ *0203/384–5810, 0203/384–6867* ⊕ *www.halongplaza.com* ⇱ *187 rooms* ⦿| *No Meals.*

Wyndham Legend

$$$$ | **HOTEL** | **FAMILY** | This ocean-facing hotel has all the amenities you'd expect and more, including a kids' pool to compliment the kids' club and a fitness center overlooking Halong Bay. The lobby is stunning, most rooms have bathtubs and balconies, and the location is prime. **Pros:** family rooms have bunk beds and a wall divider; prime location; excellent design. **Cons:** light-color carpet is easily smudged; surcharge for buffet breakfast. *[$] Rooms from: d1,700,000 ✉ 12 Ha Long, Bai Chay, Halong ☎ 0203/363–6555 🌐 www.wyndhamhalong.com 🛏 217 rooms 🍴 No Meals.*

Nightlife

Halong City has a surprisingly active nightlife, but it is not what you would call sophisticated. Divey karaoke bars are popular; there are plenty of lively spots for younger crowds. Also popular are the city's legion of bia hoi venues where cheap beer and food keep the spirits high.

Activities

The most popular sporting activity in Halong City—aside from playing or watching football—is kayaking on Halong Bay. Most of the better hotels can organize an itinerary for you, but the best approach is to book a specialized tour from one of the respected tour operators, such as the Sinh Tourist, in Hanoi.

Cat Ba Island

At the southern end of Halong Bay, 30 km (19 miles) east of Haiphong by boat.

One of Halong Bay's most remarkable formations is Cat Ba Island, 420 square km (162 square miles) of wildly steep spines of mountains, narrow valleys and waterfalls, lush wetlands, golden beaches, and one of Vietnam's most beautiful national parks, which protects about two-thirds of the island. The sea life in much of the surrounding inshore waters is also protected. Included in these ecosystems are tropical evergreen forests, 15 kinds of mammals (including wild boars and hedgehogs), 200 species of fish, 21 species of birds, and 640 species of plants. Don't expect to see many wild mammals, however, such as the endangered langur monkeys that supposedly swing from the trees.

In 1938 a French archaeologist found traces of an ancient fishing culture on the island dating from the end of the Neolithic era. Human bones alleged to be 6,000 years old were also found. More recently, during the Vietnam War, American bombers targeted the military and naval station here, causing numerous casualties and forcing hospitals to set up in nearby caves on the island to avoid the bombings. An ethnic Chinese community numbering about 10,000 settled on Cat Ba over the years, only to leave en masse in 1979 after Chinese troops invaded Vietnam in the brief but bloody border war of that year. The ethnic Chinese, or Hoa, sailed in dinghies to Hong Kong and other Asian ports, many dying along the way. Few ethnic Chinese have returned to Cat Ba.

Today the population of more than 20,000 continues to subsist on fishing and rice and fruit cultivation, but tourism is quickly becoming a primary cash crop. Walk off your seafood dinner along the harbor, where you can sip iced Vietnamese coffee and watch the shooting stars. Splendid caves, just off the road to the national park, are great for exploring. Hiking through Cat Ba can be strenuous: the mountain ridges are steep, trails are poorly marked, and roads are narrow, making blind crests somewhat dangerous. Talk to your hotel manager or one of the many local tour operators about the best hiking trails for your level. A hike through the park—through the tropical forest to a rocky peak overlooking much of the island—is best undertaken with a guide. The park is also a favorite spot for Vietnamese tourists, many of whom seem to be able to scale the slippery rocks in stiletto heels.

GETTING HERE AND AROUND

Unless you're a guest of the Vietnamese military, the only way on and off Cat Ba Island is by boat or hydrofoil. There is a ferry service from Halong City to Cat Ba, but the more common route is from Haiphong. Several companies operate the route between Haiphong's Binh Station (Ben Binh) and Cat Ba town and departure times are liberally scattered throughout the day, meaning that missing a crossing needn't be a disaster. Note, however, that services are reduced significantly during the off-season winter months. Fares vary according to each company, the most reputable of whom include Hadeco, Hoang Long, and Mekong Hoang Yen, but range from 110,000d to 240,000d. Crossing times vary from one to two hours depending on the speed and condition of the vessel. Hadeco also offers a bus-boat package from Halong City, costing around 300,000d one way; buy tickets from their office in Halong City's Luong Yen Bus Station.

Just about any of the hotels can arrange for car or minibus tours of the island and rides to the national park. You can also get to the park on your own (rent a motorbike, or take a motorbike taxi) and hire a guide there. But it's much easier to go along on one of the tours, where the park and guide fees are prepaid and a hike is mapped out. Tour packages usually include minibus transportation to the national park, where a guide leads a hike through it, down to Viet Hai village, and over to a bay where a boat is waiting to bring you back to town. This runs about 250,000d per person, with lunch included. Or you can head down to the wharf and arrange for a boat

yourself—just make sure they know what you're asking and you know what they're offering. Rates are negotiable, so be sure to bargain, and understand that sleeping on a fishing boat is not an ideal way to see the area.

TOURS Cat Ba Travel Service. ✉ *Cat Ba Town* ☎ *098/897–1685* ⊕ *www.catbatravelservice.com.* **Full Moon Party Tour.** ✉ *236 St. 1–4, Cat Ba Town* ☎ *096/310–5200* ⊕ *www.fullmoonpartytourvietnam.com.*

 ## Sights

Cannon Fort

VIEWPOINT | A French-era fort that was also used during the defense of Haiphong during the war with the United States, this hilltop landmark is also notable for offering some of the best views on Cat Ba Island. A motorbike taxi can take you most of the way up the hill from Cat Ba Town and wait while you explore the area. You will find two cannons, two bunkers, a small photography and memorabilia shop, and several lookout points that offer views of the sweeping vista that captures the karst-studded landscape in all its glory. There is also a small café serving tea and juice where you can relax if you've made the journey on foot. ✉ *Cat Ba Town* 🎫 *40,000d.*

★ Cat Ba National Park

NATIONAL PARK | Home to 32 species of mammals, including the endangered white-headed langur monkey, which lives among the jungle terrain and freshwater lakes, Cat Ba National Park covers about 263 square km (101 square miles) of Cat Ba Island. Within its tropical rain forest are 78 species of birds and 20 species of reptiles. In addition to impressive beaches and mangroves, within its boundaries are two historical caves once used as clinics during the Vietnam War. Signs outside the park offer four hiking routes; 1, 2, and 3 cost 40,000d, and 4, the Cang Viet Hai Trail, costs 80,000d. Active travelers can tackle this demanding (yet rewarding) 18-km (11-mile) trail across the park if they arrive before 10 am. For a striking vista of the surrounding scenery, the view from the park's observation tower is hard to beat. Be warned, though, the climb-up metal ladders and cliffs are not for the faint of heart. The park is about 30 minutes from Cat Ba Town. ⊠ *Trung Trang, Cat Ba Island* ☎ *0225/3121–6350* 🚢 *From 40,000d.*

Fishing Villages

TOWN | Many overnight boat tours will take you to see one or more of the four floating villages on Halong Bay, where 300 local families make a living by fishing the mystical waters. If they're not fishing or fixing their nets for the next big catch, they may be passing the time swinging on hammocks—or even rowing toward your cruise boat to sell you groceries and souvenirs in a floating "store." These impressive fishing villages have their own wooden shacks and grocery stores that stay afloat by Styrofoam platforms wrapped in waterproof tarps. ⊠ *Cat Ba Island.*

★ Hospital Cave

CAVE | One of the most intriguing sights on Cat Ba Island, Hospital Cave served as a bomb-proof medical facility during the American War. It also provided well-hidden refuge for Vietcong leaders and fighters during the conflict. Like Cu Chi Tunnels in the south and Vinh Moc Tunnels near Dong Ha, Hospital Cave is a prime example of the Communists' engineering ingenuity. Built between 1963 and 1965, the three-story facility is a labyrinth of dim chambers. Guides operate from outside the cave, which is around 10 km (6 miles) north of Cat Ba Town and will show you around the 17 rooms and point out notable features such as the old operating theater and a natural cavern that was used as a movie theater. ⊠ *Cat Ba Town* 🚢 *40,000d.*

★ Lan Ha Bay

NATURE SIGHT | Although it is technically and geologically an extension of Halong Bay, the 300 or so karst islands of Lan Ha Bay feel somewhat removed from tourist traffic. Lying south and east of Cat Ba Town, they are too distant for most of the tour boats that leave from Halong City to reach. Therefore visitors here, mostly on itineraries arranged in Cat Ba Town, can enjoy the sense of peace and isolation that Halong Bay has arguably lost. Sailing, snorkeling, and kayaking are popular activities here. Lan Ha Bay also possesses several idyllic beaches such as Hai Pai Beach (also known as Tiger Beach), and day tours are cheap, starting at 360,000d. ⊠ *Cat Ba Town.*

🏖 Beaches

Cat Co Cove

BEACH | The island's beaches are among the best in North Vietnam and the three stretches of sand at Cat Co Cove are justifiably popular with Vietnamese tourists and other sun-worshippers. Of the three beaches, the one at Cat Co 2 is the prettiest with limestone cliffs backing golden sand. Here, you will find Cat Ba Beach Resort, one of the island's more luxurious lodgings. The other two beaches are less crowded, but there tends to be more debris and trash in the water. Cat Co is an easy 15-minute walk from Cat Ba Town. **Amenities**: food and drink; parking; toilets. **Best for:** swimming; sunset. ⊠ *Cat Ba Town.*

🍽 Restaurants

In recent years, Cat Ba Island has evolved into a top tourist destination in northern Vietnam. Unfortunately, that progress has not been reflected in its hospitality sector, which remains resolutely mediocre. Identical menus that cover all the culinary bases are standard, so don't expect much in the way of gastronomic flair. For a more local experience, join the hordes of Vietnamese tourists and dine at one of the floating restaurants on the harbor. These garish neon-lighted venues tend to close and reopen under another name on a regular basis and specialize in fresh seafood.

Le Pont

$$$ | **VIETNAMESE** | The secret to having a good meal at this Cat Ba restaurant/hostel/hotel is ordering what is local and fresh. Pass on the steak and order instead whole fish, prawns, squid, or the house specialty: seafood hotpot. **Known for:** great service; large portions; seafood hotpot. [$] *Average main: d180,000* ✉ *Near Beach 3, Cat Ba Town* ☎ *097/374–8081, 096/973–2568* 🌐 *www.lepont.vn.*

Like Coffee

$ | **CAFÉ** | A small and cute café full of travelers and cats, Like Coffee is a hit with its simplicity. The chai tea latte and fluffy pancakes are excellent, but it's the milk shakes and egg coffee that bring repeat business. **Known for:** breakfast; milk shakes; sweet Vietnamese coffee. [$] *Average main: d60,000* ✉ *177 St. 1–4, Cat Ba Town* ☎ *090/247–4274.*

Hotels

CAT BA TOWN

Cat Ba Palace Hotel

$$ | **HOTEL** | You may not get much in the way of trimmings here, but rooms are spacious and spotlessly clean, and it's an easy walk from the ferry port, in an extremely convenient location in the center of town. **Pros:** honeymoon suites won't break the bank; a stone's throw from everything; centrally located. **Cons:** Wi-Fi reception can be somewhat spotty. [$] *Rooms from: d635,000* ✉ *180 Nui Ngoc St., Cat Ba Town* ☎ *0225/369–6030* 🛏 *20 rooms* 🍴 *Free Breakfast.*

Gieng Ngoc Hotel

$ | **HOTEL** | With a prime location on the seafront and many rooms with ocean-facing balconies, this is one of the better options in Cat Ba Town. **Pros:** rooms have minibar and TV; ocean-facing balconies are pleasant; nice café. **Cons:** in-house karaoke can cause a ruckus; bedding is a bit old and musty. [$] *Rooms from: d250,000* ✉ *240 St. 1–4, Cat Ba Town* ☎ *0225/388–8243* 🌐 *www.facebook.com/giengngochotelcatba* 🛏 *64 rooms* 🍴 *No Meals.*

CAT BA BEACHES AND ISLANDS

Woodstock Beach Camp

$ | **B&B/INN** | Not for everyone, this bohemian hangout away from the main strip provides great access to the beach and treats guests like family. **Pros:** great bay views; eclectic and outdoorsy; nightly "family dinner". **Cons:** far from Cat Ba town; high staff turnover; poorly equipped to deal with bad weather. [$] *Rooms from: d150,000* ✉ *Cat Ba Town* ☎ *0225/388–8599* 🛏 *57 rooms* 🍴 *No Meals.*

Nightlife

Oasis Bar

BARS | Nobody could ever call Cat Ba Town's nightlife sophisticated, but it can be fun. Nowhere is this more evident than at the Oasis Bar, where owner Miss Blue and her staff preside over a mixed crowd of travelers. Drinks are very reasonably priced and the food does an acceptable job of soaking them up. There's a pool table, and karaoke is available for those who fancy strutting their vocal stuff. ✉ *228 St. 1–4, Cat Ba Town* ☎ *0225/368–8298.*

⚲ Activities

A major factor in Cat Ba Island's emergence as a traveler favorite is the sheer variety of outdoor activities on offer. From trekking through the vivid-green jungle in Cat Ba National Park to kayaking among the karsts on Lan Ha Bay, the island has adventures to suit a range of tastes. Rock climbing is a particularly popular pursuit, and there are numerous routes up and down the limestone outcrops. These routes vary in grades of difficulty, making Cat Ba as suitable for beginners as it is for expert climbers.

★ Blue Swimmer Adventures

ENTERTAINMENT CRUISE | Formerly Blue Swimmer Sailing, this Cat Ba–based tour operator *has luxury boats that bring guests to remote areas in the bay. Sailing,*biking, and kayaking tours are also available. In addition, its overnight eco-junks are geared more toward budget-conscious travelers. ⊠ *237 Cai Beo Street, Cat Ba Island, Cat Ba Island* ☎ *0225/368–8237* ⊕ *www.blueswimmeradventures.com* ⊠ *Full day activities: kayaking from 990,000d.*

Bai Tu Long Bay

202 km (125 miles) east of Hanoi, 56 km (34 miles) east of Halong Bay.

The limestone outcrops that rise out of the waters of Bai Tu Long Bay are perhaps not as lofty as the ones at Halong, but the two seascapes are virtually interchangeable, and you would need to be a true karst aficionado to notice the difference. Clearly apparent, however, is the relative lack of tourists here, in comparison with its more famous next-door neighbor. The submerged limestone plateau, the geological phenomenon that gave rise to the scenic splendor in this part of the Gulf of Tonkin, continues all the way to the Chinese border and Bai Tu Long Bay is the easternmost extension of the chain. Having neglected it for years, tour operators are beginning to cash in on the bay's potential. Nevertheless, development is still in its infancy, which means largely unpolluted waters and a wealth of unexplored islands, caves, and immaculate sandy coves. Despite the area's undoubted beauty, there are some clouds on the horizon. Boat traffic may not be as heavy as it is in Halong Bay, but garbage from trawlers and from mainland Vietnam and China is a common and unsightly blight. For the most part, however, Bai Tu Long Bay, and islands such as Quan Lan, Tra Ban, and Van Don, offer a laid-back alternative to Halong Bay that makes traveling the extra distance from Hanoi worthwhile.

GETTING HERE AND AROUND

Frequent buses run between Halong City and Cai Rong bus station. The journey takes around 1½ hours and costs about 60,000d. Boat charters to the outlying islands and onto the bay can be organized from Cai Rong Pier. Costs vary depending on bargaining skills, but expect to pay at least 150,000d per hour. Daily ferries link Cai Rong with islands such as Quan Lan, Tra Ban, and Ngoc Vung. One-way fares range from 40,000d to 70,000d. There's also a slow boat to Co To, which costs 70,000 and leaves at 7 am and 1 pm, and a faster speedboat servicing Co To that departs from Cai Rong at 1 pm daily for 155,000d.

Kayaking is a popular activity in Bai Tu Long Bay.

Sights

Co To Island

ISLAND | Anchored comfortably in the aquamarine waters of the Gulf of Tonkin is the Co To Island District, the larger archipelago which homes Co To Island. Although it is the farthest inhabited island from the mainland in the Bai Tu Long archipelago, Co To is fast becoming the area's rising star. Good facilities including hotels and restaurants complement natural attractions that include sandy beaches and some impressive peaks.

Ngoc Vung Island

ISLAND | Skirting the boundary of Halong and Bai Tu Long bays, Ngoc Vung boasts dramatic limestone cliffs. There's also a very attractive sandy beach with some basic beach huts on its southern shore.

Quan Lan Island

ISLAND | Sunseekers disappointed by northern Vietnam's relative lack of good beaches will find succor at the beautiful stretch of sand at Minh Chau beach on the northeastern coast of Quan Lan. The water is too chilly for most during the winter months, while the summer months see a mass influx of Vietnamese tourists. Other points of interest on the island include a 200-year-old pagoda in Quan Lan Town. Beyond beach bumming, the main activities here include forest walks and leisurely cycling along the island's quiet byways.

Tra Ban Island

ISLAND | The largest island in Bai Tu Long Bay is also one of its wildest and most undeveloped. Thick jungle blankets the southern part of the island, while the offshore karsts are among the most impressive in the entire region. There's very little in the way of accommodations on the island beyond a few basic beach huts, so plan for a day trip rather than an overnight stay.

Van Don Island

ISLAND | The largest island in the Bai Tu Long archipelago is also its most populated and developed. Linked to the mainland by a series of bridges, the island mainly serves as a jumping-off point for the smaller, more idyllic destinations in the area. Cai Rong, the main town, is a bustling port with some acceptable accommodations options. There's not much else to see on Van Don, but the outlook to the offshore karst formations from Bai Dai (long beach) on the southern side of the island is stunning. The Vietnamese government has big plans for Van Don, with a special Economic Zone with an international airport in the pipeline.

🍴 Restaurants

Neither Cai Rong nor the outlying islands have much in the way of outstanding restaurants. Nevertheless, the Minh Chau Beach Resort on Quan Lan Island and Co To Lodge on Co To Island have very acceptable dining options. Elsewhere in the archipelago, simple eateries serve up fresh seafood to a predominantly Vietnamese crowd.

HANOI

8

Updated by
Joshua Zukas

● Sights	🍴 Restaurants	🛏 Hotels	💼 Shopping	🍸 Nightlife
★★★★★	★★★★★	★★★★★	★★★★★	★★★★★

WELCOME TO HANOI

TOP REASONS TO GO

⭐ **Embark on a cultural odyssey.** Delve into the thriving art scene at one of the city's contemporary galleries or at a museum highlighting Vietnam's rich culture and history.

⭐ **Take it to the streets.** Wander the narrow streets of Hanoi's Old Quarter, where cafés, bars, and shops spill onto the sidewalks and mobile vendors roam the streets.

⭐ **Go on a gastronomic adventure.** Appease your palate in a melting pot of meals, ranging from pho food carts with plastic stools to fancy fine dining restaurants offering the ultimate in refined service.

⭐ **Seek out the revolutionary.** Eye-catching propaganda art displayed in public and in small galleries to banner attractions such as Ho Chi Minh's mausoleum brings Hanoi's revolutionary past to life.

⭐ **Check out hip Hanoi.** From arty bars, where intellectual discourse flows as freely as red wine, to cutting-edge live music venues, the capital continues to stake its claim as Vietnam's most engaging cultural hub.

1 **The Old Quarter.** The logical starting point for most visitors, this ancient enclave bursts with amenities and attractions. After 1,000 years as one of Hanoi's main centers of commerce, the narrow streets are still alive with shops, markets, and bars.

2 **The French Quarter.** The wide avenues and graceful villas of this area present an alluring change of pace after the frenetic hubbub of the Old Quarter.

3 **Ho Chi Minh Mausoleum and Around.** Ba Dinh District is home to a variety of historic sights, both ancient and more contemporary, including Ho Chi Minh's monolithic mausoleum and the Temple of Literature.

4 **West Lake and Truc Bach Lake.** Hanoi's most upscale area, West Lake is home to some of the best dining and lodging options in the city.

5 **Side Trips From Hanoi.** Co Loa Citadel, Thay Pagoda and Tay Phuong Pagoda, Tam Dao Hill Station, Ho Chi Minh Trail Museum and the Perfume Pagoda, and Ba Vi National Park are all easy trips from Hanoi.

West Lake (Tay Ho)

0 ½ mi
0 500 m

BA DINH

Van Cao
Hoang Hoa Tham
Doi Can
Kim Ma
Giang Vo Lake
Giang Vo
Lieu Giai
La Thanh

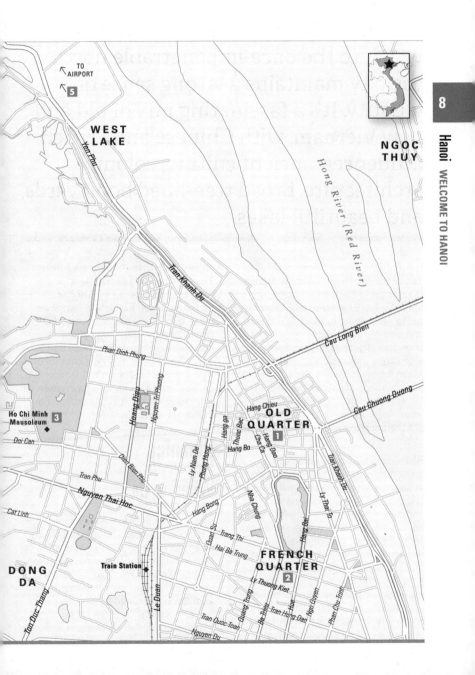

Hanoi is more than 1,000 years old, and although Western fashions, music, and food have long since elbowed their way into the once-impenetrable north, the city maintains a strong sense of identity. It's a fascinating mix of old and new Vietnam, with Chinese and French influences, ancient culture, colonial architecture, broad tree-lined boulevards, and beautiful lakes.

Full of things to see, from the architecture of the Old Quarter and the French Quarter to Ho Chi Minh's Mausoleum and the Temple of Literature, the Vietnamese capital lends itself to leisurely exploration. The city is home to one of Asia's stronger indigenous culinary traditions, with earthy markets and a rambunctious street-food culture, but also boasts a stellar range of international dining options. Hanoi is also very affordable by urban Asian standards, with the majority of hotels and restaurants offering plenty of value.

Hanoi continues to modernize at a breakneck pace. The predominant sound at an intersection was once the delicate ring of bicycle bells. Today motorcycles and cars, including luxury models such as BMWs and Bentleys, are taxing the city's antiquated road system. Like their counterparts in Ho Chi Minh City, the youth of Hanoi express themselves through an eclectic range of influences ranging from skateboard culture and envelope-pushing contemporary art to high living and luxury labels. Nonetheless, Hanoi remains a refined city of academics,

artists, diplomats—and contradictions. Timeless tableaus of "Old Asia" are easy to spot. Emerge early and you'll find old-timers practicing tai chi moves down by the banks of mist-shrouded Hoan Kiem Lake. Nearby, beret-wearing grandfathers stroke their wispy beards as they contemplate their next chess move over a cup of full-bodied Vietnamese coffee. Those looking for a city preserved in aspic won't find it in this urbane, confounding metropolis.

Planning

When to Go

In terms of weather, the ideal time to visit Hanoi is between October (with temperatures averaging 80°F) and mid-December (with temperatures ranging from the upper 60s to mid-70s), when the heat and humidity are not so oppressive. But be prepared for cold snaps and chilly nights. The brief spring from March to April is also a pleasant time.

From January to March a layer of clammy mist—the infamous *mua phun*—hovers over Hanoi. The city begins its summer swelter in May and sweats through August, when the monsoons bring heavy downpours and sudden flooding. This continues until late September, so if you choose to brave the elements at this time, bring rubber footwear and rain pants or buy them in Hanoi—you could be in it up to your knees. Temperatures range from the mid-70s to the high 90s.

FESTIVALS AND EVENTS

Tet

Late January to early February is a good time to visit if you want to breathe in the excitement of Tet, the lunar new year, a movable date based on the lunar calendar. In preparation for Vietnam's largest festival, the Old Quarter comes alive with floor-to-ceiling displays of moon cakes, red banners, joss sticks, and red envelopes for giving lucky money (*li xi*) to children. Be aware that when Tet does arrive, many shops and restaurants close for up to a week—although some restaurants and cafes have discovered the financial benefits of staying open. If you're planning to conduct any business, this is definitely not the time to do it. ✉ *Hanoi*

Pilgrimage to the Perfume Pagoda

February and March are the months to join the mass Buddhist pilgrimage to the Perfume Pagoda, but be prepared to deal with serious crowds—many thousands each day—if you make the trip during this peak season. Smaller religious festivals take place at Hanoi's temples and outlying villages in March and April. Because all Vietnamese festivals follow the lunar calendar, check online or with your tour operator for exact dates. ✉ *Hanoi*

Planning Your Time

IF YOU HAVE TWO DAYS

If you'll just be passing through, your time would be best spent exploring the Old Quarter and visiting the Ho Chi Minh Mausoleum and the adjacent museum. Since your time is limited, do as the Vietnamese do and start at the crack of dawn. Make your way down to the northern shore of **Hoan Kiem Lake** and look on as the Vietnamese limber up with tai chi routines and other exercises. You'll need some sustenance for a busy day so head to a *pho* joint for a warming bowl of Vietnam's de facto national dish. After breakfast, take a couple of hours to wander around the narrow streets of the **Old Quarter.** The sheer volume of traffic can make strolling hazardous, but it is worth the peril to experience the sights and sounds of the area. After grabbing lunch at either a smart café such as **Bancong** or **The Hanoi Social Club**, make your way to **Ba Dinh District** for a pilgrimage to **Ho Chi Minh's mausoleum** where the body of the venerated former leader of Vietnam remains on display. To find out more about his life and work, head to the nearby **Ho Chi Minh Museum**, which celebrates both the man and the onward march of revolutionary socialism. For dinner, head to one of the many contemporary restaurants in **West Lake** or **Truc Bach Lake** before going back to the Old Quarter to end a busy day with some *bia hoi*, Vietnam's legendarily cheap beer. After an action-packed first day you can afford to take things slightly easier on day two. After breakfast and some potent Vietnamese coffee, make your way to the **French Quarter** to stroll the shady tree-lined avenues and admire the lovely colonial architecture. Lunch on Vietnamese street food in a palatial setting at **Quan An Ngon** or try *cha ca*, a Hanoi specialty fish dish, at **Vua Cha Ca** before making your way back to Ba Dinh District, this time focusing on ancient relics such as the One Pillar Pagoda and the Temple of

Did You Know?

Hanoi, the capital city of Vietnam, is famously home to some of the most incredible street food in the world. You'll see vendors carrying local specialties along many bustling streets.

Literature. For another quintessentially Hanoian experience, take in an evening show at the water puppet theater before treating yourself to an upscale dinner at the **Sofitel Legend Metropole Hotel** or **Tung Dining.**

IF YOU HAVE FIVE DAYS

Five days gives you time to spread your wings beyond the obvious sights. After following the two-day itinerary, the remainder of your time can then be devoted to really exploring Hanoi's myriad nooks and crannies. Those with an interest in architecture will find it both fascinating and educational to take one of the **walking tours** organized by companies such as Hidden Hanoi. These guided explorations delve deep beyond the surface and can provide invaluable insight to everything from the unique "tube houses" in the Old Quarter to the European (and especially Gallic) influences at play in the French Quarter. Another Hanoi highlight that few short-stay visitors really have the time to get to grips with is the city's mind-blowing **street food culture.** For a comprehensive insight try one of the itineraries run by Hanoi Street Food Tours. Cultural sights beyond the big-hitters, meanwhile, include the fascinating **Vietnam Museum of Ethnology** and a growing number of contemporary art spaces. While taking it easy may seem contrary to the restless spirit of the city, there's a lot to be said for slowing down to a more leisurely pace. Enjoy the view over **Hoan Kiem Lake** from an upstairs coffee shop and spend your evening holed up in a left-field drinking den like **Tadioto** or a cocktail bar like **Leo's**. If you have a day left to spare, leave the city and take a trip out to the **Perfume Pagoda**, a complex of Buddhist temples that is one of Vietnam's most famous pilgrimage sites, or to **Ba Vi**, a national park.

Getting Here and Around

AIR

Noi Bai International Airport lies about 35 km (22 miles) north of the city. Several improvements were made to the airport in recent years that brought it up to international standards. The existing Terminal 1 was extended to encompass a new hall with a capacity for 3 million extra passengers per year. And Terminal 2, which was inaugurated in 2015, now provides capacity for 10 million passengers per year.

The somewhat arduous journey between the airport and downtown Hanoi, meanwhile, was shortened by the Nhat Tan–Noi Bai Highway, routed over the new Nhat Tan Bridge.

International airlines fly into Hanoi from other parts of Asia and also from European hubs such as Frankfurt, Paris, and London. From New York, Korean Air, Cathay Pacific, and American Airlines have daily flights to Hanoi and Ho Chi Minh City with connections in Seoul and Hong Kong. From the West Coast, similar routes connect Los Angeles and San Francisco to Vietnam. It is also possible to get flights from Australia and Canada.

Domestic destinations served from Hanoi include Danang, Dien Bien Phu, Ho Chi Minh City, Hue, Phu Quoc, and Nha Trang.

AIRPORT TRANSFERS

Vietnam Airlines has an airport shuttle located just outside the Noi Bai arrival terminal. It departs once it is full (approximately every 45 minutes) and will take you to the Vietnam Airlines office on Quang Trung in central Hanoi. It's a bit of an uncomfortable ride, but the 40,000d per person fee makes this one of the most economical options. Look for the logo on the side of the minivan. There is also a city bus, #86, which costs 30,000d per person, stops every kilometer, and finishes its route at the train station.

8

Hanoi PLANNING

A number of taxi companies operate the route between Noi Bai Airport and Hanoi city center. The largest of these is Noi Bai Taxi, which has its own parking lot at the airport. Some of these companies offer a fixed price fare for the route; others will use the meter. For a four-seat taxi the price between Noi Bai and the Old Quarter is around 300,000d. The bigger the vehicle, the higher the price.

AIRPORT CONTACTS Noi Bai International Airport. ✉ *Phu Minh, Hanoi* ☎ *04/3886–5047* ⊕ *vietnamairport.vn/noibaiairport.*

AIRPORT TRANSFER CONTACTS Noi Bai Taxi. ✉ *Hanoi* ☎ *04/326–68218* ⊕ *www. noibaiairporttaxi.org.***Vietnam Airlines Shuttle Bus.** ⊕ *www.hanoiairportshuttle.com.*

BIKE

Bikes can be rented through establishments such as Hanoi Bicycle Collective who have access to a selection of mountain and city bikes. Prices for city bikes range from 75,000d per half day to 150,000d for the full day. You can get the tires pumped up at just about any street corner for 2,000d per tire. Traffic is so congested in the Old Quarter, however, that walking is advisable.

Hanoi Bicycle Collective

While nobody would call frenetic Hanoi a cyclist's paradise, the Hanoi Bicycle Collective is doing its best to encourage the use of pedal power. As well as serving as a retail space, with several brands of bike on offer, the outlet has set itself up to become a hub of cycling life, commuting, social activity, and fitness. They can rent good quality bicycles, but make sure you call ahead. ✉ *31 Nhat Chieu, Tay Ho District* ☎ *097/817–3156* ⊕ *www.thbc.vn.*

BUS

Bus travel in Vietnam has improved immeasurably in recent times. Aside from in remote, rural destinations, public buses are generally fairly clean and comfortable. There are nine major bus stations—none of which are in the center of town—but you're likely to encounter only four of them: My Dinh, which serves the north and northwest; Gia Lam, which serves the east and northeast; Yen Nghia, which serves the southwest; and Giap Bat, which serves the south. Knowing which is the right bus station isn't straightforward, so book your bus ticket ahead of time through your hotel, direct with the bus company, or through a travel website like VeXeRe. Reputable bus companies include The Sinh Tourist and Hoang Long. Some bus companies will include transfer by minibus from your hotel to the bus station where you'll board a bigger, long-distance bus; otherwise they will specify which bus station or pick-up point you need to reach.

BUS CONTACTS Gia Lam Bus Station. ✉ *Ben Xe Gia Lam, Long Bien.***Giap Bat Bus Station.** ✉ *Km 6, Ben Xe Giap Bat, Hoang Mai.***Hoang Long Bus Company.** ✉ *28 Tran Nhat Duat, Hanoi* ☎ *024/3928–2828.* **VeXeRe.** ⊕ *vexere.com .***My Dinh Bus Station.** ✉ *20 Pham Hung, Tu Liem.***Yen Nghia Bus Station.** ✉ *Phu Lam, Dong Da District.*

CAR

As Hanoi is the largest city and a tourist hub in northern Vietnam and a major international gateway, few Western visitors actually arrive here by car. Those who do are usually coming from Ho Chi Minh City via Highway 1 or from Danang or Hue after flying there from Ho Chi Minh City. A much more common method is to tour the south by land, by car or train from Ho Chi Minh City to Hue, and then fly from there to Hanoi.

It's quite easy to arrange leaving Hanoi by car for side trips. There are any number of reputable international and local rental companies that will hire you a car and driver, and you can find them through your hotel or small travel agencies in the Old Quarter. You can count on paying around 1,000,000d per day in the city for an air-conditioned sedan and a driver. Expect to pay 1,200,000d or more per day for a minivan. You can arrange for a pickup at your hotel, although a deposit—usually 50% of the fare—is often expected. There is no need for you to leave your passport with the agency renting you the car.

FINDING YOUR WAY

Addresses in Vietnam often contain words such as district (*huyen*), road (*duong*), or street (*pho*). Odd- and even-number addresses are usually on different sides of the street. Sometimes one address is broken into several units (A, B, C, etc.).

CYCLO

Traffic in Hanoi is notorious for its chaotic mix of cars, buses, motorcycles, and bicycle rickshaws, known as cyclos.

The traditional way to explore Hanoi's Old Quarter is by cyclo. You'll feel pampered (or maybe a bit conspicuous) as you're pedaled around the bustling city on a padded tricycle. Rates start at 100,000d per hour. Tipping is not required or even expected, but giving your driver 20,000d is a nice gesture.

TAXI AND MOTORBIKE TAXI

There are several options for getting around, but taxis are generally the safest and most efficient, although a bit more expensive. Taxi scams are not uncommon, but can usually be avoided by riding only with a trusted taxi company—Mai Linh and Hanoi Taxi are two of the capital's most reputable companies.

Taxis tend to congregate at the northwest corner of Hoan Kiem Lake and outside most major hotels and shopping malls. You can also call for a cab, as all taxi dispatchers speak English.

Motorbike taxis, known as xe om, are another way to get around the city—if you're brave. Although the traffic may look a little daunting, drivers know how to navigate it.

If you decide to rent a motorbike yourself and drive around the city, keep in mind that the traffic is busy, loud, and crazy. Although the streets may be less

intimidating in Hanoi than in Ho Chi Minh City, the consensus is that drivers are worse. And visitors are paying the price: Vietnam's number one cause of injuries and death among foreigners is accidents involving a motorcycle. You can purchase an acceptable helmet at various outlets for around 500,000d. Helmets that would pass an international safety test start at 2,000,000d. Don't become a Vietnam traffic statistic—wear a good helmet.

That said, most hotels and many tour and travel agencies will find you a bike with few questions asked. Prices start at around 150,000d per day. A deposit is sometimes required, as is a passport or a photocopy, and you usually sign a short-term contract (be sure you're aware of the stipulated value of the bike in the contract). It would also be wise to consult your insurance policy; many companies refuse to cover motorcycle drivers or riders.

TAXI CONTACTS Mai Linh Taxi.
☎ *024/3833–3333* ⊕ *www.mailinh.vn.*

TRAIN

It's easiest to buy tickets at the main Hanoi train station, Ga Ha Noi, between 8 and 11 am, and between 1 and 11 pm. Another smaller train station, across the tracks from the main one, services northern routes; the foreign booking agents at the main station will direct you. Another train station, Ga Long Bien, sits buried in the Old Quarter, but is only used for getting to Haiphong.

Trains leave 10 times daily for Ho Chi Minh City but only one (SE3) is an express (32 hours). The express makes stops at most major cities, including Vinh, Hue, Danang, and Nha Trang. Purchase a day in advance if you want to ensure a seat. Other destinations include Lao Cai (two times daily; 10 hours) and Haiphong (four times daily; two hours). For the most updated train schedule and ticket fare, consult dsvn.vn. You can also book online using the website, but it may have trouble accepting an international credit card.

TRAIN CONTACT Ga Ha Noi. ⊠ *120 Le Duan, Hoan Kiem District.*

Sights

Despite being southwest of the winding Red River, Hanoi is known as a city of lakes. Daily life for much of the city centers around three of the city's many lakes: Hoan Kiem Lake, Truc Bach Lake, and the substantially larger West Lake. Hoan Kiem Lake is the undisputed heart of Hanoi and is wedged between the original city—known today as the Old Quarter—and the colonial charm of the French Quarter. Not far to the northwest of the city center, West Lake and Truc Bach Lake are where many of the booming capital's newly moneyed residents and growing expat community eat, drink, and act merrily. To fully explore Hanoi, reserve three days to visit museums, watch theater productions, stroll through the Old Quarter, and find bargains at the city's shops and markets. Tack on a day or two for a side trip to Halong Bay or to Mai Chau or Ninh Binh.

Hanoi is divided into several districts, or *quan*, but most visitors only visit four of them: Hoan Kiem, Hai Ba Trung, Ba Dinh, and West Lake.

The **Hoan Kiem District,** named after the lake at its center, stretches from the railway tracks to the Red River, north of Nguyen Du Street, and is the hub of all local and tourist activity. Just north of the lake is the **Old Quarter,** a charming cluster of ancient streets. South of the lake you'll find the modern city center, part of the **French Quarter,** which houses grand colonial-style villas that have been converted into restaurants and offices; the best examples of French-era architecture are around Dien Bien Phu and Le Hong Phong Streets, where embassies line the road.

The **Ba Dinh District** includes the zoo, the **Ho Chi Minh Mausoleum,** and other big attractions such as the Temple of Literature and the One Pillar Pagoda. Northwest of both Ba Dinh and Hoan Kiem is picturesque **West Lake** (Tay Ho District) with its wide range of dining venues, bars, and luxury hotels.

Outside these districts are other areas of interest. The **Hai Ba Trung District,** which covers the southeast part of Hanoi and largely encompasses the French Quarter, is a calm, elegant residential area; one of the primary attractions here is Thong Nhat Park, in the northwest corner of the district.

Restaurants

From curbside feasts on Lilliputian plastic chairs to superb fine dining, Hanoi's restaurant scene has something for everyone. Locals are fiercely proud of their street food culture and this is where the essence of Hanoi's food scene can be discovered. Signature northern dishes include bun cha (vermicelli with minced pork burgers), banh cuon (steamed rice rolls stuffed with minced pork, mushrooms, and shallots), and the ubiquitous pho, Vietnam's nominal national dish, which comes in chicken and beef varieties. These classics represent just a tantalizing taste of what is on offer in the city. And with a seemingly endless array of vendors slaving over hot grills, simmering alchemy in large pots, or doling out pillow-soft steamed buns from a ramshackle cart, opportunities to eat like a local are limitless. In the past, Hanoi's restaurant sector has suffered in comparison to its kingly street dining scene. That has changed significantly over the past decade or so. There is now an eclectic selection of interesting (and often excellent) eating spots that run the gamut from simple French bistros and laid-back cafés to opulent venues for multicourse blowouts and cutting-edge options that would not be out of place in the world's major gastronomic hubs.

What it Costs			
$	**$$**	**$$$**	**$$$$**
RESTAURANTS			
Under 70,000d	70,000d–270,000d	271,000d–400,000d	over 400,000d

Hotels

If there is one thing Hanoi is not short of, it's places to stay. In the Old Quarter, small family-run hotels rule the roost. While many of these remain fairly basic affairs, there has been real movement in the mid- to high-end sector. Many of the more salubrious establishments bill themselves as "boutique hotels." For Westerners used to this sobriquet referring to individualist, design-led options, the term may feel like a misnomer given the relative uniformity of most of what is on offer. Nevertheless, with opulent marble-clad lobbies coupled with excellent, personal service, and smart and luxurious bedrooms, there is little to fault about many of these places. Outside the Old Quarter, some of the biggest international hotel brands have made their mark. The leafy avenues of the area south of Hoan Kiem Lake shelter some sterling lodgings, including the city's undisputed grande dame, the Sofitel Legend Metropole. West Lake, Ba Dinh, and even some outlying areas such as Tu Liem, an enclave mooted as the city's new central business district, are also home to some excellent international-standard options.

For expanded reviews, visit Fodors.com.

What It Costs			
$	**$$**	**$$$**	**$$$$**
HOTELS			
Under 750,000d	750,000d–1,000,000d	1,100,000d–2,500,000d	over 2,500,000d

Nightlife

Hanoi has enough bars and clubs to keep you busy. They range from low-key drinking venues to more pleasant spots with extensive wine lists to raucous places where loud house music and cheap drinks keep dancers on the floor. Because many ventures are short-lived—Hanoi's nightclubs are curiously prone to electrical fires and other mysterious disasters—it is wise to call ahead when possible. For something a bit more casual, head to one of the cafés or bars in the Old Quarter, where rooftop lounges, cocktail bars, and the popular *bia hoi* beer corner cluster about in a historical setting. Upscale hotels tend to have swanky bars of their own with live jazz to accompany a dry martini. For a mellow vibe and drinks with a view, you can go to waterfront bars near West Lake. Head into town early for happy hour since most joints close by midnight.

Performing Arts

Hanoi's performing-arts legacy is impressive. As in Europe, the emperors often kept acting guilds and musicians in or around the Imperial Palace. Roving drama and musical troupes entertained citizens in the countryside. The arrival of the French and the 20th century saw an explosion of theater culture in the capital, the lingering remnants of which can be experienced at a handful of small drama houses that host troupes performing traditional folk arts.

Tuong is a classical art form developed in central Vietnam. It uses very few stage props, and the actors must conform to age-old rules of behavior concerning their specific characters. Content usually focuses on Vietnamese legends, and music is minimal. The northern folk art known as *cheo* is more of a "people's opera," incorporating both comic and tragic elements. Music and singing are prominent, as cheo developed into a loud and lively art form in order to outdo the noise and distractions of the marketplace where it was originally performed.

Cai luong, the "renovated opera" that emerged in the early 20th century, is more similar to Western dramas and operas than other Vietnamese styles. Music and singing are an important feature of these performances. Although cai luong is a southern creation, the form has endeared itself to Hanoians. The Hanoi theaters listed below stage productions; none prints schedules in English, so call or drop by the theater to see if there's something on for an evening when you're in town.

In its musical theaters and diverse nightlife, Hanoi's cultural allure comes alive when the sun goes down. Productions showcasing traditional music and theater are a great way to delve into the spirit of Vietnam. With the multimillion-dollar restoration of the Opera House in the late 1990s, Hanoi's performing-arts scene reemerged. The imposing French-built arts palace hosts Vietnam's top traditional musicians and pop stars as well as the occasional Western performer. Elsewhere in the city, you can catch a performance of Vietnamese folk opera, traditional music, or enchanting water puppetry.

Shopping

Whether they're selling clothing, pottery, silks, or souvenirs, shops in Hanoi can do some serious damage to your spending account. Tackle your wish list in the Old Quarter, where 40 streets offer every type of product imaginable, and then some. This fashion hub is a good place to find silk dresses and skirts, and if you can't find what you're looking for, a local tailor will certainly offer to create something for you. Hanoi is a good place to pick up a traditional *ao dai,* as many local women still wear these fitted silk tunics that drape over elegant pants. Throughout the city are galleries and shops selling ceramics, lacquer and silk paintings, and traditional embroidery.

Souvenir shops are easy to come by, with the best ones located in the Old Quarter and near the Temple of Literature. When buying art in Vietnam, be careful of fakes. Paintings by Vietnam's most famous painters—Bui Xuan Phai, Nguyen Tu Nghiem, and Le Thiet Cuong—are the most widely copied. Serious art collectors should consult the well-respected high-end galleries.

It's possible to have clothes made to order with enough time—one day to three weeks, depending on what you want made and the tailor's schedule. You may also need to return a couple of times to have the clothes fitted.

Tours

Reputable tour operators based in Hanoi provide detailed itineraries (often tailor-made to individual requirements), visitor information, transportation and hotel bookings, car and bus rentals, guided tours, private tour guides, and visa extensions. These companies can organize everything from an extended itinerary in northern Vietnam to shorter excursions to nearby highlights such as Ninh Binh, Halong Bay, Mai Chau, and Sapa. Types of tours, meanwhile, range from adventure to luxury and cultural tourism. Within Hanoi itself, these companies as well as a growing number of boutique operators run by local and foreign enthusiasts, can organize specialty excursions such as detailed investigations into the city's amazing street food culture, markets, and architectural heritage.

CONTACTS Handspan Travel Indochina. ⊠ *78 Ma May St., Hoan Kiem District* ☎ *024/3926–2828* ⊕ *www.handspan. com.* **Hanoi Backstreet Tours.** ⊠ *3B Hang Tre, Hoan Kiem District* ☎ *097/215–8383*

⊕ *www.hanoibackstreettours.com.*
Hanoi Street Food Tour. ⊠ *74–76 Hang Bac St., Hoan Kiem District* ⚐ *Kim's Tours Bldg.* ☎ *096/696–0188 cell phone* ⊕ *www.hanoistreetfoodtour.com.***Hidden Hanoi.** ⊠ *147 Nghi Tam, Tay Ho District* ☎ *098/724–0480 cell phone* ⊕ *hiddenhanoi.vn.***Exotic Voyages.** ⊠ *33B Pham Ngu Lao, Hoan Kiem District* ☎ *888/497–0068* ⊕ *www.exoticvoyages.com.*

Essentials

HEALTH AND SAFETY

International clinics in Hanoi offer the highest quality care but also cost more. Local hospitals are not quite up to the standards of Thailand, Hong Kong, or Singapore, but they are decent and often employ doctors who have been trained overseas, typically in France.

Temperatures in Hanoi can get extremely hot, with average daytime temperatures in late spring and summer exceeding 100 degrees Fahrenheit —drink plenty of water and use common sense to avoid dehydration and heat stroke. Sunscreen is also highly recommended. Dengue fever is a real risk in Vietnam; if not taking a prophylaxis, make sure to use mosquito repellent.

Hanoi is a generally safe city, and a little common sense should keep you out of harm's way. Traffic accidents are not uncommon in Vietnam's cities and towns—take care crossing the street. Pickpockets and thieves are an issue—keep an eye on personal belongings especially in public and avoid ostentatious displays of wealth. Bar areas can be less safe late at night compared to other parts of Hanoi.

Vietnamese usually will not initiate conflicts with foreign visitors, but if challenged they may resort to violence as a means for solving an argument. As an Asian tonal language, Vietnamese can sound aggressive to Western ears—keep in mind that someone might sound like they're angry when they're not. On the whole, the Vietnamese are usually friendly to visitors, though, many see no problem whatsoever in charging foreigners more for goods or services. There is no foolproof way to avoid being overcharged from time to time. Make sure that prices are as clear as possible before making a purchase, and ride only in taxis with meters. When booking a tour, clarify what's included in the price.

MONEY MATTERS

ATMs—many in international banks—are easy to find throughout Hanoi. U.S. dollars are the preferred currency of exchange, but other major currencies are easy to change at banks, exchange kiosks, and hotels.

Vendors or small businesses in the countryside surrounding Hanoi will frequently not have change for a 500,000d note (a common denomination issued at ATMs). Make sure you have plenty of small change on hand. Credit card transactions often involve additional surcharges, usually around 3%.

Visitor Information

The privately run Tourist Information Center can arrange tours and is a good resource for maps. They also offer free walking tours with students around the Old Quarter.

CONTACT Tourist Information Center.
⊠ *28 Hang Dau, Hoan Kiem District* ☎ *094/133–6677* ⊕ *www.north-vietnam.com.*

Hoan Kiem Lake is shrouded in myth and legend (and it's a great place to catch sunset).

The Old Quarter

Hoan Kiem Lake, Long Bien Bridge, a former city rampart, and a citadel wall surround the oldest part of Hanoi. The area was unified under Chinese rule, when ramparts were built to encircle the city. When Vietnam gained its independence from China in the 11th century, King Ly Thai To built his palace here, and the area developed as a crafts center. Artisans were attracted from all over the northern part of the country and formed cooperative living and working situations based on specialized trades and village affiliation. In the 13th century the various crafts—silversmiths, metalworkers, potters, carpenters, and so on—organized themselves into official guilds.

This area is referred to as the 36 Streets, though there are actually nearly 70. To this day many of the streets are still named after the crafts practiced by the original guilds, and most maintain their individual character despite the encroachment of more modern lifestyles. Note the slim buildings called "tunnel" or "tube" houses—with narrow frontage but deceiving depth—that combine workshops and living quarters. They were built this way because each business was taxed according to the width of its storefront. In addition to the specialty shops you'll still find here, each street has religious structures reflecting the beliefs of the village from which its original guilds came. Some are temples dedicated to the patron saint of a particular craft. Hang Bong and Hang Dao, for example, each have five of these pagodas and small temples. Many are open to the public and provide welcome relief from the intensity of the streets.

◉ Sights

★ Bia Hoi Corner

BREWERY | For some in-your-face Vietnamese chaos, venture into Hanoi's lively Old Quarter, home to cheap eats, authentic cuisine, and the *bia hoi* corner, where fresh beer is less than 50 cents a pint. The hub of this brew haven is at the intersection of Luong Ngoc Quyen and Ta Hien Streets, where you pull up a mini plastic chair and sit to watch Hanoi in action. ⊠ *Near Hoan Kiem Lake, Hoan Kiem District* ✣ *at Luong Ngoc Quyen and Ta Hien Sts.*

Dong Xuan Market

MARKET | Once conveniently accessible by riverboat, this market, the oldest and largest in the city, has seen trading with the whole of Southeast Asia. The huge structure was destroyed by a massive fire in 1994. The fire displaced 3,000 workers, caused millions of dollars in damage and losses, and took five human lives, not to mention the lives of thousands of endangered animals. The market reopened in December 1996 and today looks more like a concrete shopping mall, but continues to sell all manner of local and foreign goods. In truth, the standard of what's on offer is variable. Clothes and other miscellanea are of poor quality. Nevertheless, the atmosphere is buzzing and very much local, making this an authentic market experience. ⊠ *Dong Xuan and Hang Chieu Sts., Hoan Kiem District.*

Hang Bac Street

STREET | Hang Bac means "Street of Silver," which explains why silversmiths, jewelry shops, and money changers have dominated this strip for centuries. The Dong Cac jewelers' guild was established here in 1428, and it later erected a temple (now gone) in tribute to three 6th-century brothers whose skills, learned from the Chinese, made them the patron saints of Vietnamese jewelry. ⊠ *Hang Bac St., Hanoi.*

Hang Gai Street

STREET | The Street of Hemp now sells a variety of goods, including ready-made silk, lovely embroidery, and silver products. With plenty of art galleries, crafts stores, and souvenirs, this is a popular spot for tourists. Many trendy boutiques also line Hang Trong, which runs perpendicular to Hang Gai. ⊠ *Hang Gai, Hoan Kiem District.*

★ Hang Ma Street

STREET | Here you can find delicate paper replicas of material possessions made to be burned in tribute to one's ancestors. Expect traditional offerings, like paper money and gold (currency of the afterlife), but also modern objects, such as replica iPhones, laptops, air-conditioning units, and karaoke machines. Hang Ma is also where Hanoians go to buy decorations, so it routinely erupts in the colors of the approaching holiday: red and gold before Tet; orange and black before halloween; and red and green before Christmas. ⊠ *Hang Ma St., Hoan Kiem District.*

Hang Quat Street

STREET | Shops along the Street of Fans sell a stunning selection of religious paraphernalia, including beautiful funeral and festival flags, porcelain Buddhas, and lacquered Chinese poem boards. Giant plane trees shade the street, which is bookended by Berry Temple (Den Dau) and a traditional wooden house honoring Vietnamese soldiers (Nha Tuong Niem Liet Si). Shooting off the street is To Tich, an alley bursting with bright, lacquered water puppets, rattan and bamboo baskets, porcelain and ceramics. If you can pull your attention away from all the eye-grabbing street-level sights, above you'll discover the timeworn facades of several French colonial teahouses. ⊠ *Hang Quat St., Hoan Kiem District.*

Heritage House (*Ngoi Nha*)

HISTORIC HOME | On the southern edge of the Old Quarter's Street of Rattan stands a Chinese-style house built at the end of the 19th century. A rich dark-wood facade fronts a sparsely decorated interior. Exquisitely carved chairs, bureaus, and tea tables decorate the second floor, where a balcony overlooks a courtyard festooned with Chinese lanterns. A Chinese family that sold traditional medicines on the ground floor originally

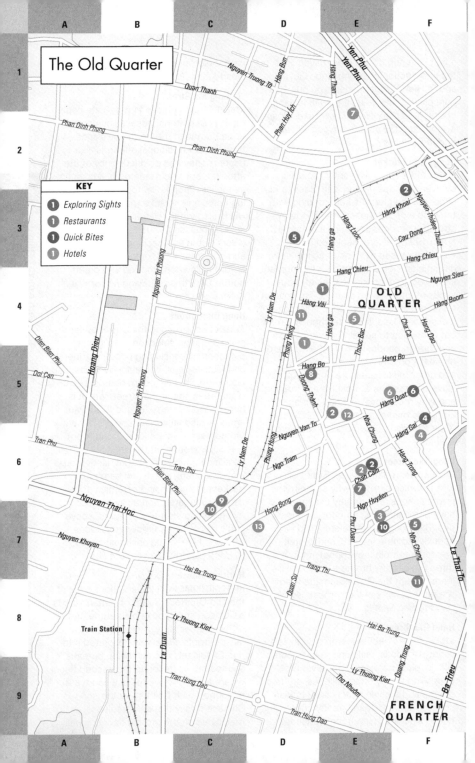

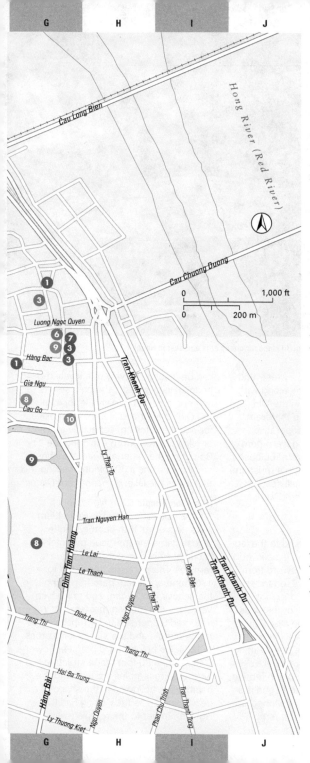

Sights ▾

1 Bia Hoi Corner G4
2 Dong Xuan Market F3
3 Hang Bac Street G5
4 Hang Gai Street F5
5 Hang Ma Street D3
6 Hang Quat Street F5
7 Heritage House G4
8 Hoan Kiem Lake G7
9 Ngoc Son Temple G6
10 St. Joseph's Cathedral E7

Restaurants ▾

1 Banh Cuon Thanh Van E4
2 Bun Bo Nam Bo
  Bach Phuong E5
3 Green Farm Restaurant G4
4 Hanoi Social Club D7
5 Mediterraneo F7
6 New Day G4
7 Ngoam E6
8 Pho Bat Dan D5
9 Puku C7
10 Salt n Pepper Kitchen C7
11 TUNG Dining F8

Quick Bites ▾

1 Bancong G5
2 Loading T E6
3 Nola Café G5

Hotels ▾

1 Calypso Premier Hotel D4
2 Camellia Hanoi Hotel E6
3 Cinnamon Hotel Hanoi E7
4 Family Holiday Hotel F6
5 Golden Art Hotel E4
6 Golden Sun Suites F5
7 Hanoi 3B Hotel E2
8 Hanoi La Selva G5
9 La Siesta Classic Ma May G5
10 La Siesta Premium Cau Go G5
11 Olympus Old Quarter Hotel D4
12 Serene Premier Hotel E5
13 Silk Path Hotel Hanoi D7

Frenetic Bia Hoi Corner is the ultimate place for cheap eats and beer in Hanoi.

occupied this house until they resettled in 1954 in southern Vietnam, along with many other Chinese living in the Old Quarter. It's hard to imagine that from 1954 until 1999, when a cooperative venture between the local government and a group of architects from Toulouse, France, turned the house into a museum, five families shared this small space. ⊠ *87 Ma May St., Hoan Kiem District* 🖅 *10,000d.*

★ Hoan Kiem Lake

PROMENADE | This lake is linked to the legend of Emperor Le Loi, who is believed to have received a magical sword from the gods, which he in turn used to repel Chinese invaders. Afterward a giant turtle reclaimed the sword for the gods from Le Loi as he boated on Hoan Kiem Lake, which derives its name ("returned sword") from the story. The sword-lifting turtle is commemorated by the lake's distinctive Turtle Tower. Ngoc Son Temple on the island at the lake's north end is a tribute to Vietnam's defeat of Mongolian forces in the 13th century. The temple

can be reached by way of a lovely red bridge. History aside, the park serves as an important part of daily life for locals in the Old Quarter and is a pleasant place for people-watching, especially at dawn, or taking a break from exploring the city. Bordering the water are park benches, small cafés, and a 30-minute walking trail that loops the lake. ⊠ *Hoan Kiem District.*

Ngoc Son Temple (*Den Ngoc Son*)

TEMPLE | On Jade Island in Hoan Kiem Lake, this quiet 18th-century shrine, whose name means "jade mountain," is one of Hanoi's most picturesque temples. This shrine is dedicated to 13th-century military hero Tran Hung Dao, the scholar Van Xuong, and to Nguyen Van Sieu, a Confucian master who assumed responsibility for repairs made to the temple and the surrounding areas in 1864. He helped build both Pen Tower (Thap But), a 30-foot stone structure whose tip resembles a brush, and the nearby rock hollowed in the shape of a peach, known as the Writing Pad (Dai Nghien). To get to the temple, walk through Three-Passage Gate (Tam Quan) and across the Flood of Morning Sunlight Bridge (Can The Huc). The island temple opens onto a small courtyard and in the pagoda's anteroom is a 6-foot-long stuffed tortoise that locals pulled from Hoan Kiem Lake in 1968. ⊠ *Dinh Tien Hoang, Hoan Kiem District* ☎ *20,000d.*

St. Joseph's Cathedral (*Nha Tho Lon*)

CHURCH | The imposing square towers of this cathedral rise up from a small square near Hoan Kiem Lake on the edge of the Old Quarter. French missionaries built the cathedral in the late 19th century and celebrated the first Mass here on Christmas Day 1886. It feels as though nothing has changed since then—the liturgy has not been modernized since the cathedral was built. The small but beautiful panes of stained glass were created in Paris in 1906. Also of note is the ornate altar, with its high gilded side walls. The government closed down the cathedral in 1975, but when it reopened 10 years later the number of returning devotees was substantial. ⊠ *40 Nha Chung St., Hoan Kiem District.*

🍴 Restaurants

★ Banh Cuon Thanh Van

$ | VIETNAMESE | This simple eatery compensates for its lack of sophistication with giant-size portions of the delicate banh cuon, steamed rice rolls stuffed with ground pork and chopped wood-ear mushrooms. Watch the resident cooks painstakingly roll out their sheets of rice noodle and spoon on the filling and feel your mouth start to water. **Known for:** freshly made banh cuon; local favorite; laid-back eating. $ *Average main: d50,000* ⊠ *12 Hang Ga, Hoan Kiem District* ▤ *No credit cards.*

★ Bun Bo Nam Bo Bach Phuong

$ | VIETNAMESE | This venue is spotlessly clean, and despite its popularity with tourists is still very much the real deal. Like all the best restaurants purveying local favorites, this place specializes in one dish only: *bun bo nam bo* (a southern beef and noodle dish). **Known for:** local favorite; generous portions of their signature dish; southern style cuisine. $ *Average main: d60,000* ⊠ *67 Hang Dieu St., Hoan Kiem District* ☎ *0243/923–0701* ▤ *No credit cards.*

Green Farm Restaurant

$$ | VIETNAMESE | This restaurant has plenty of gluten-free options and specializes in cooking classes. They operate two farms near Hanoi and grow most of their own food. **Known for:** reliable, if not exceptional, Vietnamese food; special dishes served inside whole fresh coconuts; well-priced cooking excursions. $ *Average main: d220,000* ⊠ *44B Dao Duy Tu, Hoan Kiem District* ☎ *091/640–0858.*

★ Hanoi Social Club

$$ | CAFÉ | The main draw here is the convivial, bohemian atmosphere. Housed in a stunning 1920s French-colonial villa in a quiet part of the Old Quarter, the café is rustic and warm, with original tiles, wooden furnishings, and high ceilings. **Known for:** live shows; laksa; hip decor. $ *Average main: d180,000* ⊠ *6 Hoi Vu St., Hoan Kiem District* ☎ *024/3938–2117.*

Mediterraneo

$$$ | ITALIAN | Delicious Italian food is served in this dim and romantic brick eatery in front of the cathedral. Along with exemplary bruschetta (toasted bread with olive oil and various toppings) and homemade pastas, the Italian hosts serve excellent cappuccinos, Napoli-style thin-crust pizzas cooked in a wood-burning oven, and interesting grappas—try licorice or peach. **Known for:** one of Hanoi's longest-running international restaurants; some tables have views of the church; authentic Italian. $ *Average main: d380,000* ⊠ *23 Nha Tho St., Hoan Kiem District, Hanoi* ☎ *024/3826–6288.*

New Day

$$ | VIETNAMESE | Popular with tourists and native Hanoians alike, this is one of the few restaurants in the Old Quarter that manages to unite the two demographics. There is an à la carte menu as well as set menus, but locals usually prefer to go for the "popular" dishes, which involves pointing at steaming vats containing things such as noodle soup, eggplants with salt, and fried pork ribs. **Known for:** efficient service; an enormous menu; excellent ribs. $ *Average main: d100,000* ⊠ *72 Ma May, Hoan Kiem District* ☎ *0243/828–0315.*

Ngoam

$$ | BURGER | This burger joint is a hit with worldly locals, who sit in the trendy dining rooms and chomp on artisanal French fries and what are probably Hanoi's best burgers. *Ngoam* loosely translates as "to open your mouth as wide as possible" and is therefore a fitting name for a place that serves tall burgers packed with delicious add-ons. **Known for:** kombucha soft drinks; creative wagyu beef burgers; cool and friendly staff. $ *Average main: d150,000* ⊠ *19 Chan Cam, Hoan Kiem District* ☎ *092/222–9898.*

★ Pho Bat Dan

$ | VIETNAMESE | When it comes to street food, Hanoians don't go in for much ostentation and the eating area here is decidedly prosaic; just a few communal tables under a couple of bare lightbulbs. What matters is the expertly judged broth, the light rice noodles, and the delicious meat, which is peeled in strips from hulking slabs of brisket then dunked in the broth for seconds to cook. **Known for:** best beef pho in town; lines out the door; communal dining. $ *Average main: d50,000* ⊠ *49 Bat Dan St., Hoan Kiem District* ▭ *No credit cards.*

Puku

$$ | CAFÉ | Open around the clock, Puku is nothing if not convenient. The international fare served won't have gourmands forming an orderly queue, but the quality

is decent. **Known for:** 24-hour dining; lots of egg and breakfast options; sports broadcasts. $ *Average main: d150,000* ⊠ *16-18 Tong Duy Tan St., Hoan Kiem District* ☎ *0243/938–1745.*

Salt n Pepper Kitchen

$$ | AUSTRALIAN | This is the place for comfort food, with a fabulous brunch menu, crunchy salads, tasty burgers, and good coffee, all in relaxed and convivial setting. The restaurant is staffed by youthful locals, many of whom are students, who speak good English and know how to deliver natural, personable service. **Known for:** coffee and smoothies; youthful energy; killer brunches. $ *Average main: d200,000* ⊠ *28 Tong Duy Tan, Hoan Kiem District* ☎ *033/432–1818 cell phone.*

★ TUNG Dining

$$$$ | CONTEMPORARY | One of only two restaurants in Vietnam to feature in Asia's 100 Best Restaurants in 2021 (the other being Anan in Ho Chi Minh City), TUNG Dining offers an astonishing fine-dining experience. Head chef and owner Hoang Tung worked in various Michelin star restaurants in Scandinavia before returning to his home city of Hanoi, and his experience is reflected in both the cuisine and the minimalist decor. **Known for:** superb and creative cuisine; fabulous wine; chic Scandi design. $ *Average main: d1,800,000* ⊠ *2C Pho Quang Trung, Hoan Kiem District* ☎ *085/993–3970* ⊕ *www. tungdining.com* ⊗ *Closed Mon.*

🍴 Coffee and Quick Bites

★ Bancong

$$ | ECLECTIC | Bancong means "balcony" in Vietnamese (from the French *balcon*), and this multistory 1940s art deco mansion has plenty of them. The outdoor spaces overflow with flowers and pot plants, and make good spots to watch scenes of the Old Quarter unfold below. **Known for:** historic architecture; iced coconut coffee; good bun cha. $ *Average* *main: d130,000* ✉ *2 Dinh Liet, Hoan Kiem District.*

Loading T

$ | CAFÉ | Loading T won fame in 2017 when CNN featured their egg coffee, a unique cinnamon-infused take on the Hanoi specialty drink. The cafe is notable for its extraordinary architecture; it sits within a grand colonial-era house that was appropriated and partitioned by the government in the 1950s. **Known for:** family-run; egg coffee; fresh juice. [$] *Average main: d40,000* ✉ *8 Chan Cam, Up the stairs and to the left, Hoan Kiem District* ☎ *090/334–2000 cell phone* 💳 *No credit cards.*

Nola Café

$$ | CAFÉ | Down a hidden alley in the Old Quarter, this quirky, three-tiered Hanoi hot spot has a rooftop terrace popular with travelers. Choose from a variety of coffees, teas, cocktails, and small bites. **Known for:** traveler favorite; hip decor; good bar day or night. [$] *Average main: d75000* ✉ *Alley 89 Ma May, Hanoi* ☎ *097/773–8835* ☞ *No credit cards.*

Hotels

Calypso Premier Hotel

$$$ | HOTEL | One of the Old Quarter's many boutique options, this small hotel offers a fair quotient of refinement for a relatively low price. **Pros:** some rooms have views of the leafy street; prices are very reasonable; close to Hanoi's famous train street. **Cons:** the red color scheme can be overwhelming; no lunch or dinner on site. [$] *Rooms from: d1,000,000* ✉ *27A Cua Dong, Hoan Kiem District* ☎ *024/3923–4070* 🛏 *20 rooms* 🍴 *Free Breakfast.*

Camellia Hanoi Hotel

$ | HOTEL | This well-run, well-maintained hotel in the thick of the Old Quarter has clean, bright rooms and friendly staff. **Pros:** great street life; elevator; excellent cafes nearby. **Cons:** no food; too basic for some. [$] *Rooms from: d500,000* ✉ *12C Chan Cam St., Hoan Kiem District, Hanoi* ☎ *024/3828–5936* 🛏 *17 rooms* 🍴 *No Meals.*

Cinnamon Hotel Hanoi

$$$ | HOTEL | A small boutique hotel located right next to the cathedral, this location wows with extremely high ceilings, elaborate wicker light fixtures, and detailed tile bathrooms. **Pros:** big rooms; prime location; street-facing rooms have balconies. **Cons:** rear rooms a little boxy; bells and church services can be loud. [$] *Rooms from: d1,600,000* ✉ *26 Au Trieu, Hoan Kiem District* ☎ *096/138–3416 cell phone* 🌐 *www.cinnamonhotel.net* 🛏 *10 rooms* 🍴 *Free Breakfast.*

Family Holiday Hotel

$ | HOTEL | Immaculate and homey all at once, the Family Holiday Hotel is just off Le Thai To Street, a short skip from Hoan Kiem Lake. **Pros:** just a few steps from Hoan Kiem Lake; rooms are airier than many Hanoi hotels; few rooms means personalized service. **Cons:** it's beginning to show its age; floor tiles can be a little chilly in the colder months. [$] *Rooms from: d500,000* ✉ *34 Hang Hanh St., Hoan Kiem District, Hanoi* ☎ *024/3823–2222* 🌐 *www.familyholidayhotel.com* 🍴 *Free Breakfast* 🛏 *11 rooms.*

★ Golden Art Hotel

$$$ | HOTEL | In one of the quieter Old Quarter streets, this small but lovely option provides a peaceful refuge from the bustle found elsewhere. **Pros:** attentive service; fantastic views from upper level rooms; quiet location. **Cons:** breakfast is on the simple side; nothing particularly arty about it. [$] *Rooms from: d1,365,000* ✉ *6A Hang But, Hoan Kiem District* ☎ *024/3923–4294* 🌐 *www.goldenarthotel.com* 🛏 *25 rooms* 🍴 *Free Breakfast.*

Golden Sun Suites

$$ | HOTEL | Conveniently located a stone's throw from Hoan Kiem Lake, the newest addition to the family-run Golden Sun chain is within easy walking distance of major attractions in the area. **Pros:** regularly replenished fresh flowers; excellent customer service; feels modern and fresh. **Cons:** some rooms are compact. [$] *Rooms from: d1,030,000* ✉ *35 Hang Quat, Hoan Kiem District* ☎ *078/759–0333* 🌐 *www.goldensunsuites.com* 🍴 *Free Breakfast* 🛏 *35 rooms.*

Hanoi La Selva

$ | **HOTEL** | An adorable hotel with impeccable service, the Hanoi La Selva is a great addition to the hospitality scene in Hanoi. **Pros:** reasonable prices; good location; friendly staff. **Cons:** some rooms don't have windows; fake grass in the hallways is a bit over the top; mediocre restaurant. [$] *Rooms from: d700,000* ✉ *57 Lo Su, Hanoi* ☎ *024/3266–8965* 🌐 *www.hanoilaselvahotel.com* 🛏 *20 rooms* 🍴 *Free Breakfast.*

Hanoi 3B Hotel

$ | **HOTEL** | Located just outside of the Old Quarter's center of gravity, this hotel offers serious bang for your buck. **Pros:** close to Long Bien market and Truc Bach; palatial lodgings at affordable prices; staff can help organize tours. **Cons:** surrounding restaurants aren't tourist friendly; local neighborhood won't be for everyone. [$] *Rooms from: d550,000* ✉ *20 Hong Phuc St., Hoan Kiem District* ☎ *024/3935–1080* 🍴 *Free Breakfast* 🛏 *18 rooms.*

La Siesta Classic Ma May

$$$$ | **HOTEL** | The original La Siesta is a very comfortable hotel with fine attention to detail. **Pros:** excellent breakfasts; wonderful service; diverse room configurations, including duplexes. **Cons:** Ma May can feel overwhelmed with tourists sometimes; rooms facing Ma May can be noisy. [$] *Rooms from: d3,000,000* ✉ *94 Ma May, Hoan Kiem District* ☎ *024/3926–3641* 🌐 *lasiestahotels.vn/mamay* 🍴 *Free Breakfast* 🛏 *75 rooms.*

★ **La Siesta Premium Cau Go**

$$$ | **HOTEL** | La Siesta is Hanoi's most successful boutique hotel brand, and with large rooms, an excellent location, and a fabulous sky bar, La Siesta Premium Cau Go is the best of the bunch. **Pros:** excellent food; dedicated staff; lovely location. **Cons:** city-facing rooms can be loud. [$] *Rooms from: d1,340,000* ✉ *1 Cau Go, Hoan Kiem District* ☎ *024/3938–0963* 🌐 *lasiestahotels.vn/caugo* 🍴 *Free Breakfast* 🛏 *27 rooms. .*

Olympus Old Quarter Hotel

$$$ | **HOTEL** | It's hard to find fault with this cheery minihotel. **Pros:** rooms are clean and bright; the friendly staff speak great English; very close to city center. **Cons:**; breakfast offerings could be improved. [$] *Rooms from: d1,550,000* ✉ *113 Phung Hung, Hoan Kiem District, Hanoi* ☎ *091/150–3113* 🛏 *12 rooms* 🍴 *Free Breakfast.*

Serene Premier Hotel

$$$ | **B&B/INN** | Serene might not be a word you would immediately associate with busy Hanoi, but the young and attentive staff here go out of their way to ensure a peaceful and stress-free stay in the city. **Pros:** smartly designed rooms; staff can help organize tours. **Cons:**; tucked away location can be hard for taxis to find. [$] *Rooms from: d1,240,000* ✉ *10 Yen Thai St., Hoan Kiem District* ☎ *097/219–9262* 🛏 *14 rooms* 🍴 *Free Breakfast.*

Silk Path Hotel Hanoi

$$$ | **HOTEL** | The Silk Path Hotel Hanoi was the Old Quarter's first four-star hotel, and it still gets high marks for service. **Pros:** easy transfer to La Siesta in Hue and Sapa; long-standing favorite; hand-printed wallpaper and artistic touches in each room. **Cons:** the busy outside street isn't the most charming Old Quarter spot; several rooms have internal windows that look into hallways. [$] *Rooms from: d1,760,000* ✉ *195–199 Hang Bong, Hoan Kiem District* ☎ *024/3266–5555* 🌐 *silkpathhotel.com* 🛏 *106 rooms* 🍴 *Free Breakfast.*

Ⓨ Nightlife

BARS AND PUBS

Highway 4

BARS | More of a restaurant than a bar but still good for evening drinks, this stylish spot specializes in Vietnamese rice wine, which is sometimes used in traditional medicines. The liquor, sold under the restaurant's own Son Tinh brand, is quite strong, so avoid drinking it on an empty stomach. Their other locations, such as the one at 25 Bat Su, are much larger and cater to groups. Bring your game face and try the insect dishes and creative rice wine cocktails. ⊠ *5 Hang Tre St., Hoan Kiem District, Hanoi* ☎ *024/3926–4200.*

★ Leo's

COCKTAIL LOUNGES | Hanoi is becoming somewhat of a cocktail bar hub, as demonstrated by Leo's, which opened in 2020. The bar is small, cozy, packed with locals, and boasts one of the most creative menus in the city. There is occasional live music, too. It's wise to make a booking on any evening. ⊠ *16 Lo Su, Hoan Kiem District* ☎ *033/635–6965.*

★ Ne Cocktail Bar

COCKTAIL LOUNGES | Ne is famous for its signature cocktails and luxurious atmosphere. The bartenders are professional and they take presentation seriously, so grab a seat at the bar for the full experience. The pho cocktail does not disappoint, and the blues and jazz will go on as long as customers keep up the orders. ⊠ *3B Tong Duy Tan, Hoan Kiem District* ☎ *098/884–2974 cell phone.*

Pasteur Street Brewing Company

BREWPUBS | The first brewery to open in Vietnam, PSBC has had immense success throughout the country. Serving several styles of craft beer and comfort food, this beautifully designed building is located right next to the cathedral. Get a growler of original craft beer and the Nashville hot chicken after you find a seat on the outdoor terrace. ⊠ *1 Au Trieu, Hoan Kiem District* ☎ *024/6294–9462* ⊕ *pasteurstreet.com.*

Polite & Co

COCKTAIL LOUNGES | A polished and vintage speakeasy, Polite & Co attracts a regular crowd of cocktail enthusiasts to its bar stools. This gentleman's pub is known for its stylish atmosphere and bartenders, so dress up and step out. ⊠ *5 Ngo Bao Khanh St., Hoan Kiem District* ☎ *096/894–9606 cell phone.*

DANCE CLUBS

1900 Le Theater

DANCE CLUBS | One of the only clubs in Hanoi, 1900 Le Theater has multiple stages, bars, and eccentric decor. There is generally a cover price and often live music or a DJ. Be forewarned, there is no customer limit so the dance floor is often jam-packed. If it's a night out you're looking for, it's best to reserve a table and pay for bottle service. ⊠ *8 Ta Hien, Pub St., Hoan Kiem District* ☎ *091/111–1900.*

Phuc Tan (The Lighthouse)

DANCE CLUBS | Hanoi is not a nightlife hub, but if you are looking for unreconstructed late-night fun then this is the place to go. Inside things are smoky, hot, and sweaty, but there's fresh air on the outside terrace and a river close by. Expect young backpackers on pub crawls. ⊠ *51 Tu Gian Phuc Tan St., Hoan Kiem District.*

🛍 Shopping

ART

Apricot Gallery

ART GALLERIES | Even if you have no intention of shelling out thousands of dollars for a painting, this beautiful gallery is still worth visiting. It's a great introduction to modern Vietnamese art as it displays works by the country's most famous contemporary artists. ⊠ *40B Hang Bong St., Hoan Kiem District* ☎ *024/3828–8965* ⊕ *www.apricotgallery.com.vn.*

Green Palm Gallery (*Green Palm Gallery*)
ART GALLERIES | This gallery sells works from some of Vietnam's biggest names in lacquer and oil painting, including Nguyen Thanh Chuong, Le Thanh Son, and Hong Viet Dung. The owner was an art critic in a previous life and is very reputable. ⊠ *39 Hang Gai St., Hoan Kiem District, Hanoi* ☎ *097/762–7722* ⊕ *www.greenpalmgallery.com.*

★ **Mai Gallery**
ART GALLERIES | Mai Gallery is run by the daughter of Vietnam's leading art critic, Duong Tuong. It is largely a showcase for Hanoi painters and is very popular with serious collectors. ⊠ *113 Hang Bong St., Hoan Kiem District* ☎ *024/3938–0568.*

CLOTHING AND ACCESSORIES
Ginkgo
MIXED CLOTHING | Ginkgo is one of Vietnam's most respected clothing brands. The emphasis is on print T-shirts, some made with organic cotton, that showcase eclectic aspects of Vietnamese culture. ⊠ *79 Hang Gai, Hoan Kiem District* ☎ *024/3938–2265* ⊕ *www.ginkgo-vietnam.com.*

★ **Ipa-Nima**
HANDBAGS | This is the place to get beautifully designed, funky, and fashionable handbags made of rattan, brocade, crochet, beads, and all kinds of other materials. It also sells original jewelry and accessories such as cuff links. The brand has gone international and celebrity fans are said to include actress Jamie Lee Curtis and Hillary Clinton. ⊠ *5 Nha Tho, Hoan Kiem District* ☎ *093/882–6716 cell phone (in Ho Chi Minh City)* ⊕ *www.ipa-nima.com.*

Kelly Bui
WOMEN'S CLOTHING | One of Vietnam's best-known clothing stores and designer labels, Kelly Bui specializes in daring and contemporary creations for women. ⊠ *272 Ba Trieu St., Hoan Kiem District* ☎ *024/320–4758* ⊕ *www.kellybui.vn.*

★ **Tired City**
MIXED CLOTHING | Tired City showcases a range of designs from young artists and graphic designers printed on ultra hip t-shirts and hoodies. There are also posters, postcards, playing cards, and other souvenir items. ⊠ *11A Bao Khanh, Hoan Kiem District* ☎ *024/3823–8499* ⊕ *tiredcity.com.*

EMBROIDERY
Kana Shop
CRAFTS | There's a little something for every size and taste here, though the large selection of embroidered handbags are particularly eye-catching. Other products available include dresses, skirts, knitwear, swimwear, shoes, wallets, and bags. ⊠ *41 Hang Trong, Hanoi* ☎ *024/3928–6208.*

★ **Tan My Design**
CRAFTS | Tan My is the most famous embroidery shop in Hanoi. Employees from Thuong Tin Province, which is known for its rich embroidery tradition, adorn tablecloths, silk clothing, and wall hangings with intricate designs. Ready-made work depicts everything from traditional Vietnamese floral patterns and dragon designs to scenes from Western fairy tales, or you can custom order. ⊠ *61 Hang Gai St., Hoan Kiem District, Hoan Kiem District* ☎ *024/3938–1154* ⊕ *www.tanmydesign.com.*

HANDICRAFTS
★ **Hien Van Ceramics**
SOUVENIRS | Housed in an astonishing colonial mansion, Hien Van Ceramics sells artisanal ceramic items, including vases, statues, and ornaments. ⊠ *8 Chan Cam, Head up the stairs and down the alleyway past Loading T, Hoan Kiem District* ☎ *094/468–3390 cell phone* ⊕ *facebook.com/hienvanceramics* ☉ *Closed Sun.*

MARKET
Long Bien Market
MARKET | Long Bien Market really kicks off at around 3 to 4 am and is worth seeing after a late night on the town. All of the produce from north of Hanoi lands

here before being distributed throughout the city. Just follow the crowds on the streets adjacent to the bridge ramp to witness the intense buying and selling of the freshest produce in town. ⊠ *Hang Dau St. near Long Bien Bridge, Hoan Kiem District.*

The French Quarter

The French thoroughly transformed this once-swampy southern suburb of Hanoi. In order to reflect the grandeur and aesthetic befitting the capital of their protectorate (the French called it Tonkin, from the Vietnamese *Dong Kinh,* or Eastern Capital), French developers rebuilt much of southern Hanoi from the ground up. The wide tree-lined boulevards combine with the majesty of Parisian-style villas and the shuttered elegance of government buildings to form a handsome seat of colonial power. The French are long gone, of course, and for decades Hanoians lacked the affluence to renovate or further build on the architectural contributions of the colonialists. Villas fell into disrepair, and only those buildings appropriated for state offices were even moderately maintained. This part of the city is caught in a 1920s and 1930s time warp.

Although much of the French Quarter's appeal lies in its grand but aging architecture, the area is now a leading diplomatic and commercial section of the city. As you walk through this airy, surprisingly green district, note the considerable international presence here: several embassies occupy renovated villas or compounds in the grid of avenues south of Hoan Kiem Lake, and modern office buildings have begun to shadow the streets of this lovely part of town.

◉ Sights

Ambassador's Pagoda (*Chua Quan Su*)
TEMPLE | This stately prayer house once served the many ambassadors who called on the Le kings. A hall named Quan Su was built in the 15th century to receive these guests, mostly Buddhists, and a pagoda was built for them in which they could comfortably worship. The hall burned to the ground, but the pagoda was saved. The Ambassador's Pagoda escaped destruction a second time, as it was the only pagoda not burned or ransacked in the final chaotic days of the Le dynasty. This pagoda sees more action than most in town, as it serves as headquarters for the Vietnam Buddhist Association. Government elites often make official visits to the pagoda, and people commonly hold "send-off" ceremonies here for the souls of family members who have recently died. The pagoda is also in part dedicated to a monk who is said to have saved King Ly Than Tong from his deathbed, so many older women come here to pray for good health. Dozens of young monks reside on the south side of the complex and study in the classrooms directly behind the pagoda. ⊠ *73 Quan Su St., Hoan Kiem District* 🕿 🖳 *Free.*

Cultural Friendship Palace
(*Cung Van Hoa Huu Nghi*)
CASTLE/PALACE | Never one to downplay its influence, the Soviet Union assisted with the design and construction of this "workers' cultural palace," formerly known as the Vietnam Xo Cultural Palace. Inaugurated September 1, 1985, the rigid 120-room white colossus stretches from Yet Kieu Street to Tran Binh Trong Road. The palace actually consists of three structures: the performance building houses a 1,200-seat concert hall, and the study and technology buildings contain a library, conference hall, and observatory. At the various clubs hosted here, Hanoians gather to share ideas on everything from biochemistry and chess

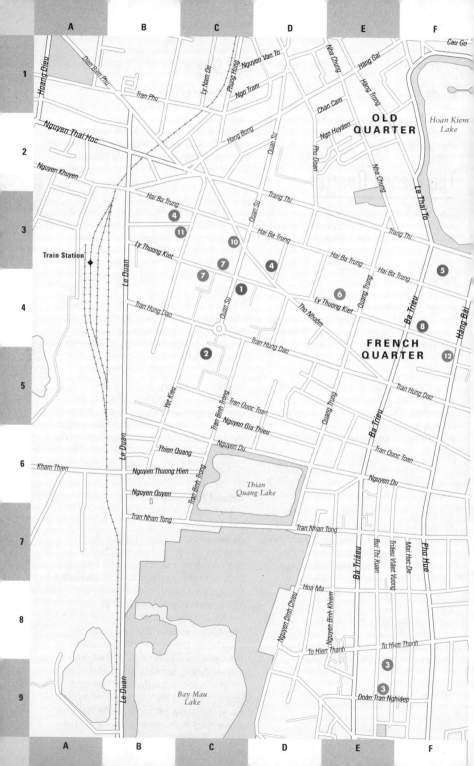

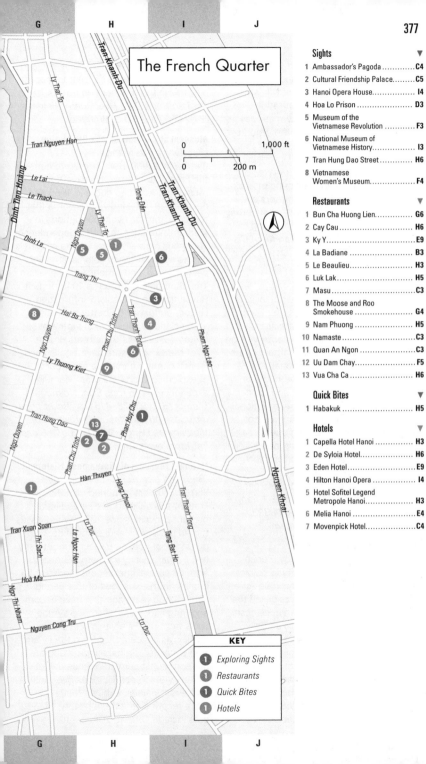

The French Quarter

Sights ▼

1 Ambassador's Pagoda C4
2 Cultural Friendship Palace C5
3 Hanoi Opera House I4
4 Hoa Lo Prison D3
5 Museum of the
   Vietnamese Revolution F3
6 National Museum of
   Vietnamese History I3
7 Tran Hung Dao Street H6
8 Vietnamese
   Women's Museum F4

Restaurants ▼

1 Bun Cha Huong Lien G6
2 Cay Cau H6
3 Ky Y E9
4 La Badiane B3
5 Le Beaulieu H3
6 Luk Lak H5
7 Masu C3
8 The Moose and Roo
   Smokehouse G4
9 Nam Phuong H5
10 Namaste C3
11 Quan An Ngon C3
12 Uu Dam Chay F5
13 Vua Cha Ca H6

Quick Bites ▼

1 Habakuk H5

Hotels ▼

1 Capella Hotel Hanoi H3
2 De Syloia Hotel H6
3 Eden Hotel E9
4 Hilton Hanoi Opera I4
5 Hotel Sofitel Legend
   Metropole Hanoi H3
6 Melia Hanoi E4
7 Movenpick Hotel C4

KEY

- **1** *Exploring Sights*
- **1** *Restaurants*
- **1** *Quick Bites*
- **1** *Hotels*

to billboard usage in the Old Quarter. The Vietnam Trade Union headquarters is just across the street, next to the Ministry of Transportation and Communication. The broad open space here known as May 1 Square is conducive to commemorating the past and present glories of the Communist Party, and you'll invariably see propaganda posters and waves of dangling street lights consisting of blinking yellow stars and red hammers and sickles. On the square's northeast corner is a beautiful Chinese-style meeting hall. ⊠ *91 Trang Hung Dao St., Hoan Kiem District* ☎ *024/3941–0590* ☞ *Closed to the public except for performances.*

★ Hanoi Opera House

PERFORMANCE VENUE | One of colonial Hanoi's most iconic edifices, the Hanoi Opera House was built by the French in the first decade of the 20th century as an Indochinese twin to Paris's largest opera house. Today it hosts traditional and modern performances by Vietnamese and international musicians and dancers and is home to the Vietnamese National Opera and Ballet. Public tours are not offered—only ticket-holding guests can enjoy the ornate architecture inside. You'll find an English-language performance schedule here: ⊕ www.ticketvn.com. Shows begin at 8 pm, and tickets generally start at around 200,000d. ⊠ *1 Trang Tien, Hoan Kiem District* ☎ *024/3933–0113* ⊕ *hanoioperahouse.org.vn.*

★ Hoa Lo Prison

JAIL/PRISON | Originally built by French colonizers to house Vietnamese political prisoners, Hoa Lo prison later held American prisoners of war and was called the "Hanoi Hilton," a name given in sarcasm because the conditions were actually quite miserable. In the 1990s more than half of the prison was demolished; the gatehouse was converted into a museum that highlights the cruelty of the occupying French but whitewashes prisoner treatment during the American War, as the Vietnam War is known locally. The prison is an important historical relic and the guidebook gives information that the placards in the museum do not. ⊠ *1 Hoa Lo, Tran Hung Dao, Hoan Kiem District* ☎ *024/3934–2253* ⊡ *30,000d.*

Museum of the Vietnamese Revolution
(*Bao Tang Cach Mang*)

HISTORY MUSEUM | Built in 1926 to house the French tax office, this cavernous museum opened its doors in 1959 and now has 29 halls, individual rooms that focus on specific events or periods in Vietnam's arduous road to independence. The focus naturally lands on the country's efforts against French colonialism, Japanese fascism, and American imperialism. The photographs from the 1945 August Revolution are particularly interesting. History buffs may do better here than at the National Museum of Vietnamese History just across the street: almost all of the exhibits here have English and French commentary, so a few hours of exploration can be a great learning experience. ⊠ *25 Tong Dan, Hoan Kiem District* ☎ *024/3825–4151* ☞ *Ticket price includes entry to National Museum of Vietnamese History* ⊡ *40,000d* ⊙ *Closed 1st Mon. every month.*

National Museum of Vietnamese History
(*Bao Tang Lich Su*)

HISTORY MUSEUM | Opened in 1932 by the French, this building has served in its present capacity since 1958, when it was turned it over to Hanoi authorities. The ground floor houses treasures from early history, particularly Vietnam's Bronze Age. Of special interest are the Ngoc Lu bronze drums, vestiges of this period some 3,000 years ago that have become enduring national Vietnamese symbols. Tools from the Paleolithic Age are on display, as are ceramics from the Ly and Tran dynasties. Painstakingly elaborate but somewhat corny dioramas depict various Vietnamese victories over hostile invaders. Upstairs, exhibits focus on more recent Vietnamese history. Standouts include 18th- to 20th-century bronze bells and *khanh* gongs (crescent-shape, decorative gongs); Nguyen-dynasty lacquered thrones, altars, and "parallel sentence" boards (Chinese calligraphy on lacquered wood carved into shapes of cucumbers, melons, and banana leaves); and an entire wing devoted to 7th- to 13th-century Champa stone carvings. As you explore the museum, be sure to consult the English-language brochure you are given with the purchase of your entrance ticket, as the information it contains about the exhibits is nearly the only information on hand. Displays provide little explanatory text, even in Vietnamese, and English-language translation is lacking. It's possible to arrange English-speaking museum guides in advance. ✉ *1 Trang Tien - No. 25, Hoan Kiem District* ☎ *024/3825–2853* 🌐 *www.baotanglichsu.vn* 🎟 *40,000d* 🕒 *Closed 1st Mon. every month* ☞ *Ticket price includes entry to Museum of the Vietnamese Revolution.*

Tran Hung Dao Street

STREET | Once called Rue Gambetta, Tran Hung Dao Street is now named after the revered Vietnamese warrior who repelled Kublai Khan's Mongol hordes three times between 1257 and 1288. This long, tree-lined boulevard is a marked example of the stateliness with which the French imbued these east–west streets. Several diplomatic missions line the boulevard; among them, fittingly, is the massive French embassy (No. 57), which takes up an entire city block. The regal Indian embassy building (No. 58-60) is also worth a look. ✉ *Tran Hung Dao, Hoan Kiem District.*

Vietnamese Women's Museum

OTHER MUSEUM | Founded in 1987, this informative and modern museum focuses on the cultural and historical aspects of Vietnamese women across 54 ethnic community groups. The three main exhibits highlight the themes of fashion, war, and family life, and the female gender role as it pertains to customs and tradition. History is told through videos, photographs, and well-presented displays of Vietnamese women in times of peace and war. The museum also covers areas of marriage, customs, and birth. There is an interesting section honoring the modern plight of the street vendor. Signage is in English, French, and Vietnamese. ✉ *36 Ly Thuong Kiet St., Hoan Kiem District* ☎ *024/3825–9936* 🌐 *baotangphunu.org.vn* 🎟 *40,000d.*

🍴 Restaurants

Bun Cha Huong Lien (*Bun Cha Obama*)

$ | **VIETNAMESE** | Bun Cha Huong Lien has wholeheartedly embraced the alias Bun Cha Obama since 2016, when the erstwhile president visited Hanoi and dined here with celebrity chef Anthony Bourdain. The *bun cha* (grilled pork and rice vermicelli noodles) and *nem hai san* (seafood spring rolls) are decent, but it's worth visiting just for the photography documenting the occasion. **Known for:** seafood spring rolls; Obama; Bourdain. [$] *Average main: d50,000* ✉ *24 Le Van Huu, Hai Ba Trung District* ☎ *024/3943–4106* 💳 *No credit cards.*

Cay Cau

$$ | **VIETNAMESE** | Serving high-quality northern Vietnamese food to a loyal following of locals (and the occasional tourist from the attached De Syloia Hotel), Cay Cau has a broad menu of meat, fish, and vegetable dishes. The tofu is particularly tasty. **Known for:** colorful staff uniforms; being long-established; huge menu. [$] *Average main: d250,000* ✉ *De Syloia Hotel, 17 Tran Hung Dao, Hoan Kiem District* ☎ *024/3933–1010.*

Ky Y

$$ | **JAPANESE** | The Japanese equivalent of your friendly neighborhood diner, this cozy restaurant is a longstanding favorite of older and affluent Hanoians. Reasonable prices encourage overindulgence in sushi or sashimi; the lunch specials are good value at around 200,000d. **Known**

Hanoi History

City of the Ascending Dragon

Hanoi residents are known for their civic pride, and it's little wonder given the history of their city. The city dates to the 7th century, when Chinese Sui dynasty settlers occupied the area and set up a capital called Tong Binh. In 1010 King Ly Thai To is said to have seen a golden dragon ascending from Hoan Kiem Lake. He relocated his capital to the shores of the lake and named his new city Thang Long, or "City of the Ascending Dragon." During the 11th century the old citadel was built, and 36 villages, each with its own specialized vocation, sprang up to serve the royal court. This is the origin of the 36 streets that define the city's Old Quarter.

In 1428 King Le Loi is said to have driven Vietnam's Chinese overlords from the country with the help of a magic sword from heaven. Celebrating his success after the war with a boating excursion on a lake, Le Loi was confronted by a gigantic golden tortoise that retrieved the sword for its heavenly owner. Thus the lake became known as the Lake of the Restored Sword, or Ho Hoan Kiem. The capital was moved to Hue under Emperor Gia Long during the Nguyen dynasty.

French capital

In the late 1800s, the French began to exert influence in Vietnam. The colonialists set up the protectorate of Annam in 1883–84, which meant the Hue royalty held the reins but only under the auspices of French rule. In the following years the French set up its administration and used Hanoi as the Eastern Capital of French Indochina.

In 1954 the French were defeated by the Vietminh at Dien Bien Phu, and France, Britain, the United States, and the Soviet Union decided at the Geneva Accords to divide the country at the 17th parallel. From 1954 until 1975, Hanoi served as the capital of the Democratic Republic of Vietnam, or North Vietnam, from which Ho Chi Minh initiated his struggle to reunify the country.

The decades after 1975 were a tough time for Hanoians and everyone else. Natural disasters and international isolation led to near mass starvation. Then in 1986 the government proclaimed *doi moi*, the move to a market economy.

Capitalism in the Capital

In the intervening 30 years the Vietnamese have learned the ways of capitalism quickly. In the 1990s Hanoi welcomed billions of dollars of foreign investment and the many international visitors eager to see this city (and nation) in the midst of renewal. One clear milestone for Vietnam was the normalization of trade relations with the United States in 2001. These market freedoms have led to a huge growth in privately run businesses such as hotels, restaurants, and tour agencies.

The move to a market-based system hasn't always been smooth. Vietnam's economy overheated in the years leading up to 2008, when the global financial crash decimated growth. Things have stabilized, but doubts remain as to how effectively the ruling party can manage reform. And as congestion increases and the government embarks on ever more ambitious building plans, the question of how Hanoi will preserve its ancient heritage remains unanswered.

for: lunch specials; fresh sushi; friendly waitstaff. $ *Average main: d220,000* ✉ *166 Trieu Viet Vuong St., Hai Ba Trung District* ☎ *024/3978–1386* 🕐 *Closed Sun.*

★ La Badiane

$$$ | FRENCH | Bringing inspired French cuisine to the heart of Hanoi, impassioned chef Benjamin Rascalou, who trained at several prestigious restaurants in Paris, has created a menu with flair. Main entrées, such as the sea bass meunière or seafood tagliatelle, will set you back more than most restaurants in Hanoi, but the flavors are worth the splurge. **Known for:** six-course tasting menu; French fusion food; bright courtyard. $ *Average main: d600,000* ✉ *10 Nam Ngu, Hoan Kiem District* ☎ *0243/942–4509* ⊕ *www.facebook.com/labadiane* 🕐 *Closed Sun.*

Le Beaulieu

$$$$ | FRENCH | Opened in 1901, Le Beaulieu was the first-ever French restaurant in Hanoi. The spacious dining room doesn't lend itself particularly well to intimacy, but an extensive wine list and expert sommelier service heighten the allure. **Known for:** Sunday brunch; French classics; delicious pan-fried foie gras. $ *Average main: d850,000* ✉ *15 Ngo Quyen, Hai Ba Trung District* ☎ *024/3826–6919* ⊕ *www.sofitel-legend-metropole-hanoi.com.*

★ Luk Lak

$$$ | VIETNAMESE | Serving countryside dishes with a refreshing modern twist, Luk Lak is a welcome addition to Hanoi's dining scene. Many of the dishes are head chef Madame Binh's take on recipes from a particular part of the country, such as the *ga nuong Tu Le* (grilled chicken with sticky rice from Yen Bai Province) and *tom xoc toi Quang Tri* (prawn with lemongrass and chili from Quang Tri Province). **Known for:** exemplary service; rare, delicious traditional dishes; modern interiors. $ *Average main: 500,000* ✉ *4A Le Thanh Tong, Hoan Kiem District* ☎ *094/314–3686 cell phone* ⊕ *luklak.vn.*

Masu

$$$$ | JAPANESE | When it comes to Japanese food in the capital, Masu has indisputably raised the bar. The menu is inspired, the ingredients are top-notch, the interior design is becoming, and the staff are appropriately attentive. **Known for:** sake; superb sashimi; crisp design. $ *Average main: d1,000,000* ✉ *60B Ly Thuong Kiet, Hoan Kiem District* ☎ *085/622–9339* ⊕ *masuvn.com* 🕐 *Closed Mon.*

The Moose and Roo Smokehouse

$$$ | AMERICAN | FAMILY | Set up in a giant courtyard full of wooden booths, deck furniture, and barrels, the Moose & Roo Smokehouse at the American Center is chock-full of those looking for delicious smoked meats and comfort food. This lively restaurant promises Texas in Hanoi, and delivers on that promise. **Known for:** family-friendly environment; barbecue; whiskey. $ *Average main: d300,000* ✉ *21 Hai Ba Trung, Hoan Kiem District* ☎ *024/3939–2470* ⊕ *www.facebook.com/mooseandroosh.*

Nam Phuong

$$ | VIETNAMESE | Aimed more at tourists than at local clientele, this restaurant within a renovated French villa provides a good introduction to Vietnamese cuisine. Just bear in mind that portions of the tasty and beautifully presented dishes, such as beef in coconut milk, can be disappointingly small. **Known for:** small portions; traditional outfits and music; Vietnamese classics. $ *Average main: d250,000* ✉ *19 Phan Chu Trinh St., Hoan Kiem District* ☎ *024/3824–0926* ⊕ *www.namphuong-restaurant.com.*

★ Namaste

$$ | INDIAN | At this authentic Indian restaurant, the owners import herbs and spices directly from India. Flatbreads like paratha and naan are cooked in a genuine clay tandoor oven, and the impressive cone-shape dosa pancake stands 2 feet tall. **Known for:** excellent kebabs; northern and southern cuisine; many vegetarian dishes. $ *Average main: d200,000* ✉ *46 Tho Nhuom, Hoan Kiem District* ☎ *024/3935–2400* 🌐 *www.namastehanoi.com* 🕒 *Closed 2–6 pm.*

Quan An Ngon

$$ | VIETNAMESE | Known among Hanoi locals for its vast menu, this eatery has specialties from northern, central, and southern Vietnam. It's almost as popular for the old courtyard setting as for the decent food. **Known for:** unparalleled variety of street food; reasonable prices; additional branches in Ho Chi Minh City and Hanoi. $ *Average main: d180,000* ✉ *18 Phan Boi Chau St., Hoan Kiem District* ☎ *090/324–6963.*

Uu Dam Chay

$$$ | VEGETARIAN | Uu Dam Chay elevates vegan food with fruity salads, interesting tofu dishes (try one of the stuffed varieties), and creative mocktails. The restaurant is huge, but bookings are still recommended. **Known for:** vegan friendly; modern interior design; pomelo salad. $ *Average main: d300,000* ✉ *34 Hang Bai, Hoan Kiem District* ☎ *098/134–9898* 🌐 *uudamchay.com.*

Vua Cha Ca

$$ | VIETNAMESE | FAMILY | This modern restaurant serves traditional *cha ca* (pan-fried fish with rice vermicelli) to multi-generational tables of lively locals. Reservations are almost essential, but if you can't get a table confirmed you can find a handful of other Vua Cha Ca locations across the city. **Known for:** popularity; must-try Hanoi specialty dish; family restaurant. $ *Average main: d150,000* ✉ *26C Tran Hung Dao, Hai Ba Trung District* ☎ *096/175–7522* 🌐 *vuachaca.vn.*

Coffee and Quick Bites

★ Habakuk

$ | CAFÉ | Serving creamy cappuccinos and delicious lattes in calm and quiet surroundings, Habakuk might be the best spot in the city for withdrawing from Hanoi's chaos with a book and a drink. Though best known for its excellent coffee, Habakuk morphs into a bistro serving delicious lasagna in the evenings. **Known for:** quiet setting; barista courses; tasty lasagna. $ *Average main: d60,000* ✉ *4 Ngo Phan Huy Chu, head down the alley, the cafe is on the right, Hoan Kiem District* ☎ *086/711–5451.*

Hotels

Capella Hotel Hanoi

$$$$ | HOTEL | Capella is Hanoi's newest, swankiest, and–in its Roaring Twenties meets opera theme–playful hotel, with some suites going for thousands of dollars a night. **Pros:** room views are unrivaled; Hanoi's most luxurious hotel; three complimentary "rituals" daily (coffee, tea, and cocktails). **Cons:** the suites have too much furniture; garish interiors won't appeal to everyone; prices are eye-wateringly steep. $ *Rooms from: d7,000,000* ✉ *11 Le Phung Hieu, Hoan Kiem District* ☎ *024/3987–8888* 🌐 *capellahotels.com* 🍴 *Free Breakfast* 🛏 *47 rooms.*

De Syloia Hotel

$$$ | HOTEL | A true French Quarter boutique hotel, the colonial–style De Syloia is small but fashionable, with wooden furniture, large beds, and cream-color linens in the well-appointed and well-maintained rooms. **Pros:** recently refurbished; friendly, attentive staff; restaurant serves good Vietnamese food. **Cons:** restaurant serves poor Western food; rooms book out quickly. $ *Rooms from: d1,840,000* ✉ *17A Trang Hung Dao St., Hoan Kiem District* ☎ *024/3824–5346, 024/3824–1083* 🌐 *www.desyloia.com* 🛏 *33 rooms* 🍴 *Free Breakfast.*

Eden Hotel

$$$ | HOTEL | Bright rooms at this top-rated hotel near Thong Nhat Park have all of the conveniences—carpeted floors, carved-wood furniture, big baths, and extras such as flat-screen televisions and classy wall hangings. **Pros:** spa and sauna; rooftop pool; close to one of Hanoi's best parks. **Cons:** pool is closed in the winter months; hotel has been known to over-charge for airport transfers; the design is beginning to look dated. $ *Rooms from: d2,100,000* ✉ *22 Doan Tran Nghiep, Hai Ba Trung District* ☎ *024/3974–8622* ⊕ *edenhotel.com.vn* ❑ *Free Breakfast* ⤴ *60 rooms.*

Hilton Hanoi Opera

$$$ | **HOTEL** | A stone's throw from the Hanoi Opera House, this was the city's top hotel long ago and it's still a solid bet today, offering easy access to the French Quarter and the Old Quarter. **Pros:** excellent restaurant; some rooms have views of the opera house; reliable service. **Cons:** sometimes there's more of a business crowd; rooms and common areas are a little dated. $ *Rooms from: d2,500,000* ✉ *1 Le Thanh Tong, Hoan Kiem District* ☎ *024/3933–0500* ⊕ *www.hilton.com* ⤴ *269 rooms* ❑ *Free Breakfast.*

★ Hotel Sofitel Legend Metropole Hanoi

$$$$ | **HOTEL** | A classic Asian colonial-era hotel in the same league as the Peninsula in Hong Kong and Singapore's Raffles Hotel, the Metropole is Hanoi's most storied accommodation, offering world-class service in a historic building nestled in the French Quarter across from the Hanoi Opera House. **Pros:** daily tours to the hotel's wartime bomb shelter; one of Hanoi's most inviting swimming pools; superb location. **Cons:** newer rooms are pleasant but lack period charm. $ *Rooms from: d7,600,000* ✉ *15 Ngo Quyen St., Hoan Kiem District* ☎ *024/3826–6919* ⊕ *www.sofitel-legend-metropole-hanoi. com* ❑ *Free Breakfast* ⤴ *364 rooms.*

Melia Hanoi

$$$ | **HOTEL** | A solid option for those who appreciate chain-hotel facilities at highly reasonable prices, there are always discounts worth bargaining for here. **Pros:** discounts available; attractive outdoor pool; well-maintained fitness facilities. **Cons:** it's not Hanoi's most charming hotel. $ *Rooms from: d1,800,000* ✉ *44B Ly Thuong Kiet St., Hoan Kiem District,*

Hanoi ☎ *024/3934–3343* ⊕ *www.melia. com* ❑ *Free Breakfast* ⤴ *306 rooms.*

Movenpick Hotel

$$$ | **HOTEL** | This well-run Swiss chain is popular with business travelers, and the pleasant rooms and efficient service are certainly a cut above average. **Pros:** state-of-the-art gym; spa and sauna facilities; good on-site restaurant Mangosteen. **Cons:** no pool, which is unusual for such an upscale name; not as much local flavor. $ *Rooms from: d1,900,000* ✉ *83A Ly Thuong Kiet St., Hoan Kiem District, Hanoi* ☎ *024/3822–2800* ⊕ *www. movenpick.com* ⤴ *151 rooms* ❑ *Free Breakfast.*

ⓨ Nightlife

BARS AND PUBS
Binh Minh's Jazz Club

LIVE MUSIC | Minh's Jazz Club is owned by one of Hanoi's best-known jazz musicians, Quyen Van Minh. Live jazz performed by both foreign and local musicians, including Minh's son, are the big draws here. Music starts at 9 nightly. ✉ *1 Trang Tien, Hoan Kiem District* ☎ *024/3933–6555.*

Kumquat Tree

COCKTAIL LOUNGES | On a small street close to French cultural center L'Espace is Kumquat Tree, one of Hanoi's first speakeasy bars. You'll need a not-so-secret code (the security guard will tell you what it is) to get into this ambient space offering on-point cocktails and regular DJ nights. ✉ *1 Nguyen Khac Can, Hoan Kiem District* ☎ *098/268–5335.*

★ Tadioto

COCKTAIL LOUNGES | Owned and operated by journalist and raconteur Nguyen Qui Duc, this Hanoi institution is now in its fourth incarnation near the Opera House. Expect a bohemian crowd, an eclectic music policy, and a nice selection of wine. They also have a reputation for great sushi. ✉ *24 Tong Dan, Hoan Kiem District* ☎ *024/6680–9124.*

🛍 Shopping

ART

Art Vietnam Gallery

ART GALLERIES | To really appreciate Hanoi's art scene this is the ideal place to start. Gallery director Suzanne Lecht is one of the leading experts on Vietnamese art and she can lead you on studio tours and advise you on major purchases. The gallery is long established, but has recently moved to a bright new space in an up-and-coming arty enclave. ✉ No.2 Alley 66 Yen Lac, Hai Ba Trung District ☎ 024/3862–3184 ⊕ www.artvietnamgallery.com.

Red Moon Gallery

ART GALLERIES | Emerging and established Vietnamese artists are showcased at this small gallery. Artworks are presented with a certificate of authenticity as well as a copy of the artist's biography. ✉ 38 Trang Tien, Hoan Kiem District ☎ 024/3934–2531 ⊕ www.redmoongallery.net.

CLOTHING AND ACCESSORIES

★ aN Store

LEATHER GOODS | Leather artisan Nguyen Mai Phuong opened aN Store on one of Hanoi's most charming colonial streets. Aside from leather purses, wallets, and bags, she also sells high quality linen clothing and home decor. ✉ 8 Ly Dao Thanh, Hoan Kiem District ☎ 091/510–7676 cell phone.

★ Magonn

WOMEN'S CLOTHING | Mixing retro and modern stylings to create items that are fresh and unique, Magonn has become one of Vietnam's leading female fashion brands with several branches throughout Hanoi and Ho Chi Minh City. ✉ 76 Ba Trieu, Hoan Kiem District ☎ 024/3633–0036 ⊕ www.magonn.com.

FOOD

Maison Marou

CHOCOLATE | Featured in international news (including the New York Times) and winner of global design awards for their chocolate wrappers, Marou now has a storefront in Hanoi. The company began by scouring the southern Vietnamese countryside for the best cacao possible. A few years after opening, their enterprise continues to grow and expose the world to Vietnamese single-origin chocolate. ✉ 91A Tho Nhuom, Hoan Kiem District ☎ 024/3717–3969 ⊕ www.marouchocolate.com.

MARKETS

Hom Market (Cho Hom)

SOUVENIRS | This is one of the biggest, busiest, and most atmospheric markets in town. It specializes in fabric, but there's a broad range of other items on sale, from candles to underwear. ✉ Pho Hue and Tran Xuan Soan Sts., Hai Ba Trung District.

The Ho Chi Minh Mausoleum and Nearby

This once-forested area west of the citadel, which is still a military base, is an expansive and refreshingly tranquil district, where stalwart buildings and monuments seem to revel in the glories of Ho Chi Minh and the Communist cause. As you travel northwest on Dien Bien Phu Street, you'll leave the tightly woven fabric of the Old Quarter behind and find yourself surrounded by sweeping French-era villas and massive ocher-color government buildings, most of which are protected from the sun by a phalanx of tall tamarind trees. Many of these villas house the embassies of socialist (or once-socialist) nations that have stood fast by Vietnam during the last few decades. Scattered among these gems are occasional anomalies of Soviet-era architecture.

Several important sights, including the final resting place of Ho Chi Minh and his former home, are close to Ba Dinh Square, where the beloved leader read his Declaration of Independence in 1945. The One-Pillar Pagoda, the underrated Fine Arts Museum, the Army Museum, and the famed Temple of Literature are within easy walking distance of the square.

If you're coming here from the French Quarter, ask a cyclo or taxi driver to take you from Hoan Kiem Lake to the Ho Chi Minh Mausoleum, in Ba Dinh District.

◉ Sights

Ba Dinh Square
PLAZA/SQUARE | Dien Bien Phu Street comes to an end at the minimally landscaped Ba Dinh Square, in the center of which flutters Hanoi's largest Vietnamese flag. This is where half a million northern Vietnamese gathered to hear Uncle Ho's Declaration of Independence on September 2, 1945, and where, after Ho's death in 1969 (also on September 2), another 100,000 Hanoians gathered to pay homage. On the west side of the square is the mausoleum itself, a cold and squat cubicle that's nonetheless arresting in its simplicity and grandeur. Across the square from the mausoleum and slightly to the left is the Ba Dinh Meeting Hall, the four-story headquarters of the Communist Party and the site where the National Assembly convenes. Across the square and to the right, where Dien Bien Phu Street meets the square, stands the huge and graceful Ministry of Foreign Affairs. Directly opposite the mausoleum and at the end of short Bac Son Road is the monument to Vietnam's revolutionary martyrs. A palm- and willow-shaded mansion to the right of the monument is the family home of former minister of defense General Vo Nguyen Giap, who orchestrated the siege at Dien Bien Phu in 1954. General Giap passed away in 2013. ⊠ *Ba Dinh Sq., Ba Dinh District.*

Botanical Gardens (*Vuon Bach Thao*)
GARDEN | This 50-acre park behind the Presidential Palace was designed by French landscape engineers in 1890. After defeating the French in Hanoi in late 1954, the state rebuilt the gardens and opened the grounds and its extensive network of trails to the public. Athletes in search of exercise congregate here for pickup soccer games, badminton, tai chi, and jogging. Lovers looking for seclusion head to the sculpture garden on the east side of the park, or cross the bridge to an island in the middle of the tree-shaded, preternaturally green lake. Unfortunately, the park doesn't have a great reputation with tourists due to its caged birds and monkeys, but it is a spot to get away from the crowds. ⊠ *3 Hoang Hoa Tham St., Hanoi* 🏠 🖃 *2,000d* ⊗ *Closes at 10 pm.*

★ **Fine Arts Museum** (*Bao Tang My Thuat*)
ART MUSEUM | Silk paintings, folk art, sculptures, artifacts, and lacquer works are among the works of art at this museum neighboring the Temple of Literature. You can see traditional paintings depicting village scenes as well as socialist-inspired works following the Vietnam War. The full collection of Cham and Buddhist art is housed in two separate buildings with signage in Vietnamese and English. Consider prearranging a tour with Sophie's Art Tour (www.sophiesarttour. com) to understand the stories behind the pieces. ⊠ *66 Nguyen Thai Hoc St., Ba Dinh District* 🏠 *0024/3823–3084* ⊕ *vn-fam.vn* 🖃 *40,000d* ⊗ *Closed during Tet.*

★ **Ho Chi Minh Mausoleum**
TOMB | Ho Chi Minh may have opposed the idea of being preserved and displayed in state after his death, but his wishes to be cremated were ignored for this Vietnamese interpretation of Lenin's mausoleum. The structure's choice of location on Ba Dinh Square was a natural one—it was here where Ho declared the founding of the Democratic Republic of Vietnam in 1945. Visits to the mausoleum

The Life of Ho Chi Minh

Early years

Ho Chi Minh (literally, "bringer of light") is the final and most memorable pseudonym in a series of more than 50 that Vietnam's intrepid leader, originally named Nguyen Sinh Cung, acquired during the course of his remarkable life. Born in 1890 in the central Vietnamese province of Nghe An, Ho received traditional French schooling and became a teacher. From his father (who abandoned the family early on), he inherited a wanderlust that became fueled by a lifelong obsession with Vietnamese independence.

Years abroad

In 1911 Ho signed on to the crew of a French freighter; two years later a stint aboard another French ship took him to the United States, where he settled for a year in Brooklyn, New York, and found work as a laborer. Ho then left for London, where he became an assistant pastry chef. He mastered several languages—among them English, French, German, Russian, Cantonese, and Japanese. He moved to Paris for six years and became increasingly active in Socialist, Communist, and Nationalist movements. After helping to found the French Communist Party, Ho left for Moscow in 1924. It soon became clear that to foment a successful workers' revolution in Vietnam, he would have to dedicate himself to organizing his countrymen. By the end of the 1920s, several poorly organized revolts had incited aggressive French retaliation, which was only compounded by economic depression. In 1930, while based in Hong Kong, Ho consolidated a number of rebellious factions under the umbrella of the Indochinese Communist Party. However, it was not until 1941—after escaping arrest in Hong Kong, forging documentation "proving" his death, shuttling between China and the Soviet Union, and disguising himself as a Chinese journalist—that he was able to sneak back into Vietnam.

Leadership in Vietnam

Shortly thereafter Ho founded the Vietminh Independence League. In July 1945, U.S. OSS officers met with Ho; impressed with Ho's operation, they agreed to supply him with arms. In August, Ho called for a general uprising, known as the August Revolution. Ho proclaimed himself president of the Democratic Republic of Vietnam in the north. The following year, Ho, in order to rid northern Vietnam of Chinese troops, agreed to an accord with the French: Vietnam would be a "free state" within the French Union and 25,000 French troops would be stationed there. Tensions between the Vietminh and the French escalated, however, and soon led to the French-Indochina War. By 1950 the United States was supplying military aid to the French, and Ho's government was recognized by the Soviet Union and China. The French-Indochina War ended in 1954 with the Vietminh's defeat of the French at Dien Bien Phu. American involvement in Vietnam escalated rapidly.

Ho died of natural causes during the Vietnam War in September 1969 at the age of 79. Ho never married—he asserted that the Vietnamese people were his family—thus he preferred the familiar "Uncle Ho." From his embalmed body in the Ho Chi Minh Mausoleum to his portrait on Vietnamese currency, he is still very present in Vietnamese life.

are expected to be quiet and respectful—skirts and shorts are forbidden, as is photography. Checking and claiming bags at the entrance can be slow, so pack lightly if possible. Lines can wind up to 2 km (a mile) long, so be prepared to wait. Hours are limited to 8 am–11 am, so arrive before 10 am to ensure entry. ⊠ *Ba Dinh Sq., Ba Dinh District* ☎ *024/3845-5168* ⏱ *Closed to public Mon. and Fri.; closes sporadically throughout the year for maintenance so call ahead.*

Ho Chi Minh Museum
(*Bao Tang Ho Chi Minh*)
HISTORY MUSEUM | With English commentary on the propagandistic and occasionally bizarre exhibits, this museum is a must-see on the Uncle Ho circuit. A collection of manifestos, military orders, correspondence, and photographs from the Communist Party's early days to the present are mixed with historical exhibits covering Vietnam's revolutionary history, the fight against fascism, Ho's revolutionary world movement, and Vietnam's struggle against imperialism. ⊠ *19 Ngoc Ha St. (also accessible from Chua Mot Cot St.), Ba Dinh District* ☎ *24/3845-5435* ⏱ *40,000d* ⏱ *Closed Mon., Fri., and lunchtime (11:30 am to 2 pm).*

★ Ho Chi Minh's Residence (*Nha Bac Ho*)
GOVERNMENT BUILDING | Just beyond Ho Chi Minh's Mausoleum is the modest wooden home where the revolutionary leader chose to live during his reign, from 1954 until his death in 1969. The lovely parklike setting offers a glimpse into the humble existence of this former ruler. Well-manicured gardens lead to a small pond where Ho Chi Minh used to clap his hands to beckon the fish for feeding time. A simple clap is enough to make these carp go wild in anticipation. Bordering the pond is the simple residence on stilts where Ho Chi Minh lived. Several rooms and his three classic cars are sectioned off for viewing. To get here, you must buy tickets next to the opulent Presidential Palace at the site's

entrance. The palace can only be viewed from the exterior; it now operates as a government building. The bomb shelter to the right of Ho Chi Minh's home is also closed to the public. ⊠ *1 Hoang Hoa Tham, Ba Dinh District* ⏱ *25,000d* ⏱ *Closed lunchtime (11 am to 1:30 pm).*

Lotte Center Observation Skydeck
VIEWPOINT | While Hanoi is famous for its ancient architecture, there are modern high-rises joining the scene as well. If you are looking for a way to take in all of Hanoi at once, head to the Lotte Center's 64th floor at sunset. There are two glass skydecks; one comes with an official photographer that will snap photos of you for a fee, but feel free to take your own. Entry to the rooftop cocktail bar is free, while the observation deck costs 230,000d. ⊠ *54 Lieu Giai, Ba Dinh District* ☎ *024/3333–6000* ⊕ *observation-deck.lottecenter.com.vn* ⏱ *230,000d.*

One-Pillar Pagoda (*Chua Mot Cot*)
TEMPLE | The French destroyed this temple on their way out in 1954. It was reconstructed by the incoming government and still commemorates the legend of Emperor Ly Thai Tong. It is said that the childless emperor dreamed that Quan Am, the Buddhist goddess of mercy and compassion, seated on a lotus flower, handed him a baby boy. Sure enough, he soon met and married a peasant woman who bore him a male heir, and in 1049 he constructed this monument in appreciation. The distinctive single pillar is meant to represent the stalk of the lotus flower, a sacred Vietnamese symbol of purity. The pillar was originally a single large tree trunk; today it's made of more durable cement. An ornate curved roof covers the tiny 10-square-foot pagoda, which rises out of a square pond. Steps leading to the pagoda from the south side of the pond are usually blocked off, but if there aren't too many people around, a monk may invite you into this miniature prayer room. Just a few yards from the One-Pillar Pagoda is Dien Huu Pagoda,

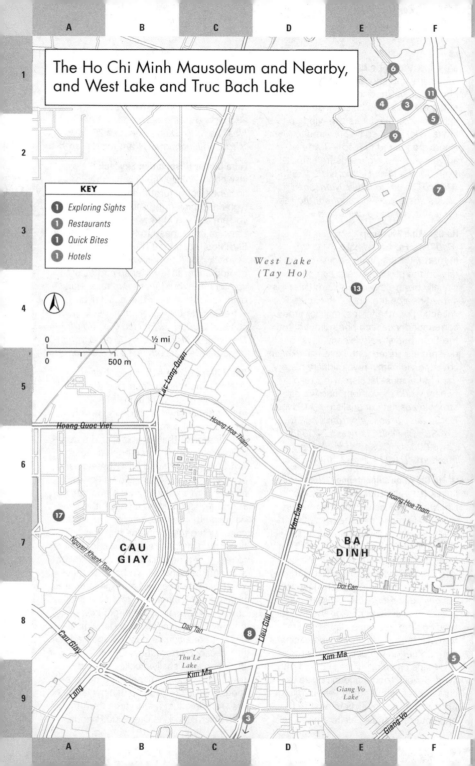

The Ho Chi Minh Mausoleum and Nearby, and West Lake and Truc Bach Lake

KEY
- ① Exploring Sights
- ① Restaurants
- ① Quick Bites
- ① Hotels

West Lake
(Tay Ho)

0 ———— ½ mi
0 ———— 500 m

Lac Long Quan

Hoang Quoc Viet

Hoang Hoa Tham

Van Cao

CAU GIAY

BA DINH

Hoang Hoa Tham

Doi Can

Nguyen Khanh Toan

Dao Tan

Thu Le Lake

Kim Ma

Kim Ma

Lang

Cau Giay

Giang Vo Lake

Giang Vo

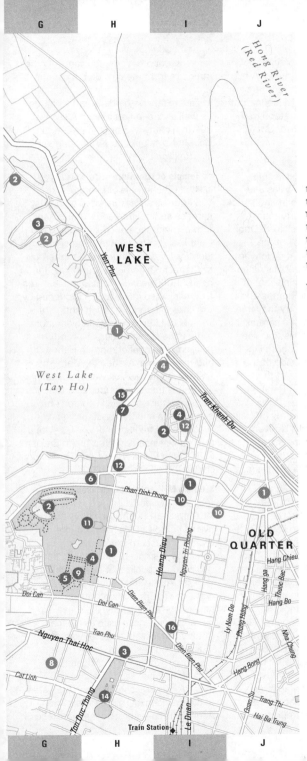

Sights ▼

1 Ba Dinh Square H7
2 Botanical Gardens G7
3 Fine Arts Museum H9
4 Ho Chi Minh Mausoleum H7
5 Ho Chi Minh Museum G7
6 Ho Chi Minh's Residence H6
7 John McCain Memorial H5
8 Lotte Center
   Observation Skydeck C8
9 One-Pillar Pagoda G7
10 Phan Dinh Phung Street I7
11 Presidential Palace H7
12 Quan Thanh Temple H6
13 Tay Ho Temple E4
14 Temple of Literature H9
15 Tran Quoc Pagoda H5
16 Vietnam Military
   History Museum I8
17 Vietnam Museum of
   Ethnology A7

Restaurants ▼

1 Bun Cha 34 .... J6
2 Chops G2
3 Cousins F1
4 Cugini E1
5 El Gaucho F2
6 The Grumpy Dumpling E1
7 Koto Villa F2
8 Ly Van Phuc (Chicken Street) G9
9 Maison de Tet Decor E2
10 Quan Cu I7
11 Sushi Dokoro Yutaka F1
12 Vege-ro I6

Quick Bites ▼

1 Bluebird's Nest I6
2 Ma Xo I6
3 Milk and Honey G3
4 Pho Cuon Chinh Thang I5

Hotels ▼

1 Hanoi Club H4
2 InterContinental Hanoi
   Westlake G3
3 JW Marriott Hotel Hanoi C9
4 Pan Pacific Hanoi I5
5 Pullman Hanoi Hotel F9

a delightful but often-overlooked temple enclosing a bonsai-filled courtyard. A tall and colorful gate opens out onto the path leading to the Ho Chi Minh Museum, but the entrance is opposite the steps to the One-Pillar Pagoda. ⊠ *Chua Mot Cot St., Ba Dinh District.*

★ Phan Dinh Phung Street

STREET | This beautiful shaded avenue leads past sprawling French villas and Chinese mandarin mansions (many occupied by long-serving party members) as well as the gracious North Door Cathedral (Nha Tho Cua Bac), at the corner of Phan Dinh Phung and Nguyen Bieu Streets. The large wheel of stained glass at the cathedral is reminiscent of Renaissance-era artwork in Europe and is enchanting from the inside; try the large front doors or ask around for a caretaker to let you in. Another option is to come on Sunday at 10 am for an English-language service. On the right side of the street stand the tall ramparts of the citadel, the military compound that once protected the Imperial Palace of Thang Long. In a surprising move, army officials in 1999 opened to the public Nguyen Tri Phuong Street, which runs straight through this once secretive space. ⊠ *Phan Dinh Phung St., Ba Dinh District.*

Presidential Palace (*Phu Chu Tich*)

CASTLE/PALACE | This imposing three-story palace just north of the Ho Chi Minh Mausoleum testifies to France's dedication to ostentatious architecture in Indochina. Constructed from 1900 to 1906, the bright, mustard-yellow building served as the living and working quarters of Indochina's governors-general. When Ho Chi Minh returned to Hanoi after the defeat of the French in 1954, he refused to live in the palace itself but chose the more modest quarters of the palace electrician. He did, however, offer use of the palace to distinguished guests during their visits to the capital. Today the building is used for formal international receptions and other important

government meetings. You can view the structure from the outside but cannot enter the palace. Surrounding the building are extensive gardens and orchards, as well as the famed Mango Alley, the 300-foot pathway from the palace to Ho Chi Minh's stilt house. ⊠ *2 Huong Vuong St., Ba Dinh District.*

★ Temple of Literature (*Van Mieu*)

TEMPLE | The Temple of Literature, or Van Mieu, is a treasure trove of Vietnamese architecture and a monument to the importance of education and Confucianism to Vietnam's national identity. Loosely modeled on the temple at Confucius's hometown in China, the nearly 1,000-year-old compound features five manicured courtyards surrounded by the Lake of Literature. Highlights of the Temple of Literature include giant stone turtles, the Constellation of Literature pavilion (a symbol of modern Hanoi), and the Imperial Academy—Vietnam's first university—which was founded in 1076. It is tradition for students to touch the stone turtles for luck, so don't be surprised to find this place packed with graduates in traditional dress. Go with a tour guide since few signs are in English. ⊠ *58 Quoc Tu Giam St., Dong Da District* ☎ *024/3747–2566* 🎫 *10,000d.*

Vietnam Military History Museum
(*Bao Tang Quan Doi*)

MILITARY SIGHT | Although not as provocative as its Ho Chi Minh City counterpart, the army museum is nonetheless an intriguing example of Vietnam's continuing dedication to publicizing its past military exploits. At the southern edge of what was once the Thang Long citadel, which housed the imperial city, the museum buildings were once used as French military barracks. In the courtyard of the museum, Chinese- and Soviet-made weaponry—including MiG fighters, antiaircraft guns, and what is said to be the tank that smashed through the gates of the Presidential Palace in Saigon on April 30, 1975—surround the wreckage of

The Temple of Literature was modeled after the temple of Confucius's hometown in China.

an American B-52 and F-4 fighter jet shot down over Hanoi. Other far-less-arresting displays include depictions of the Trung sisters' revolt against Chinese overlords in AD 40, sound-and-light shows highlighting battles and troop movements during the wars against the French and Americans, bicycles known as steel horses that were used on the Ho Chi Minh Trail, captured French and American firearms and uniforms, field maps and tables of major attacks, and the dreaded pungee sticks. Adjacent to the museum is the Hanoi Flag Pillar, a 100-foot tapered hexagonal guard tower atop a three-tier square base. Built in 1812, the pillar escaped destruction by the French when they leveled much of the citadel; instead they used the tower as an observation and communication station—much like the Vietnamese military before them. The intricate fan- and flower-shape holes allow light into the tower, which has a crisp red-and-yellow Vietnamese flag fluttering from its flagpole. ⊠ *28A Dien Bien Phu St., Ba Dinh District* ☎ *024/6253-1367* ⊠ *40,000d* ☉ *Closed Mon., Fri., and lunchtime (11:30 am to 1 pm).*

★ **Vietnam Museum of Ethnology**

OTHER MUSEUM | FAMILY | Showcasing the cultural heritage of 54 ethnic groups in Vietnam, this museum has an indoor exhibition with a large collection of photographs and artifacts, including clothing, jewelry, tools, weapons, instruments, and items related to religious beliefs and wedding and funeral ceremonies. Behind the main building is an outdoor exhibit space with winding pathways that lead to 18 replicas of life-size tombs, boats, and traditional Vietnamese homes, including the impressive Nha Rong Bana Communal House reachable by a log ladder with chiseled steps. A free water-puppet show is presented several times daily (check the times as soon as you arrive). This is one of Vietnam's very best museums, and it's especially worth visiting if you're going to or coming from the ethnically diverse northern mountains. ⊠ *Nguyen Van Huyen Rd., Nghia Do, Cau Giay* ☎ *24/3756–2193* ⊠ *40,000d* ☉ *Closed Mon. and during Tet.*

🍴 Restaurants

Bun Cha 34

$ | **VIETNAMESE** | Drawing crowds with enormous servings of *bun cha* (grilled pork with rice vermicelli), Bun Cha 34 does not fail to deliver good quality bowls for a mere 40,000d per dish. Customers rave over the charred pork and fragrant herbs. **Known for:** crispy spring rolls; pork patties grilled with lot leaves; bigger than average portions. [$] *Average main: d40,000* ✉ *34 Hang Than, Ba Dinh District* 💳 *No credit cards.*

Ly Van Phuc (Chicken Street)

$ | **VIETNAMESE** | Colloquially known as "Chicken Street," this is the place to come for delicious barbecued poultry served right off the street. The street is lined with vendors working near-identical alchemy with a limited menu of grilled chicken wings, legs, and feet; sweet potatoes; and bread that's been brushed with honey before being toasted. **Known for:** delicious barbecue chicken; open late; cold local beer. [$] *Average main: d120,000* ✉ *Ly Van Phuc, Ba Dinh District* 💳 *No credit cards.*

Quan Cu

$$ | **VIETNAMESE** | Quan Cu means "old restaurant," which is a misleading title for this clean, efficient, and well-organized Vietnamese restaurant. The staff speak little English but an attractive picture menu makes ordering easy; try the grilled chicken, any dish with tofu, and the fresh morning glory stir-fried with garlic. **Known for:** bun thang (chicken noodle soup); traditional northern cuisine; cold Hanoi beer. [$] *Average main: d200,000* ✉ *31A Phan Dinh Phung, Ba Dinh District* ☎ *024/3734–4048.*

☕ Coffee and Quick Bites

Bluebird's Nest (*To Chim Xanh*)

$ | **CAFÉ** | Full of bricks, books, and artistic locals and expats, Bluebird's Nest is a quiet oasis where you can work, study, or kick back and get some leisure reading done. This café often hosts intimate events, like film nights or acoustic music shows, and you might overhear a private English or Vietnamese lesson if you stay the afternoon. **Known for:** evening events; books; rooftop terrace. [$] *Average main: d50,000* ✉ *19 Dang Dung, Ba Dinh District* ✥ *Go into the alley and look for the signs* ☎ *034/956–5226* 💳 *No credit cards.*

🛏 Hotels

JW Marriott Hotel Hanoi

$$$$ | **HOTEL** | Although located a fair distance from the thick of the action, in an area mooted as the city's new main business district, Marriott's first Hanoi property still makes a worthwhile base. **Pros:** delightfully landscaped grounds, with a lake; the best hotel dining in the city; crisp, modern architecture. **Cons:** breakfast buffet not included in rate; less local flavor at this trusted brand; out of the way. [$] *Rooms from: d3,015,000* ✉ *8 Do Duc Duc, Tu Liem* ☎ *24/3833–5588* 🌐 *www.jwmarriotthanoilife.com* 🔑 *395 rooms* 🍽 *No Meals.*

Pullman Hanoi Hotel

$$$ | **HOTEL** | An impressive green-glass-fronted facade and attentive and professional service are indicative of the elevated ambitions of this smart business hotel. **Pros:** outdoor pool; excellent buffet breakfast; smart fitness facilities. **Cons:** somewhat lacking in character; rooms are not overly large; it's not in the most attractive neighborhood. [$] *Rooms from: d1,600,000* ✉ *40 Cat Linh St., Dong Da District* ☎ *024/3733–0688* 🌐 *pullman-hanoi.com* 🔑 *240 rooms* 🍽 *No Meals.*

🎟 Performing Arts

FILM

Goethe Institut

CULTURAL FESTIVALS | In addition to German language classes and opportunities abroad, Germany's cultural institution often hosts photography and film exhibitions. ✉ *56–60 Nguyen Thai Hoc, Ba Dinh District* ☎ *024/3200–4494* ⊕ *www.goethe.de.*

National Cinema

FILM | This refurbished cinema has 12 screens. Films are often cheaper than in the major theaters, and many film festivals are held here throughout the year. There's also an arcade on the first floor. ✉ *87 Lang Ha, Ba Dinh District.*

THEATER

Hanoi Cheo Theater

OPERA | This tiny, simple drama house seats 50 people. Cheo operas and traditional music concerts are usually staged on Friday and Saturday evenings at 8 pm, but call or stop by to confirm. Cheo is a form of satirical music theater from northern Vietnam. This theater will arrange special performances for groups of 10 or more. ✉ *1 Giang Van Minh St., Ba Dinh District, Hanoi* ☎ *024/3845–7403.*

Vietnam Opera and Ballet Theater

BALLET | Vietnam Opera and Ballet Theater is where Vietnam's up-and-coming opera singers and ballerinas train to learn the skills they will need to perform at the Hanoi Opera House and even with foreign troupes. Performances take place sporadically and online information is sparse so always call ahead. ✉ *11 Ngo Nui Truc St., Ba Dinh District, Hanoi* ☎ *024/3846–2651.*

 Shopping

ART

54 Traditions Gallery

ANTIQUES & COLLECTIBLES | Vietnam's amazing ethnodiversity is highlighted at this gallery-antiques emporium. Craft works and cultural antiques obtained from the 54 ethnic groups in Vietnam are spread over four floors. A shipping service is available. ✉ *12 Hang Bun, Tay Ho District* ☎ *091/232–1487* ⊕ *www.54traditions. com.vn.*

★ **Manzi Art Space and Cafe**

ART GALLERIES | Founders Tram Vu and Bill Nguyen opened Manzi, the first and best place to purchase contemporary Vietnamese art in Hanoi, in 2012. The gallery's focus is to support and promote up-and-coming Vietnamese artists through exhibitions, concerts, charity events, and by providing a creative space to work within. Much of the art displayed can be purchased, and the adjoining cafe serves as a great co-working space, too. They have a sister exhibition space just around the corner (2 Ngo Hang Bun). ✉ *14 Phan Huy Ich, Ba Dinh District* ☎ *024/3716–3397.*

Nguyen Art Gallery

ART GALLERIES | This prestigious gallery stocks original and quality paintings as well as sculptures. The focus is on young and emerging artists from Vietnam. Art can be viewed and ordered online and shipped worldwide. ✉ *31 Van Mieu St., Hanoi* ☎ *091/334–2887 cell phone* ⊕ *www.nguyenartgallery.com.*

HANDICRAFTS

Craft Link

SOUVENIRS | This nonprofit organization benefits local artisans by selling their handmade crafts such as textiles, bags, scarfs, clothing, and trinkets at fair-market prices. Items are of high quality and prices are reasonable. The back room on the first floor has a designated section of handbags and silk purses. ✉ *43 Van Mieu, near the Temple of Literature, Hanoi* ☎ *024/3733–6101* ⊕ *www.craftlink. com.vn.*

HOUSEWARES AND FURNISHINGS

DOME

FURNITURE | Well-designed, modern home furnishings—linens, furniture, lamps, candles, and more—are for sale here. Simple, curved designs in wrought iron are a signature style, one you'll see in restaurants and hotels throughout town. ✉ *10 Yen The St., Ba Dinh District* ☎ *024/3843–6036* ⊕ *www.dome.com.vn.*

West Lake and Truc Bach Lake

About 3 km (2 miles) northwest of Hoan Kiem Lake is West Lake (Ho Tay), a body of water that's steeped in legend. It is said that a giant golden calf from China followed the peals of a monk's bronze bell to this spot. When the ringing stopped, the calf lost its direction and kept walking in circles, creating the basin of West Lake. Like Hoan Kiem's tortoise, the calf is said still to dwell in the lake. West Lake's wealth of history takes a more tangible form in the temples and pagodas that line its shores. Development is changing the face of the shore, however, as luxury apartment buildings and high-rent villas eat away at the land of traditional flower villages like Nghi Tam, where wealthy expatriates seclude themselves behind walls of bougainvillea. As such, West Lake is home to Hanoi's most eclectic selection of international restaurants.

Next to West Lake and separated by Thanh Nien Street sits Truc Bach Lake, a smaller body of water that's become a popular weekend spot for Vietnamese couples, who paddle around the murky waters in boats shaped like ducks and swans. Afterward they stop at one of the cafes overlooking the lake or snack on banh tom (deep-fried shrimp cakes) and pho cuon (fresh spring rolls with beef), two neighborhood specialty dishes. Walking around Truc Bach Lake takes about an hour, but allow for more time if you want to peek around the temples and pagodas. Allow even more time if you want to rent a swan boat. The walk along Phan Dinh Phung Street, Hanoi's most picturesque street, back toward Old Quarter is another 15 to 25 minutes.

◉ Sights

John McCain Memorial
MONUMENT | This small memorial between West Lake and Truc Bach Lake marks the capture of one of the Vietnam War's most famous American POWs. On October 26, 1967, Navy lieutenant commander John McCain's jet fighter was shot down, sending him parachuting into Truc Bach Lake. Suffering from badly broken bones and severe beatings, he was imprisoned in the "Hanoi Hilton" and other North Vietnamese prisons for more than five years. He went on to become an Arizona senator and a vocal advocate of reconciliation between the United States and his former captors, and was a presidential candidate in 2008. The underwhelming red-sandstone memorial features a bound and suspended prisoner with his head hanging low and the letters U.S.A.F. (the memorial is incorrectly labeled, as McCain belonged to the navy and not the air force). ⊠ Thanh Nien St., Tay Ho District.

Quan Thanh Temple
(Chua Quan Thanh or Tran Vu Quan)
TEMPLE | A large black bronze statue of the Taoist god Tran Vu is housed here, protected on either side by wooden statues of civil and military mandarins. Built by King Ly Thai To in the 11th century, this much-made-over temple was once known as the Temple of the Grand Buddha; its present name translates into "Holy Mandarin Temple." An important collection of 17th-century poems can be seen in the shrine room. On the right side of this room is an altar dedicated to Trum Trong, the master bronze caster who oversaw the construction of Tran Vu's statue. Note the red, gold-stitched boots in the center of the shrine room; although such boots customarily appear in temples with figures of civil and military mandarins, Emperor Thanh Thai presented them in a vein of humor to Tran Vu's shoeless statue. Above the ornamented main gate is a 1677 replica

of the bronze bell that supposedly lured the West Lake's legendary golden calf from China. Huge mango and longan trees drape over the courtyard, keeping the temple and its environs cool and somewhat dark, even at midday. Two mounted stone elephants, symbols of loyalty, flank the entrance here. Go in the morning to avoid the afternoon crowds. ✉ *Quan Thanh St., Ba Dinh District* 🎫 *10,000d donation.*

Tay Ho Temple

TEMPLE | Phu Tay Ho, a temple dedicated to a 17th-century princess named Lieu Hanh, more popularly known here as Thanh Mau (Mother of the Nation), is attractive for its gigantic banyan trees and the view from West Lake's eastern shore. In the middle chamber of the main prayer hall is a sub-altar containing the statue of a holy tiger that protects Lieu Hanh, who is visible through the wooden slats of a locked separating wall inside the back chamber. In a second worship hall, women come to pray to another national mother figure, Nhi Thuong Ngan, for happiness and luck in motherhood and marriage. Two prayer stupas in the shady courtyard are dedicated to the guardian spirits of young boys and girls, Lau Cau and Lau Co, respectively. In spring and summer, you can sometimes catch locals treading water as far as 200 yards from the lakeside wall of the temple, fully clothed and with their conical hats glinting in the sun as they manipulate long pole-nets to collect snails from the bottom of the lake. A taxi is the easiest way to get here. ✉ *At the end of Pho Phu Tay Ho St., directly off Dang Thai Mai St., Tay Ho District* 🎫 *Free.*

★ Tran Quoc Pagoda (*Chua Tran Quoc*)

TEMPLE | Hanoi's oldest pagoda dates from the 6th century, when King Ly Nam De had a pagoda, named Khai Quoc, built on the bank of the Red River. More than a thousand years later excessive erosion of the riverbank caused King Le Kinh Tong to move the pagoda to Goldfish Islet (Ca Vang) on West Lake and rename it Tran Quoc. This modest pagoda is noted for its stelae dating from 1639, which recount the history of the building and its move from the Red River. There are also lovely brick stupas adjacent to the main temple. Tran Quoc is an active monastery where resident monks in brown robes hold daily services. Architecturally distinct from other Hanoi pagodas, Tran Quoc maintains a visitor's hall in front and various statues, including a gilded wooden depiction of Shakyamuni Buddha. In the main courtyard is a giant pink-and-green planter holding a bodhi tree, purportedly a cutting from the original bodhi tree beneath which the Buddha reached his enlightenment. The bodhi was a gift from former Indian president Razendia Prasat, who visited the pagoda in 1959. ✉ *Thanh Nien St., Tay Ho District* 🎫 *Free.*

🍴 Restaurants

Chops

$$ | **AMERICAN** | **FAMILY** | With three always-full locations, Chops is becoming a staple in Hanoi's foodie community. Their slogan, "Hops, Wheat, Meat," says it all. **Known for:** seriously good service; Australian beef and lamb burgers; beer. 💲 *Average main: d170,000* ✉ *4 Quang An, Tay Ho District* ☎ *024/6292–1044* ⊕ *www.chopsvietnam.com.*

★ Cousins

$$ | **FRENCH** | The outdoor area of this French-influenced venue is an ideal place for some very romantic dining and expat gatherings. The interior is equally convivial with stripped pine tables and wooden furniture. **Known for:** rotating menus; imported pork belly; wine and Champagne options. 💲 *Average main: d250,000* ✉ *15 Ngo 45 To Ngoc Van, Tay Ho District* ☎ *083/867–0098 cell phone.*

★ Cugini

$$$ | **ITALIAN** | The owner of Cousins (*cugini* means cousins in Italian) partnered with Italian chef Nico Ceccomoro to create an authentic dining experience at decent prices. Classy red and black interiors, sensual paintings, and a tree-shaded balcony make this location perfect for a date night. **Known for:** knowledgeable staff; slow-cooked meat; creative pasta dishes. [$] *Average main: d300,000* ✉ *67 To Ngoc Van, Tay Ho District* ☎ *088/811–6654 cell phone.*

El Gaucho

$$$$ | **STEAKHOUSE** | The West Lake branch of a chain of Argentinean steak houses with outlets in Ho Chi Minh City and Bangkok, El Gaucho Hanoi is modern and assured. A variety of cuts are imported from the United States and Australia. **Known for:** stellar service; exemplary (if expensive) steaks; familiar sides, such as mac and cheese and corn on the cob. [$] *Average main: d1,000,000* ✉ *2 Tay Ho, Tay Ho District* ☎ *0024/3718–6991* 🌐 *www.elgaucho.asia.*

The Grumpy Dumpling

$$ | **ASIAN** | Australian dumpling chef Gabby Redmond opened this trendy evening spot in 2021. With a smart selection of dumplings (steamed, pan-fried, or deep-fried), a stellar wine menu, and a cozy balcony with views of West Lake, The Grumpy Dumpling caters to young expats and hip locals. **Known for:** good wine; lake views; deep-fried cheeseburger dumplings. [$] *Average main: d180,000* ✉ *37 Ngo 52 To Ngon Van, Quan Tay Ho* ☎ *078/239–8715 cell phone* 🌐 *facebook.com/thegrumpydumpling* 🕒 *Closed Mon.*

★ Koto Villa

$$ | **ECLECTIC** | **FAMILY** | Now gracing a French-style villa in West Lake (the restaurant used to be next to the Temple of Literature), this place can get packed with tour groups. The flavors here—from baked fish in banana leaf to bamboo beef—are bold and brilliant, and the menu is a mix of creative dishes. **Known for:** creative and delicious cuisine; charity restaurant benefiting kids; tourist favorite. [$] *Average main: d250,000* ✉ *Alley 35 Dang Thai Mai, Tay Ho District* ☎ *084/438–3999* 🌐 *www.kotovilla.com.*

★ Maison de Tet Decor

$$ | **ECLECTIC** | **FAMILY** | This beautiful bohemian villa serves up excellent food and an impressive farm-to-table ethos. They own two farms, one in Sapa and one in Soc Son, so all produce is carefully grown and selected. **Known for:** freshly roasted coffee; tranquility; organic food. [$] *Average main: d200,000* ✉ *26 Quang Ba, Tay Ho District* ☎ *024/3823–9722.*

Sushi Dokoro Yutaka

$$ | **JAPANESE** | This West Lake institution serves some of the best Japanese food in Hanoi. The city has a sizeable community of Japanese expats, which means that this venue is reliably packed with homesick salarymen looking to sample an authentic taste of home. **Known for:** particularly good sushi and sashimi; lunch sets; bento boxes. [$] *Average main: d250,000* ✉ *95 Xuan Dieu, Tay Ho District* ☎ *024/3718–6344* 🕒 *Closed Mon.*

★ Vege-ro

$$ | **RAMEN** | Vegans and vegetarians descend on this hole-in-the-wall ramen joint for their tofu, tempeh, and other meat alternatives, but the rich broth will likely tickle omnivores' taste buds, too. Fewer than ten seats face the Japanese ramen chef, so you can watch him meticulously prepare your meal before slurping it up. **Known for:** rich ramen broth; creative meat alternatives; intimate atmosphere. [$] *Average main: d180,000* ✉ *105A2 Lac Chinh, Hanoi* ☎ *084/532–5729* 🌐 *facebook.com/hanoivegetarianramen* 💳 *No credit cards.*

Coffee and Quick Bites

★ Ma Xo
$$ | **CAFÉ** | Little sister to Hanoi institution The Hanoi Social Club, Ma Xo is the place to go for coffee, cocktails, and quick bites. The menu features home brunch comforts and innovative creations, such as fresh spring rolls with duck, a modern take on the neighborhood's favorite dish. **Known for:** lake views; comfort food; boho vibes. [$] *Average main: d130,000* ✉ *152 Tran Vu* ☎ *033/385–0852 cell phone* 🌐 *facebook.com/Ma.Xo.Cafe.*

Milk and Honey
$$ | **CAFÉ** | This all-day cafe serves up some of West Lake's best coffee, with freshly baked cookies, cakes, and croissants to match. Tuck into overnight oats and fresh juice for brunch or peruse a small but thoughtful selection of sandwiches for lunch. **Known for:** rotating cake selection; creamy cappuccinos; lunch set menu deals. [$] *Average main: d100,000* ✉ *46 Tu Hoa, Tay Ho District* 🌐 *facebook.com/milkandhoneyhanoi.*

Pho Cuon Chinh Thang
$ | **VIETNAMESE** | More of a snack and less of a fully fledged meal, *pho cuon* (fresh spring rolls with beef) is a Truc Bach specialty. This family-run eatery serves up some of the freshest and tastiest rolls in the neighborhood on a handful of tables that occasionally spill out onto the street. **Known for:** neighborhood specialty; mom-and-pop vibes; on-the-go snack. [$] *Average main: d70,000* ✉ *7 Mac Dinh Chi* ☎ *083/684–8819 cell phone* 🌐 *foody.vn/ha-noi/pho-cuon-chinh-thang* 💳 *No credit cards.*

Hotels

Hanoi Club
$$$ | **HOTEL** | Despite being a little outdated, well-appointed rooms at this sports club afford spectacular sunset views over West Lake and include the use of the club's facilities. **Pros:** plenty of sports facilities; lakeside setting; terrace bar. **Cons:** so much to do, you might not want to leave the property; in need of a makeover; on-site restaurant below average. [$] *Rooms from: d2,300,000* ✉ *76 Yen Phu St., Tay Ho District* ☎ *024/3823–8115, 024/3823–8390* 🌐 *www.thehanoiclub.com* 🛏 *89 rooms* 🍴 *No Meals.*

★ InterContinental Hanoi Westlake
$$$$ | **HOTEL** | **FAMILY** | In a tranquil setting, over-the-water pavilions house spacious rooms with balconies and great views of West Lake and Hanoi, helping guests feel removed from the urban bustle of the city center, even though the hotel is only a couple of miles from the Old Quarter and Hoan Kiem Lake. **Pros:** glass-walled restaurant with views; large pool; cooking classes for kids. **Cons:** spa not up to the level you would expect at this price point; breakfast buffet not included in rate. [$] *Rooms from: d2,520,000* ✉ *5 Tu Hoa, Tay Ho District* ☎ *024/6270–8888* 🌐 *hanoi.intercontinental.com* 🍴 *No Meals* 🛏 *318 rooms.*

Pan Pacific Hanoi
$$$$ | **HOTEL** | Stunning views of Truc Bach Lake and West Lake and a central location are two of the highlights of this luxury hotel, but the standout is the indoor heated swimming pool with a view over the neighboring lakes and a retractable roof for year-round swimming. **Pros:** great restaurants; club floor benefits are extremely attractive; near Truc Bach's attractions. **Cons:** not central; rooftop bar is a little dated. [$] *Rooms from: d2,675,000* ✉ *1 Thanh Nien St., Ba*

Dinh District, Hanoi ☎ 024/3823–8888, 024/3829–3888 ⊕ www.panpacific.com ⇨ 273 rooms ⦿ No Meals.

☕ Nightlife

BARS AND PUBS

The Bottle Shop

BEER GARDENS | Sister bar to Standing Bar, The Bottle Shop serves a dizzying array of bottled craft beers from Vietnam and beyond. There are a couple of pub benches at the front and a cozy beer yard out back that's popular with expats, especially on warm weekend afternoons. ✉ 25B Ngo 12 Dang Thai Mai, Quan Tay Ho ☎ 098/317–1366 ⊕ www.thebottleshop.vn ⊙ Closed Mon.

Furbrew

BEER GARDENS | The beer alone is worth the trip but it's the employees that make this bar truly special. They are passionate not only about the beer, but about customer service as well. There are always 8 to 10 beers on tap, but the brewers have created more than 50 different varieties since they opened. The pho beer has a taste profile similar to that of a spiced Christmas ale back home, and the bar is big enough to host your whole party. ✉ 52 To Ngoc Van, Tay Ho District ☎ 091/266–6736 cell phone ⊕ www.furbrew.vn.

★ Standing Bar

BREWPUBS | At Standing Bar you'll find a tempting selection of beers and ciders with which to wash down elaborate beer snacks, including smoked sausage, goat's cheese croquettes, and sun-dried tuna. The west-facing lakeside setting shines at sunset, and the second story plays host to comedy nights and live music. ✉ 170 Tran Vu, Tay Ho District ☎ 024/3266–8057 ⊕ standingbarhanoi.com/en.

🛍 Shopping

BOOKS

★ Bookworm

BOOKS | Owned by avid reader Hoang Van Truong, this is by some distance Hanoi's best bookshop. There are over 10,000 books in stock and Truong and his learned team speak excellent English. The new location doubles as a cute café. ✉ 44 Pham Hong Thai, Ba Dinh District ☎ 024/3715–3711 ⊕ www.bookwormhanoi.com.

MARKETS

Quang Ba Flower Market

FLORIST | Earlier risers and victims of jet lag will enjoy this flower market that opens at 10 pm and continues until just past sunrise. It's the floral hub for wholesalers who arrive with bundles of roses and chrysanthemums tethered to their bikes and mopeds. Even if you aren't in the market for flowers, this place is oozing with photo opportunities. ✉ Au Co St., Tay H, near West Lake, Hanoi.

🏃 Activities

Sports have been an integral and institutionalized part of the Hanoi educational system for years. Many resources are still committed to the study and improvement of martial arts such as tae kwon do and *wushu*, two disciplines in which Vietnam is world renowned. Ping-Pong and badminton are also determinedly pursued.

BIKING

★ Hanoi Bicycle Collective

BIKING | While nobody would call frenetic Hanoi a cyclist's paradise, the Hanoi Bicycle Collective is doing its best to encourage the use of pedal power. As well as serving as a retail space, with several brands of bike on offer, the outlet has set itself up to become a hub of cycling life, commuting, social activity, and fitness. They can rent good quality bicycles, but make sure you call ahead. ✉ 31 Nhat Chieu, Tay Ho District ☎ 097/817–3156 ⊕ www.thbc.vn.

BOATING

Paddleboating was once in vogue in Hanoi, but youngsters have since found other ways to entertain themselves. Nevertheless, you can still rent swan-shape paddleboats on the southwest corner of **Truc Bach Lake**. Sailing, rowing, and other water-sports are, for the most part, reserved for members of the elite Hanoi Club on the east shore of West Lake and the Olympic athletes that train on the west shore. If you're not a Hanoi Club (or the guest of a member), the only way you'll be able to use the club's catamarans and other goodies (including tennis, racquetball, squash, and exercise facilities and a swimming pool) is if you stay at the hotel or apartment facilities managed by the club.

BOWLING

Bowling is a popular activity for Vietnam's younger urbanites. If your image of bowling includes folks in matching shirts, you're in for a surprise: pumping music, lights, and local beer add a little extra excitement to this wholesome pursuit. Some of the newer malls include a bowling alley, kids' zone, and a cinema. If you're intent on bowling, call ahead to reserve a lane.

Dream Games Bowling

BOWLING | Bowling games at Dreams Games Bowling, which sits on the 4th story of Aeon Mall, a sparkling Japanese shopping center, cost less than 100,000d per person per game, including shoe rental. It's rarely busy, but you can call ahead and reserve a lane. ⊠ *Aeon Mall, 27 Co Linh, Long Bien* ☎ *024/3200–3190*.

GOLF

BRG Kings Island Golf Resort

GOLF | BRG Kings Island Golf Resort is a gorgeous course surrounded by the beautiful Tan Vien Mountain. Golf in Vietnam is not cheap, however. For members, 36 holes costs more than 2,000,000d; for nonmembers it can be more than 7,000,000d. Renting clubs will set you back at least 1,100,000d,

and there are other service charges to consider. ⊠ *Dong Mo, about 45 km (28 miles) west of Hanoi, Son Tay town* ☎ *024/3368–6555* ⊕ *brgkingsislandgolf. vn* ⊠ *Fees are updated each season: see website* ✝ *36 holes, 6454 yards, par 72.*

SOCCER

No sport captures the attention and hearts of the Vietnamese quite like soccer. The game's biggest crowds are down in Ho Chi Minh City, but the religiously followed semiprofessional national league packs them in at the 20,000-seat capacity Hang Day Stadium. The season runs roughly from January to August and when the Hanoi Police face off against the Ho Chi Minh City Police in the capital, you can bet the stadium is rocking. Smaller matches are held at the Army Stadium, in the southern portion of the citadel, with access from Hoang Dieu Street. Many Vietnamese bars in town have a soccer schedule, and with a bit of gesturing and pointing you should be able to figure out whether or not a huge match is going on while you're in town.

Hang Day Stadium

SOCCER | The national V.League packs soccer fans in at the 22,000-seat capacity Hang Day Stadium. The season runs roughly from January to August. ⊠ *9 Trinh Hoai Duc, Dong Da District* ☎ *024/3734–4923*.

THEATER AND OPERA

★ Vietnam National Tuong Theatre

THEMED ENTERTAINMENT | Rivaling the musical aspect of the famed Water Puppet Theater, but sans the water puppets, this remarkable show blends acting, music, comedy, and storytelling in an hour-long performance. This version of a Chinese opera comprises five acts, and there is English translation between each segment. Check the website to see the performance schedule. Note that the theater has another location out west in Chau Giay District. ⊠ *51 Duong Thanh, Hoan Kiem District* ☎ *098/454–5228 cell phone.*

TRADITIONAL MUSIC

As many of Vietnam's dramatic performances are closely linked with the strains of Vietnamese music, there are very few concerts of exclusively traditional music in the city. Your best bet is to see a water-puppet performance or go to the theater to watch cheo, tuong, or cai luong.

If you happen across an old man or woman on the street who's playing a one-stringed instrument in an impromptu fashion, consider yourself extremely lucky.

Xam, a type of melancholy folk music, is a dying art in Vietnam—and not because it's the music played at funerals, although xam artists are often invited to perform at such functions. Xam artists are simply dying off, and no one's replacing them. Four professional xam musicians were on hand throughout the day and evening at Hoan Kiem Lake in Hanoi—one at each corner—in the xam heyday of the early 1940s. A half century later there's not a single true xam master plying his or her trade on the streets of the capital. One aging xam professional, the unflagging Hoang Thi Cau of Ninh Binh Province, has done much to save her art from extinction by teaching xam to some cheo performing groups in and around Hanoi and by recording her performances for future generations. But the prospects for this ancient art are bleak; cheo artists are understandably concerned with preserving their own beloved art, and experts say that true xam music cannot be performed by anyone but a bona fide xam master.

WATER PUPPETRY

The thousand-year-old art of *mua roi nuoc,* or water puppetry, is unique to northern Vietnam and easily ranks as one of Southeast Asia's most beautiful and complex art forms. Long considered an art of the common people, water puppetry gained acceptance at royal celebrations and was often performed for reigning emperors and kings. Water puppetry is performed on—and under, in particular—a small pond whose surface conceals the flurry of activity beneath it. Through the near-magical use of bamboo rods and a system of pulleys and levers, master puppeteers stand waist deep at the back of the pond (usually behind a curtain) and make their lacquered marionettes literally walk on water. Shows usually depict scenes from rural life and Vietnamese legend, and the experience is positively delightful.

National Puppetry Theater

PUPPET SHOWS | The National Puppet Theater holds water-puppet shows that are more in the vein of village performances, harking back to the days when water puppets were used as political commentary right under the noses of bad kings or provincial French rulers. Traveling water-puppet theaters traditionally relayed information from village to village. You may find that you are as much of the show as the puppets. Check the website for the performance schedule. ✉ *361 Truong Chinh St., Dong Da District, Hanoi* ☎ *024/3853–4545* ⊕ *nhahatmuaroivietnam.vn* 🎫 *80,000d.*

★ Thang Long Water Puppet Theater

PUPPET SHOWS | As one of Hanoi's top tourist attractions, this entertaining performance gives you insight into Vietnam's history and traditions through water puppetry storytelling, at least three musicians, and interlude commentaries. Somewhat humorous and endearing at times, puppets are guided through the water by puppeteers hidden behind a curtain. The hour-long show, which takes place several times a day, highlights the folklore and culture of this ancient civilization. Thang Long Water Puppet is aimed only at tourists, and so is not for the cynical and disenchanted traveler. For a more authentic and intimate experience, head to the National Puppetry Theatre or catch one of the shows at the Museum of Ethnology. Flashing cameras and video

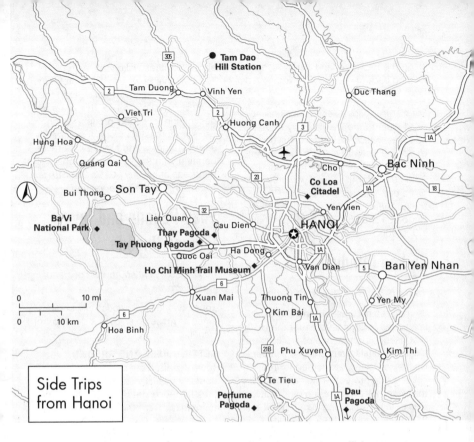

Side Trips
from Hanoi

recorders can be extremely distracting.
✉ 57B Dinh Tien Hoang, Hoan Kiem
District ☎ 091/351–1063 cell phone
⊕ thanglongwaterpuppet.com 💵 From
100,000d.

Side Trips from Hanoi

Although Hanoi is the cultural hub of
northern Vietnam, much of the city's
history and many of its legends and traditions are rooted in the region surrounding
the capital. Citadels, temples, art guilds,
and festival focal points ring the city, and
a few hours' drive in any direction will
bring you to points of interest ranging
from pagodas to idyllic valleys and national parks.

Tours organized by Hanoi's tourist cafés
and tour operators cover all of the sights

and are the most time-efficient way to
see this region. Tourist café tours are less
expensive than those run by travel agencies. If a group tour isn't available to the
site you want, arrange a private car and
driver for the day. A good example is the
silk-making village of Van Phuc, the Bat
Trang pottery village, a snake farm in Gia
Lam across the Red River, and the village
of Dong Ho, where the ancient folk art of
wood-block printing is still practiced. The
trip averages 2,500,000d for an air-conditioned car and driver for the whole day.
An English-speaking guide costs from
800,000d to 1,000,000d per day.

Another great way of escaping the city
and seeing some of its most interesting
immediate outlying areas is by taking a
day or a half-day cycling tour. Most of
the best tour operators can arrange an
itinerary that typically takes in the villages

along the Red River and Bat Trang before looping back to the Old Quarter via West Lake and Ba Dinh District.

For history, religion, and a bit of hiking, head west to the Thay and Tay Phuong pagodas, which makes for a full day of exploring. Go with a group tour or rent a private car with a driver for around 3,000,000d for the trip. If you only have half a day, take a trip to Co Loa Citadel to the northeast. A private car with driver to Co Loa and back will cost less than 1,000,000d, including waiting time.

Co Loa Citadel

15 km (9 miles) northeast of Hanoi.

30 minutes northeast of the Old Quarter is a series of large earthen ramparts that used to protect one of the country's earliest capitals from Chinese invaders. Co Loa, or "snail," so named for the spiral-shape protective walls and moats that resembled the design of a nautilus, was built by An Duong Vuong more than 2,000 years ago and remains one of northern Vietnam's important historical relics.

GETTING HERE AND AROUND
You should be able to hire a car with driver for less than 1,000,000d to go from Hanoi to Co Loa Citadel. A round-trip and a visit to the citadel takes about three hours.

◉ Sights

Co Loa Citadel
RUINS | The first fortified citadel in Vietnamese history (dating back to the 3rd century) and a onetime capital of the country, Co Loa is worth visiting for those with an interest in the nation's history. Only three of the original earthen ramparts are extant today. You can explore the site of the ancient imperial palace and nearby, under an old banyan tree, is the Ba Chua temple. A large

and colorful festival on the sixth day of Tet, the lunar new year, celebrates King An Vuong Duong, now considered the guardian spirit of Co Loa. This is a popular destination for school groups, which can sometimes transform the normally serene temples into playgrounds reverberating with the laughter and chatting of hundreds of children. ⊠ *Co Loa Citadel, Hanoi* 🖾 *10,000d per attraction.*

Thay Pagoda and Tay Phuong Pagoda

40 km (25 miles) southwest of Hanoi in Ha Tay Province.

These two lovely pagodas can be combined to make an enjoyable day trip from Hanoi.

GETTING HERE AND AROUND
Trips organized by tourist cafés and tour operators usually cover the admission fees for these sites. It's easy to arrange tours that cover both pagodas.

◉ Sights

Tay Phuong Pagoda
TEMPLE | The Tay Phuong Pagoda, or Western Pagoda, comprises three sanctuaries built into Cau Lau Mountain and surrounded by a square enclosure. Each ancient wooden structure is separated by a small pool of water that reflects an eerie soothing light into the temples. Begun in the 3rd century, the pagoda was rebuilt in the 9th century and expanded to its present size under the Tay Son dynasty in 1794. The centuries-old curved rooftops are particularly noteworthy, as are the masterpieces of wood sculpture: more than six dozen figures carved from jackfruit wood. The pagoda's rafters are elaborately carved with bas-reliefs of dragons and lotuses, and ceramic animal statues grace the rooftops. ⊠ *Thach That* 🖾 *5,000d.*

Thay Pagoda

TEMPLE | The Thay Pagoda, or Master's Pagoda, is named in honor of Tu Dao Hanh, a 12th-century monk. The grounds of the four main sanctuaries here ring shrill with the chirping of cicadas and are lush with fruit trees and a giant frangipani said to be 700 years old. In the upper pagoda (Chua Thuong) a statue of Master Hanh sits in the foreground of a large central altar that supports the statues of 18 arhats, monks who have reached enlightenment. The altar to the left of this holds Ly Nhan Tong, a king who was the supposed reincarnation of Tu Dao Hanh. Stone steps adjacent to the pagoda lead farther up the mountain to various shrines and temples and lovely vista points. The Thay Pagoda is the site of one of two ancient water-puppetry stages remaining in Vietnam. Constructed during the 15th century, this small stage sits on stilts in the middle of a pond and was used during elaborate pagoda ceremonies and royal visits. Water-puppetry shows still take place here, particularly on the annual festival of the pagoda, which is from the 5th through the 7th days of the third lunar month. ⊠ *Quoc Oai* 🚗 *5,000d.*

Tam Dao Hill Station

85 km (53 miles) northwest of Hanoi in Vinh Phuc Province.

Up in the clouds, the damp hill station of Tam Dao splits opinion. In 1907 French developers scaled the rugged 4,590-foot peaks (there are three of them) north of Hanoi and decided the cool weather of a nearby mountain retreat could serve the French well. The result was a graceful town of elegant villas surrounded by lush vegetation and sweeping views of the valley below. Since the French left in 1954, however, little grace has been bestowed on Tam Dao, whose chalet charm took a decided turn for the worse when Soviet-era architecture announced itself in the form of a monstrously square 40-room hotel. More recently, a string of developments flaunting garish colors and sometimes bizarre architectural decisions have proliferated throughout the town. Although still not what it once was, the town square and many villas around have been renovated and many Vietnamese tourists enjoy the views and food from the restaurants around town. More and more development is underway and Tam Dao is rising again as another weekend destination easy reachable from Hanoi. Tam Dao can get uncomfortably busy on Saturday and Sunday, but is rather quiet during the week. The Animals Asia Bear Rescue Center is located at the foot of the mountainous road leading to Tam Dao Hill Station.

GETTING HERE AND AROUND

Buses to the town of Vinh Yen near Tam Dao run from Gia Lam bus station in Hanoi (40,000d, one hour). From there, the easiest way to get to Tam Dao is to charter a xe om (motorbike taxi) for the 24-km (15-mile) journey to the national park. The ride should cost no more than 200,000d, but you'll need to haggle. Hiring a car and driver for the day from Hanoi will cost about 1,500,000d.

⊙ Sights

Tam Dao Hill Station

FOREST | Tam Dao's main attraction lies in its elevation and subsequent cool temperatures: it's a nice way to beat the heat of Hanoi, and the hiking is fair. Don't expect much in the way of information on trails, however, unless you have organized a tour with one of the better Hanoi tour operators. Few people, even locals, realize that Tam Dao and the surrounding peaks are in a national park, which may be one reason why logging and poaching remain a problem for the area (some of the restaurants here list supposedly protected animals on their menus). But for the most part, a hike up to the radio transmitter above the town is a walk into dense jungle. Small Buddhist temples line the concrete steps up to the tower, and a spring bubbles up from beneath the underbrush and splays out into a small waterfall. If you're spending the night up in these mountains, bring a sweater and some rain gear. People have been known to ride mountain bikes up to Tam Dao and spend the night, but the climb is extreme (a 10% gradient over long stretches). Less-active riders put their bikes in minivans on the way up and then careen down the extremely winding and dangerous—but ultimately exhilarating—route to the base of the mountain.

🛏 Hotels

Belvedere Resort

$$$ | RESORT | Like some other resorts in northern Vietnam, the Belvedere combines trappings of luxury with the odd lapse in taste. **Pros:** tennis courts and pool table on-site; terrace café is a lovely spot; outdoor pool. **Cons:** the pool gets packed on the weekends; severe markup on average restaurant food; quite dated. 💲 *Rooms from: d1,800,000* ✉ *Hamlet 2, Tam Dao* ☎ *094/787–7688 cell phone* 🌐 *www.bel.vn* 🛎 *48 rooms* 🍽 *Free Breakfast.*

Ho Chi Minh Trail Museum and the Perfume Pagoda

15 km (9 miles) and 60 km (37 miles) south of Hanoi, respectively.

One of Hanoi's less visited historic sights, perhaps due to its distance from the city center, the Ho Chi Minh Trail Museum delivers an interesting insight to the effort and determination that went into maintaining the famous supply route from the Communist north to Vietcong strongholds in the American-backed south of Vietnam. The Perfume Pagoda, meanwhile, offers interesting shrines and a romantic river journey. This trip can also be combined with a visit to the mummies in the Dau Pagoda.

GETTING HERE AND AROUND

Day trips from Hanoi to the Perfume Pagoda, leaving at about 6:30 am, are available from any number of tour operators, as well as from tourist cafés. These tours run around 800,000d per person, including all transport and entrance fees. You can also rent a car for about 1,500,000d, and a guide for 650,000d. Most tours from Hanoi skip the Ho Chi Minh Trail Museum, meaning that to combine the two attractions you'll need to rent a vehicle.

👁 Sights

Dau Pagoda

TEMPLE | This 11th-century pagoda from the Ly dynasty houses Vietnam's two most famous mummies. In 1639 the Buddhist monks Vu Khac Minh and Vu Khac Truong locked themselves in a private room to meditate, instructing their disciples not to disturb them for 100 days. On the 100th day, their disciples entered the room to find both monks seated in a lotus position, perfectly preserved in death. The monks' bodies were covered in a thin but durable red lacquer. What makes these mummies unique is that they still have all their bones and organs. Dau Pagoda contains several other noteworthy artifacts, including a giant bronze bell built in 1801, a bronze book detailing the pagoda's construction, several stone stelae dating to the 17th century, and six altars for the worship of 18 arhats (enlightened monks). The pagoda, which was partially destroyed by French forces in 1947, consists of five halls, an accessible (just barely) bell tower, and a small walking garden full of jackfruit and longan trees, birds of paradise, and a temple dedicated to local deities. Rice fields and ponds surround the pagoda, and you'll pass duck farmers and lotus vendors near the grove-shaded road that leads to the entrance. The pagoda is less

A short distance from Hanoi is Ba Vi National Park, a foggy and lush former hill station.

than an hour's ride south of Hanoi. Take a taxi or hire a private car to get here, and keep an eye peeled for a sign directing you to turn right off Highway 1 toward the pagoda. ⊠ *Hwy. 1, 24 km (15 miles) south of Hanoi* 🕮 *Free.*

Ho Chi Minh Trail Museum

HISTORY MUSEUM | The elaborate network of paths of the Ho Chi Minh Trail was used by North Vietnam to transport supplies to Vietcong strongholds in South Vietnam during the Vietnam War. The Ho Chi Minh Trail Museum (Bao Tang Duong Mon Ho Chi Minh) provides color on the trail, one of the war's most riveting symbols of dedication and perseverance. Renovated in 2017, the museum is decidedly more modern. Displays are heavy on photojournalism from the period. There's also an extensive collection of captured American ordnance and military equipment as well as personal artifacts such as helmets, IDs, and uniforms. This museum lies some distance outside of Hanoi's Old Quarter and can be hard to find, so it's best if you hire a taxi or car

and driver. ⊠ *Yen Nghia, Ha Dong, Hanoi* 🕿 *096/852–2559 cell phone* 🕮 *20,000d* 🕑 *Closed Sun. and lunchtime.*

Perfume Pagoda

TEMPLE | Considered one of Vietnam's most important Buddhist sites, the Perfume Pagoda (Chua Huong) is the largest of a cluster of shrines carved into the limestone of the Huong Tich Mountains. In late spring the trails leading up to the shrines are clogged with thousands making their pilgrimage to pray to Quan Am, the goddess of mercy and compassion. According to a Vietnamese version of the Chinese legend, Quan Am was a young wife falsely accused of trying to kill her newlywed husband. Thrown out of her mother-in-law's house, she took refuge in a monastery, posing as a monk. A reckless girl one day blamed her pregnancy on the monk, not knowing he was a she. Without a word of self-defense, the vilified monk took the child in and raised him. Only after Quan Am died did villagers discover her silent sacrifice. In the past, pilgrims came to the grottoes to pray for Quan Am's help in bearing sons and in fighting unjust accusations. From the shores of the Yen River, you are ferried to the site, 4 km (2½ miles) away, on sampans that seem to be made of flimsy aluminum. It's a spectacular ride through the flooded valley, past boats laden with fruit and farmers at work in their fields. You'll be let off at Chua Tien Chu. From there, follow a stone path uphill to the various pagodas and shrines. Three kilometers (2 miles) later you'll reach the Perfume Pagoda. A steep set of stairs takes you inside the impressive cavern, where gilded Buddhas and bodhisattvas sit nestled in rocky recesses. The air is misty from incense and the cooking fires of the Buddhist monks who tend the shrines. In early spring, from just after Tet to the middle of the second lunar month, thousands of Buddhists make their pilgrimage to the Perfume Pagoda. This is an intense—and sometimes stressful—time to visit as the crowds of Vietnamese faithful clog the Yen River with extra boats and make navigating the slippery stairs more of an exercise in caution than a journey of discovery. The atmosphere at this time of year is positively electric with thousands of Buddhists crowding into the cavern to leave offerings, catch a droplet of water from a holy stalactite, or buy Buddhist trinkets and mementos from the dozens of stall owners. Note that the climb up to the pagoda can be rough going, especially when it's muddy, and that local operators sometimes lead the climb at a very fast pace. Be careful of independent tourist agents—many have been known to take unsuspecting travelers to a smaller pagoda closer to Hanoi and tell them it's the Perfume Pagoda. Also, it's unwise to attempt this trip on your own as you will most likely be overcharged. ✉ *Huong Son, My Duc.*

Ba Vi National Park

65 km (41 miles) west of Hanoi.

With the triple-peaked Ba Vi Mountain as its towering centerpiece, this former French hill station is a popular weekend excursion for Hanoians. The park shelters several rare and endangered plants as well as plentiful birdlife. The high point (literally) of the park is a temple dedicated to Ho Chi Minh that sits at the mountain's summit.

GETTING HERE AND AROUND

Ba Vi National Park is a fair distance from Hanoi and is not commonly on the radar of most tour operators. To get there, the best option is to rent a vehicle in Hanoi for one or two days, depending on whether you want to stay overnight. A car with a driver starts around 2,000,000d per day. Another, cheaper way of visiting is to come here on motorbike. Bikes can be rented from any number of hotels, rental firms, and tourist cafés and start from 150,000d per day.

◉ Sights

★ Ba Vi National Park

NATIONAL PARK | Magnificent and (especially on one of the frequent foggy days) moody, Ba Vi offers a convenient natural refuge from the bustle of Hanoi. The national park is dominated by the triple-peaked Ba Vi Mountain, once a French hill station. The reserve around the mountain, meanwhile, boasts plentiful plant and birdlife and is ideal for hiking. The most popular walk in the area is the climb to the mountain's summit, which is a strenuous ascent up 1,320 steps through the trees. A temple dedicated to Ho Chi Minh sits at the mountain's summit. Due to its proximity to the capital, Ba Vi is one of Vietnam's most visited protected areas and numbers can be high on weekends and during holiday periods. ✉ *Ba Vi National Park, Tan Linh Commune* ☎ *096/617–3119* ⊕ *www. vuonquocgiabavi.com.vn.*

Chapter 9

THE NORTHWEST

9

Updated by
Khanh Nguyen

◉ Sights	🍴 Restaurants	🛏 Hotels	🛍 Shopping	🍸 Nightlife
★★★★★	★★☆☆☆	★★★☆☆	★★★☆☆	★☆☆☆☆

WELCOME TO THE NORTHWEST

TOP REASONS TO GO

★ **Conquer Vietnam's highest peak.** Scaling Mt. Fansipan is no small feat—it stands proud at 10,312 feet. The two-day hike to the summit can be wet and arduous, but you'll have the best vista in the country.

★ **Tackle the Ha Giang Loop by motorbike.** Vietnam has its fair share of classic road trips, but none are more epic than the so-called Ha Giang Loop, which starts in Ha Giang and entails a 805-km (500-mile) loop around the province. The most common route stops in Dong Van, Bao Lac, Be Be Lake, and Cho Ra.

★ **Treat your taste buds in Sapa.** Beyond Hanoi and Ho Chi Minh City, few destinations in Vietnam can claim as much culinary variety as Sapa. Sample contemporary takes on hill-tribe cuisine, decadent French cakes, and pizza.

★ **Bike around Mai Chau Valley.** Hard-core exploration it is not, but the flat floor of the Mai Chau Valley is ideal territory for using pedal power to propel yourself between traditional White Thai villages.

A little planning goes a long way when visiting this region. The preferred entry point for exploring the area is undoubtedly Sapa, and the traditional way of getting to the former French hill station was by overnight train from Hanoi to the border city of Lao Cai and then onward by bus. Now, however, with the opening of the Noi Bai-Lao Cai highway, a bus journey from Hanoi to Lao Cai takes just 3½ hours, making travel by road the quickest option. For travelers heading directly to Dien Bien Phu, the main airport there has daily connections with Hanoi. A bus ride from Dien Bien Phu to Hanoi can take up to 13 hours, so flying is the better option. By far the best way of experiencing the region in all its grandeur is via the Ha Giang or Northwest Loop. These grand tours, which take at least a week to do properly, kick off in Hanoi or Ha Giang.

1 Sapa. The bustling hill town and the tourist center of the Northwest, where Dao and H'mong women converge at the local market to buy, sell, and trade.

2 Bac Ha. This unhurried town makes a plausible alternative base in the area. It is famous for its Sunday market and has a growing choice of lodgings.

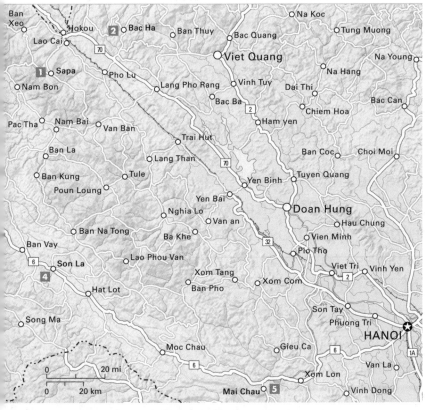

Vietnam's staggering beauty and ethnic diversity are perhaps most evident in the Northwest, where dozens of ethnic-minority groups as well as the Kinh, the ethnic majority, inhabit the imposing highlands. Physically and culturally removed from Hanoi, many communities in the remote region exist today as they have for generations, harvesting terraced rice fields or practicing slash-and-burn agriculture on the rocky hillsides. This region of imposing mountains bore witness to French ignominy at the battle of Dien Bien Phu, a crucial factor in the end of colonial rule in Indochina, which at the same time nurtured Ho Chi Minh's revolution.

The mountain town of Sapa is a star attraction for both domestic and international tourists, and with the new highway cutting journey times from Hanoi by more than half, the popularity of the former French hill station is set to increase. A large part of Sapa's appeal lies in its proximity to some of the most compelling sights in the region. It is the jumping-off point for expeditions into the nearby Hoang Lien Mountains, dubbed the Tonkinese Alps by the French. Preeminent among these mist-shrouded peaks is Fansipan, Vietnam's tallest summit at 10,308 feet. If the arduous hike up Fansipan doesn't appeal, numerous less demanding treks can be arranged from Sapa to nearby hill-tribe villages and through the bucolic surrounding scenery. Northeast of Sapa, the town of Bac Ha has a pleasant climate and one of the liveliest weekly Sunday markets in the region. From Sapa it is a glorious motorbike, car, or bus journey over the Tram Ton Pass, Vietnam's highest stretch of tarmac, to Lai Chau. This area has undergone a massive transformation. The former town of Lai Chau was flooded during construction of the Song Da Reservoir and is now known as Muong Lay. The new town of Lai Chau, formerly known as Tam Duong, has little of interest for travelers beyond the beautiful surrounding scenery and a diverting hill-tribe market.

Once considered something of an outpost, Dien Bien Phu has grown significantly since becoming a provincial capital in 2004. There are daily flights from Hanoi, and the presence of the nearby Tay Trang-Sop border crossing ensures a steady flow of tourist traffic. Beyond the historic and military sights, the main draw for visitors is the opportunity for trekking in the area. Surrounding villages make convenient hopping-off points for hikes into the hinterland. With flights from Hanoi making Dien Bien Phu simple to reach, it is perhaps the quickest and most convenient way of immersing yourself in the wondrous scenery. Southeast of Dien Bien Phu lies Son La Province, which is one of Vietnam's most ethnically diverse regions, home to more than 30 minorities including Black Thai, Meo, Muong, and White Thai. Farther southeast still is the Mai Chau Valley, an area that has boomed in popularity with tourists over the last few years. Homestays with the White Thai minority in the area are a fascinating way of experiencing traditional life, and the flat floor of the valley makes it a perfect place to explore by bicycle.

A booming business of selling handicrafts, clothing, and textiles to tourists has sprung up in many communities of the Northwest, particularly around Sapa. Increased contact between these ethnic minorities and tourists has created a flurry of interest in their cultures and lives, but has also cost them some privacy. One unfortunate casualty, for instance, has been the near disappearance of authentic Saturday-night "love markets," where young Red Dao men and women in search of a spouse or lover would pair off for an evening of socializing and possible romance. In Sapa there is a sanitized version of this every Saturday evening, but the real deal takes place only very rarely in the more remote areas of the north.

Traveling around this region often takes a long time and changing weather can make some roads quite dangerous, or even impassable. In the mountains, heavily traveled routes are paved but are still in poor condition. Though the scenery is spellbinding, travel can be physically exhausting. Still, it's a rewarding challenge to cover the region by car, from Hanoi to Sapa to Lai Chau to Dien Bien Phu to Son La then back to Hanoi. If you can handle five or more days on rutted mountain roads, this route is adventurous and allows for some great exploring.

MAJOR REGIONS

Sapa and Nearby. Although much of the Northwest remains remote and undeveloped, Sapa is the region's undisputed tourism star. Idyllically located high among the mountains, yet less than an hour's drive from the transportation hub of Lao Cai,. Sapa feels accessible yet suitably sanctuary-like. The bustling town center has plenty of hotels and shops, yet a short distance away, the rhythms of traditional mountain life beat on as they have for centuries.

Dien Bien Phu and Nearby. Its main claim to fame is as the site of one of the most significant military victories in Vietnamese history, but there's more to Dien Bien Phu than just echoes of the past. In the Muong Thanh valley, not far from the border with Laos, the town enjoys a rarefied position amid some archetypically gorgeous highland scenery, perfect for hiking.

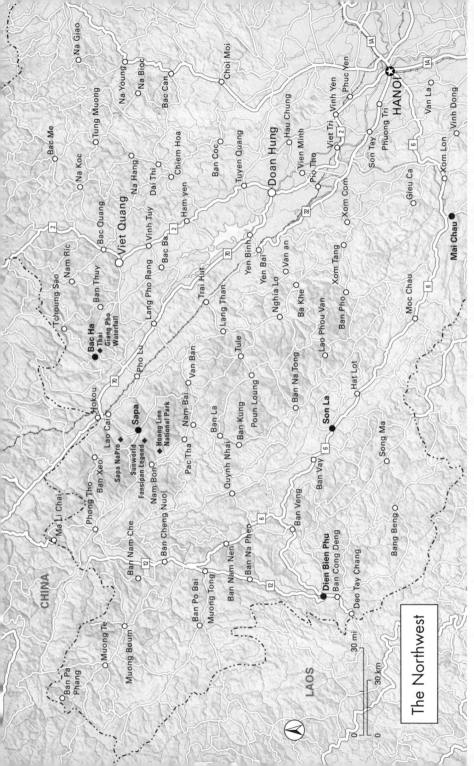

The Northwest

Planning

When to Go

The best time to tour the northern highlands is from late August to mid-December, after the summer monsoons have abated and any mudslides are likely to have been cleared.

Northwest Vietnam has a clearly defined winter, with a cold and clammy mist settling in for a few months starting in January. January and February are quite cold in the mountains, and Mt. Fansipan is occasionally dusted with snow. If you're heading into the highlands in winter and intend to do some trekking, come prepared: a light sweater, a waterproof jacket, a wool hat, long johns, and some insulated hiking boots should keep you warm.

There are also various microclimates in the Northwest. Sapa, for example, is the coldest place in Vietnam on average, with mist and cloud regularly making visibility an issue and lowering temperatures even further. Just over the Tram Ton Pass, however, the area around Lai Chau experiences much clearer weather. The best time to visit Sapa is spring and early summer (approximately March to May) and in the fall (September to November), the latter being the ideal time to see the area's rice terraces in their full verdant glory. The climate in Bac Ha is noticeably sunnier and warmer than in Sapa, making it a plausible alternative base in the region. There are not as many festivals in Dien Bien Phu as there are in the towns farther north, but you might want to time your visit to coincide with the biennial Dien Bien Phu Festival, which takes place on May 7th. The festival commemorates the battle of Dien Bien Phu, but also encompasses a host of other events and activities.

FESTIVALS

During winter, after the turn of the lunar new year, the minority tribes of the area celebrate a colorful array of festivals. Special events at this time include the Nhan Song and Nao Song Festival, celebrated by the Red Dao, and the Gau Tao Festival, marked by the H'mong ethnic group. Both festivals and others in the Sapa area are centered on themes of regeneration and longevity.

Gau Tao Festival

A H'mong festival where members of the mountain communities ask for happiness and longevity, Gau Tao is celebrated early in the lunar year, around Tet holiday in most households. Following a blessing by a H'mong holy man, the festival is marked by a series of lively traditional games and competitions. The Gau To festival is not held by the village but in households, and lasts for three to five days every year. ⊠ *Sapa*

Nhan Song and Nao Song Festival

Celebrating the coming of spring, and held in the first lunar month every year, this festival is celebrated by the Red Dao people in the village of Giang Ta Chai. People of the village indulge in a range of ceremonies with the purpose of raising awareness of deforestation. The village leader, also the forest protector, will announce regulations about deforestation that the people have to obey. ⊠ *Giang Ta Chai*

During Tet, the lunar new year, you'll find northern Vietnam cold and drizzly but extremely festive. If you're coming during this time, make plane and hotel reservations very early.

Getting Here and Around

AIR

Four times daily Vietnam Airlines flights connect Hanoi to Dien Bien Phu; the one-way fare starts at around 1,000,000d. Since the Northwest is best experienced on the ground, consider flying to Dien Bien Phu and then returning to Hanoi another way. You can rent a private car or motorbike and take Highway 6 to Hanoi, or you can head up to Sapa first on Route 70. From Sapa, jump on the Noi Bai Lao Cai Expressway to get back where you started. Talk with one of the travel agencies or tourist cafés in Hanoi to see if they have contacts that can book you a one-way trip back to the capital. They may insist, however, that you pay for the mileage for the driver's return to Dien Bien Phu or Son La.

CONTACTS Vietnam Airlines. ☎ *1900–1100* ⊕ *www.vietnamairlines.com.*

BIKE

If you've got the legs, lungs, and equipment, mountain biking is a formidable but fantastic way to experience the steep mountain ranges of Hoa Binh Province. Most people who do the Hoa Binh–Mai Chau route find alternative transportation to the provincial capital of Hoa Binh, such as an early morning public bus. Bus drivers will strap bikes to the top of their vehicles for a nominal payment of around 20,000d. From there it's about 100 km (62 miles) up and down two major sets of mountains. Hardy bikers reach Mai Chau by evening, exhausted. Slower riders can spend the night in a home in one of many roadside villages. The Hanoi Bicycle Collective rents out a variety of bikes from simple runarounds to more advanced models capable of negotiating the steep mountain roads of northern Vietnam. All-terrain sport bicycles can be rented at the listings below for anywhere from 90,000d to 150,000d ($4–$7) per day, depending on brand and type.

BIKE CONTACT Bike Plus. ⊠ *96 Yen Hoa St., Yen Phu Ward, Tay Ho District* ☎ *091/888–9981* ⊕ *bikeplus.vn.*

CAR

A sedan is a perfectly viable way to get around much of the Northwest. You can rent a car and driver in dozens of spots in Hanoi, and you'll be able to book a two-day, one-night car trip to Sapa for about 4,500,000d, all driver's expenses included. A longer excursion in a four-wheel-drive vehicle specifically suited for mountainous terrain is more expensive: the going rate for the six-day, five-night excursion through the Northwest (Hanoi–Mai Chau–Son La–Dien Bien Phu–Sapa–Hanoi) in a Toyota Innova (with a driver) is 10,200,000d. A host of rental companies in Hanoi will provide modern four-wheel-drive vehicles for such an itinerary. Popular models include Mercedes, Toyota, Ford, and Hyundai.

Set aside at least five days to visit Dien Bien Phu from Hanoi: two days traveling each way and one full day to see what you came for—although the remarkable scenery makes the trip as interesting as the history of the place. If you're coming from Mai Chau and Son La, the natural next step is to continue clockwise: through Lai Chau, on to Sapa, and then back to Hanoi. The Dien Bien Phu–Sapa road has been much upgraded and is narrow, but in good condition. It is a beautiful stretch, and although the round-trip adds a day or two to your journey, it's much more interesting than simply retracing your outward route.

The Ha Giang Loop is gaining considerable popularity with tourists, both as package excursions and solo adventures on a motorbike or with a car. The route takes you from Hanoi to Ha Giang to Quan Ba to Dong Van to Meo Vac to Mau De, then back through Quan Ba to Hanoi. A private SUV with a driver will cost 3,200,000d per day. The trip takes four to five days to complete and encompasses stunning scenery and villages.

Motorbikes are an epic way to tour the Ha Giang loop, a popular 500-mile loop through the province.

The 35-km (22-mile) stretch of road from Sapa north to the border town of Lao Cai is in good condition. If time is limited, you may prefer to go directly to Sapa, bypassing Dien Bien Phu, Son La, and Mai Chau, and heading up and down Route 70 and the main Noi Bai-Lao Cai Expressway.

Cars with drivers can be hired from travel agencies, car rental firms, and tourist cafés in Hanoi. Try Hoa Mai Tour, which can rent everything from a compact four-seater car to a Landcruiser and even a bus, with a selection of top-of-the-range modern models. The Hung Thanh Company also has a broad range of new vehicles ranging from smaller cars to Landcruisers and mini-buses.

CAR CONTACTS Hoa Mai Tour. ⊠ *No.9, Alley 92, Nguyen Khanh Toan St., 2nd fl., Hanoi* ☎ *09/8509–4455* ⊕ *hoamaitour. com.* **Hung Thanh Company.** ⊠ *287 Tran Khat Chan, Hanoi* ☎ *04/3633–7575* ⊕ *www. hungthanhtravel.com.vn.*

MOTORCYCLE

The Northwest, with its visual splendor and patchwork of ethnic minorities, has become a hotly favored destination for exploration by motorbike, although the roads are not of the highest standard. Traveling as part of a group is the best and safest option.

The Hanoi–Dien Bien Phu–Sapa route and the Ha Giang Loop are only for adventurous motorcyclists. These roads are very remote, and adequate emergency care is virtually nonexistent. Wear a helmet, take a sheet of important words and phrases (such as the Vietnamese expression for "My clutch is broken"), and go with a partner. You'll need reasonable clearance and maneuverability, however, so doubling up on one bike is not recommended. Also, be prepared to get wet in mud puddles, although at some larger washout spots enterprising locals set up ferry services on small boats for motorcycles. If you drive a motorbike from Hanoi to Mai Chau, pay extra attention on the mountain roads—the trucks that run this route are notoriously stingy when it comes to giving adequate room to two-wheelers.

Several companies specializing in motorbike tours of the north operate from Hanoi. They can supply well-maintained bikes ranging from classic to modern models and offer expert advice on worthwhile diversions and how to tackle the roads. Rental bikes vary in price, depending on the model, but start from around 250,000d per day. For beginners, however, a better option would be to join one of the group tours these companies offer, providing strength in numbers and guide expertise. Another option is to ride behind an experienced driver; for the Ha Giang Loop, this will cost around 2,700,000d per day.

Cuong's Motorbike Adventures

A founding member of Hanoi's Minsk Club, Cuong has been synonymous with motorbiking in northern Vietnam for two decades. A skilled mechanic who has provided support to high-profile Western television shows filmed in Vietnam, Cuong knows everything there is to know about bike maintenance. He and his team are also expertly versed in the best routes to take in the north. As well as group and individual tours, Cuong has a broad range of bikes for rent and is an invaluable resource for anyone looking to hit the road on two wheels. Cuong also runs tours in classic U.S. Army M151 MUTT jeeps. With his popularity and status, Cuong himself is often booked up months in advance. ✉ *Ngo 1150 Nguyen Khoai St., Hoang Mai* ☎ *0091/876–3515* ⊕ *www.cuongs-motorbike-adventure. com.*

Flipside Adventures Vietnam

Flipside is a New Zealand–owned adventure company that aims to put exploration at the heart of your Southeast Asia journey. They specialize in a four-day bike tour of the north that takes in the Ha Giang Loop called "The True North Motorbike Trip." Their staff are all highly experienced and ready to ride. They also offer kayaking tours through the jungle. ✉ *Km 7 route to Dong Van highland, Hoa Bac commune, ward Thuan Hoa, district Vi Xuyen, Giang Ta Chai* ☎ *0035/479–5803* ⊕ *www.facebook. com/flipsidevietnam.*

Motorbike Tour Expert

Founded by three Hanoian motorbike nuts, this operation is well-versed in the routes and lore of the northern mountains. The Japanese bikes they use for their tours are of the highest quality, and guides are well-trained and skilled at getting guests out of a tight spot should their machine malfunction. Tour itineraries range from bite-size options to more epic voyages through magnificent landscapes. ✉ *264 Nguyen Trai, Tay Ho District* ☎ *097/988–4588 cell phone* ⊕ *motorbiketourexpert.com.*

TRAIN

If you don't want to lose the best part of a day driving to Sapa, take the overnight train from Hanoi to Lao Cai. The most comfortable trip is on Friday night, when you get a soft sleeper in a four-person compartment on the "luxury" train. The one-way ticket costs anywhere from $31 to $78 depending on the level of comfort and luxury required. The cheapest ticket, at $31, will get you a place on a reasonably comfortable four-to-six person compartment. The most expensive, at $78, gets you one of the two beds in a private tourist compartment located in the most comfortable parts of the train. Trains leave Hanoi train station at 9:35 pm and 10 pm, and take 11 hours to reach their destination. The easiest way to buy tickets is through a Hanoi travel agency, but the Vietnam Railways System website is an ultra-handy online resource that lets you study timetables for every route in Vietnam, including the Hanoi–Lao Cai service. Tickets booked online can be delivered to your hotel or picked up at the departure train station.

Don't lose your ticket after boarding the train. You need to present it to the station guards in Lao Cai when arriving at the station and again when departing the station upon returning to Hanoi. You can purchase your round-trip ticket in Sapa (and check train and bus schedules) at the tourist office in the center of town. Hotels in Sapa can book a round-trip in a private soft-sleeper carriage.

Minibuses waiting at the Lao Cai train station can take you the 35 km (22 miles) to Sapa for 50,000d–80,000d. The buses leave when full and usually drop you in the town center. From Sapa, buses return to the Lao Cai train station every hour starting at 6 am. You can also join with other travelers and share a bus or a taxi that will leave at the time you want. If you'd like to combine a one-way train to Sapa with a return to Hanoi by car, you can arrange that in Sapa at one of the tour agencies dotting the main roads.

TRAIN CONTACT Vietnam Railways System. ⊕ *www.vietnam-railway.com.*

Money Matters

There are several ATMs in Sapa and in major towns such as Lao Cai and Dien Bien Phu. Make sure you stock up on cash if you are taking an extended trip outside these hubs, as ATMs are nonexistent in more remote areas.

Restaurants

With the exception of Sapa, with its range of international and Vietnamese options, dining in the Northwest is often more of a necessity than a delight. The mountains provide little gratification for gourmands. Life has traditionally been extremely difficult up in these high passes, and culinary flair has rarely been at the top of the agenda. Consequently,

most of the restaurants in the area purvey very similar, basic fare. Expect plenty of boiled chicken and grilled meat (mostly pork) accompanied by rice and vegetables such as corn, cassava, and greens. Don't expect much in the way of fragrant herbs or delicious marinades. Here, the staple flavoring agent is pungent fish sauce, often augmented with a boiled egg, which is mashed up and stirred into the salty condiment. Atmosphere and aesthetics are also low on the list of priorities, so you're likely to dine around stainless steel tables under unforgiving strip lighting.

One "pleasure" that you most likely will be unable to avoid while traveling through the highlands is rice wine, or *ruou* (pronounced *zee*-oo). Distilled locally, ruou is everywhere and is used as a welcoming drink. It is also drunk at lunch; before, during, and after dinner; while gathering with friends; when meeting with officials; at small and large celebrations; and as a good-luck send-off. Refusing it outright is difficult, stopping once you've started is nearly impossible, and getting sick from drinking too much is easy.

A communal twist on the ruou standard is *ruou can* (straw-rice wine), which is consumed by up to a dozen people at the same time through bamboo straws stuck into an earthenware jar. First filled halfway with manioc and rice husks, the jar is sealed tight and left to ferment for 17 days. On the day of consumption, a water-sugar mixture is added. The sweet, slightly fetid alcohol is downed at weddings and other major celebrations—such as when a couple of foreigners step into a remote village. It's beneficial that ruou can is more diluted than its bottled cousin, which can be anywhere from 60 to 110 proof.

Hotels

Lodging in the Northwest has improved immeasurably in recent years. Established tourist destinations like Sapa have added several enticing new options to their hotel portfolio, and even the budget hotels have good amenities such as free Wi-Fi, hot water, and satellite television. In the smaller towns and cities in the region, you're likely to find several decent (but no-frills) family-run minihotels. In more remote areas, such as ethnic-minority villages, you may have to share a mat or roll-away mattress in the living room of a host family; bathrooms are often a curtained shack next to a well where you draw your own water. Don't write off such an experience, however; many of the stilt houses in ethnic-minority villages are exquisitely built, cool, and comfortable, and you may find the owners to be your most gracious hosts. In fact, in Mai Chau in particular, a homestay with a local family has become an integral part of the tourist experience.

For expanded reviews, visit Fodors.com

What It Costs			
$	$$	$$$	$$$$
RESTAURANTS			
Under 60,000d	60,000d– 150,000d	151,000d– 250,000d	over 250,000d
HOTELS			
Under 600,000d	600,000d– 900,000d	901,000d– 1,500,000d	over 1,500,000d

Tours

Travel agencies and tourist cafés in Hanoi, such as Exo Travel and Handspan, can organize a variety of trips to the Northwest. One of the most popular is an overnight or two-night excursion to Mai Chau. On the very popular Mai Chau tour, you generally stay at the White Thai village where most of the homestays and guesthouses operate. Prices for this tour vary, but generally cost between 1,150,000d and 5,000,000d for the two-night version. Several tour operators conduct one- to seven-day hiking trips to Mt. Fansipan and other areas around Sapa. The Fansipan trip costs around 1,300,000d for one person in a group trip of 15 people (fewer hikers means a higher price). The company's newest routes include 2 days, 1 night hiking tours to beautiful rice terraces in **Tu Le** and **Mu Cang Chai** highlands. These prices include food, tents, and tours of remote mountain villages.

CONTACTS Handspan Indochina Travel. ✉ *78 Ma May St., Hanoi* ☎ *024/3926– 2828* ⊕ *www.handspan.com.*

Sapa

350 km (217 miles) northwest of Hanoi.

Ringed by the majestic Tonkinese Alps, Sapa is a hill town and region that has become the undisputed tourist capital of the Northwest. Make the journey here and you'll be rewarded with a glimpse of some of Vietnam's most breathtaking mountain scenery and the opportunity to discover its mosaic of ethnic-minority cultures. Overlooking a verdant valley of rice terraces, the town enjoys an outstanding location and a cool, fresh climate. It was this, and the surrounding beauty, that prompted the French to establish a hill station here in 1922.

Today, Sapa attracts an even more international crowd, who come for its selection of hotels and pampering options, complemented by bustling markets that strike a mostly pleasant balance between unashamed tourism and earthier local character. The mountains and hill-tribe villages outside the town are magnets for well-equipped hikers.

Sapa's popularity has created increasing demand for accommodations. The hotel boom that continues unchecked has created ill-conceived concrete architecture and muddied and potholed streets in certain parts of town. It has also attracted the persistent presence of H'mong and Dao traders, looking to offload handicrafts and trinkets, which can prove extremely tiresome after a few hours. These issues are easy to overlook when you're gazing in wonder as the mist rises to reveal the timeless, beguiling landscapes or learning about the region with the help of your H'mong or Red Dao guide. The key is to get out into the countryside and interact with locals.

GETTING HERE AND AROUND

The Noi Bai-Lao Cai Expressway makes travel by road the easiest and fastest way to get to Sapa. Journey times between Hanoi and the border town of Lao Cai are four hours by car and a little longer by bus. Several bus companies service the route. Buses leave from Hanoi's My Dinh Bus Station to Lao Cai Bus Station and the journey takes around 5½ hours. Ticket prices for the one-way journey start at around 250,000d. Sapa Express also operates a direct service from Hanoi to Sapa. It leaves from Hanoi's Old Quarter around 6:30 am and arrives in Sapa around 12:30 pm. The one-way fare starts from 300,000d and can go up to 350,000d. The road has also made car rental from Hanoi much more appealing with a number of rental firms offering cars with drivers.

Despite the ease of road travel, the overnight train from Hanoi to Lao Cai remains a popular way to get to Sapa. The most comfortable trip is on Friday night, when you get a soft sleeper in a four-person compartment on the "luxury" train. The one-way ticket starts from 713,971d ($31) for a soft berth in a standard four-person compartment and can go as high as 1,796,445d ($78) for a cushy bed in a "luxury" two-bed compartment. Trains leave Hanoi train station at 9:35 pm and 10 pm, and take 11 hours. The

Languages of Vietnam 👁

There are eight language groups in Vietnam. Vietic, which includes standard Vietnamese (spoken by the majority group), Muong, Churt, and Tho, have the most speakers. There's a lot of overlap in language groups between China, Vietnam, Thailand, and Laos—and sometimes other Southeast Asian and South Pacific countries, from neighboring Cambodia all the way to Tahiti. Tai languages, for example, are spoken in Vietnam, Thailand, and Laos. H'mong languages are spoken in all four countries.

easiest way to buy tickets is through a Hanoi travel agency.

Minibuses waiting at the Lao Cai train station can take you the 35 km (22 miles) to Sapa for 50,000d–80,000d. The buses leave when full and usually drop you in the town center. From Sapa, buses return to the Lao Cai train station every hour, starting at 6 am. If you'd like to combine a one-way train to Sapa with a return to Hanoi by car, you can arrange that in Sapa at one of the tour agencies dotting the main roads.

Privately run buses operate between Sapa and Dien Bien Phu. The journey takes approximately eight hours and one-way tickets cost around 300,000d.

TRANSPORTATION CONTACTS Sapa

Express. ✉ 70C Nguyen Huu Huan St., Hoan Kiem District 🕾 24/6682–1555 ⊕ www.sapaexpress.com. **Vietbus.** ✉ 28 Pham Hung, Tu Liem 🕾 097/506–5858 ⊕ www.facebook.com/ Vanchuyenhanglientinh.

Hiking in the Northwest

One of the best ways to experience northern Vietnam is by tackling the trails that lead out of the towns and into more remote areas of the highlands. These footpaths lead through more pristine terrain than you would be able to see from the back seat of a Landcruiser. Villages throughout the mountains are connected by trails, and it may not be long before someone produces a publication documenting and mapping a network of the best hiking trails in the north. Until then, however, your best bet is to pick up local maps when you arrive at a destination or to arrange a trekking itinerary with an ethical guide group. These operators have researched the hikes with knowledgeable locals and are pretty familiar with the needs and preferences of Western travelers. Dozens of trails lead out of the hillside town of Sapa, for instance, and into H'mong villages. Minority peoples have a vast knowledge of local routes, and working as guides has become a key source of income and respect for the women in these families. These local guides often speak better English than Vietnamese and homestays are a beautiful way to learn about their way of life. You can venture out independently, but communication may be a hurdle. A decent guide becomes essential if you intend on trekking to the top of Mt. Fansipan, Vietnam's highest peak.

TOURS

Ethos - The Spirit of the Community

Ethos is an ethical travel company that provides experiences with local ethnic minority families. You can choose to trek with a guide, provide lunch for a local family, stay overnight in a traditional home, or create your own experience. It was founded by Phil and Hoa Hoolihan with community development and education at the heart of everything. Theirs is a total approach to responsible tourism and their customers leave wanting to come back again and again. ✉ *79 Nguyen Chi Thanh, Sapa* ✛ *See website for complete directions* ☎ *036/689–2536, 0165/365–1093* ⊕ *www.ethosspirit.com* ✉ *Trek from 1,000,000d.*

Sapa O'Chau

Operated on a basis of social enterprise, this acclaimed tour company was started by Shu Tan, a young single mother from the Black H'mong tribe. Working with Australian volunteers she funded the first H'mong-owned homestay in Sapa and established a socially conscious trekking service. The company can organize a range of trekking itineraries, including a two-day, one-night ascent of Fansipan. Proceeds are plowed back into the community through projects such as improvements to village schools in the area and English classes for Sapa's young tour guides and street vendors. ✉ *03 Le Van Tam St., Sapa* ☎ *0214/377–1166* ⊕ *www.sapaochau.org* ✉ *Day treks from 1,240,000d per person per day; Fansipan treks from 2,140,000d per person.*

Sapa Sisters

Entirely owned and run by women, this H'mong-operated trekking group can arrange a number of programs and activities. These include everything from multiple-day treks to market tours and homestays with families in the valley. Eschewing set itineraries, Sisters offers treks tailored to guest's requirements. One of the more fulfilling aspects of Sapa Sisters is spending the night in your guide's home (if you so choose), where you will eat simple but delicious food, and get to interact with a local family.

At Hoang Lien National Park, many visitors enjoy hiking or swimming in waterfall pools.

✉ *11 Fansipan St., Sapa* ⊕ *www.sapa-sisters.com* ✆ *Day treks from 730,000đ per person.*

ESSENTIALS

VISITOR INFORMATION Sapa Tourist Office. ✉ *2 Fansipan St., Sapa* ☎ *024/387–1975* ⊕ *www.sapa-tourism.com.*

◉ Sights

Hoang Lien National Park

NATIONAL PARK | Sapa is part of this mountainous 7,400-acre landscape covered by temperate and subtemperate forests. The reserve provides a habitat for 66 species of mammals—tigers, leopards, monkeys, and bears among them—16 of which, including the Asiatic black bear, are considered endangered. An impressive 347 species of birds, including the red-vented barbet and the collared finchbill, can be found only in these mountains. Among the area's geological resources are minerals from sediments deposited in the Mesozoic and Paleozoic periods. From the Muong Hoa River to the peak of Mt.

Fansipan, the eastern boundary of the reserve is formed by a ridge of marble and calcium carbonate. Also found in this region is kaolinite, or China clay, used in the making of porcelain. Guided walking tours of the nature reserve are recommended and are easily arranged through hotels, guesthouses, and tour agencies in town. Motorbike drivers will be happy to take you down the road from Sapa for a full day of hiking, swimming in waterfall pools, and visiting H'mong and Thai villages. Hoteliers and tour companies can also make arrangements for you. ✉ *Sapa.*

Sapa Market

MARKET | Now housed in a less-than-pleasant building near the bus station, the Sapa market is still the best place in Vietnam to purchase textiles. H'mong and Red Dao women are the primary sellers, and you can rest assured their products are handmade. Most sellers walk in from surrounding villages, while a few catch rides on the backs of motorcycles. They are often dressed in their finest traditional garb: richly embroidered

Cable cars take visitors to the top of Mt. Fansipan, the tallest mountain in Vietnam.

vests and dresses, aqua-and-black cotton shirts, finely detailed silver necklaces and bracelets, and elaborate headdresses that tinkle with every movement. Many of these women have picked up a few French and English words or phrases. The real selling goes on upstairs, so skip the ground floor. ■TIP→ **Part of the fun is bargaining, but don't express too much interest up front. Hold out for as long as you can, and then ask to see the good stuff. You'll likely be shown fabric of quality superior to what was offered only moments before.** The market is at its peak on Saturday, when tourists from Hanoi flood into Sapa; you may actually find it quieter and more fun on weekdays. ☒ *Dien Bien Phu, Sapa.*

Sapa Museum

OTHER MUSEUM | The first floor of this small museum is called the Sapa Minorities Handicraft Shop, and you can indeed purchase beautiful gifts here. For the information, head up the large wooden staircase and peruse the slightly dusty exhibits. You can get a useful crash course in the ethnology of the area and view photos and artifacts used in traditional celebrations. ☒ *103 Cau May, Sapa* ⊕ *Entrance is behind tourist information center* ☜ *Free.*

Sapa NaPro

SPAS | Sapa NaPro is a locally run spa located in Ta Phin Village, which is a 40-minute taxi ride from Sapa town. You could also opt to hike here with a guide and stay the night in a local homestay. Although the owners don't speak great English, it is fairly easy to navigate. The herbal baths in this beautiful wooden house cost around 100,000d and you can stay as long as you like. The custom of herbal baths is longstanding in the Red Dao communities, and were customarily used to heal women after they gave birth. Take in the awe-inspiring views while you soak your tired bones. ☒ *Ta Phin Village, Sapa* ☎ *0214/221–6765* ☜ *100,000d.*

Sunworld Fansipan Legend

MOUNTAIN | The highlight of this mountainside compound of attractions is a cable car system, which is 6,292.5

meters (20,645 feet) long and a stunning 1,410 meters (4,626 feet) high. It is the longest nonstop three-rope cable car in the world and allows anyone to get to the top of Mt. Fansipan in just a few short minutes. Designed by Doppelmayr, a German-Swiss-Austrian group, this cable car takes you through the mountain mist over beautiful rice terraces and valleys, and delivers you to the Sapa Station where you can take a funicular or walk 300 steps to the top. Many visitors have complained that the restaurants and shops at the top are an eyesore, but the construction shows true ingenuity. ✉ *Nguyen Chi Thanh St., Sapa* ☎ *094/830–8888* 🌐 *fansipanlegend.sunworld.vn* 🎟 *700,000d adults, 600,000 for children.*

★ Victoria Spa

SPAS | There are numerous fairly basic places in town for a massage and most do a reasonable job for the money. However, for a top-class treatment to soothe tired bones and muscles after a hard day of travel, the spa at the Victoria Hotel is the pick of Sapa's pampering options. Choose from a number of treatments and luxuriate in the resort's gorgeous massage rooms. ✉ *Xuan Vien St., Sapa* ✣ *At very top of the hill* ☎ *0214/387–1522* 🌐 *www.victoriahotels.asia.*

🍴 Restaurants

Cinnamon Restaurant

$$ | VIETNAMESE | This cozy restaurant is at the bottom of the Legend Hotel. The chandeliers and bamboo curtains add to the beauty of the rustic interior. **Known for:** pork; hot rice wine; local salmon. [$] *Average main: d150,000* ✉ *024 Dong Loi, Sapa* ☎ *098/388–9798.*

Delta Italian Restaurant

$$$ | ITALIAN | Tourists gather at this restaurant near the market for the large portions of pasta and pizzas cooked in a genuine Italian pizza oven by the amiable owner-chef, Mr. Tung, who spent six months studying in Milan before opening the restaurant. Exquisite crepes satisfy a lighter appetite, and there's an extensive international wine list. **Known for:** stone pizza oven; authentic Italian fare; rustic interior. [$] *Average main: d170,000* ✉ *31 Cau May St., Sapa* ☎ *096/669–6089.*

★ Le Gecko

$$$ | BISTRO | Like Sapa itself, Le Gecko bears noticeable French influence with a menu that features a host of bistro classics. There's a comfortable bar area that is popular in the evenings, while the outside terrace is a great spot for people-watching. **Known for:** casual fare; rich beef bourguignon; cozy atmosphere. [$] *Average main: d180,000* ✉ *033 Xuan Vien, Sapa* ☎ *0214/387–1898* 🌐 *www.legeckosapa.com.*

★ Maison de Sapa

$$$ | INTERNATIONAL | The sister restaurant of the Maison de Tet in Hanoi, Maison de Sapa is the place to relax and unwind for a few hours and enjoy some delicious food and drinks. Specializing in fresh, farm-to-table ingredients, the menu is

Visiting Mu Cang Chai's Rice Terraces 👁

More than 5,000 acres of striking green and yellow rice terraces surround Mu Cang Chai, a small mountain village that's a four- to five-hour drive from Sapa (or a seven-hour drive from Hanoi). Both are a good base for multiday trips to this rural countryside, and plenty of photography, trekking, and biking tours exist, including from the reputable tour company Handspan. Sapa's Topas Ecolodge can also arrange four- to 10-day trips. If you're sticking around Mu Cang Chai, there are few better places to stay than at the Mu Cang Chai Ecolodge.

always changing to reflect the finest seasonal options. **Known for:** hiring and training local staff; great coffee blends; bohemian decor. [$] *Average main: d210,000* ✉ *18 Thac Bac, Sapa* ☎ *096/661–1383* ⊕ *facebook.com/maisondesapavilla.*

Viet Emotion

$$ | VIETNAMESE | Like most of the restaurants in Sapa, Viet Emotion has a typical Western and Vietnamese blended menu, but they go out of their way to make the building bright and colorful. If you're hungry, try the Hunter's Meal, which is sticky rice and pork marinated in a bamboo pipe. **Known for:** MSG-free food; brightly colored lanterns; sticky rice and pork. [$] *Average main: d100,000* ✉ *027 Cau May, Sapa* ☎ *0214/387–2669.*

🛏 Hotels

★ Aira Boutique Hotel & Spa

$$$$ | HOTEL | One of the highest rated hotels in Sapa, the Aira Boutique delivers fantastic service and well-designed rooms. **Pros:** thoughtful staff; great views; panoramic views of Fansipan. **Cons:** no indoor pool. [$] *Rooms from: d2,160,000* ✉ *30 Hoang Lien, Sapa* ☎ *0214/377–2268* ⊕ *www.airaboutique-sapa.com* ⇨ *52 rooms* ❑ *Free Breakfast.*

Amazing Sapa

$$$ | HOTEL | This hotel has a wonderful view of the mountains and impeccable service. **Pros:** heated rooftop pool; fantastic terrace; good location. **Cons:** rooms are a tad small; karaoke club in the basement can go till midnight on weekends. [$] *Rooms from: d1,275,000* ✉ *Dong Loi, Sapa* ✛ *Next to Chau Long Hotel* ☎ *0214/386–5888* ⊕ *www.amazinghotel.com.vn* ⇨ *82 rooms* ❑ *Free Breakfast.*

Bamboo Sapa Hotel

$$ | HOTEL | Like many of Sapa's hotels, the Bamboo Sapa enjoys a stunning location with towering views of the surrounding mountains and the valley below, and to maximize this epic outlook most rooms have private balconies.

Pros: rooms have televisions and private bathrooms; spacious; spotlessly clean. **Cons:** very noisy; lack of an elevator can be an issue for the elderly or those who are less mobile; extremely cold in winter. [$] *Rooms from: d840,000* ✉ *18 Muong Hoa St., Sapa* ☎ *091/551–0689* ⊕ *www.bamboosapahotel.com.vn* ❑ *Free Breakfast* ⇨ *55 rooms.*

BB Hotel

$$$ | HOTEL | This centrally located hotel is right next to the main town square and offers a lot of value. **Pros:** most central location in town; 24-hour gym; restaurant and rooftop bar on site. **Cons:** hot water can be inconsistent. [$] *Rooms from: d1,700,000* ✉ *8 Cau May, Sapa* ☎ *0214/387–1996* ⊕ *www.bbhotels-resorts.com.vn* ⇨ *57 rooms* ❑ *Free Breakfast.*

Chau Long Hotel

$$$ | HOTEL | The stately French villas of Sapa have nothing on this distinctive—and decidedly incongruous—crenellated mock-château containing one of the town's better hotels. **Pros:** spectacular views; deluxe rooms feel very homey; good restaurant on-site. **Cons:** gaudy architecture is not for everyone. [$] *Rooms from: d1,200,000* ✉ *24 Dong Loi St., Sapa* ☎ *091/460–2529* ⊕ *www.chaulonghotel.com* ❑ *Free Breakfast* ⇨ *67 rooms.*

Pao's Sapa Leisure Hotel

$$$$ | HOTEL | Stepping into Pao's, you may feel that you've found an otherworldly art gallery: the large structure is meant to resemble rice terraces, and the swooping architectural design is inspired. **Pros:** elegant rooms with lush carpets; each room has private balcony and garden; spa and heated pool on-site. **Cons:** rooftop bar looks a bit like an airport lobby; not a central location. [$] *Rooms from: d1,800,000* ✉ *Muong Hoa, Sapa* ☎ *0214/625–3999* ⊕ *www.paoshotel.com* ❑ *Free Breakfast* ⇨ *223 rooms.*

meters (20,645 feet) long and a stunning 1,410 meters (4,626 feet) high. It is the longest nonstop three-rope cable car in the world and allows anyone to get to the top of Mt. Fansipan in just a few short minutes. Designed by Doppelmayr, a German-Swiss-Austrian group, this cable car takes you through the mountain mist over beautiful rice terraces and valleys, and delivers you to the Sapa Station where you can take a funicular or walk 300 steps to the top. Many visitors have complained that the restaurants and shops at the top are an eyesore, but the construction shows true ingenuity. ⊠ *Nguyen Chi Thanh St., Sapa* 🕾 *094/830–8888* ⊕ *fansipanlegend. sunworld.vn* 🖃 *700,000d adults, 600,000 for children.*

★ Victoria Spa

SPAS | There are numerous fairly basic places in town for a massage and most do a reasonable job for the money. However, for a top-class treatment to soothe tired bones and muscles after a hard day of travel, the spa at the Victoria Hotel is the pick of Sapa's pampering options. Choose from a number of treatments and luxuriate in the resort's gorgeous massage rooms. ⊠ *Xuan Vien St., Sapa* ✛ *At very top of the hill* 🕾 *0214/387–1522* ⊕ *www.victoriahotels.asia.*

🍴 Restaurants

Cinnamon Restaurant

$$ | VIETNAMESE | This cozy restaurant is at the bottom of the Legend Hotel. The chandeliers and bamboo curtains add to the beauty of the rustic interior. **Known for:** pork; hot rice wine; local salmon. 🖫 *Average main: d150,000* ⊠ *024 Dong Loi, Sapa* 🕾 *098/388–9798.*

Delta Italian Restaurant

$$$ | ITALIAN | Tourists gather at this restaurant near the market for the large portions of pasta and pizzas cooked in a genuine Italian pizza oven by the amiable owner-chef, Mr. Tung, who spent six

Visiting Mu Cang Chai's Rice Terraces 👁

More than 5,000 acres of striking green and yellow rice terraces surround Mu Cang Chai, a small mountain village that's a four- to five-hour drive from Sapa (or a seven-hour drive from Hanoi). Both are a good base for multiday trips to this rural countryside, and plenty of photography, trekking, and biking tours exist, including from the reputable tour company Handspan. Sapa's Topas Ecolodge can also arrange four- to 10-day trips. If you're sticking around Mu Cang Chai, there are few better places to stay than at the Mu Cang Chai Ecolodge.

months studying in Milan before opening the restaurant. Exquisite crepes satisfy a lighter appetite, and there's an extensive international wine list. **Known for:** stone pizza oven; authentic Italian fare; rustic interior. 🖫 *Average main: d170,000* ⊠ *31 Cau May St., Sapa* 🕾 *096/669–6089.*

★ Le Gecko

$$$ | BISTRO | Like Sapa itself, Le Gecko bears noticeable French influence with a menu that features a host of bistro classics. There's a comfortable bar area that is popular in the evenings, while the outside terrace is a great spot for people-watching. **Known for:** casual fare; rich beef bourguignon; cozy atmosphere. 🖫 *Average main: d180,000* ⊠ *033 Xuan Vien, Sapa* 🕾 *0214/387–1898* ⊕ *www. legeckosapa.com.*

★ Maison de Sapa

$$$ | INTERNATIONAL | The sister restaurant of the Maison de Tet in Hanoi, Maison de Sapa is the place to relax and unwind for a few hours and enjoy some delicious food and drinks. Specializing in fresh, farm-to-table ingredients, the menu is always changing to reflect the finest seasonal options. **Known for:** hiring and training local staff; great coffee blends; bohemian decor. $ *Average main: d210,000 ✉ 18 Thac Bac, Sapa ☎ 096/661–1383 ⊕ facebook.com/maisondesapavilla.*

Viet Emotion

$$ | VIETNAMESE | Like most of the restaurants in Sapa, Viet Emotion has a typical Western and Vietnamese blended menu, but they go out of their way to make the building bright and colorful. If you're hungry, try the Hunter's Meal, which is sticky rice and pork marinated in a bamboo pipe. **Known for:** MSG-free food; brightly colored lanterns; sticky rice and pork. $ *Average main: d100,000 ✉ 027 Cau May, Sapa ☎ 0214/387–2669.*

Hotels

★ Aira Boutique Hotel & Spa

$$$$ | HOTEL | One of the highest rated hotels in Sapa, the Aira Boutique delivers fantastic service and well-designed rooms. **Pros:** thoughtful staff; great views; panoramic views of Fansipan. **Cons:** no indoor pool. $ *Rooms from: d2,160,000 ✉ 30 Hoang Lien, Sapa ☎ 0214/377–2268 ⊕ www.airaboutique-sapa.com ⤴ 52 rooms |◯| Free Breakfast.*

Amazing Sapa

$$$ | HOTEL | This hotel has a wonderful view of the mountains and impeccable service. **Pros:** heated rooftop pool; fantastic terrace; good location. **Cons:** rooms are a tad small; karaoke club in the basement can go till midnight on weekends. $ *Rooms from: d1,275,000 ✉ Dong Loi, Sapa ✛ Next to Chau Long Hotel ☎ 0214/386–5888 ⊕ www.amazinghotel.com.vn ⤴ 82 rooms |◯| Free Breakfast.*

Bamboo Sapa Hotel

$$ | HOTEL | Like many of Sapa's hotels, the Bamboo Sapa enjoys a stunning location with towering views of the surrounding mountains and the valley below, and to maximize this epic outlook most rooms have private balconies.

Pros: rooms have televisions and private bathrooms; spacious; spotlessly clean. **Cons:** very noisy; lack of an elevator can be an issue for the elderly or those who are less mobile; extremely cold in winter. $ *Rooms from: d840,000 ✉ 18 Muong Hoa St., Sapa ☎ 091/551–0689 ⊕ www.bamboosapahotel.com.vn |◯| Free Breakfast ⤴ 55 rooms.*

BB Hotel

$$$ | HOTEL | This centrally located hotel is right next to the main town square and offers a lot of value. **Pros:** most central location in town; 24-hour gym; restaurant and rooftop bar on site. **Cons:** hot water can be inconsistent. $ *Rooms from: d1,700,000 ✉ 8 Cau May, Sapa ☎ 0214/387–1996 ⊕ www.bbhotels-resorts.com.vn ⤴ 57 rooms |◯| Free Breakfast.*

Chau Long Hotel

$$$ | HOTEL | The stately French villas of Sapa have nothing on this distinctive—and decidedly incongruous—crenellated mock-château containing one of the town's better hotels. **Pros:** spectacular views; deluxe rooms feel very homey; good restaurant on-site. **Cons:** gaudy architecture is not for everyone. $ *Rooms from: d1,200,000 ✉ 24 Dong Loi St., Sapa ☎ 091/460–2529 ⊕ www.chaulonghotel.com |◯| Free Breakfast ⤴ 67 rooms.*

Pao's Sapa Leisure Hotel

$$$$ | HOTEL | Stepping into Pao's, you may feel that you've found an otherworldly art gallery: the large structure is meant to resemble rice terraces, and the swooping architectural design is inspired. **Pros:** elegant rooms with lush carpets; each room has private balcony and garden; spa and heated pool on-site. **Cons:** rooftop bar looks a bit like an airport lobby; not a central location. $ *Rooms from: d1,800,000 ✉ Muong Hoa, Sapa ☎ 0214/625–3999 ⊕ www.paoshotel.com |◯| Free Breakfast ⤴ 223 rooms.*

Sapa Dragon Hotel

$$ | **B&B/INN** | A simple budget accommodation, the Sapa Dragon Hotel gets rave reviews due to considerate service and helpful staff. **Pros:** easy walking distance to restaurants and sights; beautiful rooftop terrace; heater in room is nice on cold nights. **Cons:** not as luxurious as some other area hotels; up a fairly steep hill; no elevator. $ *Rooms from: d800,000 ⊠ 01A Thac Bac, Sapa ☎ 0214/387–1363 ⊕ www.sapadragonhotel.com ⤴ 20 rooms* ❢❂❢ *Free Breakfast.*

★ Silk Path Grand Sapa Resort & Spa

$$$$ | **RESORT** | The only five-star luxury resort in Sapa, this modern-day castle is close to perfection. **Pros:** heated indoor pool; breathtakingly beautiful; two restaurants. **Cons:** mountain views can be obscured by construction. $ *Rooms from: d2,250,000 ⊠ Doi Quan 6, Group 10, Sapa ☎ 0214/378–8555 ⊕ www. silkpathhotel.com ⤴ 152 rooms* ❢❂❢ *Free Breakfast.*

Topas Eco-Lodge

$$$$ | **HOTEL** | If Sapa town is too busy for your liking, this resort within Hoang Lien National Park has lodgings arranged around the summit of a small hill, guaranteeing absolute seclusion and some fabulous panoramic views. **Pros:** stunning views; two saltwater infinity pools and spa on-site; private balconies. **Cons:** an hour's drive from town; Wi-Fi limited to public areas; expensive restaurant, and no other nearby options. $ *Rooms from: d4,900,000 ⊠ Off QL32, Sapa ☎ 0214/387–1331, 0243/715–1005 ⊕ www.topasecolodge.com* ❢❂❢ *No Meals ⤴ 41 lodges.*

★ Victoria Sapa Resort & Spa

$$$ | **HOTEL** | The premier hotel in Sapa, the luxurious, French-designed Victoria sits on a hilltop overlooking the town and caters to the fancy of its guests with heaps of amenities. **Pros:** tour package includes travel from Hanoi; height of luxury in the mountains; rooms have inviting bathtubs and private terrace. **Cons:** steps out of the bathrooms are on the high side, so care is needed. $ *Rooms from: d1,400,000 ⊠ Xuan Vien St., Sapa ☎ 0214/387–1522 ⊕ www.victoriahotels. asia* ❢❂❢ *Free Breakfast ⤴ 77 rooms, 2 suites.*

❢ Nightlife

Color Bar

BARS | This atmospheric spot is a little out of the way, but worth the journey for its friendly, bohemian vibe. Owned by a Vietnamese artist, the venue has a mellow feel with a soundtrack of laid-back tunes and unlimited ice-cold beer of the usual local varieties along with classic cocktails. There are occasional exhibitions of live music, dance, and even art workshops, so be sure to check their Facebook page for the latest goings-on. ⊠ *56 Fansipan St., Sapa ⊕ www.facebook.com/ColorBarSapa.*

★ H'mong Sisters

BARS | Raucous and rowdy, this is by far the liveliest nightspot in Sapa. Busy every night of the week, the bar attracts an eclectic crowd that spans backpackers, locals, trekkers, and members of Sapa's small expatriate community. A pool table, sports on the TV, a great selection of music, and generously strong drinks keep the party going until late. ⊠ *31 Muong Hoa St., Sapa ☎ 097/625–9828.*

❢ Shopping

The ethnic-minority communities that surround Sapa, particularly the women, have developed sophisticated trading networks, not just among themselves but for tourists as well. And what's trading hands is positively beautiful: richly dyed textiles; hand-loomed silk scarves, headdresses, and broadcloth; brocaded vests and dresses; woven bamboo baskets of all shapes and sizes; and traditional silver jewelry. Many of these wares are on display at Sapa's main market and also at weekly markets in the area such as Can

Cau and Coc Ly. In Sapa, a smattering of boutiques is taking a more contemporary approach to marketing traditional craftsmanship. The hard-sell tactics of the Dao and H'mong women on the streets of Sapa can be a little grating. Nevertheless, if you have patience with constant attention from vendors and the ability to bargain, some rewarding purchases can be made.

★ Indigo Cat

CRAFTS | Run by a H'mong woman and her husband, this is by far the most stylish of Sapa's small boutiques. The craftsmanship of the H'mong minority is legendary, and this skill shines through in the shop's well-chosen selection of bags, clothing, pillows, and belts. Authentic batik classes can also be arranged through Indigo Cat. ✉ *46 Fansipan St., Sapa* ☎ *098/240–3647 cell phone* ⊕ *www.indigocat.shop.*

Activities

HIKING

A 30-minute hike from the center of town to the radio tower above Sapa gives you a spectacular panoramic view. Climb the stone steps from the main road. The steps lead up past well-manicured gardens and through rocky fields. A path breaks off to the right and winds around boulders to the tower. The town of Sapa is laid out below, and across the valley is Mt. Fansipan. Opportunities for trekking in the town's hinterland are limitless, either independently or in the company of a guide from one of the local hill tribes. One of the easiest (it is more of a stroll than a hike) is the downhill walk from Sapa to Cat Cat Village. The route is simple, but tour agencies in Sapa will be happy to supply a map. Local guides can be hired for around 400,000d per day and

their comprehensive knowledge of the villages in the area and the narrow paths that link them is invaluable.

Trekking through the rice terraces to local villages is one of the key features of a visit to Sapa. Although there are many Vietnamese tour guides, the best and most authentic trips employ H'mong women. They will lead you to markets and villages around Sapa including Ta Phin and Ta Van. Some guides welcome travelers to stay in their homes for the night; though these homes usually lack running water and modern comforts, a homestay is a great way to make lasting memories.

Hiking Mt. Fansipan, 10,312 feet high, requires little technical expertise, but it does take two to three days; you must depart from Sapa and hike down into the valley, then back up the other side. The summit of Fansipan is 19 km (12 miles) from Sapa, and most visitors have stopped climbing since the introduction of the cable car. For all treks, it is recommended that you bring an experienced guide to suggest the best route, help you navigate the wet, chilly mountainside, and find places to camp. If you are serious about hiking Fansipan, contact one of the many reputable travel operators in Sapa or in Hanoi, which can all organize treks to the peak. Recommended companies include Sapa O Chau, Handspan, Exo Travel, Ethos, and Sapa Sisters *(see Tours)*. The tour companies will usually be happy to customize an itinerary for you. The price for the two-day, one-night ascent of Fansipan varies on the size of your group. It can get very cold in Sapa and even colder on the mountain, so dress accordingly.

Ethnic Minorities in the North 👁

In the remote mountains and valleys of the north, ethnic-minority populations continue to live as they have for centuries, although modern society is always threatening to encroach. The history of these unique ethnic minorities is still the subject of some dispute, but many anthropologists now believe the largest of the groups, the Muong, as well as smaller groups like the Kho-mu, the Khang, the Mang, and the La Ha, have been living in the Hoang Lien Mountains and the northern foothills for thousands of years, preceding even the arrival of the Kinh—the ethnic Vietnamese who now make up 85% of the country's population.

Late migration
Most other groups migrated from Thailand, China, or Laos—some as late as the 19th century—as a result of war, lack of land, or a simple disregard for national borders. Living in the highest elevations, near the climatic limits of hill rice cultivation, are the H'mong and Dao (pronounced zow). The clothing and jewelry of these two groups, particularly the women, are among the most colorful and elaborate in the north. The Muong and Thai (with distinct Black Thai and White Thai subgroups) are two of the larger minorities, each numbering about a million. They practice wetlands cultivation on the middle and lower slopes and generally live in airy, comfortable stilt houses in village clusters ranging from a handful of houses to several dozen.

Slash-and-burn agriculture, the traditional mainstay of ethnic-minority economies, was for centuries an ideal form of natural resource management. In the 21st century, however, as the land available for such cultivation shrinks, this method has begun to generate heated controversy in Vietnam. Indeed, northern Vietnam is one of the most deforested regions of Indochina. A migration of Kinh Vietnamese from the Red River delta farther inland and into the distant valleys is also displacing many nomadic farmers as land privatization plans take hold.

Displacement controversies
Vietnam's growing energy needs are also wreaking havoc on minority life. The Hoa Binh Dam, Vietnam's first hydroelectric power project, 70 km (43 miles) southwest of Hanoi, displaced 60,000 people from the Da River valley. Most were ethnic minorities who were pushed into higher elevations, for which they had little farming experience or expertise. This form of displacement has been repeated on a larger scale at other energy initiatives, especially during the construction of the Son La Dam, currently the largest hydroelectric power station in Southeast Asia. The project required displacement of more than 91,000 ethnic minority people, the largest resettlement in Vietnam's history. There are now 71 dams in Lao Cai province and the displacement has uprooted many.

Despite odds that continue to be stacked against them, including inhospitable land, unofficial but very real bias toward the Kinh majority, and the threat of displacement, Vietnam's ethnic minorities continue to work their ancestral lands, and social enterprises are pushing for wider provisions.

Bac Ha

100 km (62 miles) northeast of Sapa, 350 km (217 miles) northwest of Hanoi.

The main reason for venturing to Bac Ha, a small town built on a desolate highland plain northeast of Lao Cai, is the century-old Sunday morning market, one of the largest in the Northwest. Ethnic-minority villagers such as the Dao and the Flower H'mong (related to the H'mong but wearing brighter and more elaborate clothing) come from miles around to buy, sell, and trade everything from horses and dogs to medicinal herbs and beautiful handmade tapestries. The market has become a firmly established part of the tourist trail in the north and the influx of day-trippers from Sapa has certainly changed the character of the market. Nevertheless, despite an increasing range of handicrafts for sale, it retains much of its authenticity. A highlight of the market are the lovely, high-pitched songs performed by Flower H'mong singers. If the market manager hasn't been able to arrange singers for that day, he plays a cassette of their songs over the public address system. The market reaches its peak around 8 am, but early birds can be seen setting up their stands and sipping pho (noodle soup) for breakfast as the sun comes up. A 3- to 6-km (2- to 4-mile) walk up the road past the Sao Mai Hotel (turn left at the fork) brings you to some ethnic-minority villages where residents will be more than happy to see you. Be aware, however, that there are very few items foreigners can purchase at this market: it is strictly a photography and tourism attraction for those not involved in the trading.

GETTING HERE AND AROUND

Many travel agencies in Sapa arrange day trips to Bac Ha, which leave at about 6 am. The going rate is around 200,000-400,000d per person in a minibus. The price includes tour guide, transportation, and lunch. The trip takes 2½ hours each way and is jam-packed with tourists—each Sunday, around 40 tour buses descend into Bac Ha. You could opt to spend Saturday night in the village where there are a few acceptable hotels, giving you a head start on the hundreds of day-trippers from Sapa. If you're heading back to Hanoi, you may want to travel to Bac Ha on a Sunday morning, then get dropped off in Sapa for the 2 pm bus to Lao Cai in the afternoon to take the train or bus back to the capital that evening.

TOURS

Bac Ha Tourist

This Bac Ha–based operator is a one-stop shop for a range of experiences in the area including market tours, trekking expeditions, and cultural explorations. They can also help arrange transport between Bac Ha and Sapa as well as other points in the vicinity. It is located inside a restaurant so you can grab a bite before or after you go. ⊠ *No. 009, 20–9 St., Hoang Yen Restaurant, Bac Ha* ☏ *091/200–5952.*

Sapa Tours

Although it specializes in Sapa tours, this outfit is adept at familiarizing guests with the wonders of Bac Ha, its market, and the surrounding scenic splendor. They have tour packages including guides, meals, transportation, and accommodations for groups or individual travelers. ⊠ *64 Phat Loc Lane, Hoan Kiem District* ☏ *090/628–8138* ⊕ *www.sapa-tours.net.*

◉ Sights

★ Bac Ha Market

MARKET | Without a doubt Bac Ha's biggest draw, the Sunday market here retains its authenticity despite a growing influx of tourists. Market day sees local hill-tribe people (most noticeably the colorfully dressed Flower H'mong) flock from the surrounding mountains to trade their wares. Handicrafts are available for tourists, but this remains a mostly local affair with goods ranging from livestock to herbs. ⊠ *Bac Ha.*

H'mong women sell colorful fabric at the Bac Ha Market.

Can Cau Market

MARKET | Taking place every Saturday, this market is a worthy precursor to the extravaganza that is Bac Ha's Sunday trading jamboree. Indeed, Can Cau possibly feels more authentic due to its remoteness—it is 20 km (12 miles) north of Bac Ha—and the relative lack of tourist numbers. Like Bac Ha Market, it is a magnet for the local tribespeople. The colorful Flower H'mong are a noticeable presence, as are the Blue H'mong, distinguished by their striking zigzag pattern costume. All manner of items are traded here, including livestock and traditional medicine. ✉ *Can Cau.*

Hoang A Tuong (*Dinh Vua Meo*)

CASTLE/PALACE | A grand palace in humble Bac Ha, this unexpected and somewhat outlandish structure was built by the French between 1914 and 1921 to keep the fractious Flower H'mong chief, the so-called Cat King, Hoang A Tuong, happy. The result is one of the more striking architectural sights in this part of Vietnam, resembling a fusion of a French château and a church. ✉ *TL 153, Bac Ha* 🕮 *Free.*

Thai Giang Pho Waterfall

WATERFALL | If you are staying in Bac Ha during the summer months, this attractive waterfall is an inviting place to cool off. Around 12 km (7 miles) east of Bac Ha, it has a large pool that is deep enough for swimming. ✉ *Tà Chai, Bac Ha.*

🍴 Restaurants

Cong Fu Restaurant

$$ | **VIETNAMESE** | Off the main road, about 200 yards from entrance to market, this restaurant, attached to a hotel of the same name, does a brisk business with lunching tourists. It serves very basic, but extremely tasty Vietnamese fare, such as pho and a variety of noodle, meat, and chicken dishes. **Known for:** affordability; pho; cold beer. 🖫 *Average main: d200,000* ✉ *152 Ngoc Uyen St., Bac Ha* ☎ *097/741–5929.*

Hoang Yen Restaurant

$$ | **VIETNAMESE** | True, there's not much in the way of competition, but this is the best dining venue in Bac Ha. The menu will be familiar to students of the region's culinary landscape, with a solid selection of Vietnamese staple noodle and rice dishes along with lots of grilled, fried, and boiled meat. **Known for:** must-try in Bac Ha; local dishes; free Wi-Fi and tourism info. $ *Average main: d120,000* ✉ *009 20/9 St., Bac Ha* ☎ *091/200–5952 cell phone* ⊕ *laocaitourism.vn/en/ nhahanghoangyen.*

🛏 Hotels

Ngan Nga Bac Ha Hotel

$ | **HOTEL** | The most modern hotel in Bac Ha makes a comfortable base in the center of town. **Pros:** rooms are clean and spacious; service from the English-speaking staff is excellent; restaurant is a good place to meet fellow travelers. **Cons:** some steep staircases; Wi-Fi is occasionally intermittent; restaurant can be noisy. $ *Rooms from: d360,000* ✉ *115–117 Ngoc Uyen St., Bac Ha* ☎ *081/780–1988, 0214/388–0286* ⊕ *www.nganngabachahotel.com* ⦿ *Free Breakfast* ➟ *15 rooms.*

Sao Mai Hotel

$$ | **HOTEL** | This is arguably the grandest place to stay in Bac Ha, with rooms that are more than adequate and clean. **Pros:** cozy restaurant with outdoor seating; new wooden houses offer an elevated standard of comfort; pleasant views. **Cons:** showers take a long time to heat up; outdated interiors. $ *Rooms from: d700,000* ✉ *004 20/9 St., Bac Ha* ☎ *0214/388–0288* ⊕ *saomaihotels.com* ⦿ *Free Breakfast* ➟ *70 rooms.*

Dien Bien Phu

284 km (176 miles) south of Sapa, 470 km (291 miles) west of Hanoi.

Hard by the Laos border in one of the most remote regions in Vietnam, it is easy to imagine that Dien Bien Phu might have remained in obscurity was it not for the seismic role it played in modern Vietnamese history. It was here, in 1954, that the Vietminh defeated the French-colonial forces in a decisive battle. The loss effectively meant the end of French-colonial power in Indochina and was another milestone in the long and bloody route toward Vietnamese independence. Even as a household name, it was not until the latter part of the 20th century that Dien Bien Phu grew into a town of any significance. It was only given town status in 1992 and was elevated to provincial capital in 2004. Nowadays, with its expansive boulevards and civic buildings, as well as its airport and proximity to Laos, the city has a slightly more bustling feel to it. The main reason to visit is to brush up on the area's evocative war history, but the surrounding Muong Thanh Valley, with its thick forests and steep terrain, is also worthy of investigation.

GETTING HERE AND AROUND

The easiest way to get to Dien Bien Phu from Hanoi is by air. Vietnam Airlines has two daily flights that start at 1,000,000d for a one-way ticket. There is no direct public bus to Dien Bien Phu, but buses to Muong Lay leave Hanoi in the morning; from Muong Lay it is possible to connect to Dien Bien Phu. Private buses run between Sapa and Dien Bien Phu and cost around 330,000d. As the buses are cramped and uncomfortable, having your own transportation—car and driver or motorbike—is infinitely preferable.

👁 Sights

Command Bunker of Colonel de Castries

MILITARY SIGHT | Within walking distance of the Dien Bien Phu Museum, the command bunker has been remade with makeshift sandbags filled with concrete. Overhead is a reproduction of the corrugated roof from which a lone Viet Minh soldier waved a victory flag—the image, re-created several hours after the fact for a documentary film, became Vietnam's enduring symbol of victory over colonial oppression. ✉ *Dien Bien Phu* ✥ *West of Ron River* 🎫 *15,000d.*

Dien Bien Phu Museum

HISTORY MUSEUM | This museum has been built on the site of the battle with the French, and although there is a section dedicated to the region's ethnic-minority communities, French ignominy and Vietnamese glory are the principal topics here. The main hall recounts the events of the siege and the battle itself, with blinking maps and legends synchronized with a recorded loop outlining the battle's chronology. Outside is a collection of weapons used in and around the garrison: the Vietnamese tanks and guns look as if they were polished yesterday afternoon, the rusting French jeeps are riddled with bullet holes, and the remains of a French plane lie in a twisted heap. The museum is designed to resemble a Vietnamese soldier's helmet. ✉ *St. 3, Muong Thanh, Dien Bien Phu* ☎ *0215/382–8208* 🎟 *15,000d.*

French War Memorial

MILITARY SIGHT | French veterans organized the construction of the small, rather forlorn-looking French War Memorial, which stands across the road from the command bunker. It commemorates the 3,000 French troops buried under the rice paddies. ✉ *Dien Bien Phu* 🎟 *Free*

Hill A1: Eliane

MILITARY SIGHT | Some of the battle's most intense combat took place at Hill A1, a position labeled Eliane by the French. Once considered impregnable by the French, it was the last key position to fall to the Viet Minh. A decrepit French tank and a monument to Viet Minh troops now stand here. ✉ *Hoang Van Thai, Dien Bien Phu* 🎟 *15,000d.*

Dien Bien Phu Memorial Cemetery

CEMETERY | Across the street from the Dien Bien Phu Museum, this spotless cemetery (also called the A1 National Martyrs Cemetery) is the final resting place for many unknown Viet Minh soldiers. Here in bas-reliefs are scenes of the battle depicted in larger-than-life-size socialist realism. One of the most emotional aspects of Dien Bien Phu is here: the names of all the Viet Minh casualties from the historic battle at Dien Bien Phu are carved on the back of the front wall of the cemetery. ✉ *1094 QL279, Dien Bien Phu* 🎟 *Free.*

🍴 Restaurants

Lien Tuoi Restaurant

$$ | **INTERNATIONAL** | Catering mostly to foreign tourists, this large restaurant, a short walk from Hill A1–Eliane, serves a wide selection of Chinese, Vietnamese, and Western dishes. **Known for:** plastic stools; chicken stewed with mushrooms; menus in English and French. [$] *Average main: d60,000* ✉ *64 Hoang Van Thai St., Dien Bien Phu* ☎ *0215/382–4919.*

★ Yen Ninh Vegetarian Restaurant

$$ | **VEGETARIAN** | With meat as the staple fare of the Northwest, it comes as some surprise to find that Dien Bien Phu's top restaurant is a wholly vegetarian affair—a delicious one at that. The owner is an English tutor, which ensures that service is much less spotty than it tends to be elsewhere in the more remote regions of Vietnam. **Known for:** fresh creations; good tofu; convivial atmosphere. [$] *Average main: d60,000* ✉ *257 Group 4, Tan Thanh, Dien Bien Phu* ☎ *098/988–7513 cell phone.*

🛏 Hotels

Muong Thanh Hotel

$$$$ | **HOTEL** | This snazzy hotel complex has cornered the (admittedly limited) business market in Dien Bien Phu due to its clean rooms and immaculate service. **Pros:** grounds include gym, karaoke, and sauna; barbecue terrace; large swimming pool (a rarity in northern Vietnam). **Cons:** on-site restaurant not highly recommended. [$] *Rooms from: d1,600,000* ✉ *514 Vo Ngueyn Giap, Dien Bien Phu* ☎ *0215/381–0043* 🌐 *muongthanh.com/en* 🔑 *144 rooms* 🍴 *Free Breakfast.*

The Si La People of Northwest Vietnam [👁]

Though there are roughly only 900 Si La people living in Lai Chau Province in northwest Vietnam, there are another 1,800 or so in Laos. The Si La people hunt, forage, and cultivate cereal. Tooth painting is common with elders; men paint their teeth red and women paint theirs black, but this has not continued with the younger generations. Si La women dress in indigo-dyed dresses with embroidered collars and sleeves. The upper part of the dress is covered in metal coinlike disks. In Vietnam, the Si La speak the Tibeto-Burmese language Sila as well as standard Vietnamese.

★ **Ruby Hotel**
$ | **HOTEL** | While some of the lodging options in Dien Bien Phu have seen better days, this hotel is spotless and relatively new. **Pros:** superlative service from owner and his team; views from the upper floors are magnificent; spacious and well-equipped rooms. **Cons:** restaurant offers only essential items; a bit basic. [$] *Rooms from: d300,000* ✉ *43 Phuong Muong Than, Dien Bien Phu* ☎ *0215/383–5568* 🍴 *Free Breakfast* 🛏 *35 rooms* 💳 *No credit cards.*

Son La

150 km (93 miles) southeast of Dien Bien Phu, 160 km (99 miles) northwest of Mai Chau, 320 km (198 miles) west of Hanoi.

Son La is a convenient overnight stop on the journey to Mai Chau or Hanoi, but there are only one or two decent hotels. Many hill tribes reside in the area, which until 1980 was considered part of the Tay Bac Autonomous Region.

GETTING HERE AND AROUND

Several buses depart from Hanoi's My Dinh bus station to Son La. The journey takes around five hours and a one-way ticket costs between 160,000d and 250,000d. In Son La, buses stop at the town's main bus station, which is around 2 km (1 mile) south of town. Frequent buses to Son La leave from Dien Bien Phu, starting at 4:30 am, and the journey takes around four hours.

👁 Sights

Hot Springs
HOT SPRING | If you feel like soaking your tired bones for awhile, have your driver or a motorbike taxi take you to the hot springs in beautiful Suoi Nuoc Nong village, a few miles south of the main road. Be warned, the rather murky communal pool is far from idyllic. ✉ *Suoi Nuoc Nong* 🎟 *From 20,000d.*

Lookout Tower (Cot V3)
VIEWPOINT | For a commanding view of the town and the surrounding area, climb the stone steps behind the Trade Union Hotel to the lookout tower known as Cot V3. The climb is steep and takes about 20 minutes, but the view is quite nice. ✉ *26–8 St., Son La.*

Old French Prison & Museum
JAIL/PRISON | Destroyed by American bombers (but partially rebuilt), this former French penal colony, with its tiny underground cells and dank corridors, leaves a strong impression of life in captivity. The ticket includes entry to the Son La Museum, housed in a moldy colonial mansion overlooking the prison. Downstairs, the museum displays pictures of life in Son La, past and present, and upstairs is a model of a Thai village and an exhibition of ethnic minority clothing. The prison and

A man plants rice in the Mai Chau Valley.

museum are on the hill in the center of town, next to the People's Committee building. You can purchase an information booklet about the prison in the gift shop for 25,000d. ✉ *QL6, Son La* ☎ *0212/385–2022* 🎫 *10,000d.*

Hotels

Hanoi Hotel
$ | **HOTEL** | With its modern design, the Hanoi Hotel is one of the better lodging options in Son La, and most of the rooms have balconies that offer decent views over the small town and out toward the surrounding rice fields and mountains. **Pros:** helpful staff; balconies are a nice extra. **Cons:** rooms are freezing in the winter; it's best to call ahead. $ *Rooms from: d300,000* ✉ *228B Truong Chinh St., Son La* ☎ *0212/375–3299* 💳 *No credit cards* 🛏 *50 rooms* 🍽 *Free Breakfast.*

Mai Chau

170 km (105 miles) southwest of Hanoi.

The Brigadoon of Vietnam, Mai Chau nestles in a serene valley of Hoa Binh Province that has been called one of the most beautiful spots in the country. Like the fictitious town that rises every 100 years, Mai Chau appears out of the mist as if in a dream. The town itself is inhabited mainly by the majority Kinh Vietnamese, but White Thai villages dot the paddy-rich valley, and this is where you're likely to spend most of your time.

The White (and later the Black) Thai migrated to Vietnam from what is now Thailand about 2,000 years ago, and they incorporate elements of both cultures. The Mai Chau Valley has a number of Thai and Muong villages where hospitality is genuine and memorable, and visiting them, either as part of a trek or independently, is easy. The valley is flat and several guesthouses, homestays, and hotels have bicycles for rent, so take off on two wheels and explore. A warm welcome and waved greeting from the children of each village is virtually guaranteed.

The homestay scene has become a burgeoning industry in recent times, and many of the tours from Hanoi include an overnight stay in a White Thai house. In fact, many of the village dwellings are closer to guesthouses than what you might associate with a homestay. Many have Western toilets and sometimes even satellite television in the common rooms. If you stay overnight in a stilt house, expect a comfortable roll-up mattress and a mosquito net. Authentic extras include unlimited use of a tobacco bong (thuoc lao) and giant vats of rice wine.

The Mai Chau market teems with villagers selling everything from hand-carved opium pipes to flayed pigs. Except for some women, most villagers have given up wearing traditional garb. Although many villagers still farm, tourism and panning for gold have become the most lucrative industries.

GETTING HERE AND AROUND

Buses from Hanoi to Mai Chau leave from Hanoi's My Dinh bus station. There are four buses a day, run by different companies. They leave at 6 am, 7:30 am, 2 pm, and 2:30 pm. The journey takes around four hours and the fare is 80,000d. The best way to get around Mai Chau is undoubtedly by bike. All of the hotels can supply decent bikes and the pedaling along the valley floor is very easy. If you need to head into Mai Chau town itself, your hotel will be able to arrange a motorbike taxi.

Tan Homestay

This homestay organized by Ms. Tan is truly an authentic way to experience Mai Chau with other travelers. The homestay is made up of four traditional wooden stilt houses, and the tour includes meals and transportation to and from Hanoi. Also included in this homestay are free

bicycle tours, in-house entertainment, and knowledgeable local guides. There are also visits to a nearby waterfall on offer. ☒ Nà Chieng, Mai Chau ☎ 034/429–0001 ☜ 3,000,000d for 2-night all-inclusive trip.

◉ Sights

A tourist alley of sorts has sprung up in Ban Lac village, accessible from the dirt road just beyond the Mai Chau Guest House. Baskets, old crossbows, and lovely weavings are laid out on tables in front of the stilt houses. Many other silk scarves and textiles hang from the windows, and they're all for sale.

Buy some bottled water in town before heading out on a long hike through the green (or golden, depending on when you go) rice fields and into the nearby hills. Countless footpaths head off into the mountains from the main valley routes and are used by minority communities (usually women) who gather wood for cooking fires or construction. Their baskets are usually extremely heavy, and it takes great skill to balance more than 90 kg (200 pounds) using only shoulder straps or a head brace.

The mountainsides have been largely denuded of their primary forest cover, forcing the villagers to hike more than a day to reach the larger trees needed for building stilt houses. The White Thai villagers here are very friendly and will often invite you into their homes to watch television together or to share some homemade rice wine or even lunch. Local children will often call out to passing hikers in Thai, "Pai la la?" (Hello, where are you going?) Your response: "Pa in!" (Just walking through!).

Heritage Tree

NATURE SIGHT | On the outskirts of the main street in Mai Chau, there is an ancient tree with historical significance. The Thai people say that their ancestors planted the tree 1,000 years ago when

The Mai Chau Valley is full of rolling green hills, rice paddies, and small villages.

they first immigrated to Vietnam. In the war with the Chinese, many women were beheaded and their heads hung in the tree to serve as a warning. For this reason, many villagers believe that the tree is full of souls that must be respected. A small pagoda used to stand next to the tree, but it was destroyed in the American war. The tree became a heritage site in 2006 and is home to a small shrine. ✉ *Mo Village, Chieng Chau Ward, Mai Chau* 🎫 *Free.*

Hoa Binh Reservoir

DAM | The Hoa Binh Dam on the Black River is the largest hydroelectric dam in Southeast Asia. Experts say it produces about 27% of Vietnam's electricity. The reservoir is an epic place to go boating, kayaking, or swimming during the summer in Mai Chau. On a darker note, the dam's construction forcibly moved more than 89,000 residents, and dam displacement can be a controversial topic in Vietnam. ✉ *Mai Chau.*

🛏 Hotels

Many people enjoy staying in one of the White Thai villages behind the Mai Chau Lodge, where any of more than 60 households will put you up. Immaculately clean and surprisingly airy and comfortable, the traditional Thai longhouse sits on stilts about 7 feet up, with barely a nail used in the construction. The split-bamboo floor is soft, smooth, and springy underfoot. The going rate is 120,000d per person per night. Your hosts would accept less, but a hefty portion of the money goes to district coffers.

★ Mai Chau Ecolodge

$$$$ | **HOTEL** | This is arguably the most relaxing retreat in the valley—surrounded by green hills and rice paddies, the property is both luxurious and sympathetic to its environment. **Pros:** thoughtfully equipped accommodations; restaurant serves local specialties; beautiful environment. **Cons:** outdoor showers are a little exposed to passing pedestrian traffic; a little pricey for the area. [$] *Rooms from:*

d2,250,000 ✉ *Na Thia Village, Na Phon Commune, Mai Chau* ☎ *0218/381–9888* 🌐 *www.maichau.ecolodge.asia* 🛏 *43 rooms* 🍴 *Free Breakfast.*

Mai Chau Lodge

$$$$ | **RESORT** | On the main road leading through the valley, this is the most luxurious lodging option in Mai Chau, with the best restaurant in the area, which specializes in Vietnamese cuisine and has a pleasant, shady dining area. **Pros:** great restaurant is a real plus. **Cons:** price is rather high for what you get. [$] *Rooms from: d1,500,000* ✉ *Mai Chau* ☎ *0218/386–8959* 🌐 *maichaulodge.com* 🛏 *16 rooms.*

Mai Chau Sunrise Village

$$ | **B&B/INN** | Located directly across the fields from the Ecolodge, these beautiful bungalows look out over rice paddies and mountains. **Pros:** attached restaurant is nice; incredible scenery; complimentary bicycles. **Cons:** the bathrooms for the communal rooms need an upgrade. [$] *Rooms from: d900,000* ✉ *Mai Chau* ✥ *Across valley from Ecolodge* ☎ *094/688–8804* 🌐 *www.maichausunrisevillage.com* 🍴 *Free Breakfast* 🛏 *16 rooms, 2 stilt-house dorms.*

Mai Chau Valley View

$$ | **HOTEL** | If you are looking for something smart and comfortable in Mai Chau but don't want to splurge, then this cozy boutique option is ideal. **Pros:** owner's inside knowledge is great for getting to know the area; open-air restaurant serves White Thai cuisine; welcoming and intimate environment. **Cons:** small number of rooms means limited availability during busy periods. [$] *Rooms from: d1,000,000* ✉ *Mai Chau* ☎ *097/205–8696 cell phone* 🌐 *maichauvalleyview.com* 🛏 *8 rooms* 🍴 *Free Breakfast.*

Sol Bungalows

$$$$ | **B&B/INN** | These bungalows are quiet and peaceful and the outdoor pool is great for traveling families. **Pros:** kind service; incredible views; nice restaurant. **Cons:** occasional power outages in the valley; rooms can get chilly in winter. [$] *Rooms from: d2,800,000* ✉ *Chieng Chau Village, Mai Chau Valley, Mai Chau* ☎ *0218/654–8709, 098/291–2999* 🌐 *www.solbungalows.com* 🍴 *Free Breakfast* 🛏 *18 rooms.*

Index

438

Photo Credits

Front Cover: Witchaphon Saengaram/Getty Images [Description: The line and pattern of rice field at Tule province, northern Vietnam].
Back cover, from left to right: 12ee12/iStockphoto, Le Thang/iStockphoto, bloodua/iStockphoto. **Spine:** Andrii Brodiahin/iStockphoto.
Interior, from left to right: Jeff_Cagle/iStockphoto (1). DuyDo/iStockphoto (2). **Chapter 1: Experience Vietnam:** HuyThoai/iStockphoto (6-7). Huy Thoai/Shutterstock (8-9). Luciano Mortula/Shutterstock (9). hadynyah/iStockphoto (9). RGB Ventures/SuperStock/Alamy (10). Hoxuanhuong/Dreamstime.com (10). Richard Taylor/Sime/eStock Photo (10). Mikolaj Michalak/Shutterstock (10). JunPhoto/Shutterstock (11). Quang nguyen vinh/Shutterstock (12). Dan Baciu/Shutterstock (12). Salajean/Dreamstime.com (12). Huy Thoai/Shutterstock (12). Judyta Jastrzebska/Shutterstock (13). DeltaOFF/Shutterstock (13). SARAH NGUYEN/Shutterstock (14). Zoonar/Galyna Andrus/Agefotostock (14). Vladimir Zhoga/Shutterstock (14). jethuynh/iStock Editorial (15). Qui Thinh Tran/iStockphoto (18). JunPhoto/Shutterstock (18). pradeep_kmpk14/Shutterstock (18). Courtesy of Vietnam Tourism Gov.vn (19). HuyThoai/iStockphoto (19). heckepics/iStock Editorial (20). R.M. Nunes/Shutterstock (20). Steve Barze/Shutterstock (20). Sergii Figurnyi/Dreamstime (21). vinhdav/iStockphoto (21). bonchan/Shutterstock (22). KOTO Villa (22). Joshua Resnick/Dreamstime (22). Ngon Restaurant (22). c8501089/iStockphoto (23). Bored Nomad/Shutterstock (23). Carolyne Parent/Shutterstock (23). KOTO Villa (23). Gina Smith/Shutterstock (24). Christian Sturzenegger/iStock Editorial (24). corradobarattaphotos/iStockphoto (24). FotoGraphik/iStock Editorial (24). Nguyen Phuc Thanh/iStockphoto (25). **Chapter 3: Ho Chi Minh City:** Nguyen Quang Ngoc Tonkin/Shutterstock (69). Joel Whalton/Shutterstock (80). Hamdan Yoshida/Shutterstock (85). Nguyen Quang Ngoc Tonkin/Shutterstock (86). Hadi [CC BY-NC 2.0]/Flickr (89). Joe Schulz [CC BY-NC 2.0]/Flickr (94). Efired/Dreamstime (96). quangpraha/iStock (102). iamtripper/Shutterstock (113). Huy Thoai/Shutterstock (119). Stelya/Dreamstime.com (124). loco75/iStock (135). **Chapter 4: The Mekong Delta:** ImaginativeGifts/Shutterstock (141). PhongTranVN/iStock (153). NguyenQuocThang/Shutterstock (156). HuyThoai/iStock (160). Tran Qui Thinh/Shutterstock (166). Vietnam Stock/Shutterstock (178). Huy Thoai/Shutterstock (182). Tran Qui Thinh/Shutterstock (184). **Chapter 5: The South-Central Coast and Highlands:** Simon Dannhauer/iStockphoto (187). Ungvari Attila/Shutterstock (195). Ungvari Attila/Shutterstock (200-201). DreamArchitect/Shutterstock (209). Dima Fadeev/Shutterstock (212). Quang nguyen vinh/Shutterstock (218). Hien Phung Thu/Shutterstock (230). Hien Phung Thu/Shutterstock (236). **Chapter 6: The Central Coast:** I am Kien. I like to take many beautiful photos about landscape./iStockphoto (239). Hel080808/Dreamstime (249). Gunter Nuyts/Shutterstock (250). Photogilio/iStockphoto (256-257). Chris Howey/Shutterstock (260). Efired/Shutterstock (270). Hien Phung Thu/Shutterstock (275). iamtripper/Shutterstock (278). TBone Lee/Shutterstock (285). Efired/Shutterstock (294). S-F/Shutterstock (297). Vietnam Stock Images/Shutterstock (309). **Chapter 7: Halong Bay and North-Central Vietnam:** Badzmanaois/Dreamstime (315). Efired/Shutterstock (324). Leotie/Shutterstock (326). Akarat Phasura/Shutterstock (328). HuyThoai/iStockphoto (340-341). SoBright7/Shutterstock (349). **Chapter 8: Hanoi:** Letloose78/Dreamstime (351). Jiayikang/Dreamstime (356). martinho Smart/Shutterstock (364). Pierre Aden/iStockphoto (368). RYOSUKEKUN/iStockphoto (391). Tony albelton/Shutterstock (405). **Chapter 9: The Northwest:** tampatra/iStockphoto (407). BenWassink/Shutterstock (415). Aivars Ivbulis/Shutterstock (421). Olga Kashubin/Shutterstock (422). QMTstudio/Shutterstock (429). Blogueandos/Dreamstime.com (433). VietNamVui/iStockphoto (435).

*Every effort has been made to trace the copyright holders, and we apologize in advance for any accidental errors. We would be happy to apply the corrections in the following edition of this publication.

Notes

Notes

Notes

Fodor's ESSENTIAL VIETNAM

Publisher: Stephen Horowitz, *General Manager*

Editorial: Douglas Stallings, *Editorial Director*; Jill Fergus, Amanda Sadlowski, Caroline Trefler, *Senior Editors*; Kayla Becker, Alexis Kelly, *Editors*; Angelique Kennedy-Chavannes, *Assistant Editor*

Design: Tina Malaney, *Director of Design and Production*; Jessica Gonzalez, *Graphic Designer*

Production: Jennifer DePrima, *Editorial Production Manager*; Elyse Rozelle, *Senior Production Editor*; Monica White, *Production Editor*

Maps: Rebecca Baer, *Senior Map Editor*; Mark Stroud (Moon Street Cartography), David Lindroth, *Cartographers*

Photography: Viviane Teles, *Senior Photo Editor*; Namrata Aggarwal, Payal Gupta, Ashok Kumar, *Photo Editors*; Rebecca Rimmer, *Photo Production Associate*; Eddie Aldrete, *Photo Production Intern*

Business & Operations: Chuck Hoover, *Chief Marketing Officer*; Robert Ames, *Group General Manager*; Devin Duckworth, *Director of Print Publishing*

Public Relations and Marketing: Joe Ewaskiw, *Senior Director of Communications & Public Relations*

Fodors.com: Jeremy Tarr, *Editorial Director*; Rachael Levitt, *Managing Editor*

Technology: Jon Atkinson, *Director of Technology*; Rudresh Teotia, *Lead Developer*; Jacob Ashpis, *Content Operations Manager*

Writers: Agnes Alpuerto, Shannon Brown, Hiezle Bual, Dan Q. Dao, Vo Thi Huong Lan, Khanh Nguyen, James Pham, Joshua Zukas

Editor: Kayla Becker

Production Editor: Jennifer DePrima

2nd Edition

ISBN 978-1-64097-366-4

ISSN 2577-5693

All details in this book are based on information supplied to us at press time. Always confirm information when it matters, especially if you're making a detour to visit a specific place. Fodor's expressly disclaims any liability, loss, or risk, personal or otherwise, that is incurred as a consequence of the use of any of the contents of this book.

SPECIAL SALES
This book is available at special discounts for bulk purchases for sales promotions or premiums. For more information, e-mail SpecialMarkets@fodors.com.

PRINTED IN CANADA

10 9 8 7 6 5 4 3 2

About Our Writers

Agnes Alpuerto is a journalist currently based in Vietnam. Her passion for written words has taken her all over Asia, including to the Philippines (her home country), Cambodia, Malaysia, and India. Her media affiliations include *ABS-CBN*, *Philippine Daily Inquirer*, *Khmer Times*, and *Vietcetera*. She worked on the Central Coast chapter of this edition.

Shannon Brown wound up in Vietnam in 2014 after stints in South Korea and Sierra Leone, and now teaches in Bangkok, Thailand. When she's not teaching and writing, she's enjoying the motorbikes, massages, and street food that are the hallmarks of Southeast Asia. For this edition, Shannon updated the Travel Smart chapter.

Hiezle Bual is a journalist originally from Cebu, Philippines. She is presently based in Ho Chi Minh City, Vietnam, where she writes news pieces on the country's business trends, economic insights, and meeting industry leaders from various sectors. Her works have appeared in *Khmer Times* and *Vietcetera*, and she's traveled to Singapore and China to cover stories. She updated the Halong Bay and North-Central Vietnam chapter of this edition.

Dan Q. Dao is a Vietnamese-American writer covering travel, food, and culture through a global Vietnamese perspective. He is currently Digital Director, International at Vietcetera, a Saigon-based digital media company. His writing has also regularly appeared in *Food & Wine*, *Vice*, *Paper*, *Saveur*, and *Condé Nast Traveler*. You can find his work at ⊕ *danqdao. com* and follow him on social media at @ danqdao. Dan updated the Experience chapter.

Vo Thi Huong Lan calls Hue City her home and paradise. This Hue native has such a great love for her own city that she decided to resign from her 10-year job in media relations to become a Hue guide. For her, this is not simply a job, it's her passion and dream-come-true. Her writing has appeared in a number of publications, and her stories can be found at lanhue.com. She has translated several English novels into Vietnamese and four of them were published by the most prestigious publishers in Vietnam, including Tre and Van Hoc. For this edition, Lan updated the Hue section.

Khanh Nguyen is a published author and award-winning screenwriter based out of Ho Chi Minh City, Vietnam. She specializes in ethnic culture, food, travel, and urban history. She wrote the script for the award-winning short movie *Other Side*, whose story revolves around a lesbian relationship in deeply conservative Vietnam.

James Pham is a writer and photographer based in Ho Chi Minh City, Vietnam. His travel stories have appeared in *Verve India*, *Oi Vietnam*, *Heritage* (Vietnam Airlines), *BBC Radio*, and many other outlets. He is also the co-author of "Eat Vietnam". James updated the Ho Chi Minh City and the South Central Coast and Highlands chapters of this edition. You can follow his travels at www.instagram.com/fly.icarus.fly.

Joshua Zukas is a Hanoi-based writer specializing in travel, culture, architecture, and innovation in Vietnam. His travel, culture, and innovation stories have been published in *The Economist*, *BBC News*, *CNN*, and many other publications, including the region's award-winning in-flight magazines. His architecture stories have been published in *Wallpaper*, *Interior Design Magazine*, *Icon*, *Wired*, and *Frame*. Joshua updated the Hanoi and Mekong Delta chapters. You can find his work at ⊕ *www.joshuazukas.com*.